W9-DEX-281

McGRAW-HILL SERIES IN POLITICAL SCIENCE

Joseph P. Harris, CONSULTING EDITOR

Political Thought in Perspective

McGRAW-HILL SERIES IN POLITICAL SCIENCE

Joseph P. Harris, CONSULTING EDITOR

ADRIAN · Governing Urban America: Structure, Politics, and Administration
BONE · American Politics and the Party System
CHASE · The United Nations in Action
EBENSTEIN · Political Thought in Perspective
FERGUSON AND McHENRY · The American Federal Government
FERGUSON AND McHENRY · The American System of Government
FERGUSON AND McHENRY · Elements of American Government
FIELD · Governments in Modern Society
FRANK · Cases on the Constitution
GOSNELL, LANCASTER, AND RANKIN · Fundamentals of American Government:
National, State, and Local
GOSNELL, LANCASTER, AND RANKIN · Fundamentals of American National
Government
GROSS · The Legislative Struggle
HAAS AND WHITING · Dynamics of International Relations
HARTMANN · Basic Documents of International Relations
HARTMANN · Readings in International Relations
HOLLOWAY · State and Local Government in the United States
LEONARD · Elements of American Foreign Policy
LEONARD · International Organization
MANGONE · A Short History of International Organization
MILLETT · Management in the Public Service
NEUMANN · European and Comparative Government
PIERSON AND GIL · Governments of Latin America
REED · Municipal Management
RIEMER · Problems of American Government
ROCHE AND STEDMAN · The Dynamics of Democratic Government
RODEE, ANDERSON, AND CHRISTOL · Introduction to Political Science
STRAUSZ-HUPÉ AND POSSONY · International Relations
SVARLIEN · An Introduction to the Law of Nations
TURNER · Politics in the United States: Readings in Political Parties and
Pressure Groups
VANDENBOSCH AND HOGAN · The United Nations: Background, Organization,
Functions, Activities
WALDO · Ideas and Issues in Public Administration: A Book of Readings
WILSON · The American Political Mind
WILSON · Police Administration

Political Thought in Perspective

WILLIAM EBENSTEIN

Professor of Politics, Princeton University

McGRAW-HILL BOOK COMPANY, INC.

1957   New York   Toronto   London

POLITICAL THOUGHT IN PERSPECTIVE

Library of Congress Catalog Card Number 57-7230

To

LANSDELL K. CHRISTIE

Books by William Ebenstein

POLITICAL THOUGHT IN PERSPECTIVE

TODAY'S ISMS
Communism, Fascism, Capitalism, Socialism

MODERN POLITICAL THOUGHT
The Great Issues

INTRODUCTION TO POLITICAL PHILOSOPHY

GREAT POLITICAL THINKERS
Plato to the Present

MAN AND THE STATE
Modern Political Ideas

THE GERMAN RECORD
A Political Portrait

THE PURE THEORY OF LAW

THE NAZI STATE

THE LAW OF PUBLIC HOUSING

FASCIST ITALY

Preface

The history of political thought is usually studied in one of two ways: either by reading the great writers themselves or by reading about them. The advantage of the first method is obvious: there is no substitute for the original words and thoughts of the great political writers, any more than an expository and interpretative summary of the contents of *Hamlet* can ever substitute for the original text. Yet the second method—the historical account and analysis of political ideas—has its advantage, too: it provides commentary and interpretation of ideas which are often difficult to grasp without the helping hand of the guide and critic.

This book tries to combine the advantages of both methods by presenting the high points of the evolution of political ideas from Plato to the present as seen by distinguished thinkers and statesmen themselves. Writing about each other, the world's leading political philosophers, statesmen, and scholars generally write with a verve and freshness that are not always present in their writing about more abstract issues of political theory. Moreover, in each selection the writer reveals as much about himself as about the man he comments upon. The kinship of greatness between author and subject adds, it is hoped, a new dimension of intimacy and understanding to the study of political ideas. In addition to critical commentaries of distinguished thinkers on each other, I have included commentaries on great political philosophers by some of the world's renowned statesmen, such as Jefferson, Woodrow Wilson, Masaryk, Lenin, Churchill, and Nehru. Vital political ideas are thus presented in the double mirror of those who either as creative political philosophers formulated them, or as leaders of peoples gave living reality to them.

It was not always possible to get the ideal pair, such as this volume contains in the case of Aristotle or Jefferson on Plato, Russell on Locke, Paine or Woodrow Wilson on Burke, Mill on Bentham, Acton on Mill, Lenin or Masaryk on Marx, and Churchill on Lenin. Not all writers included are of equal importance as creative thinkers or statesmen, and particularly in the case of the more recent writers, history alone will tell how important they are from a long-term viewpoint. Yet despite the differences in stature, originality, and outlook of the authors included in this volume, there emerges a sense of unity and progress of political thought from Plato to the present that could hardly be gained from individual works of great political thinkers or statesmen, or from a single systematic account by the historian of political thought.

In several cases, I have myself translated materials hitherto unavailable in English, revised older translations, and modernized the spelling, punctuation, and arrangement of older texts in English. In several other cases, I have been able to include materials not easily accessible, or virtually forgotten. The essay of Lord Acton on John Stuart Mill is an example. Originally published in *The Rambler* (1859–1860), it was signed only with the initial "A." Yet there is no doubt that Acton, who was the editor and who frequently signed his articles in this way, was the author.

I have prefaced each chapter with a brief introductory note; its purpose is to provide some of the salient biographical and literary facts about the writer and the subject of his essay. A full-length commentary of my own on the commentaries reproduced in this volume would be out of place, since the essays speak for themselves. Moreover, I have presented such fuller commentaries and criticisms in my earlier books, *Great Political Thinkers: Plato to the Present* (1951) and *Modern Political Thought: The Great Issues* (1954).

WILLIAM EBENSTEIN

Princeton University

Contents

Political Thought in Perspective

ARISTOTLE
ST. AUGUSTINE
HEGEL
JEFFERSON
BRANDEIS

PLATO

In the whole history of Western philosophy (perhaps of all Western thought), no one has exercised as much influence as Plato (427-347 B.C.). He is the founder of philosophical idealism, one of the two or three major schools of philosophy dominating Western thought in the past as in the present (the other two being materialism and, more recently, empiricism). Plato's ideas have had a decisive impact, not only on general philosophy and metaphysics, but also on social and political philosophy, and his imprint on Christian theology has been more vivid and enduring than that of any other pagan philosopher. His best-known work is *The Republic,* in which he inquires into the nature of the justly ordered state and society. His concepts of social and political justice are, on the whole, opposed to the ideals of democracy; yet Plato advances his arguments with such literary and artistic brilliance that *The Republic* is still the most fascinating work of political philosophy ever written, and even the most confirmed democrat can still learn a great deal from Plato's profound insights into politics, including his biting criticisms of the basic concepts of democracy.

As is so often the case, the best critique and corrective of Plato's political ideas were put forward by his own student and disciple, Aristotle (383-322 B.C.), particularly in his *Politics*. In pursuing his ideal of unity within the state, Plato was willing to sacrifice the happiness of the rulers as well as the ruled, to abolish such basic human institutions as property and the family with respect to the ruling class, and to have the ruling class govern without much concern for the consent of the governed. By contrast, Aristotle saw that "a state is not made up only of so many men, but of different kinds of men," and that "the nature of a state is to be a plurality." He therefore concluded that the principle of unity, Plato's supreme ideal, could lead to social and political self-destruction if carried to an extreme; in particular, Aristotle held that no form of government could be stable unless the principles of individual freedom and property were recognized in some genuine fashion. While no out-and-out democrat, Aristotle shows moderation and lack of fanaticism in his conservative outlook, and his defense of private property against Plato's contrary theories is probably the most convincing ever formulated, and still relevant to many of the great issues of private property today.

The continuity of Western thought from pagan antiquity to medieval Christianity can clearly be seen in the thought of St. Augustine (A.D. 354–430), the first of the great church fathers, and to this day one of the two dominant figures in the whole history of the Christian Church (the other being St. Thomas Aquinas). Baptized at the relatively late age of thirty-three, St. Augustine quickly rose in the clerical hierarchy, finally becoming bishop only eight years later. His chief work is *The City of God* (426), a monument of Christian scholarship and apologetics, rebutting, on the one hand, the pagan charges against Christianity, and formulating, on the other, the positive tenets of the Christian way of life. St. Augustine frankly, and at times enthusiastically, acknowledges his indebtedness to, and admiration for, Plato, "the most Christian of all pagan philosophers," as he calls him. This deep affinity of outlook cannot, of course, conceal or bridge the fundamental gap between the two: For Plato, justice consists essentially in the right ordering of the conflicting elements of man's soul, and in his right relations with his fellow men. St. Augustine Christianizes and transforms this secular conception into a religious one: the essence of justice is the relation between man and God, from which right relations between man and man will inevitably follow. Yet despite this difference, St. Augustine served as one of the principal gates through which Plato's thought entered the mainstream of Christian thought in medieval and modern times, and to the extent that the Augustinian interpretation of the Christian faith and philosophy has occupied a central position in the history of Christianity, Platonism has played a perpetually vitalizing and provocative role in the evolution of Western thought.

In the modern age, philosophical idealism has been most characteristically, and most influentially, represented in the work of the German philosopher Georg Wilhelm Friedrich Hegel (1770–1831). Because the political experience of Germany has been preponderantly authoritarian, its orthodox political tradition has been chiefly, though not wholly, antidemocratic. In this tradition Hegel's philosophy occupies a place of special importance. His system encompasses philosophy, metaphysics, religion, art, ethics, history, and politics. In its range alone his work is impressive and of a truly encyclopedic character. Both versions of modern totalitarianism—fascism and communism—have frankly acknowledged their intellectual indebtedness to Hegel, although for this reason alone Hegel cannot fairly be held responsible for all the barbarous excesses of modern totalitarianism. The leadership principle, central in Plato's notion of government by a superior elite, is also stressed by Hegel in his discussion of the merits of the different types of constitutions—democracy, aristocracy, and monarchy. Yet his preference is for monarchy, whereas Plato, the product of a civilization whose lifeblood was curiosity, inquiry, and reasoning, attributed to his ideal elite the right to rule on the basis of superior qualities of mind and character. Though the most powerful modern representative of Platonism, Hegel does not fully accept Plato's political philosophy in the extensive treatment of Plato in his *History of Philosophy* (1833), and, ironically, criticizes Plato for not allowing enough scope for individual liberty.

In the European tradition, the preeminence of Plato in political philosophy was due, not only to the intellectual persuasiveness of his arguments, but also (and even more so perhaps) to the historical fact that European governments and politics have been preponderantly based on undemocratic and antidemocratic ideas and practices in the last twenty-five hundred years. By contrast, Plato's concepts of superior and inferior classes, and particularly his idea that the ruling class of philosopher-kings has the right (and duty) to rule independently of the consent of the ruled, stand in opposition to the heritage of American thought and the experience of American life. For a long time, and particularly as long as the European intellectual tradition commanded a high prestige in the United States solely because it was European, many Americans joined unquestioningly (and some still do to this day) in the veneration of Plato. Yet the authentic American viewpoint on Plato has always been much more critical than the conventional attitude in Europe. In the whole intellectual history of the United States, Thomas Jefferson (1743–1826) still towers above all the rest; he is still the most universal personality the United States has brought forth on its soil and contributed to the common heritage of Western civilization. Author of the Declaration of Independence, third President of the United States (1801–1809), apostle of democracy and free thought, statesman, philosopher, scientist, architect, Jefferson minced no words in expressing his sharply critical attitude on Plato, causticly attacking his "mysticism" and "foggy mind."

As in ancient Rome, much of the creative political thinking in modern America is due to its great jurists and judges, rather than to professional political philosophers. Louis D. Brandeis (1856–1941) will always rank as one of the imaginative and illustrious American lawyers, reaching his greatest influence in national affairs while serving as an Associate Justice on the Supreme Court of the United States (1916–1939). Brandeis was one of the pioneers of "sociological jurisprudence" in theory and practice, seeking to humanize the law by exposing it more fully to the impact of common sense and, above all, the facts of modern industrial life. His comments on Plato are taken from his personal diary and notebooks. Written by Brandeis at the age of twenty, his views on Plato's *Republic* show unmistakable signs of youthfulness and simplicity, yet foreshadow the later and more mature Brandeis, who to his last day cherished the Jeffersonian image and promise of American democracy.

Aristotle on PLATO

Our purpose is to consider what form of political community is best of all for those who are most able to realize their ideal of life. We must therefore examine not only this but other constitutions, both such as actually exist in well-governed states, and any theoretical forms which are held in esteem; that what is good and useful may be brought to light. And let no one suppose that in seeking for something beyond them we are anxious to make a sophistical display at any cost; we only undertake this inquiry because all the constitutions with which we are acquainted are faulty.

We will begin with the natural beginning of the subject. Three alternatives are conceivable: The members of a state must either have (1) all things or (2) nothing in common, or (3) some things in common and some not. That they should have nothing in common is clearly impossible, for the constitution is a community, and must at any rate have a common place—one city will be in one place, and the citizens are those who share in that one city. But should a well-ordered state have all things, as far as may be, in common, or some only and not others? For the citizens might conceivably have wives and children and property in common,

[From Aristotle, *Politics* (trans. Benjamin Jowett, Clarendon Press, 1885).]

as Socrates proposes in the *Republic* of Plato. Which is better, our present condition, or the proposed new order of society?

There are many difficulties in the community of women. And the principle on which Socrates rests the necessity of such an institution evidently is not established by his arguments. Further, as a means to the end which he ascribes to the state, the scheme, taken literally, is impracticable, and how we are to interpret it is nowhere precisely stated. I am speaking of the premiss from which the argument of Socrates proceeds, 'that the greater the unity of the state the better'. Is it not obvious that a state may at length attain such a degree of unity as to be no longer a state?—since the nature of a state is to be a plurality, and in tending to greater unity, from being a state, it becomes a family, and from being a family, an individual; for the family may be said to be more than the state, and the individual than the family. So that we ought not to attain this greatest unity even if we could, for it would be the destruction of the state. Again, a state is not made up only of so many men, but of different kinds of men; for similars do not constitute a state. It is not like a military alliance. The usefulness of the latter depends upon its quantity even where there is no difference in quality (for mutual protection is the end aimed at), just as a greater weight of anything is more useful than a less (in like manner, a state differs from a nation, when the nation has not its population organized in villages, but lives an Arcadian sort of life); but the elements out of which a unity is to be formed differ in kind. Wherefore the principle of compensation, as I have remarked in the *Ethics*, is the salvation of states. Even among freemen and equals this is a principle which must be maintained, for they cannot all rule together, but must change at the end of a year or some other period of time or in some order of succession. The result is that upon this plan they all govern; just as if shoemakers and carpenters were to exchange their occupations, and the same persons did not always continue shoemakers and carpenters. And since it is better that this should be so in politics as well, it is clear that while there should be continuance of the same persons in power where this is possible, yet where this is not possible by reason of the natural equality of the citizens, and at the same time it is just that all should share in the government (whether to govern be a good thing or a bad), an approximation to this is that equals should in turn retire from office and should, apart from official position, be treated alike. Thus the one party rule and the others are ruled in turn, as if they were no longer the same persons. In like manner when they hold office there is a variety in the offices held. Hence it is evident that a city is not by nature one in that sense which some persons affirm; and that what is said to be the greatest good of cities is in reality their destruction; but surely the good of things must be that which preserves them. Again, in another point of view, this extreme unification of the state is clearly not good; for a family is more self-sufficing than an individual, and a city than a family, and a city only comes into being when the community is large enough to be self-sufficing. If then self-sufficiency is to be desired, the lesser degree of unity is more desirable than the greater.

But, even supposing that it were best for the community to have the greatest degree of unity, this unity is by no means proved to follow from the fact 'of all men saying "mine" and "not mine" at the same instant of time', which, according to Socrates, is the sign of perfect unity in a state. For the word 'all' is ambiguous. If the meaning be that every individual says 'mine' and 'not mine' at the same time, then perhaps the result at which Socrates aims may be in some degree accomplished; each man will call the same person his own son and the same person his own wife, and so of his property and of all that falls to his lot. This, however, is not the way in which people would speak who had their wives and children in common; they would say 'all' but not 'each'. In like manner their property would be described as belonging to them, not severally but collectively. There is an obvious fallacy in the term 'all': like some other words, 'both', 'odd', 'even', it is ambiguous, and even in abstract argument becomes a source of logical puzzles. That all persons call the same thing mine in the sense in which each does so may be a fine thing, but it is impracticable; or if the words are taken in the other sense, such a unity in no way conduces to harmony. And there is another objection to the proposal. For that which is common to the greatest number has the least care bestowed upon it. Every one thinks chiefly of his own, hardly at all of the common interest; and only when he is himself concerned as an individual. For besides other considerations, everybody is more inclined to neglect the duty which he expects another to fulfil; as in families many attendants are often less useful than a few. Each citizen will have a thousand sons who will not be his sons individually, but anybody will be equally the son of anybody, and will therefore be neglected by all alike. Further, upon this principle, every one will use the word 'mine' of one who is prospering or the reverse, however small a fraction he may himself be of the whole number; the same boy will be 'my son', 'so and so's son', the son of each of the thousand, or whatever be the number of the citizens; and even about this he will not be positive; for it is impossible to know who chanced to have a child, or whether, if one came into existence, it has survived. But which is better —for each to say 'mine' in this way, making a man the same relation to two thousand or ten thousand citizens, or to use the word 'mine' in the ordinary and more restricted sense? For usually the same person is called by one man his own son whom another calls his own brother or cousin or kinsman—blood relation or connexion by marriage either of himself or of some relation of his, and yet another his clansman or tribesman; and how much better is it to be the real cousin of somebody than to be a son after Plato's fashion! Nor is there any way of preventing brothers and children and fathers and mothers from sometimes recognizing one another; for children are born like their parents, and they will necessarily be finding indications of their relationship to one another. Geographers declare such to be the fact; they say that in part of Upper Libya, where the women are common, nevertheless the children who are born are assigned to their respective fathers on the ground of their likeness. And some women, like the females of other animals—for example, mares and cows—have a strong tendency to produce offspring resembling their parents, as was the case with the Pharsalian mare called Honest.

Other evils, against which it is not easy for the authors of such a community to guard, will be assaults and homicides, voluntary as well as involuntary, quarrels and slanders, all which are most unholy acts when committed against fathers and mothers and near relations, but not equally unholy when there is no relationship. Moreover, they are much more likely to occur if the relationship is unknown, and, when they have occurred, the customary expiations of them cannot be made. Again, how strange it is that Socrates, after having made the children common, should hinder lovers from carnal intercourse only, but should permit love and familiarities between father and son or between brother and brother, than which nothing can be more unseemly, since even without them love of this sort is improper. How strange, too, to forbid intercourse for no other reason than the violence of the pleasure, as though the relationship of father and son or of brothers with one another made no difference.

This community of wives and children seems better suited to the husbandmen than to the guardians, for if they have wives and children in common, they will be bound to one another by weaker ties, as a subject class should be, and they will remain obedient and not rebel. In a word, the result of such a law would be just the opposite of that which good laws ought to have, and the intention of Socrates in making these regulations about women and children would defeat itself. For friendship we believe to be the greatest good of states and the preservative of them against revolutions; neither is there anything which Socrates so greatly lauds as the unity of the state which he and all the world declare to be created by friendship. But the unity which he commends would be like that of the lovers in the *Symposium*, who, as Aristophanes says, desire to grow together in the excess of their affection, and from being two to become one, in which case one or both would certainly perish. Whereas in a state having women and children common, love will be watery; and the father will certainly not say 'my son', or the son 'my father'. As a little sweet wine mingled with a great deal of water is imperceptible in the mixture, so, in this sort of community, the idea of relationship which is based upon these names will be lost; there is no reason why the so-called father should care about the son, or the son about the father, or brothers about one another. Of the two qualities which chiefly inspire regard and affection—that a thing is your own and that it is your only one—neither can exist in such a state as this.

Again, the transfer of children as soon as they are born from the rank of husbandmen or of artisans to that of guardians, and from the rank of guardians into a lower rank, will be very difficult to arrange; the givers or transferrers cannot but know whom they are giving and transferring, and to whom. And the previously mentioned evils, such as assaults, unlawful loves, homicides, will happen more often amongst those who are transferred to the lower classes, or who have a place assigned to them among the guardians; for they will no longer call the members of the class they have left brothers, and children, and fathers, and mothers, and will not, therefore, be afraid of committing any crimes by reason of consanguinity. Touching the community of wives and children, let this be our conclusion.

Next let us consider what should be our arrangements about property: should the citizens of the perfect state have their possessions in common or not? This question may be discussed separately from the enactments about women and children. Even supposing that the women and children belong to individuals, according to the custom which is at present universal, may there not be an advantage in having and using possessions in common? Three cases are possible: (1) the soil may be appropriated, but the produce may be thrown for consumption into the common stock; and this is the practice of some nations. Or (2), the soil may be common, and may be cultivated in common, but the produce divided among individuals for their private use; this is a form of common property which is said to exist among certain barbarians. Or (3), the soil and the produce may be alike common.

When the husbandmen are not the owners, the case will be different and easier to deal with; but when they till the ground for themselves the question of ownership will give a world of trouble. If they do not share equally in enjoyments and toils, those who labour much and get little will necessarily complain of those who labour little and receive or consume much. But indeed there is always a difficulty in men living together and having all human relations in common, but especially in their having common property. The partnerships of fellow-travellers are an example to the point; for they generally fall out over everyday matters and quarrel about any trifle which turns up. So with servants: we are most liable to take offense at those with whom we most frequently come into contact in daily life.

These are only some of the disadvantages which attend the community of property; the present arrangement, if improved as it might be by good customs and laws, would be far better, and would have the advantages of both systems. Property should be in a certain sense common, but, as a general rule, private; for, when every one has a distinct interest, men will not complain of one another, and they will make more progress, because every one will be attending to his own business. And yet by reason of goodness, and in respect of use, 'Friends', as the proverb says, 'will have all things common'. Even now there are traces of such a principle, showing that it is not impracticable, but, in well-ordered states, exists already to a certain extent and may be carried further. For, although every man has his own property, some things he will place at the disposal of his friends, while of others he shares the use with them. The Lacedaemonians, for example, use one another's slaves, and horses, and dogs, as if they were their own; and when they lack provisions on a journey, they appropriate what they find in the fields throughout the country. It is clearly better that property should be private, but the use of it common; and the special business of the legislator is to create in men this benevolent disposition. Again, how immeasurably greater is the pleasure, when a man feels a thing to be his own; for surely the love of self is a feeling implanted by nature and not given in vain, although selfishness is rightly censured; this, however, is not the mere love of self, but the love of self in excess, like the miser's love of money; for all, or almost all, men love money and other such objects in a measure. And further, there is the greatest pleasure in doing a kindness or service to friends or guests or companions, which can only be rendered when a man has private property. These advantages are lost by excessive unification of the state. The exhibition of two virtues, besides, is visibly annihilated in such a state: first, temperance towards women (for it is an honourable action to abstain from another's wife for temperance sake); secondly, liberality in the matter of property. No one, when men have all things in common, will any longer set an example of liberality or do any liberal action; for liberality consists in the use which is made of property.

Such legislation may have a specious appearance of benevolence; men readily listen to it, and are easily induced to believe that in some wonderful manner everybody will become everybody's friend, especially when some one is heard denouncing the evils now existing in states, suits about contracts, convictions for perjury, flatteries of rich men and the like, which are said to arise out of the possession of private property. These evils, however, are due to a very different cause—the wickedness of human nature. Indeed, we see that there is much more quarrelling among those who have all things in common, though there are not many of them when compared with the vast numbers who have private property.

Again, we ought to reckon, not only the evils from which the citizens will be saved, but also the advantages which they will lose. The life which they are to lead appears to be quite impracticable. The error of Socrates must be attributed to the false notion of unity from which he starts. Unity there should be, both of the family and of the state, but in some respects only. For there is a point at which a state may attain such a degree of unity as to be no longer a state, or at which, without actually ceasing to exist, it will become an inferior state, like harmony passing into unison, or rhythm which has been reduced to a single foot. The state, as I was saying, is a plurality, which should be united and made into a community by education; and it is strange that the author of a system of education which he thinks will make the state virtuous, should expect to improve his citizens by regulations of this sort, and not by philosophy or by customs and laws, like those which prevail at Sparta and Crete respecting common meals, whereby the legislator has made property common. Let us remember that we should not disregard the experience of ages; in the multitude of years these things, if they were good, would certainly not have been unknown; for almost everything has been found out, although sometimes they are not put together; in other cases men do not use the knowledge which they have. Great light would be thrown on this subject if we could see such a form of government in the actual process of construction; for the legislator could not form a state at all without distributing and dividing its constituents into associations for common meals, and into phratries and tribes. But all this legislation ends only in forbidding agriculture to the guardians, a prohibition which the Lacedaemonians try to enforce already.

But, indeed, Socrates has not said, nor is it easy to decide, what in such a community will be the general form of the state. The citizens who are not guardians are the majority, and about them nothing has been determined: are the husbandmen, too, to have their property in common? Or is each individual to have his own? and are the wives and children to be

individual or common? If, like the guardians, they are to have all things
in common, in what do they differ from them, or what will they gain by
submitting to their government? Or, upon what principle would they
submit, unless indeed the governing class adopt the ingenious policy of
the Cretans, who give their slaves the same institutions as their own, but
forbid them gymnastic exercises and the possession of arms. If, on the
other hand, the inferior classes are to be like other cities in respect of
marriage and property, what will be the form of the community? Must it
not contain two states in one, each hostile to the other? He makes the
guardians into a mere occupying garrison, while the husbandmen and
artisans and the rest are the real citizens. But if so the suits and quarrels,
and all the evils which Socrates affirms to exist in other states, will exist
equally among them. He says indeed that, having so good an education,
the citizens will not need many laws, for example laws about the city or
about the markets; but then he confines his education to the guardians.
Again, he makes the husbandmen owners of the property upon condition
of their paying a tribute. But in that case they are likely to be much more
unmanageable and conceited than the Helots, or Penestae, or slaves in
general. And whether community of wives and property be necessary for
the lower equally with the higher class or not, and the questions akin to
this, what will be the education, form of government, laws of the lower
class, Socrates has nowhere determined: neither is it easy to discover this,
nor is their character of small importance if the common life of the guardians is to be maintained.

Again, if Socrates makes the women common, and retains private
property, the men will see to the fields, but who will see to the house?
And who will do so if the agricultural class have both their property and
their wives in common? Once more: it is absurd to argue, from the
analogy of the animals, that men and women should follow the same
pursuits, for animals have not to manage a household. The government,
too, as constituted by Socrates, contains elements of danger; for he makes
the same persons always rule. And if this is often a cause of disturbance
among the meaner sort, how much more among high-spirited warriors?
But that the persons whom he makes rulers must be the same is evident;
for the gold which the God mingles in the souls of men is not at one
time given to one, at another time to another, but always to the same: as
he says, 'God mingles gold in some, and silver in others, from their very
birth; but brass and iron in those who are meant to be artisans and husbandmen'. Again, he deprives the guardians even of happiness, and says
that the legislator ought to make the whole state happy. But the whole
cannot be happy unless most, or all, or some of its parts enjoy happiness.

In this respect happiness is not like the even principle in numbers, which may exist only in the whole, but in neither of the parts; not so happiness. And if the guardians are not happy, who are? Surely not the artisans, or the common people. The Republic of which Socrates discourses has all these difficulties, and others quite as great.

The same, or nearly the same, objections apply to Plato's later work, the *Laws*, and therefore we had better examine briefly the constitution which is therein described. In the *Republic,* Socrates has definitely settled in all a few questions only; such as the community of women and children, the community of property, and the constitution of the state. The population is divided into two classes—one of husbandmen, and the other of warriors; from this latter is taken a third class of counsellors and rulers of the state. But Socrates has not determined whether the husbandmen and artisans are to have a share in the government, and whether they, too, are to carry arms and share in military service, or not. He certainly thinks that the women ought to share in the education of the guardians, and to fight by their side. The remainder of the work is filled up with digressions foreign to the main subject, and with discussions about the education of the guardians. In the *Laws* there is hardly anything but laws; not much is said about the constitution. This, which he had intended to make more of the ordinary type, he gradually brings round to the other or ideal form. For with the exception of the community of women and property, he supposes everything to be the same in both states; there is to be the same education; the citizens of both are to live free from servile occupations, and there are to be common meals in both. The only difference is that in the *Laws*, the common meals are extended to women, and the warriors number 5000, but in the *Republic* only 1000.

The discourses of Socrates are never commonplace; they always exhibit grace and originality and thought; but perfection in everything can hardly be expected. We must not overlook the fact that the number of 5000 citizens, just now mentioned, will require a territory as large as Babylon, or some other huge site, if so many persons are to be supported in idleness, together with their women and attendants, who will be a multitude many times as great. In framing an ideal we may assume what we wish, but should avoid impossibilities.

It is said that the legislator ought to have his eye directed to two points—the people and the country. But neighbouring countries also must not be forgotten by him, firstly because the state for which he legislates is to have a political and not an isolated life. For a state must have such a military force as will be serviceable against her neighbours, and not merely useful at home. Even if the life of action is not admitted to be the best, either for individuals or states, still a city should be formidable to enemies, whether invading or retreating.

There is another point: Should not the amount of property be defined in some way which differs from this by being clearer? For Socrates says that a man should have so much property as will enable him to live temperately, which is only a way of saying 'to live well'; this is too general a conception. Further, a man may live temperately and yet miserably. A better definition would be that a man must have so much property as will enable him to live not only temperately but liberally; if the two are parted, liberality will combine with luxury; temperance will be associated with toil. For liberality and temperance are the only eligible qualities which have to do with the use of property. A man cannot use property with mildness or courage, but temperately and liberally he may; and therefore the practice of these virtues is inseparable from property. There is an inconsistency, too, in equalizing the property and not regulating the number of the citizens; the population is to remain unlimited, and he thinks that it will be sufficiently equalized by a certain number of marriages being unfruitful, however many are born to others, because he finds this to be the case in existing states. But greater care will be required than now; for among ourselves, whatever may be the number of citizens, the property is always distributed among them, and therefore no one is in want; but, if the property were incapable of division as in the *Laws*, the supernumeraries, whether few or many, would get nothing. One would have thought that it was even more necessary to limit population than property; and that the limit should be fixed by calculating the chances of mortality in the children, and of sterility in married persons. The neglect of this subject, which in existing states is so common, is a never-failing cause of poverty among the citizens; and poverty is the parent of revolution and crime. Pheidon the Corinthian, who was one of the most ancient legislators, thought that the families and the number of citizens ought to remain the same, although originally all the lots may have been of different sizes: but in the *Laws* the opposite principle is maintained. What in our opinion is the right arrangement will have to be explained hereafter.

There is another omission in the *Laws*: Socrates does not tell us how the rulers differ from their subjects; he only says that they should be related as the warp and the woof, which are made out of different wools. He allows that a man's whole property may be increased fivefold, but why should not his land also increase to a certain extent? Again, will the good management of a household be promoted by his arrangement of homesteads? For he assigns to each individual two homesteads in separate places, and it is difficult to live in two houses.

The whole system of government tends to be neither democracy nor oligarchy, but something in a mean between them, which is usually called a polity, and is composed of the heavy-armed soldiers. Now, if he intended to frame a constitution which would suit the greatest number of states, he was very likely right, but not if he meant to say that this constitutional form came nearest to his first or ideal state; for many would prefer the Lacedaemonian, or, possibly, some other more aristocratic government. Some, indeed, say that the best constitution is a combination of all existing forms, and they praise the Lacedaemonian because it is made up of oligarchy, monarchy, and democracy, the king forming the monarchy, and the council of elders the oligarchy, while the democratic element is represented by the Ephors; for the Ephors are selected from the people. Others, however, declare the Ephoralty to be a tyranny, and find the element of democracy in the common meals and in the habits of daily life. In the *Laws* it is maintained that the best constitution is made up of democracy and tyranny, which are either not constitutions at all, or are the worst of all. But they are nearer the truth who combine many forms; for the constitution is better which is made up of more numerous elements. The constitution proposed in the *Laws* has no element of monarchy at all; it is nothing but oligarchy and democracy, leaning rather to oligarchy. This is seen in the mode of appointing magistrates; for although the appointment of them by lot from among those who have been already selected combines both elements, the way in which the rich are compelled by law to attend the assembly and vote for magistrates or discharge other political duties, while the rest may do as they like, and the endeavour to have the greater number of the magistrates appointed out of the richer classes and the highest officers selected from those who have the greatest incomes, both these are oligarchical features. The oligarchical principle prevails also in the choice of the council, for all are compelled to choose, but the compulsion extends only to the choice out of the first class, and of an equal number out of the second class and out of the third class, but not in this latter case to all the voters but to those of the first three classes; and the selection of candidates out of the fourth class is only compulsory on the first and second. Then, from the persons so chosen, he says that there ought to be an equal number of each class selected. Thus a preponderance will be given to the better sort of people, who have the larger incomes, because many of the lower classes, not being compelled, will not vote. These considerations, and others which will be adduced when the time comes for examining similar polities, tend to show

that states like Plato's should not be composed of democracy and monarchy. There is also a danger in electing the magistrates out of a body
who are themselves elected; for, if but a small number choose to combine,
the elections will always go as they desire. Such is the constitution which
is described in the *Laws*.

Other constitutions have been proposed; some by private persons,
others by philosophers and statesmen, which all come nearer to established
or existing ones than either of Plato's. No one else has introduced such
novelties as the community of women and children, or public tables for
women: other legislators begin with what is necessary. In the opinion of
some, the regulation of property is the chief point of all, that being the
question upon which all revolutions turn. This danger was recognized
by Phaleas of Chalcedon, who was the first to affirm that the citizens of
a state ought to have equal possessions. He thought that in a new colony
the equalization might be accomplished without difficulty, not so easily
when a state was already established; and that then the shortest way of
compassing the desired end would be for the rich to give and not to
receive marriage portions, and for the poor not to give but to receive them.

Plato in the *Laws* was of opinion that, to a certain extent, accumulation should be allowed, forbidding, as I have already observed, any citizen
to possess more than five times the minimum qualification. But those who
make such laws should remember what they are apt to forget—that the
legislator who fixes the amount of property should also fix the number of
children; for, if the children are too many for the property, the law
must be broken. And, besides the violation of the law, it is a bad thing
that many from being rich should become poor; for men of ruined fortunes are sure to stir up revolutions. That the equalization of property
exercises an influence on political society was clearly understood even
by some of the old legislators. Laws were made by Solon and others pro-
hibiting an individual from possessing as much land as he pleased; and
there are other laws in states which forbid the sale of property: among
the Locrians, for example, there is a law that a man is not to sell his
property unless he can prove unmistakably that some misfortune has befallen him. Again, there have been laws which enjoin the preservation of
the original lots. Such a law existed in the island of Leucas, and the abro-
gation of it made the constitution too democratic, for the rulers no longer
had the prescribed qualification. Again, where there is equality of property, the amount may be either too large or too small, and the possessor
may be living either in luxury or penury. Clearly, then, the legislator
ought not only to aim at the equalization of properties, but at moderation in their amount. Further, if he prescribe this moderate amount

equally to all, he will be no nearer the mark; for it is not the possessions but the desires of mankind which require to be equalized, and this is impossible, unless a sufficient education is provided by the laws. But Phaleas will probably reply that this is precisely what he means; and that, in his opinion, there ought to be in states, not only equal property, but equal education. Still he should tell precisely what he means; and what, in his opinion, there ought to be in having one and the same for all, if it is of a sort that predisposes men to avarice, or ambition, or both. Moreover, civil troubles arise, not only out of the inequality of property, but out of the inequality of honour, though in opposite ways. For the common people quarrel about the inequality of property, the higher class about the equality of honour; as the poet says—

The bad and good alike in honour share.

There are crimes of which the motive is want; and for these Phaleas expects to find a cure in the equalization of property, which will take away from a man the temptation to be a highwayman, because he is hungry or cold. But want is not the sole incentive to crime; men also wish to enjoy themselves and not to be in a state of desire—they wish to cure some desire, going beyond the necessities of life, which preys upon them; nay, this is not the only reason—they may desire superfluities in order to enjoy pleasures unaccompanied with pain, and therefore they commit crimes.

Now what is the cure of these three disorders? Of the first, moderate possessions and occupation; of the second, habits of temperance; as to the third, if any desire pleasures which depend on themselves, they will find the satisfaction of their desires nowhere but in philosophy; for all other pleasures we are dependent on others. The fact is that the greatest crimes are caused by excess and not by necessity. Men do not become tyrants in order that they may not suffer cold; and hence great is the honour bestowed, not on him who kills a thief, but on him who kills a tyrant. Thus we see that the institutions of Phaleas avail only against petty crimes.

There is another objection to them. They are chiefly designed to promote the internal welfare of the state. But the legislator should consider also its relation to neighbouring nations, and to all who are outside of it. The government must be organized with a view to military strength; and of this he has said not a word. And so with respect to property: there should not only be enough to supply the internal wants of the state, but also to meet dangers coming from without. The property of the state should not be so large that more powerful neighbours may be tempted by it, while the owners are unable to repel the invaders; nor yet so small that the state is unable to maintain a war even against states of equal power, and of the same character. Phaleas has not laid down any rule; but we should bear in mind that abundance of wealth is an advantage. The best limit will probably be, that a more powerful neighbour must have no inducement to go to war with you by reason of the excess of your wealth, but only such as he would have had if you had possessed less. There is a story that Eubulus, when Autophradates was going to besiege Atarneus, told him to consider how long the operation would take, and then reckon up the cost which would be incurred in the time. 'For', said he, 'I am willing for a smaller sum than that to leave Atarneus at once'. These words of Eubulus made an impression on Autophradates, and he desisted from the siege.

The equalization of property is one of the things that tend to prevent the citizens from quarrelling. Not that the gain in this direction is very great. For the nobles will be dissatisfied because they think themselves worthy of more than an equal share of honours; and this is often found to be a cause of sedition and revolution. And the avarice of mankind is insatiable; at one time two obols was pay enough; but now, when this sum has become customary, men always want more and more without end; for it is of the nature of desire not to be satisfied, and most men live only for the gratification of it. The beginning of reform is not so much to equalize property as to train the nobler sort of natures not to desire more, and to prevent the lower from getting more; that is to say, they must be kept down, but not ill-treated. Besides, the equalization proposed by Phaleas is imperfect; for he only equalizes land, whereas a man may be rich also in slaves, and cattle, and money, and in the abundance of what are called his movables. Now either all these things must be equalized, or some limit must be imposed on them, or they must all be let alone. It would appear that Phaleas is legislating for a small city only, if, as he supposes, all the artisans are to be public slaves and not to form a supplementary part of the body of citizens. But if there is a law that artisans are to be public slaves, it should only apply to those engaged on public works, as at Epidamnus, or at Athens on the plan which Diophantus once introduced.

From these observations any one may judge how far Phaleas was wrong or right in his ideas.

St. Augustine on PLATO

Of the Socratic Philosophy

Socrates is said to have been the first who directed the entire effort of philosophy to the correction and regulation of morals, all who went before him having expended their greatest efforts in the investigation of physical, that is, natural phenomena. However, it seems to me that it cannot be certainly discovered whether Socrates did this because he was wearied of obscure and uncertain things, and so wished to direct his mind to the discovery of something manifest and certain, which was necessary in order to obtain a blessed life—that one great object toward which the labor, vigilance, and industry of all philosophers seem to have been directed—or whether (as some yet more favorable to him suppose) he did it because he was unwilling that minds defiled with earthly desires should essay to raise themselves upward to divine things. For he saw that the causes of things were sought for by them—which causes he believed to be ultimately reducible to nothing else than the will of the one true and supreme God—and on this account he thought they could only be comprehended by a purified mind; and therefore that all diligence ought to be given to the purification of the life by good morals, in order that the mind, delivered from the depressing weight of lusts, might raise itself upward by its native vigor to eternal things, and might, with purified understanding, contemplate that nature which is incorporeal and unchangeable light, where live the causes of all created natures. It is evident, however, that he hunted out and pursued, with a wonderful pleasantness of style and argument, and with a most pointed and insinuating urbanity, the foolishness of ignorant men, who thought that they knew this or that—sometimes confessing his own ignorance, and sometimes dissimulating his knowledge, even in those very moral questions to which he seems to have directed the whole force of his mind. And hence there arose hostility against him, which ended in his being calumniously impeached, and condemned to death. Afterwards, however, that very city of the Athenians, which had publicly condemned him, did publicly bewail him—the popular indignation having turned with such vehemence on his accusers, that one of them

[From St. Augustine, *The City of God* (trans. Marcus Dods, in vol. II of *A Select Library of the Nicene and Post-Nicene Fathers of the Christian Church*, ed. Philip Schaff, Buffalo, 1887).]

perished by the violence of the multitude, while the other only escaped a like punishment by voluntary and perpetual exile.

Illustrious, therefore, both in his life and in his death, Socrates left very many disciples of his philosophy, who vied with one another in desire for proficiency in handling those moral questions which concern the chief good (*summum bonum*), the possession of which can make a man blessed; and because, in the disputations of Socrates, where he raises all manner of questions, makes assertions, and then demolishes them, it did not evidently appear what he held to be the chief good, every one took from these disputations what pleased him best, and every one placed the final good in whatever it appeared to himself to consist. Now, that which is called the final good is that at which, when one has arrived, he is blessed. But so diverse were the opinions held by those followers of Socrates concerning this final good, that (a thing scarcely to be credited with respect to the followers of one master) some placed the chief good in pleasure, as Aristippus, others in virtue, as Antisthenes. Indeed, it is tedious to recount the various opinions of various disciples.

Concerning Plato, the Chief among the Disciples of Socrates, and His Threefold Division of Philosophy

But, among the disciples of Socrates, Plato was the one who shone with a glory which far excelled that of the others, and who not unjustly eclipsed them all. By birth, an Athenian of honorable parentage, he far surpassed his fellow-disciples in natural endowments, of which he was possessed in a wonderful degree. Yet, deeming himself and the Socratic discipline far from sufficient for bringing philosophy to perfection, he travelled as extensively as he was able, going to every place famed for the cultivation of any science of which he could make himself master. Thus he learned from the Egyptians whatever they held and taught as important; and from Egypt, passing into those parts of Italy which were filled with the fame of the Pythagoreans, he mastered, with the greatest facility, and under the most eminent teachers, all the Italic philosophy which was then in vogue. And, as he had a peculiar love for his master Socrates, he made him the speaker in all his dialogues, putting into his mouth whatever he had learned, either from others, or from the efforts of his own powerful intellect, tempering even his moral disputations with the grace and politeness of the Socratic style. And, as the study of wisdom consists in action and contemplation, so that one part of it may be called active, and the other contemplative—the active part having reference to the conduct of life, that is, to the regulation of morals, and the contemplative part to the investigation into the causes of nature and into pure truth—Socrates is said to have excelled in the active part of that study, while Pythagoras gave more attention to its contemplative part, on which he brought to bear all the force of his great intellect. To Plato is given the praise of having perfected philosophy by combining both parts into one. He then divides it into three parts—the first moral, which is chiefly occupied with action; the second natural, of which the object is contemplation; and the third rational, which discriminates between the true and the false. And though this last is necessary both to action and contemplation, it is contemplation, nevertheless, which lays peculiar claim to the office of investigating the nature of truth. Thus this tripartite division is not contrary to that which made the study of wisdom to consist in action and contemplation. Now, as to what Plato thought with respect to each of these parts— that is, what he believed to be the end of all actions, the cause of all natures, and the light of all intelligences—it would be a question too long to discuss, and about which we ought not to make any rash affirmation. For, as Plato liked and constantly affected the well-known method of his master Socrates, namely, that of dissimulating his knowledge or his opinions, it is not easy to discover clearly what he himself thought on various matters, any more than it is to discover what were the real opinions of Socrates. We must, nevertheless, insert into our work certain of those opinions which he expresses in his writings, whether he himself uttered them, or narrates them as expressed by others, and seems himself to approve of—opinions sometimes favorable to the true religion, which our faith takes up and defends, and sometimes contrary to it, as, for example, in the questions concerning the existence of one God or of many, as it relates to the truly blessed life which is to be after death. For those who are praised as having most closely followed Plato, who is justly preferred to all the other philosophers of the Gentiles, and who are said to have manifested the greatest acuteness in understanding him, do perhaps entertain such an idea of God as to admit that in Him are to be found the cause of existence, the ultimate reason for the understanding, and the end in reference to which the whole life is to be regulated. Of these three things, the first is understood to pertain to the natural, the second to the rational, and the third to the moral part of philosophy. For if man has been so created as to attain, through that which is most excellent in him, to that which excels all things—that is, to the one true and absolutely good God, without whom no nature exists, no doctrine instructs, no exercise profits—let Him be sought in whom all things are secure to us, let Him be discovered in whom all truth becomes certain to us, let Him be loved in whom all becomes right to us.

That It Is Especially with the Platonists That We Must Carry on Our Disputations on Matters of Theology, Their Opinions Being Preferable to Those of All Other Philosophers

If, then, Plato defined the wise man as one who imitates, knows, loves this God, and who is rendered blessed through fellowship with Him in His own blessedness, why discuss with the other philosophers? It is evident that none come nearer to us than the Platonists. To them, therefore, let that fabulous theology give place which delights the minds of men with the crimes of the gods; and that civil theology also, in which impure demons, under the name of gods, have seduced the peoples of the earth given up to earthly pleasures, desiring to be honored by the errors of men, and by filling the minds of their worshippers with impure desires, exciting them to make the representation of their crimes one of the rites of their worship, whilst they themselves found in the spectators of these exhibitions a most pleasing spectacle—a theology in which, whatever was honorable in the temple, was defiled by its mixture with the obscenity of the theatre, and whatever was base in the theatre was vindicated by the abominations of the temples. To these philosophers also the interpretations of Varro must give place, in which he explains the sacred rites as having reference to heaven and earth, and to the seeds and operations of perishable things; for, in the first place, those rites have not the signification which he would have men believe is attached to them, and therefore truth does not follow him in his attempt so to interpret them; and even if they had this signification, still those things ought not to be worshipped by the rational soul as its god which are placed below it in the scale of nature, nor ought the soul to prefer to itself as gods things to which the true God has given it the preference. The same must be said of those writings pertaining to the sacred rites, which Numa Pompilius took care to conceal by causing them to be buried along with himself, and which, when they were afterwards turned up by the plough, were burned by order of the senate. And to treat Numa with all honor, let us mention as belonging to the same rank as these writings that which Alexander of Macedon wrote to his mother as communicated to him by Leo, an Egyptian high priest. In this letter not only Picus and Faunus, and Aeneas and Romulus or even Hercules, and Aesculapius and Liber, born of Semele, and the twin sons of Tyndareus, or any other mortals who have been deified, but even the principal gods themselves, to whom Cicero, in his Tusculan questions, alludes without mentioning their names, Jupiter, Juno, Saturn, Vulcan, Vesta, and many others whom Varro attempts to identify with the parts or the elements of the world, are shown to have been men. There is, as we have said, a similarity between this case and that of Numa; for the priest being afraid because he had revealed a mystery, earnestly begged of Alexander to command his mother to burn the letter which conveyed these communications to her. Let these two theologies, then, the fabulous and the civil, give place to the Platonic philosophers, who have recognized the true God as the author of all things, the source of the light of truth, and the bountiful bestower of all blessedness. And not these only, but to these great acknowledgers of so great a God, those philosophers must yield who, having their mind enslaved to their body, supposed the principles of all things to be material; as Thales, who held that the first principle of all things was water; Anaximenes, that it was air; the Stoics, that it was fire; Epicurus, who affirmed that it consisted of atoms, that is to say, of minute corpuscles; and many others whom it is needless to enumerate, but who believed that bodies, simple or compound, animate or inanimate, but nevertheless bodies, were the cause and principle of all things. For some of them—as, for instance, the Epicureans—believed that living things could originate from things without life; others held that all things living or without life spring from a living principle, but that, nevertheless, all things, being material, spring from a material principle. For the Stoics thought that fire, that is, one of the four material elements of which this visible world is composed, was both living and intelligent, the maker of the world and of all things contained in it—that it was in fact God. These and others like them have only been able to suppose that which their hearts enslaved to sense have vainly suggested to them. And yet they have within themselves something which they could not see: they represented to themselves inwardly things which they had seen without, even when they were not seeing them, but only thinking of them. But this representation in thought is no longer a body, but only the similitude of a body; and that faculty of the mind by which this similitude of a body is seen is neither a body nor the similitude of a body; and the faculty which judges whether the representation is beautiful or ugly is without doubt superior to the object judged of. This principle is the understanding of man, the rational soul; and it is certainly not a body, since that similitude of a body which it beholds and judges of is itself not a body. The soul is neither earth, nor water, nor air, nor fire, of which four bodies, called the four elements, we see that this world is composed. And if the soul is not a body, how should God, its Creator, be a body? Let all those philosophers, then, give place, as we have said, to the Platonists, and those also who have been ashamed to say that God is a body, but yet have thought that our souls are of the same nature as God. They have not been staggered by the great changeableness of the soul—

an attribute which it would be impious to ascribe to the divine nature—but they say it is the body which changes the soul, for in itself it is unchangeable. As well might they say, "Flesh is wounded by some body, for in itself it is invulnerable." In a word, that which is unchangeable can be changed by nothing, so that that which can be changed by the body cannot properly be said to be immutable.

Concerning the Meaning of the Platonists in That Part of Philosophy Called Physical

These philosophers, then, whom we see not undeservedly exalted above the rest in fame and glory, have seen that no material body is God, and therefore they have transcended all bodies in seeking for God. They have seen that whatever is changeable is not the most high God, and therefore they have transcended every soul and all changeable spirits in seeking the supreme. They have seen also that, in every changeable thing, the form which makes it that which it is, whatever be its mode or nature, can only *be* through Him who truly *is,* because He is unchangeable. And therefore, whether we consider the whole body of the world, its figure, qualities, and orderly movement, and also all the bodies which are in it; or whether we consider all life, either that which nourishes and maintains, as the life of trees, or that which, besides this, has also sensation, as the life of beasts; or that which adds to all these intelligence, as the life of man; or that which does not need the support of nutriment, but only maintains, feels, understands, as the life of angels—all can only *be* through Him who absolutely *is.* For to Him it is not one thing to *be,* and another to live, as though He could *be,* not living; nor is it to Him one thing to live, and another thing to understand, as though He could live, not understanding; nor is it to Him one thing to understand, another thing to be blessed, as though He could understand and not be blessed. But to Him to live, to understand, to be blessed, are to *be.* They have understood, from this unchangeableness and this simplicity, that all things must have been made by Him, and that He could Himself have been made by none. For they have considered that whatever *is* is either body or life, and that life is something better than body, and that the nature of body is sensible, and that of life intelligible. Therefore they have preferred the intelligible nature to the sensible. We mean by sensible things such things as can be perceived by the sight and touch of the body; by intelligible things, such as can be understood by the sight of the mind. For there is no corporeal beauty, whether in the condition of a body, as figure, or in its movement, as in music, of which it is not the mind that judges. But this could never have been, had there not existed in the mind itself a superior form of these things, without bulk, without noise of voice, without space and time. But even in respect of these things, had the mind not been mutable, it would not have been possible for one to judge better than another with regard to sensible forms. He who is clever, judges better than he who is slow, he who is skilled than he who is unskillful, he who is practised than he who is unpractised; and the same person judges better after he has gained experience than he did before. But that which is capable of more and less is mutable; whence able men, who have thought deeply on these things, have gathered that the first form is not to be found in those things whose form is changeable. Since, therefore, they saw that body and mind might be more or less beautiful in form, and that, if they wanted form, they could have no existence, they saw that there is some existence in which is the first form, unchangeable, and therefore not admitting of degrees of comparison, and in that they most rightly believed was the first principle of things which was not made, and by which all things were made. Therefore that which is known of God He manifested to them when His invisible things were seen by them, being understood by those things which have been made; also His eternal power and Godhead by whom all visible and temporal things have been created.[1] We have said enough upon that part of theology which they call physical, that is, natural.

How Much the Platonists Are to Be Held as Excelling Other Philosophers in Logic, i.e., Rational Philosophy

Then, again, as far as regards the doctrine which treats of that which they call logic, that is, rational philosophy, far be it from us to compare them with those who attributed to the bodily senses the faculty of discriminating truth, and thought, that all we learn is to be measured by their untrustworthy and fallacious rules. Such were the Epicureans, and all of the same school. Such also were the Stoics, who ascribed to the bodily senses that expertness in disputation which they so ardently love, called by them dialectic, asserting that from the senses the mind conceives the notions (ἔννοιαι) of those things which they explicate by definition. And hence is developed the whole plan and connection of their learning and teaching. I often wonder, with respect to this, how they can say that none are beautiful but the wise; for by what bodily sense have they perceived that beauty, by what eyes of the flesh have they seen wisdom's comeliness of form? Those, however, whom we justly rank before

[1] Rom. i. 19, 20.

all others, have distinguished those things which are conceived by the
mind from those which are perceived by the senses, neither taking away
from the senses anything to which they are competent, nor attributing to
them anything beyond their competency. And the light of our understandings, by which all things are learned by us, they have affirmed to be
that selfsame God by whom all things were made.

That the Platonists Hold the First Rank in Moral Philosophy Also

The remaining part of philosophy is morals, or what is called by the
Greeks ἠθική, in which is discussed the question concerning the chief good
—that which will leave us nothing further to seek in order to be blessed,
if only we make all our actions refer to it, and seek it not for the sake of
something else, but for its own sake. Therefore it is called the end, because we wish other things on account of it, but itself only for its own
sake. This beatific good, therefore, according to some, comes to a man
from the body, according to others, from the mind, and, according to
others, from both together. For they saw that man himself consists of
soul and body; and therefore they believed that from either of these two,
or from both together, their well-being must proceed, consisting in a certain final good, which could render them blessed, and to which they might
refer all their actions, not requiring anything ulterior to which to refer
that good itself. This is why those who have added a third kind of good
things, which they call extrinsic—as honor, glory, wealth, and the like—
have not regarded them as part of the final good, that is, to be sought
after for their own sake, but as things which are to be sought for the sake
of something else, affirming that this kind of good is good to the good,
and evil to the evil. Wherefore, whether they have sought the good of
man from the mind or from the body, or from both together, it is still
only from man they have supposed that it must be sought. But they who
have sought it from the body have sought it from the inferior part of
man; they who have sought it from the mind, from the superior part;
and they who have sought it from both, from the whole man. Whether,
therefore, they have sought it from any part, or from the whole man, still
they have only sought it from man; nor have these differences, being
three, given rise only to three dissentient sects of philosophers, but to
many. For diverse philsophers have held diverse opinions, both concerning the good of the body, and the good of the mind, and the good of both
together. Let, therefore, all these give place to those philosophers who have
not affirmed that a man is blessed by the enjoyment of the body, or by
the enjoyment of the mind, but by the enjoyment of God—enjoying Him,

however, not as the mind does the body or itself, or as one friend enjoys another, but as the eye enjoys light, if, indeed, we may draw any comparison between these things. But what the nature of this comparison is, will, if God help me, be shown in another place, to the best of my ability. At present, it is sufficient to mention that Plato determined the final good to be to live according to virtue, and affirmed that he only can attain to virtue who knows and imitates God—which knowledge and imitation are the only cause of blessedness. Therefore he did not doubt that to philosophize is to love God, whose nature is incorporeal. Whence it certainly follows that the student of wisdom, that is, the philosopher, will then become blessed when he shall have begun to enjoy God. For though he is not necessarily blessed who enjoys that which he loves (for many are miserable by loving that which ought not to be loved, and still more miserable when they enjoy it), nevertheless no one is blessed who does not enjoy that which he loves. For even they who love things which ought not to be loved do not count themselves blessed by loving merely, but by enjoying them. Who, then, but the most miserable will deny that he is blessed, who enjoys that which he loves, and loves the true and highest good? But the true and highest good, according to Plato, is God, and therefore he would call him a philosopher who loves God; for philosophy is directed to the obtaining of the blessed life, and he who loves God is blessed in the enjoyment of God.

Concerning That Philosophy Which Has Come Nearest to the Christian Faith

Whatever philosophers, therefore, thought concerning the supreme God, that He is both the maker of all created things, the light by which things are known, and the good in reference to which things are to be done; that we have in Him the first principle of nature, the truth of doctrine, and the happiness of life—whether these philosophers may be more suitably called Platonists, or whether they may give some other name to their sect; whether, we say, that only the chief men of the Ionic school, such as Plato himself, and they who have well understood him, have thought thus; or whether we also include the Italic school, on account of Pythagoras and the Pythagoreans, and all who may have held like opinions; and, lastly, whether also we include all who have been held wise men and philosophers among all nations who are discovered to have seen and taught this, be they Atlantics, Libyans, Egyptians, Indians, Persians, Chaldeans, Scythians, Gauls, Spaniards, or of other nations—we prefer these to all other philosophers, and confess that they approach nearest to us.

*That the Excellency of the Christian Religion Is Above All
the Science of Philosophers*

For although a Christian man instructed only in ecclesiastical literature may perhaps be ignorant of the very name of Platonists, and may
not even know that there have existed two schools of philosophers speaking the Greek tongue, to wit, the Ionic and Italic, he is nevertheless not so
deaf with respect to human affairs, as not to know that philosophers profess the study, and even the possession, of wisdom. He is on his guard,
however, with respect to those who philosophize according to the elements
of this world, not according to God, by whom the world itself was made;
for he is warned by the precept of the apostle, and faithfully hears what
has been said, "Beware that no one deceive you through philosophy and
vain deceit, according to the elements of the world." [2] Then, that he may
not suppose that all philosophers are such as do this, he hears the same
apostle say concerning certain of them, "Because that which is known of
God is manifest among them, for God has manifested it to them. For His
invisible things from the creation of the world are clearly seen, being understood by the things which are made, also His eternal power and Godhead." [3] And, when speaking to the Athenians, after having spoken a
mighty thing concerning God, which few are able to understand, "In Him
we live, and move, and have our being," [4] he goes on to say, "As certain
also of your own have said." He knows well, too, to be on his guard
against even these philosophers in their errors. For where it has been said
by him that God has manifested to them by those things which are made
His invisible things, that they might be seen by the understanding, there it
has also been said that they did not rightly worship God Himself, because they paid divine honors, which are due to Him alone, to other
things also to which they ought not to have paid them—"because, knowing God, they glorified Him not as God: neither were thankful, but became vain in their imaginations, and their foolish heart was darkened.
Professing themselves to be wise, they became fools, and changed the
glory of the incorruptible God into the likeness of the image of corruptible
man, and of birds, and fourfooted beasts, and creeping things" [5]—where
the apostle would have us understand him as meaning the Romans, and
Greeks, and Egyptians, who gloried in the name of wisdom; but concerning this we will dispute with them afterwards. With respect, however,
to that wherein they agree with us we prefer them to all others, namely,
concerning the one God, the author of this universe, who is not only above

---

[2] Col. ii. 8.

[3] Rom. i. 19, 20.

[4] Acts xvii. 28.

[5] Rom. i. 21–23.

every body, being incorporeal, but also above all souls, being incorruptible —our principle, our light, our good. And though the Christian man, being ignorant of their writings, does not use in disputation words which he has not learned—not calling that part of philosophy natural (which is the Latin term), or physical (which is the Greek one), which treats of the investigation of nature; or that part rational, or logical, which deals with the question how truth may be discovered; or that part moral, or ethical, which concerns morals, and shows how good is to be sought, and evil to be shunned—he is not, therefore, ignorant that it is from the one true and supremely good God that we have that nature in which we are made in the image of God, and that doctrine by which we know Him and ourselves, and that grace through which, by cleaving to Him, we are blessed. This, therefore, is the cause why we prefer these to all the others, because, while other philosophers have worn out their minds and powers in seeking the causes of things, and endeavoring to discover the right mode of learning and of living, these, by knowing God, have found where resides the cause by which the universe has been constituted, and the light by which truth is to be discovered, and the fountain at which felicity is to be drunk. All philosophers, then, who have had these thoughts concerning God, whether Platonists or others, agree with us. But we have thought it better to plead our cause with the Platonists, because their writings are better known. For the Greeks, whose tongue holds the highest place among the languages of the Gentiles, are loud in their praises of these writings; and the Latins, taken with their excellence, or their renown, have studied them more heartily than other writings, and, by translating them into our tongue, have given them greater celebrity and notoriety.

How Plato Has Been Able to Approach So Nearly to Christian Knowledge

Certain partakers with us in the grace of Christ wonder when they hear and read that Plato had conceptions concerning God, in which they recognize considerable agreement with the truth of our religion. Some have concluded from this, that when he went to Egypt he had heard the prophet Jeremiah, or, while travelling in the same country, had read the prophetic scriptures, which opinion I myself have expressed in certain of my writings.[6] But a careful calculation of dates, contained in chronological history, shows that Plato was born about a hundred years after the time in which Jeremiah prophesied, and, as he lived eighty-one years, there are found to have been about seventy years from his death to that time when Ptolemy, king of Egypt, requested the prophetic scriptures of the Hebrew

[6] *De Doctrina Christiana*, ii. 43.

people to be sent to him from Judea, and committed them to seventy Hebrews, who also knew the Greek tongue, to be translated and kept. Therefore, on that voyage of his, Plato could neither have seen Jeremiah, who was dead so long before, nor have read those same scriptures which had not yet been translated into the Greek language, of which he was a master, unless, indeed, we say that, as he was most earnest in the pursuit of knowledge, he also studied those writings through an interpreter, as he did those of the Egyptians—not, indeed, writing a translation of them (the facilities for doing which were only gained even by Ptolemy in return for munificent acts of kindness, though fear of his kingly authority might have seemed a sufficient motive), but learning as much as he possibly could concerning their contents by means of conversation. What warrants this supposition are the opening verses of Genesis: "In the beginning God made the heaven and earth. And the earth was invisible, and without order; and darkness was over the abyss: and the Spirit of God moved over the waters." [7] For in the *Timaeus*, when writing on the formation of the world, he says that God first united earth and fire; from which it is evident that he assigns to fire a place in heaven. This opinion bears a certain resemblance to the statement, "In the beginning God made heaven and earth." Plato next speaks of those two intermediary elements, water and air, by which the other two extremes, namely, earth and fire, were mutually united; from which circumstance he is thought to have so understood the words, "The Spirit of God moved over the waters." For, not paying sufficient attention to the designations given by those scriptures to the Spirit of God, he may have thought that the four elements are spoken of in that place, because the air also is called spirit. Then, as to Plato's saying that the philosopher is a lover of God, nothing shines forth more conspicuously in those sacred writings. But the most striking thing in this connection, and that which most of all inclines me almost to assent to the opinion that Plato was not ignorant of those writings, is the answer which was given to the question elicited from the holy Moses when the words of God were conveyed to him by the angel; for, when he asked what was the name of that God who was commanding him to go and deliver the Hebrew people out of Egypt, this answer was given: "I am who am; and thou shalt say to the children of Israel, He who *is* sent me unto you;" [8] as though compared with Him that truly *is*, because He is unchangeable, those things which have been created mutable *are* not—a truth which Plato zealously held, and most diligently commended. And I know not whether this sentiment is anywhere to be found in the books of those who were before Plato, unless in that book

[7] Gen. i. 1, 2.   [8] Ex. iii. 14.

where it is said, "I am who am; and thou shalt say to the children of Israel, *who is* sent me unto you."

Hegel on PLATO

The only point of interest for us in Plato's philosophy of mind is his view of man's moral nature; and this real, practical side of consciousness is Plato's greatest glory, and hence must now be specially dealt with by us. Its form certainly does not suggest that Plato gave himself much trouble to discover a supreme moral principle, as it is now called, which, for the very reason that it is supposed to be all-embracing, has in it a certain lack of content. Neither did he trouble himself about a natural right, which is but a trivial abstraction foisted on to the real practical existence, the right; but it is of man's moral nature that he treats in the Republic. Man's moral nature seems to us to have little to do with the State; to Plato, however, the reality of mind—that is, of mind as opposed to nature—appeared in its highest truth as the organization of a state which, as such, is essentially moral; and he recognized that the moral nature (free will in its rationality) comes to its right, to its reality, only in an actual nation.

We must further remark that in the Republic Plato introduces the investigation of his subject with the object of showing what justice (δικαιοσύνη) is. After much discussion has taken place, and several definitions of justice have been taken into consideration only to be rejected, Plato at last says in his simple way: "The present investigation is very like the case of a man who is required to read small handwriting at a distance; if it were observed that the same letters were to be seen at a shorter distance and of a larger size, he would certainly prefer to read first the letters where they were written larger, and then would be able to read more easily the small letters also. The same plan should be followed now with justice. Justice is not only in the individual, but also in the state, and the state is greater than the individual; justice is therefore imprinted on states in larger characters, and is more easily recognizable." (This is different from what the Stoics say of the wise man.) "It is therefore preferable to consider justice as it is to be found in the state." By making this comparison Plato transforms the question anent justice into an investigation of the state; it is a very simple and graceful transition, though it

[From G. W. F. Hegel, *Lectures on the History of Philosophy*, vol. II (1833, trans. E. S. Haldane and F. H. Simson, Kegan Paul, 1897).]

seems arbitrary. It was great force of insight that really led the ancients to the truth; and what Plato brings forward as merely simplifying the difficulty, may, in fact, be said to exist in the nature of the thing. For it is not convenience which leads him to this position, but the fact that justice can be carried out only in so far as man is a member of a state, for in the state alone is justice present in reality and truth. Justice, not as the understanding, but as mind in its striving to realize itself, is the existence of freedom here and now, the actuality of the self-conscious, intelligent existence in and at home with itself and possessing activity—just as in property, for instance, I place my freedom in this particular thing. But the principle of the state again is the objective reality of justice, the reality in which the whole mind is present and not only the knowledge of myself as this individual. For as the free and reasonable will determines itself, there are laws of freedom; but these laws are nothing else than state-laws, for the Notion of the state implies the existence of a reasoning will. Thus laws have force in the state, and are there matter of practice and of custom; but because self-will is also there in its immediacy, they are not only matter of custom, but must also be a force operating against arbitrary self-will, and showing itself in the courts of justice and in governments. Thus Plato, in order to discern the features of justice, with the instinct of reason fixes his attention on their manner of representation in the state.

Justice in itself is ordinarily represented by us in the form of a natural right, right in a condition of nature; such a condition of nature is, however, a direct moral impossibility. That which is in itself is, by those who do not attain to the universal, held to be something natural, as the necessary moments of the mind are held to be innate ideas. The natural is rather what should be sublated by the mind, and the justice of the condition of nature can only emerge as the absolute injustice of the mind. In contrast with the state, which is the real spirit, the spirit in its simple and as yet unrealized Notion is the abstract implicitude; this Notion must of course precede the construction of its reality; it is this which is conceived of as a condition of nature. We are accustomed to take our start from the fiction of a condition of nature, which is truly no condition of mind, of reasonable will, but of animals among themselves: wherefore Hobbes has justly remarked that the true state of nature is a war of every man against his neighbour. This implicitude of the mind is at the same time the individual man, for in the ordinary conception the universal separates itself from the particular, as if the particular were absolutely and in and for itself what it certainly is, and the Universal did not make it that which it is in truth—as if this were not its essence, but as if the individual element were the most important. The fiction of a state of nature starts from the individuality of the person, his free will, and his relation to other persons according to this free will. Natural justice has thus been a term applied to that which is justice in the individual and for the individual; and the condition of society and of the state has been recognized only as a medium for the individual person, who is the chief end and object. Plato, in direct contrast with this, lays as his foundation the substantial, the universal, and he does this in such a way that the individual as such has this very universal as his end, and the subject has his will, activity, life and enjoyment in the state, so that it may be called his second nature, his habits and his customs. This moral substance which constitutes the spirit, life and Being of individuality, and which is its foundation, systematizes itself into a living, organic whole, and at the same time it differentiates itself into its members, whose activity signifies the production of the whole.

This relation of the Notion to its reality certainly did not come into consciousness with Plato, and thus we do not find in him a philosophic method of construction, which shows first the absolute Idea, then the necessity, inherently existent, for its realization, and this realization itself. The judgment that has been delivered respecting Plato's Republic therefore is that Plato has therein given a so-called ideal for the constitution of a state; this has become proverbial as a *sobriquet*, in the sense that this conception is a chimera, which may be mentally conceived of—and in itself, as Plato describes it, it is doubtless excellent and true—that it is also capable of being carried out, but only on the condition that men should be of an excellence such as may possibly be present among the dwellers in the moon, but that it is not realizable for men like those on the earth. But since men must be taken as they are, this ideal cannot be realized by reason of men's wickedness; and to frame such an ideal is therefore altogether idle.

As to this, the first remark to be made is that in the Christian world in general, there passes current an ideal of a perfect man which certainly cannot be carried out in the great body of a nation. We may, perhaps, see it realized in monks or Quakers, or other similar pious folk, but a set of melancholy specimens such as these could never form a nation, any more than lice or parasitic plants could exist for themselves, or otherwise than on an organic body. If such men were to constitute a nation, there would have to be an end of this lamb-like gentleness, this vanity which occupies itself exclusively with its own individual self, which pets and pampers itself, and ever has the image and consciousness of its own excellence before its eyes. For life in the universal and for the universal demands, not that lame and cowardly gentleness, but gentleness combined with a like measure of energy, and which is not occupied with itself and its own sins, but with the universal and what is to be done for it. They before whose eyes that false ideal floats of course find men to be always compassed with weakness and depravity, and never find that ideal realized. For they raise into importance the veriest trifles, which no reasonable man would give heed to; and they think such weaknesses and defects are present even when they overlook them. But we need not esteem this forbearance to be generosity; for it rather implies a perception on their part that from what they call weakness and defect proceeds their own destruction, which comes to pass from their making such defects of importance. The man who has them is immediately through himself absolved from them, in so far as he makes nothing of them. The crime is a crime only when they are real to him, and his destruction is in holding them to be something real. Such an ideal must therefore not stand in our way, whatever be the fairness of its form, and this even when it does not appear exactly as it does to monks and Quakers, but, for instance, when it is the principle of renouncing sensuous things, and abandoning energy of action, which principle must bring to nought much that would otherwise be held of value. It is contradictory to try to keep intact all our relationships, for in those that otherwise hold good there always is a side where opposition is encountered. Moreover, what I have already said regarding the relation between philosophy and the state shows that the Platonic ideal is not to be taken in this sense. When an ideal has truth in itself through the Notion, it is no chimera, just because it is true, for the truth is no chimera. Such an ideal is therefore nothing idle and powerless, but the real. It is certainly permissible to form wishes, but when pious wishes are all that a man has in regard to the great and true, he may be said to be godless. It is just as if we could do nothing, because everything was so holy and inviolable, or as if we refused to be anything definite, because all that is definite has its defects. The true ideal is not what ought to be real, but what is real, and the only real; if an ideal is held to be too good to exist, there must be some fault in the ideal itself, for which reality is too good. The Platonic Republic would thus be a chimera, not because excellence such as it depicts is lacking to mankind, but because it, this excellence, falls short of man's requirements. For what is real, is rational. The point to know, however, is what exactly is real; in common life all is real, but there is a difference between the phenomenal world and reality. The real has also an external existence, which displays arbitrariness and contingency, like a tree, a house, a plant, which in nature come into existence. What is on the surface in the moral sphere, men's action, involves much that is evil, and might in many ways be better; men will ever be wicked and depraved, but this is not the Idea. If the reality of the substance is recognized, the surface where the passions battle must be penetrated. The temporal and transitory certainty exists, and may cause us trouble enough, but in spite of that it is no true reality, any more than the particularity of the subject, his wishes and inclinations, are so.

In connection with this observation, the distinction is to be called to mind which was drawn when we were speaking above of Plato's Philosophy of Nature: the eternal world, as God holy in Himself, is reality, not a world above us or beyond, but the present world looked at in its truth, and not as it meets the senses of those who hear, see, &c. When we thus study the content of the Platonic Idea, it will become clear that Plato has, in fact, represented Greek morality according to its substantial mode, for it is the Greek state-life which constitutes the true content of the Platonic Republic. Plato is not the man to dabble in abstract theories and principles; his truth-loving mind has recognized and represented the truth, and this could not be anything else than the truth of the world he lived in, the truth of the one spirit which lived in him as well as in Greece. No man can overleap his time, the spirit of his time is his spirit also; but the point at issue is, to recognize that spirit by its content.

On the other hand, a constitution that would be perfect in respect to one nation, is to be regarded as not, perhaps, suitable for every nation. Thus, when it is said that a true constitution does not do for men as they now are, we must no doubt keep in mind that the more excellent a nation's constitution is, it renders the nation also so much the more excellent; but, on the other hand, since the morals commonly practised form the living constitution, the constitution in its abstraction is nothing at all in its independence; it must relate itself to the common morality, and be filled with the living spirit of the people. It can, therefore, certainly not be said that a true constitution suits any and every nation; and it is quite the case that for men as they are—for instance, as they are Iroquois, Russians, French—not every constitution is adapted. For the nation has its place in history. But as the individual man is trained in the state, that is, as individuality is raised into universality, and the child grows into a man, so is every nation trained; or barbarism, the condition in which the nation is a child, passes over into a rational condition. Men do not remain at a standstill, they alter, as likewise do their constitutions. And the question here is, What is the true constitution which the nation must advance towards; just as it is a question which is the true science of mathematics or of anything else, but not whether children or boys should possess this science, as they must rather be first so educated that they may be capable of understanding it. Thus the true constitution stands before the nation of history, so that it may advance towards it. Every nation in course of time makes such alterations in its existing constitution as will bring it nearer to the true constitution. The nation's mind itself shakes off its leading-strings, and the constitution expresses the consciousness of what it is in itself,—the form of truth, of self-knowledge. If a nation can no longer accept as implicitly true what its constitution expresses to it as the truth, if its consciousness or Notion and its actuality are not at one, then the nation's mind is torn asunder. Two things may then occur. First, the nation may either by a supreme internal effort dash into fragments this law which still claims authority, or it may more quietly and slowly effect changes on the yet operative law, which is, however, no longer true morality, but which the mind has already passed beyond. In the second place, a nation's intelligence and strength may not suffice for this, and it may hold to the lower law; or it may happen that another nation has reached its higher constitution, thereby rising in the scale, and the first gives up its nationality and becomes subject to the other. Therefore it is of essential importance to know what the true constitution is; for what is in opposition to it has no stability, no truth, and passes away. It has a temporary existence, but cannot hold its ground; it has been accepted, but cannot secure permanent acceptance; that it must be cast aside, lies in the very nature of the constitution. This insight can be reached through Philosophy alone. Revolutions take place in a state without the slightest violence when the insight becomes universal; institutions, somehow or other, crumble and disappear, each man agrees to give up his right. A government must, however, recognize that the time for this has come; should it, on the contrary, knowing not the truth, cling to temporary institutions, taking what—though recognized—is unessential, to be a bulwark guarding it from the essential (and the essential is what is contained in the Idea), that government will fall, along with its institutions, before the force of mind. The breaking up of its government breaks up the nation itself; a new government arises,—or it may be that the government and the unessential retain the upper hand.

Thus the main thought which forms the groundwork of Plato's Republic is the same which is to be regarded as the principle of the common Greek morality, namely, that established morality has in general the relation of the substantial, and therefore is maintained as divine. This is without question the fundamental determination. The determination which stands in contrast to this substantial relation of the individual to established morality, is the subjective will of the individual, reflective morality. This exists when individuals, instead of being moved to action by respect and reverence for the institutions of the state and of the fatherland, from their own convictions, and after moral deliberation, come of themselves to a decision, and determine their actions accordingly. This principle of subjective freedom is a later growth, it is the principle of our modern days of culture: it, however, entered also into the Greek world, but as the principle of the destruction of Greek state-life. It was looked on as a crime, because the spirit, political constitution, and laws of the Greeks were not, and could not be calculated to admit of the rise of this principle within them. Because these two elements were not homogeneous, traditional and conventional morality in Greece was overthrown. Plato recognized and caught up the true spirit of his times, and brought it forward in a more definite way, in that he desired to make this new principle an impossibility in his Republic. It is thus a substantial position on which Plato takes his stand, seeing that the substantial of his time forms his basis, but this standpoint is at the same time relative only, in so far as it is but a Greek standpoint, and the later principle is consciously banished. This is the universal of Plato's ideal of the state, and it is from this point of view that we must regard it. Investigations as to whether such a state is possible, and the best possible, which start from quite modern points of view, can only lead us astray. In modern states we have freedom of conscience, according to which every individual may demand the right of following out his own interests; but this is excluded from the Platonic idea.

a. I will now indicate more fully the main features, in so far as they possess philosophic interest. Though Plato represents what the state is in its truth, yet this state has a limit, which we shall learn to know, namely, that the individual—in formal justice—is not opposed to this universality, as in the dead constitution of the ideal states founded on the theory of legal right. The content is but the whole; the nature of the individual, no doubt, but as reflecting itself into the universal, not unbending, or as having absolute validity; so that practically the state and the individual are the same in essence. Because Plato thus takes his start from that justice which implies that the just man exists only as a moral member of the state, in dealing with his subject in greater detail, in order to show how this reality of the substantial mind is produced, he in the first place opens up before us the organism of the moral commonwealth, i.e. the differences which lie in the Notion of moral substance. Through the development of these moments it becomes living and existing, but these moments are not independent, for they are held in unity. Plato regards these moments of the moral organism under three aspects, first, as they exist in the state as classes; secondly, as virtues, or moments in morality; thirdly, as moments of the individual subject, in the empirical actions of the will. Plato does not preach the morality of reflection, he shows how traditional morality has a living movement in itself; he demonstrates its functions, its inward organism. For it is inner systematization, as in organic life, and not solid, dead unity, like that of metals, which comes to pass by means of the different functions of the organs which go to make up this living, self-moving unity.

α. Without classes, without this division into great masses, the state has no organism; these great distinctions are the distinction of the substantial. The opposition which first comes before us in the state is that of the universal, in the form of state life and business, and the individual, as life and work for the individual; these two fields of activity are so distinct that one class is assigned to the one, and another to the other. Plato further cites three systems of reality in the moral, the functions (αα) of legislation, counsel, in short, of diligence and foresight in the general behalf, in the interest of the whole as such; (ββ) of defense of the commonwealth against foes from without; (γγ) of care for the individual, the supplying of wants, agriculture, cattle-rearing, the manufacture of clothing and utensils, the building of houses, &c. Speaking generally, this is quite as it should be, and yet it appears to be rather the satisfaction of external necessities, because such wants are found without being developed out of the Idea of mind itself. Further, these distinct functions are allotted to different systems, being assigned to a certain number of individuals specially set apart for the purpose, and this brings about the separate classes of the state, as Plato is altogether opposed to the superficial conception that one and the same must be everything at one time. He accordingly represents three classes, (αα) that of the governors, men of learning and wisdom, (ββ) that of the warriors, (γγ) that of the producers of necessaries, the husbandmen and handicraftsmen. The first he also speaks of as guardians (φύλακας), who are really philosophically educated statesmen, possessing true knowledge; they have the warriors to work on their behalf (ἐπικούρους τε καὶ βοηθούς), but in such a way that there is no line of separation between the civil and military classes, both being united, and the most advanced in years are the guardians. Although Plato does not deduce this division of the classes, they follow from the constitution of the Platonic state, and every state is necessarily a system within itself of these systems. Plato then passes on to particular determinations, which are in some measure trifling, and might with advantage have been dispensed with; for instance, among other things, he goes so far as to settle for the highest rank their special titles, and he states what should be the duties of the nurses.

β. Then Plato points out that the moments which are here realized in the classes, are moral qualities which are present in individuals, and form their true essence, the simple ethical Notion divided into its universal determinations. For he states as the result of this distinction of the classes that through such an organism all virtues are present in the commonwealth; he distinguishes four of these, and they have been named cardinal virtues.

αα. Wisdom (σοφία) or knowledge appears as the first virtue; such a state will be wise and good in counsel, not because of the various kinds of knowledge therein present which have to do with the many particular ordinary occupations falling to the multitude, such as the trade of blacksmith, and the tillage of the soil (in short, what we should call skill in the industrial arts, and in finance). The state is called wise, by reason of the true knowledge which is realized in the presiding and governing class, who advise regarding the whole state, and decide upon the policy that is best, both at home and in relation to foreign states. This faculty of perception is properly the peculiar possession of the smallest class.

ββ. The second virtue is courage (ἀνδρία) which Plato defines as a firm opinion about what may justly and lawfully be considered an object of fear, courage which, in its strength of purpose, remains unshaken either by desires or pleasures. To this virtue corresponds the class of the warriors.

γγ. The third virtue is temperance (σωφροσύνη), the mastery over the desires and passions, which like a harmony pervades the whole; so that, whether understanding, or strength, or numbers, or wealth, or anything else be regarded, the weaker and the stronger work together for one and the same object, and are in agreement one with another. This virtue therefore is not, like wisdom and courage, confined to one part of the state, but like a harmony it is shared by governors and governed alike, and is the virtue of all classes. Notwithstanding that this temperance is the harmony in which all work towards one end, it is yet peculiarly the virtue of the third class, to whom it is allotted to procure the necessaries of life by work, although at the first glance the one does not appear to have much correspondence with the other. But this virtue is present precisely when no moment, no determination or particularity isolates itself; or, more closely viewed in a moral aspect, it is when no want asserts its reality and thus becomes a crime. Now work is just this moment of activity concentrating itself on the particular, which nevertheless goes back into the universal, and is for it. Therefore, if this virtue is universal, it yet has special application to the third class, which at first is the only one to be brought into harmony, as it has not the absolute harmony which the other classes possess in themselves.

δδ. Finally, the fourth virtue is justice, which was what Plato began by considering. This, as right-doing, is to be found in the state when each individual does only one kind of work for the state, that work for which by the original constitution of his nature he is best fitted; so that in this way each man is not a jack-of-all-trades, but all have their special work, young and old, women and children, bond and free, handicraftsmen, rulers and subjects. The first remark we make on this is, that Plato here places justice on a level with the other moments, and it thus appears as one of the four determinations. But he now retracts this statement and makes it justice which first gives to wisdom, courage and temperance the power to exist at all, and when they have once come into existence, the power to continue. This is the reason of his also saying that justice will be met with independently, if only the other virtues spoken of are forthcoming. To express it more definitely, the Notion of justice is the foundation, the Idea of the whole, which falls into organic divisions, so that every part is only, as it were, a moment in the whole, and the whole exists through it. Thus the classes or qualities spoken of are nothing else than the moments of this whole. Justice is only the general and all-pervading quality; but at the same time it implies the independence of every part, to which the state gives liberty of action.

In the second place, it is clear from what he says, that Plato did not understand by justice the rights of property, the meaning which the term commonly bears in jurisprudence, but rather this, that the mind in its totality makes for itself a law as evidence of the existence of its freedom. In a highly abstract sense my personality, my altogether abstract freedom, is present in property. To explain what comes under this science of law, Plato considers on the whole superfluous (De Republica, IV. p. 425 Steph.; p. 176 Bekk.). To be sure we find him giving laws concerning property, police regulations, &c., "But," he says, "to impose laws about such matters on men of noble character does not repay the trouble." In truth, how can we expect to find divine laws in what contains contingencies alone? Even in the Laws he considers ethics chiefly, though he gives a certain amount of attention to the rights of property. But as justice, according to Plato, is really the entire being, which presents itself to the individual in such a way that each man learns to do the work he is born to do as well as it can be done, and does it, it is only as determined individuality that man reaches what is law for him; only thus does he belong to the universal spirit of the state, coming in it to the universal of himself as a "this." While law is a universal with a definite content, and thus a formal universal only, the content in this case is the whole determined individuality, not this or that thing which is mine by the accident of possession; what I properly hold as my own is the perfected possession and use of my nature. To each particular determination justice gives its rights, and thus leads it back into the whole; in this way it is by the particularity of an individual being of necessity developed and brought into actuality, that each man is in his place and fulfils his vocation. Justice, therefore, according to its true conception, is in our eyes freedom in the subjective sense, because it is the attainment of actuality by the reason, and seeing that this right on the part of liberty to attain to actuality is universal, Plato sets up justice as the determination of the whole, indicating that rational freedom comes into existence through the organism of the state,—an existence which is then, as necessary, a mode of nature.

γ. The particular subject, as subject, has in the same way these qualities in himself; and these moments of the subject correspond with the three real moments of the state. That there is thus one rhythm, one type, in the Idea of the state, forms for Plato's state a great and grand basis. This third form, in which the above moments are exhibited, Plato characterizes in the following manner. There manifest themselves in the subject, first of all sundry wants and desires (ἐπιθυμίαι), like hunger and thirst, each of which has something definite as its one and only object. Work for the satisfaction of desires corresponds to the calling of the third class. But, secondly, there is also at the same time to be found in the individual consciousness something else which suspends and hinders the gratification of these desires, and has the mastery over the temptation thus to gratify them; this is reasonableness (λόγος). To this corresponds the class of rulers, the wisdom of the state. Besides these two ideas of the soul there is a third, anger (θυμός), which on one side is allied to the desires, but of which it is just as true that it resists the desires and takes the side of reason. "It may happen that a man has done wrong to another, and suffers hunger and cold at the hands of him whom he considers entitled to inflict them upon him; in this case, the nobler he is, the less will his anger be excited. But it may also happen that he suffers a wrong; if this is the case, he boils and chafes, and takes the side of what he believes to be justice, and endures hunger and cold and other hardships, and overcomes them, and will not desist from the right until he conquers or dies, or is calmed down by reason, as a shepherd quiets his dog." Anger corresponds with the class of the brave defenders in the state; as these grasp their weapons in behalf of reason within the state, so does anger take the part of reason, if it has not been perverted by an evil upbringing. Therefore wisdom in the state is the same as in the individual, and this is true of courage also. For the rest, temperance is the harmony of the several moments of what pertains to nature; and justice, as in external matters it consists in each doing his own duty, so, in the inner life, it consists in each moment of the mind obtaining its right, and not interfering in the affairs of the others, but leaving them do as they will. We have thus the deduction of three moments, where the middle place between universality and particularity is filled by anger in its independence and as directed against the objective: it is the freedom which turns back within itself and acts negatively. Even here, where Plato has no consciousness of his abstract ideas, as he has in the Timaeus, this of a truth is inwardly present to him, and everything is moulded thereby. This is given as the plan according to which Plato draws up the great whole. To fill up the outlines is a mere detail, which in itself has no further interest.

b. In the second place Plato indicates the means of maintaining the state. As, speaking generally, the whole commonwealth rests on common morality as the minds of individuals grown into nature, this question is asked: How does Plato arrange that everyone takes as his own that form of activity for which he is specially marked out, and that it presents itself as the moral acting and willing of the individual,—that everyone, in harmony with temperance, submits to filling this his post? The main point is to train the individuals thereto. Plato would produce this ethical quality directly in the individuals, and first and foremost in the guardians, whose education is therefore the most important part of the whole, and constitutes the very foundation. For as it is to the guardians themselves that the care is committed of producing this ethical quality through maintenance of the laws, in these laws special attention must be given to the guardians' education; after that also to the education of the warriors. The condition of affairs in the industrial class causes the state but little anxiety, "for though cobblers should prove poor and worthless, and should be only in appearance what they ought to be, that is no great misfortune for the state." The education of the presidents should, however, be carried on chiefly by means of philosophic science, which is the knowledge of the universal and absolute. Plato in this passes over the particular means of education, religion, art, science. Further on he speaks again and more in detail on the question of how far music and gymnastic are to be permitted as means. But the poets Homer and Hesiod he banishes from his state, because he thinks their representations of God unworthy. For then began in real earnest an inquiry into the belief in Jupiter and the stories told by Homer, inasmuch as such particular representations had been taken as universal maxims and divine laws. At a certain stage of education childish tales do no harm; but were they to be made the foundation of the truth of morality, as present law, the case would be different. The extermination of the nations which we read of in the writings of the Israelites, the Old Testament, might for instance be taken as a standard of national rights, or we might try to make a precedent of the numerous base acts committed by David, the man of God, or of the horrors which the priesthood, in the person of Samuel, practised and authorized against Saul. Then it would be high time to place these records on a lower level, as something past, something merely historical. Plato would further have preambles to the laws, wherein citizens would be admonished as to their duties, and convinced that these exist, &c. They also should be shown how to choose that which is most excellent, in short, to choose morality.

But here we have a circle: the public life of the state subsists by means of morality, and, conversely, morality subsists by means of institutions. Morals cannot be independent of institutions, that is, institutions cannot be brought to bear on morals through educational establishments or religion only. For institutions must be looked on as the very first condition of morality, for this is the manner in which institutions are subjective. Plato himself gives us to understand how much contradiction he expects to find. And even now his defect is commonly considered to lie in his being too idealistic, while his real deficiency consists in his not being ideal enough. For if reason is the universal force, it is essentially spiritual; thus to the realm of the spiritual belongs subjective freedom, which had already been held up as a principle in the philosophy of Socrates. Therefore reason ought to be the basis of law, and so it is, on the whole. But, on the other hand, conscience, personal conviction,—in short, all the forms of subjective freedom—are essentially therein contained. This subjectivity at first, it is true, stands in opposition to the laws and reason of the state-organism as to the absolute power which desires to appropriate to itself —through the external necessity of wants, in which, however, there is absolute reason—the individual of the family. Individual conscience proceeds from the subjectivity of free-will, connects itself with the whole, chooses a position for itself, and thus makes itself a moral fact. But this moment, this movement of the individual, this principle of subjective freedom, is sometimes ignored by Plato, and sometimes even intentionally disparaged, because it proved itself to be what had wrought the ruin of Greece; and he considers only how the state may best be organized, and not subjective individuality. In passing beyond the principle of Greek morality, which in its substantial liberty cannot brook the rise of subjective liberty, the Platonic philosophy at once grasps the above principle, and in so doing proceeds still farther.

c. In the third place, in regard to the exclusion of the principle of subjective freedom, this forms a chief feature in the Republic of Plato, the spirit of which really consists in the fact, that all aspects in which particularity as such has established its position, are dissolved in the universal,—all men simply rank as man in general.

α. It specially harmonizes with this particular quality of excluding the principle of subjectivity, that Plato in the first place does not allow individuals to choose their own class; this we demand as necessary to freedom. It is not, however, birth which marks off the different ranks, and determines individuals for these; but everyone is tested by the governors of the state, who are the elders of the first class, and have the education of individuals in their hands. According as anyone has natural ability and talents, these elders make choice and selection, and assign each man to a definite occupation. This seems in direct contradiction to our principle, for although it is considered right that to a certain class there should belong a special capacity and skill, it always remains a matter of inclination which class one is to belong to; and with this inclination, as an apparently free choice, the class makes itself for itself. But it is not permitted that another individual should prescribe as to this, or say, for example: "Because you are not serviceable for anything better, you are to be a labourer." Everyone may make the experiment for himself; he must be allowed to decide regarding his own affairs as subject in a subjective manner, by his own free will, as well as in consideration of external circumstances; and nothing must therefore be put in his way if he says, for instance: "I should like to apply myself to study."

β. From this determination it further follows that Plato (De Republica, III. pp. 416, 417 Steph.; pp. 162–164 Bekk.) in like manner altogether abolished in his state the principle of private property. For in it individuality, the individual consciousness, becomes absolute; or the person is looked on as implicit, destitute of all content. In law, as such, I rank as "this" implicitly and explicitly. All rank thus, and I rank only because all rank, or I rank only as universal; but the content of this universality is fixed particularity. When in a question of law we have to do with law, as such, to the judges of the case it matters not a whit whether this or that man actually possesses the house, and likewise the contending parties think nothing of the possession of the thing for which they strive, but of right for right's sake, (as in morality duty is done for duty's sake): thus a firm hold is kept of the abstraction, and from the content of reality abstraction is made. But Being to Philosophy is no abstraction, but the unity of the universal and reality, or its content. The content has therefore weight only in as far as it is negatively posited in the universal; thus only as returning into it, and not absolutely. In so far as I use things,—not in so far as I have them merely in my possession, or as they have worth for me as existent, as definitely fixed on me,—they stand in living relation to me. With Plato, then, those of the other class carry on handicrafts, trade, husbandry, and procure what will satisfy the general requirements, without acquiring personal property by means of their work, for they are all one family, wherein each has his appointed occupation; but the product of the work is common, and he receives as much as he requires both of his own and of the general product. Personal property is a possession which belongs to me as a certain person, and in which my person as such comes into existence, into reality; on this ground Plato excludes it. It remains, however, unexplained how in the development of industries, if there is no hope of acquiring private property, there can be any incentive to activity; for on my being a person of energy very much depends my capacity for holding property. That an end would be put to all strifes and dissensions and hatred and avarice by the abolition of private property, as Plato thinks, (De Republica, V. p. 464 Steph.; pp. 243, 244 Bekk.) may very well be imagined in a general way; but that is only a subordinate result in comparison with the higher and reasonable principle of the right of property: and liberty has actual existence only so far as property falls to the share of the person. In this way we see subjective freedom consciously removed by Plato himself from his state.

γ. For the same reason Plato also abolishes marriage, because it is a connection in which persons of opposite sex, as such, remain mutually bound to one another, even beyond the mere natural connection. Plato does not admit into his state family life—the particular arrangement whereby a family forms a whole by itself,—because the family is nothing but an extended personality, a relationship to others of an exclusive character within natural morality,—which certainly is morality, but morality of such a character as belongs to the individual as particularity. According to the conception of subjective freedom, however, the family is just as necessary, yea, sacred to the individual as is property. Plato, on the contrary, causes children to be taken away from their mothers immediately after birth, and has them gathered together in a special establishment, and reared by nurses taken from among the mothers who gave them birth; he has them brought up in common, so that no mother can possibly recognize her child. There are certainly to be marriage celebrations, and each man is to have his particular wife, but in such a way that the intercourse of man and wife does not pre-suppose a personal inclination, and that it should not be their own pleasure which marks out individuals for one another. The women should bear children from the twentieth to the fortieth year, the men should have wives from the thirtieth to the fifty-fifth year. To prevent incest, all the children born at the time of a man's marriage shall be known as his children. The women, whose natural vocation is family life, are by this arrangement deprived of their sphere. In the Platonic Republic it therefore follows that as the family is broken up, and the women no longer manage the house, they are also no longer private persons, and adopt the manners of the man as the universal individual in the state. And Plato accordingly allows the women to take their part like the men in all manly labours, and even to share in the toils of war. Thus he places them on very nearly the same footing as the men, though all the same he has no great confidence in their bravery, but stations them in the rear only, and not even as reserve, but only as *arrière-garde,* in order that they may at least inspire the foe with terror by their numbers, and, in case of necessity, hasten to give aid.

These are the main features of the Platonic Republic, which has as its essential the suppression of the principle of individuality; and it would appear as though the Idea demanded this, and as if this were the very point on which Philosophy is opposed to the ordinary way of looking at things, which gives importance to the individual, and thus in the state, as also in actualized mind, looks on the rights of property, and the protection of persons and their possessions, as the basis of everything that is. Therein, however, lies the very limit of the Platonic Idea—to emerge only as abstract idea. But, in fact, the true Idea is nothing else than this, that every moment should perfectly realize and embody itself, and make itself independent, while at the same time, in its independence, it is for mind a thing sublated. In conformity with this Idea, individuality must fully realize itself, must have its sphere and domain in the state, and yet be resolved in it. The element of the state is the family, that is, the family is the natural unreasoning state; this element must, as such, be present. Then the Idea of the state constituted by reason has to realize all the moments of its Notion in such a way that they become classes, and the moral substance divides itself into portions, as the bodily substance is separated into intestines and organs, each of which lives on in a particular way of its own, yet all of which together form only one life. The state in general, the whole, must finally pervade all. But in exactly the same way the formal principle of justice, as abstract universality of personality with individual Being as its existent content, must pervade the whole; one class, nevertheless, specially belongs to it. There must, then, also be a class in which property is held immediately and permanently, the possession of the body and the possession of a piece of land alike; and in the next place, a class where acquisition is continually going on, and possession is not immediate, as in the other, but property is ever fluctuating and changing. These two classes the nation gives up as a part of itself to the principle of individuality, and allows rights to reign here, permitting the constant, the universal, the implicit to be sought in this principle, which really is a principle of variability. This principle must have its full and complete reality, it must indeed appear in the shape of property. We have here for the first time the true, actual mind, with each moment receiving its complete independence, and the mind itself attaining to being-another in perfect indifference of Being. Nature cannot effect this production of independent life in her parts, except in the great system. This is, as we shall elsewhere see, the great advance of the modern world beyond the ancient, that in it the objective attains to greater, yea, to absolute independence, but for the very same reason returns with all the greater difficulty into the unity of the Idea.

The want of subjectivity is really the want of the Greek moral idea. The principle which became prominent with Socrates had been present up to this time only in a more subordinate capacity; now it of necessity became an even absolute principle, a necessary moment in the Idea itself. By the exclusion of private property and of family life, by the suspension of freedom in the choice of the class, *i.e.* by the exclusion of all the determinations which relate to the principle of subjective freedom, Plato believes he has barred the doors to all the passions; he knew very well that the ruin of Greek life proceeded from this, that individuals, as such, began to assert their aims, inclinations, and interests, and made them dominate over the common mind. But since this principle is necessary through the Christian religion—in which the soul of the individual is an absolute end, and thus has entered into the world as necessary in the Notion of the mind—it is seen that the Platonic state-constitution cannot fulfil what the higher demands of a moral organism require. Plato has not recognized the knowledge, wishes, and resolutions of the individual, nor his self-reliance, and has not succeeded in combining them with his Idea; but justice demands its rights for this just as much as it requires the higher resolution of the same, and its harmony with the universal. The opposite to Plato's principle is the principle of the conscious free will of individuals, which in later times was by Rousseau more especially raised to prominence: the theory that the arbitrary choice of the individual, the outward expression of the individual, is necessary. In this the principle is carried to the very opposite extreme, and has emerged in its utter one-sidedness. In opposition to this arbitrariness and culture there must be the implicitly and explicitly universal, that which is in thought, not as wise governor or morality, but as law, and at the same time as my Being and my thought, *i.e.* as subjectivity and individuality. Men must have brought forth from themselves the rational along with their interests and their passions, just as it must enter into reality through the necessities, opportunities, and motives that impel them.

Jefferson on PLATO

I am just returned from one of my long absences, having been at my other home for five weeks past. Having more leisure there than here for reading, I amused myself with reading seriously Plato's Republic. I am wrong, however, in calling it amusement, for it was the heaviest task-work I ever went through. I had occasionally before taken up some of his other works, but scarcely ever had patience to go through a whole dialogue. While wading through the whimsies, the puerilities, and unintelligible jargon of this work, I laid it down often to ask myself how it could have been, that the world should have so long consented to give reputation to such nonsense as this? How the *soi-disant* Christian world, indeed, should have done it, is a piece of historical curiosity. But how could the Roman good sense do it? And particularly, how could Cicero bestow such eulogies on Plato! Although Cicero did not wield the dense logic of Demosthenes, yet he was able, learned, laborious, practised in the business of the world, and honest. He could not be the dupe of mere style, of which he was himself the first master in the world. With the moderns, I think, it is rather a matter of fashion and authority. Education is chiefly in the hands of persons who, from their profession, have an interest in the reputation and the dreams of Plato. They give the tone while at school, and few in their after years have occasion to revise their college opinions. But fashion and authority apart, and bringing Plato to the test of reason, take from him his sophisms, futilities and incomprehensibilities, and what remains? In truth, he is one of the race of genuine sophists, who has escaped the oblivion of his brethren, first, by the elegance of his diction, but chiefly, by the adoption and incorporation of his whimsies into the body of artificial Christianity. His foggy mind is forever presenting the semblances of objects which, half seen through a mist, can be defined neither in form nor dimensions. Yet this, which should have consigned him to early oblivion, really procured him immortality of fame and reverence. The Christian priesthood, finding the doctrines of Christ levelled to every understanding, and too plain to need explanation, saw in the mysticism of Plato materials with which they might build up an artificial system, which might, from its indistinctness, admit everlasting contro-

[From Thomas Jefferson, letter to John Adams (July 5, 1814).]

versy, give employment for their order, and introduce it to profit, power and pre-eminence. The doctrines which flowed from the lips of Jesus himself are within the comprehension of a child; but thousands of volumes have not yet explained the Platonisms engrafted on them; and for this obvious reason, that nonsense can never be explained. Their purposes, however, are answered. Plato is canonized; and it is now deemed as impious to question his merits as those of an Apostle of Jesus. He is peculiarly appealed to as an advocate of the immortality of the soul; and yet I will venture to say, that were there no better arguments than his in proof of it, not a man in the world would believe it. It is fortunate for us, that Platonic republicanism has not obtained the same favor as Platonic Christianity; or we should now have been all living, men, women and children, pell mell together, like beasts of the field or forest. Yet "Plato is a great philosopher," said La Fontaine. But, says Fontenelle, "Do you find his ideas very clear?" "Oh no! he is of an obscurity impenetrable." "Do you not find him full of contradictions?" "Certainly," replied La Fontaine, "he is but a sophist." Yet immediately after he exclaims again, "Oh, Plato was a great philosopher." Socrates had reason, indeed, to complain of the misrepresentations of Plato; for in truth, his dialogues are libels on Socrates.

Brandeis on PLATO

Have just read this essay, judging from which (I have no other source of information) Plato's ideal republic, which he himself thought too perfect ever to be realized, must be the most theoretically nonsensical plan that human ingenuity ever invented. The plans of Government of other theorists have at least the semblance of adaptability to the nature of mankind. Locke's plan of government—though it failed so egregiously when adopted in one of the colonies of our country—was at least apparently feasible among a race of people in whom our virtues existed in a greater, our vices in a less, degree. But in order that Plato's republic should have prospered, he would have had to first create a new species of man, different in their desires, inclinations, and feelings from any who have as yet inhabited the earth—he would have to play both the part of the creator and lawgiver. The peculiarity of Plato's ideal creatures is their great dissimilarity from all other ideals of utopian theorists. When Thomas More

[From Louis D. Brandeis's unpublished notebooks, dated August 29, 1876. The entry is entitled "DeQuincy's Plato's Republic."]

pictured to himself the perfection of man, he imagined people who are affected by feelings and circumstances and events, by their education, just as we are. But to form this noble race he gave them our virtues in a greater degree and freed them from our vices.

Plato on the contrary takes us as we are (or, rather, the Greeks as they were at his time) actuated by the same base motives, the same appetites and desires, but imagines them so constituted to be quite differently affected by circumstances, education, and events than we would be—he imagines a people to whom our feelings and impulses are unknown. This is the reason why he seems so theoretical and visionary to us in his daydreams. Plato, in one word, creates a being formed as we are and possessing at his birth the same abstract virtues and vices that we do, but in every other respect an entirely different nature. He imagines a race of men who retain their respect and admiration for women with whom from the earliest youth and during their whole life gymnastic exercises are gone through in utter nudity; his creative brain presents to him a race of men who will love and honor wives whom the state has selected for them— whose company they are not allowed to enjoy, who are to be the common property of the state. Plato's fathers are to dearly love their children and sacrifice their lives for their sons and daughters—whom they have never seen, whom they can only suppose to exist. He imagines a class of men in his society who possess all the physical power, who enjoy the respect and admiration of the state, but who nevertheless have no desire to accumulate property, who have no tendency toward despotism and this though all the nobler feelings which usually fill men's breasts have been killed at their birth or eradicated, although they have had no education in what is elevating and ennobling, on the contrary, whose greatest virtue is to be violence and brutality, whose pleasures debauchery, the emoluments of whose profession unlimited concubinage and mandatory infanticide.

Such is the noble race of soldiers who are to be the guardians of Plato's Republic, who are to ensure its stability and greatness. Such are the men who are to be the terror of the enemy, the gods of their countrymen. Surely, we must either accuse the creator of such anomalous men of endless incongruities and inconsistencies, or we cannot sufficiently admire the mind which can so successfully liberate itself from everything human as to imagine a new creature unaffected by what affects us, moved to good deeds by what leaves us cold, who is not governed by our passions, appetites, and desires, nor actuated by such motives as we are, but who is blessed with our virtues and cursed with our vices, which, however, the education devised by Plato is to eradicate. Indeed we are forced to exclaim: "Such is the ingenuity of man."

2 | ST. THOMAS AQUINAS
        LUTHER
        KELSEN

ARISTOTLE

In the first few centuries of its existence, the strong mystical and idealistic tendency in Christianity found philosophical kinship and affinity in Plato. By the thirteenth century, Christian thought and church organization had changed considerably, and Platonism could no longer serve as the philosophical and metaphysical foundation of an institution in which the emphasis had changed from individual inspiration and illumination to institutional stability and sobriety. The triumph of Aristotle (see page 1) in the thirteenth century, both in secular and religious speculation, was the work of many men, schools, and universities, but above all it was due to the influence of St. Thomas Aquinas (1226–1274). He was born in a highly aristocratic Italian family, related to European kings and emperors. Against the strong opposition of his family, he joined the mendicant order of the Dominicans at the early age of sixteen and henceforth dedicated his life to philosophical and theological study and teaching. His lasting achievement is the incorporation of Aristotelianism into Christian thought. Just as Augustinianism is the fusion of Platonism and Christianity, Thomism is the synthesis of Aristotelianism and Christianity. It can thus be seen that the most decisive issue in the philosophical evolution of the church was in effect a repetition of the dialogue between Plato and Aristotle, adapted to the Christian world and its theology. Until the seventeenth century, at least, it seemed that Plato and Aristotle had laid down for all time the two possible basic philosophical systems; with all its hostility to pre-Christian pagan philosophy, medieval scholasticism was completely under the spell of Plato and Aristotle. For St. Thomas Aquinas, Aristotle was more than a great, or even the greatest philosopher; he was "the philosopher," as he usually refers to him. Throughout his works he constantly relies on the authority of Aristotle, and in his *Commentary on Aristotle's Politics* he follows his master step by step through the arguments as they progress in chapter after chapter of the *Politics*; his agreement with Aristotle is not only on fundamentals, but also on details, and while his interpretation of Aristotle's political ideas thus offers little that is new or original, it demonstrates the loyalty and devotion which St. Thomas Aquinas felt for Aristotle.

The victory of Thomism over Augustinianism was thus also a victory of Aristotle over Plato, and it was bound to produce a vehement reaction within the church, precisely because the victory had been so complete. Those who persisted in seeing Christianity as essentially love and faith, rather than as law and institution, rebelled against the Thomistic process of rationalization and systematization. The greatest leader of this rebellion was Martin Luther (1483–1546). Luther was an Augustinian monk, and his opposition to church conditions in his time was based not only on the prevalence of venality, corruption, and power among the higher clergy, but —more deeply—on the dominant tendency to transform a religion of love and faith into a church of law and power. Throughout his works he frequently refers to St. Augustine with much warmth, while seeing in the adoption of Aristotle's rationalism the source of all evil. In his *Address to the Christian Nobility of the German Nation* (1520), Luther discusses the troubled conditions of contemporary Germany, covering a wide range of subjects, from the grounds of political obedience to the reform of the universities. It is in dealing with the latter subject that he concentrates on the traditional study of Aristotle as the source of all evil in the intellectual life of his time. Here is, in a few pages, a typical example of Luther's passion and fanaticism in revolt against Aristotelian rationalism, foreshadowing the later German revolt against classicism as expressed in German romanticism in the late eighteenth and early nineteenth centuries.

Whereas Luther attacks Aristotle on the grounds of excessive rationalism, a modern political philosopher, Hans Kelsen, focuses his criticism on the argument that Aristotle's political theory was not so much a scientific analysis of government as an ideological justification for one particular form of government, namely, monarchy, and, more specifically still, the Macedonian type of monarchy, which sought to destroy Greek democracy and turn Greece into a province of a vast empire ruled by an absolute monarch. As the originator of the "pure theory of law," Kelsen (1881–   ) is one of the most influential legal philosophers of the twentieth century, his influence being more marked in Europe and Latin America than in the English-speaking world. As he progressed, his interests turned from law to politics, sociology, and anthropology; yet throughout his work there is always one central theme: the role of ideology in the formulation of legal and political philosophy, the attempt of scholars and statesmen to clothe interest in the language of ethics and philosophy and thus confer upon interest the qualities of validity and objectivity which it otherwise would not have. In the history of political philosophy, Plato and Aristotle have attracted Kelsen's main attention, and his interpretation of both diverges on many points from the conventional point of view. As one of the leading modern exponents of philosophical relativism in the social sciences, Kelsen holds that Plato's philosophical idealism also strongly permeates Aristotle's thought and that the antidemocratic conclusions of Platonism are also implicit in Aristotle's political ideas. The most systematic exposition of Kelsen's work will be found in his *General Theory of Law and State* (1945).

St. Thomas Aquinas on ARISTOTLE

As Aristotle teaches in Book II of his *Physics*, art imitates nature. The reason is that actions and their effects are related to one another in the same way as are principles among themselves. The human mind is the origin of all works of art, and it derives in a certain way from the divine mind which is the origin of natural things. Therefore works of art necessarily imitate the works of nature, and works of nature, the works of art. When the teacher of some art is making something, the pupil who is learning from him should observe how he is doing it, so that he may be able to do it with the same skill. The human mind, too, which derives the light of intelligence from the divine mind, must study natural processes in what it does and imitate them. Hence Aristotle remarks that if art were able to make things that are in nature, it would operate like nature itself. Conversely, if nature could make things proper to art, it would act like art. Nature, however, does not create works of art, but

[From St. Thomas Aquinas, *Commentary on the Politics of Aristotle* (*ca.* 1268, trans. William Ebenstein).]

merely prepares certain basic principles and offers a kind of model for the artist to follow. Art, on the other hand, while able to perceive the works of nature, is unable to create them. It is thus clear that human reason can only know the works of nature, while it can both perceive and produce works of art. The human sciences that deal with natural phenomena are thus speculative, whereas those dealing with man-made things are practical, operating by imitating nature. Nature proceeds in its operation from simple to complex things; that which, in the operation of nature, is the most complex is also, at the same time, the most perfect, and it represents the integrated goal of other things. Such is the case with regard to any whole as it relates to its parts. The operative reason of man likewise progresses from the simple to the complex, that is, from the imperfect to the perfect. But because human reason must not only have at its disposal the means of life that are useful, but must also deal with men themselves who are ruled by reason, it proceeds in both cases from the simple to the complex. In those things which are useful to man, as in building a ship out of timber or constructing a home out of timber and stone, as well as in organizing a community out of many individuals, human reason proceeds in that manner.

There are different grades and orders among such communities, but the highest form is the political community which provides whatever is necessary for human life. Among all communities, the human is therefore the most perfect. Since the means that man uses only serve his end and purpose, which are more important than the former, it necessarily follows that the totality of the political community is more important than all other institutions which the human mind can devise or construct. From these statements of political theory made by Aristotle, four conclusions follow. First, as regards the necessity of a science of politics: all that can be understood by reason must be explained for the sake of perfecting human wisdom, or philosophy, as it is called. The kind of group which constitutes a political community must be subject to the judgment of reason. The completeness of philosophy, therefore, necessarily demands a doctrine of political science. Secondly, there is the generic problem of this science. The practical sciences are distinguished from the speculative ones inasmuch as the latter aim at the knowledge of truth, whereas the former are meant to work in practice. Political science is practical, because human reason both knows and creates the political community. Reason can exercise its influence in two ways: either by creating something out of external materials (as in the case of the smith or shipwright) or by immanent action on the part of man himself (such as counseling and choosing, and whatever pertains to the science of morality).

It is manifest that political science, which deals with the organization of human relations, is one of the moral sciences rather than a mechanical craft. Thirdly, we may enlarge upon the dignity and importance of political science as compared with all the other practical sciences. The political community is the most important creation of human reason, for all other communities are subordinated to it and measured against it. All that can be produced through the mechanical arts for the sake of utility is a means to man as an end. If that science is the most important which is concerned with the noblest and most perfect, then the science of politics is the most important among all practical sciences and the foundation of all of them, because it deals with the ultimate and perfect good in human affairs. Fourthly, from what has been said so far, the method and system of political science may be seen. Just as the speculative sciences, in studying a totality, arrive at knowledge by observing its parts and principles in operation, so the science of politics studies the parts and principles of the political community in order to understand it as a whole. And because political science is a practical one, it also shows how the individual parts may be perfected, as is necessary in every practical science.

Luther on ARISTOTLE

The universities need a sound and thorough reformation. I must say so no matter who takes offence. Everything that the papacy has instituted or ordered is directed solely towards the multiplication of sin and error. Unless they are completely altered from what they have been hitherto, the universities will fit exactly what is said in the Book of Maccabees: "Places for the exercise for youth, and for the Greekish fashion." [1] Loose living is practised there; little is taught of the Holy Scripture or the Christian faith; the blind pagan teacher, Aristotle, is of more consequence than Christ. In my view, Aristotle's writings on *Physics, Metaphysics, On the Soul,* and *Ethics,* hitherto regarded as the most important, should be set aside along with all others that boast they treat of natural objects, for in fact they have nothing to teach about things natural or

[From Martin Luther, *Address to the Christian Nobility of the German Nation* (1520, in vol. I of *Reformation Writings of Martin Luther,* trans. Bertram Lee Woolf, Philosophical Library, Inc., 1953). By permission.]

[1] 2 Macc. 4:9, 12.

spiritual.[2] Remember too that no one, up to now, has understood his teaching, but much precious time and mental energy have been uselessly devoted to wasteful work, study, and effort. I venture to say that a potter has more understanding of the things of nature than is written down in those books. It pains me to the heart that this damnable, arrogant, pagan rascal has seduced and fooled so many of the best Christians with his misleading writings. God has made him a plague to us on account of our sins.

In his book, *On the Soul,* which is one of his best, the wretched fellow teaches that the soul dies with the body; and many have tried, in vain, to defend him. It is as if we did not possess the Holy Scriptures where we find a superabundance of teaching on the whole subject, of which Aristotle has not the faintest inkling. Yet this defunct pagan has attained supremacy; impeded, and almost suppressed, the Scriptures of the living God. When I think of this lamentable state of affairs, I cannot avoid believing that the Evil One introduced the study of Aristotle.

On the same principles, his book on *Ethics* is worse than any other book, being the direct opposite of God's grace, and the Christian virtues; [3] yet it is accounted among the best of his works. Oh! away with such books from any Christian hands. Let no one accuse me of overstating the case, or object that I do not understand. My dear sir, I know well enough what I am saying. Aristotle is as familiar to me as to you and your like. I have read him and studied him with more understanding than did St. Thomas Aquinas or Duns Scotus.[4] Without pride, I can make that

[2] This seemingly extraordinary judgment of Aristotle was not due to Luther's impatience or ignorance. Immediately after graduating M.A. at Erfurt, he began to teach Aristotle. This was part of his duties which he undertook on oath. He continued teaching Aristotle when he transferred to Wittenberg in 1508 and until 1512, when he was appointed Professor of Holy Scripture. Moreover, the view was shared to a large extent by Erasmus; cf. *Colloquies, passim.* Nor was it a novelty. "Roger Bacon . . . believed that Aristotle's philosophy was entirely wrong. . . . In Paris, a considerable body of opinion, in the middle of the nineteenth century, regarded Aristotelianism as mere pedantry," Sir E. Whittaker, *Space and Spirit,* 1946, p. 49. "I believe that nothing could be more absurdly said in Natural Philosophy than in . . . Aristotle's," T. Hobbes, *Leviathan,* p. 522. "The popularity of Aristotelian logic retarded the advance of physical science throughout the Middle Ages," A. N. Whitehead, *Science and the Modern World,* 1926, p. 37. Luther seems to have been in goodly company when he formed this opinion of Aristotle, though A. remains "the master of them that know", Dante, *Inferno,* IV, 131.

[3] A criticism of Aristotle's doctrine of virtue as the mean between two extremes; cf. *Nichomachean Ethics,* ed. D. P. Chase, 1877, p. 74.

[4] Both Aquinas and Scotus knew Aristotle only in a Latin translation, probably made from the Arabic.

claim, and if needs be, prove it. It makes no difference that for centuries so many of the best minds have devoted their labours to him. Such objections do not affect me as at one time they used to do. For it is plain as the day that the longer the lapse of time, the greater the errors which abound in the world and the universities.

I would gladly grant the retention of Aristotle's books on *Logic*, *Rhetoric*, and *Poetics*; or that they should be abridged and read in a useful form to train young men to speak and preach well. But the comments and notes should be set aside, and, just as Cicero's *Rhetoric* is read without notes and comments, so also Aristotle's *Logic* should be read in its simple form, and without the lengthy comments. But to-day no man learns from it how to speak or preach; the whole thing has become a mere subject of argumentation and a weariness to the flesh.

Then there are the languages: Latin, Greek, and Hebrew, the mathematical disciplines, and history. But this is a subject which I commend to men of greater knowledge than I possess; it will right itself if a reformation is undertaken seriously; much depends on that. For Christian youth, and those of our upper classes, with whom abides the future of Christianity, will be taught and trained in the universities. In my view, no work more worthy of the pope and the emperor could be carried out than a true reformation of the universities. On the other hand, nothing could be more wicked, or serve the devil better, than unreformed universities.

Kelsen on ARISTOTLE

The *Politics* of Aristotle is essentially a doctrine of the constitutions, of which the broad lines, at least, have been sketched in the *Nicomachean Ethics*. The central theme is the celebrated six-forms scheme of constitutions, which distinguishes three true forms of state rule—monarchy, aristocracy, and polity. With these there are associated three perverted forms. Thus tyranny is a perverted form of monarchy, oligarchy a perverted form of aristocracy, and democracy a perverted form of polity. This scheme provides at the same time for a fixed order of rank, in which monarchy appears as the best constitution, aristocracy comes next, then polity. After these, in reverse order, follow the perverted forms of constitution, such that democracy, though worse than any of the three true

[From Hans Kelsen, "The Philosophy of Aristotle and the Hellenic-Macedonian Policy," *Ethics*, vol. 48 (October, 1937). By permission.]

forms, is nevertheless classed as the best of the deviations. Tyranny is the worst of all forms. Monarchy, especially unlimited hereditary monarchy, is from the very outset declared to be the best form of all state rulerships. Thus the Aristotelian scheme emphatically opposes monarchy to that form which would seem most nearly to resemble it—namely, tyranny. And this opposition is chiefly effected by representing the rule of the monarch as analogous to that of the father over his sons, the rule of the tyrant as that of the master over his slaves. The former is a rulership which benefits the subjects; the latter benefits only the ruler. And this distinction is also declared to be decisive as between the true and the perverted forms, so that democracy, which is classed in the *Nicomachean Ethics* as a perverted constitution, is also characterized as a kind of despotism, i.e., as a rule over slaves.[1]

This is very unusual teaching. For in Aristotle's time royal rule was considered by the Hellenes as a barbarous form of government, a rulership over slaves, to which the republican Polis, the self-government of free men, the special constitution of the Greek nation, stood in startling contrast. He who in Hellas, and especially in Athens, declared kingly rule to be the best was faced with a prevalent opinion which regarded monarchy as a barbarian dominion over slaves. If the true significance of the Aristotelian teaching as to forms of government is to be grasped, the political and historical situation in which it was evolved and which it sought to influence must be kept in mind.

The historical situation is Athens, republican Athens, in which the proud recollection of that great epoch of Periclean democracy is still living, where the word of Euripides is still the expression of public opinion. "Nothing is more pernicious to a state than a one man rule where that which is of first importance—a common law—is inexistent. A master there is who is law unto himself—so that equality of right there is none." The heroic days of the monarchy of antiquity, it is true, are still piously held in historical remembrance. But nothing is more significant than that their mythical representative, King Theseus, is honored as the founder of the democratic form of government. Euripides puts into his mouth the words: "The city is not governed by one man, but is free. And the people rule by turn in annual succession." Writing about this city of Athens Isocrates says that it "hates monarchy most of all things."[2] The Polis democracy, indeed, had passed its culminating point when Aristotle was

---

[1] Cf. *Eth. Nic.* 1160*b*–1161*b*; *Pol.* 1278*b*–1279*b*, 1289*a*–1289*b*, and esp. 1312*b*: "The extreme form of democracy is tyranny."

[2] Isocrates, *Nikokles* 6.

living in Athens. But it was just passing through the bitterest phase of democracy's struggle against the Macedonian hereditary monarchy. Those were the years in which Demosthenes, one of the leaders of the national democratic party, in his passionate orations against Philip and Alexander, called on the Athenians to vindicate their political freedom. In these orations the Macedonian monarchy is charged with precisely those distinctive qualities, those terrifying characteristics, from which monarchy, in the Aristotelian doctrine of government, was supposed to be exempt. The Aristotelian doctrine most emphatically repudiates those very accusations which Demosthenes, in his orations, levels against the king. If the philosopher again and again declares that kingly rule is essentially different from a rule of force—that it is not a rulership over slaves as is a tyranny— the orator on the other hand warns his country against the Macedonian hereditary monarchy by stigmatizing it again and again as a form of government fit only for slaves. Thus he says in his first Olynthian oration, with reference to Macedonia, that he believes "a state ruled by force is generally an object of suspicion to free states, especially when both are neighbours"; further, it is to be presumed that "the Päonen and the Illyrians and generally all those peoples would much prefer to be free and independent than to be slaves; for they are not accustomed to obey and he [King Philip] is reported to be an imperious master." To be governed by a king is for Demosthenes synonymous with being a slave. Only in a democracy can one live as a free citizen; and therefore he represents the struggle against the Macedonian monarchy again and again, and especially in his second oration against Philip, as the defense of "free states against the encroachments of the tyrant." " 'What do you desire?' I said. 'Freedom. And you do not see that even Philip's title means just the contrary? For every king and tyrant is an opponent of freedom and an enemy to order according to law.' " King and tyrant are for Demosthenes one and the same, not, as Aristotle declares, "distinct and different." The struggle, therefore, of Athens against Philip and Alexander is a struggle of democracy against monarchy. While Aristotle is never tired of proclaiming that kingly rule guarantees the most complete community of interests between the ruler and the ruled, as the king like a father seeks only the good of his subjects, Demosthenes adjures the Athenians in his second Olynthian oration as follows: "Believe not, Oh ye men of Athens, that he [King Philip] and his subjects have a common interest. He, on his side, thirsts for glory, they, on their side, have no part in this kind of glory, rather are they harassed being exhausted by the continual and diverse campaigns." While Aristotle teaches that not monarchy but tyranny is the rule over slaves, and therefore suitable for barbarians, who are by nature slaves, Demosthenes does not cease to stigmatize the Macedonian monarchy as a barbarous form of government. "Is not Philip our enemy?" he exclaims in the third Olynthian oration. "Is he not the robber of our property, is he not a barbarian, the epitome of all thinkable evil?" He reminds Athens that Macedonia had formerly been subject to her. Nor does he omit at this point to emphasize the natural subjection of the barbarian monarchy to the Hellenic democracy.

This is the political atmosphere in which Aristotle presents his theory of constitutions. It is true he never expressly says, nor even suggests, that the monarchy which he holds up as the best form of government is the Macedonian monarchy and that the democracy to which he assigns an inferior place is the Athenian democracy. But was it possible, considering the circumstances of the town in which he lived and the time in which he wrote, to speak of the comparative values of monarchy and democracy without every word being understood as either for or against the Macedonian monarchy, for or against the Athenian democracy? Is it possible to mistake the connection between the political attitude of the greatest and most popular orator who, with all the convincing rhetoric at his disposal, hammered into the Greek brain and heart again and again the thesis: royal rule is slavery, only democracy is freedom; and the theory of government of the leading philosopher of the time, who maintained royal rule to be diametrically opposed to a rulership over slaves, the latter to be rather—as all perverted constitutions are—democracy. Aristotle's doctrine of government is not without its political background. It can be understood only by remembering the direct opposition in which it stood to the political system, which obtained its living expression in the orations of Demosthenes.

This is shown by an analysis of the chief work of the Aristotelian theory of state—the *Politics*. A complete analysis of this work would not here be possible. We shall call attention only to those points which bear directly on the historical context.

Book i of the *Politics* contains an examination of the different relationships of rule, in which a parallel is established between rule of a state and that of a family. This parallel is designed chiefly to show the principal difference between the rule of the master over his slaves and the rule of the father over his children—the mastery of the king being that of the latter, not that of the former type. Thus the whole presentation of the slave problem in this first book of the *Politics* is rather of a political than of an economic character. Aristotle is here, it is true, concerned with the justification of slavery as an economic institution, but this is certainly not his chief concern, as is generally believed. His aim above all is to

vindicate monarchy against its opponents who love to identify it with
slavery. Therefore he does not omit, especially in this connection, to insist
on the fact that the oldest and most naturally organized community
amongst men had a monarchical character and that even the community
of the Olympian gods was a kingly rule.[3] The decisive passage is the following:

> Of household management we have seen that there are three parts—
> one is the rule of a master over slaves, which has been discussed al-
> ready, another of a father, and the third of a husband. A husband
> and father, we saw, rules over wife and children, both free,—but the
> rule differs—the rule over his children being a royal, over his wife a
> constitutional [that is a republican] rule. . . . . But in most constitu-
> tional [republican] states the citizens rule and are ruled by turns, for
> the idea of a constitutional state implies that the natures of the citi-
> zens are equal, and do not differ at all. Nevertheless, when one rules
> and the other is ruled we endeavour to create a difference of outward
> forms and names and titles of respect, which may be illustrated by the
> saying of Amasis about his footpan.[4]

This is not a very flattering allusion. Herodotus relates of Amasis who,
although of modest origin, had risen to the throne, that he was rather
despised on account of his humble birth. Amasis, however, ordered the
statue of a god to be made out of a golden basin which his guests used
for washing their feet and other like purposes and thus compelled the
Egyptians to pay homage to what they had been wont to despise. Whoever has read carefully the foregoing passages in which Aristotle endeavors to show that the distinction between the ruler and those who
are ruled is according to nature, cannot help noticing the subtle thrust
directed against the democratic republic, in which he who yesterday had
to obey, today commands, and where the natural distinction between such
as are born to command and such as are born to obey is ignored. Nor is
it proper to compare the rule of the husband over the wife to the republican form of constitution. In this connection it is said that "the male is
by nature fitter for command than the female." And in fact the relationship between husband and wife never changes, for it is always the husband who rules over the wife. "Now the relation of the male to the
female is of this kind [rulership] but there the inequality is permanent."

---

[3] *Pol.* 1252*b*. Isocrates says much the
same in his praise of monarchy (*Nikokles* 6): "The Gods are also under the
royal rule of Zeus . . . we would not
say the Gods make use of monarchy, if
we did not believe it to be superior to
other constitutions."

[4] *Ibid.* 1259*a* 37 ff.

After this covert disparagement of the republican-democratic form of government Aristotle continues, expressing a thought already developed in the *Nicomachean Ethics:*

> The rule of a father over his children is royal, for he rules by virtue both of love and of the respect due to age, exercising a kind of royal power. And therefore Homer has appropriately called Zeus "father of Gods and men" because he is the King of them all. For a King is the natural superior of his subjects, but he should be of the same kin or kind with them, and such is the relation of elder and younger, of father and son.

The preference given already in the first book of the *Politics* to monarchy as being that form of government most conforming to nature, in opposition to the republican and therefore democratic form, is unmistakable.

The train of thought pursued in Book i, which seeks by examining the different forms of government to lay the foundation for a doctrine of constitutions, is continued only in Book iii. Book ii, as also the greater part of Books vii and viii, are devoted to the problem of the ideal state. They are evidently to be attributed to a youthful production of Aristotle, and were only later incorporated into his doctrine of constitutions which has been handed down to us under the name of *Politics.* And this work was certainly produced during the period of the philosopher's second stay in Athens, while the writing about the ideal state was done at the time when Aristotle was still the pupil of Plato and a member of the latter's Academy. This work is openly under the influence of Plato's *Politeia.* Therefore we cannot find it in Aristotle's real and definitive opinions about the state and the value of the constitutions. These are contained in the theory of state of Books i, iii–vi, of the so-called *Politics,* which is a very contradictory compilation of two quite different works of Aristotle. Book iii, which continues the train of thought of the first, opens with the discussion of certain preliminary questions concerning the doctrine of constitutions, especially of that problem which lay at the basis of all the political theory of the antique city-state, namely, the description of the citizen. Who is the citizen? And the further question: Is the virtue of the good man and the virtue of the good citizen one and the same? This may be said to be the core of the democratic Polis ideology, according to which man attains his full, i.e., his moral, personality in participation in government, wherefore the slave, who had no political rights, was not considered to be a full man, and therefore virtue can be developed only in political activity. Consequently the virtue of the good citizen and of the good man must be regarded, according to the official conception, as identical. But as Aristotle's object is to show by his teaching that monarchy, under which the subject is excluded from all share in government, is the best form, he must above all try to overthrow this fundamental doctrine of the democratic Polis ideology. The utmost caution, of course, had to be observed in an attack directed against a sacred political dogma. Accordingly, Aristotle first of all maintains that the conception of what constitutes the citizen must vary according to the form of government and that the usual conception of the citizen which takes its initial idea from the extent to which he shares in government is, in the main, applicable only to democracy which, as his later arguments are intended to prove, is not a true state form. "For in some states the people are not acknowledged, nor have they any regular assembly, but only extraordinary ones." [5] He is evidently thinking here of monarchy; he does not say so, however, nor does he dare to draw the final conclusion from his recognition of the connection between forms of government and the definition of a citizen. He is contented with showing the relative significance of the prevailing conception of what constitutes the citizen. But nevertheless there is no ambiguity in such statements as that "the subject is a citizen as well as the ruler." [6] Thus the conception of citizen is no longer limited exclusively to the active political qualification, but is extended to the passive condition of being ruled, and in this way adapted to the monarchical form of government. And a like tendency is perceptible in the answer to the question whether the virtue of the man is identical with that of the citizen. Aristotle was obliged to answer in the negative. Again he insists on the dependence of the ideal of virtue on the form of government:

> The virtue of the citizen must therefore be relative to the constitution of which he is a member. If then, there are many forms of government, it is evident that there is not one single virtue of the good citizen which is perfect virtue. But we say that the good man is he who has one single virtue which is perfect virtue. Hence it is evident that the good citizen need not of necessity possess the virtue which makes a good man. [7]

Thus the virtue of a good man and the virtue of a good citizen need not be identical. "But will there then be no case in which the virtue of the good citizen and the virtue of the good man coincide? To this we answer that the good ruler is a good and wise man." [8] And after calling attention to the necessity of a special education for the ruler, he arrives at the con-

[5] *Pol.* 1275*b*.
[6] *Ibid.* 1277*a*.
[7] *Ibid.* 1276*b*.
[8] *Ibid.* 1277*a*.

clusion that both virtues, the virtue of the good man and the virtue of a good citizen, are really united only in the person of the ruler, not in that of the subject. For the "virtue of a ruler differs from that of a citizen" (that is, he who is only ruled).[9] The subject "may be compared to the maker of the flute, while the ruler is like the flute player."[10] The reference to the monarchy is unmistakable.

The theory of government in the true sense of the word begins with the question "whether there is only one form of government or many, and if many, what they are, and how many, and what are the differences between them."[11] And from this in the further development of his thesis the question arises: "What is to be the supreme power in the state: Is it the multitude? Or the wealthy? Or the good? Or the one best man? Or a tyrant?"[12] Although to put the question thus is to answer it, although no disagreement is possible that the one best man, if such there be (which is assumed in this question), should have the supreme power in the state. Nevertheless the advantages and the disadvantages of the different forms of government, and particularly of democracy and of monarchy, which obviously are in the foreground, are most carefully weighed one against the other. The very certainty of the conclusion (in favor of monarchy) compels objectivity in the discussion. And such objectivity was imperative in the political conditions then prevailing in Athens, on the soil of a democracy defending itself desperately against the encroachments of a monarchy. Aristotle shows himself extremely anxious to consider sympathetically the arguments generally advanced in defense of democracy, as opposed to aristocracy and monarchy. But finally he reaches the conclusion:

> If, however, there be some one person, or more than one, although not enough to make up the full complement of a state, whose virtue is so pre-eminent that the virtues or the political capacity of all the rest admit of no comparison with his or theirs, he or they can no longer be regarded as part of a state; for justice will not be done to the superior, if he is reckoned only as the equal of those who are so far inferior to him in virtue and in political capacity. Such an one may truly be deemed a God among men.[13]

What does the cautious condition stipulated in this formula mean, since to all those to whom it is of importance it may be asserted that the condition is fulfilled? To whom else, if not to Philip or to Alexander, should

[9] Ibid.
[10] Ibid. 1277b.
[11] Ibid. 1278b.
[12] Ibid. 1281a.
[13] Ibid. 1284a.

these words refer? The former was worshipped almost as a god. A statue had been erected to him in Athens, and Isocrates had written of him— "when Philip has submitted the kingdom of Persia nothing will remain for him to do, except to become a God." [14] Theopompos had said of him that it was believed nature herself was in union with him, as with her favorite, because during his Grecian campaigns in Macedonia she caused the fig trees and the vine to bear fruit even in the middle of spring. This contemporary historian had declared Philip to be the greatest statesman Europe had yet produced, in any case the greatest who had ever sat upon a throne. Alexander too was given a place among the Olympian gods and an altar was erected to him as to a god. Kallisthenes, the nephew and disciple of Aristotle, as the official historian of Alexander maintained his divine origin. Can one seriously doubt, then, the intention, when in a work on politics appearing in Athens under the reign of Alexander a monarch is spoken of who by virtue of his pre-eminent capacity and in-comparable political gifts "may truly be deemed a God among men"? Can a general doctrine of state, such as the Aristotelian *Politics* claims to be, express this intention in plainer terms; can it set forth other than hypothetical assertions? Is it not sufficient to develop a theory—i.e., theses generally applicable and therefore necessarily formulated in hypothetical terms—a theory which may then be used as an apology applicable directly to a concrete case, that is, to a certain definite person? Are they not the most effective ideologies that employ this method?

It is very interesting to note the extreme skill with which Aristotle leads up cautiously yet persistently to his fundamental thesis—the demonstration of the superiority of hereditary monarchy over democracy. After obtaining, in the first place, the general recognition of the possible supremacy of hereditary monarchy as the best form of state government, the important point now is to deepen and strengthen this position. This cannot be achieved better than by using the proved method of producing the desired effect by contrast. Monarchy glowing in the halo of its own virtue, in which the best man exercises his rightful rule, is placed in relief against democracy as the background, painted in somber colors—democracy in which there is no room for the one best man. Democracy is attacked on one of its worst defects, on one of its worst abuses, namely, ostracism, and compared with monarchy just on this its weakest side, not without recognizing beforehand the claim of the monarch, by reason of his pre-eminent virtue, to be exempt from all legal control. "Hence we see that legislation is necessarily concerned only with those who are equal in birth and capacity; and that for men of pre-eminent virtue there is no

[14] Isocrates iii (letter).

law, they are themselves a law. Anyone would be ridiculous who attempted to make laws for them." [15] The king is himself the law, for he is the incarnation of the highest virtue. Ostracism means the elimination of the most capable. It is recognized as a necessary consequence of democracy, and therefore in a certain sense justifiable. But this concession is made only with a view to justifying monarchy more effectively and to raising it above democracy.

> It would certainly be better that the legislator should from the first so order his state as to have no need of such a remedy [as ostracism]. But if the need arise, the next best thing is that he should endeavour to correct the evil by this or some similar measure. . . . It is true that, under perverted forms of government and from their special point of view, such a measure is just and expedient; but it is also clear that it is not absolutely just. In the perfect state [and by this, in Book iii of the *Politics*, is meant the monarchy of the six-forms scheme of constitutions] there would be great doubts about the use of it; not when applied to excessive strength, wealth, popularity, or the like, but when used against some one who is pre-eminent in virtue. What is to be done with such a man? Mankind will not allow him to be banished and exiled. On the other hand, he ought not to be a subject— that would be as if mankind should claim to rule over Zeus, dividing his offices among them. The only alternative is that all should joyfully obey such a ruler, according to what seems to be the order of nature, and that men like him [the born to rule] should be kings in their state for life.

The superiority of monarchy having been thus established, it is asserted:

> The preceding discussion by a natural transition, leads to the consideration of royalty, which we admit to be one of the true forms of government. Let us see whether in order to be well governed a state or country should be under the rule of a king or under some other form of government.

All this as if the question had not already been decided, as if any other possibility were open except that of recognizing that monarchy alone was the best form of government. But the same answer to the question is to be obtained a second time and thus it is to be rendered still more affirmative and convincing. And every effort is made in this second demonstration to avoid all appearance of prejudice and to be as just as possible to de-

15 *Pol.* 1284*a*.

mocracy. But the final conclusion, which characteristically starts from the supposition that there exists in a state a family pre-eminent in capacity, runs as follows:

> But when a whole family, or some individual, happens to be so pre-eminent in virtue as to surpass all others, then it is just that they should be of the royal family and supreme over all, or that this one citizen should be king of the whole nation. For, as I said before, to give them authority is not only agreeable to that ground of right which the founders of all states, whether aristocratical, or oligarchical, or again democratical, are accustomed to put forward [for these all recognize the claim of excellence, although not the same excellence], but accords with the principle already laid down. For surely it would not be right to kill, or ostracize, or exile such a person, or require that he should take his turn in being governed. The whole is naturally superior to the part, and he who has this pre-eminence [that all others together have less virtue and political capacity than he alone] is in the relation of a whole to a part. But if so, the only alternative is that he should have the supreme power, and that mankind should obey him, not in turn, but always.[16]

The scales so long in the balance are now definitely weighed down in favor of monarchy and against democracy. But the arguments that have led up to this result are marked by an extraordinary measure of prudence and an obvious endeavor to avoid hurting democratic sensibilities. After all this is a state which is proud of its republican democracy; there is at least one powerful party, which has not given up the struggle for Athenian political self-determination.

Book iii having closed with an examination of the monarchical form of government and its cautious hypothetical justification, Book iv opens with an explanatory development of the thesis that not only an absolute, but also a relative good exists, and that therefore the doctrine of state has to propound not only the absolutely best form, but also the relatively best. Here the order of rank of the values corresponding to the six-forms scheme of constitutions comes in a general manner under discussion, and it is just in this connection that the opinion is unequivocally expressed that monarchy is the absolutely best form of government. At the beginning of chapter 2 attention is called to the distinction made between the three true and the three perverted forms, and to the discussion which has already taken place of monarchy and aristocracy: "for the inquiry into the perfect state is the same thing with the discussion of the two forms thus

[16] *Ibid.* 1288a.

named." Aristotle here treats monarchy as a kind of aristocracy, that is, as the name implies, government by the one best man, or by the best. To speak of monarchy (or aristocracy) means to speak of the best form of government. And then in conclusion he lays down most emphatically that tyranny is the worst form; that royalty, of which tyranny must be considered a perversion, is "the first and the most divine," therefore the absolutely best form of constitution.

Of the further developments which, whether directly or indirectly are intended to glorify hereditary monarchy, only two passages will be especially noted here. In Book v we find:

> The appointment of a king is the resource of the better classes against the people, and he is elected by them out of their own number, because either he himself or his family excel in virtue and virtuous actions; whereas a tyrant is chosen from the people to be their protector against the notables, and in order to prevent them from being injured.[17]

Royalty is the protection afforded to good citizens by an intellectually and morally pre-eminent man; nor in defining it thus does Aristotle neglect to associate with the praise of the king his family, for his object is the glorification of hereditary monarchy. But tyranny is the protection of the multitude, whose inferiority, even worthlessness, is sufficiently set forth. It would appear, however, that tyranny, in so far as it may be a protection for the people—safeguarding them from the notables—cannot be totally condemned. But we are reminded that most of the ancient tyrants were originally demagogues. Of these demagogues it is said:

> Sometimes the demagogues, in order to curry favour with the people, wrong the notables and so force them to combine; either they make a division of their property, or diminish their incomes by the imposition of public services, and sometimes they bring accusations against the rich that they may have their wealth to confiscate. Of old, the demagogue was also a general, and then democracies changed into tyrannies. Most of the ancient tyrants were originally demagogues. They are not so now, but they were then; and the reason is that they were generals and not orators, for oratory had not yet come into fashion. Whereas in our day, when the art of rhetoric has made such progress, the orators lead the people, but their ignorance of military matters prevents them from usurping power; at any rate instances to the contrary are few and slight.

[17] *Pol.* 1310*b*.

This passage seems to be an allusion to Demosthenes who is here, though not expressly named, stigmatized as a demagogue, and to the king of Macedonia, to whose military capacity special attention is called. The following is very important:

> And so, as I was saying, royalty ranks with aristocracy [i.e., with the rule of the best], for it is based upon merit, whether of the individual or of his family, or on benefits conferred, or on these claims with power added to them. For all who have obtained this honour have benefited, or had in their power to benefit, states and nations; some, like Codrus, have prevented the state from being enslaved in war; others, like Cyrus, have given their country freedom, or have settled or gained a territory, like the Lacedaemonian, Macedonian and Molossian kings.[18]

If it were still possible to entertain any doubt that this apology for royalty was intended to be the ideology of one definite hereditary monarchy, this passage must remove all such doubt. For it shows clearly that Aristotle applies his theoretically established category of hereditary royalty as the absolutely best constitution to real states existing in history and organized as hereditary monarchies. If he credits his reader with discerning not only in the Lacedaemonian and Molossian reigning dynasties, but even in the Persian monarchy founded by Cyrus—therefore in a barbarian rule—the realization of the highest form of virtue, or at least the most perfect statesmanship, this sacrifice to intelligence can obviously only have its foundation in the intention to combine discreetly and naturally the Macedonian with the Persian, Lacedaemonian and Molossian kings. He who offers the crown to the latter, can scarcely refuse it to the former. A witness of extraordinary significance to an ideological critical analysis of the *Politics* is furnished here. In no other passage does the extremely cautious Aristotle venture so far. Only he who is blind or shuts his eyes to the political reality can believe that Aristotle, the contemporary of Demosthenes, was not conscious of the political import of his teaching.

And it is only by keeping in view the historical situation, of which we shall have to speak later, that the full significance of the ensuing line of argument can be understood, by which Aristotle pleads the cause of hereditary monarchy in the Athenian democracy, appealing to the property class, to whom hereditary royalty alone can offer security.

> The idea of a king is to be a protector of the rich against unjust treatment, of the people, against insult and oppression. Whereas a tyrant, as has often been repeated, has no regard to any public inter-

[18] *Ibid.* 1310b.

est, except as conducive to his private ends. His aim is pleasure, the aim of a king, honour. Wherefore also in their desires they differ; the tyrant is desirous of riches, the king of what brings honour.[19]

But what is urged in favor of monarchy, as against tyranny, is also skilfully used against democracy. For in this same passage we are reminded that "tyranny has all the vices both of democracy and oligarchy." From oligarchy tyranny, the perversion of monarchy, borrows the principle that the end of government is wealth, but "from democracy tyrants have borrowed the art of making war upon the notables and destroying them secretly or openly or of exiling them." The "notables" are evidently the persons who possess any property; these are always attacked by democracy, which is the rule of those who possess nothing. To the property classes no better form of government could be proposed than one which guaranteed ownership. And it is especially as such that monarchy is represented.

The second passage is still more significant. At the opening of Book vii of the *Politics* Aristotle expresses the opinion that the best form of government is that which conduces by its organization to a happy life for the individual. In what does this happy life consist? The answer is the same as in his ethics: in virtue. Some general reflections precede the assertion that happiness consists in an interior subjective attitude of man. God himself is called to witness that true happiness consists in virtue "for He is happy and blessed, not by reason of any external good, but in Himself and by reason of His own nature.[20] The problem of virtue is then put in the form of an alternative: "which is the more eligible life, that of a citizen who is a member of a state," i.e., one who takes a share in the government and public administration, "or that of an alien, who has no political ties," [21] i.e., one who holds aloof from all political activity. This is the distinction already developed in the ethics and fundamental for Aristotle's dual morality—the distinction between the contemplative and the active life. The relevance of this problem to the question of the form of government is obvious. The opposition between autocracy and democracy which dominates Aristotle's whole doctrine of government corresponds to a hair to the opposition between the two ideals of virtue. The question as to which of the two manners of life is to be preferred from a moral point of view is almost identical with the question as to which of the two forms of government should have the preference. For the ideal of democracy presupposes that virtue is to be found in the life "of a citizen, who is a member of a state," i.e., of one who takes a share in the

[19] *Ibid.* 1311*a*.   [20] *Ibid.* 1323*b*.   [21] *Ibid.* 1324*a*.

government and public administration. The teaching of the autocratic ideal is that the individual, because he has no "political ties," is as "an alien in the state," i.e., he holds aloof from all political activity, and that this attitude must be ideologically honored as being virtue. As the ethics of the Greek Polis—at least in its official representatives—still continued to maintain the former standpoint—namely, that virtue is to be found in the active sharing in the government and that therefore democracy has the preference—extreme caution was naturally to be observed in the enunciation of the contrary opinion. The reasoning at this point, therefore, is by no means direct. To express his meaning Aristotle makes use of a parallel between the individual and the state, similar to that established by Plato in the *Politeia* to illustrate the nature of justice. The happiness and therefore the virtue of the individual is "the same as that of the state." And since that state is not the best organized, whose chief aim is to gain despotic power over its neighbors, but rather that which limits its action to establishing interior order, so also that individual life is not the best, of which the aim is directed outwardly toward others, that is, to master them, which is the aim of active political life. Indeed, it must be allowed that only an active life can be happy in the sense of being virtuous, "for happiness is activity." [22]

But perhaps someone, accepting these premises, may still maintain that supreme power is the best of all things, because the possessors of it are able to perform the greatest number of noble actions. If so, the man who is able to rule, instead of giving up anything to his neighbour, ought rather to take away his power; and the father should make no account of his son, nor the son of his father, nor friend of friend. . . . . There might be some truth in such a view if we assume that robbers and plunderers attain the chief good! [23]

Aristotle's design in propounding this strange opinion is to present the principle of the active political life., i.e., the principle of mastery over others, as highly problematical, and he does so by showing how, if generalized and pushed to its extreme limit, it would inevitably lead to the struggle of all against all. Some form of restraint, at least, is necessary and this is the state, where only some rule and the others are ruled. And here the two forms, democracy and monarchy, are opposed. "For equals the honourable and the just consist in sharing alike, as is just and equal," i.e., governing in turns, because it is impossible for all to govern at the same time, and Aristotle continues:

[22] *Ibid.* 1325a.   [23] *Ibid.*

But that the unequal should be given to equals, and the unlike to those who are like, is contrary to nature, and nothing which is contrary to nature is good. If, therefore, there is anyone superior in virtue and in the power of performing the best actions, him we ought to follow and obey, but he must have the capacity for action as well as virtue.[24]

Aristotle's mention here of the problem of democracy and monarchy would be absolutely incomprehensible did we not suppose a connection with the question whether the virtue of the individual should consist in political activity or not. If men were equal, the question would be answered in favor of political activity, that is, of democracy. But if they are not equal, and if one is pre-eminent over all the others, then monarchy, which means that from all—with the exception of the monarch—a nonpolitical life is demanded. That such is the sense of the preceding passage, the following shows: "If we are right in our view, and happiness is assumed to be virtuous activity, the active life will be the best, both for every city collectively, and for individuals." But, Aristotle adds, "not that a life of action must necessarily have relation to others, as some persons think." [25] Judging by all that has preceded this pronouncement, no doubt is possible but that the life "directed outwardly, towards others" is the active political life; participation in the government and public administration is the activity which every citizen of a democracy must, and in the fullest measure only a democracy can, exercise. Above this ideal of political activity Aristotle places here in the *Politics*, as he does also in the *Ethics*, the ideal of the contemplative life. "Nor are those ideas only to be regarded as practical which are pursued for the sake of practical results, but much more the thoughts and contemplations which are independent and complete in themselves." Also by the activity directed wholly inwardly man can attain to virtue. "Neither, again, is it necessary that states which are cut off from others and choose to live alone should be inactive; for activity, as well as other things, may take place by sections; there are many ways in which the sections of a state act upon one another." Thus Aristotle characterizes the internal activity of the state. And he adds: "The same thing is equally true of every individual." [26] Just as the state should not strive for the mastery over other states, neither ought men to seek dominion over their fellow-men. Just as the state should restrict itself to an internal activity, so ought men to renounce all activity having relation to others, i.e., all political activity. To the question, Which of the two ways of life is to be preferred, the life of active sharing in the gov-

[24] *Ibid.* 1325*b*.   [25] *Ibid.*   [26] *Ibid.*

ernment of the state, or that deprived of all such sharing? Aristotle finally gives the answer in favor of the second alternative without, it is true, totally rejecting the first. The possibility of allowing the latter as an ideal of secondary value is left open. But, nevertheless, what a contrast to the traditional ethics of the Polis democracy, according to which morality can only be realized by active sharing in the affairs of state and by which he who has no such share is considered as useless.

This whole question as to the best life for the individual is of secondary importance, and this Aristotle, from time to time, conveys. The important question is: Which is that form of government whose organization conduces most effectively to the happy life of the individual? But this question is left here without a direct answer. For the answer has been already practically given in that given to the question alleged as secondary. The political ideal of a virtue remote from all active share in political life, corresponds to monarchy alone. But for an ideal so foreign to that of the Hellenic city-state, Aristotle deems an absolutely unassailable justification necessary. As he had appealed to the Godhead in the beginning of the paragraph, so he repeats his appeal at its close. There is no need of human activity directed to others. For "if this were otherwise, God and the universe, who have no external actions over and above their own energies, would be far enough from perfection." [27] God himself justifies the ideal of a nonpolitical life. Only here, where ethics and metaphysics meet in politics, do their central ideas, the pre-eminence of theoretical over practical virtue and the self-regarding Godhead resting in himself, show their real, i.e., their political, significance.

A distinctive peculiarity of the Aristotelian theory of government, which has not hitherto been sufficiently remarked, is that it starts, in principle, from two different standpoints and consequently answers the question as to the best form of government according to two methods, each exclusive of the other. The line of argument which leads to the glorification of hereditary monarchy is carried from the premise that there exists an absolutely best form of government, which is monarchy, from which a strict rank order of constitutions follows: aristocracy, polity, democracy, oligarchy, and tyranny. This scale of values proceeding from the absolutely best to the absolutely worst form is at the foundation of the six-forms scheme, according to which the forms of government are divided into three true and three perverted forms. But already in the representation of this scheme another point of view appears. Each of the three true forms of government is only true under certain quite definite conditions, but these conditions being present, then any one of them will be the best.

[27] *Ibid.* 1325*b*.

Thus monarchy will be best when any one individual is pre-eminent over all the others, when he is more virtuous than all the others together; aristocracy when a minority fulfils the same conditions; and democracy or polity when all the citizens are equally virtuous and all together possessed of greater capacity than any one citizen or than a minority group. This is an altogether relativist principle of values which cannot be associated methodically with the apodictic thesis that royalty is always the best form of government. It is just this relativist principle that Aristotle takes up again in Book iv, after having, in Book iii, represented royalty as being always the best form of government. Here he develops in the introduction the notion that the true legislator and statesman "ought to be acquainted, not only with that which is best in the abstract, but also with that which is best relatively to circumstances," and it is not sufficient to lay down the always best, it is rather necessary "to know the form of government which is best suited to states in general," which is obviously the same as that described in another passage as "the best constitution for most states." The conception of such a constitution, relatively, because only in certain circumstances best, is not clearly expressed in the beginning of Book iv, where it is confused with other problems, e.g., how such a constitution is to be founded, how upheld, or which is the nearest attainable constitution. But in the further course of his arguments Aristotle places this principle of relative value more and more in the foreground. Thus we read: "All these forms of government have a kind of justice, but, tried by an absolute standard, they are faulty"; or, in another passage: "I say relatively to given conditions, since a particular government may be preferable, but another form may be better for some people." [28] In the same line of thought with this relativity, the rigid relation between oligarchy and democracy, according to the six-forms scheme, is relinquished in the admission of the question as to forms of governments "to whom each is suited. For democracy may meet the needs of some better than oligarchy, and conversely." And then it is said, too, that "that which most contributes to the permanence of constitutions is the adaptation of education to the form of government," and therefore it is necessary that "the young are trained by habit and education in the spirit of the constitution, if the laws are democratical, democratically, or oligarchically if the laws are oligarchical." And right in the middle of the discussion as to the cause of the change and decay of democratic and oligarchical constitutions Aristotle speaks of "virtue and justice of the kind proper to each form of government" and adds in explanation, "for, if what is just is not the same in all governments, the quality of justice must also differ." This is the

[28] *Ibid.* 1296*b*.

classical formula of a fundamental relativist principle of constitutional justice.

It is from this standpoint that Aristotle can be relatively just to democracy. That in the rigid scale of values of the six-forms scheme a more favorable place has been assigned to democracy than is its due—as a perversion of the worst of the three true forms—is clear. In the reflections contained in Books iv–vi a markedly indulgent criticism of popular government is evident. It is spoken of, not as a rulership of the poor, but of a free people, or at least of a constitution "when the free who are also poor govern." Different kinds of democracies are distinguished, but only so as to attribute to the most extreme form of this constitution—to that, namely, "in which not the law but the multitude have the supreme power and supersede the law by their decrees"—the place which, according to the original six-forms scheme, should fall expressly to democracy in general as a perversion, being a despotic, a tyrannical form of government. "This sort of democracy being relatively to other democracies what tyranny is to other forms of monarchy, the spirit of both is the same, and they alike exercise a despotic rule over the better citizens." Only of this extreme form of democracy it is said that "such a democracy is fairly open to the objection that it is not a constitution at all; for where the laws have no authority there is no constitution. . . . . So that, if democracy be a real form of government, the sort of system in which all things are regulated by decrees is clearly not even a democracy in the true sense of the word. . . . ." [29] The effort is clearly evident to draw a sharp line between moderate and extreme democracy, admitting the former as a constitution and having, therefore, at least a relative political value. This is a totally different attitude from that which led Aristotle to invent the form of polity, with a view to contrasting it with democracy as its perversion. Now Aristotle goes so far as to declare that in certain circumstances, namely, "where the number of the poor is more than proportioned to the wealth of the rich, there will naturally be a democracy, varying in form with the sort of people who compose it in each case." [30] And in speaking of a democracy in which all "elect to offices and conduct scrutinies and sit in the law-courts" but where "the great offices should be filled up by election and from persons having a qualification, the greater requiring a greater qualification, or, if there be no offices for which a qualification is required, then those who are marked out by special ability should be appointed," Aristotle declares: "Under such a form of government the citizens are sure to be governed well [for the offices will always be held by the best persons; the people are willing enough to elect them and are not jealous of the

[29] *Ibid.*; cf. also 1298*a*.   [30] *Pol.* 1296*b*.

good]. The good and the notables will then be satisfied. . . . ."[31] Democracy, this unnatural rule over slaves, has been promoted to the rank of a well-governed state, in harmony with the will of the people, always supposing, of course, that it is a moderate democracy.

And this is the constitution which under the name of polity is declared to be the best for most states. It can, obviously, only be this for the reason that the conditions under which the constitution must be considered as the best are, as a rule, most frequently given. Aristotle characterizes this polity again and again as a fusion of democracy and oligarchy. He remarks occasionally, it is true, that it approximates very nearly to the so-called aristocratic form. But everything he says about polity—and his remarks are mostly of a very general character—shows that the democratic element in it is predominant. "The government should be confined to those who carry arms." There is also a property qualification. "As to the property qualification, we must see what is the highest qualification sufficiently comprehensive to secure that the number of those who have the rights of citizens exceeds the number of those excluded." By this is emphatically laid down that when speaking of polity it is to be understood as a fusion of oligarchical and democratic elements, in which the latter prevail. Should the government incline rather toward oligarchy, then aristocracy is spoken of. If the differentiation in terminology between oligarchy and aristocracy resulting from certain political tendencies be disregarded, then what Aristotle calls a polity may be denominated as a democracy with a certain aristocratic element. Aristotle also finally allows that "polity more nearly approximates to democracy than to oligarchy." He says that according to the generally accepted doctrine which distinguishes only "two principal forms," namely, oligarchy and democracy (obviously monarchy is not here in question), "aristocracy is considered to be a kind of oligarchy, as being the rule of a few, and the so-called constitutional government"—that is polity—"to be really a democracy," and that "the states which we call constitutional governments have been hitherto called democracies."[32] Besides, Aristotle himself uses indifferently in speaking of one and the same form, at one time the term "polity," at another the term "democracy"; thus he speaks of the form of government which succeeded Gelo's tyranny as democracy, although in a former passage he had denominated it polity (constitutional government).

The characteristic feature of this moderate democracy is that the supreme power is vested in the middle class. "Now in all states there are three elements: one class is very rich, another very poor, and a third is a

[31] *Ibid.* 1318*b*.   [32] *Ibid.* 1297*b*.

mean. It is admitted that moderation and the mean are best, and therefore it will clearly be best to possess the gifts of fortune in moderation." [33] The mean being the best and the most useful for the state leads to the conclusion that

> the best political community is formed by citizens of the middle class, and that those states are likely to be well-administered, in which the middle class is large, and stronger if possible than both the other classes, or at any rate than either singly. Great then is the good fortune of a state in which the citizens have a moderate and sufficient property. . . . . The mean condition of states is clearly best, for no other is free from faction; and where the middle class is large, there are least likely to be factions and dissensions.[34]

This mean condition of states is polity, for "where the middle class is large and stronger if possible than both the other classes, or at any rate than either singly, a lasting polity is possible." It is a democracy guaranteed by the moderate fortune and therefore itself a guaranty for the same, in modern language a property class democracy, not a proletarian democracy. This is just what distinguishes it essentially from extreme democracy, which is the rule of the poorer classes over the richer, which Aristotle always reproaches with injuring the latter by confiscating their property in favor of the former. Very appropriately has Oncken remarked: "The rule of the middle-class with Aristotle is only another word for the rule of the property class." [35] Aristotle earnestly urges that "those who have the welfare of the state at heart" must above all counteract the demagogic confiscation of property in the law courts by making a law that "the property of the condemned should not be public and go into the treasury, but be sacred." [36] It is from democracy that he requires that

> the rich should be spared; not only should their property not be divided, but their incomes, also, which in some states are taken from them imperceptibly, should be protected. It is a good thing to prevent the wealthy citizens, even if they are willing, from undertaking expensive and useless public services, such as the giving of choruses, rotch-races, and the like.[37]

This requirement polity fulfils, and it is one of the chief reasons why Aristotle deems it, generally, "the best constitution for most states."

[33] *Pol.* 1295b.
[34] *Ibid.*
[35] Oncken, *Die Staatslehre des Aristoteles*, II (1875), 272.
[36] *Pol.* 1320a.
[37] *Ibid.* 1309a.

It is the Mesotes formula, according to which polity is declared to be
the best form of government. It appears therefore—although in no wise
in harmony with the six-forms scheme of constitutions—that polity as a
true form of state is the mean, or in other words the result of the fusion
of two perverted forms of government. But such a fusion should produce
a still worse constitution. And, indeed, if Aristotle speaks of tyranny as
the worst form of government, he describes it as follows: "A compound
of Oligarchy and Democracy in their most extreme forms; it is therefore
most injurious to its subjects, being made up of two evil forms of government, and having the perversions and errors of both" [38] (i.e., of the most
faulty). To tyranny he does not apply the Mesotes formula. He does so
only as regards polity. According to this formula, it must be the mean
between two evils. In answering the inquiry "What is the best constitution for most states, and the best life for most men," Aristotle declares:

> If what was said in the *Ethics* is true, that the happy life is the life
> according to virtue lived without impediment, and that virtue is a
> mean, then the life which is in a mean, and in a mean attainable by
> everyone, must be the best. And the same principles of virtue and vice
> are characteristic of cities and of constitutions, for the constitution is
> in a figure the life of the city.[39]

And thus polity, instead of being a kind of aristocracy, as it would be according to the six-forms scheme, is characterized as a mean between oligarchy and democracy, two perverted constitutions according to the six-
forms scheme. But what is good or right in the meaning of the Mesotes
formula is so not relatively but absolutely, representing the highest grade
in moral and political value. If polity is, as Aristotle here declares, a
"Meson," a mean form of constitution, it follows that in the meaning of
the Mesotes formula it is the best of all constitutions, just as monarchy,
according to the six-forms scheme of constitutions, is pre-eminent among
all others. According, therefore, to the one formula, the order of constitutions would be quite different from the order according to the other. In
fact, it appears in one passage as if Aristotle were inclined to draw this
conclusion from the application of his Mesotes formula to his doctrine of
government. He says, with reference to polity as a mean:

> What then is the best form of government and what makes it the
> best, is evident; and of other constitutions, since we say that there are
> many kinds of democracy and many of oligarchy, it is not difficult to
> see which has the first and which the second, or any other place in the

[38] *Ibid.* 1310*b*.   [39] *Ibid.* 1295*a*.

order of excellency, now that we have determined which is the best. For that which is nearest to the best must of necessity be better, and that which is furthest from it worst.[40]

But from this passage it may be seen that the scale of excellence descending from polity as the best constitution does not include all constitutions. Monarchy obviously is here not included because Aristotle wishes to make monarchy also appear as always the best form of government. But this appreciation of monarchy corresponds to a totally different scheme incompatible with the Mesotes formula. Thus he either drops at once his estimation of constitutions, determined according to the Mesotes formula, or he limits it considerably, adding the remark already quoted in another place: it may be that the value of a constitution is to be estimated according to existing conditions, i.e., on the principle that any form of government in certain circumstances, especially in respect to the nature of the people, may be the best. This means that he falls back on the principle of relative constitutional justice. This teaching, however, is not in harmony with the doctrine that in a fixed hierarchy of excellence royal rule must be assigned the first place.

All these inconsistencies, however, are the result of Aristotle's effort on the one hand to present hereditary monarchy as the highest ideal of constitution, and especially to contrast it with democracy. On the other hand, he desires, but less urgently, to assign to democracy—that is, of course, to a moderate form, protecting property, a form designated under the name of polity—a place with the best constitution. Therefore, he utilizes at one time the conception of the citizen whose essential qualification is his sharing in government, at another time that of the subject distinguished as such by his aptness to be ruled. And this dual structure of his politics, according to which on the one hand hereditary monarchy is best, on the other moderate democracy, corresponds exactly to the dual morality of his ethics, which alongside the practical virtue of deeds sets up as an ideal theoretical contemplative knowledge. It corresponds likewise to the discord in his metaphysics which, far from questioning the many gods of the official state religion, with Zeus at their head governing the world, seeks to confirm this belief, yet seeks to elevate the self-contemplating, inactive godhead above the world, a sole godhead, who by his very nature is irreconcilable with the polytheism of the Greek religion.

This parallel is not merely an apparent one; for between the religion of the Olympic gods—the traditional morality of practical life and of the

[40] *Ibid.* 1296b 3 ff.

Polis democracy on the one side—and the godhead, resting in himself—the ideal of contemplative virtue and absolute monarchy on the other side—there exists the closest connection. This whole philosophy of Aristotle culminating in the doctrine of state would give the impression of one single enormous contradiction, if no account were taken of the political background, which alone explains its true significance. The fundamental contradiction of the Aristotelian politics, to which the ethics and the metaphysics contribute, the apparently irreconcilable opposition between the two political ideals of a hereditary monarchy and of a moderate democracy, explain themselves when the Aristotelian conception is confronted with the historical reality of its time, if we remember the object of the great struggle between the Greek city republics, at the head of which Athens stood, and the Macedonian monarchy, which was in power at the time when Aristotle wrote his *Politics*.

The political aim of Philip, as of Alexander, was by no means the destruction of the Hellenic city-democracy, nor the submission of all the little state republics to the Macedonian monarchy and the incorporation of them into one uniform state. What the Macedonian government wished was only an external political protectorate over the Greek states. Their constitutions so far as internal affairs were concerned should be preserved. The monarchy did not desire to take the place of the democracy but to sit beside and only to a certain extent above it. It was indeed one of the most characteristic methods of the Macedonian imperialism to conciliate the Hellenes to its expansion by giving them a guaranty of existing constitutions (considerably diminished in their respective competence, as regarded external politics) and a guaranty of the rights of property depending on these constitutions. These aims of the Macedonian policy appear most clearly in the peace concluded with the Greek republics by Philip in 338 B.C. at Corinth, and renewed two years later by Alexander.

By this treaty an alliance was founded to which all the Greek states with the exception of Sparta and Thessaly adhered; Macedonia remained outside this League of Greek States, being joined to it only in the form of a personal union. The head of this League, as federal general-in-chief with unlimited powers, was the Macedonian king. It was he who determined the external policy of the League, and thus the policy also of the states of which it was composed. The aim of the alliance, the executive power of which lay in the hands of the king as guardian of its constitution, was the prosecution of the war against Persia, the hereditary enemy of Hellas, and last, but not least, the preservation of the constitutions of the allies against revolutionary forces within the states, especially of a social nature. The terms of the treaty, therefore, prohibited expressly the confiscation of fortunes, remittances of debt, the sharing of estates, and the liberation of slaves. The organization of the League was otherwise very loose. In addition to the executive organ there was a general assembly, having its seat in Corinth, to which every member state sent representatives. This general assembly was unimportant, especially in the domain of foreign policy, as the military forces were exclusively in the hands of the federal general-in-chief, the head of the League. The contributions of the members to the objects of the League were limited to the furnishing of contingents of land and sea forces, the strength of which was strictly prescribed to each state. Any citizen of a member state who should take military service against the League or against the Macedonian monarchy under a foreign power should be punished as a traitor with exile and the confiscation of his fortune, a measure especially directed against Persia, which in its struggle against Macedonia was thus deprived of the possibility of Grecian help.

The political significance of this League of States is obvious. The Greek republics renounced their external and military sovereignty in favor of the Macedonian monarchy and received from the latter a guaranty for the safeguarding of their more or less democratic Polis constitution, but, above all, security for the existing rights of property of the reigning classes against the attacks of those who possessed nothing.

It is not easy to see in this Corinthian alliance even a transitory national unification of the Greeks, imposed on them by the Macedonian monarchy, as this political action is sometimes interpreted. For the treaty of the union preserves most carefully the unhappy disruption of the Greeks, who were split up into numerous small states; it avoids creating any central power, which might tend to diminish these divisions. It divests the Hellenic republics of their essential forces and of their competence in foreign affairs, and this, not in order to hand them over to an organ common to all the member states, but to a third power outside the League. This is nothing but the juridical form of a protectorate of the Macedonian monarchy over the Greek republics. Moreover, how little the Macedonian government cared about this "unification" of the Greeks is shown by the action of Alexander, who as soon as he judged this rear guard no longer necessary dropped it without hesitation.

About a year after Alexander had confirmed the Treaty of Corinth concluded by his father, immediately after the destruction of Thebes, after the overthrow of Athens, and after the demand of the Macedonian government for the delivering-up of Demosthenes, Aristotle returned again to the place where he had received his philosophical training in the school of Plato, in order to found a school there himself. This was that second Athenian period in the philosopher's life during which, as we believe, his *Politics*—or, more exactly, that part of the *Politics*—was written, which represents Aristotle's realistic theory of the state. Close as may have been the intellectual ties that bound Aristotle to Athens, the city of Plato, it must not be forgotten that he never acquired the citizenship of that state, in which he always remained a metic, and that from the very first he never took any part in the political life of that community. He was a citizen of Stagira, and that town belonged to the Macedonian realm, of which he was the rightful subject. As the son of a royal physician attached to the Macedonian court, as the tutor of Alexander, who subsidized not only the scientific works of his teacher but also of his teacher's pupil Theophrastus, as the friend of the Macedonian minister, all-powerful in Hellas, Antipater, Aristotle was doubtless on the best of terms with the government and with the society of the Macedonian monarchy, which was striving to conquer Hellas not only by military but also by intellectual weapons. It was King Philip who from the very beginning attached great importance to gaining for his cause adherents and friends from among the intellectually pre-eminent personalities in the Greek states. He attracted distinguished men to his court, and among them, as is comprehensible, particularly those from whose intellectual ascendancy over their fellow-citizens he hoped to draw political profit. Nor did he disdain to use, whenever the occasion offered, blunter material means to gain the desired sympathy. Thus he won over, among others, the orators Isocrates and Aischines, whose influence in Athens was extremely great, not of course only with coarse bribes, which were openly whispered about in Athens (these means must not be overrated), but also by means of the attraction which the brilliant and successful personality of a victorious dictator exercises over the "intellectuals" of a democracy, especially when this democracy has passed its highest point of development and is evidently on the down grade. It is almost always power that makes mind subservient. Among the intellectuals so important in the Polis, because it was they who directed public opinion, Philip and Alexander knew how to create an intellectual atmosphere relatively favorable to the desired hegemony of the Macedonian monarchy. Not only Aristotle's school of philosophy but also the Platonic Academy was on the side of the Macedonian party. Extremely instructive of the whole situation is the fact that Alexander ordered from Xenocrates, who was at that time the head of the Academy, a work on monarchy, which meant an apology for this constitution. Macedonian imperialism created for itself in Hellas, partly by consciously directed action, partly without effort, an adequate ideology. Not, of course, without exciting a passionate countermovement.

The part played by Demosthenes in this opposition is well known. During Aristotle's second stay in Athens the Macedonian party had, it is true, the upper hand. They demanded and obtained a political action against Demosthenes, who was obliged to flee from Athens. But the opposing forces were also at work. Whoever in any way espoused the cause of peace or proposed a compromise with the Macedonian power, or accepted or even directly defended its political object, was suspected of being in the pay of the king. Spies were suspected everywhere. Aristotle and his school, consisting chiefly of non-Athenian scholars, were also probably regarded as the intellectual exponents of the Macedonian government. It would appear that the philosopher was even directly attacked on account of the relation in which he stood to Philip and Alexander. The national democratic party was only awaiting a favorable opportunity to renew their attacks. Scarcely had the news of Alexander's death reached Athens when immediately an action for godlessness was brought against Aristotle, of which the purely political character was obvious, and which compelled the philosopher to take refuge in Chalkis, a Macedonian fortress. The Delphians deprived him of the honors with which he had been invested in recognition of the Pythionike list which he had drawn up. Demades, the leader of the Macedonian party, was also implicated in an action. But Demosthenes returned to Athens, and was received with acclamation.

This sufficiently shows how extremely cautious a philosophical writer and a teacher of politics had to be in such a politically tense atmosphere, if he would attack the rooted traditional prejudice reigning in the Polis democracy against monarchy in general, and against the Macedonian monarchy in particular. Even Isocrates, a frankly open partisan of Philip, who used the pan-Hellenic idea in the service of the Macedonian hegemony by saluting in it the instrument for the unity of Greece, rejected monarchy as a form of government. In his more than obsequious oration addressed to Philip he thinks himself obliged to mention that the founder of the Macedonian dynasty "did not include Grecian territory in his plans," but aimed "at limiting monarchy to Macedonia, for he knew that the Greeks are not accustomed to submitting to a monarchy; but that other peoples do not know how to organize their lives without such domination." He adheres firmly to the Polis democracy at least in principle. Nevertheless, he also extols the advantages of monarchy, but he puts these words into the mouth of Nikokles, a tyrant of Cyprus, not of an Athenian.[41] This is quite in the vein of the Macedonian policy as is

[41] Isocrates, *Philippos* 44; *Nikokles* 5 ff. Cf. Kaerst, *Studien*, p. 39.

shown by the Peace of Corinth. This, alone, explains the strange attitude adopted by Aristotle in that part of his *Politics,* written during
his second stay in Athens, in which he treats of constitutions: monarchy
is the best form of government; but a moderate democracy is so too; the
former—according to the Corinthian Peace—for foreign affairs, the latter
for home matters. The former as a hereditary monarchy, the latter provided it is under the obligation to afford protection to property. Everything that the Corinthian Peace stipulates under this heading, especially
the prohibition of the confiscation of property and of the liberation of
slaves, finds its theoretical justification in the Aristotelian *Politics.*

It has always been considered as one of the incomprehensible parts of
Aristotle's teaching that in it the state is constantly identified with the
city-state, the specific Hellenic Polis, that he seems to have been blind
to the new formations in the political reality of his time. Not only were
the Asiatic states, for example, Egypt, in no wise comprehensible in terms
of the conception of the Polis, but also the Macedonian kingdom, ever
extending its frontiers, was anything but a city-state. On the soil of
Hellas also, states' unions had arisen, which had long since burst the
limits of the Polis. "The federal state," writes Beloch, "is in the middle
of the fourth century the dominant form of state in a large part of the
Grecian Peninsula." [42] If for Plato the state and the Polis are the same,
this is quite natural; for he is an Athenian and, as such, he has the
Athenian particularism in his blood. The ideological expression of this
is: The true state can be nothing but a town surrounded by plains,
necessary for the life of its inhabitants. Plato is too, above all, a speculative mind, who turns away his glance consciously from natural and
social reality. That Aristotle, still being Plato's pupil and a member of
the Academy, develops his theory of state quite within the categories of
his teacher, is surely comprehensible. But how can he still adhere to the
same after his stay in Assos, even after his activity at the court of Philip,
after having lived in the midst of a great and powerful state, he who
showed himself in his writings on natural science so close an observer of
reality, and who in conscious opposition to his former teacher accepts
also in his later theory of state an empirical method? Had he not in order
to gain the empirical material for his political theory composed a great
work—his series of constitutions—which unfortunately have almost all
been lost? It is true, one must not overlook the fact that that part of the
Politics in which the greatness of the state is discussed and answered quite
in the spirit of the city-state conception, is contained in Book vii and,

[42] Beloch, *Griechische Geschichte,* II, 525.

therefore, belongs to the work dealing with the ideal state, which is a youthful production written under Platonic influence. Nevertheless, the work produced later, during his second stay in Athens, the theory of government of Books i, iii–vi of the *Politics*, does not mention, certainly not theoretically, the existence of a territorial state. The doctrine therein developed, however generally it may be expressed in its wording, and although it occasionally refers to non-Greek states, is not really a general theory of state in the present-day sense of the word, but—as for the most part it confines itself to the consideration of Greek constitutions—a Hellenic doctrine of state. And at the same time, what is most striking, this doctrine shows no trace of a thought of the possibility or of the necessity of a national state, comprising all the Greeks, although this notion had already then gained ground, and played a certain part in the relations existing between the Macedonian kingdom and Hellas. That Aristotle was already aware of this idea in favor of a national political union of the Greeks the following well-known passage attests: "The Hellenic race . . . . if it could be formed into one state, would be able to rule the world." But it is instructive enough that this thought, from which moreover no further conclusion is drawn, is also found in Book vii, therefore in the youthful production concerning the ideal state. The later *Politics* contains not the slightest hint of this kind. If this attitude of Aristotle be compared with that of Isocrates, who was in the service of the Macedonian government and who used the national Hellenic idea directly in favor of Philip's hegemony over Greece, this comparison seems to show that Aristotle's political theory was—at this point—independent of the Macedonian policy. For it would appear as if the demand for national Greek union, which owing to the unconquerable particularism of the little states, torn asunder by internecine war, never took firm root, was never more than a rhetorical phrase having no significance except as an ideology of the Macedonia which aimed at making itself the leading power. In order to justify the protectorate claimed by Philip over the Greek republics, the Macedonian policy was interpreted as an attempt in the interests of Hellas herself to promote her national unity, and to lead her against her hereditary enemy. But in reality Philip's policy was nothing but an endeavor to gain possession of Greece before the unavoidable settlement of Macedonia with the Persian kingdom, so as himself to make use of the forces of these little states and thus to remove, once for all, the danger either of the Persian position being strengthened or of Macedonia being attacked by the Greek states. These little Greek states had no immediate reason for engaging in a war with their "hereditary" enemy. The Persian government even showed itself ready to support the

Hellenic states against Macedonia, and considering the long cherished hatred and the traditional contempt in which the Hellenes held the Macedonians, whom they considered barbarians, the latter seemed suitable for anything rather than for liberators of Greece. When an orator such as Isocrates, to justify his attitude, unfurled the pan-Hellenic flag, the Macedonian government could tolerate it, as long as behind this phraseology no real pan-Hellenic movement existed. But the real unity of Hellas, the establishment of a great Greek national state, was not in the interests of Macedonia. Quite the opposite, nothing would have been more dangerous for her than such a political constellation which, of necessity, would have been obliged to turn toward the great rival in the north. What Philip and Alexander really wanted, the Peace of Corinth shows: politically Hellas was to be kept in the *status quo,* with the addition that Macedonia extend her sovereignty over the little city republics, arrogating to herself their foreign policy and military competence.

The Aristotelian doctrine of constitutions cannot be understood if it is viewed in the light of an attempt to justify to Asia the imperialistic policy pursued by Macedonia in her efforts to subjugate that continent. Alexander had no need of such justification—and, moreover, the teaching of a Greek philosopher on the subject of government, even as an ideology, would not have been a suitable means for that purpose. The *Politics* of Aristotle is addressed solely to a Greek public. Therefore we must expect to find in this work only the reflection of the policy of the Macedonian government in Greece. That the *Politics* as a theory of city-states not united to a higher unity does justify the real aims of the Macedonian policy, in the interests of which the political system of the many little city-states was to be preserved, in no wise excludes the honest conviction of Aristotle that this policy was, under the circumstances, the best for Hellas. And also in this sense his work is the Hellenic theory of state of his time.

Especially as such—as the theory of the Hellenic state—Aristotle's political philosophy is epoch-making, for it marks a decisive turning-point in the political ideology of antiquity. With this system, deeply rooted in ethics and metaphysics, that direction in Greek political philosophy begins which proclaims monarchy, instead of the Polis democracy, as the expression of constitutional justice. It is the schools of the Cynics and of the Stoics. that, by deciding in favor of monarchy, extol the nonpolitical virtue of a life removed from all share in state affairs. It is the ideal of the sage. On the one side, the king is described as possessing all the virtues of the sage; on the other, it is taught that man—as the subject—is to hold himself aloof from all affairs of state; he, as the true philosopher, is especially adapted to obey. Between this philosophy for the subject, taught by the Cynics and likewise by the Stoics, and the absolute quietism of the Epicureans, whose political indifference had its source in the desire to avoid all conflict with the absolute monarchy, there is scarcely any essential difference. They are both the ideological reflex of that actual political condition under which, since the submission of Greece, the Macedonian power had excluded even the intellectuals from any real influence on the formation of the will of the state, and had made any share in public life appear as worthless and dangerous. This complete spiritual conversion which took place in later Greek social philosophy is clearly announced in the teaching of Aristotle, the source of which must be looked for in the beginning of the political development under the influence of which the theories of government of the later schools of philosophy were formed. Already Aristotle places monarchy above democracy; already he places the virtue of philosophical, scientific knowledge above the virtue of political activity. The Greeks of the Polis still find the expression of their will—their will to active participation—in their political destiny, in the notion of the gods, ruling in power and in justice. The Aristotelian godhead, who neither creates nor rules the world but, knowing himself, rests in himself, is already the expression of practical political resignation.

This is the decisive line of demarcation between the Aristotelian, also the post-Aristotelian, and the Platonic philosophy. The claim made by the latter to rule the state must have appeared, in face of the blunt political reality of the imperialism which was swallowing up the Greek democracies, from the standpoint of the sage, who desired only to understand the world, even the social world, no better than a Utopia. Certainly Plato's political ideal contained a deep-rooted aversion to democracy; it was rather developed toward aristocracy, even toward autocracy. But Plato wishes to give to philosophy, i.e., to his own philosophy instead of to democracy, the place of ruler; this theory of government has, from the point of view of practical politics, absolutely no, or, at most, a purely negative significance. It is but a symptom of the decline already begun of the Polis constitution. Very different is the Aristotelian, in which the real power of the state is already clearly announced, the far-reaching effects of which were destined to give to antiquity its political stamp.

CICERO

Law and administration are the two great contributions of Rome to the conceptions and practices of government and politics in the Western world. By contrast, there is not much formal political theory in the Roman heritage that compares with the brilliant masterpieces of Greek philosophers. The only Roman political writer who has had an enduring influence throughout the ages is Cicero (106–43 B.C.). He was not a professional philosopher and leader of a school or academy of his own, but a lawyer and statesman whose works are reflections on politics rather than on political theory. Like other educated Romans of his class, he owed his philosophical outlook as much to Plato and Aristotle as to Stoicism. He was the leading lawyer of his time, and rose to high office, both in Rome and in the provinces. Cicero fervently believed in moderation, concord, and constitutionalism; he was a conservative whose faith in constitutional government ran counter to the drift toward dictatorship on the Right, and whose social and economic views antagonized the radical elements on the Left. Only a year after the assassination of Caesar, Cicero, too, was murdered. His two main works on government are his *Republic* and *Laws,* written in obvious reference to Plato's two works of the same titles. Whereas for Plato the political world ended at the confines of the city-state, Cicero had a sense of the world, nurtured by the Stoic elements of his thinking and by his wide governmental experience in various parts of the world.

In modern times, Cicero exercised his greatest influence in the eighteenth century, both in Europe and in North America. Among leading modern political thinkers, perhaps no one was closer to Cicero, in temperament and outlook, than Montesquieu (1689–1755). He, too, was a conservative with a strong faith in the rule of law and constitutional government, who failed to stem the drift of his country to extremism and, finally, revolution. One of the key ideas of his principal work, *The Spirit of the Laws* (1748), is that of the balanced constitution, just as Cicero had proclaimed the balanced combination between kingship, aristocracy, and democracy as the best constitution. Montesquieu, however, went beyond Cicero and refined the concept of the balanced constitution into that of separation of powers, which became one of the guiding and inspiring concepts of the founders of the American political system. Montesquieu's oration on Cicero, reproduced in full below, was written by him in his youth; while its style shows unmistakable signs of youthful enthusiasm and exuberance, it nevertheless testifies to the deep intellectual and spiritual kinship between himself and Cicero.

Montesquieu on CICERO

Among all the ancients, Cicero is the one who had the highest personal merits, and the one whom I should most like to resemble. No one possessed a character finer and greater than he did; no one loved glory better than he did; no one attained it more firmly, or arrived at it by paths less trodden.

The reading of his works elevates the heart no less than the mind; his eloquence is all grandeur, all majesty, all heroism. One has to see him triumph over Catiline, arise against Anthony, or finally weep over the deplorable remains of dying liberty. Whether he tells us of his own actions or of the feats of the great men who fought for the Roman Republic, he becomes moved by his own glory and intoxicated by that of the great Romans. The fearlessness of his expressions enters into the vivacity of his sentiments. I feel that he carries me with him in his raptures and emotions. What portraits he draws of Brutus, Cassius, and Cato! What fire, what liveliness, what swiftness, what torrent of elo-

[Charles-Louis de Montesquieu, "Discourse on Cicero" (written in his youth and published posthumously in *Mélanges Inédits*, 1892, trans. William Ebenstein).]

quence! As for me, I do not know whether I should rather resemble Cicero the panegyrist or Cicero the hero. If he occasionally displays his talents with too much ostentation, he only makes me express that which he has already made me feel; he forestalls me with the eulogies which are due to him. I am not displeased being informed that it is not simply an orator who speaks, but the liberator of his country and the defender of freedom.

Cicero merits the title of philosopher as much as that of orator. One could even say that he has distinguished himself more in the Lyceum than on the speaker's rostrum. He is original in his books on philosophy, but has had several rivals in his eloquence. He was the first Roman who took philosophy out of the hands of the learned and freed it from the encumbrance of a foreign language. He made philosophy the common property of all men, as is reason itself, and in the ensuing applause which he received the men of letters found themselves in accord with the people. I cannot enough admire the depth of his arguments, put forward in an era in which the sages distinguished themselves only by their bizarre clothes. I only wish he could have lived in a more enlightened century, so that his happy talents might have been employed to discover truths rather than to demolish errors. It must be admitted that he left behind an awesome void in philosophy: he destroyed all that had been imagined until then; new beginnings had to be made and new thoughts conceived; the human race entered its infancy, as it were, sent back by Cicero to first principles.

What a pleasure to see Cicero, in his book on *The Nature of the Gods,* survey all sects, confound all philosophers, and point in each prejudice to its blemishes! Sometimes he fights against these monsters; sometimes he makes fun of philosophy. The champions he introduces destroy each other; this one is abashed by that one, who, in turn, is defeated by someone else. All these systems disintegrate one after another, and in the mind of Cicero's reader there remains nothing but scorn for the philosophers and admiration for their critic.

With equal satisfaction we observe Cicero, in his book *On Divination,* free the mind of the Romans of the yoke of soothsayers and the rules of their craft—the shame of pagan theology, first established among uncouth and primitive peoples by the policies of the magistrates, and later weakened, again by public policies, once the people became more enlightened.

Cicero sometimes reveals the charms of friendship and makes us feel its delights. At other times he makes us see the advantages of an age which is illuminated by reason and saves us from the violence of passions. Cultivating our morals and manners, Cicero shows us the extent of our duties and teaches us the meaning of honesty and utility: what we owe to society and what we owe to ourselves, what we must do as fathers of families or as citizens.

Cicero's character and morals were more austere than his mind. He conducted himself in his governing of Cilicia with the disinterestedness of men like Cincinnatus, Camillus, and Cato. But his virtue, which had nothing ferocious about it, did not prevent him from enjoying the refinements of his century. His works on ethics breathe an air of gaiety and a certain contentment of spirit that mediocre philosophers do not know of. He does not issue precepts to us, but makes us feel them. He does not incite to virtue, but attracts us to it. Reading his works one will become repelled by Seneca and his like forever, men who are more ill than those they seek to cure, more desperate than those they console, more tyrannized by passions than those they wish to liberate from them.

Some persons, accustomed to measure all heroes against Quintus Curtius, have formed a false conception of Cicero; they have regarded him a weak and timid man and have reproached him in a way never done even by Anthony, his greatest enemy. Cicero avoided danger, because he knew of it. But he was no longer aware of it once he could not avoid it. This great man always subordinated his passions, his fears, and his courage to prudence and reason. I dare say that perhaps no one among the Romans showed greater examples of forcefulness and courage. In delivering his Second Philippic before Anthony, did Cicero not incur the peril of certain death, generously sacrificing his life for the sake of his offended name and reputation? The courage and boldness of the orator must therefore be even more admired than his eloquence. Let us remember that Anthony was the most powerful of men, the master of the world, who dared everything and accomplished all he dared, and that he was surrounded in the Senate by his soldiers, a king rather than a consul. Covered with confusion and ignominy, thunderstruck, annihilated, Anthony was compelled to listen to the most humiliating statements from the mouth of a man from whom he could take a thousand lives.

Thus, it was not at the head of an army that Cicero was in need of firmness and courage. The tribulations he had to suffer, in times so difficult for honest men, always brought him close to the presence of death. All the enemies of the Republic were his enemies: Verres, Claudius, Catiline, Caesar, Anthony, and finally all the villains of Rome declared war on him.

True, there were occasions when the force of his spirit seemed to abandon him; when he saw Rome torn by so many factions, he gave himself up to sorrow, he let himself be beaten down, and his philosophy was less strong than his love for the Republic.

In that famous war which decided the destiny of the universe, Cicero trembled for his fatherland; he saw Caesar approach with an army that had won more battles than it had legions. But how strong was Cicero's grief when he saw that Pompey abandoned Italy and left Rome exposed to the fury of the rebels! "After such cowardice," Cicero said, "I can no longer respect that man who, rather than withdraw from his country, should have died on the ramparts of Rome and been buried under her ruins."

Cicero, who had closely watched Caesar's intentions for a long time, would have brought upon that ambitious man Catiline's fate if his counsels of prudence had been listened to. "If my advice had been followed," Cicero said to Anthony, "the Republic would flourish today, and you would be nothing. I felt strongly that Caesar should not have been permitted to continue the rule of Gaul beyond five years. I was also persuaded that during his absence he should not have been allowed to ask for the consulate. If I had been fortunate enough to convince enough people of my views, we should have never fallen into the abysm in which we are today. However, when I saw that Pompey had delivered the Republic to Caesar, realizing too late the evils that I had foreseen so long before, I did not cease to speak of accommodation and I spared no effort to unite the spirits."

After Pompey abandoned Italy, Cicero knew well that he had to flee; yet he refused to do so and stayed on for some time. Caesar met with him and sought to compel him, by pleas and threats, to ally himself with Caesar's party. But that true republican rejected his proposals with as much contempt as with pride. Once the party of liberty was destroyed, Cicero submitted to Caesar, as did the whole world. He did not put up useless resistance; he did not act like Cato who cowardly abandoned his country by taking his life. He kept himself in reserve for more auspicious times and he sought in philosophy the comfort that others had found in death.

He retired to Tusculum to find there the freedom which his country had lost. Those fields were never so gloriously fertile; we owe them the fine works that will always be admired by all schools, and throughout all changes of philosophy.

Yet once the conspirators committed that great act that even today still astonishes the tyrants, Cicero came forward as from a tomb, and that sun, eclipsed temporarily by the star of Julius Sidus, appeared in a new light. Brutus, covered with blood and glory, showed the people the dagger of liberty and he cried, "Cicero!" Whether he thus asked for his aid, or congratulated him for the freedom just restored him, or whether the new liberator of his country declared himself his rival, he expressed in that one word the most magnificent eulogy which a mortal ever received.

Cicero soon joined forces with Brutus; the perils did not dismay him. Caesar still lived in the hearts of his soldiers; Anthony, the heir to Caesar's ambitions, held in his hands the consular authority. All this did not stop Cicero from making his decision, and by his authority and example he determined in the uncertain world whether Brutus should be considered a parricide or the liberator of his nation.

But the liberality shown by Caesar in his testament became new chains for the Romans. Anthony harangued that avaricious people and, showing them Caesar's bloody robe, he aroused them so strongly that they proceeded to set fire to the houses of the conspirators. Brutus and Cassius, compelled to leave their ungrateful country, saw no other way of escaping the insults of a furious and blind populace.

Anthony became bolder and he usurped more authority in Rome than even Caesar had ever possessed. He seized the public treasury, sold provinces and public offices, made war with the Roman colonies, and finally violated all the laws. Proud of the success of his eloquence, he did not fear that of Cicero and attacked him openly in the Senate; but he was amazed to find still a Roman in Rome.

Shortly afterward, Octavius made the infamous agreement in which Anthony demanded, as price of his friendship, the head of Cicero. No war was more baneful to the Republic than this shameless reconciliation, which devoured as victims only those who had gloriously defended their country.

The detestable Popilius is vindicated by Seneca for having brought death to Cicero in this way: the odious crime was that of Anthony who had commanded it, and not that of Popilius who had carried out the command; the proscription of Cicero was to die, and that of Popilius to take his life; and therefore it was not strange that Popilius was forced to kill Cicero, the first of all Romans, because he was doomed to lose his head.

4 | MURRAY

THE STOICS

After the breakdown of the Greek city-state, a philosophy was needed which was both more individualistic and universalistic than the classical philosophy anchored in the organic community of the small city-state. This need was filled by Stoicism, the most representative and influential philosophical school of the five centuries from about 300 B.C. to about A.D. 200. On the one hand it stressed individual integrity and selfhood in an era of rapidly disintegrating social and political institutions, and on the other it put the stress on mankind rather than on one people or empire. The breadth of Stoicism is symbolically expressed by the fact that its two leading exponents were Epictetus (about A.D. 50–120), a former Phrygian slave, and Marcus Aurelius (A.D. 121–180), a Roman emperor. The Stoic doctrine that all men are brothers, inasmuch as all men have "God as maker and father and kinsman," has strongly permeated Christian thinking and has also vitally contributed to the development of the theory of international law since the sixteenth century; the Stoic concept of a "law behind the law" became the fundamental principle of the American constitutional system, jealously guarded by the judiciary and deeply revered by the American people, who have been unwilling to accept the view that laws of fallible men, exposed to the temptations of passion and interest, are binding under all circumstances.

Since the Renaissance, each age has rediscovered the ancient heritage anew, in the light of its specific needs and circumstances. In the twentieth century, no one in any country has done as much for that revival as Gilbert Murray (1866–   ), the leading British classicist of our era. He is the author of numerous new translations and studies of Aeschylus, Euripides, Sophocles, and Aristophanes, to mention but the giants of the Greek drama, and he has also summarized the meaning of Greek civilization for us today in such books as *The Five Stages of Greek Religion* (1912) and *Greek Studies* (1946). Faithfully following the message of Stoicism, Murray has also been active in helping to build an international order based on the rule of law. His lecture on "The Stoics," delivered in London in 1915, stresses their humanistic creed, of which Murray himself is a self-confessed and confirmed disciple.

Murray on THE STOICS

I propose to give here in rough outline some account of the greatest system of organized thought which the mind of man had built up for itself in the Graeco-Roman world before the coming of Christianity with its inspired book and its authoritative revelation. Stoicism may be called either a philosophy or a religion. It was a religion in its exalted passion; it was a philosophy inasmuch as it made no pretence to magical powers or supernatural knowledge. I do not suggest that it is a perfect system, with no errors of fact and no inconsistencies of theory. It is certainly not that; and I do not know of any system that is. But I believe that it represents a way of looking at the world and the practical problems of life which possesses still a permanent interest for the human race, and a permanent power of inspiration. I shall approach it, therefore, rather as a psychologist than as a philosopher or historian. I shall not attempt to trace the growth or variation of Stoic doctrine under its various professors, nor yet to scrutinize the logical validity of its arguments. I shall merely try as best I can to make intelligible its great central principles and the almost irresistible appeal which they made to so many of the best minds of antiquity.

From this point of view I will begin by a very rough general suggestion—viz. that the religions known to history fall into two broad classes, religions which are suited for times of good government and religions which are suited for times of bad government; religions for prosperity or

[Gilbert Murray, *The Stoic Philosophy* (Conway Memorial Lecture, G. P. Putnam, 1915). By permission.]

for adversity, religions which accept the world or which defy the world, which place their hopes in the betterment of human life on this earth or which look away from it as from a vale of tears. By "the world" in this connection I mean the ordinary concrete world, the well-known companion of the flesh and the Devil; not the universe. For some of the religions which think most meanly of the world they know have a profound admiration for all, or nearly all, those parts of the universe where they have not been.

Now, to be really successful in the struggle for existence, a religion must suit both sets of circumstances. A religion which fails in adversity, which deserts you just when the world deserts you, would be a very poor affair; on the other hand, it is almost equally fatal for a religion to collapse as soon as it is successful. Stoicism, like Christianity, was primarily a religion for the oppressed, a religion of defence and defiance; but, like Christianity, it had the requisite power of adaptation. Consistently or inconsistently, it opened its wings to embrace the needs both of success and of failure. To illustrate what I mean—contrast for the moment the life of an active, practical, philanthropic, modern Bishop with that of an anchorite like St. Simeon Stylites, living in idleness and filth on the top of a large column; or, again, contrast the Bishop's ideals with those of the author of the Apocalypse, abandoning himself to visions of a gorgeous reversal of the order of this evil world and the bloody revenges of the blessed. All three are devout Christians; but the Bishop is working with the world of men, seeking its welfare and helping its practical needs; the other two are rejecting or cursing it. In somewhat the same way we shall find that our two chief preachers of Stoicism are, the one a lame and penniless slave to whom worldly success is as nothing, the other an Emperor of Rome, keenly interested in good administration.

The founder of the Stoic school, Zeno, came from Cilicia to Athens about the year 320 B.C. His place of birth is, perhaps, significant. He was a Semite, and came from the East. The Semite was apt in his religion to be fiercer and more uncompromising than the Greek. The time of his coming is certainly significant. It was a time when landmarks had collapsed, and human life was left, as it seemed, without a guide. The average man in Greece of the fifth century B.C. had two main guides and sanctions for his conduct of life: the welfare of his City and the laws and traditions of his ancestors. First the City, and next the traditional religion; and in the fourth century both of these had fallen. Let us see how.

Devotion to the City or Community produced a religion of public service. The City represented a high ideal, and it represented supreme power. By 320 B.C. the supreme power had been overthrown. Athens, and all independent Greek cities, had fallen before the overwhelming force of the great military monarchies of Alexander and his generals. The high ideal at the same time was seen to be narrow. The community to which a man should devote himself, if he should devote himself at all, must surely be something larger than one of these walled cities set upon their separate hills. Thus the City, as a guide of life, had proved wanting. Now when the Jews lost their Holy City they had still, or believed that they had still, a guide left. "Zion is taken from us," says the Book of Esdras; "nothing is left save the Holy One and His Law." But Greece had no such Law. The Greek religious tradition had long since been riddled with criticism. It would not bear thinking out, and the Greeks liked to think things out. The traditional religion fell not because the people were degenerate. Quite the contrary; it fell, as it has sometimes fallen else-where, because the people were progressive. The people had advanced, and the traditional religion had not kept pace with them. And we may add another consideration. If the Gods of tradition had proved themselves capable of protecting their worshippers, doubtless their many moral and intellectual deficiencies might have been overlooked. But they had not. They had proved no match for Alexander and the Macedonian phalanx.

Thus the work that lay before the generation of 320 B.C. was twofold. They had to rebuild a new public spirit, devoted not to the City, but to something greater; and they had to rebuild a religion or philosophy which should be a safe guide in the threatening chaos. We will see how Zeno girded himself to this task.

Two questions lay before him—how to live and what to believe. His real interest was in the first, but it could not be answered without first facing the second. For if we do not in the least know what is true or untrue, real or unreal, we cannot form any reliable rules about conduct or anything else. And, as it happened, the Sceptical school of philosophy, largely helped by Plato, had lately been active in denying the possibility of human knowledge and throwing doubt on the very existence of reality. Their arguments were extraordinarily good, and many of them have not been answered yet; they affect both the credibility of the senses and the supposed laws of reasoning. The Sceptics showed how the senses are notoriously fallible and contradictory, and how the laws of reasoning lead by equally correct processes to opposite conclusions. Many modern philosophers, from Kant to Dr. Schiller and Mr. Bertrand Russell, have followed respectfully in their footsteps. But Zeno had no patience with this sort of thing. He wanted to get to business.

Also he was a born fighter. His dealings with opponents who argued against him always remind me of a story told of the Duke of Wellington when his word was doubted by a subaltern. The Duke, when he was very old and incredibly distinguished, was telling how once, at mess in the Peninsula, his servant had opened a bottle of port, and inside found a rat. "It must have been a very large bottle," remarked the subaltern. The Duke fixed him with his eye. "It was a damned small bottle." "Oh," said the subaltern, abashed; "then no doubt it was a very small rat." "It was a damned large rat," said the Duke. And there the matter has rested ever since.

Zeno began by asserting the existence of the real world. "What do you mean by real?" asked the Sceptic. "I mean solid and material. I mean that this table is solid matter." "And God," said the Sceptic, "and the soul? Are they solid matter?" "Perfectly solid," says Zeno; "more solid, if anything, than the table." "And virtue or justice or the Rule of Three; also solid matter?" "Of course," said Zeno; "quite solid." This is what may be called "high doctrine," and Zeno's successors eventually explained that their master did not really mean that justice was solid matter, but that it was a sort of "tension," or mutual relation, among material objects. This amendment saves the whole situation. But it is well to remember the uncompromising materialism from which the Stoic system started.

Now we can get a step further. If the world is real, how do we know about it? By the evidence of our senses; for the sense-impression (here Stoics and Epicureans both followed the fifth-century physicists) is simply the imprint of the real thing upon our mind-stuff. As such it must be true. In the few exceptional cases where we say that "our senses deceive us" we speak incorrectly. The sense-impression was all right; it is we who have interpreted it wrongly, or received it in some incomplete way. What we need in each case is a "comprehensive sense-impression." The meaning of this phrase is not quite clear. I think it means a sense-impression which "grasps" its object; but it may be one which "grasps" us, or which we "grasp," so that we cannot doubt it. In any case, when we get the real imprint of the object upon our senses, then this imprint is of necessity true. When the Sceptics talk about a conjuror making "our senses deceive us," or when they object that a straight stick put half under water looks as if it were bent in the middle, they are talking inexactly. In such cases the impression is perfectly true; it is the interpretation that may go wrong. Similarly, when they argue that reasoning is fallacious because men habitually make mistakes in it, they are confusing the laws of reasoning with the inexact use which people make of them. You might just as well say that twice two is not four, or that 7×7 is not 49, because people often make mistakes in doing arithmetic.

Thus we obtain a world which is in the first place real and in the second knowable. Now we can get to work on our real philosophy, our doctrine of ethics and conduct. And we build it upon a very simple principle, laid down first by Zeno's master, Crates, the founder of the Cynic School: the principle that Nothing but Goodness is Good. That seems plain enough, and harmless enough; and so does its corollary: "Nothing but badness is bad." In the case of any concrete object which you call "good," it seems quite clear that it is only good because of some goodness in it. We, perhaps, should not express the matter in quite this way, but we should scarcely think it worth while to object if Zeno chooses to phrase it so, especially as the statement itself seems little better than a truism.

Now, to an ancient Greek the form of the phrase was quite familiar. He was accustomed to asking "What is the good?" It was to him the central problem of conduct. It meant: "What is the object of life, or the element of things which makes them worth having?" Thus the principle will mean: "Nothing is worth living for except goodness." The only good for man is to *be* good. And, as we might expect, when Zeno says "good" he means good in an ultimate Day-of-Judgement sense, and will take no half-measures. The principle turns out to be not nearly so harmless as it looked. It begins by making a clean sweep of the ordinary conventions. You remember the eighteenth-century lady's epitaph which ends: "Bland, passionate, and deeply religious, she was second cousin to the Earl of Leitrim, and of such are the kingdom of heaven." One doubts whether, when the critical moment came, her relationships would really prove as important as her executors hoped; and it is the same with all the conventional goods of the world when brought before the bar of Zeno. Rank, riches, social distinction, health, pleasure, barriers of race or nation—what will those things matter before the tribunal of ultimate truth? Not a jot. Nothing but goodness is good. It is what you are that matters—what you yourself are; and all these things are not you. They are external; they depend not on you alone, but on other people. The thing that really matters depends on you, and on none but you. From this there flows a very important and surprising conclusion. You possess already, if you only knew it, all that is worth desiring. The good is yours if you but will it. You need fear nothing. You are safe, inviolable, utterly free. A wicked man or an accident can cause you pain, break your leg, make you ill; but no earthly power can make you good or bad except yourself, and to be good or bad is the only thing that matters.

At this point common sense rebels. The plain man says to Zeno: "This is all very well; but we know as a matter of fact that such things as health, pleasure, long life, fame, etc., are good; we all like them. The reverse are bad; we hate and avoid them. All sane, healthy people agree in judging so." Zeno's answer is interesting. In the first place, he says: "Yes; that is what most people say. But the judges who give that judgement are bribed. Pleasure, though not really good, has just that particular power of bribing the judges, and making them on each occasion say or believe that she is good. The Assyrian king Sardanapalus thinks it good to stay in his harem, feasting and merry-making, rather than suffer hardship in governing his kingdom. He swears his pleasure is good; but what will any unbribed third person say? Consider the judgements of history. Do you ever find that history praises a man because he was healthy, or long-lived, or because he enjoyed himself a great deal? History never thinks of such things; they are valueless and disappear from the world's memory. The thing that lives is a man's goodness, his great deeds, his virtue, or his heroism."

If the questioner was not quite satisfied, Zeno used another argument. He would bid him answer honestly for himself: "Would you yourself really like to be rich and corrupted? To have abundance of pleasure and be a worse man?" And, apparently, when Zeno's eyes were upon you, it was difficult to say you would. Some Stoics took a particular instance. When Harmodius and Aristogeiton, the liberators of Athens, slew the tyrant Hipparchus (which is always taken as a praiseworthy act), the tyrant's friends seized a certain young girl, named Leaina, who was the mistress of Aristogeiton, and tortured her to make her divulge the names of the conspirators. And under the torture the girl bit out her tongue and died without speaking a word. Now, in her previous life we may assume that Leaina had had a good deal of gaiety. Which would you sooner have as your own—the early life of Leaina, which was full of pleasures, or the last hours of Leaina, which were full of agony? And with a Stoic's eyes upon them, as before, people found it hard to say the first. They yielded their arms and confessed that goodness, and not any kind of pleasure, is the good.

But now comes an important question, and the answer to it, I will venture to suggest, just redeems Stoicism from the danger of becoming one of those inhuman cast-iron systems by which mankind may be browbeaten, but against which it secretly rebels. What *is* Goodness? What is this thing which is the only object worth living for?

Zeno seems to have been a little impatient of the question. We know quite well; everybody knows who is not blinded by passion or desire. Still, the school consented to analyse it. And the profound common sense and reasonableness of average Greek thought expressed the answer in its own characteristic way. Let us see in practice what we mean by "good." Take a good bootmaker, a good father, a good musician, a good horse, a good chisel; you will find that each one of them has some function to perform, some special work to do; and a good one does the work well. Goodness is performing your function well. But when we say "well" we are still using the idea of goodness. What do we mean by doing it "well"? Here the Greek falls back on a scientific conception which had great influence in the fifth century B.C., and, somewhat transformed and differently named, has regained it in our own days. We call it "Evolution." The Greeks called it *Phusis,* a word which we translate by "Nature," but which seems to mean more exactly "growth," or "the process of growth." [1] It is Phusis which gradually shapes or tries to shape every living thing into a more perfect form. It shapes the seed, by infinite and exact gradations, into the oak; the blind puppy into the good hunting dog; the savage tribe into the civilized city. If you analyse this process, you find that Phusis is shaping each thing towards the fulfilment of his own function—that is, towards the good. Of course Phusis sometimes fails; some of the blind puppies die; some of the seeds never take root. Again, when the proper development has been reached, it is generally followed by decay; that, too, seems like a failure in the work of Phusis. I will not consider these objections now; they would take us too far afield, and we shall need a word about them later. Let us in the meantime accept this conception of a force very like that which most of us assume when we speak of evolution; especially, perhaps, it is like what Bergson calls *La Vie* or *L'Élan Vital* at the back of *L'Évolution Creatrice,* though to the Greeks it seemed still more personal and vivid; a force which is present in all the live world, and is always making things grow towards the fulfilment of their utmost capacity. We see now what goodness is; it is living or acting according to Phusis, working with Phusis in her eternal effort towards perfection. You will notice, of course, that the phrase means a good deal more than we usually mean by living "according to nature." It does not mean "living simply," or "living like the natural man." It means living according to the spirit which makes the world grow and progress.

This Phusis becomes in Stoicism the centre of much speculation and much effort at imaginative understanding. It is at work everywhere. It is like a soul, or a life-force, running through all matter as the "soul" or life of a man runs through all his limbs. It is the soul of the world. Now,

[1] See a paper by Professor J. L. Myres, "The Background of Greek Science," *University of California Chronicle,* xvi, 4.

it so happened that in Zeno's time the natural sciences had made a great advance, especially astronomy, botany, and natural history. This fact had made people familiar with the notion of natural law. Law was a principle which ran through all the movements of what they called the *cosmos,* or "ordered world." Thus Phusis, the life of the world, is, from another point of view, the Law of Nature; it is the great chain of causation by which all events occur; for the Phusis which shapes things towards their end acts always by the laws of causation. Phusis is not a sort of arbitrary personal goddess, upsetting the natural order; Phusis is the natural order, and nothing happens without a cause.

A natural law, yet a natural law which is alive, which is itself life. It becomes indistinguishable from a purpose, the purpose of the great world-process. It is like a fore-seeing, fore-thinking power—*Pronoia;* our common word "Providence" is the Latin translation of this *Pronoia,* though of course its meaning has been rubbed down and cheapened in the process of the ages. As a principle of providence or forethought it comes to be regarded as God, the nearest approach to a definite personal God which is admitted by the austere logic of Stoicism. And since it must be in some sense material, it is made of the finest material there is; it is made of fire, not ordinary fire, but what they called intellectual fire. A fire which is present in a warm, live man, and not in a cold, dead man; a fire which has consciousness and life, and is not subject to decay. This fire, Phusis, God, is in all creation.

We are led to a very definite and complete Pantheism. The Sceptic begins to make his usual objections. "God in worms?" he asks. "God in fleas and dung beetles?" And, as usual, the objector is made to feel sorry that he spoke. "Why not?" the Stoic answers; "cannot an earthworm serve God? Do you suppose that it is only a general who is a good soldier? Cannot the lowest private or camp attendant fight his best and give his life for his cause? Happy are you if you are serving God, and carrying out the great purpose as truly as such-and-such an earthworm." That is the conception. All the world is working together. It is all one living whole, with one soul through it. And, as a matter of fact, no single part of it can either rejoice or suffer without all the rest being affected. The man who does not see that the good of every living creature is his good, the hurt of every living creature his hurt, is one who wilfully makes himself a kind of outlaw or exile: he is blind, or a fool. So we are led up to the great doctrine of the later Stoics, the Συμπαθεία τῶν ὅλων, or Sympathy of the Whole; a grand conception, the truth of which is illustrated in the ethical world by the feelings of good men, and in the world of natural science. . . . We moderns may be excused for feeling a little surprise. . . . by the fact that the stars twinkle. It is because they are so sorry for us: as well they may be!

Thus Goodness is acting according to Phusis, in harmony with the will of God. But here comes an obvious objection. If God is all, how can anyone do otherwise? God is the omnipresent Law; God is all Nature; no one can help being in harmony with Him. The answer is that God is in all except the doings of bad men. For man is free. . . . How do we know that? Why, by a *kataléptiké phantasia,* a comprehensive sense impression which it is impossible to resist. Why it should be so we cannot tell. "God might have preferred chained slaves for His fellow-workers; but, as a matter of fact, he preferred free men." Man's soul, being actually a portion of the divine fire, has the same freedom that God Himself has. He can act either with God or against Him, though, of course, when he acts against Him he will ultimately be overwhelmed. Thus Stoicism grapples with a difficulty which no religion has satisfactorily solved.

It will be observed that by now we have worked out two quite different types of Stoic—one who defies the world and one who works with the world; and, as in Christianity, both types are equally orthodox. We have first the scorner of all earthly things. Nothing but goodness is good; nothing but badness bad. Pain, pleasure, health, sickness, human friendship and affection, are all indifferent. The truly wise man possesses his soul in peace; he communes with God. He always, with all his force, wills the will of God; thus everything that befalls him is a fulfilment of his own will and good. A type closely akin to the early Christian ascetic or the Indian saint.

And in the second place we have the man who, while accepting the doctrine that only goodness is good, lays stress upon the definition of goodness. It is acting according to Phusis, in the spirit of that purpose or forethought which, though sometimes failing, is working always unrestingly for the good of the world, and which needs its fellow-workers. God is helping the whole world; you can only help a limited fraction of the world. But you can try to work in the same spirit. There were certain old Greek myths which told how Heracles and other heroes had passed laborious lives serving and helping humanity, and in the end became gods. The Stoics used such myths as allegories. That was the way to heaven; that was how a man may at the end of his life "become not a dead body, but a star." In the magnificent phrase which Pliny translates from a Greek Stoic, God is that, and nothing but that; man's true God is the helping of man: *Deus est mortali iuvare mortalem.*

No wonder such a religion appealed to kings and statesmen and Roman governors. Nearly all the successors of Alexander—we may say

all the principal kings in existence in the generations following Zeno—
professed themselves Stoics. And the most famous of all Stoics, Marcus
Aurelius, found his religion not only in meditation and religious exercises,
but in working some sixteen hours a day for the good practical government of the Roman Empire.

Is there any real contradiction or inconsistency between the two types
of Stoic virtue? On the surface certainly there seems to be; and the school
felt it, and tried in a very interesting way to meet it. The difficulty is this:
what is the good of working for the welfare of humanity if such welfare
is really worthless? Suppose, by great labour and skill, you succeed in
reducing the death-rate of a plague-stricken area; suppose you make a
starving countryside prosperous; what is the good of it all if health and
riches are in themselves worthless, and not a whit better than disease and
poverty?

The answer is clear and uncompromising. A good bootmaker is one
who makes good boots; a good shepherd is one who keeps his sheep well;
and even though good boots are, in the Day-of-Judgement sense, entirely
worthless, and fat sheep no whit better than starved sheep, yet the good
bootmaker or good shepherd must do his work well or he will cease to
be good. To be good he must perform his function; and in performing
that function there are certain things that he must "prefer" to others,
even though they are not really "good." He must prefer a healthy sheep
or a well-made boot to their opposites. It is thus that Nature, or Phusis,
herself works when she shapes the seed into the tree, or the blind puppy
into the good hound. The perfection of the tree or hound is in itself
indifferent, a thing of no ultimate value. Yet the goodness of Nature
lies in working for that perfection.

Life becomes, as the Stoics more than once tell us, like a play which
is acted or a game played with counters. Viewed from outside, the
counters are valueless; but to those engaged in the game their importance
is paramount. What really and ultimately matters is that the game shall
be played as it should be played. God, the eternal dramatist, has cast you
for some part in His drama, and hands you the role. It may turn out
that you are cast for a triumphant king; it may be for a slave who dies
in torture. What does that matter to the good actor? He can play either
part; his only business is to accept the role given him, and to perform it
well. Similarly, life is a game of counters. Your business is to play it in
the right way. He who set the board may have given you many counters;
He may have given you few. He may have arranged that, at a particular
point in the game, most of your men shall be swept accidentally off the
board. You will lose the game; but why should you mind that? It is

your play that matters, not the score that you happen to make. He is not a fool to judge you by your mere success or failure. Success or failure is a thing He can determine without stirring a hand. It hardly interests Him. What interests Him is the one thing which he cannot determine—the action of your free and conscious will.

This view is so sublime and so stirring that at times it almost deadens one's power of criticism. Let us see how it works in a particular case. Suppose your friend is in sorrow or pain, what are you to do? In the first place, you may sympathize—since sympathy runs all through the universe, and if the stars sympathize surely you yourself may. And of course you must help. That is part of your function. Yet, all the time, while you are helping and sympathizing, are you not bound to remember that your friend's pain or sorrow does not really matter at all? He is quite mistaken in imagining that it does. Similarly, if a village in your district is threatened by a band of robbers, you will rush off with soldiers to save it; you will make every effort, you will give your life if necessary. But suppose, after all, you arrive too late, and find the inhabitants with their throats cut and the village in ruins—why should you mind? You know it does not matter a straw whether the villagers' throats are cut or not cut; all that matters is how they behaved in the hour of death. Mr. Bevan, whose studies of the *Stoics and Sceptics* form a rare compound of delicate learning and historical imagination, says that the attitude of the Stoic in such a case is like that of a messenger boy sent to deliver a parcel to someone, with instructions to try various addresses in order to find him. The good messenger boy will go duly to all the addresses, but if the addressee is not to be found at any of them what does that matter to the messenger boy? He has done his duty, and the parcel itself has no interest for him. He may return and say he is sorry that the man cannot be found; but his sorrow is not heartfelt. It is only a polite pretence.

The comparison is a little hard on the Stoics. No doubt they are embarrassed at this point between the claims of high logic and of human feeling. But they meet the embarrassment bravely. "You will suffer in your friend's suffering," says Epictetus. "Of course you will suffer. I do not say that you must not even groan aloud. Yet in the centre of your being do not groan! Ἔσωθεν μέντοι μὴ στενάξῃς." It is very like the Christian doctrine of resignation. Man cannot but suffer for his fellowman; yet a Christian is told to accept the will of God and believe that ultimately, in some way which he does not see, the Judge of the World has done right.

Finally, what is to be the end after this life of Stoic virtue? Many religions, after basing their whole theory of conduct on stern duty and self-sacrifice and contempt of pleasure, lapse into confessing the unreality of their professions by promising the faithful as a reward that they shall be uncommonly happy in the next world. It was not that they really disdained pleasure; it was only that they speculated for a higher rate of interest at a later date. Notably, Islam is open to that criticism, and so is a great deal of popular Christianity. Stoicism is not. It maintains its ideal unchanged.

You remember that we touched, in passing, the problem of decay. Nature shapes things towards their perfection, but she also lets them fall away after reaching a certain altitude. She fails constantly, though she reaches higher and higher success. In the end, said the Stoic—and he said it not very confidently, as a suggestion rather than a dogma—in the very end, perfection should be reached, and then there will be no falling back. All the world will have been wrought up to the level of the divine soul. That soul is Fire; and into that Fire we shall all be drawn, our separate existence and the dross of our earthly nature burnt utterly away. Then there will be no more decay or growth; no pleasure, no disturbance. It may be a moment of agony, but what does agony matter? It will be ecstasy and triumph, the soul reaching its fiery union with God.

The doctrine, fine as it is, seems always to have been regarded as partly fanciful, and not accepted as an integral part of the Stoic creed. Indeed, many Stoics considered that if this Absorption in Fire should occur, it could not be final. For the essence of Goodness is to do something, to labour, to achieve some end; and if Goodness is to exist the world process must begin again. God, so to speak, cannot be good unless he is striving and helping. Phusis must be moving upward, or else it is not Phusis.

Thus Stoicism, whatever its weaknesses, fulfilled the two main demands that man makes upon his religion: it gave him armour when the world was predominantly evil, and it encouraged him forward when the world was predominantly good. It afforded guidance both for the saint and the public servant. And in developing this two-fold character I think it was not influenced by mere inconstancy. It was trying to meet the actual truth of the situation. For in most systems it seems to be recognized that in the Good Life there is both an element of outward striving and an element of inward peace. There are things which we must try to attain, yet it is not really the attainment that matters; it is the seeking. And, consequently, in some sense, the real victory is with him who fought best, not with the man who happened to win. For beyond all the accidents of war, beyond the noise of armies and groans of the dying, there is the presence of some eternal Friend. It is our relation to Him that matters.

A Friend behind phenomena: I owe the phrase to Mr. Bevan. It is the assumption which all religions make, and sooner or later all philosophies. The main criticism which I should be inclined to pass on Stoicism would lie here. Starting out with every intention of facing the problem of the world by hard thought and observation, resolutely excluding all appeal to tradition and mere mythology, it ends by making this tremendous assumption, that there is a beneficent purpose in the world and that the force which moves nature is akin to ourselves. If we once grant that postulate, the details of the system fall easily into place. There may be some overstatement about the worthlessness of pleasure and worldly goods; though, after all, if there is a single great purpose in the universe, and that purpose good, I think we must admit that, in comparison with it, the happiness of any individual at this moment dwindles into utter insignificance. The good, and not any pleasure or happiness, is what matters. If there is no such purpose, well, then the problem must all be stated afresh from the beginning.

A second criticism, which is passed by modern psychologists on the Stoic system, is more searching but not so dangerous. The language of Stoicism, as of all ancient philosophy, was based on a rather crude psychology. It was over-intellectualized. It paid too much attention to fully conscious and rational processes, and too little attention to the enormously larger part of human conduct which is below the level of consciousness. It saw life too much as a series of separate mental acts, and not sufficiently as a continuous, ever-changing stream. Yet a very little correction of statement is all that it needs. Stoicism does not really make reason into a motive force. It explains that an "impulse", or ὁρμή, of physical or biological origin rises in the mind prompting to some action, and then Reason gives or withholds its assent (συγκατάθεσις). There is nothing seriously wrong here.

Other criticisms, based on the unreality of the ideal Wise Man, who acts without desire and makes no errors, seem to me of smaller importance. They depend chiefly on certain idioms or habits of language, which, though not really exact, convey a fairly correct meaning to those accustomed to them.

But the assumption of the Eternal Purpose stands in a different category. However much refined away, it remains a vast assumption. We may discard what Professor William James used to call "Monarchical Deism" or our own claim to personal immortality. We may base ourselves on Evolution, whether of the Darwinian or the Bergsonian sort. But we do seem to find, not only in all religions, but in practically all philosophies, some belief that man is not quite alone in the universe, but is met in his endeavours towards the good by some external help or sympathy. We find it everywhere in the unsophisticated man. We find it in the unguarded self-revelations of the most severe and conscientious Atheists. Now, the Stoics, like many other schools of thought, drew an argument from this consensus of all mankind. It was not an absolute proof of the existence of the Gods or Providence, but it was a strong indication. The existence of a common instinctive belief in the mind of man gives at least a presumption that there must be a good cause for that belief.

This is a reasonable position. There must be some such cause. But it does not follow that the only valid cause is the truth of the content of the belief. I cannot help suspecting that this is precisely one of those points on which Stoicism, in company with almost all philosophy up to the present time, has gone astray through not sufficiently realizing its dependence on the human mind as a natural biological product. For it is very important in this matter to realize that the so-called belief is not really an intellectual judgement so much as a craving of the whole nature.

It is only of very late years that psychologists have begun to realize the enormous domination of those forces in man of which he is normally unconscious. We cannot escape as easily as these brave men dreamed from the grip of the blind powers beneath the threshold. Indeed, as I see philosophy after philosophy falling into this unproven belief in the Friend behind phenomena, as I find that I myself cannot, except for a moment and by an effort, refrain from making the same assumption, it seems to me that perhaps here too we are under the spell of a very old ineradicable instinct. We are gregarious animals; our ancestors have been such for countless ages. We cannot help looking out on the world as gregarious animals do; we see it in terms of humanity and of fellowship. Students of animals under domestication have shown us how the habits of a gregarious creature, taken away from his kind, are shaped in a thousand details by reference to the lost pack which is no longer there—the pack which a dog tries to smell his way back to all the time he is out walking, the pack he barks to for help when danger threatens. It is a strange and touching thing, this eternal hunger of the gregarious animal for the herd of friends who are not there. And it may be, it may very possibly be, that, in the matter of this Friend behind phenomena, our own yearning and our own almost ineradicable instinctive conviction, since they are certainly not founded on either reason or observation, are in origin the groping of a lonely-souled gregarious animal to find its herd or its herd-leader in the great spaces between the stars.

At any rate, it is a belief very difficult to get rid of.

5 | NIEBUHR

ST. AUGUSTINE

The strong psychological element in St. Augustine's works, most clearly seen in his *Confessions*, has revived the theological and philosophical interest in St. Augustine (see page 2) in our own day. Reinhold Niebuhr, the leading American Protestant theologian of our time, owes much of his insight into the human predicament to modern psychological and psychoanalytical theory, although his fundamental point of view is always that of the theologian. Being rooted in theological doctrine and displaying intimate familiarity with psychological analysis, Niebuhr's writings show a depth and penetration which have put him into the front rank of social and political thinkers of the twentieth century. While legitimately concerned with the troubling social, economic, and political problems of our age, Niebuhr probes beyond these specific aspects of the crisis of our age, and seeks to lay bare the human situation which underlies the specific ills dealt with by political scientists, economists, or sociologists. As his study of St. Augustine shows, there are some basic difficulties in the human predicament which are inherent in the human situation rather than in this or that institutional maladjustment, to be remedied for good by this or that specific reform. Interestingly enough, although Niebuhr's theology and metaphysics tend toward the conservative viewpoint, his social and political ideas have generally been associated with the more liberal and reformist currents in American life. His principal works of interest to the student of political philosophy are *Moral Man and Immoral Society*

(1941), *The Children of Light and the Children of Darkness* (1945), *The Irony of American History* (1952), and *Christian Realism and Political Problems* (1953).

Niebuhr on ST. AUGUSTINE

The terms "idealism" and "realism" are not analogous in political and in metaphysical theory; and they are certainly not as precise in political, as in metaphysical, theory. In political and moral theory "realism" denotes the disposition to take all factors in a social and political situation which offer resistance to established norms, into account, particularly the factors of self-interest and power. In the words of a notorious "realist," Machiavelli, the purpose of the realist is "to follow the truth of the matter rather than the imagination of it; for many have pictures of republics and principalities which have never been seen." This definition of realism implies that idealists are subject to illusions about social realities, which indeed they are. "Idealism" is, in the esteem of its proponents, characterized by loyalty to moral norms and ideals, rather than to self-interest, whether individual or collective. It is, in the opinion of its critics, characterized by a disposition to ignore or be indifferent to the forces in human life which offer resistance to universally valid ideals and norms. This disposition, to which Machiavelli refers, is general whenever men are inclined to take the moral pretensions of themselves or their fellowmen at face value; for the disposition to hide self-interest behind the facade of pretended devotion to values, transcending self-interest, is well-nigh universal. It is, moreover, an interesting human characteristic, proving that the concept of "total depravity," as it is advanced by some Christian realists, is erroneous. Man is a curious creature with so strong a sense of obligation to his fellows that he cannot pursue his own interests without pretending to serve his fellowmen. The definitions of "realists" and "idealists" emphasize disposition, rather than doctrines; and they are therefore bound to be inexact. It must remain a matter of opinion whether or not a man takes adequate account of all the various factors and forces in a social situation. Was Plato a realist, for instance, because he tried to guard against the self-interest of the "guardians" of his ideal state by divesting them of property and reducing their family responsibilities to a minimum? Does this bit of

[From Reinhold Niebuhr, *Christian Realism and Political Problems* (Charles Scribner's Sons, 1953). By permission.]

"realism" cancel out the essential unrealism, inherent in ascribing to the "lusts of the body" the force of recalcitrance against the moral norm; or in attributing pure virtue to pure mind?

Augustine was, by general consent, the first great "realist" in western history. He deserves this distinction because his picture of social reality in his *civitas dei* gives an adequate account of the social factions, tensions, and competitions which we know to be well-nigh universal on every level of community; while the classical age conceived the order and justice of its *polis* to be a comparatively simple achievement, which would be accomplished when reason had brought all subrational forces under its dominion.

This difference in the viewpoint of Augustine and the classical philosophers lies in Augustine's biblical, rather than rationalistic, conception of human selfhood with the ancillary conception of the seat of evil being in the self. Augustine broke with classical rationalism in his conception of the human self, according to which the self is composed of mind and body, the mind being the seat of virtue because it has the capacity to bring all impulses into order; and the body, from which come the "lusts and ambitions," being the cause of evil. According to Augustine the self is an integral unity of mind and body. It is something more than mind and is able to use mind for its purposes. The self has, in fact, a mysterious identity and integrity transcending its functions of mind, memory, and will. "These three things, memory, understanding, and love are mine and not their own," he declares, "for they do what they do not for themselves but for me; or rather I do it by them. For it is I who remember by memory and understand by understanding and love by love." [1] It must be observed that the transcendent freedom of this self, including its capacity to defy any rational or natural system into which someone may seek to coordinate it (its capacity for evil) makes it difficult for any philosophy, whether ancient or modern, to comprehend its true dimension. That is why the classical wise men obscured it by fitting its mind into a system of universal mind and the body into the system of nature; and that is also why the modern wise men, for all their rhetoric about the "dignity" of the individual, try to cut down the dimension of human selfhood so that it will seem to fit into a system of nature. This conception of selfhood is drawn from the Bible, rather than from philosophy, because the transcendent self which is present in, though it transcends, all of the functions and effects, is comprehensible only in the dramatic-historical mode of apprehension which characterizes biblical faith. Augustine draws on the insights of neo-Platonism to illustrate the self's power of self-transcend-

[1] *De Trin.*, 15.22.

ence; but he rejects Plotinus' mystic doctrine, in which the particular self, both human and divine, is lost in a vast realm of undifferentiated being.

Augustine's conception of the evil which threatens the human community on every level is a corollary of his doctrine of selfhood. "Self-love" is the source of evil rather than some residual natural impulse which mind has not yet completely mastered. This excessive love of self, sometimes also defined as pride or *superbia*, is explained as the consequence of the self's abandonment of God as its true end and of making itself "a kind of end." It is this powerful self-love or, in a modern term, "egocentricity," this tendency of the self to make itself its own end or even to make itself the false center of whatever community it inhabits, which sows confusion into every human community. The power of self-love is more spiritual than the "lusts of the body," of which Plato speaks; and it corrupts the processes of the mind more than Plato or Aristotle knew. That is why Augustine could refute the classical theory with the affirmation that "it is not the bad body which causes the good soul to sin but the bad soul which causes the good body to sin." At other times Augustine defines the evil in man as the "evil will"; but with the understanding that it is the self which is evil in the manifestation of its will. "For he who extols the whole nature of the soul as the chief good and condemns the nature of the flesh as if it were evil, assuredly is fleshly both in the love of the soul and in the hatred of the flesh." [2] This concise statement of the Christian position surely refutes the absurd charge of moderns that the Christian faith is "dualistic" and generates contempt for the body. It also established the only real basis for a realistic estimate of the forces of recalcitrance which we must face on all levels of the human community, particularly for a realistic estimate of the spiritual dimension of these forces and of the comparative impotence of "pure reason" against them. Compared with a Christian realism, which is based on Augustine's interpretation of biblical faith, a great many modern social and psychological theories, which fancy themselves anti-Platonic or even anti-Aristotelian and which make much of their pretended "realism," are in fact no more realistic than the classical philosophers. Thus modern social and psychological scientists are forever seeking to isolate some natural impulse such as "aggressiveness" and to manage it; with equal vanity they are trying to find a surrogate for Plato's and Aristotle's disinterested "reason" in a so-called "scientific method." Their inability to discover the corruption of self-interest in reason or in man's rational pursuits; and to measure the spiritual dimension of man's inhumanity and cruelty, gives an air of sentimentality to the learning of our whole liberal culture. Thus we have no guidance amid the intricacies

[2] *De Civ. Dei*, 15.5.

of modern power politics except as the older disciplines, less enamored of the "methods of natural science," and the common sense of the man in the street supplies the necessary insights.

II

Augustine's description of the social effects of human egocentricity or self-love is contained in his definition of the life of the "city of this world," the *civitas terrena*, which he sees as commingled with the *civitas dei*. The "city of this world" is dominated by self-love to the point of contempt of God; and is distinguished from the *civitas dei* which is actuated by the "love of God" to the point of contempt of self. This "city" is not some little city-state, as it is conceived in classical thought. It is the whole human community on its three levels of the family, the commonwealth, and the world. A potential world community is therefore envisaged in Augustine's thought. But, unlike the stoic and modern "idealists," he does not believe that a common humanity or a common reason gives promise of an easy actualization of community on the global level. The world community, declares Augustine, "is fuller of dangers as the greater sea is more dangerous." [3] Augustine is a consistent realist in calling attention to the fact that the potential world community may have a common human reason but it speaks in different languages and "Two men, each ignorant of each other's language" will find that "dumb animals, though of a different species, could more easily hold intercourse than they, human beings though they be." [4] This realistic reminder that common linguistic and ethnic cultural forces, which bind the community together on one level, are divisive on the ultimate level, is a lesson which our modern proponents of world government have not yet learned.

Augustine's description of the *civitas terrena* includes an emphasis on the tensions, frictions, competitions of interest, and overt conflicts to which every human community is exposed. Even in the family one cannot rely on friendship "seeing that secret treachery has often broken it up." [5] This bit of realism will seem excessive until we remember that our own generation has as much difficulty in preserving the peace and integrity in the smallest and most primordial community, the family, as in integrating community on the highest global level.

The *civitas terrena* is described as constantly subject to an uneasy armistice between contending forces, with the danger that factional disputes may result in "bloody insurrection" at any time. Augustine's realism prompts him to challenge Cicero's conception of a commonwealth as rooted in a "compact of justice." Not so, declares Augustine. Common-

[3] *Ibid.*, 19.7.   [4] *Ibid.*, 19.7.   [5] *Ibid.*, 19.5.

wealths are bound together by a common love, or collective interest, rather than by a sense of justice; and they could not maintain themselves without the imposition of power. "Without injustice the republic would neither increase nor subsist. The imperial city to which the republic belongs could not rule over provinces without recourse to injustice. For it is unjust for some men to rule over others." [6]

This realism has the merit of describing the power realities which underlie all large scale social integrations whether in Egypt or Babylon or Rome, where a dominant city-state furnished the organizing power for the Empire. It also describes the power realities of national states, even democratic ones, in which a group, holding the dominant form of social power, achieves oligarchic rule, no matter how much modern democracy may bring such power under social control. This realism in regard to the facts which underlie the organizing or governing power refutes the charge of modern liberals that a realistic analysis of social forces makes for state absolutism; so that a mild illusion in regard to human virtue is necessary to validate democracy. Realistic pessimism did indeed prompt both Hobbes and Luther to an unqualified endorsement of state power; but that is only because they were not realistic enough. They saw the dangers of anarchy in the egotism of the citizens but failed to perceive the dangers of tyranny in the selfishness of the ruler. Therefore they obscured the consequent necessity of placing checks upon the ruler's self-will. Augustine's realism was indeed excessive. On the basis of his principles he could not distinguish between government and slavery, both of which were supposedly the rule over man by man and were both a consequence of, and remedy for, sin; nor could he distinguish between a commonwealth and a robber band, for both were bound together by collective interest; "For even thieves must hold together or they cannot effect what they intend." The realism fails to do justice to the sense of justice in the constitution of the Roman Empire; or for that matter to the sense of justice in a robber band. For even thieves will fall out if they cannot trust each other to divide the loot, which is their common aim, equitably. But the excessive emphasis upon the factors of power and interest, a wholesome corrective to Cicero's and modern Ciceronian moralistic illusions, is not fatal to the establishment of justice so long as the dangers of tyranny are weighed as realistically as the dangers of anarchy.

Augustine's realistic attitude toward government rests partly upon the shrewd observation that social peace and order are established by a dominant group within some level of community; and that this group is not exempt from the corruption of self-interest merely because the peace

[6] *Ibid.*, 19.21.

of society has been entrusted to it. (One thinks incidentally how accurately the Augustinian analysis fits both the creative and the ambiguous character of the American hegemony in the social cohesion of the free world.) The realism is partly determined by his conception of a "natural order" which he inherited from the early Christian fathers, who in turn took it from that part of the Stoic theory which emphasized the primordial or primitive as the natural. This Stoic and Christian primitivism has the merit of escaping the errors of those natural law theories which claim to find a normative moral order amid the wide variety of historic forms or even among the most universal of these forms. The freedom of man makes these Stoic conceptions of the "natural" impossible. But it has the weakness which characterizes all primitivism, whether Stoic, Christian, or Romantic, for it makes primitive social forms normative. A primitive norm, whether of communal property relations or unorganized social cohesion, may serve provisionally as an occasion for the criticism of the institutions of an advancing civilization, more particularly the institutions of property and government; but it has the disadvantage of prompting indiscriminate criticism. This lack of discrimination is obvious in primitivistic Stoicism, in early Christianity, in seventeenth-century Cromwellian sectarianism, in Romanticism, and in Marxism and anarchism.

Augustine expressed this idea of a primitive social norm as follows: "This is the prescribed order of nature. It is thus that God created man. For 'let them,' He says, 'have dominion over the fish of the sea and the fowl of the air and over every creeping thing, which creepeth on the earth.' He did not intend that His rational creature, made in His image, should have dominion over anything but irrational creation—not man over man but man over beasts. And hence the righteous men of primitive times were made shepherds of cattle rather than kings of men." [7] This primitivism avoids the later error of the absolute sanctification of government. But its indiscriminate character is apparent by his failure to recognize the difference between legitimate and illegitimate, between ordinate and inordinate subordination of man to man. Without some form of such subordination the institutions of civilization could not exist.

III

If Augustine's realism is contained in his analysis of the *civitas terrena*, his refutation of the idea that realism must lead to cynicism or relativism is contained in his definition of the *civitas dei*, which he declares to be "commingled" with the "city of this world" and which has the "love of God" rather than the "love of self" as its guiding principle. The tension

[7] *Ibid.*, 19.15.

between the two cities is occasioned by the fact that, while egotism is "natural" in the sense that it is universal, it is not natural in the sense that it does not conform to man's nature who transcends himself indeterminately and can only have God rather than self for his end. A realism becomes morally cynical or nihilistic when it assumes that the universal characteristic in human behavior must also be regarded as normative. The biblical account of human behavior, upon which Augustine bases his thought, can escape both illusion and cynicism because it recognizes that the corruption of human freedom may make a behavior pattern universal without making it normative. Good and evil are not determined by some fixed structure of human existence. Man, according to the biblical view, may use his freedom to make himself falsely the center of existence; but this does not change the fact that love rather than self-love is the law of his existence in the sense that man can only be healthy and his communities at peace if man is drawn out of himself and saved from the self-defeating consequences of self-love. There are several grave errors in Augustine's account of love and of the relation of love to self-love; but before considering them we might well first pay tribute to his approach to political problems. The virtue of making love, rather than justice, into the norm for the community may seem, at first blush, to be dubious. The idea of justice seems much more relevant than the idea of love, particularly for the collective relationships of men. The medieval tradition which makes the justice of a rational "natural law" normative even for Christians when they consider the necessities of a sinful world, seems much more realistic than modern forms of sentimental Protestantism which regards love as a simple alternative to self-love, which could be achieved if only we could preach the idea persuasively enough to beguile men from the one to the other. Augustine's doctrine of love as the final norm must be distinguished from modern sentimental versions of Christianity which regard love as a simple possibility and which think it significant to assert the obvious proposition that all conflicts in the community would be avoided, if only people and nations would love one another. Augustine's approach differs from modern forms of sentimental perfectionism in the fact that he takes account of the power and persistence of egotism, both individual and collective, and seeks to establish the most tolerable form of peace and justice under conditions set by human sin. He inherited the tradition of monastic perfection; and he allows it as a vent for the Christian impulse toward individual perfection, without however changing the emphasis upon the duty of the Christian to perfect the peace of the city of this world. Furthermore, he raises questions about monastic perfection which, when driven home by the Reformation, were to undermine the whole system. "I venture to say," he writes, "that it is good for those who observe continence and are proud of it, to fall that they may be humbled. For what benefit is it to anyone in whom is the virtue of continence, if pride holds sway? He is but despising that by which man is born in striving after that which led to satan's fall . . . holy virginity is better than conjugal chastity . . . but if we add two other things, pride and humility . . . which is better, pride or humility? . . . I have no doubt that a humble married woman is to be preferred to a proud virgin . . . a mother holds a lesser place in the Kingdom of God because she has been married, than the daughter, seeing that she is a virgin. . . . But if thy mother has been proud and thou humble, she will have some sort of place and thou none." [8]

While Augustine's doctrine of love is thus not to be confused with modern sentimentalities which do not take the power of self-love seriously, one may well wonder whether an approach to politics which does not avail itself of the calculations of justice, may be deemed realistic. We have already noted that Augustine avails himself of the theory of the "natural law," only in the primordial version of the theory. If primordial conditions of a "natural order" are not to be defined as normative, the only alternative is to assume a "rational order" to which the whole of historical life conforms. Aquinas, in fact, constructed his theory of the natural law upon classical, and primarily Aristotelian, foundations. It was the weakness of both classical and medieval theories that they assumed an order in history, conforming to the uniformities of nature. Aristotle was aware of deviations in history, greater than those in nature; but he believed that there was nevertheless one form "which was marked by nature as the best." There is, in other words, no place in this theory of natural law for the endlessly unique social configurations which human beings, in their freedom over natural necessity, construct. The proponents of "natural law" therefore invariably introduce some historically contingent norm or social structure into what they regard as God's inflexible norm. That was the weakness of both classical and medieval social theory; and for that matter of the natural law theories of the bourgeois Parties of the eighteenth century, who had found what they regarded as a more empirically perceived "natural law"; but the modern empirical intelligence was no more capable than the deductive rational processes of classical and medieval times to construct a social norm, not colored by the interests of the constructor, thus introducing the taint of ideology into the supposed sanctities of law. We must conclude therefore that Augustine was wise in avoiding the alleged solution of a natural law theory, which was the basis of so much

[8] Sermon cccIIV, ix, 9.

lack of realism in both the classical and the medieval period, and which can persist today long after the Aristotelian idea of fixed form for historical events has been overcome, as the dogma of a religious system which makes its supposed sanctities into an article of faith. His conception of the radical freedom of man, derived from the biblical view, made it impossible to accept the idea of fixed forms of human behavior and of social organization, analogous to those of nature, even as he opposed the classical theory of historical cycles. Furthermore, his conception of human selfhood and of the transcendence of the self over its mind, made it impossible to assume the identity of the individual reason with a universal reason, which lies at the foundation of the classical and medieval natural law theories. It is in fact something of a mystery how the Christian insights into human nature and history, expressed by Augustine, could have been subordinated to classical thought with so little sense of the conflict between them in the formulations of Thomas Aquinas; and how they should have become so authoritative in Roman Catholicism without more debate between Augustinian and Thomistic emphases.

Augustine's formula for leavening the city of this world with the love of the city of God is more adequate than classical and medieval thought, both in doing justice to the endless varieties of historical occasions and configurations and in drawing upon the resources of love rather than law in modifying human behavior.

Every "earthly peace," declares Augustine, is good as far as it goes. "But they will not have it long for they used it not well while they had it." That is, unless some larger love or loyalty qualifies the self-interest of the various groups, this collective self-interest will expose the community to either an overt conflict of competing groups or to the injustice of a dominant group which "when it is victorious it will become vice's slave." Let us use some examples from current national and international problems to illustrate the Augustinian thesis. There is, or was, a marked social tension between the middle classes of industrial owners and the industrial workers in all modern industrial nations. In some of them, for instance in Germany and France, this tension led to overt forms of the class conflict. In others such as Britain, the smaller European nations and America, this tension was progressively resolved by various accommodations of interest. Wherein lay the difference? It did not lie in the possession of more adequate formulae of justice in some nations than in others. The difference lay in the fact that in some nations the various interest groups had, in addition to their collective interest, a "sense of justice," a disposition to "give each man his due" and a loyalty to the national community which qualified the interest struggle. Now, that spirit of justice is identical with the spirit of love, except at the highest level of the spirit of love, where it becomes purely sacrificial and engages in no calculation of what the due of each man may be. Two forms of love, the love of the other and the love of the community, were potent in short in modifying the acerbities and injustices of the class struggle. The two forms of love availed themselves of various calculations of justice in arriving at and defining their *ad hoc* agreements. But the facts in each nation and in each particular issue were too variable to allow for the application of any general rules or formulae of justice. Agreements were easier in fact if too much was not claimed for these formulae. Certain "principles" of justice, as distinguished from formulas or prescriptions, were indeed operative, such as liberty, equality, and loyalty to covenants; but these principles will be recognized as no more than the law of love in its various facets.

In the same manner the international community is exposed to exactly the tensions and competitions of interest which Augustine describes. There are no formulas of justice or laws which will prevent these tensions from reaching overt conflict, if the collective interest of each nation is not modified by its loyalty to a higher value such as the common civilization of the free nations. Where this common loyalty is lacking, as in our relation with Russia, no formula can save us from the uneasy peace in which we live. The character of this peace is just as tentative as Augustine described it. Whenever common loves or loyalties, or even common fears, lay the foundation for community, it must of course be our business to perfect it by calculations of justice which define our mutual responsibilities as exactly as possible.

It must be noted that the Augustinian formula for the leavening influence of a higher upon a lower loyalty or love, is effective in preventing the lower loyalty from involving itself in self-defeat. It corrects the "realism" of those who are myopically realistic by seeing only their own interests and failing thereby to do justice to their interests where they are involved with the interests of others. There are modern realists, for instance, who, in their reaction to abstract and vague forms of international idealism, counsel the nation to consult only its own interests. In a sense collective self-interest is so consistent that it is superfluous to advise it. But a consistent self-interest on the part of a nation will work against its interests because it will fail to do justice to the broader and longer interests, which are involved with the interests of other nations. A narrow national loyalty on our part, for instance, will obscure our long range interests where they are involved with those of a whole alliance of free nations. Thus the loyalty of a leavening portion of a nation's citizens to a value transcending national interest will save a "realistic" nation from defining its interests in such narrow and short range terms as to defeat the real interests of the nation.

IV

We have acknowledged some weaknesses in the Augustinian approach to the political order which we must now define and examine more carefully. Non-Catholics commonly criticize Augustine's alleged identification of the *civitas dei* with the visible Church. But we must absolve him of this charge or insist on a qualification of the criticism. He does indeed accept the Catholic doctrine, which had grown up before his day; and he defines the visible Church as the only perfect society. There are passages in which he seems to assume that it is possible to claim for the members of the Church that they are solely actuated by the *amor dei*. But he introduces so many reservations to this assertion that he may well be defined in this, as in other instances, as the father of both Catholicism and the Reformation. Of the Church, Augustine declared, "by faith she is a virgin. In the flesh she has few holy virgins" [9] or again: "God will judge the wicked and the good. The evil cannot now be separated from the good but must be suffered for a season. The wicked may be with us on the threshing floor . . . in the barn they cannot be." [10] The reservations which he made upon the identification of the Church and the kingdom laid the foundations for the later Reformation position. But these reservations about the sinners who might be present in the visible Church cannot obscure a graver error in his thought. This error is probably related to his conception of grace which does not allow for the phenomenon, emphasized by the Reformation, that men may be redeemed in the sense that they consciously turn from self to Christ as their end, and yet they are not redeemed from the corruption of egotism which expresses itself, even in the lives of the saints. This insight is most succinctly expressed in Luther's phrase *"justus et peccator simul"* (righteous and sinners at once). When Augustine distinguished between the "two loves" which characterize the "two cities," the love of God and the love of self, and when he pictured the world as a commingling of the two cities, he does not recognize that the commingling is due, not to the fact that two types of people dwell together but because the conflict between love and self-love is in every soul. It is particularly important to recognize this fact in political analyses; for nothing is more obvious than that personal dedication is no guarantee against the involvement of the dedicated individual in some form of collective egotism.

We have frequently referred to Augustine's definition of the "two

[9] Sermon ccxiii, vii, 7.   [10] *Comm. on Ps.* cxi, 9.

loves" which inform the "two cities" of which "the one is selfish and the other social," the one loving self to the point of the contempt of God and the other loving God to the point of contempt of self. The question is whether Bishop Nygren [11] is right in defining the Augustinian conception of *amor dei* as rooted in a classical rather than a biblical concept.

In defense of Augustine it must be said that he is not insensible to the two facets of the love commandment and therefore does not define the *amor dei* in purely mystical terms as a flight from this world. He insists on the contrary that the *amor dei* is "social" and he offers the concord among brethren as a proof of the love of God. But nevertheless Nygren is right in suggesting that the thought of Plotinus has colored Augustine's conceptions sufficiently so that the *agape* of the New Testament is misinterpreted by Augustine's conception of *charitas* and *amor dei*. The *agape* form of love in the New Testament fails to be appreciated particularly in two of its facets: A) the equality of the "two loves," the love of the neighbor and the love of God (enforced in the Scripture by the words "the Second is like unto it") is violated by Augustine under the influence of Plotinus even as a later medieval Catholic mystic, St. John of the Cross, violates it when he regarded the love of the creature as a ladder which might lead us to the love of God, but must be subordinated to the latter. Augustine wants us to love the neighbor for the sake of God, which may be a correct formulation; but he wants us to prove the genuineness of our love of God in the love of the neighbor, or by leading him to God. Thus the meeting of the neighbor's need without regard to any ultimate religious intention is emptied of meaning. The love of the neighbor is for him not part of a double love commandment but merely the instrument of a single love commandment which bids us flee all mortality including the neighbor in favor of the immutable good. B) The second facet of the *agape* concept of the New Testament which tends to be obscured is the notion of sacrificial love, the absurd principle of the Cross, the insistence that the self must sacrifice itself for the other. It is not fair to Augustine to say that he neglects this facet of meaning for he seems to emphasize it so constantly. He comes closest to its meaning when he deals with the relation of humility to love. Yet it seems fair to say that he was sufficiently imbued by classical mystical thought forms so that the emphasis lies always upon the worthiness or unworthiness of the object of our love; the insistence is that only God and not some mutable "good" or person is worthy of our love. This is a safeguard against all forms of idolatry. But it does not answer another important question: when I love a person or a community do I love myself in them or do I truly love

[11] Anders Nygren, in *Agape and Eros*.

them? Is my love a form of alteregoism? The Augustinian *amor dei* assumes that the self in its smallness cannot contain itself within itself and therefore it is challenged to go out from itself to the most ultimate end. But it hardly reveals the full paradox of self-realization through self-giving which is a scandal in the field of rational ethics as the Cross is a scandal in the field of rational religion. Yet it is the source of ultimate wisdom. For the kind of self-giving which has self-realization as its result must not have self-realization as its conscious end; otherwise the self by calculating its enlargement will not escape from itself completely enough to be enlarged. The weakness of Augustine in obscuring these facets of the *agape* principle may be illustrated, without unfairness I hope, by referring to his treatment of family love. He questions the love of mate or children as the final form of love, but not for New Testament reasons. He does not say: "When you love your wife and children are you maybe really loving yourself in them and using them as the instruments of your self-aggrandisements?" He declares instead, in effect, you must not love your family too unreservedly because your wife and children are mortal. They also belong to the "rivers of Babylon," and, if you give them absolute devotion, the hour of bereavement will leave you desolate. Of course Augustine is too much the Christian to engage in a consistent mystic depreciation of the responsibilities and joys of this earthly life. After all, his whole strategy for the "commingling" of the two cities revolves around the acceptance of the ordinary responsibilities of home and state but in performing these tasks for the ultimate, rather than the immediate end. "What then?" he asks. "Shall all perish who marry and are given in marriage, who till the fields and build houses? No, but those who put their trust in these things, who prefer them to God, who for the sake of these things are quick to offend God, these will perish. But those who either do not use these things or who use them as though they used them not, trusting more in Him who gave them than in the things given, understanding in them His consolation and mercy, and who are not absorbed in these gifts lest they fall away from the giver. These are they whom the day will not overtake as a thief unprepared." [12] We must not, in criticizing Augustine for neo-Platonic elements in his thought, obscure the Christian elements which will be equally an offense to modern men who regard the world as self-sufficing and self-explanatory, who reject as absurd the Christian faith that there is not only a mystery behind and above the world of observed phenomena and intelligible meanings, but that it is a mystery whose meaning has been disclosed as a love which elicits our answering love. This modern generation with its confidence in

[12] *Comm. on Ps.* cxx, 3.

a world without mystery, and without meaning beyond simple intelligibility, will not be beguiled from its unbelief by a reminder that its emancipation from God has betrayed it into precisely those idolatries, the worship of false gods, the dedication to finite values as if they were ultimate, of which Augustine spoke. But it must be recorded nevertheless as a significant fact of modern history. While it is an offense to regard communism as the inevitable end-product of secularism, as some Christians would have us believe, it is only fair to point out that the vast evils of modern communism come ironically to a generation which thought it would be easy to invest all the spiritual capital of men, who mysteriously transcend the historical process, in some value or end within that process; and communism is merely the most pathetic and cruel of the idolatrous illusions of this generation.

We must be clear about the fact that all the illusions about man's character and history which made it so difficult for either the classical or the modern age to come to terms with the vexing problems of our togetherness, seem to stem from efforts to understand man in both his grandeur and his misery by "integrating" him into some natural or rational system of coherence. Thereby they denied the mystery of his transcendence over every process which points to another mystery beyond himself without which man is not only a mystery to himself but a misunderstood being.

We cannot deny that from a Christian standpoint the world is like a "river of Babylon" to use Augustine's symbol; and that Augustine is right in suggesting that ultimately we cannot find peace if we are merely tossed down the river of time. We must find security in that which is not carried down the river. "Observe however," declares Augustine in a simile which will seem strange to generations which have made the "rivers of Babylon," the stream of temporal events, into forces of redemption; but which will not seem so strange as the modern experience proves history as such to be less redemptive than we had believed. "The rivers of Babylon are all things which are here loved, and pass away. For example, one man loves to practice husbandry, to grow rich by it, to employ his mind on it, to get his pleasure from it. Let him observe the issue and see that what he has loved is not a foundation of Jerusalem, but a river of Babylon. Another says, it is a grand thing to be a soldier; all farmers fear those who are soldiers, are subservient to them, tremble at them. If I am a farmer, I shall fear soldiers; if a soldier, farmers will fear me. Madman! thou hast cast thyself headlong into another river of Babylon, and that still more turbulent and sweeping. Thou wishest to be feared by thy inferior; fear Him Who is greater than thou. He who fears thee may on a sudden become greater than thou, but He Whom thou oughtest to fear will never become less. To be an advocate, says another, is a grand thing; eloquence is most powerful; always to have clients hanging on the lips of their eloquent advocate, and from his words looking for loss or gain, death or life, ruin or security. Thou knowest not whither thou hast cast thyself. This too is another river of Babylon, and its roaring sound is the din of the waters dashing against the rocks. Mark that it flows, that it glides on; beware, for it carries things away with it. To sail the seas, says another, and to trade is a grand thing—to know many lands, to make gains from every quarter, never to be answerable to any powerful man in thy country, to be always travelling, and to feel thy mind with the diversity of the nations and the business met with, and to return enriched by the increase of thy gains. This too is a river of Babylon. When will the gains stop? When wilt thou have confidence and be secure in the gains thou makest? The richer thou art, the more fearful wilt thou be. Once shipwrecked, thou wilt come forth stripped of all, and rightly wilt bewail thy fate *in* the rivers of Babylon, because thou wouldest not sit down and weep *upon* the rivers of Babylon.

"But there are other citizens of the holy Jerusalem, understanding their captivity, who mark how human wishes and the diverse lusts of men, hurry and drag them hither and thither, and drive them into the sea. They see this, and do not throw themselves into the rivers of Babylon, but sit down upon the rivers of Babyon and upon the rivers of Babylon weep, either for those who are being carried away by them, or for themselves whose deserts have placed them in Babylon." [13]

Whatever the defects of the Augustine approach may be, we must acknowledge his immense superiority both over those who preceded him and who came after him. A part of that superiority was due to his reliance upon biblical rather than idealistic or naturalistic conceptions of selfhood. But that could not have been the only cause, else Christian systems before and after him would not have been so inferior. Or were they inferior either because they subordinated the biblical-dramatic conception of human selfhood too much to the rationalistic scheme, as was the case with medieval Christianity culminating in the thought of Thomas Aquinas? or because they did not understand that the corruption of human freedom could not destroy the original dignity of man, as was the case with the Reformation with its doctrines of sin, bordering on total depravity and resulting in Luther's too pessimistic approach to political problems? As for secular thought, it has difficulty in approaching Augustine's realism without falling into cynicism or in avoiding nihilism without falling into

[13] *Comm. on Ps.* cxxxvi, 3, 4.

sentimentality. Hobbes' realism was based on an insight which he shared with Augustine, namely, that in all historical encounters the mind is the servant and not the master of the self. But he failed to recognize that the self which thus made the mind its instrument was a corrupted and not a "normal" self. Modern "realists" know the power of collective self-interest as Augustine did; but they do not understand its blindness. Modern pragmatists understood the irrelevance of fixed and detailed norms; but they do not understand that love must take the place as the final norm for these inadequate norms. Modern liberal Christians know that love is the final norm for man; but they fall into sentimentality because they fail to measure the power and persistence of self-love. Thus Augustine, whatever may be the defects of his approach to political reality, and whatever may be the dangers of a too slavish devotion to his insights, nevertheless proves himself a more reliable guide than any known thinker. A generation which finds its communities imperiled and in decay from the smallest and most primordial community, the family, to the largest and most recent, the potential world community, might well take counsel of Augustine in solving its perplexities.

6 | MARITAIN

St. Thomas AQUINAS

By church law and intellectual tradition, St. Thomas Aquinas (see page 50) has become the most important single authority on the doctrine of the Roman Catholic Church, and his influence has always been strongly felt outside of his church as well. A reappraisal of St. Thomas Aquinas, "the first Whig," as he has been called, in the light of the twentieth century is to be found in *St. Thomas Aquinas: Angel of the Schools* (1931) by Jacques Maritain (1882–   ), the outstanding liberal Catholic writer since Lord Acton, and one of the leading Thomist philosophers. Liberalism has a long background and tradition in Maritain's native country, France, stronger probably than in any other major Catholic country. It is Maritain's firm belief that "St. Thomas wrote not for the thirteenth century but for our own time," and that he is "preeminently the apostle and teacher of our time." Maritain also believes that the message of Thomism should not be confined to the realm of theology and metaphysics, but also has an important bearing on the pressing social, economic, and political problems of our time. Maritian's unflinching opposition to totalitarianism of any kind, whether fascist or communist, is more fully elaborated in his books *True Humanism* (1938), *Scholasticism and Politics* (1940), and *Christianity and Democracy* (1945). In these books Maritain develops his concept of "personalist democracy," in which he seeks to combine Thomism and modern democratic thought. His main charge against classical Western individualism is that the latter is too atomistic and mechanistic, while suppressing the "social organic totality." By contrast, his main opposition to totalitarianism is that it engulfs the human personality. After the fall of France in 1940, Maritain migrated to the United States, where he taught at Princeton University, while continuing his literary activities as a prolific and encyclopedic writer.

Maritain on St. Thomas AQUINAS

Thanks to Thomas Aquinas, the thirteenth century achieved in the sphere of metaphysics and theology what the fifteenth and sixteenth centuries failed to do in the sphere of art and the allurements of the senses. It did not excommunicate Aristotle and the whole effort of reason; it did not yield or apostatize before them; it converted them. St. Thomas transformed, without deforming, Aristotle; not content with restoring his true meaning where the commentators had perverted it, with completing and correcting him wherever he was mistaken or hesitated, he worked the miracle of extricating from the Aristotle of history—"*tel qu'en lui-même enfin* Théologie *le change*"—a pure Aristotelian form much more purely Aristotelian than Aristotle himself had ever known. Aristotle was for St. Thomas above all the treasurer of natural reason; with Aristotle it was the whole of antiquity that he adopted, at the same time retaining whatever valuable elements had been imported by Jew and Arab. So also he gathered together every testimony contained in Holy Scripture and the Fathers, the whole of Christian speculation, in such a way that "because he had the utmost reverence for" the Fathers and holy Doctors who had preceded him, "he seems to have inherited the intellect of all." [1] The novelty he introduced was thus a novelty not of destruction but of achievement. His originality consists in having his philosophy taught by everyone. He is not merely the disciple of uncreated Wisdom, of the wisdom of the saints and the wisdom of the philosophers—did he not once allow himself to be instructed at Cologne by an ignorant fellow-pupil?—he is also the disciple of the human race.

The universal inheritance taken up in its entirety and in its entirety reconstructed, born again in the intellect, is quite the opposite of eclecticism and a mosaic of opinions. An immaterial word, infinitely complex

[From Jacques Maritain, *St. Thomas Aquinas: Angel of the Schools* (Sheed and Ward, Inc., 1931). By permission.]

[1] An observation of Cajetan's adopted by Pope Leo XIII and Pope Pius XI.

in structure and perfectly one in essence, was vitally begotten in the womb of the mind. Nothing could be loftier than such a synthesis, nothing could require greater independence and a more precise personal vigour of thought. But, again, no work is in itself more impersonal. The philosophy of St. Thomas is not the property of St. Thomas. It is the common property of the Church and mankind. It is the only philosophy whose peculiar characteristic is that it is peculiar to nobody, strictly impersonal, absolutely universal. "Common truth," said Giacomo di Viterbo even in his day to Bartolommeo di Capua, "common clarity, common enlightenment, common order, and a philosophy which quickly leads to perfect understanding." That is the reason why "it is not Catholicism which is Thomist, but Thomism which is Catholic; and it is Catholic because it is universalist." [2] And the whole of reality is to be found in it unimpaired. If Friar Thomas dwelt in the deep seclusion of his philosophy, the eyes of his reflection were open wide on things—and with what innocent simplicity! He never forces them, never arranges them with artful care, never plays any tricks of light and shade or indulges in exaggerations of relief, tricks which all philosophers, Aristotle excepted, play in secret. He employs his great artistic gifts solely for precision of expression and exactitude of judgement. He knows no compromise with truth: he sets it forth in all its grandeur. Men may say: "A harsh doctrine!" It makes no difference. Such pacific wisdom carries the investigations of reason—absolutely human in philosophy, superelevated by faith in theology—through the whole range of the created and the uncreated, but it measures the spirit everywhere against what is, compelling it to respect both the twilight below due to the obscurity of matter, and the night above due to the too lucid transparency of divine things. Fundamentally opposed to agnosticism and rationalism, opposite engines which both divorce the mind from mystery, Thomist realism weds mind and mystery in the heart of being.

Theology makes use of philosophy and illuminates it by judging it in its own light. So St. Thomas transplanted Aristotelian concepts to a new climate—a supernatural climate—in which faith forces them to produce in our minds some knowledge of the mysteries of God. There is a Thomist philosophy—based upon the sole evidence of reason. St. Thomas achieved a great philosophical work, he had an extraordinary metaphysical genius. But he is not simply, or primarily, a philosopher, he is essentially a theologian. It is as a theologian, from the summit of knowledge which is architectonic *par excellence,* that he definitively establishes the order of Christian economy.

Against the old scholasticism, incapable of recognizing in him the

[2] H. Woroniecki.

true heir of Augustine, he defends the rights of truth in the natural sphere and the value of reason; against the Averroists, incapable of recognizing in him the true interpreter of Aristotle, he defends the rights of revealed truth and the value of faith. Affirming both the essential naturality of metaphysics and the essential *super*naturality of the infused virtues, and the essential subordination of the natural to the supernatural, proclaiming both that grace perfects, without destroying, nature and that the specifically divine life, which grace implants in us, can alone heal the wounds of nature and must take hold of nature absolutely, his peculiar achievement was to bring all the virtues of the mind into the service of Jesus Christ. The whole problem of culture and humanism presented itself in him and his answer was: *sanctity*. Man becomes perfect only supernaturally: he develops only on the cross. A humanism is possible, but on condition that its ultimate end is union with God through the humanity of the Mediator and that it proportions its means to that essentially supernatural end, a humanism of the Incarnation: on condition that it orders itself entirely to love and contemplation; that it entirely subordinates, like the holy soul of Thomas Aquinas itself, mere knowledge to wisdom, and metaphysical wisdom to theological wisdom and theological wisdom to the wisdom of the saints; that it realizes that the form of reason can subject the world only if it is itself subject to the supra-rational and supra-human order of the Holy Ghost and His gifts. Otherwise humanism, even Christian humanism, will inevitably tend to the destruction of man and a universal ruin.

If it be a question thereafter of ethical values and the conduct of human life, then it is only too easy to see to what extent the modern world is the world of selfishness, meanness, and insensibility. Once man undertook to be self-sufficient, what was there to prevent everything in him becoming dissociated and desiccated in irremediable antagonisms? Such at any rate appears to be the case as regards the residue of the near past. And, in truth, love lives only by God and by what it deifies, and when it perceives that what it has deified is but a mere fragment of nothing it turns to contempt and hatred. For this reason the love of humanity without God could not end otherwise than in a state in which the last resource of everyone is merely self-worship or suicide.

As far as the second historical element, the dynamic element above referred to, is concerned, what the contemporary world reveals to us precisely by reason of the kind of impossibility to live which anthropocentric egotism creates, is the need and presentiment of a vast effusion of love. Here again we must be on our guard against counterfeits; as we must be on our guard against false systems of metaphysics, so we must also be on our guard against the delusive forms of love.

A false humanitarian mysticism, pseudo-Buddhist, theosophical or anthroposophical, a false reign of the heart which claimed to install itself at the expense of the mind, in contempt of the Word which creates and forms and Its laws, a sort of quietist heresy which reduced us to a condition below the level of man, because we should then have lost the very idea of truth, and dissolved us in an equivocal poetic sensuality, unworthy of the name of truth, are a few of the evils which threaten us from that point of view. We are far removed from the materialism of the nineteenth century: it is from a pseudo-spiritualism and a pseudo-mysticism that we may expect the greatest dangers of deviation in our time.

The Angelic Doctor shows us the direct road, reminds us that order dwells in the heart of holy love, and that if in God subsisting Love proceeds from the Father and the uncreated Word, love in our case also must proceed from truth and pass through the lake of the Word; otherwise its diffusion only means destruction.

He reminds us also that there is only one effective and authentic way of loving our brethren and that is to love them with that same charity which makes us first love God above all. Thus—according to the admirable order of charity described in the second part of the *Summa*, which embraces all men without injuring the native privileges of any—love which unites us, above being, to the principle of being, descends again upon the creature with a divine force, shatters every obstacle and rekindles every coldness, opens up a new world which reveals the divine attributes in a more profound, unsuspected way, a world in which beings not only know one another but also recognize one another, and makes us wish well to our enemies. So we must assert against the deliquescences of sentimentality and the naturalist worship of the human race the true nature of the divine love.

And against the hardening due to the worship of force, the naturalist worship of the individual, the class, the race or the nation, it is the primacy of that same love which must be asserted. *Caritas major omnium*. Need it be observed that the whole ethical theory of St. Thomas is based upon that doctrine which he derives from the Gospel and St. Paul? He has erected upon that teaching of the Gospel an infrangible theological synthesis, in which he shows how Love, which makes us undeviatingly desire our last end, enjoys an absolute practical primacy over the whole of our individual and social life and constitutes the very bond of perfection, how it is better for us to love God than to know Him, and how no virtue, lacking such love, is truly virtuous or attains its perfect form, not even justice. And St. Thomas knows that such love really dominates human life, is effective love of God above all things and of one's neighbour as of one's self, only if it is supernatural, rooted in faith, proceeding from the grace of Christ, which makes us, in the image of the Crucified, sons and heirs of the God Who is Love. If we follow the Angelic Doctor, we shall realize that peace in man and among men (the direct work of charity, *opus charitatis*, "for love is a unifying force and the efficient cause of unity") descends from that superessential Peace and from that eternal Love which resides in the heart of the Trinity.

The distress of modern times, it was observed in the beginning of this essay, derives from the fact that culture, which is a certain perfection of man, has come to consider itself an ultimate end. It began by despising in its Cartesian or philosophical phase everything above the level of reason; it ends by despising reason itself, suffers both the law of the flesh and the spiritual vertigo which irrationality inevitably precipitates in the case of man. "The error of the modern world consists in its claim to ensure the dominance of reason over nature while refusing the dominance of supernature over reason." [3] This is the reason why, even in the order of knowledge, the metaphysics referred to a moment ago remains an inadequate remedy. Another wisdom, more exalted and more divine, is born of love itself, through the gifts of the Holy Ghost. And it is for that mystical wisdom in the first place that our misery hungers and thirsts, because it alone is capable of satisfying our hunger and our thirst, being union in experience with divine things and a beginning of beatitude. And yet it still leaves us hungry and thirsty, because vision alone can fully satiate our desire with God.

St. John of the Cross is the great experimental doctor of such wisdom; St. Thomas Aquinas is its great theologian. And because he has defined more accurately than any other doctor the central truth which cannot be disregarded without dealing a mortal blow to contemplation, and Christianity itself—I mean the distinction between nature and grace, and their active compenetration, and the whole organism of the infused gifts—he provides a better explanation than any other of the true nature of mystical wisdom, and defends it better than any other against every counterfeit.

That is the greatest benefit we may expect from him from the point of view of the restoration of Christian culture; for, in the last resort, it is from that wisdom and contemplation that the whole Christian order on this earth depends.

[3] Cf. *The Things that are not Caesar's* (Sheed & Ward), p. xxv.

The unity of a culture is determined in the first place and above all by a certain common philosophical structure, a certain metaphysical and moral attitude, a certain common scale of values, in a word, a certain common conception of the universe, of man and human life, of which social, linguistic, and juridical structures are, so to speak, the embodiment.

This metaphysical unity has long been broken—not certainly completely destroyed, but broken and as it were obliterated in the West. The drama of Western culture consists in the fact that its stock of common metaphysics has been reduced to an utterly inadequate minimum, so that only matter now holds it together, and matter is incapable of keeping anything together. The drama is all the more tragic for us because everything at the moment has to be recreated, everything to be put in place again in our European house. If a common philosophy succeeded in securing acceptance by an élite in Europe, it would be the beginning of the cure of the Western world.

As Thomas Aquinas united in his marvellously tempered constitution the talents of the men of the North and South, Norman and Lombard, as he integrated in his doctor's mission the Italy of the Popes, the Germany of Albert the Great, the France of St. Louis and the University of Paris, as he combined the treasures of the Greeks and the Latins, the Arabs and the Jews, with the inheritance bequeathed by the Fathers and Christian wisdom, in a word the entire contribution of the known world of his time, so his marvellously synthetic and organic theology, open to every aspect of reality, offers the intellectual tendencies peculiar to the various nations, and more particularly to the three just mentioned, the means of exercising themselves freely, not in mutual destruction, but in mutual completion and consolidation.

The reason is that St. Thomas succeeded in constructing a philosophical and theological wisdom so elevated in immateriality that it is really free of every particularization of race or environment. Alas! what we have witnessed during the past few centuries is an absolutely opposite phenomenon, a kind of racial materialization of philosophy. Descartes is one of the glories of France, but he hypostasizes certain defects, certain temptations peculiar to the French intellectual temperament. Hegel does the same for Germany; William James, the pragmatists and the pluralists, for the Anglo-Saxon countries. It is time to turn to truth itself, which belongs to no particular country, time to turn to the universality of human reason and supernatural wisdom. The necessity is all the more urgent because it appears as though the advent of a new era in philosophy were imminent.

Imagine for a moment that Catholics in the various countries realized the primordial importance of intellectual questions, of metaphysics and theology, that they discarded senseless prejudices against scholasticism, that they considered it, not as a mediaeval mummy to be examined with archaeological curiosity, but as a living armour in the mind and the indispensable equipment for the boldest enterprises of discovery; imagine that they fulfilled in practice the ardent aspiration of the Church, which is not to conquer adherents as though Catholicism were a human undertaking, but to serve divine Truth everywhere in the souls of men and the universe; imagine that they transcended intestine divisions and the petty rivalries of schools which everywhere sterilize their activity, finally, that they became conscious of the necessity of a serious and sustained intellectual co-operation among Catholics of all nations.

The common Doctor of the Church would then become in all truth their common master; with him to lead them, they might work effectively for the restoration of the West and its unity. Then there would be workers for the harvest. Then in the speculative sphere, Thomist metaphysics might assimilate into a true intellectual order the immense body of the individual sciences, abandoned at the moment to chaos and in danger of having their admirable progress exploited by aberrant philosophies. In the moral sphere, Thomist metaphysics and theology might architectonically preside over the elaboration of the new social order, the Christian economy, the Christian politics which the present state of the world so urgently requires. Finally, to revert to the great primitive symptoms and the great primitive causes of the divisions afflicting us, humanism, Protestantism, rationalism, at the end of their tether, having had time to suffer to the extreme the process of self-destruction developed by their initial error, and to experience also the value of many a reality which that error fails to take into account, would be astonished to find in the treasury of the Angelic Doctor the very truths which they coveted with no clear perception of their nature and which they have only been able to ruin.

I would add that Greek and Russian piety, which differs apparently from Catholic piety not so much in divergences of dogma as in certain characteristics of spirituality, is much less hostile, in my opinion, to the philosophy of St. Thomas than might at first be supposed. It approaches the problems from another angle and the scholastic presentation as a rule irritates and offends it. These are merely questions of modality; and I am convinced that a proper understanding of the Thomist system would dispel innumerable misunderstandings and facilitate many unexpected encounters. I am also convinced that when our separated brethren are driven, under pressure of contemporary errors, to a more systematic and developed theological defence, they will be constrained to seek in the principles elaborated by St. Thomas trusty weapons against vain philosophy.

In all this St. Thomas appears to us as the great intellectual renovator of the West.

Need it be added that it would argue a very imperfect acquaintance with human nature to believe in the possibility of such a Utopia? Nevertheless, if a serious effort is not made in such a direction, one may as well proclaim that culture in the West is doomed. It may be hoped, in spite of everything, that such an effort will be made.

Not every philosophy is fit for baptism as it stands. It must first be corrected and in most cases transformed. And in many cases all that can be done is to destroy it. The reason why Aristotle could be baptized by Saint Thomas is that his metaphysical principles were based upon objective reality. And if the great metaphysical systems of ancient civilization differ from modern systems in having *being* for their object, and are therefore capable of being universally adopted, by that very fact they have a sort of longing, as it were, to be corrected by Aristotelianism and Thomism. How much more gratifying it would be to our indolence, how much more soothing to our spirit of adventure, what a relief to play truant and to dispense with the discipline of the *philosophia perennis*! But culture cannot dispense with such a discipline, and will never more be able to dispense with Aristotle the Greek transfigured by the Angelic Doctor.

I do not say that the wisdom of Saint Thomas must be imposed as a dogma. The Gospel is not bound up with such wisdom. Nor do I say that all that is to be retained of the spiritual treasures of the East is what may have already been literally formulated in a system thenceforth deemed to be complete. The case is quite the reverse! What I say is that out of regard and respect for such treasures, and so that they shall assume their proper dimensions, and to co-operate loyally in preserving them against the forces of destruction, those who desire to integrate them in a permanent cultural achievement must equip themselves with an indefectible doctrinal apparatus.

And Thomist philosophy itself will be the better therefor. It will emerge from the everlasting controversies of the School, it will run the highways, take the air. What Saint Dominic said with regard to men is equally applicable to ideas: "Grain rots in the heap but is fruitful when sown." Thomist philosophy in itself is a progressive and assimilative philosophy, a missionary philosophy, a philosophy constantly at the service of primary Truth. And Saint Thomas is not a relic of the Middle Ages, a mere object for the consideration of history and erudition. He is in all the fulness of the expression the Apostle of our time.

All religions other than the Catholic religion are in more or less narrow and servile fashion, according as their metaphysical level is high or low, integral parts of certain definite cultures, particular to certain ethnic climates and certain historical formations. Only the Catholic religion, because it is supernatural and proceeds from the riven Heart of God dying upon the cross, is absolutely and rigorously transcendental, supra-cultural, supra-racial and supra-national.

That is one sign of its divine origin. It is also one of the signs of contradiction which until the end of time will be a cause of the passion of the Church, raised like her Master between earth and sky. It is conceivable from this point of view that the world is entering a phase of particularly stern conflicts which may, perhaps, be compared to the conflicts of apostolic times in the Rome of the Caesars. On the one hand the non-Christian nations are incapable of distinguishing between their autochthonous culture, with all its human values in themselves deserving of respect and filial piety, and the errors and superstitions of their religions. And Christian universalism will have to show them how such a distinction can be made and how the Gospel respects and superelevates— and by slow degrees transforms—such particular values. The demonstration is, as a rule, not unattended with bloodshed. And the imbecile dogma of positivist sociologism, which is taught in all countries in the name of European science and according to which every religion is merely the specific product of the social clan (and Christianity therefore a specific product of the European races) will not make it any the easier.

The disease afflicting the modern world is in the first place a disease of the mind; it began in the mind, it has now attacked the roots of the mind. Is it surprising that the world should seem to us shrouded in darkness? *Si oculus tuus fuerit nequam, totum corpus tuum tenebrosum erit.*

Just as at the moment when the original sin was committed all the harmony of the human being was shattered, because the order that insists that the reason shall be subject to God had first been violated, so at the root of all our disorders there is apparent, in the first place and above all, a rupture in the supreme ordinations of the mind. The responsibility of philosophers in this respect is enormous. In the sixteenth century, and more particularly in the age of Descartes, the interior hierarchies of the virtue of reason were shattered. Philosophy abandoned theology to assert its own claim to be considered the supreme science, and, the mathematical science of the sensible world and its phenomena taking precedence at the same time over metaphysics, the human mind began to profess independence of God and being. Independence of God: that is to say, of the supreme Object of all intelligence, Whom it accepted only half-heartedly until it finally rejected the intimate knowledge of Him supernaturally procured by grace and revelation. Independence of being: that is to say, of the connatural object of the mind as such, against which it ceased to measure itself humbly, until it finally undertook to deduce it entirely from the seeds of geometrical clarity which it conceived to be innate in itself.

We have difficulty in realizing that the ordered relation of the mind to its object should be thus shattered; we have difficulty in realizing—so material have we become—the frightful significance, sodden with blood and tears, of those few abstract words; we have difficulty in realizing the tremendous upheaval, the tremendous invisible catastrophe, thereby indicated. The mind is that 'divine' activity, as Aristotle said, that prodigy of light and life, that supreme glory and perfection of created nature, through which we become immaterially all things, through which we shall one day possess our supernatural beatitude, the cause of all our actions on earth so far as they are human actions and of the rectitude of everything we do. Can we conceive what is the meaning for man of the disturbance of that life, which he carries in him and in which the divine light has its share? The revolution inaugurated by Descartes and continued by the philosophers of the eighteenth and nineteenth centuries, which merely let loose the destructive forces for ever active in the minds of the children of Adam, is an infinitely greater historical cataclysm than the most formidable upheavels of the crust of the earth or the economy of the nations.

Indocile to the object, to God, to being, the mind becomes also and to the same extent indocile to all human authority, a rebel against all tradition and spiritual continuity. It retires within its shell, shuts itself up in the incommunicability of the individual. And if you consider that *docibilitas,* the faculty of being taught, is an essential characteristic of the created mind—nay, rather of animal faculties themselves, inasmuch as they imitate and prepare the mind, so much so that Aristotle classifies animals according to that criterion, placing those that refuse to be taught on the lowest rung; if you also consider that such *docibilitas* is in our case the real root of social life—man being a political animal primarily because he needs other men to make progress in the work of the speculative and practical reason, which is his specific work—the inevitable conclusion is, on the one hand, that by losing its docility to human teaching and its docility also to the object, the mind in our time has proceeded in the direction of an absolutely brutal hardening and a progressive weakening of reason; and, on the other hand, that the most profound and at the same time most human bonds of social life must have simultaneously become by an unavoidable consequence gradually loosened and undone.

Three main symptoms of the disease afflicting the mind at the present day down to its very roots may be discerned at the point of evolution which speculation has reached since the great changes inaugurated by the Cartesian reform.

The mind imagines that it is giving proof of its own native strength by denying and rejecting as science first theology and then metaphysics; by abandoning any attempt to know the primary Cause and immaterial realities; by cultivating a more or less refined doubt which is an outrage both to the perception of the senses and the principles of reason, that is to say the very things on which all our knowledge depends. Such a presumptuous collapse of human knowledge may be described in one word: agnosticism.

The mind at the same time refuses to recognize the rights of primary Truth and repudiates the supernatural order, considering it impossible—and such a denial is a blow at all the interior life of grace. That may be described in a word as naturalism.

Lastly, the mind allows itself to be deceived by the mirage of a mythical conception of human nature, which attributes to that nature conditions peculiar to pure spirit, assumes that nature to be in each of us as perfect and complete as the angelic nature in the angel and therefore claims for us, as being in justice our due, along with complete domination over nature, the superior autonomy, the full self-sufficiency, the αὐτάρκεια appropriate to pure forms. That may be described as individualism, giving the word its full metaphysical meaning, although *angelism* would be a more accurate description; such a term is justified by historical no less than by doctrinal considerations, because the ideal origin and metaphysical type of modern individualism are to be found in the Cartesian confusion between substance of whatever sort and the angelic monad.

I say that these three great errors are the symptoms of a really radical disease, for they attack the very root, the triple root, rational, religious and moral, of our life.

They were, to begin with, singularly latent and dissimulated, in the state of pure spiritual intentions. They are before us to-day, sparkling, oppressive, ubiquitous. Everybody sees and feels them, because their sharp unsparing point has passed from the mind into the very flesh of humanity.

Let it be observed once more, it is the integrity of natural reason, the singleness of the eye of the mind, to adapt the expression in the Gospel, the fundamental rectitude of common sense which is outraged by such errors. What a strange fate has befallen rationalism! Men emancipated themselves from all control to conquer the universe and reduce all things to the level of reason. And in the end they come to abandon reality, no longer dare to make use of ideas to adhere to being, forbid themselves the knowledge of anything beyond the sensible fact and the phenomenon of consciousness, dissolve every object of speculation in a great fluid jelly called Becoming or Evolution, conceive themselves barbarous if they do not suspect every first principle and every rational demonstration of naïveté, substitute for the effort of speculation and logical discernment a sort of refined play of instinct, imagination, intuition, visceral emotions, have lost the courage to form a judgement.

Now it is important to realize that nothing below the level of the mind can remedy this disease, which affects the mind and derives from it: the mind alone can cure itself. If the mind is not saved, nothing will be saved. However ailing it may be, it always conceals in its depths an essential vitality which nothing can injure or corrupt, and always remains, in the metaphysical order, the most exalted faculty of the human being. Because of the indefectible energy of its spiritual nature, the disease that afflicts it, however radical it may be, is still of the accidental order, of the operative order, and is incapable of affecting its essential constitution; and it is precisely when that disease has become most manifest that one is entitled to hope for the salutary reaction: only let it become conscious of the disease and it will immediately rouse itself against it.

It is useless, however, to be constantly carping: we are faced with an ineluctable necessity. The evils afflicting us have spread so far in the substance of humanity, have wrought such general havoc, that every means of defence and every extrinsic support, due in the first place to the fabric of society, to established institutions, to the moral order of the family and the State—and truth no less than the highest acquisitions of culture is in vital need of them among men—are, if not actually destroyed, at any rate shaken to their foundation. Everything which was humanly solid is compromised, 'the mountains slide and leap.' Man stands alone before the ocean of being and the transcendentals. It is an abnormal state for human nature and as perilous as can be. But it is at all events proof that everything henceforth depends on the restoration of the mind. The metaphysical truths which Pascal thought too remote for the common feeling of mankind are henceforth beyond a doubt the sole refuge and safeguard of the common life and the most immediate interests of humanity. It is no longer a question of wagering heads or tails. It is a question of judging, truth or falsehood, and affronting eternal realities.

The attempts at political and social reconstruction, amid the universal disorder, which the instinct of preservation urges the nations to make, will merely degenerate into a brutal and ephemeral despotism, will be incapable of producing anything stable, if the mind is not restored; the movement of religious revival apparent in the world will be permanent and truly efficacious, only if the mind is restored. Truth in the first place; *veritas liberabit vos.* Woe betide us, if we fail to realize that now as in the days of the creation of the world, the Word is in the beginning of the works of God.

What is the most striking characteristic of that which is most exalted, most divine, most efficacious in St. Thomas Aquinas, the most striking characteristic of the very sanctity of St. Thomas? "The chief characteristic of the sanctity of St. Thomas is what St. Paul calls *sermo sapientiae,* 'the word of wisdom,' and the union of the two forms of wisdom, the acquired and the infused. . . ." [4] Let us say that the sanctity of St. Thomas is the sanctity of the mind; and I wish I could vividly convey all the reality contained in those words.

Not only does the *philosophy* of St. Thomas maintain better than any other the rights and nobility of the mind—affirming its natural preeminence over the will; gathering under its light all the hierarchized diversity of being; itself identifying it, when it finds it in pure act, with the infinitely holy nature of the living God; unceasingly reminding us in the practical order that the life of man, and the Christian life preeminently, 'are based upon the mind'—but also, and this goes ever so much further, the very *sanctity* of Thomas Aquinas, his charity, his sacrifice of praise, his consummation in Jesus, are all accomplished and radiant in him at the summit of the spirit, in that life of the mind which Aristotle declared to be superior to human life, where the activity of man borders on the activity of pure forms; and it is thence that everything pours out in waves of light, down to the lowliest faculties of the created being. That is the sense in which we should understand the age-old title of *Doctor Angelicus,* so appropriately bestowed on Thomas Aquinas. St. Thomas is in a super-eminent sense the pure intellectual, because the intellect itself is his means *par excellence* of serving and loving God, because the intellect itself is the host which he adores.

His chief work, every schoolboy knows, was, with the approbation and encouragement, nay, rather at the instigation, of the papacy, to make

[4] Pius XI, Encyclical *Studiorum Ducem.*

room in the Christian mind for Aristotle, by completing and perfecting him, by purging him of all accretions, and for all the natural wisdom of the philosophers whom Tertullian called 'glorious animals.' He fought a very hard fight to achieve it. For if there is between Aristotle and the Gospel, between human wisdom which grew up on the soil of Greece and revelation which came down from the sky of Judaea, a preestablished harmony, which is in itself an admirable apologetic symbol, nevertheless, to realize that harmony, to make it actual, by triumphing over the obstacles which arose from the limitations of the human subject, all the strength of the great dumb ox of Sicily was required over and above the maturity of the civilization of St. Louis's age. As Pascal saw so clearly, it is the mediocrity of our intellectual capacity in the first place which makes us fall into error, because we are incapable of comprehending simultaneously apparently opposite truths which are in reality complementary. 'Exclusion' is thus 'the cause of heresy' and more generally of error. The self-styled Augustinians of the thirteenth century, confusing, in their material attachment to the literal interpretation of their master, the formal objects of faith and reason, of metaphysical wisdom and the wisdom of the saints—inclining, in short, to what we should nowadays describe as anti-intellectualism—what else were they doing, after all, but denying the rights of truth in the natural order? That tendency culminated later in formal heresy, with Luther and his inhuman hatred of reason. The Averroists who, in their fanatical devotion to an Aristotle corrupted by the Arabs, were incapable of perceiving the peculiar light and the supremacy of faith and theology—inclining, in short, to rationalism—denied the rights of supernatural truth; and we know only too well where that tendency was to culminate. St. Thomas shattered them both, and he will shatter them again, for it is always the same battle. And at the same time he determined by conclusive principles the rational theory of that distinction and harmony between the natural and the supernatural orders which are integral to the Catholic Faith and more important to the life of the world than the cycle of the stars and the seasons.

But that double battle against the Averroists and the old belated Scholasticism, that immense achievement of integrating Aristotle in Catholic philosophy, is merely the manifestation and the indication of an interior struggle, still greater and more formidable. The peculiar task of St. Thomas, the undertaking to which he was appointed by the Lord, was to bring the proudest and most intractable (because the most spiritual) of powers—I mean the mind, in all its apparel of riches and majesty, armed with all its speculative energies, all its logic and science and art, all the harness of its fierce virtues which are rooted in being itself—to bring the mind (by compelling it to sobriety but never to abdication) whole and entire into the holy light of Christ, to the service of the Child-God lying in the manger between the ox and the ass. He has all the Magi behind him for the rest of time.

Such considerations enable us, I think, to catch a glimpse of the mystery of the very vocation of St. Thomas. A very surprising vocation, it has often been observed. For the place which Thomas Aquinas was called upon to leave in obedience to the summons received from God was not the world, but the cloister, not the society of his time, but Monte Cassino. It was not what the Church calls the ignominy of the habit of the world, *ignominia saecularis habitus,* but the holy Benedictine habit which he discarded to don the white robe of St. Dominic. It was not the danger of the world that he quitted for the state of perfection: he moved from one state of perfection to another, and a more difficult one. He had to leave the house of the Blessed Father Benedict from whom, as a little oblate in a black habit, he had learned the twelve degrees of humility and of whom, as a Doctor, dazzled with ecstasy after the completion of his work, he asked hospitality in order to die. And knowing that such was the pleasure of the Lord, he persisted in taking his departure with all the tenacity of an indomitable will.

Brothers, mother, prison, guile and violence, nothing could shake his determination. Why was he so obstinate? He had to be about his Father's business. What is God? He had to teach us the spelling of divine things, and that was what Countess Theodora could not understand.

St. Dominic had asked St. Benedict for him in Heaven, because the Word of God had asked St. Dominic for him, to entrust him with a mission to the Christian mind. His duty was to serve the mind, but as the priest serves the creature of God. His duty was to teach it, to baptize it, to nourish it with the Body of the Lord, to preside at the nuptials of the Mind and the Lamb. On the white pebble given to him, which was also the live coal that purified his lips, there was written the word: *Truth.*

St. Thomas is peculiarly and above all the *apostle of the mind:* that is the first reason why he is to be considered the *apostle of our time.*

The second reason is what may be described as the absolutism of truth in his soul and in his work, with the triple consequence of absolute purity in intellectual quality, absolute rigour of logic and at the same time of harmonious complexity in doctrine, and absolute docility of obedience to reality. All philosophers and theologians doubtless seek and desire truth. But do they desire it with such vehemence and so exclusively? Not to mention particularist preoccupations and other vices of all kinds, vanity, curiosity, the vain desire for originality and novelty pursued for their own sakes, which so often spoil the quest, may not a philosopher in his search for truth address himself *also* to something else? It is in reality very rare for Truth *alone* to attract everything to itself in the heaven of the mind. Other transcendentals, giant stars, mingle their allurements also and divert speculation. And this is a grave disorder, for science as such should be regulated only by what is true. Is there not deep down in the metaphysics of Platonism, as in the Scotist theology, a secret collusion between Beauty or the Good and Truth, between Love and Knowledge? Other philosophers are affected by more mundane influences, convenience, complaisance, conformity to the needs of the day or to the exigencies of a teaching curriculum or more generally to the frailty of the human subject—and by an ill-controlled anxiety as to the practical consequences, an effort to strike a balance between opposite opinions which is taken to be wisdom, whereas in reality it is merely the attempt to discover a *medium virtutis* between truth and error, as though truth and error were two opposite vices. So truths are diminished by the sons of men.

St. Thomas, on the other hand, leaves truth all its grandeur intact, and its grandeur is to be estimated by the Son of God. He is a philosopher and a theologian and he knows nothing but Truth and is that not the way in which Philosophy and Theology, considered as such, must know nothing but Jesus crucified? He finds his whole standard of regulation in being, he is in absolutely direct relation to his object. Nothing but the intelligible necessities and exigencies of the supreme principles ever determines his solutions, even though they should be so rendered the more difficult for us, even though they should make men exclaim: *durus est hic sermo.* And if his doctrine is based entirely, in the analytical order, *in via inventionis,* on the idea of being, the primary datum of the mind, it is nevertheless entirely suspended, in the synthetic order, *in via judicii,* from the idea of God, of primary Truth, the supreme object of every mind. St. Thomas cast his net upon the universe and carried off all things, transformed into life in the mind, towards the beatific vision. This theology of the pacific is, under the light of faith, an immense movement of speculation between two intuitions, the intuition of being and the first principles of reason, whence it takes its departure and which is granted to it on this earth, and the intuition of God clearly perceived, towards which it proceeds and which will be granted to it later. Ordering the whole discourse to an ineffable supreme end, it remains perpetually rational, but at the same time teaches reason not to look for its standard in itself and in face of the mysteries below, such as matter and potentiality; just as in face of the mysteries above, such as the influence of divine premonition on created liberty, it asks us to do homage to the rights of being over our spirit as to the divine sublimity. That is the reason why it is so serene and universal, so open and so free, most boldly affirmative and humbly prudent, most systematic and least partial, most intractable and hospitable to every delicate shade of difference in reality, richest in certitudes and yet most sedulously careful to make allowance for probabilities and opinions, most resolute and uncompromising and most detached from human knowledge. So transcendent is the object in which its ardent desire is to lose itself!

Now I say that in this respect also St. Thomas answers in a special fashion the needs of the present time. The spirit nowadays is exposed to such extreme dangers that no palliative can possibly be sufficient for it. Many compromises which might formerly have been successful are now utterly futile to help minds ploughed to their very depths by modern controversies and the more exacting therefore in their criticisms.

To mention only philosophy, this is specially apparent when you come to consider certain primary questions such as the distinction between essence and existence, or the analogy of being, or the nature of intellection, or the value of the intuition of exterior sensibility, or the relation of pre-eminence between the mind and the will.

The work of the negative forces goes so far forward at the present day that an inexorably rigorous philosophy is required to get the better of it, one so comprehensive at the same time that it can do justice to all the diversities in which contemporary speculation, for lack of a controlling light, exhausts itself. So it comes about that what is most apt to our needs is precisely the absolutism of truth, what is most opportune and 'practical' is doctrinal radicalism, but a radicalism devoid of all narrowness and brutality, all partiality and fanaticism, and suspended therefore from the only true Absolute, from the transcendence of primary Truth, whence all things proceed in being. A thousand doctrines can aggravate the state of the mind, only one can cure it.

Thomism—and this is the third reason why St. Thomas should be described as the apostle of our time—is alone capable of delivering the mind from the radical errors mentioned in the beginning of this chapter.

Scrutinizing knowledge metaphysically, while respecting—it is the only system which does so—the original nature and mysterious immateriality of knowledge, placing our ideas in continuity with things through the intuition of the senses and resolving all our learning in the evidence of being and first principles, whose transcendental value enables it to ascend to God, the philosophy of St. Thomas is a form of wisdom sufficiently exalted to save the mind from the enchantments of agnosticism and to counter the devil of idealism (already far advanced in age) with a realism which is not naïve but soundly critical.

Conscious of the infinite elevation and the infinite liberty of the Creator, as of the radically contingent basis of the created being, assuring, through a sound conception of the universal, the value of nature and its laws, and pointing out that nature still remains in the sight of God immensely ductile and immensely perfectible—penetrable throughout by the divine influence—it reduces to absurdity the naturalist postulate and the metaphysical hypocrisy which, concealed behind the curtain of the positive sciences, attempts to endow the creature with the aseity of divinity.

Understanding all the grandeur and servitude involved in the very idea of rational animal, placing the human mind on the lowest rung of the ladder of spirits, abruptly dismissing all its pretensions to play at being pure spirit, making proper allowance for the autonomy which becomes us as spirits and the dependence which becomes us as creatures, as material creatures and as wounded creatures, it destroys by the root, by its *angelist* root, an individualism which in reality sacrifices human personality to an illusory and devouring image of man.

The reason is that St. Thomas—and this is the most immediate benefit he confers—brings the mind back to its object, orientates it towards its end, restores it to its nature. He tells it that it is made for being. How could it possibly not give ear? It is as though you were to tell the eye that it is made for seeing or the wings that they are made for flying. It is itself it rediscovers when it finds its object; it orders itself entirely to being; in accordance with the sovereign inclination which things have for their first principle, it tends, above all, to subsisting Being itself.

Simplicity of perception is at the same time restored to it; artificial obstacles no longer obtrude to make it hesitate before the natural evidence of first principles and the continuity between philosophy and common sense is re-established.

Submissive to the object, but in order to attain its true liberty, because it is in such submission that it acts with the most spontaneous and living activity; docile to the teaching of masters, but in order to make its own grasp of the object more intense and complete, because it is for the love of being that it invites the labour of the ages to succour and fortify it, it restores within itself its own essential hierarchies and the order of its virtues.

What constitutes the nobility of philosophers, of modern philosophers in particular, is that in spite of their aberrations they are genuinely devoted to the mind, even when they ruin it. But their devotion to the mind has for the most part been greater than their love of God. St. Thomas loves God more than the mind, but his devotion to the mind is greater than the devotion of all the other philosophers. That is the reason why he can restore it, by reminding it of its duties. He shames it out of its cowardice, gives it back the courage to affront the supreme truths. He shames it out of its vain glory, forces it to measure itself against things and to listen to a tradition. He teaches it again simultaneously the two complementary virtues it had lost together, magnanimity and humility.

The apostle of the mind, the doctor of truth, the restorer of the intellectual order, St. Thomas wrote not for the thirteenth century but for our time. His own time is the time of the spirit, which dominates the ages. I say that he is a contemporary writer, the most modern of all philosophers. He adheres so purely to the high light of wisdom that as regards the inferior sciences and their moving shadows he enjoys such liberty as no philosopher ever knew: all the sensible vesture borrowed from the science of the thirteenth century may be discarded, his philosophical and metaphysical doctrine remains as intact as the soul once it has departed from the body. And the divestiture effected by the revolutions which have taken place in the science of phenomena since the time of Nicole Oresme, Leonardo da Vinci and Galileo, was perhaps necessary to bring Thomism to the state of spirituality, and therefore of effectiveness, truly corresponding to the spiritual elevation of the authentic thought of St. Thomas. He stands at the cross-roads before us; he holds the key to the problems which oppress our hearts; he teaches us how to triumph over anti-intellectualism and rationalism alike, over the disease which depresses the reason below the level of reality and the disease which exalts it above that level; he communicates to us the secret of true humanism, of the supreme development of human personality and the intellectual virtues, but in sanctity, not in concupiscence, through the spirit and the cross, not through the grandeurs of the flesh. At a time sorely tormented by the desire (too frequently erratic and dispersed over the things of this world) for a kingdom of the heart and a life of love, he teaches the only doctrine which affirms the absolute practical primacy of charity in our life and which invites us to the banquet of true love, of supernatural charity, I mean, yet without repudiating the mind and its metaphysical superiority or adulterating charity itself by contaminating it with pragmatism, humanitarianism or animal sensibility. Charity should always increase in virtue of the first commandment, and the perfection of charity for this reason falls under the commandment, as the end to which everyone is bound to tend according to his condition. Such is the law of gravitation that the Angelic Doctor teaches to a world all the more haunted by the idea of progress because it is ignorant for the most part of the meaning of progress.

William of Tocco even in his day dwelt unceasingly upon the *modernity* of Friar Thomas. That modernity is in truth at opposite poles to the modernity pursued nowadays and found so captivating. For St. Thomas is only accidentally an innovator; his one desire is the truth: whereas innovations are made nowadays for the sake of novelty as such, and truth has become a mere accident. Such being the case, the object is not so much to improve what is old as to destroy it and to exalt the originality of every thinking subject rather than to make thought conform to the object. It is a complete reversal of the proper order, an essentially particularist and negative method, which is in reality essentially retrograde. All acquired truths are thus inevitably bound to be annihilated one after the other.

The method practised by St. Thomas is, on the contrary, essentially universalist and positivist. Its object is to preserve all the acquired knowledge of humanity in order to add to and perfect it; and it involves the more and more absolute effacement of the philosopher before the truth of the object. If he devotes himself to Aristotle, it is not because he considers Aristotle a fashionable philosopher, recently imported by the Arabs, but because he recognizes him to be the best interpreter of natural reason, the philosopher who based philosophy on foundations in conformity with what is. And he follows him, yet criticizing him at every step, correcting and purifying him by a higher light, which is not the light of Aristotle but of Wisdom incarnate. If he opposes the too materialist disciples of St. Augustine, it is not for the purpose of destroying St. Augustine, but with the object of following and understanding him in a more vivid, more profoundly faithful, manner, in a more perfect commerce of spirit. And no theologian was ever more sedulously devoted to the common secular wisdom with which the Church is divinely instructed. That is the reason why the Angelic Doctor is also the Common Doctor of the Church. The Common Doctor! What an admirable title, indicative of a truly superhuman grandeur, a title which puts all our sorry vanities in their place and answers the most pressing needs of the moment! It is not a special Doctor or a particular Doctor or an original Doctor, or a Doctor peculiar to our person or our family, it is not an illuminate Doctor, or a devout or subtle or irrefragable Doctor, or a

Doctor *facundus* or *resolutissimus* or *eximius,* or a *venerabilis inceptor,* but a Common Doctor, the Common Doctor of the Church that we need. There he stands on the threshold of modern times offering us in the elaborately ornamented basket of his thousands of arguments the sacred fruits of wisdom.

Now something very much more important is taking place in our time than many material events more easily noticeable. As the voice of the Church, the philosophy of St. Thomas is not only restored or in process of being restored in Catholic schools and in the education of aspirants to the priesthood, but it has also emerged from the old folios in which it was kept in reserve, not itself old but as youthful as truth, it speaks to the world and claims its place, that is to say the first place, in the intellectual life of the age, it cries in the market-place, as it is said of wisdom: *sapientia foris praedicat, in plateis dat vocem.* After the long idealist aberration due to Descartes and the great Kantian heresy, we are now spectators of an attempt to reintegrate the philosophy of being in Western civilization. Lovers of paradox and novelty should be the first to rejoice.

7 | GILSON

DANTE

The struggle between ecclesiastical and political authority, between church and empire, is one of the dominant themes of medieval thought and life. It was a struggle of both conflicting ideas and interests, and like so many deep-seated conflicts in Western history, it was never fully resolved. In recent times, the issue flared up again when Bismarck tried to subjugate the Catholic element in Germany in his *Kulturkampf,* and more recently still the fascist and communist types of totalitarianism have sought to destroy the influence of church and religion, both of which are opposed, and must be opposed, to the total domination of man by the state. During the Middle Ages, religion in the Western world was represented by one united church, and political authority, too, was reflected (frequently in theory more than in practice) by one institution, the Holy Roman Empire of the German dynasties. The polarization of the two rival forces added to the bitterness of the struggle, and it was hard to maintain a middle ground. St. Augustine and St. Thomas Aquinas were among the foremost spokesmen of the supremacy of the church over mundane authority; the most important antipapalist writer of the Middle Ages is Dante Alighieri (1265–1321), whose book *On Monarchy,* or *On World Government* (about 1310) firmly asserted the political unity of mankind under a political ruler, sovereign in his authority and independent of any ecclesiastical interference in the realm of government. The greatest poet of the medieval period, Dante was also, with varying success, a diplomat, soldier, politician, philologist, theologian, and philosopher. As an artist and thinker, Dante clearly announces the dawn of the Renaissance. By his use of the vernacular in *The Divine Comedy* he helped to create a national Italian language and thus break the monopoly of Latin as the only means of literary communication.

In his *De monarchia,* Dante was primarily concerned with three questions: whether there was need for world government; whether such government for the whole human race should be a monarchy; and whether the authority of the emperor derives directly from God or from some minister or vicar of God, that is, the Pope. On all three questions his answer was in the affirmative. Yet as a modern student of Dante, the Frenchman Etienne Gilson (1884-   ), shows in his study of *Dante the Philosopher* (1949), the latter's political philosophy was based on a more general metaphysics, in which man's life on earth was sharply divided from his ultimate life in Heaven. Philosophy and government expressed the first, whereas theology and church expressed the second. By affirming the independence of philosophy from theology, Dante was inevitably led to the separation of church and empire. Writing from the Thomist viewpoint, Gilson feels that this separation of philosophy from theology in Dante's thought has had even more far-reaching effects in Western intellectual history than his affirmation of the independence of political authority in relation to the church. Like Maritain, Gilson is a leading exponent of modern French Thomism, concentrating on the Middle Ages, on which he has written copiously and illuminatingly, as in *The Spirit of Medieval Philosophy* (1936) and *Reason and Revelation in the Middle Ages* (1938).

Gilson on DANTE

If we admit that universal peace is the goal of the human race, it remains for us to seek the means to attain it. This is one of the questions on which Dante is most readily compared to St. Thomas Aquinas. Nevertheless, the first fact to be noted—and it is probably not without some significance—is that St. Thomas never propounded the problem of the relationship of the Empire to the Papacy. So far as I know, he never

[From Etienne Gilson, *Dante the Philosopher* (Sheed & Ward, Inc., 1948). By permission.]

once went so far as to write the word *imperator*. This theologian, then, views everything as if the Emperor did not exist. Those of whom he always speaks in his writings are the "princes", that is to say chiefs of States, varying in extent, men who themselves hold different titles—kings, dukes, princes, etc.—the sole qualification being that they should possess supreme temporal authority in their respective countries. The fact is accounted for by two things of which the historians tell us. First, the majority of theologians defend the supreme authority of the Pope in temporal matters against the Emperor; they are therefore the natural allies of the local temporal powers over which the Emperor claims to have authority.[1] Consequently, it was not in the interest of the theologians to attribute to the Emperor a theoretical importance greater than his real importance. A sole spiritual head could more easily exercise his rights over a sprinkling of petty States and petty princes than over a sole universal Empire which set up in opposition to the Pope a temporal sovereign having a jurisdiction co-extensive with his own. Even if there were an Emperor it would be better to act as if there were none. In fact—and this is the second reason—we may say that in practice there was none. "The humiliation of the Empire is so profound," wrote H. Pirenne of these times, "that for a moment after 1250 it may have seemed on the point of disappearing."[2] Moreover, this is the very thing that makes Dante's attitude such a great one. Writing in an age when there is no longer an Emperor of any kind, he does not fight for a man, but for an idea. One understands the fact that St. Thomas did not think it his duty to galvanize this corpse or to join battle with the phantom authority when it was in the Church's interest that it should remain so.

In examining St. Thomas's doctrine we must therefore confine ourselves to what he says of the relations between the prince of a specific country and the Pope who presides over the universal Church. Now Dante differs from him here in the emphasis of his demonstration that the existence of a universal monarch, supreme temporal sovereign of all mankind, is absolutely essential in the name of philosophical principles which are themselves universal and necessary. As it is here a question of Dante's most original personal contribution to the history of political philosophy, this primary difference cannot be regarded as negligible. Moreover, one gravely suspects that it will have consequences. St. Thomas, who cannot imagine a Church without a Pope, makes do admirably with

---

[1] See the remarks of H. Pirenne, in L. Halphen and P. Sagnac, *La fin du moyen âge* (*Peuples et Civilisations,* Vol. VII, 1), Paris, F. Alcan, 1931, pp. 6–7.

[2] H. Pirenne, *op. cit.,* p. 7.

a world without an Emperor, but Dante can no more accept a world without an Emperor than a Church without a Pope, precisely because he desires that, when a Pope takes a hand in the affairs of Florence,[3] he should find himself faced with someone to whom he may speak. Florence alone against the Pope faces defeat, but Florence represented by a universal Emperor against the Pope finds the chances once more in her favour. It was with the object of assuring all States of this protector and supreme temporal arbiter that Dante invoked all the principles of Aristotle and produced from them this universal monarchy which even the tutor of Alexander of Macedon certainly never dreamed of.

In this matter, therefore, Dante's achievement consisted in reviving the principal arguments which St. Thomas and Aristotle had used, in order to prove that a single head is required in every political community, these arguments being applied, however, to that universal political community for the existence of which he craved—a human fellowship. Since there exists a *propria operatio humanae universitatis* ("an activity characteristic of all humanity"), this universal community must also exist for the purpose of leading men to that goal. Now let us note carefully that here Dante is thinking particularly of the question of ensuring the complete actualization of the human intellect in the sphere of action. Not that he regards the practical function of reason as superior to its speculative function. As I have said, Dante never called in question the hierarchies of dignity established by Aristotle and confirmed by St. Thomas. Speculation is nobler than action and the practical arts, the moral order of action and the technical order of creation are subordinate to the theoretical order of knowledge, and contemplation remains the supreme goal assigned by the supreme Good to the human race. That is even the reason, notes Dante in this connection, why Aristotle says in his *Politics* "that those who prevail by virtue of understanding naturally have authority over others." [4] Only, ethics and politics, though mere concomitants of contemplation, are its essential concomitants. No peace, no philosophy. Therefore universal peace, if not our beatitude, is at any rate the loftiest of its concomitants. In other words it is supreme and transcendent in the sphere of ways and means. That is why we should regard this universal

[3] It is impossible to explain Dante in terms of the history of Florence, for many other Florentines have lived that history, and yet there is only one Dante; but the events of which he was a witness were certainly the origin of the course which he adopted and of which his doctrine is professedly a universally valid justification. Cf. F. Ercole, *Il pensiero politico di Dante*, Vol. II, pp. 274–296.

[4] Dante, *De Monarchia*, I, 3, end. Cf. Aristotle, *Pol.*, I, 2, 1252 a 31–32; but Dante is inclined to follow St. Thomas Aquinas, *In XII lib. Metaph. Aristot.*, Prooemium.

peace, which was heralded by the Angels on the birth of Christ, as the best means whereby the human race may accomplish its special task. Looked upon in this way, universal peace should therefore be regarded as the first essential for the attainment of the goal assigned by God to humanity.[5] Now if there is no universal monarch there will be no peace. Therefore a universal monarch is necessary for the existence, order and peace of a politically organized human race.

However interesting they may be in themselves, the arguments which Dante uses to justify his thesis concern rather the content of his philosophy than his general attitude towards philosophy. Let us, then, merely recall that, supported by the "venerable authority" of Aristotle as voiced in his *Politics,* Dante lays down as a principle that "when several things are directed towards a single goal, it is imperative for one of them to control or rule, and for the others to be controlled and ruled." [6] Not only does the authority of Aristotle prescribe this law, but inductive reasoning establishes it. In the individual, everything must be subject to the intellect if he desires to be happy. In a family, everything must be subject to the father of the family if it is desired that its members should attain the object of family life, which is readiness to live a good life. Similarly, in a village, a city, a kingdom, there must be a single head if it is not desired that the word of the Infallible Truth should prove correct: "Every kingdom divided against itself is brought to desolation" (*Matt.,* XII, 25). If, then, the entire human race is directed towards a single goal, it is essential to the well-being of the world that there should exist a Monarchy, in other words a sole command—that of the Emperor.[7]

Of the numerous arguments of this kind which Dante piles up seemingly at random in order to establish his thesis, there is one which

[5] Dante, *De Monarchia,* I, 4.

[6] Dante, *De Monarchia,* I, 5. Cf. Aristotle, *Pol.,* I, 5, 1254 a 28–32; or better St. Thomas Aquinas, *In XII libros Metaph. Aristot.,* Incipit.

[7] Dante, *De Monarchia,* I, 6. Dante next proves that the unity of command which obtains in the parts of the human race should, *a fortiori,* obtain in the human race as a whole (I, 6); that, as the parts of which it is the whole are joined to it by single heads, the human race should be joined by a single head to the whole of which it forms part, viz. the universe, of which God is the Monarch (I, 7); that the human race, of which God is the cause, should tend to become assimilated in the highest degree possible to its cause: it should therefore be one, as God is one (I, 8); that the son should follow in his father's footsteps; now the human race traces its origin, partially at least, to heaven, which is moved by a single Monarch (I, 9); that wherever conflict is possible there should be a judge; now there may be conflict among princes; consequently there should be an Emperor to decide between them (I, 10). It is at this point in his argumentation that Dante comes to his decisive proof, which is derived from the idea of justice.

should be examined with particular attention, for it is bound up with what is deepest and most personal in the poet's thought—his ideal of justice. Wishing to praise the era which he saw taking shape in his day, Virgil had already sung in his *Bucolics: Iam redit et Virgo, redeunt Saturnia regna.* ("Already too the Virgin returns, and the days of Saturn's dominion.") [8]

By the word *Virgo* ("Virgin") we must understand Justice; by *Saturnia regna* ("Saturn's dominion") Virgil signified that age of excellence which was also called the "golden age". But the world is in its most perfect state only when justice reigns, and justice reigns without question only under the authority of a single Monarch; thus the world can only be in its most perfect state under a Monarchy or Empire. What is justice in fact? Considered in itself and with respect to its special character, it is a certain rectitude, or standard, which rules out everything that deviates from righteousness. It is analogous to those forms which, according to Gilbert de la Porrée, consist of simple and unvarying essences —abstract whiteness, for instance—and which, being in themselves incapable of increase or decrease, grow or diminish only in terms of the entities that embody them. Thus, considered in itself, justice is an absolute, but there may be varying degrees of it in the world, and it is when the minimum of injustice goes to its making and its mode of operation that the maximum of justice is to be found in the world. When it shines forth in the world, we may indeed say, with the Philosopher, that "neither in Hesperus nor in Lucifer is there anything so admirable".[9] What prevents men's wills from being imbued with a sense of justice is "greed", which is its antithesis; what prevents the just will from acting in accordance with justice is lack of power, or of strength: what is the use of wishing to assign to every man his due, if one cannot do so? "The more powerful the just man is, the more amply will his justice be able to express itself in deeds." In order, therefore, that the world's state may be of the best, justice must reside in it in a supremely active and supremely powerful will. There is none that can be more so than that of a single monarch; it is only, then, if justice resides in such a monarch, or Em-

---

[8] Virgil, *Buc.*, IV, 6. The reader will notice in the passage one of those frequently recurring indications which enable us to understand in what sense Dante was able to regard Virgil as a "sage". It was no slight praise, especially coming from Dante, to represent him as the prophet of Justice in a world pacified by the Emperor Augustus. With regard to the mediaeval conceptions of Virgil, see D. Comparetti, *Virgilio nel Medio Evo*, La Nuova Italia, Florence, 1937–XV; as to the idea which Dante himself formed of him, see in particular two excellent pages, Chap. XV, pp. 274–275.

[9] Aristotle, *Eth. Nic.*, V, 3, 1129 b 28–29. Cf. Thomas Aquinas, *In X lib. Ethic.*, lib. V., lect. 2, ed. Pirotta, No. 906.

peror, that it will reach its highest point in the world and the world will be supremely well ordered (I, 11).

The most important point in this proof is undoubtedly the definition which Dante offers of the antithesis of justice: "Where the will is not free from all greed, even if justice is in it, it is nevertheless not present in the full splendour of its purity: it is, in fact, present in an entity which, however little, in some measure resists it" (I, 11). This *cupiditas* ("greed"), of which the She-wolf of the *Divine Comedy* is most certainly a symbol,[10] does not at first appear in Dante as a religious and Christian notion. He borrows it from the Philosopher, or at any rate the Philosopher suggests it to him: *Justitiae maxime contrariatur cupiditas, ut innuit Aristoteles in quinto ad Nicomachum.* ("The greatest enemy of justice is greed, as Aristotle indicates in the fifth book of the *Ethica ad Nicomachum.*")[11] Eliminate greed, and there remains nothing in opposition to justice. Now it happens that the only way to procure a man free from all greed is to install in power one who, possessing all, can no longer covet anything.

Such, to be exact, would be the single Monarch of Dante's dreams: a sovereign whose jurisdiction ends only at the edge of the ocean, that is to say—since in Dante's time fleets count for hardly anything—a sovereign whose jurisdiction is limitless. The universal Monarch exercises an author-

---

[10] Cf. M. Barbi, *Nuovi problemi di critica dantesca*, in *Studi Danteschi*, 1938–XVII, p. 29.

[11] Dante, *De Monarchia*, I, 11. Aristotle in fact distinguishes legal justice, which is not a particular virtue, but virtue in its entirety, and of which the antithesis is injustice (*Eth. Nic.*, V, 3, 1130 a 9–10), from justice regarded as a particular virtue, the antithesis of which is that particular farm of injustice which is called "avarice". (Regarding πλεονεξία, see V, 2, 1129 b 9.) The notions of greed and avarice are, moreover, closely related; but Dante seems to have preferred that of greed, because, as is clearly indicated by what is to follow, the evil of which he is thinking is specifically the active avarice of princes who covet for themselves the territories of others. Let us note, moreover, that *cupiditas* translates better than *avaritia* the fundamental meaning of πλεονεξία: the desire to have more than others, avidity, greedy desire, the tendency to usurp. Cf. in this connection the work of Allan H. Gilbert, *Dante's Conception of Justice*, Duke University Press, Durham (North Carolina), 1925. This book has the merit not only of dealing with what is truly a fundamental point in Dante's doctrine, but also of having, by an obligatory reference to St. Thomas's commentary on the *Ethica ad Nicomachum*, shed light on the exact meaning of the notions of justice and avarice (or greed) in the works of Dante. Even if, as is natural, we do not regard as justified all the parallels between the *Banquet* and St. Thomas's commentary which the author suggests, enough of them remain established for the thesis of Mr. A. H. Gilbert to be considered proven. Consult especially Chap. I, *The Materials for Dante's Treatise on Justice: St. Thomas' Commentary on Ethics V*, 1–9, pp. 3–66.

ity that knows no frontiers: there is therefore no frontier for him to violate. The universal Monarch can have no feeling of greed: he therefore has feelings only of love and charity. Now just as the slightest trace of greed is enough to obscure justice, so too charity, that is to say integrity in love (*recta dilectio*), refines and clarifies justice. It is therefore certain that under a Monarch free from all greed justice must reign without constraint. Expressing himself with rare vigour, Dante notes that greed consists essentially of scorn for the unique dignity of each man and covets everything else, whereas charity scorns everything else, seeking only God and man, and consequently the good of man. Now the most precious good within the reach of all men is to live in peace. Justice alone can enable them to enjoy it, and the charity, unmarred by covetousness, which a universal Monarch alone can reveal for all men is the necessary condition of the reign of justice. The world therefore needs a single Emperor, who shall stand in relation to the entire universe as a kind of universal cause. The nearer such a cause approaches to universality, the more truly will it be a cause, and the more truly it is a cause, the more pregnant will it be with love. That such a Monarch would be eminently disposed to act in accordance with justice who can doubt, unless he is ignorant of the meaning of the word "monarch"? If he is truly Monarch, he can have no enemies (I, 12).

Having reached this point, Dante will now hurl himself into the thick of the fray, for the moment has come for him to reveal to the world the very foundation of that freedom to which greed of any kind is a menace. Men say that this foundation is free will and that free will is free judgment as to what one should desire. And what they say is true; but, adds Dante, people repeat these formulas without understanding what they are saying any more than do our logicians when they cram their logic with mathematical examples—for instance, that the three angles of a triangle are equal to two right angles. What it is important to understand here is that a judgment is free in so far as it comes near to being purely rational, i.e. in so far as it approaches complete emancipation from the appetite and the desires. Freedom is the possession of the rational judgment which actuates the appetite and which is in no way actuated by it. Now this capacity for making up our minds through reason is the greatest good with which God has endowed human nature, since it alone enables us to be happy on earth as men and to be so as gods in the afterlife. Only the Monarch of the human race can desire the good of the human race—namely, that all men, existing each for his own sake, should be as good as it is possible for them to be. Such is not the goal that single States have in view. Whether democracies, oligarchies, or tyrannies are involved, each pursues some particular interest to which it subjects men, although this goal is not theirs. That, moreover, is why Aristotle in his *Politics* says that "in a perverted community the honest man is a bad citizen, whereas, in a righteous community, the honest man and the good citizen are one and the same". Thus, good communities are those which understand freedom aright, that is to say those which desire that men should exist for their own sakes, not for that of the State of which they form part. The authority of a single Monarch is therefore absolutely essential if it is desired that men should be governed with a view to their own good instead of being exploited for particular ends which are not their own.[12]

These are only a few of the philosophical arguments accumulated by Dante, with a vigour and a richness of invention that are remarkable, to justify the necessity of a universal monarchy, and we cannot even consider the historical and juridical arguments of which Book II of the *Monarchy* is entirely composed. The essential thing is, indeed, for us to notice the profound gulf that separates the actual nature of the problem propounded by Dante from the apparently similar problem in St. Thomas Aquinas to which it is often compared. Sometimes, indeed, scholars argue as if the Thomistic question of the relationship between princes and Popes were identical with the Dantesque question of the relationship between the Emperor and the Pope. It is not entirely so. Not only does St. Thomas never speak of an Emperor of any kind, but, even if he did, the head of the Romano-Germanic Empire of whom he might be thinking would only be in a general sense comparable to this supreme master of the human race for whom Dante clamours. By a curious paradox, Dante was able to raise up a universal Monarch vis-à-vis to the universal Pope only by imagining this Monarch himself as a kind of Pope.[13] To be sure, a temporal Pope,

---

12 Dante, *De Monarchia*, I, 12. Cf. Aristotle, *Pol.*, III, 2, 1276 b 40–1277 a 1, or better St. Thomas Aquinas, *In X lib. Ethic. Aristotelis*, lib. V, lect. 3, ed. Pirotta, No. 926.

13 So true is this that theologians were able to accept Dante's attitude without any modification, provided only that the Pope was substituted for the Emperor. That is what was done by the Franciscan François de Mayronnes in the writings in which he dealt exclusively with this problem, especially in his *Tractatus de Principatu Temporali*, Bib. Nat., Fonds latin, 3655 and 14195. It is true to say that François de Mayronnes, like Dante, believed that "in universo nostro est dare unum monarcham qui ita praesit omni-

bus temporaliter, quod nulli in temporalibus sit subjectus" (*op. cit.*, MS. 3655, fol. 44 vo.), although in his eyes this universal temporal Monarch is the Pope; if it is insisted that he should be the Emperor, it is better to do without him: "In universo, secundum optimam dispositionem sui, non est dare, secundum rectam rationem, aliquem monarcham sui principem, videlicet in temporalibus, quando ille subsit temporaliter et etiam in temporalibus principe spirituali, ut puta Papae" (*op. cit.*, Explicit). An edition of this treatise and of the chief passages in François de Mayronnes dealing with this problem has just been prepared by M. Pierre de Lapparent.

but nevertheless the head of a kind of natural Catholic community deriving its dogma from the ethics of Aristotle and guided towards its specific goal by the authority of a single pastor. If the *genus humanum* ("human race") of Dante is really the first known expression of the modern idea of Humanity, we may say that the conception of Humanity first presented itself to the European consciousness merely as a secularized imitation of the religious notion of a Church. This, moreover, is why Dante portrays his Monarch as a temporal father compelled by his position and his functions to practise charity and justice no less absolutely than the Pope, the spiritual father of mankind, is compelled by his function and his position —if, that is, he respects them—to practise spiritual fatherhood and sanctity. Like the head of an immense religious community, Dante's Monarch, precisely because he is responsible for subjecting others to the laws which lead them to their goal, is in reality merely their servant: *Monarcha, qui minister omnium habendus est* ("The Monarch, who must be regarded as the servant of all") (I, 12). This Emperor is therefore a minister, almost as St. Bonaventure had been a minister of the Franciscan Order, and this indeed is what will shortly invest the problem with an entirely new urgency, a scope quite different from that which it had in the *De regimine principum* of St. Thomas Aquinas, not only because of the formidable power that this leader of Humanity will wield in the presence of the leader of Christendom, but especially because of the right that he too will henceforth have to speak as one invested with supreme moral authority in his sphere and charged with leading to a clearly defined goal the entirety of mankind, which God has entrusted to him. In thus investing temporal society with all the attributes of the Church Dante was transposing the classic controversy between the Priesthood and the Empire into a new key. Any comparison between Dante's doctrine and those of his predecessors or contemporaries must necessarily take this fact into account; otherwise it is bound to fall into errors of perspective which themselves suggest doctrinal pseudo-similarities and misinterpretations.

Independence of the Empire

It follows from Book II of the *Monarchy* that the Roman Empire, in the form in which it survives in the Middle Ages, is a lawful power, the existence of which is desired by God with a view to the happiness of mankind. Now the Papacy likewise claims to be a universal authority of divine origin. The question, consequently, is how to reconcile the authority of "those two great luminaries, the Roman Pontiff and the Roman Prince". And first of all "we ask whether the authority of the Roman Monarch, who is by right the Monarch of the world, as the Second Book has proved, is directly subject to God's will or whether it is subject to that of some vicar or minister of God, by which I mean the successor of Peter, who is in truth the key-bearer of the Kingdom of Heaven".[14] It is, I think, unnecessary to stress the word *directly*. That the authority of the Emperor of the world is in the long run subject to the will of God goes without saying; the only question is whether it is subject to it directly or through the Pope, but it is a very important question.

In approaching the matter, it is of some interest to note that the Third Book of the *Monarchy* begins with a quotation from the Scriptures, with which Dante in a sense covers himself as with a shield, because it places him under the protection of justice: *Conclusit ora leonum, et non nocuerunt mihi; quia coram eo justitia inventum est in me* ("My God . . . hath shut the lions' mouths, and they have not hurt me: forasmuch as before him justice was found in me") (*Dan.*, VI, 22). If collected, the sentences in which Dante stresses this virtue would form a very long list, but they would lose their meaning. In his work justice resembles, indeed, a kind of theme, or *leit-motiv*, which is never long in reappearing, sometimes in the least expected forms. If he wishes to base his argument on natural reason, Dante has recourse to the *Ethica ad Nicomachum,* Book V, where the two kinds of justice, legal and personal, receive such unreserved homage. If he is thinking of that definite form of human justice whose reign is associated with the supremacy of the Roman Empire, Dante has recourse to Virgil, the prophet of the golden age in which felicity will reign in peace under the authority of Rome; [15] if only as the singer of Roman justice realized in the triumph of law. Virgil would already have amply deserved the honour of suggesting, as a theme of Dante's thought, the glory of the sage in addition to that of the poet. But if he wishes to reveal the religious, sacred and truly divine character of the virtue of justice, Dante turns to the Scriptures, and not only to its text, but to its heroes and sages. As a counter to the presumptuous Popes, Dante disposes in paradise of an ally whose holiness renders him immune to their attacks and whose justice judges them: the most wise King Solomon, in whose behalf David

---

[14] Dante, *De Monarchia*, III, 1. Several other equivalent formulas occur in the same treatise: "Isti vero ad quos erit tota disputatio sequens, asserentes auctoritatem Imperii ab auctoritate Ecclesiae dependere, velut artifex inferior dependet ab architecto. . . ." (III, 4). Cf. "Quod autem auctoritas Ecclesiae. . . ." (III, 13).

[15] Dante, *De Monarchia*, II, 3; note that King Aeneas is here mentioned as the father of the sovereign people on account of his justice: "Quo justior alter nec pietate fuit . . ." Cf. *op. cit.*, II, 6, for Rome's natural capacity for government: "Tu regere imperio populos, Romane, memento", and II, 8: "Certe hinc Romanos olim volventibus annis hinc fore ductores . . ." Cf. *Epist.* to the Emperor Henry, on the justice of Augustus.

had entreated God: "Give to the king thy judgments, and thy justice unto the king's son." [16] Every form of justice—the philosophical, the poetic and the Christian—is here brought into operation in the service of the Emperor.

The fundamental principle propounded by Dante as the basis of all his reasoning is that *God does not desire that which contradicts the intention of nature* (III, 2); for it was God Himself Who desired the existence of nature; if, then, God, desiring the existence of nature, did not desire that which is necessarily desired by nature, one would have to say that God does not desire that which He does desire. Furthermore, Dante does not think there is any real uncertainty as to the correct answer to be given to this question. At heart all know what they should think; if there is any argument on the point, ignorance is not the cause of it, but rather it is the cause of ignorance. Passions and feelings of all kinds here come between truth and the light of reason, inciting against it three main adversaries:

1. The Sovereign Pontiff, vicar of Our Lord Jesus Christ and successor of Peter, to whom we owe, not all that is due to Christ, but all that is due to Peter, and who perhaps allows himself to be led astray by his zeal for the power of the keys. Let us place in the same category certain Christian pastors who do not gainsay the truth out of pride, but only out of zeal for the Church.

2. There are others, on the contrary, in whom an inveterate greed has extinguished the light of reason; true sons of the devil, these self-styled sons of the Church do not content themselves with sowing on earth universal discord; to such a degree do they abhor even the thrice sacred name of the Imperial Principate that they do not hesitate shamelessly to deny the very principles on which it rests.

3. Last come the Decretalists, folk whose ignorance of theology, as of philosophy, is complete; these know nothing but their famous Decretals. To be sure, no one denies that the latter are venerable, but they count on their ultimate victory and take their stand on them in order to belittle the Empire.

Of these three kinds of adversary Dante begins by eliminating the last, for it is not on the Decretals, but on the Scriptures, that he for his part intends to rely in order to find the truth of the Church. He likewise

[16] Dante, *De Monarchia*, I, 13, quoting Psalm LXXI, 1–3: "Deus judicium tuum regi da, et justitiam tuam filio regis;—judicare populum tuum in justitia, et pauperes tuos injudicio.—Suscipiant montes pacem populo, et colles justitiam." Solomon is again quoted in support of justice (with Daniel, David and St. Paul) in *De Monarchia*, III, pending the time when Dante will crown him in heaven, with detailed introductory notes of the greatest possible clarity on the symbolism assigned to him, in the *Divine Comedy*, *Par.*, X, 109–114.

eliminates, as being impervious to persuasion, those who are blinded by greed. The only enemies remaining to him are therefore the Pope and those prelates who, led astray by their very zeal for our mother the Church, do not know the truth in question (III, 3). But even as Dante thus defines his adversary he dismisses his claims in advance. No doubt the reader has noticed the skilful formula which the poet uses in the passage in order to limit, even while he proclaims it, the extent of his obedience to the Pope: All that he owes not to Christ, but to Peter. To propound this article as something beyond discussion was equivalent to regarding the question as settled in advance, for it was an affirmation that there are privileges belonging to Christ which neither Peter nor his successors have inherited. More precisely still, it was tantamount to excluding privileges belonging to Christ which Peter and his successors have inherited—that very temporal primacy which Dante was making ready to refuse to them. The simplest way to convince oneself of the importance of the issue at stake is to collate the two formulas in which Dante and St. Thomas have expressed the essence of their positions:

DANTE
De Monarchia (III, 3)

"Summus namque Pontifex, Domini nostri Jesu Christi vicarius et Petri successor, cui non quicquid Christo sed quicquid Petro debemus."

"For the Sovereign Pontiff, vicar of Our Lord Jesus Christ and Peter's successor, to whom we owe what is the due, not of Christ, but of Peter."

THOMAS AQUINAS
De regimine principum (I, 14)

". . . summo Sacerdoti successor Pontifici, cui omnes reges populi Petri, Christi vicario, Romano christiani oportet esse subditos, sicut ipsi Domino nostro Jesu Christo."

". . . the Sovereign Priest Peter's successor, the Vicar of Christ, the Roman Pontiff, to whom all the kings of the Christian people owe submission, as to Our Lord Jesus Christ Himself."

The whole problem is there, concentrated in those two sentences, the almost word-for-word opposition between which is so striking that one cannot help wondering whether, when he wrote his, Dante was not recalling St. Thomas's. Whatever the truth may be in this matter, the theses which these two formulas define flagrantly contradict each other. Undoubtedly both admit without question the supremacy of the temporal power of Christ; but St. Thomas teaches that Christ bequeathed His two-fold kingship, spiritual and temporal, to Peter and to all the successors of Peter, to whom all the kings of the Christian people should consequently be subject as to Jesus Christ Himself; in Dante's eyes, on the contrary, if Jesus Christ possessed, like God, a temporal sovereignty which, as it happens, He never used, that temporal authority returned to heaven with Him. The Popes have not inherited it. Between St. Thomas's Pope, *qui utriusque potestatis apicem tenet* ("who holds the supreme authority in either sphere"), and Dante's Pope, who is entirely without control of the temporal power, a choice must be made: they cannot be reconciled.[17]

Dante's doctrine touching the relations between the Priesthood and the Empire has been interpreted in almost every conceivable way. Some conceive it as teaching the total isolation of the two powers: each is competent in its own sphere and owes absolutely nothing to the other. Others maintain that, whatever he may seem to say, Dante recognizes the subordination of the Emperor to the Pope. Others maintain, on the contrary, that Dante subordinates the Pope to the Emperor. Finally, some, disturbed at all these contradictions, come to the conclusion that the historians would agree more wholeheartedly if *Dante* had not contradicted

[17] With regard to the problem of the temporal power of the Popes, and that we may confine ourselves strictly to introductions to the study of it, see the mainly doctrinal work of Charles Journet, *La juridiction de l'Eglise sur la Cité*, Paris, Desclée de Brouwer, 1931 (especially two most excellent pages, pp. 117–118), and the mainly historical work of M. Grabmann, *Studien über den Einfluss der aristotelischen Philosophie auf die mittelalterlichen Theorien über das Verhältnis von Kirche und Staat*, Munich, 1934. If I do not here undertake to interpret the Thomistic doctrine for its own sake, it is not that I disclaim interest in it; rather is it that, even if to St. Thomas it is only a question of an "indirect power", essentially spiritual, exercised by the Popes over temporal things, I think that Dante is at variance with him *on this point*. For the thesis here upheld to be affected by it, one of the following two propositions would have to be maintained: 1. that St. Thomas did not recognize any Papal authority, indirect or direct, in temporal things, whatever the pretext; 2. that Dante recognized some sort of temporal Papal authority direct or indirect, over the Emperor, whatever the pretext. No one, I think, would to-day uphold the first of these two theses; the second still has its champions, but we shall see that it is difficult to uphold it in the precise sense of a jurisdiction which, whatever its nature and its cause, implies some kind of limitation of the universal, exclusive and absolute temporal authority that belongs by divine right to the Emperor. If I have made a mistake, it concerns this last point, and if I have made it, the reason is that I do not see how one can agree with St. Thomas while denying the Pope a temporal authority that one concedes to Jesus Christ. St. Thomas's doctrine rests in fact on this principle—that Peter and his successors have inherited the whole power of Christ. See the passage in the *Contra errores Graecorum* (in *Opuscula*, ed. P. Mandonnet, Vol. III, p. 324) where St. Thomas bases this thesis on the authority of the Pseudo-Cyril, quoting his *Liber Thesaurorum*: "Cui [*sc.* Petro] omnes jure divino caput inclinant et primates mundi tanquam ipsi domino Jesu obediunt."

himself.[18] Before resigning ourselves to this despairing solution, we must ascertain the exact nature of the apparently discordant theses which it is sought to reconcile.

In fact, Dante has several times asserted that the Emperor is subject to the influence of the Pope and even that he needs to come under it because of the beneficial effects that it produces on him. The care which Dante exercises in stressing this point as clearly as possible whenever he seems to force the contrary viewpoint to its extreme limit is a very sure guarantee that the co-existence of these two apparently contradictory theses does not result from any negligence on his part. It is because he wishes to uphold them as being simultaneously valid that Dante simultaneously affirms them. For instance, when in the *Monarchy* he discusses the classic comparison of the two powers with the two great luminaries created by God on the fourth day (*Gen.*, I, 15–16), Dante does not deny that one may, in a certain sense, liken the Empire to the moon and the Papacy to the sun; he therefore does not deny either that, in a certain sense, the Empire benefits by the action exerted on it by the Papacy, as the moon profits by the illuminative action of the sun. On the contrary, Dante expressly affirms it: "The moon receives from the sun the means to function better and more strongly (*virtuosius*), to wit, an abundant light through which it functions with greater intensity after receiving it; so, too, the temporal government . . . receives from the spiritual the means to function more strongly, through the light of grace which God, in heaven, and, on earth, the blessing of the Sovereign Pontiff, infuse into it" (III, 4). This, moreover, is the sense in which we must interpret the famous final article of the *Monarchy,* which scholars have already discussed at such great length without reaching agreement: "The truth with regard to this last question should not be taken in the strict sense that the Roman Prince is not subject in any respect to the Roman Pontiff, since this mortal felicity is somehow designed as a means to immortal felicity. Let Caesar therefore show for Peter that reverence which a first-born shows for his father, in order that, illuminated by the light of paternal grace, he may shine forth more strongly (*virtuosius*) upon the terrestrial orb, of which he has been appointed ruler by Him alone Who orders all things, both spiritual and temporal" (III, 16, end).

This last sentence shows us at the same time the other aspect of Dante's thought. In the first place, God is absolutely without peer as

---

[18] Hans Kelsen, *Die Staatslehre des Dante Alighieri* (Wiener Staatswissenschaftliche Studien, VI Bd., 3 Heft), Vienna and Leipzig, F. Deuticke, 1905, Chap. VIII, pp. 97–98.

sovereign both of the spiritual and of the temporal worlds; we may therefore be sure that neither the Emperor nor the Pope may aspire to the exercise of this twofold authority. Furthermore, Dante is careful to make it clear, in this final sentence of his work, and at the very moment when he is recalling Caesar to a feeling of filial respect for Peter, that the Emperor derives his universal authority from God alone: *Orbem terrae . . . , cui ab Illo solo praefectus est, qui est omnium spiritualium et temporalium gubernator* ("The earth . . . , of which he has been put in command by *Him alone,* Who is the Lord of all things, both spiritual and temporal") (III, 16, end). If we go back from this to the first of the two sentences which have just been quoted, we shall see that together they form a perfect whole.

Indeed, even if we leave aside the skilful exegesis with which Dante disposes of the Biblical argument of the two "great luminaries" created by God on the fourth day, we should note that he argues at the end as if this allegorical reasoning were valid. Now, even if we admit that it is so, the thesis that Dante wishes to prove remains unaffected. In the first place, the moon does not owe its existence to the sun: *Quantum est ad esse, nullo modo luna dependet a sole.* ("As regards its existence, the moon is in no wise dependent on the sun"). It follows clearly from this that the Imperial power likewise does not owe its existence to the Pope, but to God alone, Who created these two powers unaided, as He created the moon unaided to be an accompaniment to the sun. Moreover, speaking generally, the moon is likewise independent of the sun so far as its own energy and functioning are concerned: it owes its movement to its own driving force (which is not the sun's), and the influence which it exerts proceeds from its own rays (not from the solar rays), for it possesses a certain luminosity of its own, as may be seen whenever it is in eclipse: *Habet enim aliquam lucem ex se* (III, 4). Dante's intention is therefore clear: he desires an Imperial authority which owes its existence directly to God, not to the Pope; which wields a power whose course is in itself, not in the authority of the Pope, and which, finally, is capable of moving and acting of itself, by itself, of its own volition, without borrowing from the Pontifical authority the mainspring of its resolutions. In short—and this is the decisive point—the influence exerted by the Pope over the Emperor is analogous to that of a blessing, i.e. of a form of grace: *Lucem gratiae, quam in coelo Deus et in terra benedictio summi Pontificis infundit illi* ("The light of grace, which in heaven God, and on earth the blessing of the Sovereign Pontiff, shed upon him") (III, 4).

There are, then, two errors to be avoided in interpreting Dante's doctrine. One might at first think that, if the Pope's influence over the

Emperor extends no further, it amounts to very little. This would be a grave error. Dante's Christianity was certainly somewhat personal; this son of the Church liked to reason with his mother about the conditions of his obedience, but he was not an indifferent Christian any more than our own Charles Péguy. Such men desire to know the exact nature of that to which they bow the knee, but, the decision once taken, their genuflexions are complete. For a Pope who is faithful to his office and who acts only as the spiritual father of mankind Dante's respect and love are boundless. The proof is that, unyielding though he is in these matters, he made a point of explicitly pardoning those among them whom "zeal of the keys", not greed, so unfortunately led astray. And not only them, but those of their fellow crusaders against the temporal power whom the same zeal had deluded: the "good friar Thomas" seems indeed to have profited by this indulgence in Dante's heart, and Dante must have loved him greatly to have forgiven him on this point. But this is not all. By reducing the problem of the two powers to a particular case of the general problem of nature and grace Dante was, incontestably, locating it in its true sphere. He knew, having derived the notion from St. Thomas, whose fundamental thesis it is, that the peculiar effect of grace is not to vindicate nature or to suppress it, but to perfect it. He knew also that in the eyes of that same St. Thomas the temporal order exists as a natural order created by God as such, endowed with special powers for the purpose of attaining its special goal, and that the Church is not there to destroy it by taking its place, but to give it new vigour and consolation, and to guide it to its ultimate supernatural goal through grace. In imagining that the work of grace thus conceived was in Dante's eyes a superfluous work we cannot be attributing to him his true conception of it. To walk in Dante's world as a pagan is to walk as a stranger. Conversely, to live in it as a Thomist is, if not to live as a stranger, at all events to propagate a misapprehension, for the special achievement of Dante's thought is to have eliminated the hierarchical gradations essential to Thomism and replaced them merely with a system of equal authorities. In St. Thomas, the actual distinction between the orders justifies and necessitates their gradation; in Dante, it excludes it. Here, then, we are faced not with a Christian world and a pagan world, but with two different dispositions of the Christian world and even with two dispositions which clash only by virtue of an identical principle: Grace presupposes nature; hence, without rendering itself purposeless, it cannot suppress nature.

In order to understand the structure of the Christian world as Dante understood it, we must return once more to his doctrine whereby the world is divided into three orders, unequal in dignity but mutually independent in their respective spheres—namely, the human order, the political order, the order of the Church. Dante and the hierocrats are agreed as to the absolute validity of the fundamental principle implicit in the philosophy of Aristotle, viz. that everything which falls within a given genus is reduced to a single term, the measure of everything which falls within that genus: *Omnia quae sunt unius generis reducuntur ad unum, quod est mensura omnium quae sub illo genere sunt.* The antagonism between Dante and the hierocrats arises from the fact that they do not agree as to the number and nature of the genera which should be thus reduced to uniformity.

Whenever Dante has to settle a conflict of authorities, his first care is to define the *genus* of the authorities in question. Indeed, in his eyes the independence and the autonomy of the genera constitute an invariable rule. Let us, for instance, suppose we are seeking that which possesses authority over man; we shall have to propound the question in terms of man *qua* man, *and in no other sense.* Man is what he is *qua* man by virtue of his substantial form, which places him in a genus (animal), in a species of that genus (reasonable), and makes him a substance. He who has authority in the genus "man" is therefore the unit of measure by which the worth of those substances which we call men is estimated. For all men fall within one and the same genus; they are therefore reduced to a single term which is their measure. What is this term? It is the perfect man, the Idea of man, if one may so put it; in other words, it is the pattern of the virtuous man as described in the final books of the *Ethica ad Nicomachum.* If, therefore, we wish to know who has authority to say how man should live *qua man,* it is fitting that we should turn to him who most perfectly realizes in himself human nature, the substance "man". The rule has no exceptions and applies to every man, including Popes and Emperors: *Nam, prout sunt homines, habent reduci ad optimum hominem, qui est mensura omnium aliorum et idea, ut dicam, quisquis ille sit, ad existentem maxime unum in genere suo: ut haberi potest ex ultimis Ethica ad Nicomachum* ("For, in so far as they are men, their standard must be the most excellent man (whoever he may be) who is the measure and ideal of all others, so to say—he who is in the highest degree one in his own kind, as may be inferred from the end of the *Ethica ad Nicomachum*") (III, 12).

It inevitably follows from this that if, *qua* men, the Pope and the Emperor ought to be reduced to uniformity, both are amenable to a principle and a measure other than the Papacy and the Empire. Both should in that case be judged by the norm of Aristotle's virtuous man, whose human perfection measures and judges their degree of human excellence. It is quite another matter in the case of the two distinct genera which they themselves represent. To be Emperor, or to be Pope, is not the same as to be a man. To be an Emperor, *as such,* is to be a master; to be a Pope, *as such,* is to be a spiritual father. Now, just as a man is a man by virtue of the substantial form which causes him to be such, he is a master, or he is a father, by virtue of the incidental forms which cause a specific human being to be also a master or a father. In other words, one is a man and is judged as such in the category of substance, but one is a master, or a father, and is judged as such, in the category of relationship. Thus, the Pope regarded as a Pope is such by virtue of the incidental form of Papacy, which confers on him the relationship, incidental to the human substance, of spiritual fatherhood. The Emperor, regarded as an Emperor, is such by virtue of the incidental form of the Imperial authority (*imperiatum*), which confers on him the relationship, incidental to the substance "man", of sovereign lordship of men's wills. If, therefore, one wishes to reduce the two genera to uniformity, it is useless to seek a measure common to them both, for it does not exist; one can hope to find a principle of uniformity and of measure only in each of these two orders of relationship taken separately: *Altera sub ambitu paternitatis et altera sub ambitu dominationis* ("The one in the sphere of fatherhood and the other in the sphere of authority") (III, 12). Hence three distinct orders, whose independence is in Dante such that one can never generalize from one to another: All men are governed and measured by the ideal man of Aristotle; all spiritual sons are governed and measured by the supreme father, who is the Pope; all subordinates are governed and measured by the supreme sovereign, who is the Emperor. The fatal error which it is important not to commit would be to wish to subordinate one of these principles to another, as if it were possible for them to fall within a single genus or a single species. Dante is categorical on this point, for his whole doctrine is bound up with it: *Non potest dici quod alterum subalternetur alteri* ("It cannot be said that the one is subordinate to the other") (III, 12). Thus, just as the Pope has no superior *qua* Pope, the Emperor has no superior *qua* Emperor, nor the wise man *qua* man.

None—let us be clear—in this world. For God is the measure and the supreme authority that governs, measures and judges all substances and all relationships. If we assemble these notions, we obtain the following scheme, which summarizes the disposition of the authorities in the Dantesque universe:

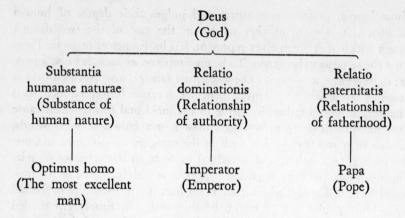

This is how the tripartite scheme of authorities which the *Banquet*
suggests is reconstituted and completed in the *Monarchy*.

FREDERICK THE GREAT
MORLEY
MUSSOLINI
CROCE

MACHIAVELLI

Modern political philosophy begins with Niccolò Machiavelli (1469–1527). Before him all political writing—from Plato and Aristotle through the Middle Ages—had one central question: the end of the state. Political power was assumed to be a means only, in the service of a higher end, such as justice, the good life, freedom, or God. Machiavelli ignores the issue of the end of the state in nonpolitical terms. He assumes that power is an end in itself, and he confines his inquiries to the means that are best suited to acquire, retain, and expand power. Machiavelli thus separates power from morality, ethics, religion, and metaphysics and sets up the state as an autonomous system of values independent of any other source. Under this concept of the "reason of state," acts are permissive, even obligatory, that would be considered heinous crimes if judged in the court of morality or religion. Statecraft is no longer, as in the previous Western tradition, the servant of higher ethical goals, but an independent master serving only his own interests. Machiavelli's influence has reached beyond the purely political field, and his *Prince* (1513) is destined to remain one of the half-dozen political writings that have entered the general body of world literature.

The Prince was meant to be a practical guide to statecraft rather than a general theory of politics, and many rulers from Machiavelli's days to our own have followed its precepts. One of the most faithful practitioners of Machiavellian principles in government and diplomacy was King

Frederick II (or the Great) of Prussia, who, more than any other Prussian monarch, transformed Prussia from a small state into a great power. In his youth, Frederick (1712–1786) was deeply attached to the ideas of the Enlightenment, and he maintained close personal relations with its most illustrious representatives, above all with Voltaire, whom he admired the most. His personal attachment to the Enlightenment went so far that he used exclusively the French language in his writings, because in his eyes German was a language fit only for horses. In his phase of youthful enthusiasm for the ideas of the age of reason, Frederick wrote the *Anti-Machiavel* (1740), one of the *curiosa* in the vast literature dealing with Machiavelli. By a twist of fate, Frederick ascended the Prussian throne in the same year 1740, and from that moment on he vigorously and consistently practiced the principles of Machiavellianism in expanding the power of Prussia. His opposition to torture and his espousal of religious toleration showed that the ideas of the Enlightenment had some lasting impact on him; also, unlike later German self-styled disciples of Machiavelli (like Emperor William II or Hitler), Frederick II rarely forgot that excessive Machiavellianism is self-defeating, as Machiavelli himself warned his followers.

English political thought has never taken kindly to Machiavelli's theory of statecraft, and a typical English view of Machiavelli will be found in John Morley's Romanes Lecture on "Machiavelli," delivered before the British Academy in 1897. Morley (1838–1923) was one of the leading figures of English letters and politics in the late nineteenth and early twentieth centuries. In 1883 he was elected a Member of the House of Commons, and he quickly became one of the foremost Liberals of his day. In 1886, Morley became Secretary of State for Ireland, and in 1905, Secretary of State for India, being sympathetic to both the Irish and Indian movements for self-government. In temperament and philosophical outlook, Morley resembled John Stuart Mill (1806–1873), whom he knew and admired. In addition to his practical experience in high political office over many decades, Morley was an outstanding literary figure throughout his career and the author of many biographies, such as *Rousseau* (1878), *Voltaire* (1878), *Diderot and the Encyclopaedists* (1878), *Burke* (1879), *Cobden* (1881), *Oliver Cromwell* (1900), and *Gladstone* (1903). In 1908, Morley was given a peerage in recognition of his political and literary services, and in the House of Lords his personal integrity and rich political experience increasingly made him the dean of English letters and politics.

One of the main reasons why self-confessed followers of Machiavelli among rulers of states have failed is to be found in their fanaticism.

Machiavelli counsels the ruler to be prudent, temperate, and not uselessly cruel and arrogant, "for to incur hatred without any advantage is the greatest temerity and imprudence." This Machiavellian precept of prudence and moderation was not, and perhaps could not be, observed by a modern fanatic, Benito Mussolini (1883–1945), fascist dictator of Italy from 1922 to 1943, who died in 1945 by assassination—the very method he had used on his opponents. Mussolini's article on Machiavelli was published in 1924 in *Gerarchia* (Hierarchy), the official intellectual organ of Italian fascism at the time. Mussolini thought that the practice of Machiavellianism would not only increase his own personal power as a dictator, but that it would also transform Italy from a respectable middle-grade power into a feared great power. Yet after more than twenty years of fascist dictatorship, Italy was in ruins, defeated and humiliated in war, and Mussolini himself assassinated.

The strength of Machiavelli's impact on Italian thinking can be seen in the fact that the more liberal element in Italian life has also been fascinated by its appeal. One of the leading Italian philosophers of the twentieth century, Benedetto Croce (1866–1952), maintained a liberal position throughout his life, and even under the difficult circumstances of the fascist censorship and thought control he made very few compromises. Yet Croce felt much sympathy toward Machiavelli as the founder of a realistic science of politics. Croce was one of the most prolific writers of his age in the fields of philosophy, literary criticism, aesthetics, history, ethics, and political studies. His political thought can be found in such (translated) works as *Historical Materialism and the Economics of Karl Marx* (1922), *History as the Story of Liberty* (1941), *Politics and Morals* (1945), and *My Philosophy and Other Essays on the Moral and Political Problems of Our Time* (1949).

Frederick the Great on MACHIAVELLI

Machiavelli's *Prince* is in point of morality, what Spinoza's work is with regard to faith: Spinoza sapped the foundations of faith, and aimed at nothing less than overturning the whole fabric of religion; Machiavelli corrupted politics, and undertook to destroy the precepts of sound morality. The errors of the one were but errors in speculation; those of the other regarded practice. We find, nevertheless, that divines have called out

[From Frederick the Great, *Anti-Machiavel* (1740).]

to arms and sounded the charge against Spinoza; that his work has been formally refuted, and his attacks opposed upon principles of divinity, while Machiavelli has only been annoyed by a few moralists, and has been able, in spite of them, and of his pernicious doctrines, to maintain his political system down to our days.

I venture to undertake the defense of humanity against this monster, who would destroy it, to oppose reason and justice to criminal sophistry. I have always looked upon Machiavelli's *Prince* as one of the most dangerous works that ever appeared in the world. It is a book that must naturally come into the hands of princes, and of those who have a taste for politics. A young, ambitious man, whose heart and judgment are not yet sufficiently formed to distinguish exactly between right and wrong, is but too liable to be corrupted by maxims which so greatly flatter his passions.

But if it is criminal to debauch the sentiments of a private person, who has but a small influence upon the affairs of the world, it is infinitely more so to corrupt the morals of princes, whose business it is to govern nations, to administer justice, and to set examples of justice to their subjects, and who by their magnanimity, mercy, and goodness ought to be the living images of the deity.

Inundations which ravage countries, thunder and lightning that reduce cities to ashes, the pestilence which lays whole provinces waste, are less fatal to the world than the vicious morals and unbridled passions of princes. The plagues of heaven continue but for a time; they only ravage some countries; and these losses, however grievous, are nevertheless repaired; whereas the crimes of kings entail a lasting misery upon whole nations. As kings have the power to do good or evil according to their choice and inclination, how deplorable is the condition of the people who have everything to fear from the abuse of majesty, whose properties are a prey to the avarice of their prince, their liberty to his caprice, their repose to his ambition, their safety to his perfidiousness, and their lives to his cruelty? Such would be the tragic situation of a country governed by a prince of Machiavelli's forming.

I must say a few words to those who believe that Machiavelli rather describes what princes do, than what they ought to do: a notion which has pleased many, purely because it is satirical. Those who pass this peremptory judgment upon sovereigns, are no doubt misled by the examples of some wicked princes, the contemporaries of Machiavelli who cites them, and by the lives of some tyrants who have indeed been the disgrace of human nature. I beseech these censorious persons to consider that, as the temptations to which a king is liable are very powerful, it requires a more than ordinary degree of virtue to resist them; and that, therefore, it is not surprising if, in so great a number of princes, there should be a mixture of bad ones among the good. In the list of Roman emperors, where a Nero, a Caligula, and a Tiberius appear, the world still reflects with pleasure on the sacred names of a Titus, a Trajan, and an Antoninus.

It is therefore a cruel injustice to impute to a whole body of men what is only applicable to some of them. As in history the names of good princes ought to be preserved, so those of all others should be allowed to sink in oblivion, with their indolence, acts of injustice, and other crimes. This indeed would lessen the number of historical books, but mankind would gain by it. The honor of living in history, and of seeing one's name transmitted to all future ages, would then only be the reward of virtue. Machiavelli's book would no longer infect the schools of politics. His continual contradictions would be treated with contempt, and the world would be persuaded that the true policy of kings, which is solely grounded on justice, prudence, and goodness, is in all respects preferable to that inconsistent and horrible system which Machiavelli has been bold enough to offer to the public.

How Far Princes Ought to Fulfil Their Engagements

Machiavelli, the preceptor of tyrants, has the boldness to affirm that princes may impose on the world by dissimulation. This is the first position that I shall endeavor to refute. The extreme curiosity of the public is well known; it is a being that sees everything, hears everything, and divulges whatever it has seen or heard. If its curiosity examines the conduct of particular men, it is only to fill up idle hours; but if it considers the characters of princes, it is with an eye to its own interest. And indeed princes are more exposed than all other men to the conjectures, comments, and judgment of the world; they are a sort of stars, at which a whole people of astronomers are continually levelling their telescopes. Courtiers who are near them are daily making their observations; a single gesture, a single glance of the eye, discovers them; and the people who observe them at a greater distance magnify them by conjectures. In short, as well may the sun hide its spots, as great princes their vices and their genuine character from the eyes of so many curious observers.

If the mask of dissimulation should cover, for a time, the natural deformity of a prince, yet he could never keep his mask always on; he would sometimes be obliged, were it only for a breathing, to throw it off; and one view of the naked features would be sufficient to content the curious. It will therefore be in vain for dissimulation to dwell in the

mouths of princes. Craftiness in their discourses and actions will have
no effect: to judge of men by their words and professions would be the
way to be always mistaken. We therefore compare their actions with
one another, and then with their words; and against this repeated examination, falsity and deceit will find no refuge. No man can well act any
part but his own; he must really have the same character which he would
bear in the world. Without this the man who thinks to impose upon the
public imposes upon none but himself.

Sixtus Quintus and Philip II passed for hypocrites and enterprising
men, but not for being virtuous. Let a prince be as artful as he would,
he will never be able, even by following all of Machiavelli's maxims, to
gain the character of virtue which he has not, and avoid the scandal of
crimes which belong to him. Machiavelli argues no better in the reasons
he assigns for employing trick and hypocrisy. The ingenious but fallacious
application of the fable of the Centaur proves nothing. For if that animal
were half man, half horse, does it follow that princes ought to be crafty
and false? A man must have a strong inclination to inculcate crime who
employs arguments so weak and far-fetched as that of the Centaur.

But here follows a reasoning as false as any we have yet met with.
Our politician affirms that a prince ought to have the qualities both of
the lion and the fox; of the lion, to destroy the wolves; and of the fox,
to avoid snares. From which he infers that a wise prince neither can nor
should fulfil his engagements: here is a conclusion without premises.
Would not any other man blush to throw out such impious sophistry?

If Machiavelli's confused notions could be strained into good sense
and sound morality, they might be represented thus: the world resembles
a match at gaming, where sharpers and fair players are promiscuously
engaged. A prince therefore who is in the game, and would not be cheated
himself, should be well acquainted with all the ways of cheating others;
not in order to put any of these lessons in practice, but only that he may
hinder them from being practiced upon him by gamesters.

But to return to Machiavelli's sophistry. Because all men, says he, are
wicked and at all times break their faith and promise to you, there is no
obligation upon you to keep yours with them. Now here is a manifest
contradiction; for he says a few lines later that dissemblers will always
find people simple enough to be imposed upon. How can this be reconciled with the other? All men are wicked, and yet you find men simple
enough to be imposed upon! But it is not true that all men are wicked;
one must have a strange misanthropic turn not to perceive that in every
society there are a great many honest men, and that the major part are
neither good nor bad. But without supposing all the world to be wicked,

how could Machiavelli have supported his detestable maxims? Nay, granting that men are as wicked as he represents them, would it follow that we ought to imitate their example? If any man robs or commits murder, I conclude that he deserves to be hanged, not that I must act accordingly. If honor and virtue were to be banished from the world, said Charles the Wise, they ought to find an asylum with princes.

After endeavoring to prove the necessity of vice, our author would encourage his disciples by showing them the facility of succeeding in it. Those who are skilled in the art of dissimulation, he affirms, will never be at a loss to find men simple enough to be duped by them. His meaning is, your neighbor is a blockhead, and you are a man of sense; wherefore you must cheat him. These are syllogisms for which some of Machiavelli's disciples have been hanged and broken on the wheel.

Not content with attempting to show the necessity and facility of being vicious, our author endeavors to point out the felicities that attend vice. But it unfortunately happens that his hero, Caesar Borgia, the greatest and most perfidious of all villains, was in effect extremely miserable. Machiavelli takes great care not to touch upon this part of his life, and is forced to have recourse to the history of wicked popes and emperors. He maintains that Pope Alexander VI, the most false and impious man of his time, was always successful in deceit, because he perfectly knew the weakness of mankind with regard to credulity. Now I will venture to affirm that the success of Pope Alexander was due not so much to the credulity of man as to certain events and circumstances of that time, and especially to the rivalry between France and Spain, to the divisions and animosities that prevailed among the chief families of Italy, and to the passions and weakness of Louis XII.

Don Louis de Haro, an able politician, looked upon deceit as an error in politics. He used to say of Cardinal Mazarin that his Eminence had one great fault in his political character, which was that he was always cheated. When the same Mazarin wanted to employ the Marshal de Faber in making a slippery treaty, Faber said, "Permit me, my Lord, to refuse cheating the Duke of Savoy, especially in a trifling affair. The world knows that I am an honest man; be pleased therefore to preserve my integrity for some other occasion, when it may do good to my country."

To say nothing either of honor or virtue, but only to consider the interest of princes: I say it is bad policy for them to impose upon and dupe the world, for they are never sure of succeeding but once, and by one act of deceit they lose the confidence of all their neighbors.

A certain Power very lately published a manifesto setting forth the reasons of her conduct, and presently afterward acted in a manner quite opposite to all her pretenses. It must be owned that such glaring deceitfulness must make one forfeit the confidence of others, for the sooner the contradiction follows the protestation, it is the more palpable. The Church of Rome, to avoid the like inconsistency, has very wisely prescribed a novitiate of a hundred years to those whom it places in the number of saints, in which time the memory of their faults and extravagances is entirely lost. Those who knew them personally when living, and could swear against them, are dead and gone; and nothing obstructs the notion of saintship which the Church would impose upon the public.

The reader, I hope, will pardon the digression. To return to Machiavelli: I own there are some unhappy cases, when a prince cannot help breaking his treaties and alliances. But he ought to do this with as much honor as he can, by giving timely notice of it to his allies, and showing that he is forced to it by the greatest necessity, and for the preservation of his people, which are the only cases wherein it is allowable.

I shall conclude by making one more remark. Observe how fertilely one vice propagates another in the hands of Machiavelli. It is not enough for his prince to be cruel, perfidious, and irreligious; he must crown all his vices with that of hypocrisy. Machiavelli thinks the people will be more won over by his devotion than offended by his oppressions. There are others of the same opinion. For my own part, the world, methinks, is very indulgent as to errors in speculation, when they are such as do not necessarily corrupt and vitiate the heart. A people will always be better affected to an unbelieving prince, if he is an honest man, than to one who is orthodox, but a villain or tyrant. It is not upon a prince's opinions, but upon his actions only that the happiness of his people depends.

Morley on MACHIAVELLI

Like most of those who take a pride in seeing human nature as it is, Machiavelli only saw half of it. We must remember the atmosphere of craft, suspicion, fraud, violence, in which he had moved, with Borgias, Medici, Pope Julius, Maximilian, Louis xii., and the reckless factions of Florence. His estimate was low. Mankind, he says, are more prone to evil than to good. We may say this of them generally, that they are ungrate-

[From John Morley, "Machiavelli" (Romanes Lecture, 1897, Macmillan, 1897).]

ful, fickle, deceivers, greedy of gain, runaways before peril. While you
serve them, they are all yours—lives, goods, children—so long as no danger is at hand: when the hour of need draws nigh, they turn their backs.
They are readier to seek revenge for wrong, than to prove gratitude for
service: as Tacitus says of people who lived in Italy long ages before,
readier to pay back injury than kindness. Men never do anything good,
unless they are driven; and where they have their choice, and can use
what licence they will, all is filled with disorder and confusion. They are
taken in by appearances. They follow the event. They easily become corrupted. Their will is weak. They know not how to be either thoroughly
good or thoroughly bad; they vacillate between; they take middle paths,
the worst of all. Men are a little breed.[1]

All this is not satire, it is not misanthropy; it is the student of the
art of government, thinking over the material with which he has to deal.
These judgments of Machiavelli have none of the wrath of Juvenal, none
of the impious truculence of Swift. They cut deeper into simple reality
than polished oracles from the moralists of the boudoir. They have not
the bitterness that hides in the laugh of Molière, nor the chagrin and disdain with which Pascal broods over unhappy man and his dark lot. Least
of all are they the voice of the preacher calling sinners to repentance. The
tale is only a rather grim record, from inspection, of the foundations on
which the rulers of states must do their best to build.

Goethe's maxim that, if you would improve a man, it is no bad thing
to let him suppose that you already think him that which you would have
him to be, would have seemed to Machiavelli as foolish for his purpose
as if you were to furnish an architect with clay, and bid him to treat it as
if it were iron. He will suffer no abstraction to interrupt positive observation. Man is what he is, and so he needs to be bitted and bridled with
laws, and now and again to be treated to a stiff dose of *'medicine forti,'*
in the shape of fire, bullet, axe, halter, and dungeon. At any rate, Machiavelli does not leave human nature out, and this is one secret of his hold.
It is not with pale opinion that he argues, it is passions and interests in
all the flush of action. It is, in truth, in every case,—Burke, Rousseau,
Tocqueville, Hobbes, Bentham, Mill, and the rest—always the moralist
who interests men most within the publicist. Machiavelli was assuredly
a moralist, though of a peculiar sort, and this is what makes him, as he
has been well called, a contemporary of every age and a citizen of all
countries.

To the question whether the world grows better or worse, Machiavelli
gave an answer that startles an age like ours, subsisting on its faith in

[1] 'However we brave it out, we men are a little breed.'—Tennyson's *Maud*, i, 5.

progress. The world, he says, neither grows better nor worse; it is always the same. Human fortunes are never still; they are every moment either going up or sinking down. Yet among all nations and states, the same desires, the same humours prevail; they are what they always were. Men are for travelling on the beaten track. Diligently study bygone things, and in every State you will be able to discover the things to come. All the things that have been, may be again. Just as the modern physicist tells us that neither physical nor chemical transformation changes the mass nor the weight of any quantity of matter, so Machiavelli judged the good and evil in the world to be ever identical.

'This bad and this good shift from land to land,' he says, 'as we may see from ancient empires; they rose and fell with the changes of their usage, but the world remained as it was. The only difference was that it concentrated its power (*virtù*) in Assyria, then in Media, then in Persia, until at last it came to Italy and Rome.'

In our age, when we think of the chequered course of human time, of the shocks of irreconcilable civilisation, of war, trade, faction, revolution, empire, laws, creeds, sects, we look for a clue to the vast maze of historic and pre-historic fact. Machiavelli seeks no clue to his distribution of good and evil. He seeks no moral interpretation for the mysterious scroll. We obey laws that we do not know, but cannot resist. We can only make an effort to seize events as they whirl by; to extort from them a maxim, a precept, or a principle, that may serve our immediate turn. Fortune, he says,—that is, Providence, or else Circumstance, or the Stars, —is mistress of more than half we do. What is her deep secret, he shows no curiosity to fathom. He contents himself with a maxim for the practical man (*Prince,* xxv.),—that it is better to be adventurous than cautious, for Fortune is a woman, and to master her, she must be boldly handled.

Whatever force or law may control this shifting distribution of imperial destinies, nothing, said Machiavelli, could prevent any native of Italy or of Greece, unless the Greek had turned Turk, or the Italian Transalpine, from blaming his own time and praising the glories of time past. 'What,' he cries, 'can redeem an age from the extremity of misery, shame, reproach, where there is no regard to religion, to laws, to arms, where all is tainted and tarnished with every foulness. And these vices are all the more hateful, as they most abound in those who sit in the judgment-seat, are men's masters, and seek men's reverence, I, at all events,' he concludes, with a glow that almost recalls the moving close of the *Agricola,* 'shall make bold to say how I regard old times and new, so that the minds of the young who shall read these writings of mine, may shun the new examples and follow old. For it is the duty of a good man, at least to strive that he may teach to others those sound lessons which the spite of time or fortune hath hindered him from executing, so that many having learned them, some better loved by heaven may one day have power to apply them.'

What were the lessons? They were in fact only one, that the central secret of the ruin and distraction of Italy was weakness of will, want of fortitude, force, and resolution. The abstract question of the best form of government—perhaps the most barren of all the topics that have ever occupied speculative minds—was with Machiavelli strictly secondary. He saw small despotic states harried by their petty tyrants, he saw republics worn out by faction and hate. Machiavelli himself had faith in free republics as the highest type of government; but whether you have republic or tyranny matters less, he seems to say, than that the governing power should be strong in the force of its own arms, intelligent, concentrated, resolute. We might say of him that he is for half his time engaged in examining the fitness of means to other people's ends, himself neutral. But then, as nature used to be held to abhor a vacuum, so the impatience of man is loth to tolerate neutrality. He has been charged with inconsistency, because in the *Prince* he lays down the conditions on which an absolute ruler, rising to power by force of genius backed by circumstance, may maintain that power with safety to himself and most advantage to his subjects; while in the *Discourses* he examines the rules that enable a self-governing State to retain its freedom. The cardinal precepts are the same. In either case, the saving principle is one: self-sufficiency, military strength, force, flexibility, address,—above all, no half-measures. In either case, the preservation of the State is equally the one end, reason of State equally the one adequate test and justification of the means. The *Prince* deals with one problem, the *Discourses* with the other, but the spring of Machiavelli's political inspirations is the same, to whatever type of rule they are applied—the secular State supreme; self-interest and self-regard avowed as the single principles of State action; material force the master key to civil policy. Clear intelligence backed by unsparing will, unflinching energy, remorseless vigour, the brain to plan and the hand to strike—here is the salvation of States, whether monarchies or republics. The spirit of humility and resignation that Christianity had brought into the world, he contemns and repudiates. That whole scheme of the Middle Ages in which invisible powers rule all our mortal affairs, he dismisses. Calculation, courage, fit means for resolute ends, human force,—only these can rebuild a world in ruins.

Some will deem it inconsistent, that with so few illusions about the weaknesses of human nature, yet he should have been so firm, in what

figures in current democracy as trust in the people. Like Aristotle, he held
the many to be in the long-run the best judges; but, unlike Goethe, who
said that the public is always in a state of self-delusion about details
though scarcely ever about broad truths, Machiavelli declared that the
public may go wrong about generalities, while as to particulars they are
usually right. The people are less ungrateful than a prince, and where
they are ungrateful, it is from less dishonourable motive. The multitude
is wiser and more constant than a prince. Furious and uncontrolled
multitudes go wrong, but then so do furious and uncontrolled princes.
Both err, when not held back by fear of consequences. The people are
fickle and thankless, but so are princes. 'As for prudence and stability, I
say that a people is more prudent, more stable, and of better judgment
than a prince.' Never let a prince, he said—and perhaps we might say,
never let a parliament—complain of the faults of a people under his rule,
for they are due either to his own negligence, or else to his own example,
and if you consider a people given to robbery and outrages against law,
you will generally find that they only copy their masters. Above all and
in any case the ruler, whether hereditary or an usurper, can have no
safety unless he founds himself on popular favour and goodwill. This
he repeats a hundred times. 'Better far than any number of fortresses, is
not to be hated by your people.'

It is then to the free Roman commonwealth that Machiavelli would
turn his countrymen. In that strong respect for law, that devotion to
country, that unquailing courage, that energy of purpose, which has been
truly called the essence of free Rome, he found the pattern that he wanted.
Modern Germans, for good reasons of their own, have taken to praise
him, but Machiavelli has nothing to do with that most brilliant of German scholars, who idolises Julius Caesar, then despatches Cato as a
pedant and Cicero as a coxcomb. You will hardly find in Machiavelli a
good word for any destroyer of a free government. Let nobody, he says,
be cheated by the glory of Caesar. Historians have been spoiled by his
success, and by the duration of the empire that continued his name. If
you will only follow the history of the empire, then you will soon know,
with a vengeance, what is the debt of Rome, Italy, and the world, to
Caesar.

Nobody has stated the argument against the revolutionary dictator
more clearly or tersely than Machiavelli. He applauded the old Romans
because their policy provided by a regular ordinance for an emergency, by
the institution of a constitutional dictator for a fixed term, and to meet a
definite occasion. 'In a republic nothing should be left to extraordinary
modes of government; because though such a mode may do good for the

moment, still the example does harm, seeing that a practice of breaking the laws for good ends lends a colour to breaches of law for ends that are bad.' Occasions no doubt arise when no ordinary means will produce reform, and then you must have recourse to violence and arms: a man must make himself supreme. But then, unfortunately, if he make himself supreme by violence, he is probably a bad man, for by such means a good man will not consent to climb to power. No more will a bad man who has become supreme in this way be likely to use his ill-gotten power for good ends. Here is the eternal dilemma of a State in convulsion. (*Disc.* i. 34, 18, 10; ii. 2.)

He forbids us in any case to call it virtue to slay fellow-citizens, to betray friends, to be without faith, without mercy, without religion; such practices may win empire, but not fair fame. A prince who clears out a population—here we may think of James i. and Cromwell in Ireland, and the authors of many a sweeping clearance since—and transplants them from province to province, as a herdsman moves his flock, does what is most cruel, most alien, not only to Christianity, but to common humanity. Far better for a man to choose a private life, than be a king on the terms of making havoc such as this with the lives of other men (*Disc.* i. 26).

It may be true, as Danton said, that 'twere better to be a poor fisherman than to meddle with the government of men. Yet nations and men find themselves inexorably confronted by the practical question. Government they must find. Given a corrupt, a divided, a distracted community, how are you to restore it? The last chapter of the *Prince* is an eloquent appeal to the representative of the House of Medici to heal the bruises and bind up the wounds of his torn and enslaved country. The view has been taken that this last chapter has nothing to do with the fundamental ideas of the book; that its glow is incompatible with the iron harshness of all that has gone before; that it was an afterthought, dictated partly by Machiavelli's personal hopes, and then picked up later by his defenders as whitewashing guilty maxims by ascribing them to large and lofty purpose. The balance of argument seems on the whole to lean this way, and Machiavelli for five-and-twenty chapters was thinking of new princes generally, and not of a great Italian deliverer. Yet he was not a man cast in a single mould. It may be that on reviewing his chapters, his heart became suddenly alive to their frigidity, and that the closing words flowed from the deeps of what was undoubtedly sincere and urgent feeling.

However this may be, whether the whole case of Italy, or the special case of any new prince, was in his contemplation, the quality of the man required is drawn in four chapters (xv.-xviii.) with piercing eye and a hand that does not flinch. The ruler's business is to save the State. He cannot practise all virtues, first because he is not very likely to possess them, and next because, where so many people are bad, he would not be a match for the world if he were perfectly good. Still he should be on his guard against all vices, so far as possible; he should scrupulously abstain from every vice that might endanger his government. There are two ways of carrying on the fight—one by laws, the other by force. The first is the proper and peculiar distinction of man; the second is the mark of the brute. As the first is not always enough, you must sometimes resort to the second. You must be both lion and fox, and the man who is only lion cannot be wise. A wise prince neither can, nor ought to, keep his word, when to keep his word would injure either himself or the State, or when the reasons that made him give a promise have passed away. If men were all good, a maxim like this would be bad; but as men are inclined to evil, and would not all keep faith with you, why should you keep faith with them? *Nostra cattività, la lor*—our badness, their badness (*Mandrag.* ii. 6). There are some good qualities that the new ruler need not have; yet he should seem to have them. It is well to appear merciful, faithful, religious, and it is well to be so. Religion is the most necessary of all for a prince to seek credit for. But the new prince should know how to change to the contrary of all these things, when they are in the way of the public good. For it is frequently necessary for the upholding of the State—and here is the sentence that has done so much to damn its writer—to go to work against faith, against charity, against humanity, against religion. It is not possible for a new prince to observe all the rules for which men are reckoned good.

The property of his subjects he will most carefully leave alone; a man will sooner forgive the slaying of his father than the confiscation of his patrimony. He should try to have a character for mercy, but this should never be allowed to prevent severity on just occasion. He must bear in mind the good saying reported in Livy, that many people know better how to keep themselves from doing wrong, than how to correct the wrong-doing of others. Never ought he to let excess of trust make him careless, nor excess of distrust to make him intolerable. He would be lucky if he could make himself both loved and feared; but if circumstance should force a choice, then of the two he had better be feared. To be feared is not the same as to be hated, and the two things to be most diligently avoided of all are hatred on the one hand, and contempt on the other.

Test there is none, save reason of State. We should never condemn a man for extraordinary acts to which he has been compelled to resort in establishing his empire or founding a republic. In a case where the safety of a country is concerned, whether it be princedom or republic, no regard is to be paid to justice or injustice, to pity or severity, to glory or shame; every other consideration firmly thrust aside, that course alone is to be followed which may preserve to the country its existence and its freedom. Diderot pithily put the superficial impression of all this, when he said that you might head these chapters as 'The circumstances under which it is right for a Prince to be a Scoundrel.' A profounder commentary of a concrete kind is furnished by Mommsen's account of Sulla [2]—an extraordinary literary masterpiece, even in the view of those who think its politics most perverse. Such a Sulla was the real type of Machiavelli's reformer of a rotten State.

It has been a commonplace of reproachful criticism that Machiavelli should have chosen for his hero Caesar Borgia. Not only was Borgia a monster, it is said, but he failed. For little more than four years the baleful meteor flamed across the sky, then vanished. If only success should command admiration, Borgia and his swiftly shattered fortunes might well be indifferent to Machiavelli and the world for which he was writing. What Machiavelli says is this—'I put him forward, as a model for such as climb to power by good fortune and the help of others. He did everything that a long-headed and capable man could do, who desires to strike root. I will show you how broad were the foundations that he laid for the fabric of his future power. I do not know what better lessons I could teach a new prince (*i.e.* an usurper) than his example. True, what he did failed in the end; that was due to the extreme malignity of fortune.' He makes no hero of him, except as a type of character well fitted for a given task.

Machiavelli knew him at close quarters. He was sent on a mission to Borgia in the crisis of his fortunes, and he thought that he discerned in Caesar those very qualities of action, force, combat, calculation, resolution, that the weakness of the age required. Machiavelli was in his train when terrible things were done. Caesar was close, solitary, secret, quick. When any business is on foot, said Machiavelli, he knows nothing of rest or weariness or risk. He no sooner reached a place, than you heard that he had left it. He was loved by his troopers, for though he meted stern punishment for an offence against discipline, he was liberal in pay and put little restraint on freedom. Though no talker, yet when he had to make a case he was so pressing and fluent, that it was hard to find an answer. He was a great judge of occasion. Bold, crafty, resolute, deep, and above

[2] *Hist. of Rome,* iv. x. vol. iii. 380–91 (Eng. Trans.).

all well known never to forget or forgive an injury, he fascinated men
with the terror of the basilisk. His firm maxim was to seek order by
giving his new subjects a good and firm government, including a civil
tribunal with a just president. Remiro was his first governor in the
Romagna. It is uncertain how Remiro incurred his master's displeasure,
but one morning Machiavelli walked out into the market-place at Cesena,
and saw Remiro, as he puts it, in two pieces, his head on a lance, and his
body still covered with his fine clothes, resting on a block with a blood-
stained axe by the side of it. His captains, beginning to penetrate Caesar's
designs, and fearing that he would seize their petty dominions one by one
—like the leaves of an artichoke, as he said—revolted. Undaunted, he
gathered new forces. Fresh bands of mercenaries flocked to the banners
of a chief who had money, skill, and a happy star. The conspirators were
no match for him in swiftness, activity, or resource; they allowed him to
sow the seeds of disunion; he duped them into making a convention
with him, which they had little thought of keeping. Everybody who knew
his revengeful and implacable spirit was sure that the conspirators were
doomed. When Machiavelli came near one of them he felt, he says, the
deadly odour of a corpse. With many arts, the duke got them to meet him
at Sinigaglia. He received their greetings cordially, pressed their hands,
and gave them the accolade. They all rode into the town together, talking of military things. Caesar courteously invited them to enter the palace,
then he quitted them and they were forthwith seized. 'I doubt if they
will be alive tomorrow morning,' the Florentine secretary wrote without
emotion to his government. They went through some form of trial,
before daybreak two of them were strangled, and two others shared the
same fate as soon as Caesar was sure that the Pope had carried out his
plans for making away by poison with the Cardinal who headed the rebellious faction at Rome.

Let us pause for a moment. One of the victims of Sinigaglia was
Oliverotto da Fermo. His story is told in the eighth chapter of the *Prince*.
He had been brought up from childhood by an uncle; he went out into
the world to learn military service; in course of time, one day he wrote to
his uncle at Fermo that he should like once more to see him and his
paternal city, and, by way of showing his good compatriots that he had
won some honour in his life, he proposed to bring a hundred horsemen
in his company. He came, and was honourably received. He invited his
uncle and the chief men of Fermo to a feast, and when the feast was over,
his soldiers sprang upon the guests and slew them all, and Oliverotto
became the tyrant of the place. We may at any rate forgive Caesar for
making sure work of Oliverotto a year later. When his last hour came,

he struggled to drive his dagger into the man with the cord. Here indeed were lions, foxes, catamounts.

This is obviously the key to Machiavelli's admiration for Borgia's policy. The men were all bandits together. Romagna is not and never was, said Dante two hundred years before, without war in the hearts of her tyrants (*Inf.* xxvii. 37). So it was now. It was full, says Machiavelli, of those who are called gentlemen, who live in idleness and abundance on the revenues of their estates, without any care of cultivating them, or of incurring any of the fatigue of getting a living; such men are pernicious anywhere, most of all when they are lords of castles, and have subjects under obedience to them. These lords, before the Pope and his terrible son took them in hand, were poor, yet had a mind to live as if they were rich, and so there was nothing for it but rapine, extortion, and all iniquity. Whether Caesar and the Pope had wider designs than the reduction of these oppressors to order, we can never know. Machiavelli and most contemporaries thought that they had, but the various historians of to-day differ. Probably the contemporaries knew best, but nothing can matter less.

We may as well finish Caesar's story, because we never know until a man's end, whether the play has been tragedy or comedy. He seemed to be lord of the ascendant, when in the summer after the transaction of Sinigaglia (1503) the Pope and he were one evening both stricken with malarious fever at Rome. There was talk of poison, but the better opinion seems to be that this is fable. Alexander vi. died; Caesar in the prime of his young man's strength, made a better fight for it, but when he at last recovered, his star had set. Machiavelli saw him and felt that Fortune this time had got the better of *virtù*. His subjects in the Romagna stood by him for a time, and then tyranny and disorder came back. The new Pope, Julius ii., was not his friend; for though Caesar had made the Spanish cardinals support his election, Julius had some old scores to pay, and as Machiavelli profoundly remarked, anybody who supposes that new services bring great people to forget old injuries, makes a dire mistake. So Caesar found his way to Naples, with a safe-conduct from Gonsalvo, the Great Captain. He reaped as he had sown. Once he had said, 'It is well to cheat those who have been masters in treachery.' He now felt the force of his maxim. At Naples he was cordially received by Gonsalvo, dined often at his table, talked over all his plans, and suddenly one night as he was about to pass the postern, in spite of the safe-conduct an officer demanded his sword in the name of the King of Aragon. To Spain he was sent. For some three years he went through strange and obscure adventures, fighting fortune with the aid of his indwelling demon to the very last. He was struck down in a fight at Viana in Navarre (1507), after a furious resistance; was stripped of his fine armour by men who did not know who he was; and his body was left naked, bloody, and riddled with wounds, on the ground. He was only thirty-one. His father, who was quite as desperate an evil-doer, died in his bed at seventy-two. So history cannot safely draw a moral.

From this digression let us return to mark some of the problems that Machiavelli raises, noting as we pass, how besides their profound effect upon active principles of statesmanship and progress, they lie at the very root of historic judgment on conspicuous men and memorable movements in bygone times. In one sense we are shocked by his maxims in proportion to our forgetfulness of history. There have been, it is said, only two perfect princes in the world—Marcus Aurelius and Louis IX. of France. If you add to princes, even presidents and prime ministers, the percentage might still be low. Among the canonised saints of the Roman Church there have only been a dozen kings in eight centuries, and no more than four popes in the same period. So hard has it been 'to govern the world by paternosters.' It is well to take care lest in blaming Machiavelli for openly prescribing hypocrisy, men do not slip unperceived into something like hypocrisy of their own.

Take the subordination of religious creed to policy. In the age that immediately followed Machiavelli, three commanding figures stand out, and are cherished in the memories of men—William the Silent, Henry of Navarre, and Elizabeth of England. It needs no peevish or pharisaic memory to trace even in these imposing personalities some of the lineaments of Machiavelli's hated and scandalous picture. William the Silent changed from Lutheran to Catholic, then back to Lutheran, and then again from Lutheran to Calvinist. His numerous children were sometimes baptized in one of the three communions, sometimes in another, just as political convenience served. Henry of Navarre abjured his Huguenot faith, then he returned to it, then he abjured it again. Our great Elizabeth, of famous memory, notoriously walked in tortuous and slippery paths. Again, the most dolorous chapter in all history is that which recounts how men and women were burned, hanged, shot, and cruelly tormented, for heresy; and there is a considerable body of authors, who through the sixteenth and seventeenth centuries used against heretics Machiavelli's arguments for making short work with rebels, and asked with logical force why their reason of Church was not just as good as his reason of State. What is the real difference between the practices

tolerated in the *Prince* for the self-preservation of a secular State, and all
the abominations perpetrated in the name and for the sake of religious
unity? Again, how many of the wars of faith, from Monophysite, Arian,
Iconoclast, downwards, have been at bottom far less concerned with
opinion than with conflicts of race, nationality, property, and policy, and
have been conducted on maxims of purely secular expediency?

Frederick the Great is the hero of the most picturesque of modern
English historians. That strong ruler, as we all know, took it into his
head to write a refutation of the *Prince*. 'Sir,' said Voltaire, 'I believe the
very first advice that Machiavelli would have given to a disciple, would
have been that he should begin by writing a refutation of his book.'
Carlyle contemptuously regrets that his hero should have taken any
trouble about the Italian's 'perverse little book' and its incredible sophistries; pity he was not refuted by a kick from old Frederick William's
jackboot; he deserved no more. Thus Carlyle does not let us forget that
nobody so quickly turns cynic as your high-flying transcendentalist, just
as nobody takes wickedness so easily as the Antinomian who holds the
highest doctrine about the incorruptibility of man's spiritual nature. The
plain truth is that Frederick, alike on his good side and his bad side,
alike as the wise law-maker, the thrifty steward, the capable soldier, and
as the robber of Silesia, and a leading accomplice, if not the inspirer, of
the partition of Poland, was the aptest of all modern types of the perverse
book. It was reserved for the following century to see even that type depraved and distorted by the mighty descendant of a fugitive family from
Tuscany, who found their way to Corsica about the time of Machiavelli's
death.

The most imposing incarnation of the doctrine that reason of State
covers all, is Napoleon. Tacitus, said Napoleon, writes romances; Gibbon
is no better than a man of sounding words; Machiavelli is the only one
of them worth reading. No wonder that he thought so. All those maxims
that have most scandalised mankind in the Italian writer of the sixteenth
century, were the daily bread of the Italian soldier who planted his iron
heel on the neck of Europe in the nineteenth. Yet Machiavelli at least
sets decent limits and conditions. The ruler may under compulsion be
driven to set at nought pity, humanity, faith, religion, for the sake of the
State; but though he should know how to enter upon evil when compelled, he should never turn from what is good when he can avoid it.
Napoleon sacrificed pity, humanity, faith, and public law, less for the
sake of the State than to satisfy an exorbitant passion for personal domination. Napoleon, Charles ix., the Committee of Public Safety, would all

have justified themselves by reason of State, and the Bartholomew massacre, the September massacres, and the murder of the Duc d'Enghien, only show what reason of State may come to in any age, in the hands of practical logicians with a knife in their grasp.

Turn from the Absolutist camp to the Republican. Mazzini is in some respects the loftiest moral genius of the century, and he said that though he did not approve the theory of the dagger, nay he deplored it, yet he had not the heart to curse the fact of the dagger. 'When a man,' he says, 'seeks by every possible artifice to betray old friends to the police of the Foreign Ruler, and then somebody arises and slays the Judas in broad daylight in the public streets—I have not the courage to cast the first stone at one who thus takes upon himself to represent social justice and hatred of tyranny.' [3]

Even in modern democracy, many a secret and ugly spring works under decorous mechanism, and recalls Machiavelli's precept to keep the name and take away the thing. Salvagnoli, minister for religion and public instruction in a liberal government of modern Italy, laid it down broadly to the scandal, real or affected, of reactionary opponents, *Colla verità non si governa.* What shall we say of two great rival Powers, each professing with no little sincerity its earnest desire to spread all the boons of civilisation, yet adjusting their own quarrel by solemn bargain and mutual compact that binds down some weak buffer-state in backwardness and barbarism? Yet such inconsistency between practice and profession may be detected in the newspaper telegrams any month by a reader who keeps his eye upon the right quarter. Is our general standard really so far removed at last from Sir Walter Raleigh's description, which has a Machiavellian twang about it,—'*Know ye not,* said Ahab, *that Ramoth Gilead is ours?* He knew this before, and was quiet enough, till opinion of his forces made him look unto his right. Broken titles to kingdoms or provinces, maintenance of friends and partisans, pretended wrongs, and indeed whatsoever it pleaseth him to allege, that thinks his own sword sharpest.' An eminent man endowed with remarkable compass of mind, not many years ago a professor in this university, imagined a modern writer with the unflinching perspicacity of Machiavelli, analysing the party leader as the Italian analysed the tyrant or the prince. Such a writer, he said, would find that the party leader, though possessed of every sort of private virtue, yet is debarred by his position from the full practice of the great virtues of veracity, justice, and moral intrepidity; he can seldom tell the full truth; can never be fair to anybody but his followers and his as-

[3] *Life and Writings of Mazzini* (ed. 1891), vi. 275–6.

sociates; can rarely be bold except in the interests of his faction. This hint of Maine's is ingenious and may perhaps be salutary, but we must not overdo it. Party government is not the Reign of the Saints, but we should be in no hurry to let the misgivings of political valetudinarianism persuade us that there is not at least as good a stock of veracity, justice, and moral intrepidity inside the world of parliaments or congress, as there is in the world without. But these three or four historic instances may serve to illustrate the ἀπορίαι and awkward points that Machiavelli's writings have propounded for men capable of political reflection in Europe, for many generations past.

If one were to try to put the case for the Machiavellian philosophy in a modern way, it would, I suppose, be something of this kind:—Nature does not work by moral rules. Nature, 'red in tooth and claw,' does by system all that good men by system avoid. Is not the whole universe of sentient being haunted all day and all night long by the haggard shapes of Hunger, Cruelty, Force, Fear? War again is not conducted by moral rules. To declare war is to suspend not merely *habeas corpus* but the Ten Commandments, and some other good commandments besides. A military manual, by an illustrious hand of our own day, warns us: 'As a nation we are brought up to feel it a disgrace even to succeed by falsehood. We keep hammering along with the conviction that honesty is the best policy, and that truth always wins in the long run. These sentiments do well for a copy-book, but a man who acts upon them had better sheath his sword for ever.' This, by the way, may be one reason among others why we should keep the sword sheathed as long as we can.

Why should the ruler of a State be bound by a moral code from which the soldier is free? Why should not he have the benefit of what has been called the evolutionary beatitude,—Blessed are the strong, for they shall prey on the weak? Right and wrong, cause and effect,—are they not two sides of one question? Has it not been well said that 'morality is the nature of things'? We must include in the computation the whole sum of consequences, and consider acts of State as worked out to their furthest results. Bishop Butler tells you that we cannot give the whole account of any one single thing whatever,—not of all its causes, its ends, its necessary adjuncts. In short, means and end are only one transaction. You must regard policy as a whole. The ruler as an individual is, like other men, no more than the generation of leaves, fleeting, a shadow, a dream. But the State lives on after he shall have vanished. He is a trustee for times to come. He is not shaping his own life only; he guides the distant fortunes of a nation. Leaves fall, the tree stands.

Such, I take it, is the defence of reason of State, of the worship of nation and empire. Everything that policy requires, justice sanctions. Success is the test. There are no crimes in politics, only blunders. 'The man of action is essentially conscienceless' (Goethe). 'Praised be those,' said one, in words much applauded by Machiavelli, 'who love their country rather than the safety of their souls.' 'Let us be Venetians first,' said Father Paul, 'and Christians after.'

We see now the deep questions that lie behind these sophistries, and all the alarming propositions in which they close. How are we to decide the constant question in national concerns, when and whether one duty overrules another that points the contrary way? It is easy to assert that the authority of moral law is paramount, but who denies that cases may arise of disputable and conflicting moral obligations? Do you condemn Prussia for violating in 1813 the treaties imposed by Napoleon after Jena? Does morality apply only to end and not to means? Is the State means or end? What does it really exist for? For the sake of the individual, his moral and material well-being, or is he mere cog or pinion in the vast thundering machine? How far is it true that citizenship dominates all other relations and duties, and is the most important of them? Are we to test the true civilisation of a State by anything else than the predominance of justice, right, equality, in its laws, its institutions, its relations to neighbours? Is one of the most important aspects of national policy its reaction upon the character of the nation itself, and can States enter on courses of duplicity and selfish violence, without paying the penalty in national demoralisation? What are we to think of such sayings as d'Alembert's motto for a virtuous man, 'I prefer my family to myself, my country to my family, and humanity to my country'? Is this the true order of honourable attachments for a man of self-respect and conscience? To Machiavelli all these questions would have been futile. Yet the world, in spite of a thousand mischances, and at tortoise-pace, has steadily moved away from him and his Romans.

The modern conception of a State has long made it a moral person, capable of right and wrong, just as are the individuals composing it. Civilisation is taken to advance, exactly in proportion as communities leave behind them the violences of external nature, and the unspeakable brutalities of man in a state of war. The usages of war are constantly undergoing mitigation. The inviolability of treaties received rude shocks between the first Napoleon and Prince Bismarck. 'You are always talking to me of principles,' said Alexander I. to Talleyrand, 'as if your public law were anything to me. I do not know what it means. What do you suppose that all your parchments and your treaties signify to me?' Yet

the sanctity of national faith has gained ground rather than lost, and
even naked invasions of it seek the decorum of a diplomatic fig-leaf.
Though it is said even now not to be wholly purged of lying, fraud, and
duplicity, diplomacy still is conscious of having a character to keep up
for truth and plain dealing, so far as circumstances allow. Such confer-
ences, again, as those at Berlin and Brussels in our own day, imperfectly
as they have worked, mark the recognition of duty towards inferior races.
All these improvements in the character of nations were in the minds of
the best men in Machiavelli's day. Reason of State has always been a
plea for impeding and resisting them. Las Casas and other churchmen,
Machiavelli's contemporaries, fought nobly at the Spanish court against
the inhuman treatment of Indians in the New World, and they were
defeated by arguments that read like maxims from the *Prince*. Grotius
had forerunners in his powerful contribution towards assuaging the
abominations of war, but both letter and spirit in Machiavelli made all
the other way. Times have come and gone since Machiavelli wrote down
his deep truths, but in the great cycles of human change he can have no
place among the strong thinkers, the orators, the writers, who have elevated the conception of the State, have humanised the methods and
maxims of government, have raised citizenship to be 'a partnership in
every virtue and in all perfection.' He turned to the past, just as scholars,
architects, sculptors, turned to it; but the idea of reconstructing a society
that had once been saturated with the great ruling conceptions of the
thirteenth century—as seen and symbolised in Dante, for example—by
trying to awaken the social energy of ancient Rome, was just as much of
an anachronism as Julian the Apostate. 'Our religion,' said Machiavelli of
Christianity, 'has glorified men of humble and meditative life, and not
men of action. It has planted the chief good in lowliness and contempt
of mundane things; paganism placed it in highmindedness, in bodily
force, in all the other things that make men strong. If our religion calls
for strength in us, it is for strength to suffer rather than to do. This seems
to have rendered the world weak.' This 'discarding of presuppositions
of Christianity,' as it has been well described, marks with exactitude the
place of Machiavelli in the development of modern European thought.
The *Prince*—the most direct, concentrated, and unflinching contribution
ever made to the secularisation of politics—brings into a full light, never
before shed upon it, the awful manicheism of human history, the fierce
and unending collision of type, ideal, standard, and endeavour.

Machiavelli has been supposed to put aside the question of right and
wrong, just as the political economist or the analytical jurist used to do.
Truly has it been said that the practical value of all sciences founded on

abstractions, depends on the relative importance of the elements rejected and the elements retained in the process of abstraction. The view that he rejected moral elements of government for a scientific purpose and as a hypothetical postulate, seems highly doubtful. Is he not more intelligible, if we take him as following up the divorce of politics from theology, by a divorce from ethics also? He was laying down certain maxims of government as an art; the end of that art is the security and permanence of the ruling power; and the fundamental principle from which he silently started, without shadow of doubt or misgiving as to its soundness, was that the application of moral standards to this business, is as little to the point as it would be in the navigation of a ship.

The effect was fatal even for his own purpose, for what he put aside, whether for the sake of argument or because he thought them in substance irrelevant, were nothing less than the living forces by which societies subsist and governments are strong. A remarkable illustration occurred in his own century. Three or four years before all this on secular and ecclesiastical princedoms was written, John Calvin was born (1509). With a union of fervid religious instinct and profound political genius, almost unexampled in European history, Calvin did in fact what Machiavelli tried to do on paper; he actually created a self-governed state, ruled it, defended it, maintained it, and made that little corner of Europe both the centre of a movement that shook France, England, Scotland, America, for long days to come, and at the same time he set up a bulwark against all the forces of Spanish and Roman reaction in the pressing struggles of his own immediate day. In one sense, Florence, Geneva, Holland, hold as high a place as the greatest States of Europe in the development of modern civilisation; but anybody with a turn for ingenious or idle speculation might ask himself whether, if the influence of Florence on European culture had never existed, the loss to mankind would have been as deep as if the little republic of Geneva had been wiped out by the dukes of Savoy. The unarmed prophet, said Machiavelli, thinking of Savonarola, is always sure to be destroyed, and his institutions must come to nought. If Machiavelli had been at Jerusalem two thousand years ago, he might have found nobody of any importance in his eyes, save Pontius Pilate and the Roman legionaires. He forgot the potent arms of moral force, and it was with these that, in the main, Calvin fought his victorious battle. We need not, however, forget that Calvin never scrupled to act on some of these Italian maxims that have been counted most hateful. He was as ready to resort to carnal weapons as other people. In spite of all the sophistries of sectarian apologists, Calvin's vindictive persecution of political opponents, and his share in the crime of burning Servetus, can only be justified on principles that are much the same as, and certainly not any better than, those prescribed for the tyrant in the *Prince*. Still the republic of Geneva was a triumph of moral force. So was the daughter system in Scotland. It is true that tyrannical theocracy does not in either case by any means escape the familiar reproaches addressed by history to Jesuits and Inquisitors.

In Italy Savonarola had attempted a similar achievement. It was the last effort to reconcile the spirit of the new age to the old faith, but Italy was for a second time in her history in the desperate case of being able to endure *nec vitia nec remedia,* neither ills nor cure. In a curious passage (*Disc.* iii. 1), Machiavelli describes how Dominic and Francis in older days kindled afresh an expiring flame. He may have perceived that for Italy in this direction all was by his time over.

The sixteenth century in Italy in some respects resembles the eighteenth in France. In both, old faiths were assailed and new lamps were kindled. But the eighteenth century was a time of belief in the better elements of mankind. An illusion, you may say. Was it a worse illusion than disbelief in mankind? Machiavelli and his school saw only cunning, jealousy, perfidy, ingratitude, dupery; and yet on such a foundation as this they dreamed that they could build. What idealist or doctrinaire ever fell into a stranger error? Surrounded by the ruins of Italian nationality, says a writer of genius, 'Machiavelli organises the abstract theory of the country with all the energy of the Committee of Public Safety, supported on the passion of twenty-five millions of Frenchmen. He carries in him the genius of the Convention. His theories strike like acts' (Quinet). Yet after all has been said, energy as an abstract theory is no better than a bubble.

'The age of Machiavel,' it has been said, 'was something like ours, in being one of religious eclipse, attended by failure of the traditional foundation of morality. A domination of self-interest without regard for moral restriction was the result' (Goldwin Smith). We may hope to escape this capital disaster. Yet it is true to say that Machiavelli represents certain living forces in our actual world; that Science, with its survival of the fittest, unconsciously lends him illegitimate aid; that 'he is not a vanishing type, but a constant and contemporary influence' (Acton). This is because energy, force, will, violence, still keep alive in the world their resistance to the control of justice and conscience, humanity and right. In so far as he represents one side in that unending struggle, and suggests one set of considerations about it, he retains a place in the literature of modern political systems and of Western morals.

Mussolini on MACHIAVELLI

One day I happened to receive word from Imola—the black legions of Imola—that a sword had been presented to me incised with Machiavelli's motto, "States are not maintained with words." This cut short any delay on my part and determined immediately the choice of the theme which I now submit to your judgment. I could call it the comment of the year 1924 on Machiavelli's *The Prince*, the book which I should like to call the "Vade mecum for the Statesman." For reasons of intellectual honesty I must add that my essay has a sparse bibliography, as will be seen in what follows. I have reread *The Prince* and the rest of the works of the great Secretary, but I have lacked both the time and the desire to read all that has been written on Machiavelli in Italy and abroad. I wanted to put the smallest number of intermediaries, old or new, Italian or foreign, between Machiavelli and myself, in order not to spoil the direct contact between his doctrine and my life, between his observations of men and affairs and mine, between his practice of government and mine. What I have to say here is therefore not a cold and scholastic dissertation, bristling with quotations from others, but rather a drama, if, as I believe, it is a dramatic attempt to throw a bridge of the spirit over the abyss of generations and events.

I shall say nothing new.

The question arises: over the distance of four centuries, what is there in *The Prince* that is still alive? Could the counsels of Machiavelli still have any usefulness for the rulers of modern states? Is the value of the political system of *The Prince* confined to the epoch in which the book was written, and therefore necessarily limited and partly obsolete, or is it universal and still timely? Especially timely? My thesis seeks to answer these questions. I affirm that Machiavelli's doctrine is today more alive than four centuries ago, because although the exernal aspects of our life have greatly changed, there have been no profound changes in the spirit of individuals or peoples.

If politics is the art of governing men, that is, of orienting, utilizing, educating their passions, their egoisms, and their interests toward purposes of a more general order that nearly always transcend the individual life because they look to the future—if that is what politics is about, then

[Benito Mussolini, "Prelude to Machiavelli," *Gerarchia*, vol. 3 (April, 1924, trans. William Ebenstein).]

there is no doubt that the fundamental element of that art is man. This is the point of departure. What is man in the political system of Machiavelli? What does Machiavelli think of man? Is he an optimist or pessimist? And using the term "man," are we to interpret it in a narrow sense, that is, as relating to the Italians whom Machiavelli knew and carefully examined as his contemporaries, or are we to interpret the meaning of man beyond time and space (*"sub specie aeternitatis,"* to put it in acquired jargon)? It seems to me that, before we undertake an analytical examination of the Machiavellian system of politics, as it appears in a condensed form in *The Prince*, we have to establish exactly Machiavelli's concept of man in general, and perhaps of the Italians in particular. What clearly emerges even from a superficial reading of *The Prince* is Machiavelli's acute pessimism with regard to human nature. Like all those who have had occasion to maintain continuous and close relations with men, Machiavelli despises them, and likes to present them—as I shall soon show—in their most negative and mortifying aspects.

Men are, according to Machiavelli, sad, more attached to things than to their own blood, and ready to change sentiments and passions. In Chapter XVII of *The Prince*, Machiavelli expresses himself as follows:

It may be said of men in general that they are ungrateful, voluble deceivers, anxious to avoid dangers, and covetous of gain; as long as you benefit them, they are entirely yours, offering you their blood, their goods, their life, and their children, when the danger is remote. But when danger approaches, they revolt. And the prince who has relied solely on their words, without making other provisions, is ruined. For the friendship which is gained by purchase and not through grandeur and nobility of spirit is bought but not secured. Men have less scruple in offending one who makes himself loved than one who makes himself feared; for love is held by a chain of obligation which, men being selfish, is broken whenever it serves their purpose; but fear is maintained by a dread of punishment which never fails.

With regard to man's egoism, I find the following in Machiavelli's *Miscellaneous Papers:*

Men grieve more over the loss of a power than over the death of a brother or father, because they can sometimes forget death, but the loss of material things, never. The reason is readily understandable: everybody knows that a change in a state cannot revive a dead brother, but may bring back lost power.

And in Chapter III of *The Discourses*, he writes as follows:

All those who have written on civil institutions demonstrate (and history is full of examples to support them) that whoever desires to found a state and give it laws, must start with assuming that all men are bad and always ready to display their vicious nature, whenever they may find occasion for it. Men act rightly only upon compulsion; where liberty and licence abound, everything becomes immediately filled with confusion and disorder.

The quotations could go on, but it is not necessary to continue. The cited passages are sufficient to demonstrate that Machiavelli's negative judgment of men is not incidental, but fundamental to his mind. It is to be found in all his works. It represents a worthwhile and disconsolate conviction. This initial and essential viewpoint must be taken into account if one is to follow the successive developments of Machiavelli's mind. It is also evident that, in judging men as he did, Machiavelli did not refer solely to Florentines, Tuscans, or Italians who lived between the fifteenth and sixteenth centuries, but to men in general without limitation of space or time. Much time has passed by since then, but if I were allowed to judge my own contemporaries, I could not in any way attenuate Machiavelli's judgment. Perhaps I might even have to aggravate it. Machiavelli does not delude himself and does not delude the ruler. The antithesis between ruler and people, between state and individual is, in Machiavelli's concept, a fatal one. What were called utilitarianism, pragmatism, or Machiavellian cynicism—they all derive logically from that initial position. The word "Prince" must be understood to mean "State." In Machiavelli's concept the ruler is the state. Whereas individuals tend, driven by their selfishness, toward social atomism, the state represents organization and limitation. The individual tends to evade continuously. He tends to disobey the laws, not pay taxes, and not go to war. Few are those—heroes and saints—who sacrifice their own on the altar of their fatherland. All the rest are in a condition of potential revolt against the state.

The revolutions of the seventeenth and eighteenth centuries attempted to resolve this discord, which is the basis of all state organization, by creating power as the emanation of the free will of the people. This is a fiction and another illusion. First of all, the people has never been defined. As a political entity, it is a pure abstraction. One does not know exactly where it begins and where it ends. The adjective "sovereign," when applied to the people, is a tragic jest. The whole people at the most delegates authority, but cannot, itself, exercise any sovereignty. The representative systems belong more to mechanics than to morality. Even in countries where these mechanisms have been intensely used for centuries, there come solemn hours when the people are not asked any questions, because of the feeling that the reply might be fatal; the paper-made crowns of sovereignty—good for normal times—are torn from the heads of the people, and they are ordered to accept a revolution or a peace or to march into the unknown of war. All that is left to the people is a monosyllable to say yes and obey. The sovereignty graciously granted to the people is taken away in moments when the people could feel its need. The people is allowed to keep it only when it is innocuous or believed to be such, that is, in times of ordinary administration. Has a war ever been proclaimed by referendum? The referendum works excellently if the issue at stake deals with the most suitable place for the village fountain, but when the supreme interests of the nation are in jeopardy, the ultrademocratic governments, too, refrain from submitting them to the judgment of the people. Even the regimes that were brought into being by the *Encyclopédie* (suffering, through Rousseau, from an incommensurate excess of optimism) contain within themselves the discord between the organized force of the state and the fragmentation of individuals and groups. Regimes based exclusively on consent have never existed, do not exist now, and probably will never exist. Long before my now famous article on "Force and Consent" Machiavelli wrote in *The Prince:*

> *Thus it comes about that all armed prophets have conquered and unarmed ones failed*; for the character of peoples varies, and it is easy to persuade them of a thing, but difficult to keep them in that persuasion. *And it is thus necessary to order things so that when they no longer believe, they can be made to believe by force. Moses, Cyrus, Theseus, and Romulus would not have been able to keep their constitutions observed for so long had they been disarmed.*

Croce on MACHIAVELLI

The name of Machiavelli has become almost the symbol of pure politics and it certainly marks a sharp crisis in the development of the science. Not that antiquity did not have some inkling of the distinction and contrast between politics and ethics: this is shown in the very fact that their subject

[From Benedetto Croce, *Politics and Morals* (trans. Salvatore J. Castiglione, Philosophical Library, Inc., 1946). By permission.]

matter was attributed to two different disciplines; and debates like those on just and unjust law, on natural and conventional law, on force and justice, etc., show how the contrast was sometimes felt and how the correlative problem appeared in outline. But the contrast never came to the forefront and never became the focus of deep study and meditation. This did not even happen in the long centuries of the domination of Christian thought, because the contrast between the *civitas Dei* and the *civitas terrena*, and later between Church and Empire, had its solution in the doctrine of the double rule instituted by God, or possibly in the doctrine of the supremacy of Church over Empire or of Empire over Church; and it was not sharpened by philosophical dissension. But there is no doubt that Christian thought, in which the examination of the moral consciousness plays so great a part, was preparing, by making this consciousness more keen, the dissension that was to break out. Niccolò Machiavelli is considered a pure expression of the Italian Renaissance; but he should also be connected in some way with the movement of the Reformation, with that general need, which asserted itself in his time, in Italy and elsewhere, to know man and to study the problem of the soul.

It is known that Machiavelli discovered the necessity and autonomy of politics, of politics which is beyond or, rather, below moral good and evil, which has its own laws against which it is useless to rebel, politics that cannot be exorcized and driven from the world with holy water. This is the concept which pervades all his works. Although this concept is not formulated with that didactic and scholastic exactness which is usually mistaken for philosophy, and although it is sometimes disturbed by fantastic idols, by figures that waver between political virtue and wicked lust of power, it must nevertheless be termed a profoundly philosophical concept, and it represents the true foundation of a philosophy of politics.

But what usually passes unobserved is the decided bitterness with which Machiavelli accompanies this assertion of politics as an intrinsic necessity. "If all men were good," he says, these precepts "would not be good." But men are "ungrateful and fickle; they flee from dangers and are eager for gains." Therefore it is well to see to it that you are feared rather than loved, to provide first for fear and then, if possible, for love. You must learn "to be not good." You must fail to keep your word when it is to your advantage to do so, because otherwise others would fail to keep their word to you; you must defeat those who are waiting for the opportunity to defeat you. Machiavelli yearns for an unattainable society of good and pure men; and he fancies it to be found in the distant past. In the meantime he prefers the less civilized peoples to the more civilized, the people of Germany and the mountaineers of Switzerland to the

Italians, the French and the Spanish (then at the height of their glory), who are the "corruption of the world." It is his feeling, and he expresses it with a shudder, that whoever reads of the horrors which history relates to us "will undoubtedly, if he is born of man, be frightened by every imitation of the evil times and will be kindled by the great desire to follow the good times." In the face of such evident signs of a stern and sorrowful moral conscience, it is amazing that there has been so much idle talk about Machiavelli's immorality; but the common people term as moral only moralistic unctuosity and bigoted hypocrisy. The lack of this bitter pessimism distinguishes Guicciardini from Machiavelli. The former feels only a sort of contempt toward men in whom he finds so "little goodness," and he settles down peacefully in this discredited world, aiming only at the advantage of his own "personal being." If he had not had to serve the Medici popes because of this "personal being" of his, he would have loved "Martin Luther more than himself," because he would have hoped that the rebel friar might undo the ecclesiastic state and destroy the "wicked tyranny of the priests." Guicciardini's man is different in temperament from Machiavelli's man.

It is still more important to observe that Machiavelli is as though divided in spirit and mind with respect to the politics whose autonomy he has discovered. At times it seems to him a sad necessity to have to soil his hands by dealing with ugly people, and at times it seems to him a sublime art to found and support that great institution which is the State. Quite often he speaks of the State in a religious tone, as when he recalls the saying that one must be prepared for the sake of the State to lose not only one's reputation, but also the salvation of one's own soul; or as when he looks back, with ill-concealed envy, at the pagan religion, which exalted, as the highest good, honour in this world, extolling human glory, and praising greatness of spirit, strength of body, and all the virtues which make man powerful; whereas the Christian religion, by showing the truth and the real way to the world beyond, despises this world, and praises abjection, setting contemplative men above the others, and endurance above action. Is politics diabolical or divine? Machiavelli imagines it in the guise of the Centaur, described by poets as a very beautiful creature, part man part beast, and he describes his prince as half man and half beast. In order that there may be no doubt as to the integrity of the human self of this creature, he assigns even the subtleties of the mind, such as craftiness, to the animal self, recommending that it be part fox and part lion, because the lion does not defend himself against traps and the fox does not defend himself against wolves. One would be acting as a novice in the art of ruling if one wished "always to carry on as a lion." The art and science of politics, of pure politics, brought to maturity by the Italians, were to him a source of pride. For this reason he answered Cardinal de Rohan, who used to tell him that the Italians knew nothing about war, by saying that "the French knew nothing about the State."

The continuation of Machiavelli's thoughts must not be sought among the Machiavellians, who continue his political casuistry and body of maxims and write about the *"raison d'état,"* frequently mixing moralizing trivialities with these maxims: nor among the anti-Machiavellians, who proclaim the fusion and identification of politics with morality and conceive States founded on pure dictates of goodness and justice: nor among the eclectics, who place in juxtaposition theories of morality and theories of politics, and take the edge off antinomies and make them empirical, instead of solving them, and change them to misfortunes and inconveniences which happen in life but have the character of accidental things. It must be sought in those who made an effort to classify the concept of "prudence," of "shrewdness" and, in short, of "political virtue," without confusing it with the concept of "moral virtue" and, also, without in the least denying the latter. (One of these was Zuccolo, a seventeenth century writer.) And it must be sought in some powerful spirits who, beyond the shrewdness and sagacity of the individual, as analyzed by Machiavelli, asserted the divine work of Providence. Such a person was Tommaso Campanella. But Machiavelli's true and worthy successor, the powerful intellect who gathered together and strengthened both these scattered suggestions of criticisms and the immortal thought of the Florentine secretary, was another Italian, Vico. In truth, the whole philosophy of politics in its central idea is symbolized in two Italians. Vico is not kind to Machiavelli, yet is full of his spirit which he tries to clarify and purify by integrating Machiavelli's concept of politics and of history, by settling his theoretical difficulties and by brightening his pessimism.

LUTHER

From the viewpoint of the expansion of political liberty, the first Protestant church, the Lutheran, had little effect either in Germany or elsewhere. Luther himself (see page 51) stressed the inner aspect of religious experience. In his assertion of the equality of all Christians as Christians, he was of revolutionary import, and his doctrine of the priesthood of all Christians contained immense possibilities that were more fully exploited later in England, Scotland, Holland, Switzerland, and North America. His bold break with Rome was not paralleled by a new social or political philosophy. On the contrary, Luther's religious radicalism was matched in Germany by extreme conservatism in social and political affairs. Supported by the absolutist princes of northern Germany, Luther stressed the duty of the subject to obey unflinchingly the commands of his ruler.

The relations of Luther's doctrines to social and political ethics and institutions is more fully elaborated in Ernst Troeltsch's *The Social Teaching of the Christian Churches* (1912, English translation, 1931). Troeltsch (1865–1923) belonged to a generation of German scholarship which, in addition to himself, produced giant figures like Ulrich von Wilamowitz-Moellendorff in classics and Max Weber in sociology. At first, Troeltsch taught theology at the Universities of Bonn and Heidelberg, but later he became professor of philosophy at the University of Berlin. A confirmed democrat, he was elected a member of the Prussian Diet in 1919, and he became Parliamentary Undersecretary of Education, gaining an influence in the shaping of educational and religious policies of the government. His interests in sociology, theology, philosophy, and history found their most comprehensive and mature expression in his monumental work on *The Social Teaching of the Christian Churches*, which, from its first German publication in 1912 to this day, has remained the authoritative treatise on the subject. His treatment of Luther and Lutheranism shows their devastating effect on German social and political development, and as a profoundly believing Lutheran himself, he looked with admiration to the English-speaking countries in which the Protestant Revolution led to an expansion of social and political liberty. In his *Christian Thought: Its History and Application* (1923) Troeltsch approached his main field of interest, the relationship of Christianity to history and social forces, from an analytical and systematic viewpoint rather than from an historical one, as he had done in his earlier work.

Troeltsch on LUTHER

The Lutheran Ethic and the State

The Lutheran conception of the State presents the same characteristics as that of the Family, and the difficulties which it presents are regarded from the same point of view. In each case the State has come into existence in very different ways—through creatures as "channels" and instruments of the Divine Reason, and in each case its existence has been confirmed and authorized by the Gospel, above all in the 13th chapter of the Epistle to the Romans. The State is a product of Reason, and is therefore, by its nature, restricted to the aims of mere Reason, the preservation of external discipline and order, and the securing of human well-being. It is the same "police" and utilitarian idea of the State as in Catholicism, only now, in accordance with the circumstances, there is a greater emphasis upon unity of authority. The means which the State has at its disposal for this purpose is authority, which therefore forms its most peculiar attribute, which it always preserves, and which may not be destroyed by any of its subjects. It is, however, the duty of the State to use this authority according to the Divine Law of Nature and for the purpose of reason, and if the powers that be refuse to observe this Law, just as in scholasti-

[From Ernst Troeltsch, *The Social Teaching of the Christian Churches*, vol. II (trans. Olive Wyon, George Allen & Unwin, Ltd., 1931). By permission.]

cism, they are to be regarded as "tyrants", who may be deposed from their office. According to Luther's own logical doctrine, however, the only resistance to these "tyrants" which he will countenance is that of passive resistance, or endurance, or in a case of religious persecution he would recommend those who are oppressed to go into exile. In this sense the State is always justified, both by Natural and by Divine Law, even among Turks and pagans; indeed, in its natural sense, it is even particularly excellent among pagans, and the ancient doctrine of the State and examples drawn from it can still be used to the profit of the State at the present day.

To this extent the State is something really Divine. Now, however, it is its duty to establish order by force and violence as well as by law and justice, and this is completely opposed to the real Christian spirit of love. The Christian ought to love his enemies and to go to law as little as possible; indeed, at first Luther taught that no Christian should go to law at all; later on he conceded the right to go to law as a means of self-protection against "knaves", with whom it is impossible to come to an understanding in a Christian way. In this concession, however, there is no ethical recognition of justice as such, whether in the form of law, or merely as a general sense of justice. Rather it is the duty of the Government to take the initiative in the administration of the law and of the police force, in order to prevent a Christian from being obliged to make too much use of the law for his own sake. There is just as little ethical value in patriotic and "Fatherland" sentiments. In cases where the Government is unchristian a Christian must either refrain from resistance or the Government must be changed. The truly Christian ideal is that of a pure fellowship of love, apart from State or Law. This implies that the State—in spite of its Divine character and its basis in Reason—is still only an institution rendered necessary by and against sin, a product of the merely relative Natural Law, reacting against sin under the conditions of the fallen State. Here, then, there reappear all the Augustinian views about the State as the product of sin, which, however, can only be rightly understood if the State is regarded as a product of Reason working with concessions to sinful brutality and evil, and itself set up by Reason against sin.

From this point of view, however, the State again seems to be something unchristian, directly opposed to a genuine Christian ethic, and it would seem to be quite natural and justifiable for Christian men to seek to contract out of the State, not only by refusing to claim the aid of the State in legal matters or to take part in military service, or in swearing an oath, etc., but also by refusing to take part in the official administration of the government, and in the execution of its laws. Faced by such scruples, however (just as in the case of the Family), Luther appeals with great emphasis to the belief that the powers that be are ordained by God, and confirmed in their position by Him. It is a duty of obedience towards God to exercise authority, to obey the Government, and to use authority for the purpose of justice; God Himself bears the responsibility for His institutions, and does not intend them to be interfered with by human sophistry and argument. The practice of government and the administration of justice are offices appointed by Divine command, and Luther describes with great vigour the contrast between the system of law which is carried out from the ruling prince down to the gaoler and the hangman, in which the work of government, administration, and punishment, including hanging, breaking on the wheel, and beheading, is all a service to God, and the non-official purely personal morality, in which, on the other hand, the true service of God consists in loving one's enemies, in sacrifice, renunciation and endurance, in loving care for others, and self-sacrifice.

It is very evident that he delights in the paradox of these two ways of serving God, and he boasts with great satisfaction that no one has yet proved so clearly from the Scriptures the Divine Right of a government, which is independent, dominated by no Church, and bewildered by no scruples. It is at this point that Luther inserts the most characteristic and remarkable tenet in his whole system of ethics, the distinction between private and public morality, in which, in his own way, he had solved the great problem which had exercised the minds and hearts of the Christian thinkers of an earlier era. In this demand for obedience to a positive command of God all the Augustinian conceptions of the State disappear, and the State is regarded entirely as the Divinely-appointed authority based on reason, whose business it is to execute all the tasks which affect public order and the common weal; by that very fact the State is distinct from the Church, which is dependent solely upon spiritual influence and vital personal fellowship.

From this point of view war also is justified. It may only be waged by the civil authority, for secular purposes, as part of its official duty, when it is necessary to protect the peace and welfare of its citizens against attack. Victory can only be expected if war is waged in self-defence. Further, war must be waged in a spirit of humility, ascribing nothing to one's own efforts, but all to the Grace of God. This excludes, therefore, all ideas of "holy" wars or Crusades; where religious interests are involved only spiritual weapons may be used, and even the war against the Turks may only be waged by the Emperor as one who is called to that duty, and then only in the secular interest of the protection of his people. This position, however, excludes all specific political thought and activity. Even a "secular" war must be waged for a righteous cause, and if a Prince should undertake an unjust oppressive war his subjects are to refuse to support him, accepting with Christian patience the suffering they will have to endure as the penalty for their disobedience. A just war also requires that those who take part in it should have the right moral and Christian spirit; they must prepare themselves by attendance at church, for God will not grant victory to the proud. In all this there is no question of treaties and political combinations. Every country stands alone, and defends itself when it is threatened, trusting in the providence of God. This is an extremely naïve kind of political idea, dependent in particular instances upon politics of the prophetic moralizing kind. Luther is convinced that all wars which are not undertaken in this spirit are permitted to fail, and that Providence uses defeats as a rod of correction and as a religious method of education. Thus the thing Luther admires most in the Romans is that they were obliged to wage war; everyone wished to force himself on them and to gain a knight's renown from them, so that they had to defend themselves; even Hannibal failed because he began the war, "for it is God who does it. He will have peace, and He is against those who begin war and break peace".

It is easy to see what a disastrous effect this kind of outlook would have upon Lutheranism in the political sphere, and although the Lutheran princes, diplomats and jurists, and later on even Luther himself, did not bind themselves to follow this policy, it was still everywhere a dangerous drag on Lutheran politics; it determined the expansion and the fate of Lutheranism, which was unable to extend beyond the land of its birth. What a contrast was presented by Calvinist politics, with their treaties and alliances and their Wars of Religion.

When, however, we inquire into the relation of the State to the Church, and to the life of the Christian community, we see the question from a fresh angle. For if the State is controlled by a Christian government, then it is no longer merely an institution based on Divine and Natural Law through the order of Creation, but it is one of the forms used for the realization of the Christian fellowship of love and redemption. This means that submission to its institutions and associations is a Christian duty of love to the whole of Society, and indeed one of the most necessary and immediate duties, since it is precisely the utilization of the forms of life within the State which helps our fellow-men more than the self-sought holiness of monastic separation from the world. Then it becomes especially the duty of the Government, as a service of love, to undertake the education and preservation of Society, Christian unity of faith, discipline, and order, and also to care for the Word of God, for purity and for the prosperity of the Church. The Government serves the Church freely, from love, creates its church-order and its financial basis, exercises the office of censor and defender of the Faith, and excludes from its sphere all expressions of false doctrine, measures which are not required of a non-Christian government. The Turks may tolerate several religions at the same time, but a Christian government must place itself at the disposal of the loving service of the Truth. Thus it will take upon itself, it is true, all kinds of secular matters, including education and the care of the poor, but it will deal with them all in a Christian spirit, and with consideration for the progress of the Christian life of faith. The religious end of Society, therefore, is exalted above the end of Natural Law, not, however, in the Catholic sense, with its graded organization, regulated in case of need by the supreme authority of the Church, but in the sense of an agreement between the activity of the State and the Christian exercise of love. Thus we have again reached an Augustinian idea, the idea of a Theocracy. Only this theocracy is not a Hierocracy, not the supremacy of the international hierarchy, and it is not a relationship which can be legally formulated; but it is the free agreement in love between the purely spiritual Church built upon the Word, and the secular authority, freely serving the Church, receiving voluntary advice from the theologians; both Church and State, however, are controlled and impelled by the Word of God, and by its miraculous and spontaneous power, which achieves its own end.

In this question, too, Luther was fully conscious that in spite of all his concessions to the State as an institution of fallen humanity, he was promulgating a highly idealistic doctrine, far removed from reality. We only have to read Luther's Catechism to see how the Christian ruler will desire nothing save to use his office with all strictness, in might and right, as God's representative to serve the cause of love and faith; and how, on the other hand, Christians ought to lead a humble and peaceful life, in unlimited love and readiness to help others, without legal proceedings or special privileges, without insistence on their formal rights, and with the greatest possible toleration of injustice. It is quite clear that this ideal of the State is superidealistic, almost utopian, in a Christian sense. On the other hand, we only need to read his angry and vehement complaints of princes and jurists, feudal lords and magistrates, as well as, above all, his complaints of the masses, "so unteachable, so coarse and brutal", to see that Luther was far removed from the opinion that the existing condition of things in the State corresponded to his ideal. However hard he tried, in contradistinction from the Baptists, to make his ideal fit into the conditions of actual life, it was as little at home in this coarse and brutal world as was his spiritual ideal of the Church, which made no provision for its extension.

This was not due, as is often said, to Luther's lack of political ability, a defect which might perhaps have been remedied. It is inherent in the religious idea itself, which cannot be combined with the political spirit. When a fusion of this kind does take place, the religious expression will also be different; Calvinism is a good example of this fact. With the modern Conservatives, who are certainly not without the political spirit, the political element (which is founded upon the essence of a policy of force based on might) and the religious element (with its spirituality which finds its chief happiness in waiting on God) diverge so far in opposite directions that there is a complete severance and disharmony.

In the Lutheranism of more recent times the tension between public and private morality disappeared more and more, and there arose that type which is usually described as Lutheran: that is, unconditional obedience towards the central government, and the subordinate officials, both of whom represent God, and only hold their office by virtue of God's permission; the belief that these authorities are based on Natural and Divine Law, which appear more and more as the fundamental laws of a true Christian Society, and which co-operate without difficulty; the duty of the Government to look after all secular and natural affairs, and, so far as it is possible, with its secular means, and in agreement with the ecclesiastical government, also to promote the Christian virtues; the preservation of external peace at any price, and of internal peace by a thorough guardianship over the restricted understanding of its subjects. The sinful origin and the sinful character of law and of force disappeared in the harmony between the Natural and the Divine Law, and this harmony made possible an ideal of Christian Society, which, in itself, was quite possible to realize, although it was constantly being obscured by sin. In this ideal, revelation and natural science and reason unite to form one great ideal of human society.

L. von Seckendorff gave classic expression to this ideal in the dedication of his *Teutscher Fürstenstaat:* "The wisdom by which Kingdoms, Principalities, and lands are happily governed is, according to its origin Divine, in itself glorious and incomparable, and includes in its breadth and universality all that which in other sciences is found only in fragments. Within the sphere of each land it is the absolutely necessary sun, by means of which all is illumined, warmed, and nourished. It may be compared with an inexhaustible ocean into which all other wisdom and art flow, and in a high and secret manner, to the welfare of all, it is again spread abroad and shared throughout the whole land. It is a Paradise which is ever green with all the most beautiful and useful plants of the virtues and good ordinances, of which each in his time and place brings forth pleasant fruits. This wisdom King Solomon besought the only Wise God for his office of government, by which in addition he receiveth the greatest treasures and riches of the world also." The pessimism and idealism of original Lutheranism have disappeared, and the doctrine of society bears the traces of a hearty and inwardly strong, but homely and commonplace, paternal government.

Social Ideal of Luther

The whole social ideal of Luther—the organization and construction of Society in general—is finally explained by political and economic and ethical ideas. As in mediaeval Catholicism, it was the ideal of the social hierarchy, as a "cosmos of callings"; the only difference is that the duty of the "calling" is now extended to all, which involves the direct incorporation of the idea of "the calling" into the very heart of Christian ethics. The "callings" are in part those which proceed from the economic organization of Society, in which a rigid guild organization would be desirable. In part they are vocations to the Church and to the work of education, to which (as is constantly repeated) it is a Christian duty to lead talented children. Then there are the callings of the prince, the noble, the official, the soldier, and last of all, the surplus of those who cannot find a place within the established organization, but who can still be used to serve in various ways as they are needed. Serfdom, which had not ceased to exist, and which was extended at the close of the sixteenth century, from this point of view was regarded in precisely the same way as slavery was regarded in the Early Church, as a class, that is, in which men may enjoy the inner liberty of Redemption, but in which they have no right to seek external legal freedom. In Lutheranism there was no idea at all of any new anti-slavery movements, and even down to the present day neither agrarian nor industrial serfdom raises any kind of misgiving in its mind. The reason for all this is perfectly clear. The social hierarchy does away with competition, so far as that is possible in the fallen state, and in so doing it harmonizes both with the ideal of love, and with the ideal of Natural Law which aims at law and order. It is in this sense that Stahl has made a new defence of the class theory as part of the theory of Christian Natural Law. A blind faith in Providence assures the community that a principle of this kind would meet all the needs of the whole population. This system can only be disturbed by unusual accidents and Divine chastisements; when this happens those whose lives have been thrown out of gear by these events are commended to the care of Christian philanthropy, and to the care of the civil authority, firmly believing that these methods will suffice to heal all social evils. At bottom, no one doubts that the Government can achieve all this, provided that it obeys conscientiously both the Law of Nature and the Law of God: that is the characteristic difference between this point of view and that of the present day. The reason for this lies partly in the fact that in reality conditions were—in a quite remarkable way—much simpler than they are now; owing to the lack of all statistical information, there was a total absence of scientific knowledge of the complicated character of the social situation, which was conditioned by and dependent on so many different factors; the right of location did not yet exist, and the problem of population had only just begun to appear as a subject for discussion. Hence a naïve conception of that kind was possible. The later theological ethic therefore, on the side of its social theories, was simply concerned with the vocational system as a whole; in particular it dealt only with the question of the family and the household, which, it felt, ought to constitute the chief sphere for the development of the ethical virtues of Christianity. The regulation of the whole is left to the Government, which, strongly supported by Lutheranism, takes supreme control. It is then the duty of the Government to see to it that in harmony with Christian and Natural Law the different classes are maintained in their suitable way of living, that social evils are remedied, and that whatever progress is necessary, is achieved. These matters come under the province of political economy and police administration; thus the Lutheran theory merges into mercantilism, since, where the good of the community is concerned, the Government is permitted to do that which is forbidden to the individual, that is, to gain an increase of property and profit, to initiate new industrial enterprises, monopolies and royalties, immunities, and alterations in the social structure and its compulsory character. In connection with this subject Seckendorff has given a classic description of the Christian "police".

Social Policy, Social Reform, and Philanthropy

When we gather up all these various particulars and summarize them it then becomes possible to answer the question: to what extent did Lutheranism attempt to mould Society according to Christian ideals, or to introduce a scheme of social reform? The answer is simpler than we would expect when we consider that Lutheranism has been interwoven with an amazingly varied social history. Lutheranism has been mainly interwoven with a social process which extends from the advanced stage of the German civilization of the sixteenth century, through the desolation of the Thirty Years War, the formation of the German States, and finally, through the politics of the Enlightenment and the Restoration periods, down to the great social problems of the present day. The simplicity of the answer is due to the fact that down to the present time the Lutheran position is based essentially upon the religious theory of the purely spiritual nature and "inwardness" of the Church, while all external secular matters are handed over to reason, to the ruling Princes, to the civil authority. At the beginning, certainly, there was combined with that the assumption that Natural and Divine Law, both issuing from the same source, will always naturally supplement each other, and that a Christian government will always desire and be able to govern and to mould secular affairs in harmony with Natural and Divine Law, in the spirit of the religious and ethical ideal.

The idea of moulding Society according to Christian ideals certainly existed; but it was left entirely to the Government, to be carried out in accordance with natural reason, which harmonized with the Gospel and was adapted to the fallen state. When, however, the modern conception of Natural Law arose which differed from the Christian Natural Law of the fallen state and of its comparative harmony with reason, then certainly a new situation had been created. Lutheran thinkers found a solution by accepting the new Natural Law just as they had accepted the old, seconding the reforming activity of the State with a partially secularized religious enthusiasm: when, moreover, the political and social development, which had also been emancipated from this idea, passed into the modern conditions of the pure struggle for power and of competition, then the social theory of Lutheranism was in a position of great embarrassment; henceforth it could only preach its doctrine, with scarcely a hope of realizing it, since, unlike Catholicism and Calvinism, Lutheranism possessed no organ by which it could put its theories into practice apart from the State, and the modern State, for its part, no longer feels itself—as in early Lutheranism—to be the secular aspect of the organism of Christian Society. This was the beginning of the social impotence of Lutheranism, in so far as it has not adopted Calvinistic and modern ideas. In its actual primitive sense it only finds support among the Conservatives; and it therefore combines its dogmatic renewal with the political and social views of the Conservatives. Its hopes of a social transformation in accordance with Natural and Divine Law are pinned no longer to the Christian State, but to the Christian Party. As we can understand very well, this brings Conservative Lutheranism into touch with the other Christian Party— against which it had once fought so ardently—that of Catholicism, in a community of "Christian world-outlook", and of opposition to the modern militaristic and bureaucratic sovereign State, with its indifference towards the Church and religion in general.

At first, however, Luther did not exhort the Church to this passive attitude in social questions. At the moment when the seething ferment of German life came into touch with the reform of religion, and when it seemed as though this combination were about to lead to the goal of a Christian commonwealth, renewed in its political, social, and Church-life, Luther, in his appeal *To the Christian Nobility of the German Nation*, outlined a programme of ecclesiastical and socio-political reform for the whole Empire, in which he had interwoven all the suggestions which had come from the opposition and the reform parties with his new ecclesiastical ideal of a Church based upon the priesthood of all believers. In this treatise, however, Luther was carried farther than he intended by the impetus of the whole movement; and even here his theory was foreshadowed, to this extent, that he does not suggest that the spiritual authority should bring about the reforms and thus impose on the nation a new Christian law, but that the princely rulers alone are to bring about the reforms outside the Church, in the strength of reason and love for the pure Gospel.

"Reasonable Regents alongside of Holy Scripture"—these are the separate powers, which, however, each within its own sphere, work together for the reform "of the Body of Christ". But an enthusiastic optimism still conceived both tasks as essentially united and destined to achieve a common victory. After these preparations had been made a General Council would then finally take in hand the reform of Christendom as a whole. Nothing came of this idea of a collective reform, so in the times of ferment the Reformation movement turned to the particular local and communal authorities, which each in its own way undertook the work of "social betterment", and during this experimental period they were supported by Luther's "group-ideal". The municipalities and the magistrates, who already possessed considerable ecclesiastical rights, and a tradition of a kind of ethical "police" supervision, now issued new regulations, which made arrangements for the system of public worship, administration of the Poor Law, and the organization of the police force in the new Protestant sense. The Wittenberg Ordinance of January 1522, and the Leisnig Ordinance of 1523, were endeavours (which have often been imitated) to institute a Christian social order which was to use the money formerly locked up in endowments and benefices for the benefit of church and school, for poor relief in general, and also in time of famine, and which desired to leave the administration of these funds in the hands of elected stewards of Church revenues. These "ordinances" were based on similar police organizations in the towns, which had previously exercised similar powers, but they were coloured by the evangelical Protestant Church spirit, and this ecclesiastical flavour certainly entitled them to be described as Christian Socialism on local and communal lines. These "ordinances" were, however, Utopian and visionary, and they were never carried out in practice. Indeed, under the influence of the disillusionment of the Peasants' War, and with the possibility which had now arisen of instituting a new order on territorial and not on local lines, Luther turned away from the dubious "group-ideal" altogether, and henceforth, in accordance with his essential main idea, he handed over all political and social matters, as external secular affairs, entirely to the Government, to reason, and to the jurists, that triad which he praised as much as he scolded it! With his eyes open Luther now maintained that the Church ought to dominate solely the purely spiritual spheres of edification and instruction. Under the influence of the Gospel, he argued, a Christian Government should then be able to settle all social questions which appeared on the horizon of that day on its own authority. These social questions were mainly concerned with the problem of the support of those who, for some reason or another, were unable to earn their living within the social hierarchy, conceived as a system of "callings".

This might have been the end of all direct ecclesiastical social activity, and the beginning of a policy of purely secular social welfare and care of the poor. The territorial Princes, however, whose authority was still far from being centralized, and the communes (free cities) which were burdened with heavy tasks, undertook this vocation very imperfectly. Luther's helpers therefore intervened, above all Bugenhagen, who was a good organizer, and they took over the task of the care of the sick and the poor, which lay so near to the heart of the Church. This service was undertaken, however, no longer in the Utopian, Christian-Socialist spirit of the "Ordinances" of Wittenberg and Leisnig, but—and in this matter it was essentially the towns which were concerned—in a very matter-of-fact combination of communal-police activity and the ecclesiastical activity of pastoral work and of charity. In accordance with municipal organizations for the care of the poor in the towns, and under the stimulus of the reform of the Poor Law by Ludovico Vives, which started in Belgium, the means were created out of endowments, the poor were controlled by the co-operation of the spiritual and the secular authorities, vagabondage was restricted, hospitals were created, and a fixed system of book-keeping was introduced in which particular care was taken to avoid the confusion caused by mixing up these accounts with those which belonged to the administration of the Church and to education. In the end, however, these new "ordinances" for administering the funds from the "common chest" were not carried out permanently. This was partially due to the fact that the problems connected with the Poor Law had been underestimated, and partially also to their failure to centralize the endowment monies which they did control; another cause was the lack of voluntary officials who could serve in turn upon the board of administration; above all, however, the new religion itself was too much engrossed with the personal interior life, too much imbued with the idea that everyone ought to work, and too much alienated from the old ideal of charity, to succeed in creating the necessary new methods. Thus the Lutheran "Chests" (*Kasten* or funds) merely became meagre funds in support of the poor alongside of other similar institutions.

Thus, in this form also, ecclesiastical Socialism came to nothing, and the task of caring for the common weal was entrusted to the various governments, which were becoming more and more centralized, and were increasingly taking control of all the interests within their sphere; these governments, however, felt that the ecclesiastical arrangements for poor relief relieved them of responsibility, and they therefore did nothing on their side. But, still, the permanent principle had been finally formulated: that all secular and political affairs, and therefore also the question of social welfare, belong to the province of the Government, while the Church is concerned solely with the salvation of the soul and the interior life of personal piety.

Thus the Lutheran social programme merged into the social politics of patriarchal mercantilism. Then, when the State accepted the modern movement of thought, and moved away from a patriarchal Absolutism to an Absolutism of the Enlightenment, the whole system of Christian social effort slipped into the modern policy of social welfare, and Lutheranism lost all inner connection with, and all influence upon, the Government, which was certainly far from being a "Christian" government.

The more, however, that the social policy became purely secular, and the more clear it became that a purely class and vocational system does not enable everyone to gain their livelihood, but that it was always surrounded by a multitude of people who had become *déclassés*, and of people in distress, and especially when the more restless social movement of modern life brought bewilderment and confusion into many lives, Lutheranism was obliged to give up its attitude of simple trust in Providence and in the vocational system; and the Christian desires to express love which it did possess were again exercised in the form of voluntary philanthropy, in institutions, fellowships, clubs, and charities. Under the influence of Pietism, Lutheranism returned to the religious-social policy of charity, without the glorification of mendicancy, and at first without permitting this practice of charity to have any connection with the Church; in every other respect, however, this meant the resumption of the charity of Catholicism and of the Early Christian Church. This has been the position ever since, and, under English influences, during the ninetenth century, as the "Innere Mission" (Home Mission) movement, this Christian social service has developed and flourished in a quite remarkable way. Orthodox ecclesiastical Lutheranism has only taken part in this movement in a rather hesitating way, but it has to-day finally become fairly sympathetic to it as a whole. Strict Lutheranism, which was renewed at the time of the Restoration and which has since then been dominant, refused to entertain any further ideas of social reform. It has maintained the position which Stahl represented, i.e. that the social order should be entrusted to a Christian Government, whose duty it should be to ensure the maintenance of the class organization of callings with the restriction of the modern life movement. Wichern's attempt to go beyond the mere exercise of charity and to introduce a Christian social reform from the side of the Church, and in the grand manner to combine organically an ecclesiastical religious philanthropy with the social policy of the State, broke down because Lutheranism was unprepared, inwardly, for action of this kind, and also because his ideas were captured by the Conservative reactionary party. The transformation of the programme of Wichern by Stöcker only led to the demand for a greater independence and power for the Church, and thus to an imitation of modern Catholic social reform; otherwise, so far as the general social ideal was concerned, it was obliged to connect itself with Conservative and middle-class principles in the true Lutheran sense; its rejection by the Conservatives finally drove it back into very small groups.

Thus, down to the present time, the Lutheran Church has never advanced farther than the renewed ideal of charity; it has never made any effort to initiate a real social transformation at all. Most Lutherans simply repeat the old doctrine of the inwardness of the Church and of the duty of leaving all external matters of legislation and social welfare to the State. Others, like the Christian Socialists of the Naumann school, discard the principles of Lutheranism altogether, and feel forced to return to the general political, economic, and social foundations of present-day Society. Others, like those who represent the point of view of the Evangelical Social Congress, fully aware that the situation has entirely changed, discuss from differing points of view the possibility of striking out along new paths.

Wherever the earlier Lutheranism is still a real force—among the

Conservatives, that is to say—all social reform consists in breaking up the rationalistic, individualistic nature of modern Society, and in the revival of a society organized on aristocratic lines, bound together by class bonds, i.e., in the struggle against the Liberal world-outlook, and against the creations of Liberalism in the political, economic, and social sphere; alongside of this, then, the "Innere Mission" (Home Mission) may indeed exercise its charitable activity among the poor and the sick, but it must guard against any possibility of shattering the idea of authority. Within these limits the "Innere Mission" has certainly achieved splendid things, although the Christian-social element certainly predominates less within it than the propaganda and the evangelistic element.

The Lutheran Ethic and the General Situation

This completes the analysis of Lutheranism. Now, however, we have to answer the final question: to what extent are these social doctrines the reflection of existing political and social conditions? So far as the actual ideal is concerned which floated before the minds of Lutheran thinkers, we must give a directly negative reply to this question. The social doctrines of Lutheranism are, like the whole of Lutheran piety, a genuine branch of the whole Christian religion and ethic of love, which either rejects or is indifferent to the world, with its law, property, might, and force, and of that monotheism which proclaims that the religious aims of the personality united to God are the only true and lasting values of life, and from that derives the idea of the union of mankind in love, through the common exercise of these values. To a far greater extent than Catholicism, certainly, Protestantism has accepted the life of the world, and it is therefore similarly determined by the spirit of general social development, which forced itself upon the attention of the Church and found itself in a situation in which this was possible without any particular difficulty. In so doing, however, Protestantism has carefully preserved the dualism of the Christian ideal which arises out of this conception, and which, in contrast with Catholicism, it has both deepened and intensified. Since Protestantism supported the mediaeval ideal of a social hierarchy and the anti-capitalistic spirit, expressed in agrarian and middle-class ways of living, along with a patriarchalism based on authority and reverence, as the right way of reconciling both sides, it drew its conclusions from the ethical and religious ideal, and not from the circumstances which happened to prevail at the time. If we reflect upon Luther's idealistic plans, and remember his bitter complaints of the non-Christian character even of the new Protestant evangelical world, we receive far more the impression of a Christian Utopia than of the justification and glorification of existing conditions, and not without reason. One of the finest and most original Lutheran thinkers, J. V. Andreä, has described Luther's social ideal (in imitation of Sir Thomas More and Campanella) in a Utopia, called *Christianopolis*.

Whenever the social doctrines of Lutheranism are treated solely as the religious sanction of the existing situation, as often happens in orthodox Lutheranism, this always means that Lutheran thought has been weakened and despiritualized; the main impulse of the real Lutheran ethic in its mystics and spiritual thinkers, in its ethical reformers, and finally in the Pietists, has always reacted against this tendency with great vigour. By the very vigour of its protest, however, this opposition often lost its connection with the real leading ideas of Lutheranism, and landed in the other extreme of asceticism. The same applies to the exaltation of Luther's doctrine of the "calling", which is a favourite idea of writers of modern books on the subject, which they try to interpret as a certain religious consecration and sanction of modern civilization. It is not due to thoughtlessness, therefore, when the idea is suggested that modern civilization means essentially an anti-Catholic freedom from sacerdotalism and from monasticism, and that otherwise it is a conservative middle-class restriction or weakening of the modern life-movement.

The religious and ethical ideas of Lutheranism are not a glorification and intensification of definite class and power interests by means of a world outlook based upon those interests. This might perhaps apply to the peculiarly irrational idea of Natural Law which enabled Lutheranism to accept the existing conditions of authority, regarding the Law of Nature as though these conditions of authority, together with sin and inequality, were all part of the unchanging Divine Order, to which the soul (which remains inwardly free) gives itself up to labour and to endure. The reason for this lay, at least originally, and in Luther himself, not in any kind of class interest, but in the authoritative conservative temperament of Luther himself, and in his peculiarly penetrating conception of the nature of authority and power, as well as the essential inequality of the fundamental elements in all human social groupings. In this he is only perpetrating the patriarchal side of the scholastic Natural Law, while he discards the individualistic rationalistic elements. This, however, is the reason why Luther also called these elements directly unchristian and the product of sin, and he only recognized them as a Divine institution within the sphere of sinful reason, under the impression of their unalterable nature and their absolute necessity. He was only able to combine this idea of Natural Law with his own general Christian idea by inculcating the spirit of humility, trust in God, readiness to suffer, and the fact that man, owing to the taint

of Original Sin, deserves to be punished. When, later on, this idea of
Natural Law was used simply to justify existing conditions, and the chief
heirs of the Lutheran spirit at the present day, the Conservatives, developed this Natural Law into an aristocratic naturalism which is related to
Darwin's doctrine of selection and to Nietzsche's ethic of the Super-Man,
these are certainly applications of the idea in the interest of political and
social domination, in which they display their flagrant opposition to the
real Christian ideas and their "class" spirit. Further, this inconsistency is
not usually apparent to most people, since they conclude that the non-
Christian character of those principles is due to the situation created by
sin, and therefore they do not merely retain them in spite of their unchristian character, but they are convinced that they ought to use them,
as results of inequality and means of repression willed by God against the
individualistic atomistic evil. This theory also undoubtedly contains right
views about the "nature" of man, and it contains no less incontrovertible
ethical values in the ideas of obedience and of authority, just as in patriarchalism itself. Thus here also the ultimate cause is the old ideological
basis, which only nowadays is so visibly useful to "the sectional interests"
and is now associated with them to make some thoroughly impure combinations.

It is more difficult to answer the opposite question: What influence
has Lutheranism had upon social history? Here, from the very outset, we
must distinguish between the effects of its spiritual individualism, which
manifest themselves plainly in the spiritual and ethical development of
German culture right down to Kant and Goethe, and which has left
traces of its influence in the idea and development of family life, and in
the realm of political, social, and economic institutions. It is essentially
the latter with which we are here concerned.

The gist of the matter is this: in itself the late mediaeval tendency in
the development of the State and the general social classification was not
altered by Lutheranism. The only changes were the disappearance of the
priesthood, which was replaced by the Protestant ministry, as well as the
abolition of the supreme control by the Church, and the establishment of
the system of purely State control which took its place; the process of
secularization and the abolition of monasticism were also changes which
cut deeply into the social fabric, but they did not initiate new social developments. The social fabric was more profoundly affected by the rise
of a Humanistic educated class, which was encouraged by the didactic
character of the new religion, and its close connection with education; yet
this was rather an effect of Humanism combined with the Reform Movement than an effect produced by the religious spirit itself.

Its political influence was more central. This does not mean that Lutheranism developed a new idea of the State, or even created a new State; but, by its renunciation of ecclesiastical independence, by its deification of the Government and its loyal passivity, it provided a most favourable setting for the development of the territorial State, which was then engaged in the process of self-development. It smoothed the way for territorial absolutism; to the feudal lords of the manor it made easier the development of the manorial estate with its privileges and the growth of a new kind of serfdom, and it fostered the patriarchal attitude and the corporate class spirit.

In relation with foreign countries, however, the same Lutheran spirit hindered the action and expansion of the various States, and finally caused terrible defeats. Its only service to the actual modern State has been to encourage the spirit of absolutism; once that was supreme, however, it became strong enough to strike out on a modern line of its own, and it has thus gone far beyond the Lutheran principles of peace, protection and punishment based on Natural Law as well as the duty of the Government to promote Christian charity.

The influence of Lutheranism in the economic sphere has been equally indirect. Here its essential spirit is that of traditionalism and agrarian middle-class production, which, by means of corporate solidarity, excludes competition, as far as possible combining simplicity in one's requirements with simplicity of the conditions of production and consumption. Since it also abolished mendicancy, urged the masses to work, and by its individualism stimulated individuals, even on the non-religious side, and created a certain elasticity of mind by its system of education (which at first certainly only affected the middle classes), it has, in spite of everything, helped to develop economic life in a more vital way. Here, however, also the chief element in the whole process was the making of the secular authority independent, which, entrusted with social welfare and exalted to supreme power, introduced Western methods of production, and in so doing it profited by the fact that the Lutheran sections of the population were more inclined to work hard than the rest. Otherwise it was not for nothing that mercantilistic rulers introduced Calvinist or Pietist settlers wherever they wished to raise the level of trade or manufactures. The modern economic situation—even in the modest range which it had attained in Germany until the nineteenth century—has been created by the State, and is not due to the influence of Lutheranism. Lutheranism opposed the modern development of the State only one degree less ardently than Catholicism.

Finally, so far as its main social tendencies are concerned, and its theoretical conception of Society, Lutheranism has always represented the principle of patriarchalism and conservatism. This was caused in part by the fact that the fundamental religious temper of trust in God and distrust of human effort and industry, the relation of the sense of sin with suffering and endurance, in itself tended to foster a conservative spirit, and in part by the fact that the bases of the earlier social constitution, with its class organization and the greater simplicity of the relation to the Divine gifts of Nature, are firmly retained by Lutheranism as the presupposition of its ethical ideas. Thus Lutheranism is inclined to endure existing conditions humbly and patiently, even when they are bad, and to glorify them when they agree with those earlier ideals. If, speaking generally, the Protestant countries are the most progressive at the present time, we must not forget, on the other hand, that during the period when the Protestant churches were being formed the mother-lands of modern civilization—Italy, France, and Spain—were Catholic, and that their exhaustion has no connection with their Catholicism—that, thus, on the other hand, the Protestant countries too, and especially the Lutheran, cannot in any case ascribe their present position primarily to their religious bases, however important these may be in particular.

The passivity of Lutheranism involved the habit of falling back upon whatever power happens to be dominant at the time. When it was suggested that this attitude left Christians at the mercy of every rogue and brutal tyrant, Luther replied that the Government ought to see that this did not happen, and that if it failed to prevent it, then certainly the Christian must simply suffer for it. Thus everywhere Lutheranism came under the influence of the dominant authority. The yielding spirit of its wholly interior spirituality adapted itself to the dominant authority of the day. This meant, however, that the form Lutheranism took was controlled by the various forms of government with which it was connected. It had no theoretical tendency towards monarchism or absolutism at all; this theory was only an invention of the modern Conservatives. It was only because absolutism and the system of manorial estates arose in Central and North Germany that it there developed the loyal spirit which characterizes *Ostelbiertum*.[1] In the imperial towns it glorified aristocratic-republican rule. In Württemberg, where there was no corresponding nobility, although it held the ruling prince in all honour, it did not hinder bourgeois and peasant democratic ideas, but even fused itself with them. In the military national State of Sweden it justified the aggressive policy of Gustavus Adolfus, and in the class struggles in the Austrian territories

---

[1] Translator.—I.e. the Nationalist spirit, which is the distinctive feature of the landed aristocracy in the agricultural districts east of the Elbe.

it justified the rise of the Lutheran nobility; in Denmark and Norway a very firmly established peasant democracy is to-day united most closely with a sturdy Lutheranism, which is certainly tinged with Pietism; and in America the most orthodox Lutheranism one can imagine flourishes under the wing of democracy.

We must, however, admit that by its very nature Lutheranism adapts itself most easily to political conditions of a monarchical and aristocratic kind, and to an economic social situation which is predominantly agrarian and middle class. Hence it has found its strongest form of expression in the politics and world-outlook of the Prussian and German Conservatives, through whom to-day Lutheranism still helps to determine the destinies of the German people.

Social and Political Significance of Lutheranism

In the aggressive position which, after the eighteenth century had culminated in the French Revolution, the older spiritual forces again adopted towards the modern world, and in which they, with the union of ideological and practical politico-social powers, advanced victoriously against the new world, the restoration of Prussian-German Lutheranism was one of the most important events in social history. It united with the reactionary movement the monarchical ideas of agrarian patriarchalism, of the militaristic love of power; it gave an ideal to the political Restoration and its ethical support. For this reason, then, it in its turn was supported by the social and political forces of reaction, by all the means of power at their disposal. Finally, Lutheranism of this type hallowed the realistic sense of power, and the ethical virtues of obedience, reverence, and respect for authority, which are indispensable to Prussian militarism. Thus Christianity and a Conservative political attitude became identified with each other, as well as piety and love of power, purity of doctrine, and the glorification of war and the aristocratic standpoint. Thus all attempts at Church reform were suppressed along with the world of Liberal thought; the representatives of modern social and spiritual tendencies were forced into an attitude of strong hostility to the Church, and all whose sympathies were Christian and religious were enlisted on the Conservative side. As an essential element in the forces of the Restoration, Lutheranism played an important part in the political and military development of German Prussia which arose out of the forces of the Restoration; and it was thus in violent opposition to all those other elements which worked together to produce a new Germany, the democratic-union elements and modern social and economic movements. Along with the international Catholic Restoration policy which was akin to it, and yet so very different from it, and with which it is in contact, sometimes friendly, sometimes hostile—Lutheranism occupies the key position of the most difficult and pregnant problems affecting the life of Germany, and does its part towards widening the gulf between the forces which support the patriarchalism of the Restoration and those which support the cause of democracy and progress, a gulf in which all moderate attempts at reconciliation are drowned; the longing to bridge over this gulf in Germany with a Christian-Social programme was an idealistic and praiseworthy but fleeting and swiftly refuted dream.

For the great majority of orthodox Christians in Germany the traditions and the spiritual constitution of Lutheranism made any such reconciliation impossible; and on the other hand, the unrestrained hatred towards the Church which characterized all progressive and democratic elements belonging to that group of movements also made any kind of union impossible. Thus Lutheranism naturally does little towards building up a new social structure. In the main its efforts are confined to the philanthropic activity of the Home Mission Movement; otherwise its tendency is to alleviate but not to re-create. Wherever the Christian-Social ethic and social policy strikes out in another direction we may be sure that other influences are at work than those of genuine Lutheranism. As a rule these influences are due to Calvinism.

CALVIN

Although Protestantism failed to become the religion of the majority of Frenchmen, it produced in John Calvin (1509–1564) a Protestant leader whose influence became decisive in other countries and particularly in the English-speaking world. In 1534 Calvin was forced to leave France, and he went to Switzerland, where Protestantism had spread rapidly. With only a few short interruptions, he stayed in Switzerland for the rest of his life; he governed Geneva with an iron hand from 1536 to 1538, and again from 1541 to 1564, the year of his death. Unlike Luther, Calvin admitted—in exceptional cases only, to be sure—the right of resistance to tyrannical rulers, provided that resistance was in the hands of the magistrates and organized estates rather than lawless mobs, or in the hands of a secular savior selected by God to deliver the people from tyranny. In Holland Calvinism was allied with the national movement of liberation from Spain, and in the end it won over the majority of the nation. In England, Scotland, and the English colonies of North America, Calvinism for a long time shaped the social and economic thought and practices of the people struggling to develop self-government.

The impact of Calvinism on economic development, and in particular its relation to capitalism, is one of the main themes of R. H. Tawney's *Religion and the Rise of Capitalism* (1926). Tawney (1880–   ) is best known as an authority on medieval economic history and on the early modern period. He held the chair of economic history at the University of

London from 1931 to 1949, training a whole generation in developing a
hitherto neglected field of historical study. His book on *The Agrarian
Problem in the Sixteenth Century* (1912) is his most outstanding contribution to his chosen field of specialization. To the general public in
Britain and abroad, Tawney is best known for his contributions to socialist thought, above all his *Acquisitive Society* (1921) and *Equality* (1931).
Yet his *Religion and the Rise of Capitalism* is likely to remain his best-
known work, combining the literary brilliance of his speculative writings
with the masterly scholarship of his more erudite works.

Tawney on CALVIN

The most characteristic and influential form of Protestantism in the two
centuries following the Reformation is that which descends, by one path
or another, from the teaching of Calvin. Unlike the Lutheranism from
which it sprang, Calvinism, assuming different shapes in different countries, became an international movement, which brought, not peace, but
a sword, and the path of which was strewn with revolutions. Where
Lutheranism had been socially conservative, deferential to established
political authorities, the exponent of a personal, almost a quietistic, piety,
Calvinism was an active and radical force. It was a creed which sought,
not merely to purify the individual, but to reconstruct Church and State,
and to renew society by penetrating every department of life, public as
well as private, with the influence of religion.

Upon the immense political reactions of Calvinism, this is not the
place to enlarge. As a way of life and a theory of society, it possessed from
the beginning one characteristic which was both novel and important.
It assumed an economic organization which was relatively advanced,
and expounded its social ethics on the basis of it. In this respect the
teaching of the Puritan moralists who derive most directly from Calvin
is in marked contrast with that both of medieval theologians and of
Luther. The difference is not merely one of the conclusions reached,
but of the plane on which the discussion is conducted. The background,
not of most medieval theory, but also of Luther and his English contemporaries, is the traditional stratification of rural society. It is a natural,
rather than a money, economy, consisting of the petty dealings of peas-

[From R. H. Tawney, *Religion and the Rise of Capitalism* (Harcourt, Brace
and Company, Inc., 1926). By permission.]

ants and craftsmen in the small market town, where industry is carried
on for the subsistence of the household and the consumption of wealth
follows hard upon the production of it, and where commerce and finance
are occasional incidents, rather than the forces which keep the whole system in motion. When they criticize economic abuses, it is precisely
against departures from that natural state of things—against the enterprise, the greed of gain, the restless competition, which disturb the stability of the existing order with clamorous economic appetites—that their
criticism is directed.

These ideas were the traditional retort to the evils of unscrupulous
commercialism, and they left some trace on the writings of the Swiss
reformers. Zwingli, for example, who, in his outlook on society, stood
midway between Luther and Calvin, insists on the oft-repeated thesis that
private property originates in sin; warns the rich that they can hardly
enter the Kingdom of Heaven; denounces the Councils of Constance and
Basel—"assembled, forsooth, at the bidding of the Holy Ghost"—for showing indulgence to the mortgaging of land on the security of crops; and,
while emphasizing that interest must be paid when the State sanctions
it, condemns it in itself as contrary to the law of God. Of the attempts
made at Zürich and Geneva to repress extortion something is said below.
But these full-blooded denunciations of capitalism were not intended
by their authors to supply a rule of practical life, since it was the duty
of the individual to comply with the secular legislation by which interest was permitted, and already, when they were uttered, they had
ceased to represent the conclusion of the left wing of the Reformed
Churches.

For Calvin, and still more his later interpreters, began their voyage
lower down the stream. Unlike Luther, who saw economic life with the
eyes of a peasant and a mystic, they approached it as men of affairs,
disposed neither to idealize the patriarchal virtues of the peasant community, nor to regard with suspicion the mere fact of capitalist enterprise in commerce and finance. Like early Christianity and modern socialism, Calvinism was largely an urban movement; like them, in its
earlier days, it was carried from country to country partly by emigrant
traders and workmen; and its stronghold was precisely in those social
groups to which the traditional scheme of social ethics, with its treatment
of economic interests as a quite minor aspect of human affairs, must have
seemed irrelevant or artificial. As was to be expected in the exponents
of a faith which had its headquarters at Geneva, and later its most influential adherents in great business centers, like Antwerp with its industrial hinterland, London, and Amsterdam, its leaders addressed their

teaching, not of course exclusively, but none the less primarily, to the classes engaged in trade and industry, who formed the most modern and progressive elements in the life of the age.

In doing so they naturally started from a frank recognition of the necessity of capital, credit and banking, large-scale commerce and finance, and the other practical facts of business life. They thus broke with the tradition which, regarding a preoccupation with economic interests "beyond what is necessary for subsistence" as reprehensible, had stigmatized the middleman as a parasite and the usurer as a thief. They set the profits of trade and finance, which to the medieval writer, as to Luther, only with difficulty escaped censure as *turpe lucrum,* on the same level of respectability as the earnings of the laborer and the rents of the landlord. "What reason is there," wrote Calvin to a correspondent, "why the income from business should not be larger than that from land-owning? Whence do the merchant's profits come, except from his own diligence and industry?" [1] It was quite in accordance with the spirit of those words that Bucer, even while denouncing the frauds and avarice of merchants, should urge the English Government to undertake the development of the woollen industry on mercantilist lines.[2]

Since it is the environment of the industrial and commercial classes which is foremost in the thoughts of Calvin and his followers, they have to make terms with its practical necessities. It is not that they abandon the claim of religion to moralize economic life, but that the life which they are concerned to moralize is one in which the main features of a commercial civilization are taken for granted, and that it is for application to such conditions that their teaching is designed. Early Calvinism, as we shall see, has its own rule, and a rigorous rule, for the conduct of economic affairs. But it no longer suspects the whole world of economic motives as alien to the life of the spirit, or distrusts the capitalist as one who has necessarily grown rich on the misfortunes of his neighbor, or regards poverty as in itself meritorious, and it is perhaps the first systematic body of religious teaching which can be said to recognize and applaud the economic virtues. Its enemy is not the accumulation of riches, but their misuse for purposes of self-indulgence or ostentation. Its ideal is a society which seeks wealth with the sober gravity of men who are conscious at once of disciplining their own characters by patient labor, and of devoting themselves to a service acceptable to God.

[1] "Quid si igitur ex negociatione plus lucri percipi possit, quam ex fundi cuiusvis proventu? Unde vero mercatoris lucrum? Ex ipsius inquies, diligentia et industria" (quoted by Troeltsch, *Die Soziallehren der Christlichen Kirche,* p. 707).

[2] Bucer, *De Regno Christi.*

It is in the light of that change of social perspective that the doctrine of usury associated with the name of Calvin is to be interpreted. Its significance consisted, not in the phase which it marked in the technique of economic analysis, but in its admission to a new position of respectability of a powerful and growing body of social interests, which, however irrepressible in practice, had hitherto been regarded by religious theory as, at best, of dubious propriety, and, at worst, as frankly immoral. Strictly construed, the famous pronouncement strikes the modern reader rather by its rigor than by its indulgence. "Calvin," wrote an English divine a generation after his death, "deals with usurie as the apothecarie doth with poyson."[3] The apologetic was just, for neither his letter to Oecolampadius, nor his sermon on the same subject, reveal any excessive tolerance for the trade of the financier. That interest is lawful, provided that it does not exceed an official maximum, that, even when a maximum is fixed, loans must be made *gratis* to the poor, that the borrower must reap as much advantage as the lender, that excessive security must not be exacted, that what is venial as an occasional expedient is reprehensible when carried on as a regular occupation, that no man may snatch economic gain for himself to the injury of his neighbor—a condonation of usury protected by such embarrassing entanglements can have offered but tepid consolation to the devout moneylender.

Contemporaries interpreted Calvin to mean that the debtor might properly be asked to concede some small part of his profits to the creditor with whose capital they had been earned, but that the exaction of interest was wrong if it meant that "the creditor becomes rich by the sweat of the debtor, and the debtor does not reap the reward of his labor." There have been ages in which such doctrines would have been regarded as an attack on financial enterprise rather than as a defense of it. Nor were Calvin's specific contributions to the theory of usury strikingly original. As a hard-headed lawyer, he was free both from the incoherence and from the idealism of Luther, and his doctrine was probably regarded by himself merely as one additional step in the long series of developments through which ecclesiastical jurisprudence on the subject had already gone. In emphasizing the difference between the interest wrung from the necessities of the poor and the interest which a prosperous merchant could earn with borrowed capital, he had been anticipated by Major; in his sanction of a moderate rate on loans to the rich, his position was the same as that already assumed, though with some hesitation, by Melanchthon. The picture of Calvin, the organizer and disciplinarian, as the par-

[3] Roger Fenton, *A Treatise of Usurie*, 1612, p. 61.

ent of laxity in social ethics, is a legend. Like the author of another revolution in economic theory, he might have turned on his popularizers with
the protest: "I am not a Calvinist."

Legends are apt, however, to be as right in substance as they are wrong
in detail, and both its critics and its defenders were correct in regarding
Calvin's treatment of capital as a watershed. What he did was to change
the plane on which the discussion was conducted, by treating the ethics
of money-lending, not as a matter to be decided by an appeal to a special
body of doctrine on the subject of usury, but as a particular case of the
general problem of the social relations of a Christian community, which
must be solved in the light of existing circumstances. The significant
feature in his discussion of the subject is that he assumes credit to be a
normal and inevitable incident in the life of society. He therefore dismisses the oft-quoted passages from the Old Testament and the Fathers
as irrelevant, because designed for conditions which no longer exist, argues
that the payment of interest for capital is as reasonable as the payment of
rent for land, and throws on the conscience of the individual the obligation of seeing that it does not exceed the amount dictated by natural
justice and the golden rule. He makes, in short, a fresh start, argues that
what is permanent is, not the rule *"non foenerabis,"* but *"l'équité et la
droiture,"* and appeals from Christian tradition to commercial common
sense, which he is sanguine enough to hope will be Christian. On such a
view all extortion is to be avoided by Christians. But capital and credit
are indispensable; the financier is not a pariah, but a useful member of
society; and lending at interest, provided that the rate is reasonable and
that loans are made freely to the poor, is not *per se* more extortionate than
any other of the economic transactions without which human affairs cannot be carried on. That acceptance of the realities of commercial practice
as a starting-point was of momentous importance. It meant that Calvinism
and its offshoots took their stand on the side of the activities which were
to be most characteristic of the future, and insisted that it was not by renouncing them, but by untiring concentration on the task of using for the
glory of God the opportunities which they offered, that the Christian life
could and must be lived.

It was on this practical basis of urban industry and commercial enterprise that the structure of Calvinistic social ethics was erected. Upon their
theological background it would be audacious to enter. But even an ama-
teur may be pardoned, if he feels that there have been few systems in
which the practical conclusions flow by so inevitable a logic from the
theological premises. "God not only foresaw," Calvin wrote, "the fall of

the first man, . . . but also arranged all by the determination of his own will." [4] Certain individuals he chose as his elect, predestined to salvation from eternity by "his gratuitous mercy, totally irrespective of human merit"; the remainder have been consigned to eternal damnation, "by a just and irreprehensible, but incomprehensible, judgment." [5] Deliverance, in short, is the work, not of man himself, who can contribute nothing to it, but of an objective Power. Human effort, social institutions, the world of culture, are at best irrelevant to salvation, and at worst mischievous. They distract man from the true aim of his existence and encourage reliance upon broken reeds.

That aim is not personal salvation, but the glorification of God, to be sought, not by prayer only, but by action—the sanctification of the world by strife and labor. For Calvinism, with all its repudiation of personal merit, is intensely practical. Good works are not a way of attaining salvation, but they are indispensable as a proof that salvation has been attained. The central paradox of religious ethics—that only those are nerved with the courage needed to turn the world upside down, who are convinced that already, in a higher sense, it is disposed for the best by a Power of which they are the humble instruments—finds in it a special exemplification. For the Calvinist the world is ordained to show forth the majesty of God, and the duty of the Christian is to live for that end. His task is at once to discipline his individual life, and to create a sanctified society. The Church, the State, the community in which he lives, must not merely be a means of personal salvation, or minister to his temporal needs. It must be a "Kingdom of Christ," in which individual duties are performed by men conscious that they are "ever in their great Taskmaster's eye," and the whole fabric is preserved from corruption by a stringent and all-embracing discipline.

The impetus to reform or revolution springs in every age from the realization of the contrast between the external order of society and the moral standards recognized as valid by the conscience or reason of the individual. And naturally it is in periods of swift material progress, such as the sixteenth and eighteenth centuries, that such a contrast is most acutely felt. The men who made the Reformation had seen the Middle Ages close in the golden autumn which, amid all the corruption and tyranny of the time, still glows in the pictures of Nürnberg and Frankfurt drawn by Aeneas Silvius and in the woodcuts of Dürer. And already a new dawn of economic prosperity was unfolding. Its promise was splen-

---

[4] Calvin, *Institutes of the Christian Religion*, trans. by J. Allen, 1838, vol. ii, p. 147 (bk. iii, ch. xxiii, par. 7).

[5] *Ibid.*, vol. ii, pp. 128–9 (bk. iii, ch. xxi, par. 7).

did, but it had been accompanied by a cynical materialism which seemed a denial of all that had been meant by the Christian virtues, and which was the more horrifying because it was in the capital of the Christian Church that it reached its height. Shocked by the gulf between theory and practice, men turned this way and that to find some solution of the tension which racked them. The German reformers followed one road and preached a return to primitive simplicity. But who could obliterate the achievements of two centuries, or blot out the new worlds which science had revealed? The Humanists took another, which should lead to the gradual regeneration of mankind by the victory of reason over superstition and brutality and avarice. But who could wait for so distant a consummation? Might there not be a third? Was it not possible that, purified and disciplined, the very qualities which economic success demanded—thrift, diligence, sobriety, frugality—were themselves, after all, the foundation, at least, of the Christian virtues? Was it not conceivable that the gulf which yawned between a luxurious world and the life of the spirit could be bridged, not by eschewing material interests as the kingdom of darkness, but by dedicating them to the service of God?

It was that revolution in the traditional scale of ethical values which the Swiss reformers desired to achieve; it was that new type of Christian character that they labored to create. Not as part of any scheme of social reform, but as elements in a plan of moral regeneration, they seized on the aptitudes cultivated by the life of business and affairs, stamped on them a new sanctification, and used them as the warp of a society in which a more than Roman discipline should perpetuate a character the exact antithesis of that fostered by obedience to Rome. The Roman Church, it was held, through the example of its rulers, had encouraged luxury and ostentation; the members of the Reformed Church must be economical and modest. It had sanctioned the spurious charity of indiscriminate almsgiving; the true Christian must repress mendicancy and insist on the virtues of industry and thrift. It had allowed the faithful to believe that they could atone for a life of worldliness by the savorless formality of individual good works reduced to a commercial system, as though man could keep a profit and loss account with his Creator: the true Christian must organize his life as a whole for the service of his Master. It had rebuked the pursuit of gain as lower than the life of religion, even while it took bribes from those who pursued gain with success: the Christian must conduct his business with a high seriousness, as in itself a kind of religion.

Such teaching, whatever its theological merits or defects, was admirably designed to liberate economic energies, and to weld into a disciplined social force the rising *bourgeoisie*, conscious of the contrast between its own standards and those of a laxer world, proud of its vocation as the standardbearer of the economic virtues, and determined to vindicate an open road for its own way of life by the use of every weapon, including political revolution and war, because the issue which was at stake was not merely convenience or self-interest, but the will of God. Calvinism stood, in short, not only for a new doctrine of theology and ecclesiastical government, but for a new scale of moral values and a new ideal of social conduct. Its practical message, it might perhaps be said, was *la carrière ouverte* —not *aux talents*, but *au caractère*.

Once the world had been settled to their liking, the middle classes persuaded themselves that they were the convinced enemies of violence and the devotees of the principle of order. While their victories were still to win, they were everywhere the spear-head of revolution. It is not wholly fanciful to say that, on a narrower stage but with not less formidable weapons, Calvin did for the *bourgeoisie* of the sixteenth century what Marx did for the proletariat of the nineteenth, or that the doctrine of predestination satisfied the same hunger for an assurance that the forces of the universe are on the side of the elect as was to be assuaged in a different age by the theory of historical materialism. He set their virtues at their best in sharp antithesis with the vices of the established order at its worst, taught them to feel that they were a chosen people, made them conscious of their great destiny in the Providential plan and resolute to realize it. The new law was graven on tablets of flesh; it not merely rehearsed a lesson, but fashioned a soul. Compared with the quarrelsome, self-indulgent nobility of most European countries, or with the extravagant and half-bankrupt monarchies, the middle classes, in whom Calvinism took root most deeply, were a race of iron. It was not surprising that they made several revolutions, and imprinted their conceptions of political and social expediency on the public life of half a dozen different States in the Old World and in the New.

The two main elements in this teaching were the insistence on personal responsibility, discipline and asceticism, and the call to fashion for the Christian character an objective embodiment in social institutions. Though logically connected, they were often in practical discord. The influence of Calvinism was not simple, but complex, and extended far beyond the circle of Churches which could properly be called Calvinist. Calvinist theology was accepted where Calvinist discipline was repudiated. The bitter struggle between Presbyterians and Independents in England did not prevent men, to whom the whole idea of religious uniformity was fundamentally abhorrent, from drawing inspiration from the conception of a visible Christian society, in which, as one of them said, the Scripture was "really and materially to be fulfilled." [6] Both an intense individualism and a rigorous Christian Socialism could be deduced from Calvin's doctrine. Which of them predominated depended on differences of political environment and of social class. It depended, above all, on the question whether Calvinists were, as at Geneva and in Scotland, a majority, who could stamp their ideals on the social order, or, as in England, a minority, living on the defensive beneath the suspicious eyes of a hostile Government.

In the version of Calvinism which found favor with the English upper classes in the seventeenth century, individualism in social affairs was, on the whole, the prevalent philosophy. It was only the fanatic and the agitator who drew inspiration from the vision of a New Jerusalem descending on England's green and pleasant land, and the troopers of Fairfax soon taught them reason. But, if the theology of Puritanism was that of Calvin, its conception of society, diluted by the practical necessities of a commercial age, and softened to suit the conventions of a territorial aristocracy, was poles apart from that of the master who founded a discipline, compared with which that of Laud, as Laud himself dryly observed,[7] was a thing of shreds and patches. As both the teaching of Calvin himself, and the practice of some Calvinist communities, suggest, the social ethics of the heroic age of Calvinism savored more of a collectivist dictatorship than of individualism. The expression of a revolt against the medieval ecclesiastical system, it stood itself, where circumstances favored it, for a discipline far more stringent and comprehensive than that of the Middle Ages. If, as some historians have argued, the philosophy of *laissez faire* emerged as a result of the spread of Calvinism among the middle classes, it did so, like tolerance, by a route which was indirect. It was accepted, less because it was esteemed for its own sake, than as a compromise forced upon Calvinism at a comparatively late stage in its history, as a result of its modification by the pressure of commercial interests, or of a balance of power between conflicting authorities.

The spirit of the system is suggested by its treatment of the burning question of Pauperism. The reform of traditional methods of poor relief was in the air—Vives had written his celebrated book in 1526 [8]—and, prompted both by Humanists and by men of religion, the secular authorities all over Europe were beginning to bestir themselves to cope with

---

[6] Gerrard Winstanley, *A New-Yeer's Gift for the Parliament and Armie*, 1650 (Thomason Tracts, Brit. Mus., E. 587 [6], p. 42).

[7] *The Works of William Laud, D.D.*, ed. Wm. Scott, vol. vi, pt. i, 1857, p. 213.

[8] *De Subventione Pauperum.*

what was, at best, a menace to social order, and, at worst, a moral scandal. The question was naturally one which appealed strongly to the ethical spirit of the Reformation. The characteristic of the Swiss reformers, who were much concerned with it, was that they saw the situation not, like the statesmen, as a problem of police, nor, like the more intelligent Humanists, as a problem of social organization, but as a question of character. Calvin quoted with approval the words of St. Paul, "If a man will not work, neither shall he eat," condemned indiscriminate alms-giving as vehemently as any Utilitarian, and urged that the ecclesiastical authorities should regularly visit every family to ascertain whether its members were idle, or drunken, or otherwise undesirable.[9] Oecolampadius wrote two tracts on the relief of the poor.[10] Bullinger lamented the army of beggars produced by monastic charity, and secured part of the emoluments of a dissolved abbey for the maintenance of a school for the assistance of the destitute.[11] In the plan for the reorganization of poor relief at Zürich, which was drafted by Zwingli in 1525, all mendicancy was strictly forbidden; travellers were to be relieved on condition that they left the town next day; provision was to be made for the sick and aged in special institutions; no inhabitant was to be entitled to relief who wore ornaments or luxurious clothes, who failed to attend church, or who played cards or was otherwise disreputable. The basis of his whole scheme was the duty of industry and the danger of relaxing the incentive to work. "With labor," he wrote, "will no man now support himself. . . . And yet labor is a thing so good and godlike . . . that makes the body hale and strong and cures the sicknesses produced by idleness. . . . In the things of this life, the laborer is most like to God." [12]

In the assault on pauperism, moral and economic motives were not distinguished. The idleness of the mendicant was both a sin against God and a social evil; the enterprise of the thriving tradesman was at once a Christian virtue and a benefit to the community. The same combination

[9] "Quod ad maiores natu spectat, a nobis quotannis repetitur in spectio cuiusque familiae. Distribuimus inter nos urbis regiones, ut ordine singulas decurias excutere liceat. Illic novi incolae examinantur. Qui semel recepti sunt, omittuntur; nisi quod requiritur sitne domus pacata et recte composita, num lites cum vicinis, num qua ebrietas, num pigri sint et ignari ad conciones frequentendas" (quoted by H. Wiskemann, *Darstellung der in Deutschland zur Zeit der Refor-* *mation herrschenden nationaloekonomischen Ansichten*, 1861, p. 80 n.).

[10] *De non habendo Pauperum Delectu* (1523), and *De Erogatione Eleemosynarum* (1524). See K. R. Hagenbach, *Johann Oekolampad und Oswald Myconius, die Reformatoren Basels*, 1859, p. 46.

[11] Carl Pestalozzi, *Henrich Bullinger, Leben und ausgewählte Schriften*, 1858, pp. 50–1, 122–5, 340–2.

[12] Wiskemann, *op. cit.*, pp. 70–4.

of religious zeal and practical shrewdness prompted the attacks on gambling, swearing, excess in apparel and self-indulgence in eating and drinking. The essence of the system was not preaching or propaganda, though it was prolific of both, but the attempt to crystallize a moral ideal in the daily life of a visible society, which should be at once a Church and a State. Having overthrown monasticism, its aim was to turn the secular world into a gigantic monastery, and at Geneva, for a short time, it almost succeeded. "In other places," wrote Knox of that devoted city, "I confess Christ to be duly preached, but manners and religion so sincerely reformed I have not yet seen in any place besides." [13] Manners and morals were regulated, because it is through the *minutiae* of conduct that the enemy of mankind finds his way to the soul; the traitors to the Kingdom might be revealed by pointed shoes or golden ear-rings, as in 1793 those guilty of another kind of *incivisme* were betrayed by their knee-breeches. Regulation meant legislation, and, still more, administration. The word in which both were summarized was Discipline.

Discipline Calvin himself described as the nerves of religion, [14] and the common observation that he assigned to it the same primacy as Luther had given to faith is just. As organized in the Calvinist Churches, it was designed primarily to safeguard the sacrament and to enforce a censorship of morals, and thus differed in scope and purpose from the canon law of the Church of Rome, as the rulers of a private society may differ from the code of a State. Its establishment at Geneva, in the form which it assumed in the last half of the sixteenth century, was the result of nearly twenty years of struggle between the Council of the city and the Consistory, composed of ministers and laymen. It was only in 1555 that the latter finally vindicated its right to excommunicate, and only in the edition of the *Institutes* which appeared in 1559 that a scheme of church organization and discipline was set out. But, while the answer to the question of the constitution of the authority by whom discipline was to be exercised depended on political conditions, and thus differed in different places and periods, the necessity of enforcing a rule of life, which was the practical aspect of discipline, was from the start of the very essence of Calvinism. Its importance was the theme of a characteristic letter addressed by Calvin to Somerset in October 1548, the moment of social convulsion for which Bucer wrote his book, *De Regno Christi*. The Protector is reminded that it is not from lack of preaching, but from failure to enforce compliance with it, that the troubles of England have sprung. Though crimes of violence are punished, the licentious are spared, and the licentious have no

---

[13] Quoted by Preserved Smith, *The Age of the Reformation*, 1921, p. 174. [14] Calvin, *Inst.*, bk. iv, ch. xii, par. 1.

part in the Kingdom of God. He is urged to make sure that "les hommes soient tenus en bonne et honneste discipline," and to be careful "que ceulx qui oyent la doctrine de l'Evangile s'approuvent estre Chrestiens par sainctité de vie." [15]

"Prove themselves Christians by holiness of life"—the words might be taken as the motto of the Swiss reformers, and their projects of social reconstruction are a commentary on the sense in which "holiness of life" was understood. It was in that spirit that Zwingli took the initiative in forming at Zürich a board of moral discipline, to be composed of the clergy, the magistrates and two elders; emphasized the importance of excommunicating offenders against Christian morals; and drew up a list of sins to be punished by excommunication, which included, in addition to murder and theft, unchastity, perjury and avarice, "especially as it discovers itself in usury and fraud." [16] It was in that spirit that Calvin composed in the *Institutes* a Protestant *Summa* and manual of moral casuistry, in which the lightest action should be brought under the iron control of a universal rule. It was in that spirit that he drafted the heads of a comprehensive scheme of municipal government, covering the whole range of civic administration, from the regulations to be made for markets, crafts, buildings and fairs to the control of prices, interest and rents.[17] It was in that spirit that he made Geneva a city of glass, in which every household lived its life under the supervision of a spiritual police, and that for a generation Consistory and Council worked hand in hand, the former excommunicating drunkards, dancers and contemners of religion, the latter punishing the dissolute with fines and imprisonment and the heretic with death. "Having considered," ran the preamble to the ordinances of 1576, which mark the maturity of the Genevese Church, "that it is a thing worthy of commendation above all others, that the doctrine of the Holy Gospel of our Lord Jesus Christ shall be preserved in its purity, and the Christian Church duly maintained by good government and policy, and also that youth in the future be well and faithfully instructed, and the Hospital well ordered for the support of the poor: Which things can only be if there be established a certain rule and order of living, by which each man may be able to understand the duties of his position. . . ." [18]

[15] Printed in Paul Henry, *Das Leben Johann Calvins*, vol. ii, 1838, *Appx.*, pp. 26–41.

[16] R. Christoffel, *Zwingli, or the Rise of the Reformation in Switzerland*, trans. by John Cochran, 1858, pp. 159–60.

[17] Printed in Paul Henry, *op. cit.*, vol. ii, *Appx.*, pp. 23–5.

[18] E. Choisy, *L'Etat Chrétien Calviniste à Genève au temps de Théodore de Bèze*, 1902, p. 145. I should like to make acknowledgments to this excellent book for most of the matter contained in the following paragraphs.

The object of it all was so simple. "Each man to understand the duties of his position"—what could be more desirable, at Geneva or elsewhere? It is sad to reflect that the attainment of so laudable an end involved the systematic use of torture, the beheading of a child for striking its parents, and the burning of a hundred and fifty heretics in sixty years.[19] *Tantum religio potuit suadere malorum.*

Torturing and burning were practised elsewhere by Governments which affected no excessive zeal for righteousness. The characteristic which was distinctive of Geneva—"the most perfect school of Christ that ever was on earth since the days of the Apostles"[20]—was not its merciless intolerance, for no one yet dreamed that tolerance was possible. It was the attempt to make the law of God prevail even in those matters of pecuniary gain and loss which mankind, to judge by its history, is disposed to regard more seriously than wounds and deaths. "No member [of the Christian body]," wrote Calvin in his *Institutes*, "holds his gifts to himself, or for his private use, but shares them among his fellow members, nor does he derive benefit save from those things which proceed from the common profit of the body as a whole. Thus the pious man owes to his brethren all that it is in his power to give."[21] It was natural that so remorseless an attempt to claim the totality of human interests for religion should not hesitate to engage even the economic appetites, before which the Churches of a later generation were to lower their arms. If Calvinism welcomed the world of business to its fold with an eagerness unknown before, it did so in the spirit of a conqueror organizing a new province, not of a suppliant arranging a compromise with a still powerful foe. A system of morals and a code of law lay ready to its hand in the Old Testament. Samuel and Agag, King of the Amalekites, Jonah and Nineveh, Ahab and Naboth, Elijah and the prophets of Baal, Micaiah the son of Imlah, the only true prophet of the Lord, and Jeroboam the son of Nebat, who made Israel to sin, worked on the tense imagination of the Calvinist as did Brutus and Cassius on the men of 1793. The first half-century of the Reformed Church at Geneva saw a prolonged effort to organize an economic order worthy of the Kingdom of Christ, in which the ministers played the part of Old Testament prophets to an Israel not wholly weaned from the fleshpots of Egypt.

---

[19] Paul Henry, *op. cit.*, pp. 70–75. Other examples are given by Preserved Smith, *op. cit.*, pp. 170–4, and by F. W. Kampschulte, *Johann Calvin, seine Kirche und sein Staat in Genf*, 1869. Statistical estimates of the bloodthirstiness of Calvin's régime vary; Smith (p. 171) states that in Geneva, a town of 16,000 inhabitants, 58 persons were executed and 76 banished in the years 1542–6.

[20] Knox, quoted by Preserved Smith, *op. cit.*, p. 174.

[21] Calvin, *Inst.*, bk. iii, ch. vii, par. 5.

Apart from its qualified indulgence to interest, Calvinism made few innovations in the details of social policy, and the contents of the program were thoroughly medieval. The novelty consisted in the religious zeal which was thrown into its application. The organ of administration before which offenders were brought was the Consistory, a mixed body of laymen and ministers. It censures harsh creditors, punishes usurers, engrossers and monopolists, reprimands or fines the merchant who defrauds his clients, the clothmaker whose stuff is an inch too narrow, the dealer who provides short measure of coal, the butcher who sells meat above the rates fixed by authority, the tailor who charges strangers excessive prices, the surgeon who demands an excessive fee for an operation.[22] In the Consistory the ministers appear to have carried all before them, and they are constantly pressing for greater stringency. From the election of Beza in place of Calvin in 1564 to his death in 1605, hardly a year passes without a new demand for legislation from the clergy, a new censure on economic unrighteousness, a new protest against one form or another of the ancient sin of avarice. At one moment, it is excessive indulgence to debtors which rouses their indignation; at another, the advance of prices and rents caused by the influx of distressed brethren from the persecutions in France; at a third, the multiplication of taverns and the excessive charges demanded by the sellers of wine. Throughout there is a prolonged warfare against the twin evils of extortionate interest and extortionate prices.

Credit was an issue of moment at Geneva, not merely for the same reasons which made it a burning question everywhere to the small producer of the sixteenth century, but because, especially after the ruin of Lyons in the French wars of religion, the city was a financial center of some importance. It might be involved in war at any moment. In order to secure command of the necessary funds, it had borrowed heavily from Basle and Berne, and the Council used the capital to do exchange business and make advances, the rate of interest being fixed at 10, and later at 12, per cent. To the establishment of a bank the ministers, who had been consulted, agreed; against the profitable business of advancing money at high rates of interest to private persons they protested, especially when the loans were made to spendthrifts who used them to ruin themselves. When, ten years later, in 1580, the Council approved the project advanced by some company promoters of establishing a second bank in the city, the ministers led the opposition to it, pointed to the danger of covetousness as revealed by the moral corruption of financial cities such as Paris, Venice and Lyons, and succeeded in getting the proposal quashed. Naturally, however, the commoner issue was a more simple one. The capitalist who

[22] Choisy, *op. cit.*, pp. 442-3.

borrowed in order to invest and make a profit could take care of himself, and the ministers explained that they had no objection to those "qui baillent leur argent aux marchands pour emploier en marchandise." The crucial issue was that of the money-lender who makes advances "simplement à un qui aura besoin," and who thereby exploits the necessities of his poorer neighbors.[23]

Against monsters of this kind the ministers rage without ceasing. They denounce them from the pulpit in the name of the New Testament, in language drawn principally from the less temperate portions of the Old, as *larrons, brigands, loups et tigres*, who ought to be led out of the city and stoned to death. "The poor cry and the rich pocket their gains: but what they are heaping up for themselves is the wrath of God. . . . One has cried in the market-place, 'curse on those who bring us dearth.' . . . The Lord has heard that cry . . . and yet we are asking the cause of the pestilence! . . . A cut-purse shall be punished, but the Lord declares by his prophet Amos . . . 'Famine is come upon my people of Israel, O ye who devour the poor.' The threats there uttered have been executed against his people." [24] They demand that for his second offense the usurer shall be excommunicated, or that, if such a punishment be thought too severe, he shall at least be required to testify his repentance publicly in church, before being admitted to the sacrament. They remind their fellow-citizens of the fate of Tyre and Sidon, and, momentarily despairing of controlling the money-lender directly, they propose to deprive him of his victims by removing the causes which create them. *Pour tarir les ruisseaux il faut escouper la source.* Men borrow because of "idleness, foolish extravagance, foolish sins, and law suits." Let censors be established at Geneva, as in Republican Rome, to inquire, among rich as well as among poor, how each household earns its livelihood, to see that all children of ten to twelve are taught some useful trade, to put down taverns and litigation, and to "bridle the insatiable avarice of those who are such wretches that they seek to enrich themselves by the necessities of their poor neighbors." [25]

The Venerable Company advanced their program, but they were not sanguine that it would be carried out, and they concluded it by expressing to the City Fathers the pious hope, not wholly free from irony, that "none of your honorable fellowship may be found spotted with such vices." Their apprehensions were justified. The Council of Geneva endured many things at the hands of its preachers, till, on the death of Beza, it brought them to heel. But there were limits to its patience, and it was in the field of business ethics that they were most quickly reached. It did not venture to question the right of the clergy to be heard on matters of commerce

[23] *Ibid.*, pp. 35–37.   [24] *Ibid.*, pp. 189, 117–19.   [25] *Ibid.*, pp. 935, 165–7.

and finance. The pulpit was press and platform in one; ministers had the public behind them, and, conscious of their power, would in the last resort compel submission by threatening to resign *en masse*. Profuse in expressions of sympathy, its strategy was to let the cannon balls of Christian Socialism spend themselves on the yielding down of official procrastination, and its first reply was normally *qu'on y pense un peu*. To the clergy its inactivity was a new proof of complicity with Mammon, and they did not hesitate to declare their indignation from the pulpit. In 1574 Beza preached a sermon in which he accused members of the Council of having intelligence with speculators who had made a corner in wheat. Throughout 1577 the ministers were reproaching the Council with laxity in administration, and they finally denounced it as the real author of the rise in the prices of bread and wine. In 1579 they addressed to it a memorandum, setting out a new scheme of moral discipline and social reform.

The prosperous *bourgeoisie* who governed Geneva had no objection to discouraging extravagance in dress, or to exhorting the public to attend sermons and to send their children to catechism. But they heard denunciations of covetousness without enthusiasm, and on two matters they were obdurate. They refused to check, as the ministers concerned to lower prices had demanded, the export of wine, on the ground that it was needed in order to purchase imports of wheat; and, as was natural in a body of well-to-do creditors, they would make no concession to the complaint that debtors were subjected to a "double usury," since they were compelled to repay loans in an appreciating currency. Money fell as well as rose, they replied, and even the late M. Calvin, by whom the ordinance now criticized had been approved, had never pushed his scruples to such lengths. Naturally, the ministers were indignant at these evasions. They informed the Council that large sums were being spent by speculators in holding up supplies of corn, and launched a campaign of sermons against avarice, with appropriate topical illustrations. Equally naturally, the Council retorted by accusing Beza of stirring up class hatred against the rich.[26]

The situation was aggravated by an individual scandal. One of the magistrates, who regarded Beza's remarks as a personal reflection, was rash enough to demand to be heard before the Council, with the result that he was found guilty, condemned to pay a fine, and compelled to forfeit fifty crowns which he had lent at 10 per cent. interest. Evidently, when matters were pushed to such lengths as this, no one, however respectable, could feel sure that he was safe. The Council and the ministers had already had words over the sphere of their respective functions, and were to fall out a year or two later over the administration of the local

[26] *Ibid.*, pp. 119–21.

hospital. On this occasion the Council complained that the clergy were interfering with the magistrates' duties, and implied politely that they would be well advised to mind their own business.

So monstrous a suggestion—as though there were any human activity which was not the business of the Church!—evoked a counter-manifesto on the part of the ministers, in which the full doctrine of the earthly Jerusalem was set forth in all its majesty. They declined to express regret for having cited before the Consistory those who sold corn at extortionate prices, and for refusing the sacrament to one of them. Did not Solomon say, "Cursed is who keeps his corn in time of scarcity"? To the charge of intemperate language Chauvet replied that the Council had better begin by burning the books of the Prophets, for he had done no more than follow the example set by Hosea. "If we should be silent," said Beza, "what would the people say? That they are dumb dogs. . . . As to the question of causing scandals, for the last two years there has been unceasing talk of usury, and, for all that, no more than three or four usurers have been punished. . . . It is notorious everywhere that the city is full of usurers, and that the ordinary rate is 10 per cent. or more." [27] The magistrates renewed their remonstrances. They had seen without a shudder an adulterer condemned to be hanged, and had mercifully commuted his sentence to scourging through the town, followed by ten years' imprisonment in chains.[28] But at the godly proposal to make capitalists die the death of Achan their humanity blenched. Besides, the punishment was not only cruel, but dangerous. In Geneva, "most men are debtors." If they are allowed to taste blood, who can say where their fury will end? Yet, such is the power of the spoken word, the magistrates did not venture on a blunt refusal, but gave scripture for scripture. They informed the ministers that they proposed to follow the example of David, who, when rebuked by Nathan, confessed his fault. Whether the ministers replied in the language of Nathan, we are not informed.

Recent political theory has been prolific in criticisms of the omnicompetent State. The principle on which the collectivism of Geneva rested may be described as that of the omnicompetent Church.[29] The religious

[27] *Ibid.*, pp. 189–94.

[28] Paul Henry, *op. cit.*, vol. ii, p. 70 n.

[29] See the description of the Church given in Calvin, *Inst.*, bk. iv, ch. i, par. 4: "Quia nunc de ecclesia visibili disserere propositum est discamus vel matris elogio, quam utilis sit nobis eius cognitio, immo necessaria, quando non alius est in vitam ingressus nisi nos ipsa concipiat in utero, nisi pariat, nisi nos alat suis uberibus, denique sub custodia et gubernatione sua nos tueatur, donec excuti carne mortali, similes erimus angelis. Neque enim patitur nostra infirmitas a schola nos dimitti, donec toto vitae cursu discipuli fuerimus. Adde quod extra eius gremium nulla est esperanda peccatorum remissio nec ulla salus."

community formed a closely organized society, which, while using the secular authorities as police officers to enforce its mandates, not only instructed them as to the policy to be pursued, but was itself a kind of State, prescribing by its own legislation the standard of conduct to be observed by its members, putting down offenses against public order and public morals, providing for the education of youth and for the relief of the poor. The peculiar relations between the ecclesiastical and secular authorities, which for a short time made the system possible at Geneva, could not exist to the same degree when Calvinism was the creed, not of a single city, but of a minority in a national State organized on principles quite different from its own. Unless the State itself were captured, rebellion, civil war or the abandonment of the pretension to control society was the inevitable consequence. But the last result was long delayed. In the sixteenth century, whatever the political conditions, the claim of the Calvinist Churches is everywhere to exercise a collective responsibility for the moral conduct of their members in all the various relations of life, and to do so, not least, in the sphere of economic transactions, which offer peculiarly insidious temptations to a lapse into immorality.

The mantle of Calvin's system fell earliest upon the Reformed Churches of France. At their first Synod, held in 1559 at Paris, where a scheme of discipline was adopted, certain difficult matters of economic casuistry were discussed, and similar questions continued to receive attention at subsequent Synods for the next half-century, until, as the historian of French Calvinism remarks, "they began to lax the reins, yielding too much to the iniquity of the time." [30] Once it is admitted that membership of the Church involves compliance with a standard of economic morality which the Church must enforce, the problems of interpretation which arise are innumerable, and the religious community finds itself committed to developing something like a system of case law, by the application of its general principles to a succession of varying situations. The elaboration of such a system was undertaken; but it was limited in the sixteenth century both by the comparative simplicity of the economic structure, and by the fact that the Synods, except at Geneva, being concerned not to reform society, but merely to repress the grosser kinds of scandal, dealt only with matters on which specific guidance was demanded by the Churches.

Even so, however, the riddles to be solved were not a few. What is to be the attitude of the Churches towards those who have grown rich on ill-

---

[30] John Quick, *Synodicon in Gallia Reformata: Or the Arts, Decisions, Decrees and Canons of those famous Na-* *tional Councils of the Reformed Churches in France,* 1692, vol. i, p. 99.

gotten wealth? May pirates and fraudulent tradesmen be admitted to the Lord's Supper? May the brethren trade with such persons, or do they share their sin if they buy their goods? The law of the State allows moderate interest: what is to be the attitude of the Church? What is to be done to prevent craftsmen cheating the consumer with shoddy wares, and tradesmen oppressing him with extortionate profits? Are lotteries permissible? Is it legitimate to invest at interest monies bequeathed for the benefit of the poor? The answers which the French Synods made to such questions show the persistence of the idea that the transactions of business are the province of the Church, combined with a natural desire to avoid an impracticable rigor. All persons who have wrung wealth unjustly from others must make restitution before they be admitted to communion, but their goods may be bought by the faithful, provided that the sale is public and approved by the civil authorities. Makers of fraudulent wares are to be censured, and tradesmen are to seek only "indifferent gain." On the question of usury, the same division of opinion is visible in the French Reformed Church as existed at the same time in England and Holland, and Calvin's advice on the subject was requested. The stricter school would not hear of confining the prohibition of usury to "excessive and scandalous" exactions, or of raising money for the poor by interest on capital. In France, however, as elsewhere, the day for these heroic rigors had passed, and the common-sense view prevailed. The brethren were required to demand no more than the law allowed and than was consistent with charity. Within these limits interest was not to be condemned.[31]

Of the treatment of questions of this order by English Puritanism something is said in a subsequent chapter. In Scotland the views of the reformers as to economic ethics did not differ in substance from those of the Church before the Reformation, and the Scottish Book of Discipline denounced covetousness with the same vehemence as did the "accursed Popery" which it had overthrown. Gentlemen are exhorted to be content with their rents, and the Churches are required to make provision for the poor. "Oppression of the poor by exactions," it is declared, "[and] deceiving of them in buying or selling by wrong mete or measure . . . do properly appertain to the Church of God, to punish the same as God's word commandeth."[32] The interpretation given to these offenses is shown by

[31] *Ibid.*, vol. i, p. 9 (pirates and fraudulent tradesmen), pp. 25, 34, 38, 79, 149 (interest and usury), p. 70 (false merchandise and selling of stretched cloth), p. 9 (reasonable profits), pp. 162, 204 (investment of money for the benefit of the poor), pp. 194, 213 (lotteries).

[32] *The Buke of Discipline*, in *Works of John Knox*, ed. D. Laing, vol. ii, 1848, p. 227.

the punishment of a usurer and of a defaulting debtor before the Kirk Sessions of St. Andrews.[33] The relief of the poor was in 1579 made the statutory duty of ecclesiastical authorities in Scotland, seven years after it had in England been finally transferred to the State. The arrangement under which in rural districts it reposed down to 1846 on the shoulders of ministers, elders and deacons, was a survival from an age in which the real State in Scotland had been represented, not by Parliament or Council, but by the Church of Knox.

Of English-speaking communities, that in which the social discipline of the Calvinist Church-State was carried to the furthest extreme was the Puritan theocracy of New England. Its practice had more affinity with the iron rule of Calvin's Geneva than with the individualistic tendencies of contemporary English Puritanism. In that happy, bishopless Eden, where men desired only to worship God "according to the simplicitie of the gospel and to be ruled by the laws of God's word," [34] not only were "tobacco and immodest fashions and costly apparel," and "that vain custom of drinking to one another," forbidden to true professors, but the Fathers adopted towards that "notorious evil . . . whereby most men walked in all their commerce—to buy as cheap and sell as dear as they can," [35] an attitude which possibly would not be wholly congenial to their more businesslike descendants. At an early date in the history of Massachusetts a minister had called attention to the recrudescence of the old Adam—"profit being the chief aim and not the propagation of religion"— and Governor Bradford, observing uneasily how men grew "in their outward estates," remarked that the increase in material prosperity "will be the ruin of New England, at least of the Churches of God there." [36] Sometimes Providence smote the exploiter. The immigrant who organized the first American Trust—he owned the only milch cow on board and sold the milk at 2d. a quart "being after at a sermon wherein oppression was complained of . . . fell distracted." [37] Those who escaped the judgment of Heaven had to face the civil authorities and the Church, which, in the infancy of the colony, were the same thing.

Naturally the authorities regulated prices, limited the rate of interest, fixed a maximum wage, and whipped incorrigible idlers; for these things

---

[33] Scottish History Soc., *St. Andrews Kirk Session Register*, ed. D. H. Fleming, 1889–90, vol. i, p. 309; vol. ii, p. 822.

[34] W. B. Weeden, *Economic and Social History of New England*, 1890, vol. i, p. 11. The words are Governor Bradford's.

[35] *Winthrop's Journal "History of New England," 1630–49*, ed. J. K. Hosmer, 1908, vol. i, pp. 134, 325; vol. ii, p. 20.

[36] Weeden, *op. cit.*, vol. i, pp. 125, 58.

[37] Winthrop, *op. cit.*, vol. ii, p. 20.

had been done even in the house of bondage from which they fled. What was more distinctive of the children of light was their attempt to apply the same wholesome discipline to the elusive category of business profits. The price of cattle, the Massachusetts authorities decreed, was to be determined, not by the needs of the buyer, but so as to yield no more than a reasonable return to the seller.[38] Against those who charged more, their wrath was that of Moses descending to find the chosen people worshipping a golden calf. What little emotion they had to spare from their rage against religious freedom, they turned against economic license. Roger Williams touched a real affinity when, in his moving plea for tolerance, he argued that, though extortion was an evil, it was an evil the treatment of which should be left to the discretion of the civil authorities.[39]

Consider the case of Mr. Robert Keane. His offense, by general consent, was black. He kept a shop in Boston, in which he took "in some . . . above 6d. in the shilling profit; in some above 8d.; and in some small things above two for one"; and this, though he was "an ancient professor of the gospel, a man of eminent parts, wealthy and having but one child, having come over for conscience' sake and for the advancement of the gospel." The scandal was terrible. Profiteers were unpopular—"the cry of the country was great against oppression"—and the grave elders reflected that a reputation for greed would injure the infant community, lying as it did "under the curious observation of all Churches and civil States in the world." In spite of all, the magistrates were disposed to be lenient. There was no positive law in force limiting profits; it was not easy to determine what profits were fair; the sin of charging what the market could stand was not peculiar to Mr. Keane; and, after all, the law of God required no more than double restitution. So they treated him mercifully, and fined him only £200.

Here, if he had been wise, Mr. Keane would have let the matter drop. But, like some others in a similar position, he damned himself irretrievably by his excuses. Summoned before the church of Boston, he first of all "did with tears acknowledge and bewail his covetous and corrupt heart," and then was rash enough to venture on an explanation, in which he argued that the tradesman must live, and how could he live, if he might not make up for a loss on one article by additional profit on another? Here was a text on which no faithful pastor could refrain from enlarging. The minister of Boston pounced on the opportunity, and took occasion in

---

[38] J. A. Doyle, *The English in America*, vol. ii, 1887, p. 57; the price of cattle "must not be judged by urgent necessity, but by reasonable profit."

[39] Roger Williams, *The Bloudy Tenent of Persecution*, 1644, chap. lv.

his public exercise the next lecture day to lay open the error of such false principles, and to give some rules of direction in the case. Some false principles were these:—

1. That a man might sell as dear as he can, and buy as cheap as he can.

2. If a man lose by casualty of sea, etc., in some of his commodities, he may raise the price of the rest.

3. That he may sell as he bought, though he paid too dear, and though the commodity be fallen, etc.

4. That, as a man may take the advantage of his own skill or ability, so he may of another's ignorance or necessity.

5. Where one gives time for payment, he is to take like recompense of one as of another.

The rules for trading were not less explicit:—

1. A man may not sell above the current price, i.e., such a price as is usual in the time and place, and as another (who knows the worth of the commodity) would give for it if he had occasion to use it; as that is called current money which every man will take, etc.

2. When a man loseth in his commodity for want of skill, etc., he must look at it as his own fault or cross, and therefore must not lay it upon another.

3. Where a man loseth by casualty of sea, etc., it is a loss cast upon himself by Providence, and he may not ease himself of it by casting it upon another; for so a man should seem to provide against all providences, etc., that he should never lose; but where there is a scarcity of the commodity, there men may raise their price; for now it is a hand of God upon the commodity, and not the person.

4. A man may not ask any more for his commodity than his selling price, as Ephron to Abraham: the land is worth thus much.

It is unfortunate that the example of Ephron was not remembered in the case of transactions affecting the lands of Indians, to which it might have appeared peculiarly appropriate. In negotiating with these children of the devil, however, the saints of God considered the dealings of Israel with Gibeon a more appropriate precedent.

The sermon was followed by an animated debate within the church. It was moved, amid quotations from 1 Cor. v. 11, that Mr. Keane should be excommunicated. That he might be excommunicated, if he were a covetous person within the meaning of the text, was doubted as little as that he had recently given a pitiable exhibition of covetousness. The question was only whether he had erred through ignorance or carelessness, or whether he had acted "against his conscience or the very light of nature"—whether, in short, his sin was accidental or a trade. In the end he escaped with his fine and admonition.[40]

If the only Christian documents which survived were the New Testament and the records of the Calvinist Churches in the age of the Reformation, to suggest a connection between them more intimate than a coincidence of phraseology would appear, in all probability, a daring extravagance. Legalistic, mechanical, without imagination or compassion, the work of a jurist and organizer of genius, Calvin's system was more Roman than Christian, and more Jewish than either. That it should be as much more tyrannical than the medieval Church, as the Jacobin Club was than the *ancien régime*, was inevitable. Its meshes were finer, its zeal and its efficiency greater. And its enemies were not merely actions and writings, but thoughts.

The tyranny with which it is reproached by posterity would have been regarded by its champions as a compliment. In the struggle between liberty and authority, Calvinism sacrificed liberty, not with reluctance, but with enthusiasm. For the Calvinist Church was an army marching back to Canaan, under orders delivered once for all from Sinai, and the aim of its leaders was the conquest of the Promised Land, not the consolation of stragglers or the encouragement of laggards. In war the classical expedient is a dictatorship. The dictatorship of the ministry appeared as inevitable to the whole-hearted Calvinist as the Committee of Public Safety to the men of 1793, or the dictatorship of the proletariat to an enthusiastic Bolshevik. If it reached its zenith where Calvin's discipline was accepted without Calvin's culture and intellectual range, in the orgies of devil worship with which a Cotton and an Endicott shocked at last even the savage superstition of New England, that result was only to be expected.

The best that can be said of the social theory and practice of early Calvinism is that they were consistent. Most tyrannies have contented themselves with tormenting the poor. Calvinism had little pity for poverty; but it distrusted wealth, as it distrusted all influences that distract the aim or relax the fibers of the soul, and, in the first flush of its youthful austerity, it did its best to make life unbearable for the rich. Before the Paradise of earthly comfort it hung a flaming brand, waved by the implacable shades of Moses and Aaron.[41]

---

[40] Winthrop, *op. cit.*, vol. i, pp. 315–18. A similar set of rules as to the conduct of the Christian in trade are given by Bunyan in *The Life and Death of Mr. Badman*, 1905 ed., pp. 118–22.

[41] I owe this phrase to the excellent book of J. T. Adams, *The Founding of New England*.

11 | M^CILWAIN

BODIN

The national state is the central concept of modern political thought, its tacit assumption, just as the city-state was that of antiquity, and universal empire that of the Middle Ages. An essential aspect of the modern national state is "sovereignty," a term first coined and elaborated by the French publicist Jean Bodin (1530–1596). Bodin was of middle-class origin, and represented the Third Estate in the Estates-General in 1576. He is the best known of the *Politiques*, a group of French administrators, lawyers, and publicists who sought to save France amidst the political and religious strife of their time. In the opinion of the *Politiques*, fanaticism and radicalism threatened to ruin the nation, and they therefore urged moderation and compromise if France was to survive. Bodin also strongly urged religious toleration, on philosophical grounds as well as on those of political prudence and expediency. His most famous work is his *Six Books on the State* (1576), in which he laid the groundwork for all future discussion of the concept of sovereignty. Although Bodin attributes to the sovereign absolute authority in relation to human laws, he was still close enough to medieval sentiment in his conviction that the ruler has no authority to violate the laws of God and nature. Much of the later exaggeration and abuse of Bodin's concept of sovereignty was due to practical political needs and their rationalization by subservient political writers, rather than to the original meaning as developed by Bodin himself.

Another tendency in modern political thought, pluralism, has aimed at the elimination of the whole idea of sovereignty as dangerous and incompatible with free government. This issue is dealt with by Charles H. McIlwain in his essay, "A Fragment on Sovereignty" (1925). McIlwain (1871–   ) demonstrates in his argument that there can be a sound middle ground in dealing with the problem of sovereignty: that it was not meant as a justification of totalitarian government, and that political analysis cannot do without it in analyzing and interpreting the nature of the modern state. After a teaching career at Princeton, McIlwain went to Harvard, where he taught history and government from 1911 to his retirement in 1946. His best known work is *The Growth of Political Thought in the West* (1932). His other writings include *The High Court of Parliament* (1910), *The American Revolution* (1923), and *Constitutionalism and the Changing World* (1949).

McIlwain on BODIN

It requires considerable courage, or presumption, as some might prefer to style it, to ask a reader's attention once more to so well-worn a topic as sovereignty. Few political conceptions have been the subject of so much discussion amongst us in the last hundred years. But this very fact is proof of its vital importance in our modern world; and the wide variety of the views held concerning its essence, as well as the conflicting conclusions to which these views still lead, may furnish sufficient excuse for another attempt to clarify some of our ideas touching this central formula under which we try to rationalize the complicated facts of our modern political life.

If sovereignty were an idea purely abstract we should be closer than we are to unanimity as to its character; but it is traditional as well as abstract, and no attempt to analyze it can have hope of success which ignores the stages and factors in its growth.

Sovereignty is no essential part of the abstract conception of a state, but to every modern man but the anarchist some kind of supremacy is essential, if his concept is to be consistent with itself; though the idea of this supremacy may at some periods of its growth have been so blurred and indistinct as to be almost undiscoverable, as during the long sway of the feudal theory of *dominion* in the middle ages.

[Charles H. McIlwain, "A Fragment on Sovereignty," *Political Science Quarterly*, vol. 48 (March, 1933). By permission.]

Sovereignty, in fact, is a supremacy conceived in a particular way and in particular terms; but supremacy itself is a broader concept, and it may be conceived and in certain periods has been conceived in ways and in terms which are quite different. The Greeks, for example, had a very definite idea of supremacy, but for reasons which will presently appear, it would seem better to distinguish it clearly from modern sovereignty.

Supremacy is central in the political thought of Aristotle, but it is a supremacy held in a state by a ruling class not in terms of that state's constitution as in the case of a modern sovereign: Aristotle's ruling class exercises this supremacy simply by virtue of the fact that it is able actually to maintain it and only so long as it has the power to do so. Supremacy is a control enjoyed in fact, not a lawful authority defined as the "sovereign's" is, by a constitution. The constitution is dictated to the state by the class in power, it is not imposed by the state upon the rulers; while a modern "sovereign", on the other hand, is constituted and defined by the constitution itself. For the Greeks, the ruling class makes the constitution; for the modern, the constitution makes the "sovereign". The Greeks were thinking of law in terms of the state; we habitually think of the state in terms of law. No word was oftener on Aristotle's lips than the word "constitution", but he meant by it the whole complex of aims, ethical, social and economic, as well as legal, toward which the common life of the citizens was guided under the dictation and direction of the rulers or class in power; we think of a constitution merely as the sum of the provisions under which the ruler is set up and his lawful authority defined, limited and regulated. For Aristotle the constitution of a state is the ideal of social and political life which its ruling class prefers and actually imposes upon the whole body of citizens because it is physically able to enforce its will over them. The ruling class, he says, determines the constitution, and the constitution *is* the state. But compare for a moment such an assertion with any modern definition of a constitution and the vast difference between them will be apparent at once. Professor Dicey, for example, in his *Law of the Constitution,* distinguishes a constitutional law from another by restricting it to those rules which are concerned with the definition or the distribution of the sovereign power in a state.

How and when did this fundamental difference arise between antique and modern thought, and what are the new elements in our modern conception of the political relation which result from this difference?

It was in the Hellenistic period apparently that "supremacy" began to take on the distinctive characteristics which mark our modern concept of sovereignty. The Stoics saw in the world of human relations a law coeval and coextensive with man himself; a law, therefore, which no state can make, nor any ruling class within a state: that law was in existence before there were any states; and no state, in the only proper sense of the term, can ever even come into being if it does not incorporate this eternal law in its framework. The state has become a *vinculum juris*; consent to a preëxistent law (*juris consensus*) is the origin and the badge of a true commonwealth; the state does not make law, law makes the state. "Modern" political thought has in fact begun, in the habit of thinking of the state in terms of law, not of law in terms of the state; and the legalistic approach, which has been the chief theoretical characteristic of politics from Roman times to our own, is already clearly apparent.

That these newer habits of thought persisted throughout the whole period of the Roman Republic and Empire is a fact which needs no proof, and in Rome we have the first actual "sovereign". We should probably have had at the same time a definite theory of sovereignty to account for this fact if the jurists of the Empire had possessed a capacity for political speculation commensurate even in slight degree with their genius in formulating the specific rules of law. But, unlike the Greeks, they show few signs of such capacity, and a clearcut conception of political supremacy in terms of law had therefore to wait for its next great opportunity, an opportunity which, however, was not to come to the western world again for a thousand years, when actual political relations in the nation-states of western Europe had once again assumed somewhat the same form at the end of the middle ages which had characterized the Roman state under the *imperium* of the emperors.

In the long interval of the middle ages which lies between, conditions were unfavorable for the formulation of any theory of sovereignty, largely because there was scarcely discernible among strictly political institutions a supremacy of any kind. In the earlier centuries of this period government, usually in the form of monarchy, was taken for granted and the medieval mind was not yet mature enough to take the step from tacit acceptance to self-conscious analysis of political relations. In the eleventh century political speculation was reborn in defense or denial of papal claims to a political authority over the whole of the *Respublica Christiana,* and an authority which was fast developing into a true *plenitudo potestatis*; but in the lower sphere of secular political relations specifically, the chief new doctrine stimulated by these ecclesiastical controversies was the theory of dominion, which reflected more of the decentralization of feudalism than of the strong monarchy of the canonists.

From the thirteenth century to the sixteenth *dominium* is the prevailing formula under which men habitually think about secular government.

But in essence this *dominium* is a theory of superiority rather than supremacy. For Beaumanoir, writing in the thirteenth century, the king is "sovereign" in his kingdom, but so is an earl in his earldom, and even a baron in his barony. If the king's authority is greater than the earl's or the baron's, this is primarily because it is wider than theirs, not so much because it is higher in kind. The king alone has the care (*garde*) of the whole kingdom and must have an authority commensurate with his broader responsibilities. It is true, as Luchaire has remarked, that in this whole period the conception of true kingship was never lost entirely, but it was without doubt obscured greatly by conceptions of the political relation drawn from actual conditions under feudal tenure with its graduated rights and interests enjoyed by a hierarchy of lords in the same fief and over the same tenants. In the feudal monarchy every king was *dominus* as well as *rex,* and as *dominus* his rights were scarcely distinguishable in kind from those of inferior lords.

In such circumstances the development of a clear-cut theory of any single supreme political authority over all subjects is not to be looked for. *Dominium,* as a theory of government drawn in largest part from a rationalization of the feudal relation, was destined to stand in the way of any true theory of sovereignty as long as the feudal institutions which gave life to the formula retained their own vitality. It remained until modern times a barrier to sovereignty, because it was inconsistent with a complete supremacy of any sort.

At times it has been said that the chief reason for the lateness of the appearance of a theory of sovereignty was not this dominion, but rather the prevalence in the middle ages of the conception of natural law, but such an explanation entails a misinterpretation of the history of the theory and implies some misunderstanding of the original notion of sovereignty itself. The earliest forms of the theory, as everyone knows, freely incorporated natural law in it, and they were entirely consistent in so doing; for sovereignty is a supreme authority not deducible from might, according to this theory, but defined by law; and if so, there is nothing to prevent the inclusion in this law of provisions which men believe to be dictated by nature, as well as those arising from custom or created by enactment. The theoretical obstacle to sovereignty was not the law of nature, except in so far as it contributed to retard men's awareness of the fact of law-making. In reality the main obstacle was twofold: the prevalence in the middle ages of the theory of dominion and the absence of any clear notion of legislation. What characterizes a modern "sovereign" is supreme authority to make law, but in medieval Europe it was not easy to find any authority supreme in all respects, and even if found, it was an authority merely to promulgate, administer and interpret a law already in being, not to make a new one. The legal rules issued in a king's name might be *stabilimenta, établissements* or *statuta*—something "established", as such terms imply; but these are not the creations of a ruler legally competent to enact legislation at will.

By the sixteenth century, however, these medieval conditions had largely been replaced in some parts of western Europe by the ones we are familiar with today, and before the end of that century a few keener minds had begun to discard older formulae explanatory of phenomena already outworn and to reshape the theory of the state in light not merely of traditional doctrines but of newer political conditions which they were beginning to discover in existence about them. In the more centralized states the king had at length outgrown the feudal stage and had become the true head of a nation, once more a monarch ruling over subjects instead of a lord over vassals, and ruling in accordance with a law which was truly national in scope and character. Moreover, such substantial additions and changes were now being made in the law itself, and with such frequency, that it was scarcely possible longer to conceal this fact under the older medieval doctrine that a monarch can only administer or interpret a law but not make it. The world was ripe for a new theory of the state. It finally came in the recognition that a state consists essentially in a supreme legislative authority over subjects.

Apparently the first definite and comprehensive statement of the new doctrine was by Jean Bodin. In his *Methodus ad Facilem Historiarum Cognitionem,* first published in 1566, he asserted the principle that an authority truly supreme is essential to every state and when present constitutes a state, though he still retained the medieval doctrine that the chief and the typical form of this supreme authority is the judicial—control over the administration and interpretation of law. But ten years later, in his more famous *République,* he has begun to see that it is supremacy in the making of law rather than its administration which marks the sovereign. In that epoch-making book he defines a republic as *un droit gouvernement de plusieurs mesnages, & de ce qui leur est commun,* AVEC PUISSANCE SOUVERAINE; and *puissance souveraine,* or sovereignty, as *la puissance absoluë & perpetuelle d'une République,* or, as in his Latin version of 1586, *suprema in cives ac subditos legibusque soluta potestas*; a power or authority of which the first and foremost element (*primum ac praecipuum caput*), to which all others are incidental, is *la puissance de donner loy à tous en general, & à chacun en particulier.* In these few statements the whole of the theory of modern sovereignty is expressed in its classical form. Bodin is no doubt entitled to his claim to be the first among philosophers and jurisconsults to formulate this theory, and Sir F. Pollock is probably justified in saying that this formulation could not have come much earlier than it did.

For an understanding of the later history of the theory a careful consideration of every important part of Bodin's statement of it is, of course, necessary; but in this paper attention will be confined practically to one part alone, and the first: *République est un* DROIT *gouvernement.* It is a government defined by law, and though the sovereign authority in it is *legibus soluta,* is "free of the laws", yet these laws can never include the fundamental rules upon which the state itself rests and by which the sovereign is constituted and his authority defined, whether these fundamental rules be thought to be drawn from the law of God or from the law of nature, or come actually from the ancient custom of the nation or from a distinct and definite expression of the nation's will. If we assume that sovereignty is not might but authority, then a definition of such authority is an absolute necessity, and the terms of that definition will fix a limit beyond which the holder of the sovereignty can never pass without negating his very existence. Bodin did so assume, and was compelled by the logic of that assumption to place beyond the sovereign's control all the essential principles which form and enter into *un droit gouvernement,* though as sovereign he is free of all laws whatsoever made or to be made in accordance with these principles.

In Bodin's day it was generally accepted that a government could never be *"droit"* if it violated the principles of justice founded upon the law of nature and the law of God. Every association of men is held together by some bond of law, but if such an association is to be better than a band of robbers this must be a law based on justice, and justice comes from the nature of man himself and from the mind of God. So there never could be a true republic except one founded in justice, nor any legitimate authority within such a republic.

But the *jus civile,* public as well as private, within a particular state will consist, as Gaius said, partly of laws common to all mankind and partly of laws peculiar to that state alone. And if the fundamentals of the common law of mankind must always be incorporated in the definition of any true commonwealth which man makes, so in a particular commonwealth this definition may in addition include some peculiar principles not necessarily present in every state, but fundamental in that particular one, and an integral part of the very definition of the state itself, of its government, and of the supreme authority therein. Such particular principles Bodin saw in France in the so-called Salic Law, and in the inalienability of the royal domain and authority. These principles did not have their source in man's nature or in God's law, but they were no less essential than such to the integrity of the French kingdom and in France were therefore "fundamental" in the same sense. When, then, Bodin declares that his sovereign is "free of the laws", he restricts such laws to the ordinary rules enacted in the state pursuant to these fundamental principles and never inconsistent with them. By these fundamental principles even the highest authority is always bound; it is only of all others that he is wholly free. It has been the fashion of most modern interpreters of Bodin in England and America to condemn this reservation of fundamental law as a fatal inconsistency in his theory and a sign of failure fully to grasp the essential principle of sovereignty. In reality this condemnation is proof of their own inability to understand his true meaning, resulting usually from imperfect knowledge of the historical basis, ancient and medieval, upon which Bodin's theory actually rests.

The fundamental law of a state as Bodin conceived it must therefore embody the laws of nature and of God and may also include particular rules which are no less an integral part of that state's "constitution". For him, as was natural at the time, all such particular rules actually come from immemorial custom. But there is no logical necessity for restricting them in this way, and therefore in after times, as men became more self-conscious politically and as law-making more and more tended to replace mere law-declaring, these particular "fundamental" rules were extended to comprise new provisions as well as ancient customs, and thus the foundations of the modern "written constitution" were finally laid. The bedrock upon which all such modern written constitutions rest—all at least which originate in the people—and the only one upon which they may rest consistently, is this distinction, in essence identical with Bodin's, between those laws which a government makes and may therefore change, and the ones which make the government itself. It is immaterial whether the latter rules be drawn from the law of nature or immemorial custom as in Bodin's day, or be made by definite act of the people's will, as they usually are now; in any case they must inevitably be superior to the government they create and beyond the reach even of the sovereign organ within it whose authority they define. This is a theory of law not of might, the theory of the *Rechtsstaat*; and it is this theory which has dominated Continental thought to the present day, and for two generations after Bodin dominated even English thought, the theory of Hooker, Eliot, Twysden, Philip Hunton and Sir Matthew Hale.

It remains briefly to consider the changes which in England ultimately replaced this theory by a newer one, and to compare this new theory with the old on the basis of their respective merits theoretical and practical.

It was Thomas Hobbes, the keenest and shortest-sighted of modern political philosophers, who put this newer theory in clean-cut terms as Bodin had put the older. In the struggle which became concrete in England in the summer of 1642 with the issuance of the militia ordinance, behind all the ponderous arguments from ancient precedent employed on either side, Hobbes saw clearly the true nature of the issue and its inevitable outcome, and he saw them earlier and more distinctly than most of his contemporaries, and set them forth in his *Behemoth,* or history of the civil wars. Though it was the ancient constitution which both parties were still professing to defend, the struggle between king and parliament was at bottom a struggle not for law but for mastery, and it could end only in the actual mastery of one or the other. In his more theoretical works, especially the *De Cive* and later in the more celebrated *Leviathan,* Hobbes reduced his observations of these actual conditions in England to a formula purporting to have universal application. The supreme authority in any state is the one which can compel actual obedience. Might, not law, makes right. It is authority, and not reason, which makes a law, as he tells us in his *Dialogue of the Common Laws of England,* written to refute the traditional doctrines of Sir Edward Coke.

Like Aristotle's supremacy in Athens of the fifth century B.C., and Bodin's sovereignty in France of the sixteenth A.D., this is a rationalization of actual political conditions; in this case, conditions as they existed in England in the period of political strife and civil war between 1640 and 1660. The core of such a rationalization is naturally actual might, not legitimate authority. But the disturbed conditions of civil war furnish poor material for a general theory of settled government. It is the unlaw of the English civil wars and Interregnum to which we are indebted for that particular type of supremacy, the sovereignty of Hobbes and Filmer and John Austin, which still prevails in the political thought of England, and, strange to say, of America as well; although it was rejected by James Otis, Samuel Adams and other Americans in the eighteenth century, and notwithstanding the fact that it is utterly incompatible with the fundamental conceptions upon which our American governments were originally established and indeed with all written constitutions and bills of rights wherever and whenever they are found, those few alone excepted which proceed from the concession of a ruler.

Nothing could show more plainly the nakedness of the might which lies at the center of Austin's theory than his well-known reformulation of Hobbes's sovereignty in *The Province of Jurisprudence Determined.*

He tells us there that when in any society a determinate person (or persons) "*habitually*" receives the obedience of "the bulk" of the members of the society, such person (or persons) must be considered to be the sovereign in that society. There is no question here of law or right. It is the mere physical fact of mastery, the actual existence and continuance of obedience whether induced by consent, fear or force, which clothes those who obtain it, no matter how or why they obtain it, with the supreme authority in a state. And furthermore, the actual submission of "the bulk" of the people is, in this theory, complete justification for a supremacy with unlimited power over all, even over those who have never consented to it. Minorities look in vain for protection under such a theory, and there is no right of an individual too sacred to be overridden with the assent of "the bulk" of the people.

If anyone should doubt the practical effects of this truly slavish theory of the state, a very slight review of certain periods of English and American history would be enough to undeceive him. It was largely by an appeal to it that Lord Mansfield defended and obtained the passage in 1766 of the Declaratory Act which affirmed that Englishmen in America were completely subject to the power of a legislative body in which they had no representatives whatever, a perfect example of Austinianism in operation; it was its influence which enabled conservatives like Lord Eldon to justify and secure the retention, even in the nineteenth century and by an unreformed parliament, of such notorious abuses as Catholic disabilities and the Test and Corporation acts, and to enact class legislation of the type of the Combination acts.

It is little wonder that such a theory should in time provoke reaction among liberal minds and meet with the opposition it deserved. The most interesting and important theoretical aspect of this opposition at the present time is the recent growth and rapid extension of the theory usually known as "pluralism".

The underlying principle of pluralism is simple in the extreme. Under it, as its name implies, it is not necessary that there be in the state any supreme authority at all. There may be one person, or institution, association, or body such as a church or guild or trade union, to whose authority a citizen defers if he chooses, or there may be more than one; and if more, the citizen himself freely determines which shall receive his obedience should their claims conflict. In effect, there is and can be no "sovereign", because sovereignty itself is a wholly inadmissible concept.

It is, however, far more than sovereignty that pluralism repudiates; it denies the existence or the right to exist of a supremacy of any kind whatsoever. There is no "sovereignty" in the state because there can be no supremacy. But such a rejection of supremacy is equivalent to a repudiation of all control over the individual citizen except that which he voluntarily imposes upon himself, a flat denial of the legitimacy of any coercive power whatever; and it is more than questionable whether anyone but a professed anarchist could make such denial without incurring the just charge of inconsistency and confusion of thought. For adherents of the theory of philosophic anarchy pluralism is an eligible explanation of political relations. How it could possibly form an integral part of any other theory of the state, it is rather difficult to see, or how anyone holding any other theory could consistently espouse it. Yet many have espoused it who are apparently unwilling to subscribe to the anarchistic creed. For most persons pluralism will contain too little and too much: too little in its assumption that all sovereignty must of necessity be Austinian sovereignty, too much in the denial that sovereignty of any kind, or supremacy even, can ever be a legitimate political concept. Political ideals are one thing; actual political phenomena often quite another. Pluralism unquestionably fits in perfectly with the high ideal of the anarchist, but he would probably be the first to admit that it accounts for no actual government existent now or hitherto.

Few countries have made more significant contribution to the modern world's stock of political institutions than the United States, but to the theory underlying them all, our contribution is negligible. Our theory, such as it is, has been mainly a theory of lawyers who were usually content to accept their explanation of government at secondhand from later English legal sources such as the *Commentaries* of Sir William Blackstone, himself a political theorist far from profound or consistent, as Jeremy Bentham had little trouble in showing. Modern federalism, for example, has been largely our work, but no thoroughgoing theory of it ever appeared till after the foundation of the new German Empire in 1871.

In short, we have hitherto been satisfied to borrow and to retain, with little discrimination and no adequate examination, a traditional theory inconsistent with our national origin, outworn when we took it and tenfold more outworn now; a theory originally built upon actual conditions of civil strife instead of national well-being, and itself unfailingly productive of new strife, except when fiction or fact has stood in the way of its full operation. The time seems ripe again for a new theoretical appraisal of our political institutions which will take complete account of present-day conditions and needs. If a satisfactory theory should ever be the outcome, such a theory would, of course, have to meet and furnish explanation of actual political conditions which are vastly more intricate

and perplexing than those of the simple unitary national monarchy of
France which gave Bodin the principal data for his rationalization in the
sixteenth century. Even if we should start with Bodin, we could certainly not end with him. But it is none the less true that no theory which
proves to be unsound for a simple state can ever form the basis for a
valid explanation of a complex one; the essentials must be the same in
both.

It is the purpose of this brief fragment merely to give a few illustrations of the importance, for a proper testing of these essentials, of a careful
review of the past development and practical results of some of the
theories of government which we still employ. Such review as the writer
himself has been able to make has seemed to him to show that the
Rechtsstaat of which Jean Bodin gave us the first analysis, is after all
probably a sounder foundation on which to build than either the assertions
of Hobbes or the negations of the modern Pluralists. From such a survey
others may and some no doubt will be led to a different conclusion, but
few are likely to dissent from the general principle that in any serious
attempt to reach an adequate synthesis of present-day political relations,
or a sound analysis, past experience cannot safely be ignored.

12

HOBBES

The turbulent first half of the seventeenth century in England provides the background for the political ideas of a lonely and complex figure, Thomas Hobbes (1588–1679). The son of an impecunious vicar, Hobbes was able to become closely associated with high aristocratic families by dint of sheer intellectual brilliance. In 1640, he fled to France, fearing that his intimate associations with royalist circles might endanger his safety. He spent about twenty years on the Continent, both before and after his escape from England, and had many opportunities to meet the leading scientists and philosophers of his time. Most of his stay abroad was in Paris, where he also instructed Charles II, the son of the executed Charles I, during the years 1646 to 1648. In 1651, Hobbes returned to England, where he declared his submission to the new republican regime of Oliver Cromwell. His principal work is the *Leviathan* (1651), a defense of strong government, but not of totalitarianism. In the English-speaking countries he has remained a great, yet isolated, figure in the history of political ideas. On the one hand, adherents of parliamentary government have felt little sympathy for his defense of the strong state, with little regard for self-government and individual freedom of expression. On the other hand, conservatives, too, have rejected Hobbes because of the contractual foundation of government in the Hobbesian scheme, and his preference for monarchy on purely expedient grounds rather than on those of its divine origin. Moreover, the charge of atheism or, at least, agnosticism against Hobbes made him unacceptable to traditional conservatives. By contrast, where, as on the European Continent, the tradition of conservatism was weak, and that of despotic government strong, Hobbes was frequently interpreted, or misinterpreted, as an intellectual forerunner of royal despotism and, later, modern totalitarianism.

The incompatibility of Hobbesianism with traditional, true conservatism was clearly seen by the greatest conservative statesman of the period, Edward Hyde, the first Earl of Clarendon (1609–1674). First allied with the popular party, he soon became associated with the royalist party, the staunchest defender of episcopacy and monarchy against the new, and more liberal, principles in church and government. His best known work is his *History of the Rebellion and Civil Wars in England* (1707), which is still of interest for its presentation of the authentic conservative viewpoint on a crucial period of English history, although less dependable for historical accuracy. His views on Hobbes are developed in great detail in *A Brief View and Survey of the Dangerous and Pernicious Errors to Church and State in Mr. Hobbes's Book Entitled Leviathan* (1676). Unlike Continental conservatives, who frequently embraced Hobbesianism with fervent enthusiasm for reasons of partisan (and often short-lived) political advantage, Clarendon is guided by his conservative instinct and reason in rejecting Hobbes from the standpoint of both religion and politics.

The Earl of Clarendon on HOBBES

Mr. Hobbes is so great an enemy to freedom that he will not allow man that which God has given him, the freedom of his will. But he shall not entangle me in that argument which he has enough exercised himself in with a more equal adversary who, I think, has been much too hard for him at his own weapon, reason, the learned Bishop of Derry, who was afterwards Archbishop of Armagh, and by which he has put him into greater choler than a philosopher ought to subject himself to, the terrible strokes whereof I am not willing to undergo and therefore shall keep

[From Edward, Earl of Clarendon, *A Brief View and Survey of the Dangerous and Pernicious Errors to Church and State in Mr. Hobbes's Book Entitled Leviathan* (1676). Spelling and punctuation have been modernized for this selection.]

myself close to that freedom and liberty only that is due to subjects and of which his business in the *Leviathan* is to deprive them totally.

A man would have expected from Mr. Hobbes's inventory of the several rights and powers of his Sovereign in his eighteenth chapter, of which one was to prescribe rules "whereby every man might know what goods he may enjoy and what actions he might do without being molested by any of his fellow subjects," which, he says, "men call propriety," that some such rule should be established as might secure that propriety, how little soever. But he has now better explained himself and finds that liberty and property are only fences against the invasion or force of fellow-subjects, but towards the Sovereign of no use or signification at all. No man has a propriety in any thing that can restrain the King from taking it from him, and the liberty of a subject "lies only in those things which in regulating their actions the Sovereign has pretermitted, such as is the liberty to buy and sell and otherwise contact with one another; to choose their own abode, their own diet, their own trade of life; and to institute their children as they think fit; and the like." I wonder he did not insert the liberty to wear his clothes of that fashion which he likes best, which is as important as most of his other concessions. And yet he seems to be jealous that even this liberty should make men imagine that the sovereign power should be in any degree limited or that anything he can do to a subject and upon what pretense soever may be called injustice or injury, the contrary whereof he says he has shown already. For he takes it as granted that all that he has said he has proved: and if he has not, he has done it now substantially by the example of Jepthah, in causing his daughter to be sacrificed (of which he is not sure) and by David's killing Uriah, which, he says, though it was against equity, yet it was not an injury to Uriah because the right was given him by Uriah, which I dare swear Uriah never knew he had done.

And by such unnatural arguments he would persuade men to be willing to be undone, very like those which the Stoics as obstinately maintained, that a wise man could not be injured because he was not capable nor sensible of it. But I wonder more than he does not discern what every other man cannot but discern, that by his so liberal taking away he has not left the subject anything to enjoy even of those narrow concessions which he has made to him. For how can any man believe that he has liberty to buy and sell when the sovereign power can presently take away what he has sold from him who has bought it, and consequently no man can sell or buy to any purpose? Who can say that he can choose his own abode, or his own trade of life, or anything when, as soon as he has chosen either, he shall be required to go to a place where he has no mind to go and to do somewhat he would not choose to do? For his person is no more at his own disposal than his goods are, so that he may as graciously retain to himself all that he has granted.

Whether the sovereign power or the liberty of the subject receive the greater injury and prejudice by this brief state and description he makes of the no-liberty, that is, the portion he leaves to the subject, would be a great question if he had not been pleased himself to determine that his subject (for God forbid that any other Prince should have such a subject) is not capable of an injury; by which the whole mischief is likely to fall upon the Sovereign. And what greater mischief and ruin can threaten the greatest Prince than that their subjects should believe that all the liberty they have consists only in those things which the Sovereign has hitherto pretermitted, that is, which he has not yet taken from them. But when he pleases, in regulating their actions, to determine the contrary, they shall then have neither liberty to buy or sell nor to contract with each other, to choose their own abode, their own diet, their own trade of life, or to breed their own children. To make their misery complete and their life as little their own as the rest, nothing the Sovereign can do to his subject, on what pretense soever, as well in order to the taking away his life as his estate, can be called injustice or injury; I say, what greater insecurity can any Prince be in or under than to depend upon such subjects? And alas! what security to himself or them can the sword in his hand be if no other hand be lifted up on his behalf or the swords in all other hands be directed against him, that he may not cut off their heads when he hath a mind to it? And it is not Mr. Hobbes's authority that will make it believed that he who desires more liberty demands an exemption from all laws by which all other men may be masters of their lives and that every subject is author of every act the Sovereign does, upon the extravagant supposition of a consent that never was given, and if it were possible to have been given must have been void at the instant it was given, by Mr. Hobbes's own rules, as shall be made out in its place. He himself confesses, and says it is evident to the meanest capacities, that "men's actions are derived from the opinions they have of the good and evil which from those actions redound unto themselves, and consequently men that are once possessed of an opinion that their obedience to the sovereign power will be more hurtful to them than their disobedience will disobey the laws and thereby overthrow the Commonwealth and introduce confusion and civil war for the avoiding whereof all civil government was ordained." If this be true (as there is no reason to believe it to be), is it possible that any man can believe that the people, for we speak not of convincing the philosophers and the mathematicians, but of the general affections of the people which must dispose them to obedience, can be persuaded by a long train of consequences from the nature of man and the end of government and the institution thereof by contracts and covenants, of which they never heard, to believe that it is best for them to continue in the same nakedness in which they were created, for fear their clothes may be stolen from them, and that they have parted with their liberty to save their lives?

There is no question but of all calamities the calamity of war is greatest and the rage and uncharitableness of civil war most formidable of all war. Indeed foreign war seldom destroys a nation without domestic combinations and conspiracies which makes a complication with civil war; surely nothing can more inevitably produce that than a universal opinion in the people that their Sovereign can take from them all they have whenever he has a mind to it, and their lives, too, without any injustice, and consequently that their obedience to him will be more hurtful to them than their disobedience—so well has Mr. Hobbes provided for the security of his Sovereign if his doctrine were believed.

Mr. Hobbes is too much conversant in both those learned languages to wish that the Western world were deprived of the Greek and Latin tongues for any mischief they have done. Upon my conscience, whatever errors may have been brought into philosophy by the authority of Aristotle, no man ever grew a rebel by reading him. If the greatest monarch that has ever been in the world, except the Monarch of the world, had thought his tutor Aristotle had been so great an enemy to monarchy (yet he knew he was born and bred in a republic) and that his works contribute so much to sedition as Mr. Hobbes supposes, he would not have valued his person so much, nor read his works with such diligence as he did. And if Mr. Hobbes would take a view of the insurrections and the civil wars which have at any time been stirred up in the western parts, he will not find that they have been contrived or fomented by men who had spent much time in the reading of Greek and Latin authors or that they have been carried on upon the maxims and principles which they found there. Jack Straw and Wat Tyler, whose insurrection, in respect of the numbers and the progress it made, was as dangerous as has happened in any age or climate, had never read Aristotle or Cicero. I believe had Mr. Hobbes been of this opinion when he taught Thucydides to speak English, which book contains more of the science of mutiny and sedition and teaches more of that oratory that contributes thereunto than all that Aristotle and Cicero have published in all their writings, he would not have communicated such materials to his countrymen. But if this new philosophy and doctrine of policy and religion should be introduced, taught, and believed, where Aristotle and Cicero have done no harm, it would undermine monarchy more in two months than those two great men have done since their deaths, and men would reasonably wish that the author of it had never been born in the English climate nor been taught to write and read.

It is a very hard matter for an architect in state and policy who despises all precedents and will not observe any rules of practice to make such a model of government as will be in any degree pleasant to the governor, or governed, or secure for either. Mr. Hobbes finds it, and though he takes a liberty to raise his model upon a supposition of a very formal contract that never was or ever can be in nature and does the drawing and preparing of his own form of contract, he is forced to allow such a latitude in obedience to his subject as shakes the very pillars of his government. And therefore, though he be contented that by the words of his contract, "Kill me, and my fellow if you please," the absolute power of all men's lives shall be submitted to the disposal of the governor's will and pleasure without being obliged to observe any rules of justice and equity, yet he will not admit into his contract the other words, "I will kill myself or my fellow," and therefore that he is not bound by the command of his Sovereign to execute any dangerous or dishonorable office. In such cases, men are not to resort so much to the words of the submission as to the intention, which distinction surely may be as applicable to all that monstrous authority which he gives his governor to take away the lives and estates of his subjects without any cause or reason upon an imaginary contract which, if never so real, can never be supposed to be with the intention of the contractor in such cases. And the subtle distinctions he finds out to excuse subjects from yielding obedience to their sovereigns and the prerogative he grants to fear for a whole army to run away from the enemy without the guilt of treachery or injustice leaves us some hope that he will at last allow such a liberty to subjects that they may not in an instant be swallowed up by the prodigious power which he pleases to grant to his Sovereign. And truly, he degrades him very dishonorably when he obliges him to be the hangman himself of all those malefactors which by the law are condemned to die, for he gives every man authority, without the violation of his duty or swearing from the rules of justice, absolutely to refuse to perform that office.

Nor has he provided much better for his security than he has for his honor when he allows it lawful for any number of men "who have rebelled against the Sovereign or committed some capital crime for which every one of them expects death then to join together and defend each other, because they do but defend their lives, which the guilty man," he says, "may do as well as the innocent." And surely, no man can legally take his life from him who may lawfully defend it, and then the murderer or any other person guilty of a capital crime is more innocent and in better condition than the executioner of justice, who may be justly murdered in the just execution of his office. And it is a very childish security that he provides for his Sovereign against this rebellion and defense of themselves against the power of the law, that he declares "it to be lawful only for the defense of their lives, and that upon the offer of pardon for themselves that self-defense is unlawful," as if a body that is lawfully drawn together with strength enough to defend their lives against the power of the law, are likely to disband and lay down their arms without other benefit and advantage than only of the saving of their lives.

But, though he be so cruel as to divest his subjects of all that liberty which the best and most peaceable men desire to possess, yet he liberally and bountifully confers upon them such a liberty as no honest man can pretend to, and which is utterly inconsistent with the security of prince and people. This unreasonable indulgence of his cannot but be thought to proceed from an unlawful affection to those who he saw had power enough to defend the transcendent wickedness they had committed, though they were without an advocate to make it lawful for them to do so till he took that office upon him in his *Leviathan,* as is evident by the instance he gives. He thinks it lawful for every man to have as many wives as he pleases if the King will break the silence of the law and declare that he may do so, which is a prerogative he vouchsafes to grant to the Sovereign to balance that liberty he gave to the subject to defend himself and his companion against him and is the only power that may enable him to be too hard for the other.

If Mr. Hobbes did not believe that the authority of his name and the pleasantness of his style would lull men asleep from enquiring into the logic of his discourse, he could not but very well discern himself that this very liberty which he allows the subject to have and which he does without scruple enjoy, to sue the Sovereign, to demand the hearing of his cause, and that sentence be given according to the law, results only from that condescension and contract which the Sovereign has made with his subject and which can as well secure many other liberties to them as their power to sue the King. For there could be no law precedent to that resignation of themselves and all they had at the institution of their supreme governor. If there had been, it had been void and invalid, it not being possible that any man who has right to nothing and from whom anything that he has may be taken away can sue his Sovereign for a debt which he might take if it were due from any other man, but can by no means be due from him to whom all belongs and who has power to forbid any judge to proceed upon that complaint, were it not for the subsequent contract which he calls a precedent law by which the Sovereign promises and obliges himself to appoint judges to exercise justice even where he himself is a party, and that he will be sued before those judges if he does not pay what he owes to his subjects. This is the contract which gives that capacity of suing and which, by his own consent and condescension, lessens his sovereignty so that his subjects may require justice from him.

Yet all these promises and lessenings Mr. Hobbes pronounces as void and to amount to contradictions that must dissolve the whole sovereign power and leave the people in confusion and war. Whereas the truth is that these condescensions and voluntary abatements of some of that original power that was in them have drawn a cheerful submission and been attended by a ready obedience to sovereignty from the time that subjects have been at so great a distance from being considered as children and that sovereigns have been without those natural tendernesses in the exercise of their power and which in the rigor of it could never have been supported. Where these obligations are best observed, sovereignty flourishes with the most luster and security, kings having still all the power remaining in them that they have not themselves parted with and released to their subjects, and their subjects having no pretense to more liberty or power than the King has granted and given to them. Both their happiness and security consists in containing themselves within their own limits, that is, for kings not to affect the recovery of that exorbitant power which their ancestors wisely parted with as well for their own as the people's benefit, and for subjects to rejoice in those liberties which have been granted to them and not to wish to lessen the power of the King, which is not greater than is necessary for their own preservation. And to such a wholesome division and communication of power as this is, that place of Scripture (with which Mr. Hobbes is still too bold), "a Kingdom divided in itself cannot stand," cannot be applied.

But that this supreme Sovereign, whom he has invested with the whole property and liberty of all his subjects and so invested him in it that he has not power to part with any of it by promise or donation or release, may not be too much exalted with his own greatness, Mr. Hobbes has humbled him sufficiently by giving his subjects leave to withdraw their obedience from him when he has most need of their assistance, for "the obligation of subjects to the Sovereign is understood to last as long and no longer than the power lasts to protect them." So that, as soon as any town, city, or province of any prince's dominions is invaded by a foreign enemy or possessed by a rebellious subject that the prince for the present cannot suppress the power of the one or the other, the people may lawfully resort to those who are over them and, for their protection, perform all the offices and duties of good subjects to them: "For the right that men have by nature to protect themselves when none else can protect them can by no covenant be relinquished, and the end of obedience is protection which, wherever a man sees it, either in his own or in another's sword, nature applies his obedience to it and his endeavors to maintain it." And truly it is no wonder if they do so, and that subjects take the first opportunity to free themselves from such a sovereign as Mr. Hobbes has given them and choose a better for themselves. Whereas the duty of subjects is, and all good subjects believe they owe, another kind of duty and obedience to their sovereign than to withdraw their subjection because he is oppressed, and they will prefer poverty and death itself before they will renounce their obedience to their natural prince or do anything that may advance the service of his enemies. Mr. Hobbes gives so ill a testimony of his government (which, by the severe conditions he would oblige mankind to submit to for the support of it, ought to be firm and not to be shaken) "that it is in its own nature not only subject to violent death by foreign war, but also from the ignorance and passion of men that it has in it from the very institution many seeds of natural mortality by intestine discord." Since Mr. Hobbes cannot say anything worse of any government, we may very reasonably prefer the government we have, and under which we have enjoyed much happiness, before his, which we do not know nor anybody has had experience of, and which by his own confession is liable to all the accidents of mortality which any others have been, and reject his, that promises so ill and exercises all the action of war in peace and when war comes is liable to all the misfortunes which can possibly attend or invade it.

Whether the relation of subjects be extinguished in all those cases which Mr. Hobbes takes upon him to prescribe as imprisonment, banishment, and the like, I leave to those who can instruct him better in the law of nations by which they must be judged, notwithstanding all his appeals to the law of nature. I presume if a banished person "during which," he says, "he is not subject," shall join in an action under a foreign power against his country wherein he shall with others be taken prisoner, the others shall be proceeded against as prisoners of war, when he shall be judged as a traitor and rebel, which he could not be if he were not a subject, and this not only in the case of an hostile action and open attempt but of the most secret conspiracy that comes to be discovered. And, if this be true, we may conclude it would be very unsafe to conduct ourselves by what Mr. Hobbes "finds by speculation and deduction of sovereign rights from the nature, need, and designs of men." Surely this woeful desertion and defection in the cases above mentioned, which has been always held criminal by all law that has been current in any part of the world, received so much countenance and justification by Mr. Hobbes's book and more by his conversation that Cromwell found the submission to those principles produced a submission to him, and the imaginary relation between protection and allegiance so positively proclaimed by him prevailed for many years to extinguish all visible fidelity to the King. Mr. Hobbes persuaded many to take the engagement as a thing lawful and to become subjects to the usurper as to their legitimate sovereign. Of that great service he could not abstain from bragging in a pamphlet he set forth in that time that he alone and his doctrine had prevailed with many to submit to the government who would otherwise have disturbed the public peace, that is, to renounce their fidelity to their true Sovereign and to be faithful to the usurper.

It appears at last why by his institution Mr. Hobbes would have the power and security of his sovereign wholly and only depend upon the contracts and covenants which the people make one with another to transfer all their rights to a third person (who shall be sovereign) without entering into any covenant with the Sovereign himself, which would have divested them of that liberty to disobey him which they have reserved to themselves, or without receiving any covenant from him that might have obliged him to have kept his promise to them, by which they might have had somewhat left to them that they might have called their own, which his institution will not bear, all such promises being void. But, if he be so tenderhearted as to think himself obliged to observe all the promises and make good all the grants he has made by which he may be disabled to provide for their safety, which is the ground that has made all those grants and promises to be void, he has granted him power to remedy all this by "directly renouncing or transferring the sovereignty to another: and that he might openly and in plain terms renounce or transfer it." Then he says, "if a monarch shall relinquish the sovereignty both for himself and his heirs, his subjects return to the absolute liberty of nature because, though nature may declare who are his sons and who are the nearest of his kin, yet it depends on his own will who shall be his heir, and if he will have no heir there is no sovereignty or subjection." This seems the hardest condition for the poor subject that he can be liable unto. When he has divested himself of all the right he had, only for his Sovereign's protection, that he may be redeemed from the state of war and confusion that nature has left him in, and when he has paid so dear for that protection, it is left still in his Sovereign's power to withdraw that protection from him, to renounce his subjection, and without his consent to transfer the sovereignty to another, to whom he has no mind to be subject. One might have imagined that this new trick of transferring and covenanting had been a universal remedy that, being once applied, would forever prevent the ill condition and confusion that nature had left us in, and that such a right would have been constituted by it that sovereignty would never have failed to the world's end, and that, when the subject can never retract or avoid the bargain he has made, how ill soever he likes it, or improve it by acquiring any better conditions in it, it shall notwithstanding be in the sovereign's power without his consent—and it may be without his privity—in an instant to leave him without any protection, without any security, and as a prey to all who are too strong for him. This, indeed, is the greatest prerogative that he has conferred upon his Sovereign when he had given him all that belongs to his subjects, that when he is weary of governing he can destroy them by leaving them to destroy one another. For kings and princes to resign and relinquish their crown and sovereignty is no new transaction, nor may it be the better for being old. Some have left them out of melancholy and devotion and, when they have ceased to be kings, made themselves monks and repented the change of their conditions afterwards. Some, out of weakness and bodily infirmities, have not been able to sustain the fatigue that the well exercising the government required and therefore have desired to see those in the quiet possession of it to whom it would of right belong when they were dead; and the more reasonably if they foresaw any difficulties likely to arise about their admission in those seasons, as Charles the Fifth apprehended with reference to some of his dominions in Italy, if his son Philip was not in possession of them before his brother Ferdinando came to be Emperor. Some princes have been so humorous as, upon the frowardness and refractoriness of their subjects and because they could not govern in that manner they had a mind to do, to abdicate the government, and would have been glad afterwards to have resumed it. And others have been so wanton as to relinquish their crown because they did not like the climate in which their dominions lay, and only that they might live in a better air and enjoy the delights and pleasures of a more happy situation. But all these generally never attempted it or imagined they could do it without the approbation and consent of their subjects, which was always deferred and yielded to with great formality. And it is very strange that in those seasons of abdication which supposes a suspension of sovereignty (especially in elective kingdoms, for in hereditary ones the immortality of the king, who never dies, may make a difference) this invention of Mr. Hobbes's of transferring one another's right and covenanting with one another has never been heard of, and, though the sovereignty is invested by election, the people have very little share in that election.

If Mr. Hobbes would have exercised his talent in that spacious field, as he might have done with more innocence and, it may be, more success, and have undertaken "by his speculation and deduction of sovereign rights from the nature, need, and designs of men," to prove that it is not in the just power of a monarch to relinquish and renounce his sovereignty, with what formality and consent soever; nor more in the authority and power of the King to abdicate and relinquish his sovereignty over his people than it is in the authority of the people to withdraw their submission and obedience from him; and that the practice of such renunciations, though never very frequent, has been the original and introduction of that mischievous doctrine sowed among the people of their having a coordinate power with the Sovereign, which will be much cherished by his new institution, since men are easily persuaded to believe that they can mar what they can make and may lawfully destroy what they create, that is, the work of their own hands. I say, if he would have laid out his reason upon that argument, he could have made it shine very plausibly and might have made many proselytes to his opinion, since many learned men are so much in their judgment against that right of relinquishing and transferring in princes that they believe it to be the only cause wherein subjects may lawfully take up defensive arms that they may continue subjects and to preserve their subjection and obedience from being alienated from him to whom it is due, and that no consent or concurrence can make such an alienation more lawful than it can dissolve the bonds of wedlock and qualify both parties to make a new choice for themselves that may be more grateful to them. But Mr. Hobbes thinks it to be more glory to discover that to be right reason which all other men find to be destructive to it and "that the sudden and rough bustling in of a new truth" will raise his fame as it has done that of many other heretics before, and which, he says, "does never break the peace, but only sometimes awake the war," which, to use his own commendable expression is "like handing of things from one to another with many words making nothing understood."

I should be very glad that Mr. Hobbes might have a place in Parliament, and sit in Council, and be present in courts of justice and other tribunals, whereby it is probable he would find that his solitary cogitation, how deep soever, and his too peremptory adhering to some philosophical notions and even rules of geometry had misled him in the investigation of policy, and would rather retire to his quiet quarter in the Peak, without envy of those whom he left in employment, than keep them longer company in so toilsome, uneasy, and ungrateful transactions. And possibly this might, and I doubt only could, prevail upon him to make such recollection and acknowledgment of all the falsehood, profaneness, impiety, and blasphemy in his book, as may remove all those rubs and disturbances which he may justly apprehend, as well in the way to his last journey as at the end of it if he be not terrified with that dismal pronunciation, "If we sin willfully after we have received knowledge of the truth, there remains no more sacrifice for sins but a certain fearful looking for of judgment and fiery indignation, which shall devour the adversaries."

13 | LINDSAY

SPINOZA

Of all European nations, Holland was probably the first that practiced religious and political toleration in modern times, and from the seventeenth century onward she has remained a haven of refuge for the victims of oppression and discrimination. It is, therefore, no accident that the first modern Jewish philosopher, Baruch Spinoza (1632–1677), was born and lived in Holland. Spinoza came of a Spanish-Jewish family that was forced to flee Spain during the Inquisition. Although making a living by grinding lenses, Spinoza early in life became interested in philosophy, ethics, and religion, and his reputation as a philosopher spread throughout the world, despite the modesty of his personality and circumstances. Philosophers from all over Europe visited him, and he was offered a tempting position as a professor of philosophy in the University of Heidelberg. Yet he preferred his independence to economic affluence if the latter was to be bought at the price of any restriction of his freedom of thought and expression. In his *Ethics* (1677) he sought to construct an ethical system *more geometrico* (in the manner of geometry), and in his *Tractatus theologico-politicus* (1670) he tried to combine the tenets and inspiration of religious idealism with the principles and maxims of scientific rationalism. A strong defender of religious toleration and freedom of speech and opinion, Spinoza strongly influenced later philosophers and writers, such as Montesquieu in France and Lessing and Goethe in Germany.

The meaning and impact of Spinoza on modern political thought is examined by A. D. Lindsay, a leading British political thinker of the twentieth century, in his essay on "Benedict Spinoza" (1926). Lindsay (1879–1952) was Master of Balliol College at Oxford and a confirmed socialist from his undergraduate days at Oxford. Like Spinoza, Lindsay was keenly interested in the relations of religion and politics, and in his *Modern Democratic State* (1943), of his works the one most likely to endure longest, he stresses the impact of religious nonconformity on the development of English democracy. His other writings include *Essentials of Democracy* (1929) and *Religion, Science, and Society in the Modern World* (1943).

Lindsay on SPINOZA

Spinoza was born at Amsterdam in 1632. His parents belonged to a community of Jews from Portugal and Spain who had settled in the Netherlands a generation before, a small and closely knit people, who kept up their use of Portuguese and Spanish, but were full of gratitude for the liberty they had found in Holland. They were a learned community, and the young Spinoza was brought up both in Jewish learning and in the ordinary secular studies of the time. He was taught Latin by a certain Van der Ende, a doctor. He it was probably who introduced him to Descartes and to the science of the time. His community had learnt the lesson of toleration as ill as persecuted minorities usually learn it, and when Spinoza showed signs of unorthodoxy he was expelled and excommunicated in 1656, when he was twenty-three. He left Amsterdam and settled outside the city with a family of Remonstrants. He removed with them to near Leyden in 1661 and then moved to Voorburg, a suburb of The Hague, in 1664, and finally to The Hague itself, where he lived till his death in 1677. He maintained himself by the trade of making and polishing lenses for optical instruments, the practical side of the great sciences of the day, and gained great repute among the scientists of the time as an optician. In 1663 he published an exposition of Descartes' philosophy, and in 1670 not under his own name, the *Tractatus Theologico-Politicus*. The book was prohibited by the States-

[A. D. Lindsay, "Benedict Spinoza," in F. J. C. Hearnshaw (ed.), *The Social and Political Ideas of Some Great Thinkers of the Sixteenth and Seventeenth Centuries* (George G. Harrap and Co., Ltd., 1926). By permission.]

General. He published nothing else in his lifetime, but his other writings and particularly the *Ethic* were circulated in manuscript to such friends as were thought trustworthy.

Though Spinoza led a singularly quiet and retired life, he was yet in touch with the philosophical and scientific speculations of the time. Oldenburg, the first Secretary of the Royal Society, knew him well and corresponded with him regularly. Huygens and Leibnitz became acquainted with him and sought his advice on optical questions.

Spinoza's system is sometimes thought of as the glorification of an impersonal abstraction: yet there is no philosopher whose personality shines out so commandingly in his works. Many readers who have neither the patience nor the ability to master much of the argumentation of parts of the *Ethic* are nevertheless mastered by the serenity, strength, and beauty of the personality which shines through a rather repellent form. No one can read the fourth and fifth books of the *Ethic* without feeling that he is being brought into contact with a singularly great and good man. All that we learn of him from his letters and from his biography confirms that impression. He lived simply and frugally, supporting himself by his craft, and devoting all his spare time to study and philosophic discussion. All who knew him seem to have been devoted to him. He was uniformly kind, cheerful, and without thought of personal advantage or resentment. The impression that his letters and his biography give is not merely that he was a good man, but that he was a saint.

Yet this man raised against himself a greater storm of abuse than perhaps any other seventeenth-century writer. It became a commonplace that his works were "blasphemous, atheistic, deceitful, soul-destroying." Sir Frederick Pollock relates that a certain Dr. Bontekoe, writing two years after Spinoza's death, replied to the charge of atheism by saying: "I will one day show the world what sort of an atheist I am, when I refute the godless works of Spinoza, and likewise those of Hobbes and Machiavelli, three of the most cursed villains that ever walked the earth." The eighteenth century was no better than the seventeenth in this regard. Hume refers to Spinoza's "hideous hypothesis" and "the sentiments for which Spinoza is so universally infamous." Universally infamous he was—his religious seriousness disgusted the French rationalists as much as his apparent materialism disgusted the orthodox, and universally infamous he remained for rather over a hundred years, when there were suddenly found persons who could understand the depth and greatness of his teaching, and the ordinary estimate of Spinoza changed completely. The German Romantics discovered Spinoza: first Lessing, then Jacobi, Herder, and above all Goethe. The atheist of the early eighteenth century became the God-intoxicated philosopher to the early nineteenth. Ever since that time Spinoza's reputation has steadily grown, and he has been recognised more and more as the most religious of philosophers.

That is a strange reversal of reputation, and I mention it at once, for if we understand the reason for it, we shall understand the greatness of Spinoza's achievement and the relation in which it stood to the thought of the seventeenth century.

This philosopher-saint was in his century more execrated and abused than even Hobbes. The reason is not far to seek, paradoxical as the fact may seem. For no one can read the *Leviathan* without being at once aware that the doctrines he finds there are immoral, and aware also that the author knows that they are. The reader may not be able to answer Hobbes, but his moral sense, being directly and honestly assailed, will encourage him to resist or to refuse to take seriously the speculations which he cannot refute. He will find in Hobbes' respectful if curious references to religion the homage which vice pays to virtue, and the tone of the author will make him feel that he has to do with ingenious speculations, which need not be taken seriously. Hobbes on the whole, like most genuine sceptics of the time, leaves theology alone. He encourages the general attitude by which the science of the seventeenth century found room to continue its work undisturbed—an attitude which kept science and theology as far as possible in two distinct worlds. "The truths of our religion," says Hobbes in one of his inimitable sentences, "are like wholesome pills for the sick, which if swallowed whole do oft effect a cure, but if chewed, are cast up again without effect." That sentence respects the informal truce between philosophy and theology which both sides on the whole respected. If the philosopher and the scientist left theology alone, however much their works might undermine its fundamental presuppositions, they might hope that the theologians would leave them alone. With this working arrangement Spinoza will have nothing to do. His first original published work, the only original work of his published in his lifetime, is called the *Tractatus Theologico-Politicus*. It laid the foundations of nineteenth-century Biblical criticism by calmly announcing that the Scriptures are to be interpreted by precisely the same scientific methods as any secular books. It categorically refuted the possibility of miracles and of everything which was ordinarily thought of as supernatural. Above all, Spinoza did all this with immense seriousness, was clearly a man who cared intensely for religion and the affairs of the spirit. The ordinary religious man was bound to feel that he had been wounded in the house of his friends: he could not dismiss Spinoza lightly as an ingenious sophist or a lighthearted scoffer. It was inevitable that he should treat him as a traitor. The philosophers and the scientists for their part felt that Spinoza had let the cat out of the bag. With the religious significance of the consequences he had deduced from their assumptions they were not concerned. They could only too well see the trouble into which those consequences would get them. They saw that their only hope of being allowed to carry on their work in peace and to maintain the truce with theology which was of so much importance to them, was to dissociate themselves from Spinoza's conclusions and join in the hue and cry to make him "universally infamous."

The qualities which made Spinoza execrated by his generation were just the qualities which make his philosophy so profound and far-reaching. They were the qualities which made Socrates a martyr and the true originator of philosophy. Spinoza combined in a peculiar degree the scientific and the religious temper. He was a rationalist through and through and he was also a mystic. He felt, as no one else of his generation did, the immense significance of the new view of the world which the sciences of the seventeenth century introduced. Because he was a saint, who believed that man's happiness lay only in the knowledge and love of God, he was concerned above all to ask how this new view of the world affected the assumptions of conduct and religion. He was determined to hold on to both science and religion, and the nature of his scientific and of his religious temper alike made it impossible for him to escape the difficulties with which he was faced by any theory of separate spheres or watertight compartments. God was One. That was the great message of his race to religion, and no one ever believed that more earnestly than Spinoza: and because God was One, He was to be found in science as well as in religion, and science was bound to be religious and religion scientific. Both his science and his religion were to be uncompromising, and in their uncompromising form they were to be brought together.

This bringing together of science and religion in a form which was to be faithful to both was Spinoza's problem, and what a problem it was we shall understand better if we consider for a little how revolutionary and far-reaching the implications of the new sciences were.

The scheme of the world which had been built up by Greek thought in the fourth century B.C.—which, unaltered in its essential features, had furnished ever since a background for men's thought about themselves and the world in which they lived, was essentially pluralistic. It thought of the world as consisting of a number of separate individual substances. No doubt these substances were in relation with one another. But their relations were accidental to their nature. Their natures or essences were peculiar to themselves, and their properties and behaviour were deducible from their essences. They were explainable from themselves alone. Further, the key to the relations between these separate entities or substances was purpose or final cause. The relations of man and other substances to one another were thought of in terms of human action. When this general scheme found expression in theology, God was necessarily thought of as separate and distinct from the other substances in the world—infinitely greater and more perfect than these, but a substance distinct, and the relations which governed the world were the relations determined by God's purposes; and because the world and all that it contained was thought of as having been set there and created to serve the purpose of God—a purpose conceived of as being like a human purpose—the world was pictured as finite, with earth, man's dwelling-place, the centre of it. This conception of the world when applied to physics had assumed that motion was to be explained in terms of the specific properties or qualities of bodies that moved. Bodies fell to the earth because of some essential kinship between their nature and that of the earth. If the moon controlled the tides, its nature must have some peculiar affinity with water.

Now the result of the physical discoveries of Galileo and Descartes was that the motion of bodies was now explained in virtue of their position in the one physical system. Temporal and spatial relations assumed an importance in scientific investigation which they had never had before. Science began now with the system as a whole and explained the motion of bodies in terms of their relations. Final causes were abandoned, and proximity in time and space became the leading principle of causal explanation. Further, the astronomical discoveries of the time destroyed the picture of the finite world set round the earth as its centre and put in its place a world of infinite extension. Things were now what they were and behaved as they did because of their place in this vast infinite system: they were constituted by their external relations—mere links in chains of connexions infinitely prolonged; and they came thus to be thought of as nothing but their external relations, mere points or meeting-places of relations.

Descartes, who first thought out the implications of the new physics, had taught that everything which happened in the world, except man's actions—even the behaviour of animals—had a mechanical explanation and that the essence of matter, which formed this infinite physical system, was extension. In the physical world everything was determined by what was external to it, and the ultimate nature of everything physical was quantitative. Final purposes and individual qualities had both disappeared.

The mind of man was not, according to Descartes, a part of this system, but was known directly as a quite independent substance, not determined but free, and so entirely different in its whole nature from the outside world and from its own body that no rational or natural explanation could be given of the relation between mind and body or between mind and the external bodies which it perceived.

This absolute distinction between mind and body had the curious effect on the prevailing philosophy of the seventeenth century that its scheme of the world demanded perpetual miracles, and miracles of a foolish and perverse kind. The general upshot of the rejection of final causes and of the acceptance of the principles of mechanical explanation had been to give a picture of the physical world from which the notion of God's direct intervention and therefore of miracle was debarred. God had made the physical world so that it could run of itself. But the dualism of body and mind implied that this machine was of such a nature that God had continuously to intervene to establish any connexion between that world and mind. Miracle was banished from nature to reappear in a most capricious and arbitrary form in the connexion between body and mind. For mind in its essence was conceived of as rational and therefore, like the external world, ruled by order and necessity. But all connexion between the two worlds and all that depends upon that connexion, perception and qualities, was the region of perpetual miracle. On the one side was a world of pure thought, on the other a world of pure extension, and in a miracle-sustained limbo between them—perception, action, qualities—in short, life. The central thought in Spinoza is the denial of this dualism: the demonstration that there can be only one substance, that that substance has infinite attributes—two of which are mind and extension; that every attribute is, so to speak, self-contained, *i.e.,* has its own necessary order and sequence, so that there is no passage from a mode in one attribute to a mode in another—no passage from a thought to a body, but that there is no such passage because there is no need for it. The thought is just the thought side of the body, and the body is just the extension side of the thought. The *ordo et connexio idearum* and the *ordo et connexio rerum* are one and the same. God is One and His attributes are infinite, and God is His attributes and all the modes which they imply; and the attributes and all their modes flow from the nature of God as the properties of a triangle flow from its nature—by the necessity of reason.

It follows that all theories or doctrines which describe God as standing apart from nature—whether as creating it or controlling it from out-side to His purposes—or standing toward it as a man stands toward the things on which he acts, are figurative and strictly speaking unmeaning. All things are in God and must be in God: they are all alike manifesta-tions or consequences of His nature.

That is Spinoza's central doctrine. Whether it is a blasphemous and soul-destroying atheism, as most of his contemporaries thought it, or an uplifting and elevating pantheism, as Goethe found it, depends on how it is interpreted. But in any case it makes unmeaning most theological lan-guage which was thought out under the ruling conception of a pluralistic world of substances. It may be that the only difference is that that con-ception started with diversity and sought unity, while this starts with unity and seeks diversity, but the imaginative difference between the two conceptions is very great. It may be that the vital truths which the old theology was trying to express can be restated in the new scheme—but they would have to be restated. However true it may be that Spinoza's central doctrine denies, not the vital truths of Christian theology, but the intellectual framework in which they were stated, nevertheless he did, by his unfaltering acceptance of the new view of the universe implied in the new sciences, entirely destroy that intellectual framework. Most of his contemporaries had never realised how the new scientific theories which they had accepted involved the destruction of that earlier framework. To them Spinoza's system seemed gratuitous destruction. By the beginning of the nineteenth century the implications of the new sciences had become common property and changed the background of men's minds. Thus men were ready to notice, not that Spinoza had a conception of the world fitted to modern thought, but that he found God in it.

The greatness of Spinoza's intention must be clear enough. To be true both to the discoveries of science and the facts of religious experience, to insist that somehow these apparently different worlds were one world, was a great conception. But the value of such an attempt will largely de-pend on how the unity is actually achieved. On the assumptions of the case the philsopher will start with a science and a religion which have been kept sharply separate and are therefore each defective. So when he tries to bring them together, will the scientific narrowness of his science pervert his view of religion or the religious narrowness of his religion pervert his view of science, or will he be great enough to divine just how each suffered from abstraction and will gain from being brought to-gether? As we have seen, Cartesianism had worked out a dualistic view of the world with an abstract physical world which was nothing but extension on the one side and an abstract mental world which was nothing but reasoning on the other, with perceptions and qualities in an unexplained and miraculous limbo between. When Spinoza took these two abstract worlds of mind and extension and put them together, did he put them together as they were and leave out the limbo in the middle—which was no doubt full of irrational miracle but was also full of life—or did he conceive the attributes of mind and extension differently because he conceived them both as attributes of one substance—God?

The answer to that question, I think, is that he partly did both of those things—that there are two tendencies struggling in Spinoza, neither of which is completely dominant, and it is this division in his thought which makes the difficulty not only of his metaphysics, but of his politics.

The question the answering of which is vital for the understanding of Spinoza is how he worked out his doctrine that the order and connexion of ideas is the same as the order and connexion of things. The doctrine is manifestly not true. To take even Spinoza's favourite example of the connexion between the definition of a triangle and its properties, the necessity seems to be the same in the thinking and in what is thought: but in the thinking there is a succession in time, and in the properties of a triangle there is not.

Actually Spinoza has in mind three kinds of connexion—the mathematical relation of implication we have referred to; physical causation, the determination of one event or, as Spinoza says, one mode by another in an infinite chain; and a third and quite different connexion which he never so clearly distinguishes, but which inspires all his finest work, the relation by which a mind somehow expresses or is conscious of its unity with itself and with the whole of which it is a part. Man's universal nature flows from the nature of God with the universal necessity of geometrical implication. Had we adequate knowledge we could so deduce it. The particular nature and existence of this or that man is on the other hand determined by his relation to external causes—determined as part of the infinite chain of physical causation. These are both forms of necessary relation, and between them the nature and character of all men are determined inexorably through and through, and determined though in different ways by the nature of God; and yet the central thought in Spinoza's *Ethic* is the difference between human bondage and human freedom, or between the extent to which man is determined by his passions—*i.e.*, by the working of external causes upon him—or by his own inner nature. Spinoza in his account of human action is trying to hold together three truths: (1) that man is part of the external world, and cannot escape from the conditions which that fact imposes or act save through external means; (2) that man's powers and man's good and evil are determined by his general nature—a man has to be a man, and humanity has its definite conditions and its limits; and (3) that yet consistently with that double necessity man may let himself be dominated by his passions so that his individuality is destroyed and he becomes a mere concourse of external relations, or he may act more and more completely from his own individual nature until he becomes more and more like God, whose essence it is to be entirely determined by His own nature.

There is already a contradiction between the two first forms of necessity as Spinoza states them. For if the nexus of physical causation is absolute and all-embracing, then the individual is unreal—only a concourse of relations with nothing to relate. The physical system which Spinoza took over from Descartes was a purely quantitative system which left no room for individuality because it left no room for qualitative differences. If that part of Spinoza's system is taken literally, it is atheism and it is in the most literal sense soul-destroying. But the central thought of Spinoza's ethics is the individual, who necessarily seeks to preserve his own nature and who can preserve it only by freeing himself from passions, his dependence on the external world, and finding himself by the knowledge of God. Knowledge is for Spinoza the key to liberty. For man can come to know God. By pursuing knowledge he will come to union with his fellows and so to greater power. If men would be led by reason, they would all attain blessedness. The distinction between human bondage and human freedom is for Spinoza the distinction between a man's being determined by the passions—that is, by the influence of external things upon him—and being determined by his own nature; and a man's own nature is to know God. No man can entirely escape the domination of the passions, for man is necessarily a part of an external nature which is greater than him; but blessedness consists in such freedom from passions and such self-determination as is possible to man.

It would be idle to maintain that Spinoza manages to reconcile satisfactorily the different points of view to which he seeks to do justice. Nevertheless, much of his strength comes from his combining a high degree of moral insight with a resolute determination to take men as he finds them: he is consistently idealist and matter-of-fact at the same time.

This combination of the matter-of-fact and the ideal is the distinguishing feature of his political theory. "Philosophers," he says in the first paragraph of his *Tractatus Politicus*, "regard the passions from which we suffer as vices into which men fall through their own fault. They are therefore accustomed to laugh at them, lament or blame them, or, if they desire a reputation for more than usual piety, to detest them. They think therefore that their action is divine and that they attain the height of wis-

dom when they praise in all kinds of ways a human nature which nowhere exists and pour reproaches on human nature as it actually is. For
they conceive men not as they are, but as they would like them to be.
Whence it has come about that they mostly write satire instead of ethics
and have never conceived a politics which could be of any practical use.
Their politics is a chimera, a political theory which could be realised in
Utopia or in the Golden Age the poets write of, where it would not be
needed. The result is that of all the sciences which are intended for use,
the theory of politics differs more from its practice than any other, and
no men are thought less fit for governing a state than the theorists or
political philosophers!" Spinoza's politics are to be scientific. He is going to
study human nature with the same freedom of mind as men study mathematics. He has tried "not to laugh at human actions or to weep over them
or alter them but to understand them."

The first result of this attitude of impartial scientific inquiry is a
position curiously like that of Hobbes. In some ways no two men are
more unlike than Hobbes and Spinoza, but they are agreed in this that
the business of the political theorist is to take men as he finds them, to
describe political society as it arises out of men's actual needs and desires.
Mr. Laski has pointed out that Hobbes was the first political theorist to
try to found the State not on what men ought to do, but on what they
wanted. The old basis of the State had been one of moral authority and,
because it had been that, it required a common recognition of moral authority. "Toleration of divers religions" had been a political impossibility.
In the seventeenth century it had become a political necessity, and political
theory, if it was to have any reality, had to recognise the new situation.
Hobbes no doubt had met the new situation by a theory which really
denied morality. But for much of what he says he had more immediate
justification than is ordinarily admitted. He might well have replied to
his critics that he was trying (as they were not) to meet the facts of the
situation: that it was no use appealing to moral authority when men
would not acknowledge a common authority, and that in his account of
the Laws of Nature he had admitted to the full the importance of moral
behaviour for the State. "The Laws of Nature are immutable and eternal:
for injustice, ingratitude, arrogance, pride, iniquity, acceptance of persons,
can never be made lawful. For it can never be that war shall preserve life
and peace destroy it." But at the same time he would have said moral
laws only make for peace when they are commonly observed, and in all
the confusion of moral standards and moral behaviour we can find a sure
basis for the State not in a moral authority about which men squabble,
but in the common need for security of which all men are conscious.

Spinoza had a far profounder view of human nature than had Hobbes. Because he had that, he displays a far more consistent realism. He sees through Hobbes' curious legal pedantry at a glance. But for all that he begins where Hobbes begins, by taking human nature as he finds it for the fact with which he has to deal: by insisting that the business of the political theorist is not to judge, but to understand and to see how the situation as he understands it can be dealt with.

The fundamental fact for the political theorist according to Spinoza is man's desire for self-preservation. "The endeavour after self-preservation," he says in the *Ethic*, "is the primary and only foundation of virtue." No doubt he means by self-preservation far more than Hobbes had meant by it. When he says, "Since reason demands nothing which is opposed to nature, it demands therefore that every person should love himself, should seek his own profit," so much Hobbes might have said; but Spinoza goes on, "what is truly profitable to him, should desire everything that leads man to greater perfection." But if that difference in the meaning of self-preservation is forgotten, Spinoza's statements seem little else than a repetition of Hobbes'. Man always desires to increase his power. That is a necessary fact which is neither right nor wrong, good nor bad. Men have therefore as much right as they have might. The sole object of men's actions, and in particular the sole object of their social relations, is increase in human power or might. That is a position not unlike Hobbes' when he describes men as actuated by "a restless desire of power after power."

Spinoza agrees also with Hobbes that you cannot turn men from following the bent of their nature by a contract or promise, if that would make them act against their own interests. Men cannot in the nature of things act against their interests as they conceive them. Further, Spinoza holds that, so far as men act under the domination of their passions, they seek not what will really give them happiness, but conflicting interests. If men understood the real nature of things, they would see that nothing increases a man's power or might so much as other men, and that men acquire power in so far as they seek a common good and are weak and impotent when they seek rival goods. That is what reason teaches, and if men were all guided by reason, they would be in harmony and form an ideal society. But few men are so guided by reason. Most men seek not their real interests, but the objects which their passions incite them to desire. Because they do that, their interests clash, and therefore Spinoza like Hobbes can say that men are naturally enemies. Thus we get a picture of the origin of society not unlike that of Hobbes. Men are naturally enemies, because led by their passions to conflicting ends, and reduced by that mutual conflict to impotence. The purpose of the State is to increase men's power. It does that in two ways: positively by enabling men to unite together for common purposes and thus giving them an immensely greater power over nature; negatively by restraining men from the conflicts into which their passions drive them, applying to passionate men the sort of sanctions which alone passionate men can understand. To effect this end government is necessary, and government is impossible without power. From the institution of government alone actions become just and unjust: for justice is what aids the ends of government and injustice what hinders them. A state or a Government, like an individual, has right in so far as it has might. There is no sense in saying that a state can act in such and such a way, but it has no right so to do. If it has might, it has right. A state, like an individual, must act according to its own interests as it conceives them, and can therefore no more than an individual be bound by a promise when its interests and the keeping of the promise conflict.

So far Spinoza and Hobbes use the same language. Because Spinoza did so he seemed to his contemporaries to take his stand along with Hobbes and Machiavelli as a cynical realist, to join with them in seeking to overthrow all the noble structure of moral authority and the Law of Nature which have been for so long regarded as the basis of the State. But in truth the agreement is only on the surface. Spinoza thought that might was right, but he had a far other view than Hobbes of the real sources of might, and that difference transforms his political theory.

Passion is impotence, and reason is might. Men are weak when their passions incite them to conflict, strong when reason unites them in pursuit of a common good. If we are to be realists and proclaim that "things are what they are and their consequences will be what they will be," we must recognise this most fundamental law which governs all human nature and human relations. Unity alone is strength, and unity is impossible without unity of mind, and unity of mind is found in the knowledge of God alone.

Man has right in so far as he has might, but he only has might in so far as he understands human nature in himself or in others. The State has a right to do all that it has power to do; but there are many things which States attempt which in the nature of things they cannot do and which they have therefore no right to do.

Spinoza, I have said, is a greater realist than Hobbes. This is seen at once in his treatment of Hobbes' doctrine of the unlimited right of the sovereign power. Hobbes had seen the necessity of a Government with power enough to enforce peace. He had realised that men's natural powers are so equal that no man can of himself "keep other men in awe." He had seen therefore that the power wielded by the sovereign could not be his own power but must somehow be given him by his subjects. But he had treated that giving of power to the sovereign as a mysterious legal process, a giving over of power which must be absolute and unconditioned and cannot be retracted. Spinoza dismisses with ease all the legal sophistry on which the doctrine of absolute sovereignty is based. The sovereign has right in so far as he has might; but his might is grounded on the support men give him, on his success in making men seek common aims, in strengthening concord and furthering their real purposes. If he so governs that men would rather risk the evil consequences of civil war than go on tolerating the oppression of an evil sovereign, he has reached the limits of his might and therefore of his right. The power of a sovereign may be legally unlimited, but that means little or nothing. His power has real and actual limitations rooted in the facts of human nature. "For we must notice in the first place that as in the State of Nature that man is most powerful and has most right over himself who is led by reason, so too that State will be most powerful and have most right which is founded on and directed by reason. For the right of the State is the power of the common people when they are led and determined as by a single mind. And union of minds is only possible where the State aims always at that which sound reason teaches to be useful for all men."

From this standpoint Spinoza develops a doctrine of the limits of State action which is of universal application and of which men still need to be reminded. The limitations of State action are determined by the nature of that action. "Subjects are in the power of the State in so far as they fear its power or threats or love the civil State. From which it follows that all those things to which men cannot be induced by rewards or threats are not in the power of the State." The State ought not to control opinion, because it cannot control opinion: it ought not to enforce religion, because religion cannot be enforced. We cannot object to this argument that if the State cannot control opinion, it does not matter whether it tries to do so or not. For the real force of Spinoza's argument is that, though a State cannot make men moral or religious, it can only be strong if men are moral and religious, and they can be that only or more easily if the State will do its proper work. "Liberty of mind or fortitude is a private virtue. The virtue of government is security." Spinoza's teaching separates ethics and politics, but it also insists that politics depends upon ethics: and just because it depends upon ethics it cannot do the work of ethics; it cannot and therefore has no right to make men moral.

The union of mind which gives the State its strength comes not from men being forced together in external bonds, but from each man being true to his own inner nature. It is men's external relations—their passions —which disunite them. The external action of the State may control these passions in the interests of reason. The action of the State is the action of men united by reason against men disunited by passion: it is therefore man's rational nature controlling his irrational nature. But however true it may be to say that the State represents man's rational nature, it is rational nature using irrational because external instruments, and it can never have power over the real nature of the individual. His springs of happiness and sources of power are in himself.

Thus Spinoza's political theory, which seems on the surface but to reproduce the barren individualism of Hobbes, proves on closer examination to contain the core of that idealist theory of the State which is ordinarily thought to have been first proclaimed by Rousseau and was developed by Hegel and the Hegelians, and yet it never countenances that exaltation of the State over the individual which is the defect of much idealist theory of the State. "The right of the State is the power of the common people when they are led and determined as by a single mind." That contains the essence of Rousseau's theory of the general will and of the organic conception of the State. But Spinoza combines with that idealism Hobbes' respect for mere facts and actual difficulties, which makes him more anxious than most idealists to do justice to the legal and external side of the State. To that combination he adds the message—which is perhaps peculiarly his own—that the purpose of all institutions is to control external relations by reason, but especially to promote in their members the greatest of all goods—liberty of mind.

LOCKE

The spirit of rational liberalism underlying Anglo-American civilization is best reflected in John Locke (1632–1704). Locke was born of a middle-class Puritan family, and his father had fought in the civil war on the side of the Parliamentary party. Locke became early associated with the leaders of the Whig party, and helped one of them, Lord Ashley, in the drawing up of the *Fundamental Constitutions of Carolina* (1669), of which colony Lord Ashley was one of the founders and chief owners. From 1675 to 1679 Locke lived in France, mostly in Montpellier and Paris. After his return to England in 1679, the outlook for Liberal sympathizers became increasingly grim and uncertain, and late in 1683 Locke was forced to flee to Holland, where he stayed until early 1689. He was captivated by the spirit of manliness and freedom prevailing there, and he envied the country that had become the center for political and religious refugees from all over Europe, including the British Isles. Locke's liberality of outlook was formed in its fundamentals before he set foot on Dutch soil, but his experience there showed him that liberalism in religion and politics could work, and it reinforced his determination to help rid England of the illiberal government of Charles II and—later—the despotic obscurantism of James II. The first of Locke's *Letters Concerning Toleration* (1689) was composed and first published in Holland, and an abstract of his chief philosophical work, the *Essay Concerning Human Understanding* (1690), the foundation of modern empiricism, was also first published there. Shortly after his return to England, Locke published his most famous work in political theory, the *Two Treatises of Government* (1690). Its philosophical rationalism, luminous common sense, and liberality of spirit have made it the Bible of modern liberalism, and its influence in America, particularly in the period immediately preceding the American Revolution, has been no less profound than in England itself. In addition to his central interests in free government and religious toleration, Locke concerned himself with political economy and education, and his *Thoughts Concerning Education* (1693) is still considered a milestone in the development of modern educational thinking, emphasizing the free development of the individual personality, rather than the traditional (and authoritarian) methods of stereotyped learning by rote. In the whole history of English thought he is the most English of all English writers: his respect for fact, rather than abstract speculation; his acceptance of probability as a guide for thought and action, in lieu of the futile quest for certainty; and, above all, his moderation and fairness in approaching problems of philosophy or practical affairs.

By stressing labor as the source of property and value, Locke had an immense influence on later socialist thought. In his own time, and for two centuries later, Locke's economic philosophy helped to liberate the ingenious and industrious entrepreneur from the paralyzing interference of government and custom. The socialists used the same Lockean theory of property to demand communal control or ownership of the basic means of production, since in their view the collective nature of work in advanced industry required collective ownership. It thus became fashionable to decry Locke as a bourgeois economist, reflecting only the interests of the capitalist classes rather than of the people as a whole. This interpretation of Locke is to be found in Karl Marx's *A History of Economic Theories from the Physiocrats to Adam Smith* (1952), published posthumously as the fragmentary remains of the fourth volume of *Das Kapital*, which Marx never finished. Karl Marx (1818–1883) was born in the Rhineland, which, more than any other part of Germany, had been strongly permeated with democratic and revolutionary ideas by the French Revolution and the long French occupation during the revolutionary and Napoleonic wars. In 1843 Marx was forced to leave Germany because of the oppressive political atmosphere, and he spent several years in France and Belgium before he went to England in 1849. He planned to stay there for a few weeks, but changed his mind and stayed there until his death in 1883. His *Communist Manifesto* (1848), written with the aid of his friend and collaborator, Frederick Engels, is still the briefest exposition of the communist creed, and it has made history as perhaps no other pamphlet has done in the last hundred years. His monumental analysis of the capitalist system, based mostly on English conditions and source materials, was *Das Kapital*, the first volume of which was published in 1867; the second and third volumes appeared posthumously in 1885-1895, edited by Engels. Marx's writings show little understanding of English political ideas and ways of thought, and his lack of insight into the forces and motivation of English politics would have been little better or worse had he stayed in Germany all his life. By contrast, his writings demonstrate a profound knowledge of the English economic system of his time. Much of his source material was derived from official English government reports. Yet it never occurred to him that the self-analysis of English capitalism, to which he owed the documentary sources of his grand indictment, might eventually evolve into peaceful self-improvement and change.

The impact of Locke on British politics is examined by Sir Frederick Pollock in an address on "Locke's Theory of the State" (1904). Pollock (1845-1937) was a leading jurist of his time, teaching common law at the Inns of Court (1884-1890) before his appointment as professor of jurisprudence at Oxford (1883-1903). His best-known books are his *Spinoza* (1880), *Introduction to the History of the Science of Politics* (1890), and *The Genius of the Common Law* (1912). Pollock's appraisal of Locke shows how the originally liberal political theory of Locke so completely permeated British political thinking and practice that it became the generally accepted, and even conservative, viewpoint.

In the twentieth century Bertrand Russell (1861-   ) is considered by many the outstanding philosopher of the time. The incisiveness and sharpness of his thinking are matched by the brilliance of his style, and he received in 1950 the Nobel Prize for literature in recognition of his literary merits. Russell has written widely on many subjects outside his dominant interest in philosophy and the theory of knowledge, covering the whole range of human relations from marriage to world organization. His sympathy for Locke is stronger than for any other philosopher who preceded him, as is clearly manifest in his *A History of Western Philosophy* (1945), one of the few histories of philosophy written by one who is an original and distinguished philosopher himself. His numerous writings on political philosophy include *Roads to Freedom* (1918), *The Practice and Theory of Bolshevism* (1920), *Freedom and Organization, 1814-1914* (1934), *Power: A New Social Analysis* (1938), *Philosophy and Politics* (1947), and *Human Society in Ethics and Politics* (1954).

Marx on LOCKE

One need but compare the works of North and Locke with the writings of Petty (*Quantulumcumque*, 1682; *A Treatise of Taxes and Contributions*, 1662; and *The Political Anatomy of Ireland*, 1672) to gain a clear picture of their close connection and to establish undeniably, especially as regards the regulating of the rate of interest, that North's and Locke's reasonings are based on Petty.

In 1691, impelled by the same circumstances, Locke published *Some Considerations of the Consequences of the Lowering of Interest* and North his *Discourses Upon Trade*. Yet the viewpoints they defended were diametrically opposed. Locke believed high interest to be caused by a shortage of money, while North thought it caused by a shortage of capital or revenue. North was the first to develop a clear idea of "stock" or capital or, rather, of money considered as a simple form of capital instead of a means of circulation. Opposed to the ideas which Locke held, Sir Dudley North was the first to formulate a correct concept of interest.

* * *

If we compare Locke's doctrine of labor with his doctrine of the origin of rent and interest—surplus value assumed only these two fixed forms to him—surplus value resembles nothing other than alienated labor, surplus labor which certain individuals can appropriate because they possess both land and capital, the prerequisites of labor. To permit any man to possess more means of production than a single person can utilize in his work is, according to Locke, a political conception contradicting the natural basis of property, the law of private property.

These are the passages which interest us:

Though the earth and all inferior creatures be common to all men, yet every man has a property in his own person; this nobody has any right to but himself. The labour of his body and the work of his hands we may say are properly his. Whatsoever, then, he removes out of the state that nature hath provided and left it in, he hath mixed his labour with and joined to it something that is his own, and thereby makes it his property. [*Of Government*, Book 2, Chapter V, *Works*, ed. 1768, II, p. 229.]

[From Karl Marx, *A History of Economic Theories from the Physiocrats to Adam Smith* (1863, trans. Terence McCarthy, Langland Press, 1952). By permission.]

His labour hath taken it out of the hands of Nature where it was common, and belonged equally to all her children, and hath thereby appropriated it to himself. [*Ibid.*, p. 230.]

The same law of nature that does by this means give us property, does also bound that property too . . . As much as anyone can make use of to any advantage of life before it spoils, so much he may by his labour fix a property in; whatever is beyond this, is more than his share, and belongs to others. [*Ibid.*, p. 230.]

And hence subduing or cultivating the earth, and having dominion, we see are joined together. [*Ibid.*, p. 231.]

The measure of property nature has well set by the extent of men's labour and the conveniency of life. No man's labour could subdue or appropriate all, nor could his enjoyment consume more than a small part; so that it was impossible for any man, this way, to entrench upon the rights of another or acquire to himself a property to the prejudice of his neighbour. . . . Which measure did confine every man's possession to a very modest proportion, and such as he might appropriate to himself without injury to anybody in the first ages of the world. . . . The same measure may be allowed still, without prejudice to anybody, full as the world seems. . . . We shall find that the possessions he could make himself, upon the measures we have given, would not be very large, nor, even to this day, prejudice the rest of mankind or give them reason to complain or think themselves injured by this man's encroachment, though the race of men have now spread themselves to all the corners of the world. [*Ibid.*, pp. 231, 232.]

Almost all the value of things is bestowed by labor. (Value is here to be taken as meaning use value and labor as concrete labor without allusion to quantity; but if labor is the measure of exchange value, it is so only because labor is the creator of use values.) Use value which cannot be reduced to labor is a gift of nature and is, therefore, common property. In this way Locke tries to prove, not that property can be acquired other than by labor, but that, even if property is held in common, nature, through the labor of individuals, can create private property.

For it is labour indeed that puts the difference of value on everything. . . . I think it will be but a very modest computation to say that of the products of the earth useful to the life of man nine-tenths are the effects of labour; nay, if we will rightly estimate things as they come to our use, and cast up the several expenses about them—what in them is purely owing to nature, and what to labour—we shall find that in most of them ninety-nine hundredths are wholly to be put on account of labour. [*Ibid.*, p. 235.]

'Tis labour, then, which puts the greatest part of value upon land. [*Ibid.*, p. 235.]

Though the things of nature are given in common, yet man, by being master of himself and proprietor of his own person and the actions or labour of it, had still in himself the great foundation of property. [*Ibid.*, p. 235.]

The two limits of property thus arise from the physical limitation upon the amount of labor an individual can perform and from the fact that no one should amass beyond his needs. Apart from other exchanges, this later is extended by the exchange of perishable products for money.

He might heap up as much of these durable things as he pleased, the exceeding of the bounds of his just property not lying in the large-ness of his possessions, but the perishing of anything uselessly in it. And thus came in the use of money—some lasting thing that men might keep without spoiling, and that, by mutual consent, men would take in exchange for the truly useful but perishable supports of life. [*Ibid.*, p. 236.]

In this way, comes about the inequality of private property. The meas-ure of personal labor nevertheless holds good.

But since gold and silver, being little useful to the life of man in pro-portion to food, raiment, and carriage, has its value only from the consent of men, whereof labour yet makes, in great part, the measure, it is plain that the consent of men have agreed to a disproportionate and unequal possession of the earth—I mean out of the bounds of society and compact; for in governments the laws regulate it; they having, by consent, found out and agreed in a way how a man may rightfully and without injury possess more than he himself can make use of by receiving gold and silver, which may continue long in a man's possession, without decaying for the overplus, and agreeing those metals should have a value. [*Ibid.*, p. 237.]

Against what Locke states in this passage must be set his argument in the following one, which deals with interest. Meanwhile, it should be remembered that Locke believed the laws of nature to establish personal labor as the natural limit of private property.

Money therefore, in buying and selling, being perfectly in the same condition with other commodities, and subject to all the same laws of value, let us next see how it comes to be of the same nature with land, by yielding a certain yearly income, which we call use, or interest. For land produces naturally something new and profitable, and of value to mankind; but money is a barren thing, and produces nothing, but by compact transfers that profit, that was the reward of one man's labour, into another man's pocket. That which occasions this, is the unequal distribution of money; which inequality has the same effect too upon land, that it has upon money. . . . For as the unequal distribution of land (you having more than you can, or will manure, and another less), brings you a tenant for your land; and the same unequal distribution of money (I having more than I can, or will employ, and another less), bring me a tenant for my money: so my money is apt in trade, by the industry of the borrower, to produce more than six per cent. to the borrower, as well as your land, by the labour of the tenant, is apt to produce more fruits, than his rent comes to. [Locke, *Considerations of the Lowering of Interest.*]

In this passage, Locke, polemicizing against private ownership of the soil, shows ground rent to differ in no respect from usury. Because of the unequal distribution of the means of production, each "transfers that profit, that was the reward of one man's labour, into another man's pocket."

Locke's distinction is the more important since he is the classic voice of the juridical theories of bourgeois society as opposed to feudalism, and because, moreover, his philosophy served as the basis upon which the thinking of all subsequent English economists rested.

Pollock on LOCKE

Locke's *Essay on Civil Government* is well known, and is probably the most important contribution ever made to English constitutional law by an author who was not a lawyer by profession; certainly there is nothing to be compared to it until we come to Bagehot in our own time. Still I do not know that it has ever been analysed by an English lawyer with reference to its immediate purpose and circumstances. In fact Locke's political

[Sir Frederick Pollock, "Locke's Theory of the State," *Proceedings of the British Academy, 1903–1904* (Oxford University Press, 1904). By permission.]

doctrine holds quite a secondary place in such accounts of Locke as are generally current in the hands of the educated public. The *Essay on Civil Government* has been overshadowed by the *Essay on the Human Understanding* and the *Letters on Toleration*. This, together with the special occasion, may perhaps be a sufficient excuse for the present attempt.

The first thing to bear in mind about the *Essay on Civil Government* is that it is essentially an apologia for the Convention Parliament, no less than Hobbes's *Leviathan* and *Behemoth* were an indictment of the Long Parliament. It is true that in the body of the work the language employed is studiously general. But the date of publication, 1690, would alone be enough to remove any doubts of the intention, and moreover that intention is clearly stated in the Preface to the two treatises of which the Essay is the second. It may be well to cite Locke's own words. 'Reader, Thou hast here the Beginning and End of a Discourse concerning Government; what Fate has otherwise disposed of the Papers that should have filled up the Middle, and were more than all the rest, 'tis not worth while to tell thee. These which remain, I hope are sufficient to establish the Throne of our great Restorer, our present King *William*; to make good his Title, in the Consent of the People; which being the only one of all lawful Governments, he has more fully and clearly, than any Prince in *Christendom*; and to justify to the World the People of *England*, whose love of their just and natural Rights, with their Resolution to preserve them, saved the Nation when it was on the very brink of Slavery and Ruin.' The doctrine which Locke had to confute was, as is well known, that of absolute monarchy; the champion whom he attacked by name and elaborately demolished in the first of the *Two Treatises of Government* was, however strange it may seem to us nowadays, not Thomas Hobbes but Sir Robert Filmer. For us Hobbes is the recognized founder of the English school of politics and jurisprudence; while Filmer, as the late Prof. Croom Robertson incidentally observed in discussing Hobbes (and I see no reason to doubt the soundness of the remark), is saved by Locke from oblivion. In Locke's time Sir Robert Filmer was fashionable among royalists and Hobbes was not. Hobbes's uncompromising rejection of ecclesiastical claims made it, in fact, impossible for a party bound up with Anglican prelacy to have anything to do with him; and his justification of obedience to any *de facto* government in being was hardly less distasteful to maintainers of the divine right of kings. Express controversy with Hobbes was therefore quite useless for Locke's purpose. Nevertheless Locke must have seen that, apart from the party strife of the moment, Hobbes was the really formidable adversary. Moreover Filmer, with all his absurdities, had one fundamental point in common with Hobbes. Indeed he was the only publicist of the time, so far as I know, who mentioned Hobbes with approval, though a limited approval. 'With no small Content,' says Filmer, 'I read Mr. Hobs's Book *De Cive*, and his *Leviathan*, about the Rights of Sovereignty, which no man, that I know, hath so amply and judiciously handled: I consent with him about the Rights of *exercising* Government, but I cannot agree to his means of *acquiring* it [1].' Again: 'We do but flatter ourselves, if we hope ever to be governed without an Arbitrary Power. No: we mistake, the Question is not, Whether there shall be an Arbitrary Power; but the only point is, Who shall have that Arbitrary Power, whether one man or many? There never was, nor ever can be any People govern'd without a Power of making Laws, and every Power of making Laws must be Arbitrary: For to make a Law according to Law, is *Contradictio in adjecto* [2].' This, I need hardly say, is pure Hobbism. The impossibility of a limited government or 'mixarchy [3]' is the very burden of Hobbes's *Behemoth*.

We need not be surprised, therefore, either at the lack of specific dealing with Hobbes in Locke's *Essay*, or at the ample internal evidence that Locke had in fact studied Hobbes's doctrine with quite as much critical attention as Filmer's.

There is no occasion for us to trouble ourselves with Locke's polemic against Filmer, even so far as it runs over from the First Treatise into the Essay. King Charles I's imaginary title as right heir of Adam is as grotesque to any modern lawyer as Adam's imaginary political dominion over the world can be to any modern publicist. Good Sir Robert wholly failed, as Locke was at the pains to show at large, to prove what was the rule of succession to Adam's original title, why it should have been primogeniture rather than equal division, and whether it is discoverable by the light of nature or imparted to us by any and what revelation. It would be too curious, perhaps, to consider whether he supposed the course of descent to be in fee simple, tail male, or how otherwise, and whether after the Deluge Noah took by a new grant and became a new stock of descent, or was in as of Adam's old estate. I have known only one man capable of doing full justice to that theme, my lamented and most learned friend Mr. Challis. Locke does point out that the whole of Filmer's theory falls to the ground unless he can make out that Shem was universal monarch. Adam's original title, moreover, had already been relied on to quite the

[1] Preface to *Observations Concerning the Original of Government* (1679).
[2] Preface to *The Anarchy of a Limited or Mixed Monarchy* (1679).
[3] This word was restored by Dr. Tönnies from Hobbes's MS.

opposite purpose by the section of the Independents known as Levellers. They deduced to all men, as sons of Adam, 'a natural property, right, and freedom' which could be duly exercised only in a pure democracy. Sir Robert Filmer, then, is out of the story; nor is it worth while to guess what kind of reply he could or would have attempted if he had been living; and we may proceed to Locke's own account of political power.

At the outset the object of inquiry is thus defined: 'Political Power . . . I take to be a Right of making Laws with Penalties of Death, and consequently all less Penalties, for the regulating and preserving of Property, and of employing the Force of the Community, in the Execution of such Laws, and in the Defence of the Commonwealth from foreign Injury, *and all this only for the publick Good.*' The last clause, which I have italicized, gives the keynote of the whole Essay. Princes and rulers hold their powers, whatever may be their legal form, not by an absolute right founded on grant, covenant, or otherwise, but on conditions in the nature of a trust, and under liability to forfeiture if the conditions are not fulfilled. Locke was no lawyer; but it is allowable to believe that the peculiar doctrines of the English Common Law as to conditional estates, and of English Courts of Equity as to the duties of trustees, although the latter was still in its infancy, had a distinct influence in moulding his dialectic. For absolute originality there was no room. Every kind of material for political construction was ready to hand in the polemics of the Reformation controversy, not to speak of the mediaeval writers who had become to Locke's contemporaries far more obscure than they are to us. The researches of modern scholars, among whom the first place is undoubtedly Gierke's, have shown that all possible theoretical combinations, except the much later system of Cabinet Government which has democratized our monarchy, were anticipated, if not developed, by the political writers of the sixteenth century. Locke's work was inevitably eclectic, and must have been so even if it had not been conditioned by a definite practical aim. He is so far from professing to be original that he is almost ostentatious in following Hooker, whom he vouches at several points in fairly copious extracts. Hooker, of course, was an authority whom Anglicans were bound to treat with respect. The skill and judgement of Locke's performance were proved in the most conclusive manner by the commanding position which the doctrine formulated by him acquired forthwith and held for nearly a century.

Locke's political system, like all such systems for a long time before and a long time after him, purports to be founded on natural law; that is to say, on rules of conduct which the light of reason, without aid of any special revelation, and without assuming the existence or authority of any form of society, can discover as generally applicable to man as a rational being. This, I think, is a sufficient account for our purpose of what Locke's contemporaries understood by the law of nature, however widely they differed in their methods of ascertaining its principles, and in the results which they derived. Hobbes was as ready as any man to declare that the laws of nature are immutable and eternal; which however did not prevent his laws of nature from being unlike other people's, or other people from regarding several of Hobbes's immutably true propositions as not only mischievous but demonstrably false. It is important for any fair appreciation of Locke to remember that, although the mediaeval tradition was interrupted, the mediaeval assumption that there is a law of nature, and that when ascertained it is supreme, was still prevalent. This indeed had never been contradicted, save so far as any Protestant controversialists maintained with Dumoulin that the text of Scripture came first. Possibly both Locke and his English opponents would have accepted the Reformers' position on that point; it was not one which they had occasion to consider. But Locke does not confine the obligations of the law of nature to mortal men. He proves *a fortiori* that those obligations are binding on princes (§ 195). They 'are so great, and so strong, in the Case of *Promises*, that Omnipotency itself can be tied by them. *Grants, Promises,* and *Oaths* are *Bonds* that *hold the Almighty.*' Locke may or may not have read in an earlier writer rediscovered for modern readers by Gierke that 'Deus ipse ex promissione obligatur.'

Thus Locke was bound to begin with the 'state of nature.' No other way of answering either Hobbes or Filmer would have given formal satisfaction. But this state, for Locke as for the Schoolmen, is rather a perfectly conscious abstraction than an attempt to construct the actual origin of society. The question is what a man's rights would be in the absence of any positive institutions. Nevertheless an actual state of nature exists between independent princes and rulers, and between any subjects of different states (or jurisdictions) who may meet in a place where there is no civilized government (§ 14). Under what law (to put a modern example) are a Scot and a French Canadian in the Khaibar Pass? Modern jurisprudence can in most cases lay hold of some circumstance to obtain a working answer. But the topic may not be pursued here. Hobbes is met with flat contradiction (though not explicitly, for the reasons already given) at the earliest possible point. All men are equal by nature in the sense that no one man has an original claim on any other's political obedience; not in any other sense, and so far we are at one with Hobbes. Every man is entitled and bound to preserve the existence which God has given him. But (contrary to Hobbes) he is no less bound to preserve other men, being his fellow creatures and fellow servants, 'when his own preservation comes not in competition.' This amounts to saying that the problem is not to account for the existence of society, but to ascertain its best or normal mode of existence. I should be the first to admit that Locke's way of saying it is both less frank and less sound than Aristotle's. As against the opponents he had to reckon with, it was effective and ingenious, being so framed that no one who accepted the authority of Scripture could well traverse it without manifest risk of impiety. Hence every man's natural power over others is already not arbitrary, as Hobbes would have it, but quasi-judicial. Every man has natural judicial and executive power until such powers are regularly constituted. Hence, again, the law of nature authorizes all necessary acts of self-defence; and this, even under the rule of settled law, is the only ground for the jurisdiction of any government over resident aliens: a curious opinion which seems to be peculiar to Locke, and gratuitous; for one does not see why the theory of submission by tacit consent, on which Locke has to rely later, is less applicable to temporary than to permanent allegiance. This doctrine of the executive power is doubtless open, says Locke, to the objection that it makes every man a judge in his own cause. That is so, and the use of civil government is to remedy such inconvenience. But absolute monarchy fails just in this respect, for the absolute monarch so dear to Hobbes and Filmer remains in a state of nature with respect to his own subjects, and therefore judge in his own cause.

Further, there is a 'plain difference between the state of Nature, and the state of War, which however some men have confounded': for 'men living together according to reason, without a common superior on earth with authority to judge between them' may live in peace if they will, and such is their will so long as they are reasonable. 'Want of a common judge with authority puts all men in a state of nature'; but it is only some act of aggression, 'force without right upon a man's person,' that makes a state of war. Political authority is instituted to avoid the risk of a state of war, not to put an end to a state of war necessarily existing. In short, in the state of nature there may be peace, though a precarious peace. This is, of course, intended as a mortal stroke against Hobbes's theory, and implicitly denies his position that the worst of governments is always more tolerable than the state of nature. Slavery is the result of conquest in a state of war; and freedom is not the absence of all rule, but 'is to have a standing rule to live by' as opposed to being subject to an arbitrary power like a conqueror's. Not that even a conqueror's power is unlimited of right; for Locke argues in a later chapter, the connexion of which with his main purpose is not made very clear, that a conqueror does not acquire general dominion over the property of the conquered, but is entitled at most to a charge upon it for an indemnity.

Locke thinks it prudent to establish a natural right of property (chap. v) antecedent to political institutions. His solution of the problem is that appropriation is the reward of labour. A man acquires a right in severally to that which 'he hath mixed his labour with.' The preceding assumption that 'every man has a property in his own person' appeared safe and easy to Locke, but it is certainly not good law, and was expressly contradicted by Ulpian ('dominus membrorum suorum nemo videtur'). The rights of every man to personal safety, reputation, and so forth, are not marketable or transferable, and are wholly distinct in kind from rights of property. Locke's attempt to make an extended conception of Occupation bear the whole burden of Property was eminently that of an ingenious layman. It is far from obvious, assuming Locke's premises, how any one can claim the sanction of the law of nature for appropriating more than is necessary to support himself and his family. Locke sees the difficulty, but cannot be said to remove it. This economic digression, however, is now of little interest. It is explained by Locke's anxiety to set up as many barriers as possible against arbitrary interference on the part of the State. He seems even to ignore the doctrine of Eminent Domain, of which he must have heard. We cannot suppose that he would have actually denied the moral right of the State to take private property for public purposes on payment of just compensation, but he may have thought it so liable to abuse as to be best kept in the background.

Property cannot be made secure by natural right alone, and for the better securing of their properties men have entered into civil society. The will of the body politic, when formed, is determined by the will of the majority, and of a bare majority if there be no different express agreement. For this Locke does not give any reason but the necessity of the case; it is certain that much worse ones have been given. As a matter of fact, we now know that a majority vote has not been generally recognized in archaic societies; the difficulty of obtaining nominal unanimity was overcome (as in special cases it still has to be) by various methods, including varying elements of force and fiction. This does not apply to the original agreement to form a society, which is assumed to be unanimous, and includes only the actual parties to it. Any one who stands out may go his ways and provide for himself elsewhere. It would seem that the community is entitled to enforce his departure; it is certain, on Locke's principles, that it has not the right to detain him against his will. Could he agree to stay in an inferior capacity like that of a resident alien? But it is needless to pursue the auxiliary fictions which might be devised. A body politic, then, is formed by consent; the essential term of the agreement is that every member gives up his natural judicial and executive power to the community (not, as Hobbes maintains, to an irresponsible sovereign); and this consent is renewed, tacitly if not expressly, in the person of every new member; for one cannot accept the benefit of a settled government except on those terms on which it is offered. Locke is bold to assert that 'a child is born a subject of no country or government,' and may choose his allegiance for himself at the age of discretion: this is another opinion which no modern lawyer will accept, least of all a continental one. It is however necessary to Locke's theory, and is one of the many details in which his individualism, and every scheme of individualism, breaks down. He guards himself to a certain extent by adding that a man does not make himself a member of an existing commonweal merely by accepting the protection of its government. Nothing short of 'positive engagement and express promise and compact' will confer citizenship.

As to the historical objection for want of proof that governments were in fact originally founded by consent, Locke answers, first that historical evidence of what men did before the beginning of history is not to be expected, and secondly that examples of states being founded by consent, such as Rome and Venice, are not wanting. More recent and more striking examples might have been drawn from the settlement of New England, but the fact that the colonists remained and professed to remain subjects of the king of England would have given too much of a handle for controversy; not to mention that the Pilgrim Fathers, whose deliberate constitution of themselves into a body politic is on record, were not at all like primitive or prehistoric men. This last consideration, however, would have had no weight among seventeenth-century disputants. The general prevalence of monarchy in early times is admitted as a fact, but not admitted to be any argument against the origin of government in consent. Why should not the consent and intention of the founders have followed the precedent set by the existing usage of families? We may suppose if we like that 'a family by degrees grew into a commonwealth, and the fatherly authority being continued on to the elder son, every one in his turn growing up under it tacitly submitted to it, and the easiness and equality of it not offending any one, every one acquiesced, till time seemed to have confirmed it and settled a right of succession by prescription' (§ 110). This is of some interest as showing exactly how near Locke could come to a historical point of view.

Summing up his argument (in chaps. vii and viii; I have not closely followed the order, as it is somewhat clumsy to a modern reader) Locke states (chap. ix) the reasons which move men to restrict their natural rights by mutual agreement, and unite into commonwealths 'for the mutual preservation of their lives, liberties, and estates, which I call by the general name, Property.' In the state of nature this cannot be assured. The defects of merely natural society are—

1. Want of established and known law. 'For tho the Law of Nature be plain and intelligible to all rational Creatures; yet Men being biassed by their Interest, as well as ignorant for want of Study of it, are not apt to allow of it as a Law binding to them, in the application of it to their particular Cases.'

2. The want of 'a known and indifferent Judge.'

3. Power to execute sentences; for though every man is, in default of positive law, 'both Judge and Executioner of the Law of Nature,' the ability is often not proportionate to the right.

Locke, then, admits that mankind are 'but in an ill condition' when left to the state of nature; he is not really very far from Hobbes's well-known description of the state of war. Some surrender of natural right is necessary; where Locke differs with Hobbes is in holding that, as the surrender is for a definite purpose, it is not unlimited, but conditional on that purpose being fulfilled. Accordingly the natural powers of self-preservation and punishment are put 'into the hands of the Society' not absolutely but 'to be so far disposed of by the Legislative, as the good of the Society shall require'; and the power of the Commonwealth or its legislative organ 'can never be supposed to extend farther than the Common Good.' Whatever be the form of government, it must be administered according to known law, and 'directed to no other End, but the Peace, Safety, and publick Good of the People.' Towards the end of the *Essay* (chap. xvii 'Of Tyranny') Locke cites an unexpected witness, no other than King James I, in support of this fundamental position.

The legislative power, once constituted by consent, is the supreme power in the Commonwealth, but not arbitrary (chap. xi). We find the reason of its supremacy given very shortly in a later passage (§ 150): 'what can give laws to another must needs be superior to him.' But the legislative authority is bound by its trust and by the law of nature to govern by established laws, to act in good faith for the common advantage, not to raise taxes without the consent of the people by themselves or their deputies, and not to transfer its power of making laws (being only a delegated power) to any other hands.

This is the most meagre and least satisfying part of Locke's work. He does not seem to conceive the possibility of a legislature having powers limited by express convention but plenary within those limits; nor does he consider at all the partial exercise of legislative power by bodies having a merely delegated authority. He could not be expected to anticipate the constitutions of self-governing colonies, but he must have known that the University of Oxford and his own House had statutes: and he must have desired to see the latter, at any rate, better secured from arbitrary inter-ference than they had been in his own case. Yet he does make a very apt reference, in distinguishing absolute from arbitrary power, to the example of military discipline, where the officer may have power of life and death over the soldier, but cannot 'dispose of one farthing of that soldier's estate, or seize one jot of his goods.' Neither does Locke touch at all on what is now called constitutional amendment, except negatively. He seems to as-sume that nothing of the kind can be done, in any form of government, without express provision for that purpose. What makes the omission of argument on this point the more remarkable is that Sir Thomas Smith, writing a century and a quarter earlier, had enounced the unqualified sov-ereignty of Parliament in terms so full and explicit that Blackstone, after the lapse of just two centuries, could add nothing to them; while on the other hand the necessity of unalterable 'fundamentals' in any scheme of government had been much discussed under the Commonwealth, and maintained by Cromwell himself among others. Sir Thomas Smith's *Com-monwealth of England* is now, for want of a modern edition, not so well known as it ought to be; but it was more than once reprinted in the seventeenth century, and one can hardly suppose Locke to have been un-acquainted with it.

In fact there was in Locke's time respectable authority for three dif-ferent theories of the supreme power in England. The King was absolute, according to the ultra-royalists and Hobbes: Locke demolished this con-tention once for all, whatever we may think of his constructive work. Parliament, or the King in Parliament, was absolute according to Sir Thomas Smith and the practice of the Tudor reigns: this view was ac-cepted by Blackstone and has been the only tenable one among English lawyers ever since. According to a third doctrine prevalent among stu-dents of the Common Law down to the early part of the eighteenth cen-tury, there are bounds set by natural justice or 'common right' even to what the King in Parliament can do; that is to say, the judges ought to disregard an Act of Parliament if it is manifestly contrary to natural justice, and perhaps if it attempts to subvert the foundations of the con-stitution; for example, if it purported to abolish the Monarchy or the House of Commons. Locke's opinion is in substance a less technical ver-sion of this last; and it is worth while to observe that existing legal authorities were in his favour. Sir Thomas Smith, whose opinion ultimately prevailed, was not a common lawyer but a civilian.

Locke touches on the separation of legislative from executive power, which was to become a constitutional dogma for his eighteenth-century followers; he gives only the practical reason that there is no need for the legislative to be always in being, but executive power for both domestic and foreign affairs must be constantly ready for action. The foreign department of government is distinguished by the not very happy epithet of 'federative,' which was not adopted, so far as I know, by any one.

We have now seen the whole of Locke's principles of polity. The last seven chapters of the *Essay* are a justification in detail, but by way of elaborate allusion, of their application to English affairs in the Whig theory of the Constitution, and in particular of the Revolution of 1688. Power being entrusted to rulers only on condition, that condition is enforceable at need, whatever be the legal forms of government: 'there remains still in the People a supreme power to remove or alter the Legislative, when they find the Legislative act contrary to the Trust reposed in them.' In this sense the Community is supreme, 'but not as considered under any form of government, because the power of the people can never take place till the government be dissolved.' In other words, the ultimate reserved power is extra-legal and superior to the positive forms of the Constitution. Blackstone, whose criticism of Locke is in the main intelligent and fair, does not do him complete justice on this point. In a constitutional Monarchy the 'single Person' at the head of the Executive may 'in a very tolerable sense' be called supreme; and he is entitled to personal allegiance not 'as supreme legislator, but as supreme executor of the law, made by a joint power of him with others.' The 'power of assembling and dismissing the Legislative' may be vested in the Executive by the Constitution, but, like all governmental powers, it is held in trust for the public, and abuse of it may justify the people in recourse to their ultimate rights. On the other hand, Locke suggests that the representation of the people in the Legislative may perhaps be amended at the discretion of the Executive, provided that such action is taken in good faith. Parliamentary reform by Order in Council was not so obviously remote from practical politics two centuries ago as it is now; but what English princes down to Elizabeth had done in the way of creating new boroughs was not of encouraging example; and I do not know that Locke's suggestion was taken seriously by any one. The failure of Temple's plan to establish an efficient and independent Privy Council had in truth made it impossible beforehand. It is an important question, but a question of modern politics and far outside Locke's field of view, whether the latent capacities of the Privy Council may not yet be developed for the purposes of co-ordinating the resources of the Empire and giving the self-governing colonies an effective share—all the more effective for not being too rigidly defined—in the handling of affairs of common interest.

Prerogative is identified by Locke with executive discretion, includ-ing some (he avoids saying how much) extraordinary discretion in emergencies; tempered, like legislative power, by the possibility of forfei-ture. Selden's way with the supposed mysteries of prerogative was more straightforward and profitable; but Locke wanted to conciliate moderate royalists.

It is obvious that Locke's position as to the reserved power of dis-solving government is not formally unassailable. A Hobbist would say that a political power 'not as considered under any form of government' is a contradiction in terms, and is not only extralegal but anarchical. Dissolve existing government, under whatever pretence, and you are remitted to the state of war which we set out to avoid at all costs. Locke's reply is indicated later (§§ 224, 225). Its effect is that neither Hobbes's nor any other dialectic will make men tolerate an intolerably bad govern-ment. In extremity they will act on the belief that institutions perverted to ends other than the public good 'are so far from being better, that they are much worse, than the state of Nature, or pure Anarchy.' To this no further answer seems possible. Nowadays we should all agree with Locke as against Hobbes that government is the instrument and not the creator of society. We should also have something to say of the force of custom as a fly-wheel in the social machine, steadying and maintaining the common course of affairs notwithstanding technical or even sub-stantial abeyance of legality. But of this Hobbes takes no account at all, and Locke only just touches upon it ('People are not so easily got out of their old Forms, as some are apt to suggest,' § 223).

The final chapter 'Of the Dissolution of Government' undertakes to show, but still under a transparent disguise of verbal generality, that the conduct of James II was in fact such a breach of 'the fundamental Ap-pointment of the Society' as justified the people in exercising their ulti-mate right of self-preservation. It does not seem useful to follow Locke through the details of his propositions, as nothing short of a minute his-torical commentary would illustrate them to any material extent.

The subsequent influence of Locke's *Essay* may be traced, as the President of Corpus has hinted, not only throughout the formal political philosophy of the eighteenth century, but in the doctrine received among English constitutional lawyers, and in the principles enounced by the promoters of American independence and the conductors of the French

Revolution in its early stages. Blackstone substantially followed Locke, though he borrowed some ornamental phrases, not to be taken too seriously, from continental writers. He was prudent enough, indeed, to repudiate the assumption of mankind having actually lived in a state of nature, and proceeded to form society by a 'convention of individuals'[4]; and, writing as a lawyer, he was naturally more anxious than Locke to vindicate the Revolution settlement as not only justifiable but legal. It is none the less true that Bentham, when he sounded the note of destructive criticism in his 'Fragment on Government,' was really attacking Locke's theory of the State through Blackstone. Again, Blackstone's *Commentaries* were a vehicle of Locke's doctrine (though not the only one) to a numerous and public-spirited audience in the American colonies; and that doctrine was at the foundation of the several Bills of Rights of the American States, among which Virginia gave the first example, and of the Declaration of Independence itself. More than this, it has been shown by modern American scholars that these instruments became well known in France, and served as precedents for the Declaration of the Rights of Man. On the whole it seems that Locke had as much to do as Rousseau with the Principles of 1789, or more. The fatal domination of Rousseau's ideas belongs to a later stage. It would be idle to consider what Locke himself would have thought of his latest spiritual posterity.

Russell on LOCKE

A. The Hereditary Principle

In the years 1689 and 1690, just after the Revolution of 1688, Locke wrote his *Two Treatises on Government,* of which the second especially is very important in the history of political ideas.

The first of these two treatises is a criticism of the doctrine of hereditary power. It is a reply to Sir Robert Filmer's *Patriarcha: or The Natural Power of Kings,* which was published in 1680, but written under Charles I. Sir Robert Filmer, who was a devout upholder of the

[From Bertrand Russell, *A History of Western Philosophy* (Simon and Schuster, Inc., 1945). By permission.]

[4] *Comm.* i. 47; as to the ultimate remedy of dissolving government, *ib.* 162; Blackstone seems to have thought 'theo- retical writers' a term peculiarly apt to include Locke; as to the Convention of 1688, *ib.* 152.

divine right of kings, had the misfortune to live till 1653, and must have suffered acutely from the execution of Charles I and the victory of Cromwell. But *Patriarcha* was written before these sad events, though not before the Civil War, so that it naturally shows awareness of the existence of subversive doctrines. Such doctrines, as Filmer points out, were not new in 1640. In fact, both Protestant and Catholic divines, in their contest with Catholic and Protestant monarchs respectively, had vigorously affirmed the right of subjects to resist tyrannical princes, and their writings supplied Sir Robert with abundant material for controversy.

Sir Robert Filmer was knighted by Charles I, and his house is said to have been plundered by the Parliamentarians ten times. He thinks it not unlikely that Noah sailed up the Mediterranean and allotted Africa, Asia, and Europe to Ham, Shem, and Japheth respectively. He held that, by the English Constitution, the Lords only give counsel to the king, and the Commons have even less power; the king, he says, alone makes the laws, which proceed solely from his will. The king, according to Filmer, is perfectly free from all human control, and cannot be bound by the acts of his predecessors, or even by his own, for "impossible it is in nature that a man should give a law unto himself."

Filmer, as these opinions show, belonged to the most extreme section of the Divine Right party.

Patriarcha begins by combating the "common opinion" that "mankind is naturally endowed and born with freedom from all subjection, and at liberty to choose what form of government it please, and the power which any one man hath over others was at first bestowed according to the discretion of the multitude." "This tenet," he says, "was first hatched in the schools." The truth, according to him, is quite different; it is, that originally God bestowed the kingly power upon Adam, from whom it descended to his heirs, and ultimately reached the various monarchs of modern times. Kings now, he assures us, "either are, or are to be reputed, the next heirs to those first progenitors who were at first the natural parents of the whole people." Our first parent, it seems, did not adequately appreciate his privilege as universal monarch, for "the desire of liberty was the first cause of the fall of Adam." The desire of liberty is a sentiment which Sir Robert Filmer regards as impious.

The claims made by Charles I, and by his protagonists on his behalf, were in excess of what earlier times would have conceded to kings. Filmer points out that Parsons, the English Jesuit, and Buchanan, the Scotch Calvinist, who agree in almost nothing else, both maintain that sovereigns can be deposed by the people for misgovernment. Parsons, of course, was thinking of the Protestant Queen Elizabeth, and Buchanan of the Catholic Mary Queen of Scots. The doctrine of Buchanan was sanctioned by success, but that of Parsons was disproved by his colleague Campion's execution.

Even before the Reformation, theologians tended to believe in setting limits to kingly power. This was part of the battle between the Church and the State which raged throughout Europe during most of the Middle Ages. In the battle, the State depended upon armed force, the Church upon cleverness and sanctity. As long as the Church had both these merits, it won; when it came to have cleverness only, it lost. But the things which eminent and holy men had said against the power of kings remained on record. Though intended in the interests of the Pope, they could be used to support the rights of the people to self-government. "The subtle schoolmen," says Filmer, "to be sure to thrust down the king below the Pope, thought it the safest course to advance the people above the king, so that the papal power might take the place of the regal." He quotes the theologian Bellarmine as saying that secular power is bestowed by men (i.e., not by God), and "is in the people unless they bestow it on a prince"; thus Bellarmine, according to Filmer, "makes God the immediate author of a democratical estate"—which sounds to him as shocking as it would to a modern plutocrat to say that God is the immediate author of Bolshevism.

Filmer derives political power, not from any contract, nor yet from any consideration of the public good, but entirely from the authority of a father over his children. His view is: that the source of regal authority is subjection of children to parents; that the patriarchs in Genesis were monarchs; that the kings are the heirs of Adam, or at least are to be regarded as such; that the natural rights of a king are the same as those of a father; and that, by nature, sons are never free of paternal power, even when the son is adult and the parent is in his dotage.

This whole theory seems to a modern mind so fantastic that it is hard to believe it was seriously maintained. We are not accustomed to deriving political rights from the story of Adam and Eve. We hold it obvious that parental power should cease completely when the son or daughter reaches the age of twenty-one, and that before that it should be very strictly limited both by the State and by the right of independent initiative which the young have gradually acquired. We recognize that the mother has rights at least equal to those of the father. But apart from all these considerations, it would not occur to any modern man outside Japan to suppose that political power should be in any way assimilated to that of parents over children. In Japan, it is true, a theory closely similar to Filmer's is still held, and must be taught by all professors and school-teachers. The Mikado can trace his descent from the Sun Goddess, whose heir he is; other Japanese are also descended from her, but belong to cadet branches of her family. Therefore the Mikado is divine, and all resistance to him is impious. This theory was, in the main, invented in 1868, but is now alleged in Japan to have been handed down by tradition ever since the creation of the world.

The attempt to impose a similar theory upon Europe—of which attempt Filmer's *Patriarcha* is part—was a failure. Why? The acceptance of such a theory is in no way repugnant to human nature; for example, it was held, apart from Japan, by the ancient Egyptians, and by the Mexicans and Peruvians before the Spanish conquest. At a certain stage of human development it is natural. Stuart England had passed this stage, but modern Japan has not.

The defeat of theories of divine right, in England, was due to two main causes. One was the multiplicity of religions; the other was the conflict for power between the monarchy, the aristocracy, and the higher bourgeoisie. As for religion: the king, since the reign of Henry VIII, was the head of the Church of England, which was opposed both to Rome and to most of the Protestant sects. The Church of England boasted of being a compromise: the Preface to the Authorized Version begins "it hath been the wisdom of the Church of England, ever since the first compiling of her public liturgy, to keep the mean between two extremes." On the whole this compromise suited most people. Queen Mary and King James II tried to drag the country over to Rome, and the victors in the Civil War tried to drag it over to Geneva, but these attempts failed, and after 1688 the power of the Church of England was unchallenged. Nevertheless, its opponents survived. The Nonconformists, especially, were vigorous men, and were numerous among the rich merchants and bankers whose power was continually increasing.

The theological position of the king was somewhat peculiar, for he was not only head of the Church of England, but also of the Church of Scotland. In England, he had to believe in bishops and reject Calvinism; in Scotland, he had to reject bishops and believe in Calvinism. The Stuarts had genuine religious convictions, which made this ambiguous attitude impossible for them, and caused them even more trouble in Scotland than in England. But after 1688 political convenience led kings to acquiesce in professing two religions at once. This militated against zeal, and made it difficult to regard them as divine persons. In any case, neither Catholics nor Nonconformists could acquiesce in any religious claims on behalf of the monarchy.

The three parties of king, aristocracy, and rich middle class made different combinations at different times. Under Edward IV and Louis XI, king and middle class combined against the aristocracy; under Louis XIV, king and aristocracy combined against the middle class; in England in 1688, aristocracy and middle class combined against the king. When the king had one of the other parties on his side, he was strong; when they combined against him, he was weak.

For these reasons among others, Locke had no difficulty in demolishing Filmer's arguments.

So far as reasoning is concerned, Locke has, of course, an easy task. He points out that, if parental power is what is concerned, the mother's power should be equal to the father's. He lay stress on the injustice of primogeniture, which is unavoidable if inheritance is to be the basis of monarchy. He makes play with the absurdity of supposing that actual monarchs are, in any real sense, the heirs of Adam. Adam can have only one heir, but no one knows who he is. Would Filmer maintain, he asks, that, if the true heir could be discovered, all existing monarchs should lay their crowns at his feet? If Filmer's basis for monarchy were accepted, all kings, except at most one, would be usurpers, and would have no right to demand the obedience of their *de facto* subjects. Moreover paternal power, he says, is temporary, and extends not to life or property.

For such reasons, apart from more fundamental grounds, heredity cannot, according to Locke, be accepted as the basis of legitimate political power. Accordingly, in his Second Treatise on Government he seeks a more defensible basis.

The hereditary principle has almost vanished from politics. During my lifetime, the emperors of Brazil, China, Russia, Germany, and Austria have disappeared, to be replaced by dictators who do not aim at the foundation of a hereditary dynasty. Aristocracy has lost its privileges throughout Europe, except in England, where they have become little more than a historical form. All this, in most countries, is very recent, and has much to do with the rise of dictatorships, since the traditional basis of power has been swept away, and the habits of mind required for the successful practice of democracy have not had time to grow up. There is one great institution that has never had any hereditary element, namely, the Catholic Church. We may expect the dictatorships, if they survive, to develop gradually a form of government analogous to that of the Church. This has already happened in the case of the great corporations in America, which have, or had until Pearl Harbor, powers almost equal to those of the government.

It is curious that the rejection of the hereditary principle in politics has had almost no effect in the economic sphere in democratic countries. (In totalitarian states, economic power has been absorbed by political power.) We still think it natural that a man should leave his property to his children; that is to say, we accept the hereditary principle as regards economic power while rejecting it as regards political power. Political dynasties have disappeared, but economic dynasties survive. I am not at the moment arguing either for or against this different treatment of the two forms of power; I am merely pointing out that it exists, and that most men are unconscious of it. When you consider how natural it seems to us that the power over the lives of others resulting from great wealth should be hereditary, you will understand better how men like Sir Robert Filmer could take the same view as regards the power of kings, and how important was the innovation represented by men who thought as Locke did.

To understand how Filmer's theory could be believed, and how Locke's contrary theory could seem revolutionary, we have only to reflect that a kingdom was regarded then as a landed estate is regarded now. The owner of land has various important legal rights, the chief of which is the power of choosing who shall be on the land. Ownership can be transmitted by inheritance, and we feel that the man who has inherited an estate has a just claim to all the privileges that the law allows him in consequence. Yet at bottom his position is the same as that of the monarchs whose claims Sir Robert Filmer defends. There are at the present day in California a number of huge estates the title to which is derived from actual or alleged grants by the king of Spain. He was only in a position to make such grants (*a*) because Spain accepted views similar to Filmer's, and (*b*) because the Spaniards were able to defeat the Indians in battle. Nevertheless we hold the heirs of those to whom he made grants to have a just title. Perhaps in future this will seem as fantastic as Filmer seems now.

B. *The State of Nature, and Natural Law*

Locke begins his second *Treatise on Government* by saying that, having shown the impossibility of deriving the authority of government from that of a father, he will now set forth what he conceives to be the true origin of government.

He begins by supposing what he calls a "state of nature," antecedent to all human government. In this state there is a "law of nature," but the law of nature consists of divine commands, and is not imposed by any human legislator. It is not clear how far the state of nature is, for Locke, a mere illustrative hypothesis, and how far he supposes it to have had a historical existence; but I am afraid that he tended to think of it as a stage that had actually occurred. Men emerged from the state of nature by means of a social contract which instituted civil government. This also he regarded as more or less historical. But for the moment it is the state of nature that concerns us.

What Locke has to say about the state of nature and the law of nature is, in the main, not original, but a repetition of medieval scholastic doctrines. Thus St. Thomas Aquinas says:

"Every law framed by man bears the character of a law exactly to that extent to which it is derived from the law of nature. But if on any point it is in conflict with the law of nature, it at once ceases to be a law; it is a mere perversion of law." [1]

Throughout the Middle Ages, the law of nature was held to condemn "usury," i.e., lending money at interest. Church property was almost entirely in land, and landowners have always been borrowers rather than lenders. But when Protestantism arose, its support—especially the support of Calvinism—came chiefly from the rich middle class, who were lenders rather than borrowers. Accordingly first Calvin, then other Protestants, and finally the Catholic Church, sanctioned "usury." Thus natural law came to be differently conceived, but no one doubted there being such a thing.

Many doctrines which survived the belief in natural law owe their origin to it; for example, laissez-faire and the rights of man. These doctrines are connected, and both have their origins in puritanism. Two quotations given by Tawney will illustrate this. A committee of the House of Commons in 1604 stated:

"All free subjects are born inheritable, as to their land, and also as to the free exercise of their industry, in those trades whereto they apply themselves and whereby they are to live."

And in 1656 Joseph Lee writes:

"It is an undeniable maxim that every one by the light of nature and reason will do that which makes for his greatest advantage. . . . The advancement of private persons will be the advantage of the public."

Except for the words "by the light of nature and reason," this might have been written in the nineteenth century.

In Locke's theory of government, I repeat, there is little that is original. In this Locke resembles most of the men who have won fame for their ideas. As a rule, the man who first thinks of a new idea is so much ahead of his time that every one thinks him silly, so that he remains obscure and is soon forgotten. Then, gradually, the world becomes ready

[1] Quoted by Tawney in *Religion and the Rise of Capitalism.*

for the idea, and the man who proclaims it at the fortunate moment gets all the credit. So it was, for example, with Darwin; poor Lord Monboddo was a laughing-stock.

In regard to the state of nature, Locke was less original than Hobbes, who regarded it as one in which there was war of all against all, and life was nasty, brutish, and short. But Hobbes was reputed an atheist. The view of the state of nature and of natural law which Locke accepted from his predecessors cannot be freed from its theological basis; where it survives without this, as in much modern liberalism, it is destitute of clear logical foundation.

The belief in a happy "state of nature" in the remote past is derived partly from the biblical narrative of the age of the patriarchs, partly from the classical myth of the golden age. The general belief in the badness of the remote past only came with the doctrine of evolution.

The nearest thing to a definition of the state of nature to be found in Locke is the following:

"Men living together according to reason, without a common superior on earth, with authority to judge between them, is properly the state of nature."

This is not a description of the life of savages, but of an imagined community of virtuous anarchists, who need no police or law-courts because they always obey "reason," which is the same as "natural law," which, in turn, consists of those laws of conduct that are held to have a divine origin. (For example, "Thou shalt not kill" is part of natural law, but the rule of the roads is not.)

Some further quotations will make Locke's meaning clearer.

"To understand political power right [he says], and derive it from its original, we must consider what state men are naturally in, and that is, a state of perfect freedom to order their actions and dispose of their possessions and persons, as they think fit, within the bounds of the law of nature; without asking leave, or depending upon the will of any other man.

"A state also of equality, wherein all the power and jurisdiction is reciprocal, no one having more than another; there being nothing more evident, than that creatures of the same species and rank, promiscuously born to all the same advantages of nature, and the use of the same faculties, should also be equal one amongst another without subordination or subjection; unless the lord and master of them all should, by any manifest declaration of his will, set one above another, and confer on him, by an evident and clear appointment, an undoubted right to dominion and sovereignty.

"But though this [the state of nature] be a state of liberty, yet it is not a state of licence: though man in that state has an uncontrollable liberty to dispose of his person or possessions, yet he has not liberty to destroy himself, or so much as any creature in his possession, but where some nobler use than its bare preservation calls for it. The state of nature has a law of nature to govern it, which obliges every one: and reason, which is that law, teaches all mankind, who will but consult it, that being all equal and independent, no one ought to harm another in his life, health, liberty, or possessions"[2] (for we are all God's property).[3]

It presently appears, however, that, where most men are in the state of nature, there may nevertheless be some men who do not live according to the law of nature, and that the law of nature provides, up to a point, what may be done to resist such criminals. In a state of nature, we are told, every man can defend himself and what is his. "Who so sheddeth man's blood, by man shall his blood be shed" is part of the law of nature. I may even kill a thief while he is engaged in stealing my property, and this right survives the institution of government, although, where there is government, if the thief gets away I must renounce private vengeance and resort to the law.

The great objection to the state of nature is that, while it persists, every man is the judge in his own cause, since he must rely upon himself for the defence of his rights. For this evil, government is the remedy, but this is not a *natural* remedy. The state of nature, according to Locke, was evaded by a compact to create a government. Not any compact that ends the state of nature, but only that of making one body politic. The various governments of independent States are now in a state of nature towards each other.

The state of nature, we are told in a passage presumably directed against Hobbes, is not the same as a state of war, but more nearly its opposite. After explaining the right to kill a thief, on the ground that the thief may be deemed to be making war upon me, Locke says:

"And here we have the plain 'difference between the state of nature and the state of war,' which, however some men have confounded, are as far distant, as a state of peace, good-will, mutual assistance and preservation, and a state of enmity, malice, violence and mutual destruction are from one another."

Perhaps the *law* of nature must be regarded as having a wider scope than the *state* of nature, since the former deals with thieves and mur-

---

[2] Cf. the Declaration of Independence.

[3] "They are his property, whose workmanship they are, made to last during his, not another's pleasure," as Locke puts it.

derers, while in the latter there are no such malefactors. This, at least, suggests a way out of an apparent inconsistency in Locke, consisting in his sometimes representing the state of nature as one where every one is virtuous, and at other times discussing what may rightly be done in a state of nature to resist the aggressions of wicked men.

Some parts of Locke's natural law are surprising. For example, he says that captives in a just war are slaves by the law of nature. He says also that by nature every man has a right to punish attacks on himself or his property, even by death. He makes no qualification, so that if I catch a person engaged in petty pilfering I have, apparently, by the law of nature, a right to shoot him.

Property is very prominent in Locke's political philosophy, and is, according to him, the chief reason for the institution of civil government:

"The great and chief end of men uniting into commonwealths, and putting themselves under government, is the preservation of their property; to which in the state of nature there are many things wanting."

The whole of this theory of the state of nature and natural law is in one sense clear but in another very puzzling. It is clear what Locke thought, but it is not clear how he can have thought it. Locke's ethic, as we saw, is utilitarian, but in his consideration of "rights" he does not bring in utilitarian considerations. Something of this pervades the whole philosophy of law as taught by lawyers. *Legal* rights can be defined: broadly speaking, a man has a legal right when he can appeal to the law to safeguard him against injury. A man has in general a legal right to his property, but if he has (say) an illicit store of cocaine, he has no legal remedy against a man who steals it. But the lawgiver has to decide what legal rights to create, and falls back naturally on the conception of "natural" rights, as those which the law should secure.

I am attempting to go as far as is possible towards stating something like Locke's theory in untheological terms. If it is assumed that ethics, and the classification of acts as "right" and "wrong," is logically prior to actual law, it becomes possible to restate the theory in terms not involving mythical history. To arrive at the law of nature, we may put the question in this way: in the absence of law and government, what classes of acts by A against B justify B in retaliating against A, and what sort of retaliation is justified in different cases? It is generally held that no man can be blamed for defending himself against a murderous assault, even, if necessary, to the extent of killing the assailant. He may equally defend his wife and children, or, indeed, any member of the general public. In such cases, the existence of the law against murder becomes irrelevant, if, as may easily happen, the man assaulted would be dead before the aid of the police could be invoked; we have, therefore, to fall back on "natural" right. A man also has a right to defend his property, though opinions differ as to the amount of injury he may justly inflict upon a thief.

In the relations between States, as Locke points out, "natural" law is relevant. In what circumstances is war justified? So long as no international government exists, the answer to this question is purely ethical, not legal; it must be answered in the same way as it would be for an individual in a state of anarchy.

Legal theory will be based upon the view that the "rights" of individuals should be protected by the State. That is to say, when a man suffers the kind of injury which would justify retaliation according to the principles of natural law, positive law should enact that the retaliation shall be done by the State. If you see a man making a murderous assault upon your brother, you have a right to kill him, if you cannot otherwise save your brother. In a state of nature—so, at least, Locke holds—if a man has succeeded in killing your brother, you have a right to kill him. But where law exists, you lose this right, which is taken over by the State. And if you kill in self-defence or in defence of another, you will have to prove to a law-court that this was the reason for the killing.

We may then identify "natural law" with moral rules in so far as they are independent of positive legal enactments. There must be such rules if there is to be any distinction between good and bad laws. For Locke, the matter is simple, since moral rules have been laid down by God, and are to be found in the Bible. When this theological basis is removed, the matter becomes more difficult. But so long as it is held that there is an ethical distinction between right actions and wrong ones, we can say: Natural law decides what actions would be ethically right, and what wrong, in a community that had no government; and positive law ought to be, as far as possible, guided and inspired by natural law.

In its absolute form, the doctrine that an individual has certain inalienable rights is incompatible with utilitarianism, i.e., with the doctrine that right acts are those that do most to promote the general happiness. But in order that a doctrine may be a suitable basis for law, it is not necessary that it should be true in every possible case, but only that it should be true in an overwhelming majority of cases. We can all imagine cases in which murder would be justifiable, but they are rare, and do not afford an argument against the illegality of murder. Similarly it may be—I am not saying that it is—desirable, from a utilitarian point of view, to reserve to each individual a certain sphere of personal liberty. If so, the doctrine of the Rights of Man will be a suitable basis for the appropriate laws, even though these rights be subject to exceptions. A utilitarian will have to examine the doctrine, considered as a basis for laws, from the point of view of its practical effects; he cannot condemn it *ab initio* as contrary to his own ethic.

C. The Social Contract

In the political speculation of the seventeenth century, there were two main types of theory as to the origin of government. Of one type we have had an example in Sir Robert Filmer: this type maintained that God had bestowed power on certain persons, and that these persons, or their heirs, constituted the legitimate government, rebellion against which it is not only treason, but impiety. This view was sanctioned by sentiments of immemorial antiquity: in almost all early civilizations, the king is a sacred person. Kings, naturally, considered it an admirable theory. Aristocracies had motives for supporting it and motives for opposing it. In its favour was the fact that it emphasized the hereditary principle, and that it gave august support to resistance against the upstart merchant class. Where the middle class was more feared or hated by the aristocracy than the king was, these motives prevailed. Where the contrary was the case, and especially where the aristocracy had a chance of obtaining supreme power itself, it tended to oppose the king, and therefore to reject theories of divine right.

The other main type of theory—of which Locke is a representative —maintained that civil government is the result of a contract, and is an affair purely of this world, not something established by divine authority. Some writers regarded the social contract as a historical fact, others as a legal fiction; the important matter, for all of them, was to find a terrestrial origin for governmental authority. In fact, they could not think of any alternative to divine right except the supposed contract. It was felt by all except rebels that *some* reason must be found for obeying governments, and it was not thought sufficient to say that for most people the authority of government is convenient. Government must, in some sense, have a *right* to exact obedience, and the right conferred by a contract seemed the only alternative to a divine command. Consequently the doctrine that government was instituted by a contract was popular with practically all opponents of divine right of kings. There is a hint of this theory in Thomas Aquinas, but the first serious development of it is to be found in Grotius. *& all of middle ages*

The contract doctrine was capable of taking forms which justified tyranny. Hobbes, for example, held that there was a contract among the citizens to hand over all power to the chosen sovereign, but the sovereign

was not a party to the contract, and therefore necessarily acquired unlimited authority. This theory, at first, might have justified Cromwell's
totalitarian State; after the Restoration, it justified Charles II. In Locke's
form of the doctrine, however, the government is a party to the contract,
and can be justly resisted if it fails to fulfill its part of the bargain. Locke's
doctrine is, in essence, more or less democratic, but the democratic element is limited by the view (implied rather than expressed) that those
who have no property are not to be reckoned as citizens.

Let us now see just what Locke has to say on our present topic.

There is first a definition of political power:

"Political power I take to be the right of making laws, with penalty
of death, and consequently all less penalties for the regulating and
preserving of property, and of employing the force of the community in
the execution of such laws, and in the defence of the commonwealth
from foreign injury, and all this only for the public good."

Government, we are told, is a remedy for the inconveniences that
arise, in the state of nature, from the fact that, in that state, every man
is the judge in his own cause. But where the monarch is a party to the dispute, this is no remedy, since the monarch is both judge and plaintiff.
These considerations lead to the view that governments should not be
absolute, and that the judiciary should be independent of the executive.
Such arguments had an important future both in England and in America, but for the moment we are not concerned with them.

By nature, Locke says, every man has the right to punish attacks on
himself or his property, even by death. There is political society there,
and there only, where men have surrendered this right to the community
or to the law.

Absolute monarchy is not a form of civil government, because there
is no neutral authority to decide disputes between the monarch and a
subject; in fact the monarch, in relation to his subjects, is still in a state
of nature. It is useless to hope that being a king will make a naturally
violent man virtuous.

"He that would have been insolent and injurious in the woods of
America would not probably be much better in a throne, where perhaps
learning and religion shall be found out to justify all that he shall do to
his subjects, and the sword presently silence all those that dare question
it."

Absolute monarchy is as if men protected themselves against pole-
cats and foxes, "but are content, nay think it safety, to be devoured by
lions."

Civil society involves the rule of the majority, unless it is agreed that a greater number shall be required. (As, for example, in the United States, for a change in the Constitution or the ratification of a treaty.) This sounds democratic, but it must be remembered that Locke assumes the exclusion of women and the poor from the rights of citizenship.

"The beginning of politic society depends upon the consent of the individuals to join into and make one society." It is argued—somewhat half-heartedly—that such consent must, at some time, have actually taken place, though it is admitted that the origin of government antedates history everywhere except among the Jews.

The civil compact which institutes government binds only those who made it; the son must consent afresh to a compact made by his father. (It is clear how this follows from Locke's principles, but it is not very realistic. A young American who, on attaining the age of twenty-one, announces "I refuse to be bound by the contract which inaugurated the United States" will find himself in difficulties.)

The power of the government by contract, we are told, never extends beyond the common good. A moment ago I quoted a sentence as to the powers of government, ending "and all this only for the public good." It seems not to have occurred to Locke to ask who was to be the judge of the common good. Obviously if the government is the judge it will always decide in its own favour. Presumably Locke would say that the majority of the citizens is to be the judge. But many questions have to be decided too quickly for it to be possible to ascertain the opinion of the electorate; of these peace and war are perhaps the most important. The only remedy in such cases is to allow to public opinion or its representatives some power—such as impeachment—of subsequently punishing executive officers for acts that are found to have been unpopular. But often this is a very inadequate remedy.

I quoted previously a sentence which I must now quote again:

"The great and chief end of men uniting into commonwealths, and putting themselves under government, is the preservation of their property."

Consistently with this doctrine Locke declares that:

"The supreme power cannot take from any man any part of his property without his own consent."

Still more surprising is the statement that, although military commanders have power of life and death over their soldiers, they have no power of taking money. (It follows that, in any army, it would be wrong to punish minor breaches of discipline by fines, but permissible to punish them by bodily injury, such as flogging. This shows the absurd lengths to which Locke is driven by his worship of property.)

The question of taxation might be supposed to raise difficulties for Locke, but he perceives none. The expense of government, he says, must be borne by the citizens, but with their consent, i.e., with that of the majority. But why, one asks, should the consent of the majority suffice? Every man's consent, we were told, is necessary to justify the government in taking any part of his property. I suppose his tacit consent to taxation in accordance with majority decision is presumed to be involved in his citizenship, which, in turn, is presumed to be voluntary. All this is, of course, sometimes quite contrary to the facts. Most men have no effective liberty of choice as to the State to which they shall belong, and very few have liberty, nowadays, to belong to no State. Suppose, for example, you are a pacifist, and disapprove of war. Wherever you live, the government will take some of your property for warlike purposes. With what justice can you be compelled to submit to this? I can imagine many answers, but I do not think any of them are consistent with Locke's principles. He thrusts in the maxim of majority rule without adequate consideration, and offers no transition to it from his individualistic premisses, except the mythical social contract.

The social contract, in the sense required, is mythical even when, at some former period, there actually was a contract creating the government in question. The United States is a case in point. At the time when the Constitution was adopted, men had liberty of choice. Even then, many voted against it, and were therefore not parties to the contract. They could, of course, have left the country, and by remaining were deemed to have become bound by a contract to which they had not assented. But in practice it is usually difficult to leave one's country. And in the case of men born after the adoption of the Constitution their consent is even more shadowy.

The question of the rights of the individual as against the government is a very difficult one. It is too readily assumed by democrats that, when the government represents the majority, it has a right to coerce the minority. Up to a point, this must be true, since coercion is of the essence of government. But the divine right of majorities, if pressed too far, may become almost as tyrannical as the divine right of kings. Locke says little on this subject in his *Essays on Government*, but considers it at some length in his *Letters on Toleration*, where he argues that no believer in God should be penalized on account of his religious opinions.

The theory that government was created by a contract is, of course, pre-evolutionary. Government, like measles and whooping-cough, must have grown up gradually, though, like them, it could be introduced suddenly into new regions such as the South Sea Islands. Before men had studied anthropology they had no idea of the psychological mechanisms involved in the beginnings of government, or of the fantastic reasons which lead men to adopt institutions and customs that subsequently prove useful. But as a legal fiction, to *justify* government, the theory of the social contract has *some* measure of truth.

D. Property

From what has been said hitherto about Locke's views on property, it might seem as though he were the champion of the great capitalists against both their social superiors and their social inferiors, but this would be only a half-truth. One finds in him, side by side and unreconciled, doctrines which foreshadow those of developed capitalism and doctrines which adumbrate a more nearly socialistic outlook. It is easy to misrepresent him by one-sided quotations, on this topic as on most others.

I will put down, in the order in which they occur, Locke's principal dicta on the subject of property.

We are told first that every man has private property in the produce of his own labour—or, at least, should have. In pre-industrial days this maxim was not so unrealistic as it has since become. Urban production was mainly by handicraftsmen who owned their tools and sold their produce. As for agricultural production, it was held by the school to which Locke belonged that peasant proprietorship would be the best system. He states that a man may own as much land as he can till, but not more. He seems blandly unaware that, in all the countries of Europe, the realization of this programme would be hardly possible without a bloody revolution. Everywhere the bulk of agricultural land belonged to aristocrats, who exacted from the farmers either a fixed proportion of the produce (often a half), or a rent which could be varied from time to time. The former system prevailed in France and Italy, the latter in England. Farther East, in Russia and Prussia, the workers were serfs, who worked for the landowner and had virtually no rights. The old system was ended in France by the French Revolution, in northern Italy and western Germany by the conquests of the French revolutionary armies. Serfdom was abolished in Prussia as a result of the defeat by Napoleon, and in Russia as a result of defeat in the Crimean War. But in both countries the aristocrats retained their landed estates. In East Prussia, this system, though drastically controlled by the Nazis, has survived to the present day; in Russia and what are now Lithuania, Latvia, and Esthonia, the aristocrats were dispossessed by the Russian Revolution. In Hungary, Rumania, and Poland they survived; in Eastern Poland they were "liquidated" by the Soviet government in 1940. The Soviet government, however, has done everything in its power to substitute collective farming rather than peasant proprietorship throughout Russia.

In England the development has been more complex. In Locke's day, the position of the rural labourer was mitigated by the existence of commons, on which he had important rights, which enabled him to raise a considerable part of his food himself. This system was a survival from the Middle Ages, and was viewed with disapproval by modern-minded men, who pointed out that from the point of view of production it was wasteful. Accordingly there was a movement for enclosure of commons, which began under Henry VIII and continued under Cromwell, but did not become strong until about 1750. From that time onward, for about ninety years, one common after another was enclosed and handed over to the local landowners. Each enclosure required an Act of Parliament, and the aristocrats who controlled both Houses of Parliament ruthlessly used their legislative power to enrich themselves, while thrusting agricultural labourers down to the verge of starvation. Gradually, owing to the growth of industry, the position of agricultural labourers improved, since otherwise they could not be prevented from migrating to the towns. At present, as a result of the taxation introduced by Lloyd George, the aristocrats have been compelled to part with most of their rural property. But those who also own urban or industrial property have been able to hang on to their estates. There has been no sudden revolution, but a gradual transition which is still in progress. At present, those aristocrats who are still rich owe their wealth to urban or industrial property.

This long development may be regarded, except in Russia, as in accordance with Locke's principles. The odd thing is that he could announce doctrines requiring so much revolution before they could be put into effect, and yet show no sign that he thought the system existing in his day unjust, or that he was aware of its being different from the system that he advocated.

The labour theory of value—i.e., the doctrine that the value of a product depends upon the labour expended upon it—which some attribute to Karl Marx and others to Ricardo, is to be found in Locke, and was suggested to him by a line of predecessors stretching back to Aquinas. As Tawney says, summarizing scholastic doctrine:

"The essence of the argument was that payment may properly be demanded by the craftsmen who make the goods, or by the merchants who transport them, for both labour in their vocation and serve the common need. The unpardonable sin is that of the speculator or middleman, who snatches private gain by the exploitation of public necessities.

tawney

The true descendant of the doctrines of Aquinas is the labour theory of value. The last of the schoolmen was Karl Marx."

The labour theory of value has two aspects, one ethical, the other economic. That is to say, it may assert that the value of a product *ought* to be proportional to the labour expended on it, or that *in fact* the labour regulates the price. The latter doctrine is only approximately true, as Locke recognizes. Nine tenths of value, he says, is due to labour; but as to the other tenth he says nothing. It is labour, he says that puts the difference of value on everything. He instances land in America occupied by Indians, which has almost no value because the Indians do not cultivate it. He does not seem to realize that land may acquire value as soon as people are *willing* to work on it, and before they have actually done so. If you own a piece of desert land on which somebody else finds oil, you can sell it for a good price without doing any work on it. As was natural in his day, he does not think of such cases, but only of agriculture. Peasant proprietorship, which he favours, is inapplicable to such things as large-scale mining, which require expensive apparatus and many workers.

but equals 99/100

The principle that a man has a right to the produce of his own labour is useless in an industrial civilization. Suppose you are employed in one operation in the manufacture of Ford cars, how is any one to estimate what proportion of the total output is due to your labour? Or suppose you are employed by a railway company in the transport of goods, who can decide what share you shall be deemed to have in the production of the goods? Such considerations have led those who wish to prevent the exploitation of labour to abandon the principle of the right to your own produce in favour of more socialistic methods of organizing production and distribution.

The labour theory of value has usually been advocated from hostility to some class regarded as predatory. The Schoolmen, in so far as they held it, did so from opposition to usurers, who were mostly Jews. Ricardo held it in opposition to landowners, Marx to capitalists. But Locke seems to have held it in a vacuum, without hostility to any class. His only hostility is to monarchs, but this is unconnected with his views on value.

Some of Locke's opinions are so odd that I cannot see how to make them sound sensible. He says that a man must not have so many plums that they are bound to go bad before he and his family can eat them; but he may have as much gold and as many diamonds as he can lawfully get, because gold and diamonds do not go bad. It does not occur to him that the man who has the plums might sell them before they go bad.

He makes a great deal of the imperishable character of the precious metals, which, he says, are the source of money and inequality of fortune. He seems, in an abstract and academic way, to regret economic inequality, but he certainly does not think that it would be wise to take such measures as might prevent it. No doubt he was impressed, as all the men of his time were, by the gains to civilization that were due to rich men, chiefly as patrons of art and letters. The same attitude exists in modern America, where science and art are largely dependent upon the benefactions of the very rich. To some extent, civilization is furthered by social injustice. This fact is the basis of what is most respectable in conservatism.

E. Checks and Balances

The doctrine that the legislative, executive, and judicial functions of government should be kept separate is characteristic of liberalism; it arose in England in the course of resistance to the Stuarts, and is clearly formulated by Locke, at least as regards the legislature and the executive. The legislative and executive must be separate, he says, to prevent abuse of power. It must of course be understood that when he speaks of the legislature he means Parliament, and when he speaks of the executive he means the king; at least this is what he means emotionally, whatever he may logically intend to mean. Accordingly he thinks of the legislature as virtuous, while the executive is usually wicked.

The legislative, he says, must be supreme, except that it must be removable by the community. It is implied that, like the English House of Commons, the legislative is to be elected from time to time by popular vote. The condition that the legislative is to be removable by the people, if taken seriously, condemns the part allowed by the British Constitution in Locke's day to King and Lords as part of the legislative power.

In all well-framed governments, Locke says, the legislative and executive are separate. The question therefore arises: what is to be done when they conflict? If the executive fails to summon the legislative at the proper times, we are told, the executive is at war with the people, and may be removed by force. This is obviously a view suggested by what happened under Charles I. From 1628 to 1640 he tried to govern without Parliament; this sort of thing, Locke feels, must be prevented, by civil war if necessary.

"Force," he says, "is to be opposed to nothing but unjust and unlawful force." This principle is useless in practice unless there exists some body with the legal right to pronounce when force is "unjust and unlawful." Charles I's attempt to collect ship-money without the consent of

Parliament was declared by his opponents to be "unjust and unlawful," and by him to be just and lawful. Only the military issue of the Civil War proved that his interpretation of the Constitution was the wrong one. This same thing happened in the American Civil War. Had States the right to secede? No one knew, and only the victory of the North decided the legal question. The belief—which one finds in Locke and in most writers of his time—that any honest man can know what is just and lawful, is one that does not allow for the strength of party bias on both sides, or for the difficulty of establishing a tribunal, whether outwardly or in men's consciences, that shall be capable of pronouncing authoritatively on vexed questions. In practice, such questions, if sufficiently important, are decided simply by power, not by justice and law.

To some degree, though in veiled language, Locke recognizes this fact. In a dispute between legislative and executive, he says, there is, in certain cases, no judge under Heaven. Since Heaven does not make explicit pronouncements, this means, in effect, that a decision can only be reached by fighting, since it is assumed that Heaven will give the victory to the better cause. Some such view is essential to any doctrine that divides governmental power. Where such a doctrine is embodied in the Constitution, the only way to avoid occasional civil war is to practise compromise and common sense. But compromise and common sense are habits of mind, and cannot be embodied in a written constitution.

It is surprising that Locke says nothing about the judiciary, although this was a burning question in his day. Until the Revolution, judges could at any moment be dismissed by the king; consequently they condemned his enemies and acquitted his friends. After the Revolution, they were made irremovable except by an Address from both Houses of Parliament. It was thought that this would cause their decisions to be guided by the law; in fact, in cases involving party spirit, it has merely substituted the judge's prejudice for the king's. However that may be, wherever the principle of checks and balances prevailed the judiciary became a third independent branch of government alongside of the legislative and executive. The most noteworthy example is the United States' Supreme Court.

The history of the doctrine of checks and balances has been interesting.

In England, the country of its origin, it was intended to limit the power of the king, who, until the Revolution, had complete control of the executive. Gradually, however, the executive became dependent upon Parliament, since it was impossible for a ministry to carry on without a majority in the House of Commons. The executive thus became, in effect, a committee chosen in fact, though not in form, by Parliament, with the result that legislative and executive powers became gradually less and less separate. During the last fifty years or so, a further development took place, owing to the Prime Minister's power of dissolution and to the increasing strictness of party discipline. The majority in Parliament now decides which party shall be in power, but, having decided that, it cannot in practice decide anything else. Proposed legislation is hardly ever enacted unless introduced by government. Thus the government is both legislative and executive, and its power is only limited by the need of occasional general elections. This system is, of course, totally contrary to Locke's principles.

In France, where the doctrine was preached with great force by Montesquieu, it was held by the more moderate parties in the French Revolution, but was swept into temporary oblivion by the victory of the Jacobins. Napoleon naturally had no use for it, but it was revived at the Restoration, to disappear again with the rise of Napoleon III. It was again revived in 1871, and led to the adoption of a constitution in which the President had very little power and the government could not dissolve the Chambers. The result was to give great power to the Chamber of Deputies, both as against the government and as against the electorate. There was more division of powers than in modern England, but less than there should be on Locke's principles, since the legislature overshadowed the executive.

The country where Locke's principle of the division of powers has found its fullest application is the United States, where the President and Congress are wholly independent of each other, and the Supreme Court is independent of both. Inadvertently, the Constitution made the Supreme Court a branch of the legislature, since nothing is a law if the Supreme Court says it is not. The fact that its powers are nominally only interpretative in reality increases those powers, since it makes it difficult to criticize what are supposed to be purely legal decisions. It says a very great deal for the political sagacity of Americans that this Constitution has only once led to armed conflict.

Locke's political philosophy was, on the whole, adequate and useful until the industrial revolution. Since then, it has been increasingly unable to tackle the important problems. The power of property, as embodied in vast corporations, grew beyond anything imagined by Locke. The necessary functions of the State—for example, in education—increased enormously. Nationalism brought about an alliance, sometimes an amalgamation, of economic and political power, making war the principal means of competition. The single separate citizen has no longer the power and independence that he had in Locke's speculations. Our age is one of organization, and its conflicts are between organizations, not between separate individuals. The state of nature, as Locke says, still exists as between States. A new international Social Contract is necessary before we can enjoy the promised benefits of government. When once an international government has been created, much of Locke's political philosophy will again become applicable, though not the part of it that deals with private property.

15 | HOLMES

MONTESQUIEU

Next to Locke, probably no political thinker had as much influence on the makers of the American political system in the eighteenth century as Montesquieu (see page 88). Montesquieu went to England in 1729 and stayed there until 1731. He was much impressed by the combination of orderliness and freedom in English public life, and, turning to the English political system, he thought that the principle of separation of powers was one of the chief clues to the success of free government. Yet Montesquieu's own countrymen failed to pay much attention to his discovery, and, as far as England was concerned, the development of cabinet government even by 1730, not to speak of later dates, made the concept of separation of powers an unrealistic analysis of English politics. It was in America that Montesquieu found his devoted disciples in theory and practice, and the American political system as conceived by the makers of the Constitution and as it exists today is still the closest approximation to Montesquieu's political ideas. The unique position of the judiciary in the American political system is partly due to the remarkable perseverance of the concept of separation of powers in the United States, as is evidenced by the appraisal of Montesquieu in an essay (1900) by one of the greatest American judges, Oliver Wendell Holmes (1841–1935). Holmes had a distinguished military record in the Civil War, and, after a short career of practicing and teaching law, he became an Associate Justice, and later Chief Justice, of the Supreme Court of Massachusetts (1882–

Judicial

1902). In 1902 he became Associate Justice of the Supreme Court of the
United States, where he served until his retirement in 1932. Although his
personal views on social and economic matters tended to be rather conservative, he frequently sided with the liberal minority of the Supreme
Court, not because he was motivated by a positive and active zeal to reform the world, but because he was imbued with a kind of aristocratic
skepticism that made him unwilling to substitute his own judgment for
that of Congress in matters upon which honest men could disagree without clearly violating the Constitution. His civilizing and humanizing effect on American public life was also greatly aided by his style of diction,
full of wit and irony, as can be seen in the many judicial opinions he
wrote as well as in his books, such as *The Common Law* (1881) and
Collected Legal Papers (1920). As a result, much of Holmes's writing
has become a part, not only of American jurisprudence and political
thought, but also of American literature.

Holmes on MONTESQUIEU

"There is no new thing under the sun." It is the judgment of a man of
the world, and from his point of view it is true enough. The things which
he sees in one country he sees in another, and he is slightly bored from
the beginning. But the judgment is quite untrue from the point of view
of science or philosophy. From the time of Pericles to now, during the
whole period that counts in the intellectual history of the race, the science
or philosophy of one century has been different from that of the one
before, and in some sense further along. By a corollary easy to work out,
we have the paradox that the books which are always modern, the
thoughts which are as stinging today as they were in their cool youth,
are the books and thoughts of the men of the world. Ecclesiastes, Horace,
and Rochefoucauld give us as much pleasure as they gave to Hebrew or
Roman or the subject of Louis XIV. In this sense it is the second rate
that lasts. But the greatest works of intellect soon lose all but their historic significance. The science of one generation is refuted or outgeneral-
ized by the science of the next; the philosophy of one century is taken up
or transcended by the philosophy of a later one; and so Plato, St.

[Oliver Wendell Holmes, Introduction to Montesquieu's *Spirit of the Laws*
(Appleton and Company, 1900).]

Augustine, and Descartes, and we almost may say Kant and Hegel, are not much more read than Hippocrates or Cuvier or Bichat.

Montesquieu was a man of science and at the same time a man of the world. As a man of science he wrote an epoch-making book. And just because and in so far as his book was a work of science and epoch-making, it is as dead as the classics. The later investigations which it did so much to start have taken up what was true in it and have refuted what needed refutation, and without the need of controversy they have killed many pale shoots of fancy and insufficient knowledge simply by letting in light and air. For a beginner to read Montesquieu with the expectation that there he is to find his understanding of the laws of social being, would be as ingenuous as to read Plato at eighteen expecting to find in him the answers to the riddles of life when they begin to perplex and sadden the mind of youth. He would learn a good deal more from Lecky. Montesquieu is buried under his own triumphs, to use his own words with a different application.

But Montesquieu also was a man of the world and a man of *esprit*. That wit which deals with the daily aspect of life and offers trenchant solutions in two or three lines is a dangerous gift. It hardly is compatible with great art, and Flaubert is not without reason when he rails at it in his letters. It is no less dangerous to great thinking, to that profound and sustained insight which distrusts the dilemma as an instrument of logic, and discerns that a thing may be neither A nor not A, but the perpendicular, or, more plainly, that the truth may escape from the limitations of a given plane of thought to a higher one. Montesquieu said that Voltaire had too much *esprit* to understand him. Nevertheless, Montesquieu had enough of it to have sustained the *Saturday Review* when Maine and Fitzjames Stephen or Venables were its contributors, and as a man of wit he still is fresh and pleasant reading. When one runs through the *Lettres Persanes* one feels as he does after reading Swift's *Polite Conversation,* struck with a wondering shame at the number of things he has been capable of feeling pleased with himself for saying, when they had been noted as familiar two hundred years before. He is in the realm of the ever old which also is the ever new, those middle axioms of experience which have been made from the beginning of society, but which give each generation a fresh pleasure as they are realized again in actual life. There is a good deal more than this, because Montesquieu was a good deal more than a man of the world, but there is this also in which we escape from the preliminary dulness of things really great.

We find the same thing in the *Esprit des Lois,* and one might read that work happily enough simply as literature. One may read it also as a first step in studies intended to be carried further and into later days. But to read it as it should be read, to appreciate the great and many-sided genius of the author and his place in the canonical succession of the high priests of thought, one must come back to it in the fulness of knowledge and the ripeness of age. To read the great works of the past with intelligent appreciation, is one of the last achievements of a studious life. But I will postpone what more I have to say of this book until we come to it in following the course of the author's career.

Charles de Secondat, Baron de la Brède, was born at the Château de la Brède, near Bordeaux, on January 18, 1689. His family had gained distinction both by the sword and in the law. His father was a magistrate, and intended that he should be one. His mother was pious, and no doubt hoped that he might be like her. Neither wish was entirely fulfilled.

At the moment of his birth a beggar presented himself at the château, and was retained that he might be god-father to the young noble, and so remind him all his life that the poor were his brothers. He was nursed by peasants, and he kept through life a touch of Gascon speech, and, the Frenchmen say, something of the Gascon in his style. His early education was by churchmen, but at twenty he showed a tendency of his mind by composing an essay to prove that the pagan did not deserve to be eternally damned. The essay has not been preserved, but perhaps an echo of his reflections is to be found in the thirty-fifth of the *Lettres Persanes,* in which Usbek, who, not without dispute, has been taken for the author, asks the "sublime dervish" Gemchid whether he thinks that the Christians are to be damned forever for not having embraced the true religion of which they never have heard.

He studied law. "When I left college," he said, "they put law books into my hands. I tried to find their inner meaning" (*J'en cherchais l'esprit*). The *Esprit de Lois* was the outcome, but not the immediate outcome, of his studies. The immediate result was that, at twenty-five, on February 24, 1714, he was admitted to the Parlement de Bordeaux as conseiller. On July 13, 1716, he succeeded to the office (*président à mortier*) and fortune of an uncle, on condition of assuming the name of Montesquieu. Meantime he had married, and he had a son this same year, and later two daughters. As a magistrate he seems to have been not without weight. In 1722 he was intrusted with the shaping of a remonstrance to the king against a tax on wines, which for the time was successful. As a husband he was not wanting in decorum. But neither magistracy nor marriage seems to have filled his life.

He made a reasonable amount of love in his day, I infer not wholly before 1715. (Whether or not he would have said that the society of women makes us "subtle and insincere," he did say that it spoils our morals and forms our taste.) I suspect also that it added a poignancy to his phrase when he came to write, as it certainly gave him a freedom and alertness of interest in dealing with matters of sex. He took his passions easily. As soon as he ceased to believe that a woman loved him, he broke with her at once, he says, and elsewhere he tells us in more general terms that he never had a sorrow which an hour's reading would not dispel. At times his detachment seems to have been too visible, as one lady reproached him with writing his book in society. Perhaps it was timidity, which he says was a plague of his life. So much for his relations, domestic and otherwise, with women. As to the magistracy, he resigned his place in 1726. He found procedure hard to master, and it disgusted him to see men upon whose talents he justly looked down excelling in a matter that was too much for him.

About the same time that he succeeded his uncle he joined a society in Bordeaux, in which for a while he devoted himself to science. He made some experiments, wrote some scientific memoirs, planned a physical history of the earth, and sent out circulars of inquiry in 1719, but happily it all came to nothing, and this failure, combined with the shortness of his outward and the reach of his inward sight, helped to fix his attention upon his kind. He had the "disease of book-making," and as early as 1721 he published his *Lettres Persanes*. The putting of the criticism of his own times into the mouth of an intelligent foreigner, and all the Oriental coloring, seem a trifle faded nowadays. But these are merely the frame or excuse for a series of essays—somewhat like those in the early contemporary *Spectator*—on social subjects and subjects of social interest, running all the way from God to the Fashions.

In almost every letter there are things which have been quoted so often that one is afraid to repeat them. In one he makes a few reflections upon suicide that are hard to answer, and which had a practical aim, in view of the monstrous condition of the law. In another he is equally outspoken with regard to divorce, and says, not without some truth, that wishing to tighten the knot the law has untied it, and instead of uniting hearts, as it proposed, has separated them forever. Before Adam Smith he remarks the activity of dissenting sects, and he points out with unorthodox candor their service in reforming the abuses of the established faith.

In the person of Usbek he says: "Everything interests me, everything excites my wonder. I am like a child whose immature organs are keenly struck by the most insignificant objects." Montesquieu proves it in these letters. Alongside of such grave discussions as the foregoing he has portraits, or rather types, that still live. The *parvenu* tax farmer, the father confessor, the old soldier who can not hope for preferment "because we" (very sensibly) "believe that a man who has not the qualities of a general at thirty never will have them," the *homme à bonnes fortunes* who has hair, little wit, and so much impertinence, the poet (Montesquieu despised the poets, at least those whom he saw)—the poet, with grimaces and language different from the others, who would stand a beating better than the least criticism, the grand seigneur who personates himself. "He took a pinch of snuff so haughtily, he wiped his nose so pitilessly, he spit with so much phlegm, he fondled his dogs in a way so insulting to men, that I could not weary of wondering." The *décisionnaire:* "In a quarter of an hour he decided three questions of morals, four problems of history, and five points of physics. . . . They dropped the sciences and talked of the news of the day. . . . I thought that I would catch him, and spoke of Persia. But I hardly had said four words when he contradicted me twice. . . . Ah! *bon Dieu!* said I to myself, what sort of man is this? Soon he will know the streets of Ispahan better than I."

The letter on fashion ought to be quoted entire. When he says in the next one that what is foreign always seems ridiculous to the French, of course he is only noticing an instance of the universal law, but he makes us remember that Little Pedlington is everywhere, and that this day there is no more marked Little Pedlingtonian than the Parisian boulevardier man of letters. It is true that Montesquieu limits his remarks to trifles. They readily will admit that other people are wiser, he says, if you grant them that they are better dressed. His talk about the Spaniards is equally good. The Spaniards whom they do not burn, he says, seem so attached to the Inquisition that it would be ill-nature to deprive them of it. But at the end he gives them their revenge. He imagines a Spaniard in Paris and makes him say that they have a house there in which they shut up a few madmen in order to persuade the world that the rest are not mad. After things of this sort, two pages further on we read that the most perfect government is that which attains its ends with the least cost, so that the one which leads men in the way most according to their inclination is best. What have two hundred years added? What proximate test of excellence can be found except correspondence to the actual equilibrium of force in the community—that is, conformity to the wishes of the dominant power? Of course, such conformity may lead to destruction, and it is desirable that the dominant power should be wise. But wise or not, the proximate test of a good government is that the dominant power has its way.

There are considerations upon colonies, upon population, upon monarchy, a striking prophecy that the Protestant countries will grow richer and more powerful and the Catholic countries weaker. There is, in short, a scattering criticism of pretty nearly everything in the social order, of a sceptically radical kind, but always moderate and rational, with hints and germs of his future work, interspersed with many little sayings not too bright or good for human nature's daily food, and with some which are famous, such as, "It sometimes is necessary to change certain laws, but the case is rare, and when it occurs one should touch them only with a trembling hand"; or, "Nature always acts slowly and, so to speak, sparingly; her operations are never violent." This last is said by Sorel to be the whole philosophy of the *Esprit des Lois,* and suggests a more extensive philosophy still, which no doubt was more or less in the air, which found expression a little later in Linnaeus's *Nutura non facit saltus,* and which nowadays in its more developed form we call evolution.

The *Lettres Persanes* came out anonymously, ostensibly from Amsterdam, when Montesquieu was little more than thirty, and ran through four editions in the first year. The name of the author became known to everybody. He went to Paris, and there frequented the society of men and women whose names to us of this country and time are but foam from the sea of oblivion, but who were the best of their day. There, to please the ladies, or a lady, he wrote in 1725 the *Temple de Gnide* and *Cephise et l'Amour,* which need not delay us. He says that only well-curled and well-powdered heads will understand them. At the beginning of 1728 he was elected to the Academy, which he, like other Frenchmen, had made sport of but desired to enter. He had been elected before, but had been refused by the king. This time he had better luck. Voltaire and D'Alembert tell a tale of how it was managed. Entrance to the Academy is apt to be an occasion for the display of malice on the one side or the other; the address of welcome twitted him with having no recognized works to justify the election, under the form of a compliment on the certainty that the public would give him the credit of clever anonymous ones. For this or other reasons he did not go much to the Academy, and he soon set out upon a tour of Europe. He went to Vienna, and there met the Prince Eugene. He applied for a post as a diplomat, and again, luckily for the world, he failed. He visited Hungary, then Venice, where he met the famous John Law and became a friend of Lord Chesterfield; then Switzerland and Holland by way of the Rhine. From Holland he went with Lord Chesterfield to England, where he remained for nearly two years, returning in August, 1731, to La Brède, his family, and his writing.

In 1734 he published his *Considérations sur les causes de la grandeur des Romains et de leur décadence.* He was drawing nearer to his great work; from sporadic *aperçus* he was turning to systematic exposition. It often is said, and with a good deal of truth, that men reach their highest mark between thirty and forty. Perhaps the statement seems more significant than it really is, because men generally have settled down to their permanent occupation by thirty, and in the course of the next ten years are likely to have found such leading and dominant conceptions as they are going to find; the rest of life is working out details. Montesquieu and Kant either are exceptions to the rule or illustrate the qualification just suggested. In their earlier life as you look back at it you see the *Critique* and the *Esprit de Lois* coming, but the fruit did not ripen fully until they were in the neighborhood of sixty. In 1734 Montesquieu was already forty-five.

Roman history has been rewritten since his day by Niebuhr and his successors. But Montesquieu gives us the key to his mode of thought and to all fruitful thought upon historic subjects when he says that "there are general causes, moral or physical, at work in every monarchy, which elevate and maintain it or work its downfall; all accidents are the result of causes; and if the chance of a battle—that is, a special cause—has ruined a state, there was a general cause at work which made that state ready to perish by a single battle. In a word, the main current carries with it all the special accidents."

Montesquieu the ladies' man, Montesquieu the student of science, Montesquieu the lover of travel both real and fictitious, Montesquieu the learned in the classics and admirer of that conventional antiquity that passed so long for the real thing in France—all these Montesquieus unite in the *Esprit des Lois*, as is pointed out most happily by Faguet, whose many-sided and delicate appreciation of the author I read just as I was writing this sentence. The book, he says, is called *Esprit des Lois*; it should have been called simply *Montesquieu*. Perhaps the fact is due in part to the subject's not having become a specialty. In the same way Adam Smith's *Wealth of Nations* has many interesting and penetrating remarks that, alas! hardly would be allowed in a modern political economy, even if the writer had the wit to make them. At all events, after his Roman history, the rest of Montesquieu's life may be summed up as the production of this volume. In the preface he calls it the labor of twenty years. It appeared in 1748. When it was done his hair had whitened over the last books, and his eyes had grown dim. "It seems to me," he said, "that the light left to me is but the dawn of the day on which my eyes shall close forever." He published a defence of the work in 1750, attended to the sale of wine from his vineyards, noticed with pleasure that the sale seemed to have been increased in England by the publication of his book, and died in Paris on February 10, 1755, watched, if not like Arthur by weeping queens, at least by the Duchess d'Aiguillon and a houseful of loving and admiring friends. According to Maupertuis, he was well proportioned, careless in dress, modest in demeanor, candid in speech, simple in his mode of life, and welcomed in society with universal joy. The medallion gives him a distinguished face.

It would be out of place to offer an analysis of a book which is before the reader, and it would take a larger book to contain all the thoughts which it suggests. The chapters on the feudal law are so far separable from the rest that it had been thought a mistake of Montesquieu to add them. The modern student naturally would turn to Roth or whatever still later man may displace Roth. With regard to the main body of the work, one might say that it expressed a theory of the continuity of the phe-nomenal universe at a time when, through no fault of the author, its facts were largely miraculous. He was not able to see history as an evolution, he looked at all events as if they were contemporaneous. Montesquieu's Rome was the Rome of fable uncritically accepted. His anthropology was anecdotic. His notion of a democracy suggests a Latin town meeting rather than the later developements in the United States and France. He made the world realize the influence of the climate and physical environ-ment—which in our day furnished the already forgotten Buckle a sug-gestive chapter—but had not the data to be more than a precursor.

His England—the England of the threefold division of power into legislative, executive and judicial—was a fiction invented by him, a fiction which misled Blackstone and Delolme. Hear Bagehot in his work upon the subject: "The efficient secret of the English Constitution may be de-scribed as the close union, the nearly complete fusion of the executive and legislative powers." And again: "The American Constitution was made upon a most careful argument, and most of that argument assumes the king to be the administrator of the English Constitution, and an un-hereditary substitute for him—viz., a president—to be peremptorily neces-sary. Living across the Atlantic, and misled by accepted doctrines, the acute framers of the Federal Constitution, even after the keenest atten-tion, did not perceive the Prime Minister to be the principal executive of the British Constitution, and the sovereign a cog in the mechanism."

It is worth remarking that, notwithstanding his deep sense of the inevitableness of the workings of the world, Montesquieu had a possibly exaggerated belief in the power of legislation, and an equally strong con-viction of the reality of abstract justice. But it is vain to attempt to criticise the book in detail. Indeed, it is more important to understand its relation to what had been done before than to criticise. There is not space even to point out how many seeds it sowed. Montesquieu is a precursor, to repeat the word, in so many ways. He was a precursor of political economy. He was the precursor of Beccaria in the criminal law. He was the precursor of Burke when Burke seems a hundred years ahead of his time. The Frenchmen tell us that he was the precursor of Rousseau. He was an authority for the writers of *The Federalist*. He influenced, and to a great extent started scientific theory in its study of societies, and he hardly less influenced practice in legislation, from Russia to the United States. His book had a dazzling success at the moment, and since then probably has done as much to remodel the world as any product of the eighteenth century, which burned so many forests and sowed so many fields.

And this was the work of a lonely scholar sitting in a library. Like Descartes or Kant, he commanded the future from his study more than Napoleon from his throne. At the same time he affects no august sovereignty, but even gives us one or two discreet personal touches full of a sort of pathetic charm—the *"Italiam! Italiam!"* when the long day's work was done and the author saw his goal before darkness closed upon him; the suppressed invocation at the beginning of Book XX; the proud epigraph, *"Prolem sine matre creatam"*; and above all the preface, that immortal cheer to other lonely spirits. It is the great sigh of a great man when he has done a great thing. The last words of that are the words with which this introduction should end. "If this work meets with success, I shall owe it largely to the majesty of my subject. However, I do not think that I have been wholly wanting in genius. When I have seen what so many great men in France, England, and Germany have written before me, I have been lost in admiration, but I have not lost my courage. 'And I too am a painter,' I have said with Correggio."

16 | LASKI

ROUSSEAU

The eighteenth century in France was a race between reform and revolution. During the first half of the century, criticism was directed more openly against the church than against the state, although once the principle of ecclesiastical authority was undermined, the issue of political authority was bound to be raised, too. The social centers of the era were the elegant Paris *salons*, in which the sparkling wit of the *philosophes* mingled with the charm of beautiful women and the skeptical nonchalance of leisurely aristocrats. The people were still inarticulate; Voltaire spoke of them as *la canaille*, and not a few of the early leaders of the Enlightenment felt the same disdain toward the masses, whom they encountered only as untutored servants, workers, or peasants. This world of relative tranquillity was shaken in its foundations by the meteoric appearance of Jean Jacques Rousseau (1712–1778). Rousseau was born in Geneva of a poor family of pure French background that had migrated there in the sixteenth century as religious refugees. At sixteen he ran away from Geneva, and for years he traveled through Europe, living on his wits more than anything else, and leading the life of a penniless vagabond, rather than that of a well-established bourgeois. In 1744, he settled in Paris, where he remained for the rest of his life. Obscurity was replaced by instantaneous international fame when he published his *Discourse on the Moral Effects of the Arts and Sciences* (1751), followed by the *Discourse on the Origin of Inequality* (1755) and *The Social Contract* (1762), the most

famous of all his writings. He struck a new note in the feeling and thinking of men everywhere, although his influence was perhaps due more to
the boldness and passion of his ideas than to their logical consistency; the
complexity of his thought has led to the paradoxical result that both
democrats and totalitarians, both bourgeois and socialists, have hailed him
as their apostle. His *Confessions* (1782) reveal Rousseau as one of the
most colorful and contradictory personalities in the history of political
thought, and throw much light on the birth and development of his ideas.

In "A Portrait of Jean Jacques Rousseau" (1928), Harold J. Laski, a
twentieth-century socialist descendant of Rousseau, appraises him as man
and as thinker. Laski (1893–1950) was one of the prodigies of his generation; after a teaching career at McGill and Harvard Universities, he returned to his native land, where he was associated with the London
School of Economics and Political Science from 1920 to his death in 1950.
He took an active part in the British labor movement for many years, and
was Chairman of the Labor party shortly after World War II. His outstanding contribution to political thought is his *Grammar of Politics*
(1925), likely to endure for a long time as a significant treatise of general
political theory; *The Problem of Sovereignty* (1917) and *Liberty in the
Modern State* (1930) are among his more notable publications. He was
perhaps more influential as a teacher than as a scholar or active promoter
of political causes.

Laski on ROUSSEAU

If the world was amazed at the appearance of Rousseau, it has not ceased
to wonder at him since his death. Few men have ever aroused emotions
more vivid or more various. He has been regarded as the philosopher
who, since Plato, has seen most deeply into the nature of the state; and
his politics have been condemned for their lack of clarity in form and
logic in substance. To some, he has seemed to penetrate more clearly the
nature of faith than any of its more orthodox defenders; while other
critics attack him as the main author of a reaction against the authority of
dogma more profound than any since the Reformation. He has been
praised as the chief element in the flowering of Romanticism, the man
who above all others, made possible the recognition of emotions and sensi-

[Harold J. Laski, "A Portrait of Jean Jacques Rousseau," *Yale Review*, vol. 17
(July, 1928). By permission.]

bilities which are part of the ultimate richness of human nature. Yet this has been as ardently condemned as the parent of an impossible anarchy which robs the intellectual realm of order and of harmony.

No man, certainly, has exercised so wide an empire in fields so disparate. Religion, politics, aesthetic, fiction, education, upon each of these he has left an unmistakable impress. If, in them all, he was something of a magnificent sciolist, in all, quite as certainly, he showed that swift power of immediate penetration which is of the essence of genius. There are not half a dozen men in the history of the modern world who have so ultimately affected the ways of its mind.

Great effort, of course, has been expended upon the discovery of those thinkers to whom he is most in debt. It is sometimes even argued that he lacked originality, and Plato and Hobbes, Locke and Montesquieu, Montaigne and Diderot, are instanced as men from whom he had drunk deeply. It is true that Rousseau was far more widely read than he liked it to be supposed; and the note-books which remain testify a little pathetically to the care with which he read. He had, moreover, in a supreme degree that gift for taking immediate seisin of a great man's thoughts which, as with Descartes, Hobbes, and Shelley, so often has momentous consequence. But the ultimate originality of Rousseau is beyond all dispute. He was shaped by his life, not by what he read. Books merely revealed to him the already half-conscious direction of his thoughts. His real genius lay in his capacity for looking inwards and reporting, with unsurpassed eloquence, how the world impinged upon his personality. What life does to a temperament more uniquely capable of self-expression than any other in the records of man—this it was his art to depict with a completeness that altered the power of self-revelation among others. Where the art of his predecessors lay in its ability to conceal or to omit, Rousseau's genius lay in his capacity to reveal and to announce. His work thus becomes a kind of autobiography externalized into a programme. So that while the influences of other men upon him are important, they are negligible beside the influence of Rousseau himself. For him, the true events of his life were his own emotions; these he had cherished and analyzed and dissected as a botanist the flowers in his garden. What, therefore, others brought to him of suggestion is as nothing compared with his power to transmute what they brought. There is, in fact, no other writer whose originality can so little be brought into question.

To grasp what he taught, we must understand what he was, and that in its historic context. He came to a Paris in which social life had attained a degree of art more perfectly proportioned than in any previous period. Its angularities had been softened, its differences harmonized, with a skill of which the secret has still an exquisite enchantment. The elegant minuet of the salon, its delicate refinement, its grace, its charm, its blending of diverse chords to harmony, these encountered a man less capable of adaptation to their nuances than any other it is possible to conceive. He was infinitely ambitious, infinitely sensitive, and infinitely proud. But his power was in a realm where external success in the life of Paris was obviously beyond him. He could not, like Diderot, dominate the company he adorned; he was tongue-tied, aloof, embarrassed. He had no capacity, like Marmontel, for meeting what sneers or contradictions he might encounter as essential elements in the art of life. He could not brook the superiority of his patrons, or meet it with the mordant irony of Fontenelle or Voltaire. When his critics pricked him he bled; and a nature given, in any case, to the passion for isolation grew ever less capable of social intercourse. Nor was the tenderness which could be evoked to tears by a sunset or a note of music, likely to find happiness in a society which he had not yet taught to make of its emotions the master of its intelligence.

He came to this society, moreover, a foreigner and a plebeian. Both of these elements are vital to the grasp of Rousseau. He was as inherently and permanently a citizen of Geneva, as Sophocles a citizen of Athens or Dante a Florentine. He never lost his pride in his birth there, nor the peculiar flavor of its Puritan temper. There was ever present in him a Calvin who measured and condemned the skeptic and pleasure-loving city he yearned to conquer. From the outset of his sojourn in Paris he was a stranger to its essence. The Puritain moralist had an Athanasius in him which drove him, as in the letter to D'Alembert, to judge and to deny. If he had lost the formalism of Calvinist dogma, he retained its substance; and there was in him always a self which never lost the craving for simplicity and clung to it the more, the more the complexity of Paris drove him in upon himself. If, as with Diderot, he had possessed the chameleon-like quality which would have enabled him to fit whatever environment he encountered, the whole ethos of his life would have been different. But, though he did not know it in those early years of passionate creation when Diderot and Voltaire seemed to him God-like beings made for emulation, he had brought Geneva with him to Paris. Its spiritualism was in conflict with the materialism of the philosophers; its sense of the omnipresence of God was in conflict with the ardent skepticism of the Encyclopedists. It was Geneva which triumphed; and his very pride and sensitiveness only made its victory more complete.

For Rousseau was also plebeian; the depth of his pride was only intensified by the consciousness of the difference this made between himself and his environment. There is hardly a line in Voltaire which suggests even a dim capacity to grasp the mind of the peasant or the urban proletariat. His sophistication, his culture, his pleasure in the refinements at the command of a man of the world, made him revolt from those who, by definition, lacked these things. For him, accordingly, the workers are the canaille, doomed to superstition and necessarily subordinate because the work of the world requires a multitude of servants to wait upon free-minded masters. Diderot, indeed, understood the people and sympathized, by the intense imaginative insight with which he was endowed, with their half-articulate wants; but Diderot, like almost all the intellectuals of the eighteenth century, was essentially déclassé, and his heart was anywhere that argument was afoot.

Rousseau was in a different category. He never lost the sense of anger against an order the tradition of which forced him at every step to fight for himself. He felt the burden of the whole proletariat upon his shoulders. He had the proud indignation of the man who feels that he embodies and voices the suffering of the world. He felt that a kindness offered him was either the prelude to insult or the forerunner of control. He lived every day of his life in that mood of Dr. Johnson when he waited in the anteroom of Chesterfield. He resented alike what was offered and what was denied. He disliked the suspicion that his time was at the disposal of the aristocracy, who could deny him entrance as they pleased. He rejected all the principles upon which his own advancement depended. His insistence, for instance, upon earning his living as a copyist was essentially a challenge to those who, as he instinctively felt, regarded him as a mountebank of genius to be cultivated as the ornament of their salon. On any terms in which he could suspect such patronage, for him an alliance with the fashionable world was impossible. To him, the proletarian, that milieu of grace with its easy mockery and ironic wit, left a dumb sense of barbarous crudity, which was as poignant an experience as so sensitive a mind could know. He believed in the goodness of the poor; and the world about him regarded them as a canaille his genius permitted him to desert. He claimed rights, and he was offered privilege; he demanded equality and he was offered alternative patrons. So that he was driven by the law of his being to deny the foundations of the world he had hoped to conquer. He saw between himself and its spirit a fundamental contradiction of principle which neither compromise nor recognition could bridge.

This perception two other things intensified. No portait of Rousseau would be adequate which failed to take account of the degree to which his perceptiveness was disorganized by the malady from which he suffered. His letters, his "Dialogues" written in the last years, the sense of a whole world in conspiracy against him, the belief that humanity has become, as it were, a gigantic gaoler, all these make it clear that the insight he had was too feverish and too passionate to be capable of the philosopher's perspective. And that insight is, in any case, less the insight of ordered and coherent logic than of a lyrical intuition to which is suddenly revealed a secret incapable of systematic statement. He himself has told us that reflection was a painful thing to him, and, as he believed, unnatural to mankind. The truths he saw were not worked out by a patient analysis of experience, but caught suddenly as a landscape breaks upon us when we have breasted the summit of a mountain. And they came to him with an emotional penumbra which gave them the force of a mystic faith incapable of brooking denial. Whatever, therefore, he saw, he had like Blake to pronounce with the majestic oratory of organ music, which depends upon sweeping us out of ourselves for the conviction it can bring. Things go to Rousseau's heart before they penetrate his mind; they are absorbed before they are analyzed. The reasons, therefore, that he reveals are always, as with the tortured soul of Pascal, those of which Reason itself is unaware. They are affirmations of the central verities of one richly lived life, irrelevant to any experience which is not in communion with them. But for those who, like Rousseau, find in them the quintessence of life's meaning, all else, whatever its logic, seems in turn puny and irrelevant. They are the outpourings of revelation, not the reasoning of philosophy, the vision of the poet, not the logic of the scientist. Their unity, therefore, is poetic in character, and it is the poet's temperament that is the core of their being.

So that the essence of Rousseau is, above all, an affirmation of himself. He could be happy, and he is miserable; he could be good, and life has made him evil; he could be free, and he is the prisoner of life. And because each of these prospects should be open to him, that is what nature intended, what accordingly, society, civilization, institutions deny. These are the cause of his degradation, and the root of their wrong is in the inequalities they ordain. For these mean pain for the many, and pleasure for the few. They make the masses the slaves of a handful of oppressors. They give the gains of life to a few who do not labor, and its toil to the many who never know its gains. The whole problem of evil is thus the outcome of the central antithesis of rich and poor. This it is which, once we have left nature for civilization, ordains disharmony by its provocation of inequalities. And the more intense the civilization, the deeper must the disharmony become. The creations of intelligence, the work of the arts and sciences, are accessible only to the few; they are appreciable only for those who have the leisure to enjoy, and the means to acquire them. So the riches of civilization are a means of degrading the mass of men. The wealthy are ever more privileged, ever more separated by their privileges from their fellows. The principle of our life is clearly wrong if what makes for the happiness of the few thus separates the many from its attainment. We seem to hear the plea of Marx set out in ethical terms.

This, in fact, is Rousseau's central theme. Nature has made man for freedom, and the device of inequality has fastened him in chains; it is no accident that the first sentence of the "Social Contract" should be the final exhortation of the "Communist Manifesto." We have therefore to abolish inequality. This does not mean a return to the pre-civil state. Rousseau believed with passion in progress; "human nature," he wrote, "does not retrogress," and there are benefits in civil society infinitely greater than the primitive condition of mankind can afford. But to secure those advantages, we must give to nature room that she may find play for the impulses of man. We must make over the elements in society which deny the good in those impulses. A restoration is required which shall at once re-fashion the individual and the institutions which to-day degrade him.

The three great books of Rousseau are all constructive essays upon this theme. The "Emile" is, above all, an effort to discover how the individual may be remade. It seeks to find a form of education in which the impulses of nature may take hold of the child before the influence of civilization destroys the goodness they confer. Nature makes us solitary, and the child is withdrawn from society. Nature feeds our instincts and reason is to be secondary to their satisfaction. Men learn by their needs, and not by books; and literature is to be withheld until the character is strong enough to resist the influence of a drug so potent. So, too, with religious experience. The child may know God since in nature the savage sees the power of a Supreme Being; but he must know neither ritual nor dogma since these are social creations and the nurse only of corruption. So that when Emile enters the world, he is safeguarded by character against its vices. He may be what the "Nouvelle Héloïse" seeks to argue we may make of ourselves if we do but follow nature. For it is the thesis of Rousseau that Julie frees herself from the dangers that surround her by a return to nature. She re-establishes the family, "the first model of a political society." In a life sweetened by the duty and affection which arise from a natural relationship, she can repel the danger of an adultery upon which society does not frown. In the life thus opened before her, her duty and her faith in God give her the chance to realize herself without the stain of hypocrisy and illusion that civilized life involves.

But this is not enough. It opens a way of escape for the few; it re-makes the few fortunate to whom the privileges of inequality give avenues to freedom. It still leaves the many in the corruption of the present society. Here, it may be argued, we may see the purpose of that "Social Contract" which, it must never be forgotten, is but a fragment of a larger work. Even in its incomplete form, it is difficult not to regard it as the essential complement of the "Emile" and the "Nouvelle Héloïse." It is a body of principles out of which, if applied, might grow the ideal society. It is a technique for restoring equality to civilization and thus making possible a civil life in which its virtues without its vices may be realized. Let men renounce their unequal freedoms, which, to-day, mean the servitude of the many. Let them constitute of themselves a common will in which all equally participate. Let all be subject to that common will in equal degree. Then all equally will be free since what is ordained will be imposed freely and equally upon all. The sovereign of the society will not be one or a few but the whole, seeking in its acts to realize the common good. The magistrate will not be a master but a servant. Political organization will no longer repress, but, by the law it applies, will liberate; for what it applies will be the law each freely imposes upon himself. And as the last and vital sanction of this new construction, there is the civil religion. God is the *deus ex machina* invoked to keep man faithful to the principles he has thus asserted. Without Him, all would be valueless; with Him, the will and promise of men is strengthened and sanctified. For it is God who made nature beneficent, and to invoke His aid is to give to man the power to maintain that pledge of self-sacrifice which is the condition of his freedom. The Savoyard Vicar is emancipated because he has confided himself to the ultimate magistracy of God.

If the edifice of principle which Rousseau affirmed is regarded in this light, the "Confessions" becomes not only intelligible, but also the cornerstone of the edifice. For it is then possible to admit that it is time and again erroneous and malign, and yet to see in it a body of essential truth without which the real bearing of Rousseau is necessarily lost. The "Confessions" becomes a self-portrait of one who, as he believed, was fashioned by nature for good, and turned to evil ways by social institutions. It is a vindication, not only of himself, but of his doctrines. It is an argument that he might have been happy had the original endowment of his character been given opportunity for social expression. But the society he did in fact encounter is one of competing wills striving fiercely with one another and succeeding only at each other's cost. It is the record of the defeat of one who sought happiness and asked but little for the constitution of that happiness. He was born free, and the chains had been fastened upon him. He had asked only to see the sunlight on Mont Blanc, to wander with Madame d'Houdetot in the woods, as Julie and Saint-Preux had wandered. The social system of Rousseau, in a word, is simply an effort to make explicit what he believed to be the whole import of his tortured wanderings.

It would not be difficult to formulate a requisitory against this corpus of doctrine the answer to which the defenders of Rousseau have thus far failed to make. The implications of the "Emile" alone show how little relation it has to the facts of life. We are to suppose a child without parents, rich so that every requirement of the system may be satisfied, upon whom neither heredity nor temperament has left a trace; and he is in the hands of a tutor for whom his education is not a means but an end. Or, as in the "Social Contract," we are to assume a power of all exercised without tyranny, upon terms the administrative character of which is never even stated. We have a picture of the working of man's mind in society which omits at least the half of what is significant, and denatures the rest. We have a religious tyranny in which the new presbyter is not merely written larger than the ancient priest, but has exactly those weapons at his disposal against the use of which most of modern history is a protest. The "Nouvelle Héloïse" is an idyl which, even after a century and three-quarters, retains almost all its original grace; yet its essence is the creation of a world within a world into which the major problems of actual life do not enter. Julie solves her problems only by assuming that outside her household there is the void which existed upon the first day of creation.

Yet, important as it is to understand the essential inadequacies of Rousseau, it is still more important to see what he did. Above all, we have to guard against the dismissal of his theories because they remain incapable of realization. This, at least, none knew better, or stated more clearly, than Rousseau himself; and none would have been more anxious to affirm that they offer less a possible, immediately achievable society than a criterion by which to expose and, it may be, to modify the evils of the present. And, certainly, much of the basis of his construction is neither utopian nor sophistical. There is nothing incredible in making socialism the outcome of individualism; that, in a broad sense, is happening before our eyes. There is nothing educationally reprehensible in making original virtue, instead of original sin, the foundation of training in childhood. There is no ultimate psychological error in making Julie undergo a moral crisis in which her whole being is re-born; no one familiar with the history of religious conversion will be inclined to deny either the truth of the evolution that Rousseau records, or the immense social significance of its ultimate outcome. And, if we omit the supernatural element, there will not be many anxious to deny that a social philosophy must make the impact of intense religious faith if it is to maintain any permanent hold upon the minds of men.

It is more fruitful to discuss the character of Rousseau's influence, and to inquire, as best we may, why it was so extensive. Here, it may be argued, the essential influence of Rousseau was fourfold. He was, above all, the author of a vast religious revival of which, even yet, we are far from the end. Its profit, maybe, was to creeds he did not share, since the effort to found a civil faith was obviously premature. But by opposing the certainty of non-rational conviction to a world puzzled and tormented by a generation of rational abstraction and argument, he carried the incomplete work of Pascal to its inevitable conclusion. He gave to the will to believe rights of which the Encyclopedists had seemed to deprive it; and men like Chateaubriand and Lamennais reaped for Catholicism the harvest he had sown.

He revived, in the second place, the ethical foundations of his period. He gave to the simple virtues a self-respect which the manners of a decaying society had taken away. He made the sanctity of marriage, the beauty of family life, the duty of so living that a man might be at peace with himself, seem important as they had not seemed for more than a generation. He made it an honorable thing for mothers to nurse their children; and it became possible to deny that it was necessary to commit adultery in order to be a man of the world. He reformed, too, the educational habits of his period, and he made men see that the future of humanity depends upon giving to the educational system a primary place in the national economy. He impressed upon society the folly of a discipline which neglects the correlation of body and mind; and he reduced the training of intelligence to its proper proportions as a lever of civic virtue. And if it is claimed that in this realm what he accomplished was but a magistral commingling of what Plato and Locke and Condillac had already said, Rousseau's is the final answer that to impose important truth upon mankind is not less important than to discover it.

In the political field, his influence is far more complicated, and, therefore, much less easy to define. For there was a Rousseau whose political influence was in the direction of an extreme individualism, as there was a Rousseau whose work produced a collectivism of a certainty not less extreme. In a sense, the latter aspect has been the more enduring. It was born of that passion to discover a unity in society which, in the Western world, goes back to the very origins of political thought. It reduces the individual to an instrument of a greater whole whose end has to seek realization as the larger whole realizes itself. That vision has had consequences in two directions. On the one hand, as with Hegel, it became the parent of an intensely conservative doctrine, of which Rousseau himself would have denied almost every principle; on the other, as it was inherited by Marx, it regained its revolutionary purposes and became again a weapon against the inequality he abhorred. The relation between Rousseau and Marx has been too little investigated, though the analogies of doctrine are obvious and striking. What, in this aspect, is especially notable is the exaltation of the state by each that, in a supreme and prolonged effort of will, inequality may perish; with the inference that with its disappearance a mild and natural anarchism may well become the settled form of social organization. But with both Hegel and Marx, as with their disciples, Rousseauism has essentially meant the sacrifice of the individual to an end beyond himself. With both, of course, it is proclaimed that the individual is the richer for his self-abnegation, that he realizes thereby an end which, more fully than otherwise might be, achieves the personality he possesses. But with each, it is difficult not to feel that the problem of freedom has been wrongly conceived, its methodology, accordingly, stated in terms that lack relation to the essence of what freedom involves.

The individualism of Rousseau is related, above all, to the lyrical character of his temperament. Rousseau, of course, did not originate the Romantic spirit; the success of La Chaussée and the theorizing of Dubos and Levesque show clearly that its time had come. But Rousseau gave it its letters of credit, and his own triumph assured its victory. What essentially his individualism did was to erect his personal experience into an argument and insist that this was valid against the historic tradition of mankind. He exalted, moreover, this experience until, for him and for his readers, it had the impelling claim of religious ecstasy. His impressions are true because they are passionately perceived. They can reject older and more sombre disciplines because they are so intimate a part of himself. On this side, at least, Rousseau is the eternal revolutionary, whose emotions are his conscience and whose conscience will not brook denial whatever the challenge it may encounter. It is subjectivism *in excelsis*— the feeling not only that the sensation of the moment is the whole of reality, but the intimate conviction that the sensation makes the reality and that, without it, reality itself would be meaningless.

Much could be said of the aesthetic consequence of the way in which Rousseau's personal life colored the substance of his Romanticism; not for nothing had he wandered amid the lakes and mountains of Geneva and Italy. But it is here more profitable to think of the passionate color he lavished on things which, before he idealized them, had seemed of little import to his contemporaries. The intimate details of a simple country

life, the cows in the field, the peasants returning home at the end of a day
—it is always the homeliest and the tenderest of virtues that he seems to
reserve for the most passionate poetic form. He was, of course, not the
first to realize how profoundly they belonged to art; the brush of van
Ostade had idealized them in a thousand different forms. But it was as
though the vision of van Ostade had suddenly burgeoned into the colorful
brilliance of a Titian so that no man could forget their clamant ecstasy. It
is not merely that nature becomes a part of art; it is, also, and emphatically, that nature in its simplest form becomes a claim on the soul of man;
and whatever is a part of nature has, accordingly, a claim on him too.
The individualism of Rousseau is, in a subtle way, an expression of that
plebeian temper which he forced upon the notice of his generation. He
invests with new dignity and new claims things that, before, men had
hardly realized as compatible with either claims or dignity. His eloquence
invests the grimness of rude plebeian effort with a splendor men had
never before seen. La Bruyère, Voltaire, above all, Diderot, had cried out
against brutalization of the people. But Rousseau asserted not his difference from them but his kinship with them. He claimed for them their
inheritance. He gave them thereby a new meaning for their lives. For he
put into words what they had dumbly felt. Thereby he became the prophet
of their future.

That there is in Rousseau a trumpet-call to revolutionary acts, a hundred events can be cited to testify. Yet to regard him only in that context
would be to falsify the man he was. As his life seems a permanent conflict
between precept and practice, so there is a singular and ultimate disharmony between what he experienced and what he was prepared to urge.
The first "Discourse" is a resounding attack upon the arts and sciences;
the second preaches with passion the case for egalitarian anarchy. Yet the
conclusion of the first seems the establishment of academies, and, if the
second has any conclusion, it is the need for submission to the will of
God from whom all governments derive their authority. So, also, with
the "Nouvelle Héloïse." Never has the glory of passion been more flam-
ingly proclaimed; never has revelation been so earnestly destroyed as in
the Savoyard Vicar's profession of faith. But Julie submits to the claim
of the marriage tie, and the Vicar's disciple is bidden to worship in the
church of his fathers. In the more purely political texts, the temper is
similar. The sovereignty of the people is proclaimed in the "Social Contract"; in the "Letters from the Mountain" civil war appears the necessary
outcome of popular right. But, in the one, all governments are given a
just authority, and, in the other, compromise is recommended to the
people of Geneva. So, also, when he was asked for advice from Poland

and from Corsica. He trembles before the need for action, and his counsels are a warning against the perils of change. To the Calas case, he has nothing to say save that time heals all things and that resignation is a virtue. To his myriad correspondents who seek to frame their lives by his principles, he is timid and hesitant and evasive; it is as though he sought to deny in life all the principles he drew from experience. There is nothing in him of the man of action, no gift of any kind for measuring the deed to the need.

The antinomy is a real one, and it is, doubtless, no small part of the seeming contradiction that his critics have seen in his work. Yet, also, it is important to remember that in so vast an edifice consistency cannot be looked for; that, in any case, the life of Rousseau is in the glimpses of truth he caught and fearlessly recorded rather than in his effort to act the part of statesman. What, after all, remains important is the fact that he was a prophet to his generation. It was, as his contemporaries well understood, a gospel that he taught; and wherever men experience the needs he experienced, to them, also, he is an evangel. It is not that he originated in any special field. It is not that he discovered in the field of social constitution laws that we can compare with similar hypotheses in the natural sciences. His contribution is a different one. It is that he gave new power and enhanced prestige to all he proclaimed as truth, that whatever passed through the crucible of his heart, emerged re-fashioned and re-created as a living and ardent thing. That is the point of Madame de Staël's famous saying; "il n'a rien découvert," she wrote, "mais il a tout enflammé." And to know what that fire meant, we have to try to catch the sudden vision of new horizons which, for the young Marie Philipon, made all of life seem different. We have to envisage the young Marat on his chair in the Paris garden reading out the "Social Contract" to humble men who hear in its music the song that is in their hearts. We have to think of the young Swiss pastor, Roustan, who can write to him that his teaching is a precious commentary on the Beatitudes, or of the young girl who begs from him the secret of a peaceful heart. Whatever his wrongs, his errors, his hestitations, the man to whom a whole epoch turned for help and comfort, was a very great man.

The greater because he was infinitely unhappy, and yet did not, in his misery, cease to proclaim a message which gave new hope and made possible new dreams. Nor must we forget his genius for sincerity. If we know the sins he committed, it is because he did not strive to conceal them, and he admitted frankly his shame. It is we, indeed, who benefit from that shame and suffering. Had he stayed in Geneva, or rested with Madame de Warens, instead of coming to Paris, he might have remained the happy wanderer, to whom the height of enchantment was plucking cherries in an autumn garden. But he came to Paris; and he was not afraid to challenge there a group of men who dominated the intellectual life of their country as it had never before been dominated. From that challenge, in no small part, there came the experiences from which his most bitter moments and ultimate disease arose. Yet he did not fear either to issue the challenge or to maintain his ground. There was courage in that.

For the men he confronted were the corporate mind of Europe in his time. Voltaire, Holbach, Grimm, Diderot, D'Alembert, Helvétius, they are, after all, a formidable company. We can still catch the fascination of their talk, its sense of power, its keen pleasure in the art of making life gracious, its zest for knowledge, its refusal any longer to be duped by the superstitution of the past, the wealth it commanded, the great personages devoted to its wants. They were a brotherhood of immense influence, devoted to a great task which was, at least in part, his own. Nothing would have been easier, as his first years in Paris make clear, than to have been admitted to the freedom of their fellowship. But their message was not Rousseau's. Theirs was the mind which denies, his was the heart which affirms. Theirs was to bound by reason an empire which sought to overpass its frontiers; his was the effort to remake its boundaries to a plan in which the sovereignty of reason had only a part to play. So, in the face of criticism and envy and hate, he took once more to the road. And whatever allowance we make against him for pride and self-pity and misinterpretation, the courage of the choice is undeniable. It was to court disaster from the only men who could have understood, and might have defended, the plea he was driven to utter. It was to choose isolation instead of friendship, persecution instead of alliance.

We have to remember that ours is the fruit of his decision. What he experienced in sorrow, we have inherited in knowledge; what he in his personal happiness lost, we in our collective tradition have gained. For him it was a tragedy the bitterness of which his utmost eloquence could hardly express. But for us it invokes the memory less of its sadder moments than of those magic hours where we seem to share the hope of his enchanted dream.

| **PAINE**
WILSON

BURKE

The English Revolution of 1640, the American Revolution of 1776, and the French Revolution of 1789 are the three main pillars of the Atlantic community as a way of life dedicated to a common ideal—liberty. The French Revolution, the third act in the drama of modern democratic revolution, began two years after the Constitution of the United States was framed. Peaceful reform would have been possible until the last minute, and the Anglophile, liberal-conservative element was at first in the ascendancy. But the *ancien régime* lacked the most elementary prudence and foresight and thus made revolution inevitable. In the early stages of the French Revolution few understood its long-term impact and significance. Some of the conservative forces in Europe even welcomed the Revolution as a sign of French weakness and decay; they failed to understand the fresh vitality and vigorous ability of the new democratic leaders, whose aim was to make France not only free but great. The first to raise the issues of the French Revolution from the plane of immediate policy to that of philosophical principle was Edmund Burke (1729-1797), whose *Reflections on the Revolution in France* (1790) was an immediate literary success in England and on the Continent. Against the individualist conception of Locke and the French philosophers, Burke put forward the organic theory of society, with its emphasis on concrete, historical group interests rather than on abstract rights of man. While Burke proved wrong in the case of the French Revolution, it ought to be remembered that he was on the side of the future on three other key issues of his time: Ireland, India, and the American colonies. In all three instances his sympathies were magnanimous and his judgment farsighted, and, as a result, his impact on liberal statesmanship and thought has been no less important than on conservatism, with which his name is associated as its greatest exponent in any language in the modern world.

Burke's *Reflections* were at once answered by a mass of prorevolutionary and prodemocratic books and pamphlets. The most famous is Tom Paine's *Rights of Man* (1791-1792), a fiery answer to the *Reflections*, and —as a defense of French democracy—a worthy successor to his *Common Sense* (1776), which had an immense effect on the writing of the Declaration of Independence. Whereas Burke was shocked and shaken by the sufferings of Queen Marie Antoinette in a "nation of men of honor, and of cavaliers," Paine remarked in the *Rights of Man* that Burke "pities the plumage, but forgets the dying bird." Paine (1737-1809) was born in England, but migrated to America in 1774, where he immediately became involved in politics. His *Common Sense* was not only a radical defense of the nascent American democracy, but also helped to strengthen the feeling for complete separation from England. During the Revolutionary War he contributed greatly to maintaining the spirit of hope and confidence in ultimate victory through a series of pamphlets on *The American Crisis*, establishing himself as the foremost pamphleteer of the American Revolution. In 1787 he returned to England and wrote the *Rights of Man* (1791-1792); in England he was prosecuted for libelous statements on English institutions allegedly contained in his book, and in September, 1792, he fled to France, where he had been elected a Member of the National Convention. Yet in revolutionary France he seemed too conservative, and was imprisoned there in 1793. While in France, he wrote *The Age of Reason* (1794-1795), which lost him much sympathy among erstwhile friends in England and America because the book attacked the Bible and defended deism as a foundation of religious belief. In 1802 he returned to America, where he lived the last seven years of his life in relative alienation and ostracism because of his political and religious views, considered too radical at that time.

As time went on and the immediate issues of the French Revolution faded into the background, even liberal thinkers developed a more sympathetic attitude toward Burke, as can be seen from Woodrow Wilson's appraisal of Burke in the *Century Magazine* in 1901. Wilson (1856-1924) graduated from Princeton in 1879 and received his Ph.D. degree from Johns Hopkins in 1886. After teaching history and politics at Bryn Mawr and Wesleyan University, he was appointed professor of jurisprudence and political economy at Princeton University, and became its president in 1902. His strong democratic sentiments were clearly—and often combatively—displayed during his administration at Princeton; in 1910 he gained national reputation after his election as Governor of New Jersey, and in 1912 he was elected President of the United States (1913–1921). His "New Freedom" foreshadowed many of the domestic policies continued twenty years later by President Franklin D. Roosevelt in his New Deal, and his advocacy of an international organization, frustrated in his own lifetime by the American failure to join the League of Nations, was vindicated in 1945, at the end of World War II, when the United States became one of the main architects of the United Nations. Wilson's many writings include *Congressional Government* (1885), *A History of the American People* (5 vols., 1902), and *Constitutional Government in the United States* (1908). His writings and speeches reveal his deep admiration for classical liberal thought in the grand Anglo-American tradition, and his conception of liberalism was broad enough to include Edmund Burke, the greatest of all liberal-conservatives.

Paine on BURKE

TO
GEORGE WASHINGTON
PRESIDENT OF THE UNITED STATES OF AMERICA

Sir,

I present you a small Treatise in defence of those Principles of Freedom which your exemplary Virtue hath so eminently contributed to establish. That the Rights of Man may become as universal as your Benevolence can wish, and that you may enjoy the Happiness of seeing the New World regenerate the Old, is the prayer of

Sir,

Your much obliged, and

Obedient humble Servant,

THOMAS PAINE.

Among the incivilities by which nations or individuals provoke and irritate each other, Mr. Burke's pamphlet on the French Revolution is an extraordinary instance. Neither the people of France, nor the National

[From Thomas Paine, *Rights of Man* (1791–1792).]

Assembly, were troubling themselves about the affairs of England, or the English Parliament; and why Mr. Burke should commence an unprovoked attack upon them, both in Parliament and in public, is a conduct that cannot be pardoned on the score of manners, nor justified on that of policy.

There is scarcely an epithet of abuse to be found in the English language, with which Mr. Burke has not loaded the French Nation and the National Assembly. Everything which rancour, prejudice, ignorance or knowledge could suggest, is poured forth in the copious fury of near four hundred pages. In the strain and on the plan Mr. Burke was writing, he might have written on to as many thousands. When the tongue or the pen is let loose in a phrenzy of passion, it is the man, and not the subject, that becomes exhausted.

Hitherto Mr. Burke has been mistaken and disappointed in the opinions he had formed of the affairs of France; but such is the ingenuity of his hope, or the malignancy of his despair, that it furnishes him with new pretences to go on. There was a time when it was impossible to make Mr. Burke believe there would be any Revolution in France. His opinion then was, that the French had neither spirit to undertake it nor fortitude to support it; and now that there is one, he seeks an escape by condemning it.

Not sufficiently content with abusing the National Assembly, a great part of his work is taken up with abusing Dr. Price (one of the best-hearted men that lives) and the two societies in England known by the name of the Revolution Society and the Society for Constitutional Information.

Dr. Price had preached a sermon on the 4th of November, 1789, being the anniversary of what is called in England the Revolution, which took place in 1688. Mr. Burke, speaking of this sermon, says, "The political Divine proceeds dogmatically to assert, that by the principles of the Revolution, the people of England have acquired three fundamental rights:

1. To choose their own governors.
2. To cashier them for misconduct.
3. To frame a government for ourselves."

Dr. Price does not say that the right to do these things exists in this or in that person, or in this or in that description of persons, but that it exists in the *whole*; that it is a right resident in the Nation. Mr. Burke, on the contrary, denies that such a right exists in the Nation, either in whole or in part, or that it exists anywhere; and, what is still more strange and marvellous, he says, "that the people of England utterly disclaim such a right, and that they will resist the practical assertion of it with their lives and fortunes." That men should take up arms and spend their lives and fortunes, *not* to maintain their rights, but to maintain they have *not* rights, is an entirely new species of discovery, and suited to the paradoxical genius of Mr. Burke.

The method which Mr. Burke takes to prove that the people of England have no such rights, and that such rights do not now exist in the Nation, either in whole or in part, or anywhere at all, is of the same marvellous and monstrous kind with what he has already said; for his arguments are that the persons, or the generation of persons, in whom they did exist, are dead, and with them the right is dead also. To prove this, he quotes a declaration made by parliament about a hundred years ago, to William and Mary, in these words: "The Lords Spiritual and Temporal, and Commons, do, in the name of the people aforesaid [meaning the people of England then living], most humbly and faithfully *submit* themselves, their *heirs* and *posterities*, for EVER." He also quotes a clause of another act of Parliament made in the same reign, the terms of which, he says "bind us [meaning the people of that day], our *heirs* and our *posterity*, to *them*, their *heirs* and *posterity*, to the end of time."

Mr. Burke conceives his point sufficiently established by producing those clauses, which he enforces by saying that they exclude the right of the Nation for *ever*. And not yet content with making such declarations, repeated over and over again, he farther says, "that if the people of England possessed such a right before the Revolution [which he acknowledges to have been the case, not only in England, but throughout Europe, at an early period], yet that the *English Nation* did, at the time of the Revolution, most solemnly renounce and abdicate it, for themselves, and for *all their posterity, for ever.*"

As Mr. Burke occasionally applies the poison drawn from his horrid principles (if it is not prophanation to call them by the name of principles) not only to the English Nation, but to the French Revolution and the National Assembly, and charges that august, illuminated and illuminating body of men with the epithet of *usurpers*, I shall, *sans cérémonie*, place another system of principles in opposition to his.

The English Parliament of 1688 did a certain thing, which, for themselves and their constituents, they had a right to do, and which it appeared right should be done: but, in addition to this right, which they possessed by delegation, *they set up another right by assumption*, that of binding and controuling posterity to the end of time. The case, therefore, divides itself into two parts; the right which they possessed by delegation, and the right which they set up by assumption. The first is admitted; but with respect to the second, I reply—

There never did, there never will, and there never can, exist a Parliament, or any description of men, or any generation of men, in any country, possessed of the right or the power of binding and controuling posterity to the *"end of time,"* or of commanding for ever how the world shall be governed, or who shall govern it; and therefore all such clauses, acts or declarations by which the makers of them attempt to do what they have neither the right nor the power to do, nor the power to execute, are in themselves null and void. Every age and generation must be as free to act for itself *in all cases* as the ages and generations which preceded it. The vanity and presumption of governing beyond the grave is the most ridiculous and insolent of all tyrannies. Man has no property in man; neither has any generation a property in the generations which are to follow. The Parliament or the people of 1688, or of any other period, had no more right to dispose of the people of the present day, or to bind or to controul them *in any shape whatever*, than the Parliament or the people of the present day have to dispose of, bind or controul those who are to live a hundred or a thousand years hence. Every generation is, and must be, competent to all the purposes which its occasions require. It is the living, and not the dead, that are to be accommodated. When man ceases to be, his power and his wants cease with him; and having no longer any participation in the concerns of this world, he has no longer any authority in directing who shall be its governors, or how its Government shall be organised, or how administered.

I am not contending for nor against any form of Government, nor for nor against any party, here or elsewhere. That which a whole Nation chooses to do, it has a right to do. Mr. Burke says, No. Where, then, does the right exist? I am contending for the rights of the *living*, and against their being willed away, and controuled and contracted for, by the manuscript assumed authority of the dead; and Mr. Burke is contending for the authority of the dead over the rights and freedom of the living. There was a time when Kings disposed of their Crowns by will upon their deathbeds, and consigned the people, like beasts of the field, to whatever successor they appointed. This is now so exploded as scarcely to be remembered, and so monstrous as hardly to be believed; but the Parliamentary clauses upon which Mr. Burke builds his political church are of the same nature.

The laws of every country must be analogous to some common principle. In England no parent or master, nor all the authority of Parliament, omnipotent as it has called itself, can bind or controul the personal freedom even of an individual beyond the age of twenty-one years. On what ground of right, then, could the Parliament of 1688, or any other Parliament, bind all posterity for ever?

Those who have quitted the world, and those who are not yet arrived at it, are as remote from each other as the utmost stretch of mortal imagination can conceive. What possible obligation, then, can exist between them; what rule or principle can be laid down that of two non-entities, the one out of existence and the other not in, and who never can meet in this world, the one should controul the other to the end of time?

In England it is said that money cannot be taken out of the pockets of the people without their consent. But who authorised, or who could authorise, the Parliament of 1688 to controul and take away the freedom of posterity (who were not in existence to give or to withhold their consent), and limit and confine their right of acting on certain cases for ever?

A greater absurdity cannot present itself to the understanding of man than what Mr. Burke offers to his readers. He tells them, and he tells the world to come, that a certain body of men who existed a hundred years ago, made a law, and that there does not now exist in the Nation, nor ever will, nor ever can, a power to alter it. Under how many subtilties or absurdities has the divine right to govern been imposed on the credulity of mankind! Mr. Burke has discovered a new one, and he has shortened his journey to Rome by appealing to the power of this infallible Parliament of former days; and he produces what it has done as of divine authority, for that power must certainly be more than human which no human power to the end of time can alter.

But Mr. Burke has done some service, not to his cause, but to his country, by bringing those clauses into public view. They serve to demonstrate how necessary it is at all times to watch against the attempted encroachment of power, and to prevent its running to excess. It is somewhat extraordinary that the offence for which James II. was expelled, that of setting up power by *assumption*, should be re-acted, under another shape and form, by the Parliament that expelled him. It shows that the rights of man were but imperfectly understood at the Revolution; for certain it is that the right which that Parliament set up by *assumption* (for by delegation it had it not, and could not have it, because none could give it) over the persons and freedom of posterity for ever, was of the same tyrannical unfounded kind which James attempted to set up over the Parliament and the Nation, and for which he was expelled. The only difference is (for in principle they differ not) that the one was an usurper over the living, and the other over the unborn; and as the one has no better authority to stand upon than the other, both of them must be equally null and void, and of no effect.

From what, or from whence, does Mr. Burke prove the right of any human power to bind posterity for ever? He has produced his clauses, but he must produce also his proofs that such a right existed, and show how it existed. If it ever existed it must now exist, for whatever appertains to the nature of man cannot be annihilated by man. It is the nature of man to die, and he will continue to die as long as he continues to be born. But Mr. Burke has set up a sort of political Adam, in whom all posterity are bound for ever; he must, therefore, prove that his Adam possessed such a power, or such a right.

The weaker any cord is the less will it bear to be stretched, and the worse is the policy to stretch it, unless it is intended to break it. Had any one proposed the overthrow of Mr. Burke's positions, he would have proceeded as Mr. Burke has done. He would have magnified the authorities, on purpose to have called the *right* of them into question; and the instant the question of right was started, the authorities must have been given up.

It requires but a very small glance of thought to perceive that altho' laws made in one generation often continue in force through succeeding generations, yet that they continue to derive their force from the consent of the living. A law not repealed continues in force, not because it *cannot* be repealed, but because it *is not* repealed; and the non-repealing passes for consent.

But Mr. Burke's clauses have not even this qualification in their favour. They become null, by attempting to become immortal. The nature of them precludes consent. They destroy the right which they *might* have, by grounding it on a right which they *cannot* have. Immortal power is not a human right, and therefore cannot be a right of Parliament. The Parliament of 1688 might as well have passed an act to have authorized themselves to live for ever, as to make their authority live for ever. All, therefore, that can be said of those clauses is that they are a formality of words, of as much import as if those who used them had addressed a congratulation to themselves, and in the oriental stile of antiquity had said: O Parliament, live for ever!

The circumstances of the world are continually changing, and the opinions of men change also; and as Government is for the living, and not for the dead, it is the living only that has any right in it. That which may be thought right and found convenient in one age may be thought wrong and found inconvenient in another. In such cases, Who is to decide, the living, or the dead?

As almost one hundred pages of Mr. Burke's book are employed upon these clauses, it will consequently follow that if the clauses themselves, so far as they set up an *assumed usurped* dominion over posterity for ever, are unauthoritative, and in their nature null and void; that all his voluminous inferences, and declamation drawn therefrom, or founded thereon, are null and void also; and on this ground I rest the matter.

We now come more particularly to the affairs of France. Mr. Burke's book has the appearance of being written as instruction to the French Nation; but if I may permit myself the use of an extravagant metaphor, suited to the extravagance of the case, It is darkness attempting to illuminate light.

While I am writing this there are accidentally before me some proposals for a declaration of rights by the Marquis de la Fayette (I ask his pardon for using his former address, and do it only for distinction's sake) to the National Assembly, on the 11th of July, 1789, three days before the taking of the Bastille; and I cannot but remark with astonishment how opposite the sources are from which that gentleman and Mr. Burke draw their principles. Instead of referring to musty records and mouldy parchments to prove that the rights of the living are lost, "renounced and abdicated for ever," by those who are now no more, as Mr. Burke has done, M. de la Fayette applies to the living world, and emphatically says, "Call to mind the sentiments which Nature has engraved in the heart of every citizen, and which take a new force when they are solemnly recognised by all: For a Nation to love Liberty, it is sufficient that she knows it; and to be free, it is sufficient that she wills it." How dry, barren, and obscure is the source from which Mr. Burke labours; and how ineffectual, though gay with flowers, are all his declamation and his arguments compared with these clear, concise, and soul-animating sentiments! Few and short as they are, they lead to a vast field of generous and manly thinking, and do not finish, like Mr. Burke's periods, with music in the ear, and nothing in the heart.

As I have introduced M. de la Fayette, I will take the liberty of adding an anecdote respecting his farewell address to the Congress of America in 1783, which occurred fresh to my mind, when I saw Mr. Burke's thundering attack on the French Revolution. M. de la Fayette went to America at an early period of the war, and continued a volunteer in her service to the end. His conduct through the whole of that enterprise is one of the most extraordinary that is to be found in the history of a young man, scarcely then twenty years of age. Situated in a country that was like the lap of sensual pleasure, and with the means of enjoying it, how few are there to be found who would exchange such a scene for the

woods and wildernesses of America, and pass the flowery years of youth
in unprofitable danger and hardship! But such is the fact. When the war
ended, and he was on the point of taking his final departure, he presented
himself to Congress, and contemplating, in his affectionate farewell, the
Revolution he had seen, expressed himself in these words: "May this
great monument raised to Liberty, serve as a lesson to the oppressor, and
an example to the oppressed!" When this address came to the hands of
Dr. Franklin, who was then in France, he applied to Count Vergennes
to have it inserted in the French Gazette, but never could obtain his consent. The fact was that Count Vergennes was an aristocratical despot at
home, and dreaded the example of the American Revolution in France, as
certain other persons now dread the example of the French Revolution in
England; and Mr. Burke's tribute of fear (for in this light his book must
be considered) runs parallel with Count Vergennes' refusal. But to return more particularly to his work—

"We have seen," says Mr. Burke, "the French rebel against a mild
and lawful Monarch, with more fury, outrage, and insult, than any people
has been known to rise against the most illegal usurper, or the most san-
guinary tyrant." This is one among a thousand other instances, in which
Mr. Burke shows that he is ignorant of the springs and principles of the
French Revolution.

It was not against Louis XVI., but against the despotic principles of
the government, that the Nation revolted. These principles had not their
origin in him, but in the original establishment, many centuries back;
and they were become too deeply rooted to be removed, and the Augean
stable of parasites and plunderers too abominably filthy to be cleansed,
by anything short of a complete and universal Revolution. When it becomes necessary to do a thing, the whole heart and soul should go into
the measure, or not attempt it. That crisis was then arrived, and there
remained no choice but to act with determined vigour, or not to act at
all. The King was known to be the friend of the Nation, and this circumstance was favourable to the enterprise. Perhaps no man bred up in the
style of an absolute King, ever possessed a heart so little disposed to the
exercise of that species of power as the present King of France. But the
principles of the Government itself still remained the same. The Monarch
and the Monarchy were distinct and separate things; and it was against
the established despotism of the latter, and not against the person or principles of the former, that the revolt commenced, and the Revolution has
been carried.

Mr. Burke does not attend to the distinction between *men* and *principles*; and, therefore, he does not see that a revolt may take place against

the despotism of the latter, while there lies no charge of despotism against the former.

The natural moderation of Louis XVI. contributed nothing to alter the hereditary despotism of the Monarchy. All the tyrannies of former reigns, acted under that hereditary despotism, were still liable to be revived in the hands of a successor. It was not the respite of a reign that would satisfy France, enlightened as she then was become. A casual discontinuance of the *practice* of despotism, is not a discontinuance of its *principles*; the former depends on the virtue of the individual who is in immediate possession of the power; the latter, on the virtue and fortitude of the nation. In the case of Charles I. and James II. of England, the revolt was against the personal despotism of the men; whereas in France, it was against the hereditary despotism of the established government. But men who can consign over the rights of posterity for ever on the authority of a mouldy parchment, like Mr. Burke, are not qualified to judge of this Revolution. It takes in a field too vast for their views to explore, and proceeds with a mightiness of reason they cannot keep pace with.

But there are many points of view in which this Revolution may be considered. When despotism has established itself for ages in a country, as in France, it is not in the person of the King only that it resides. It has the appearance of being so in show, and in nominal authority; but it is not so in practice and in fact. It has its standard everywhere. Every office and department has its despotism, founded upon custom and usage. Every place has its Bastille, and every Bastille its despot. The original hereditary despotism resident in the person of the King, divides and subdivides itself into a thousand shapes and forms, till at last the whole of it is acted by deputation. This was the case in France; and against this species of despotism, proceeding on through an endless labyrinth of office till the source of it is scarcely perceptible, there is no mode of redress. It strengthens itself by assuming the appearance of duty, and tyrannises under the pretence of obeying.

When a man reflects on the condition which France was in from the nature of her Government, he will see other causes for revolt than those which immediately connect themselves with the person or character of Louis XVI. There were, if I may so express it, a thousand despotisms to be reformed in France, which had grown up under the hereditary despotism of the monarchy, and became so rooted as to be in great measure independent of it. Between the Monarchy, the Parliament, and the Church, there was a *rivalship* of despotism; besides the feudal despotism operating locally, and the ministerial despotism operating everywhere.

But Mr. Burke, by considering the King as the only possible object of a revolt, speaks as if France was a village, in which everything that passed must be known to its commanding officer, and no oppression could be acted but what he could immediately controul. Mr. Burke might have been in the Bastille his whole life, as well under Louis XVI. as Louis XIV., and neither the one nor the other have known that such a man as Mr. Burke existed. The despotic principles of the Government were the same in both reigns, though the dispositions of the men were as remote as tyranny and benevolence.

What Mr. Burke considers as a reproach to the French Revolution (that of bringing it forward under a reign more mild than the preceding ones) is one of its highest honours. The Revolutions that have taken place in other European countries, have been excited by personal hatred. The rage was against the man, and he became the victim. But, in the instance of France we see a revolution generated in the rational contemplation of the rights of man, and distinguishing from the beginning between persons and principles.

But Mr. Burke appears to have no idea of principles when he is contemplating Governments. "Ten years ago," says he, "I could have felicitated France on her having a Government, without inquiring what the nature of that Government was, or how it was administered." Is this the language of a rational man? Is it the language of a heart feeling as it ought to feel for the rights and happiness of the human race? On this ground, Mr. Burke must compliment all the Governments in the world, while the victims who suffer under them, whether sold into slavery, or tortured out of existence, are wholly forgotten. It is power, and not principles, that Mr. Burke venerates; and under this abominable depravity he is disqualified to judge between them. Thus much for his opinion as to the occasions of the French Revolution. I now proceed to other considerations.

I know a place in America called Point-no-Point, because as you proceed along the shore, gay and flowery, as Mr. Burke's language, it continually recedes and presents itself at a distance before you; but when you have got as far as you can go, there is no point at all. Just thus it is with Mr. Burke's three hundred and fifty-six pages. It is therefore difficult to reply to him. But as the points he wishes to establish may be inferred from what he abuses, it is in his paradoxes that we must look for his arguments.

As to the tragic paintings by which Mr. Burke has outraged his own imagination, and seeks to work upon that of his readers, they are very well calculated for theatrical representation, where facts are manufactured for the sake of show, and accommodated to produce, through the weakness of sympathy, a weeping effect. But Mr. Burke should recollect that he is writing history, and not *plays*, and that his readers will expect truth, and not the spouting rant of high-toned exclamation.

When we see a man dramatically lamenting in a publication intended to be believed that *"The age of chivalry is gone! that The glory of Europe is extinguished for ever! that the unbought grace of life* (if any one knows what it is), *the cheap defence of nations, the nurse of manly sentiment and heroic enterprise is gone!"* and all this because the Quixote age of chivalry nonsense is gone, what opinion can we form of his judgment, or what regard can we pay to his facts? In the rhapsody of his imagination he has discovered a world of windmills, and his sorrows are that there are no Quixotes to attack them. But if the age of Aristocracy, like that of Chivalry, should fall (and they had originally some connection), Mr. Burke, the trumpeter of the order, may continue his parody to the end, and finish with exclaiming: *"Othello's occupation's gone!"*

Notwithstanding Mr. Burke's horrid paintings, when the French Revolution is compared with the Revolutions of other countries, the astonishment will be that it is marked with so few sacrifices; but this astonishment will cease when we reflect that *principles*, and not *persons*, were the meditated objects of destruction. The mind of the nation was acted upon by a higher stimulus than what the consideration of persons could inspire, and sought a higher conquest than could be produced by the downfall of an enemy. Among the few who fell there do not appear to be any that were intentionally singled out. They all of them had their fate in the circumstances of the moment, and were not pursued with that long, cold-blooded, unabated revenge which pursued the unfortunate Scotch in the affair of 1745.

Through the whole of Mr. Burke's book I do not observe that the Bastille is mentioned more than once, and that with a kind of implication as if he were sorry it was pulled down, and wished it were built up again. "We have rebuilt Newgate," says he, "and tenanted the mansion; and we have prisons almost as strong as the Bastille for those who dare to libel the Queens of France." As to what a madman like the person called Lord G—— G—— might say, to whom Newgate is rather a bedlam than a prison, it is unworthy a rational consideration. It was a madman that libelled, and that is sufficient apology; and it afforded an opportunity for confining him, which was the thing that was wished for. But certain it is that Mr. Burke, who does not call himself a madman (whatever other people may do), has libelled in the most unprovoked manner, and in the grossest stile of the most vulgar abuse, the whole representative authority of France, and yet Mr. Burke takes his seat in the British House of Commons! From his violence and his grief, his silence on some points and his excess on others, it is difficult not to believe that Mr. Burke is sorry, extremely sorry, that arbitrary power, the power of the Pope and the Bastille, are pulled down.

Not one glance of compassion, not one commiserating reflection that I can find throughout his book, has he bestowed on those who lingered out the most wretched of lives, a life without hope in the most miserable of prisons. It is painful to behold a man employing his talents to corrupt himself. Nature has been kinder to Mr. Burke than he is to her. He is not affected by the reality of distress touching his heart, but by the showy resemblance of it striking his imagination. He pities the plumage, but forgets the dying bird. Accustomed to kiss the aristocratical hand that hath purloined him from himself, he degenerates into a composition of art, and the genuine soul of nature forsakes him. His hero or his heroine must be a tragedy-victim expiring in show, and not the real prisoner of misery, sliding into death in the silence of a dungeon.

There is a general enigma running through the whole of Mr. Burke's book. He writes in a rage against the National Assembly; but what is he enraged about? If his assertions were as true as they are groundless, and that France, by her Revolution, had annihilated her power, and become what he calls a *chasm*, it might excite the grief of a Frenchman (considering himself as a national man), and provoke his rage against the National Assembly; but why should it excite the rage of Mr. Burke? Alas! it is not the Nation of France that Mr. Burke means, but the COURT; and every Court in Europe, dreading the same fate, is in mourning. He writes neither in the character of a Frenchman nor an Englishman, but in the fawning character of that creature known in all countries, and a friend to none, a COURTIER. Whether it be the Court of Versailles, or the Court of St. James, or of Carlton House, or the Court in expectation, signifies not; for the caterpillar principle of all courts and courtiers are alike. They form a common policy throughout Europe, detached and separate from the interest of Nations; and while they appear to quarrel, they agree to plunder. Nothing can be more terrible to a Court or courtier than the Revolution of France. That which is a blessing to Nations is bitterness to them: and as their existence depends on the duplicity of a country, they tremble at the approach of principles, and dread the precedent that threatens their overthrow.

Conclusion

Reason and Ignorance, the opposite to each other, influence the great bulk of mankind. If either of these can be rendered sufficiently extensive in a country, the machinery of Government goes easily on. Reason obeys itself; and Ignorance submits to whatever is dictated to it.

The two modes of Government which prevail in the world, are—
First, Government by election and representation.
Secondly, Government by hereditary succession.

The former is generally known by the name of Republic; the latter by that of Monarchy and Aristocracy.

Those two distinct and opposite forms erect themselves on the two distinct and opposite bases of Reason and Ignorance.

As the exercise of Government requires talents and abilities, and as talents and abilities cannot have hereditary descent, it is evident that hereditary succession requires a belief from man to which his reason cannot subscribe, and which can only be established upon his ignorance; and the more ignorant any country is, the better it is fitted for this species of Government.

On the contrary, Government, in a well-constituted Republic, requires no belief from man beyond what his reason can give.

He sees the *rationale* of the whole system, its origin and its operation; and as it is best supported when best understood, the human faculties act with boldness, and acquire under this form of Government a gigantic manliness.

As, therefore, each of those forms acts on a different base, the one moving freely by the aid of reason, the other by ignorance, we have next to consider, what it is that gives motion to that species of Government which is called Mixed Government, or, as it is sometimes ludicrously stiled, *a Government of this, that, and t'other.*

The moving power in this species of Government is of necessity Corruption. However imperfect election and representation may be in Mixed Governments, they still give exercise to a greater portion of reason than is convenient to the hereditary part; and therefore it becomes necessary to buy the reason up.

A Mixed Government is an imperfect everything, cementing and soldering the discordant parts together by corruption, to act as a whole. Mr. Burke appears highly disgusted that France, since she had resolved on a Revolution, did not adopt what he calls *"A British Constitution;"* and the regretful manner in which he expresses himself on this occasion implies a suspicion that the British Constitution needed something to keep its defects in countenance.

In Mixed Governments there is no responsibility: the parts cover each other till responsibility is lost; and the Corruption which moves the machine, contrives at the same time its own escape. When it is laid down as a maxim, that *a King can do no wrong*, it places him in a state of similar security with that of idiots and persons insane, and responsibility is out of the question with respect to himself.

It then descends upon the Minister, who shelters himself under a majority in Parliament, which by places, pensions, and corruption, he can always command; and that majority justifies itself by the same authority with which it protects the Minister. In this rotatory motion, responsibility is thrown off from the parts, and from the whole.

When there is part in a Government which can do no wrong, it implies that it does nothing; and is only the machine of another power, by whose advice and direction it acts.

What is supposed to be the King in a Mixed Government is the Cabinet; and as the Cabinet is always a part of the Parliament, and the members justifying in one character what they advise and act in another, a Mixed Government becomes a continual enigma; entailing upon a country, by the quantity of corruption necessary to solder the parts, the expence of supporting all the forms of Government at once, and finally resolving them into a Government by committee; in which the advisers, the actors, the approvers, the justifiers, the persons responsible, and the persons not responsible, are the same persons.

By this pantomimical contrivance, and change of scene and character, the parts help each other out in matters which neither of them singly would assume to act.

When money is to be obtained, the mass of variety apparently dissolves, and a profusion of parliamentary praises passes between the parts. Each admires with astonishment, the wisdom, the liberality, and disinterestedness of the other; and all of them breathe a pitying sigh at the burdens of the Nation.

But in a well-constituted Republic, nothing of this soldering, praising, and pitying, can take place; the representation being equal throughout the country, and compleat in itself, however it may be arranged into legislative and executive, they have all one and the same natural source. The parts are not foreigners to each other, like Democracy, Aristocracy, and Monarchy. As there are no discordant distinctions, there is nothing to corrupt by compromise, nor confound by contrivance. Public measures appeal of themselves to the understanding of the Nation, and resting on their own merits, disown any flattering applications to vanity. The continual whine of lamenting the burden of taxes, however successfully it may be practised in Mixed Governments, is inconsistent with the sense and spirit of a Republic. If taxes are necessary, they are of course advantageous, but if they require an apology, the apology itself implies an impeachment. Why, then, is man imposed upon, or why does he impose upon himself?

When men are spoken of as Kings and subjects, or when Government is mentioned under the distinct or combined heads of Monarchy, Aristocracy, and Democracy, what is it that *reasoning* man is to understand by the terms? If there really existed in the world two or more distinct and separate *elements* of human power, we should then see the several origins to which those terms would descriptively apply; but as there is but one species of man, there can be but one element of human power, and that element is man himself. Monarchy, Aristocracy, and Democracy, are but creatures of imagination; and a thousand such may be contrived as well as three.

From the Revolutions of America and France, and the symptoms that have appeared in other countries, it is evident that the opinion of the world is changed with respect to systems of Government, and that Revolutions are not within the compass of political calculations.

The progress of time and circumstances, which men assign to the accomplishment of great changes, is too mechanical to measure the force of the mind, and the rapidity of reflection, by which Revolutions are generated: All the old Governments have received a shock from those that already appear, and which were once more improbable, and are a greater subject of wonder, than a general Revolution in Europe would be now.

When we survey the wretched condition of Man, under the monarchical and hereditary systems of Government, dragged from his home by one power, or driven by another, and impoverished by taxes more than by enemies, it becomes evident that those systems are bad, and that a general Revolution in the principle and construction of Governments is necessary.

What is Government more than the management of the affairs of a Nation? It is not, and from its nature cannot be, the property of any particular man or family, but of the whole community, at whose expence it is supported; and though by force and contrivance it has been usurped into an inheritance, the usurpation cannot alter the right of things. Sovereignty, as a matter of right, appertains to the Nation only, and not to any individual; and a Nation has at all times an inherent, indefeasible right to abolish any form of Government it finds inconvenient, and to establish such as accords with its interest, disposition, and happiness. The romantic and barbarous distinction of men into Kings and subjects, though it may suit the conditions of courtiers, cannot that of citizens; and is exploded by the principle upon which Governments are now founded. Every citizen is a member of the sovereignty; and, as such, can acknowledge no personal subjection: and his obedience can be only to the laws.

When men think of what Government is, they must necessarily suppose it to possess a knowledge of all the objects and matters upon which its authority is to be exercised. In this view of Government, the Republican system, as established by America and France, operates to embrace the whole of a Nation; and the knowledge necessary to the interest of all the parts, is to be found in the centre, which the parts by representation form; but the old Governments are on a construction that excludes knowledge as well as happiness; Government by monks, who know nothing of the world beyond the walls of a convent, is as inconsistent as Government by Kings.

What we formerly called Revolutions, were little more than a change of persons, or an alteration of local circumstances. They rose and fell like things of course, and had nothing in their existence or their fate that could influence beyond the spot that produced them. But what we now see in the world, from the Revolutions of America and France, are a renovation of the natural order of things, a system of principles as universal as truth and the existence of man, and combining moral with political happiness and national prosperity.

"I. *Men are born, and always continue, free and equal in respect of their rights. Civil distinctions, therefore, can be founded only on public utility.*

II. *The end of all political associations is the preservation of the natural and imprescriptible rights of man; and these rights are liberty, property, security, and resistance of oppression.*

III. *The Nation is essentially the source of all sovereignty; nor can* ANY INDIVIDUAL, *or* ANY BODY OF MEN, *be entitled to any authority which is not expressly derived from it.*"

In these principles there is nothing to throw a Nation into confusion by inflaming ambition. They are calculated to call forth wisdom and abilities, and to exercise them for the public good, and not for the emolument or aggrandisement of particular descriptions of men or families. Monarchical sovereignty, the enemy of mankind, and the source of misery, is abolished; and sovereignty itself is restored to its natural and original place, the Nation. Were this the case throughout Europe, the cause of wars would be taken away.

Wilson on BURKE

Much has been said and written about Edmund Burke, and all the world knows his fame; but it is not necessary to repeat all in order to see him live again. It is not necessary to tell the whole story of his life to make it clear what manner of man he was, or of what force and consequence in his day. It is possible to look at him from a single point of view and in a single situation, and yet see him complete and whole, in his habit as he lived. There is often to be found in the life of a great man some point of eminence at which his powers culminate and his character stands best revealed, his characteristic gifts brought to light and illustrated with a sort of dramatic force. Generally it is a moment of success that reveals him, when his will has had its way and his genius its triumph. But Edmund Burke gave the most striking proofs of his character and genius in the evil days in which his life ended—not when he was a leader in the Commons, but when he was a stricken old man at Beaconsfield. That Burke was a great statesman, no thinking man who reads his pamphlets and speeches can deny; but a man may be a great statesman and yet fall very far short of being a great man. Burke makes as deep an impression upon our hearts as upon our minds. We are taken captive, not so much by his reasoning, strongly as that moves to its conquest, as by the generous warmth that steals out of him into our hearts. There is a tonic breath of character and of generous purpose in what he writes—the fine sentiment of a pure man; and we are made aware that he who could write thus was great, not so much by reason of what he said or did, as by reason of what he was. What a man was you may often discover in the records of his days of bitterness and pain better than in what is told of his seasons of cheer and hope; for if the noble qualities triumph then and show themselves still sound and sweet, if his courage sink not, if he show himself still capable of self-forgetfulness, if he still stir with a passion for the service of causes and policies which are beyond himself, his stricken age is even greater than his full-pulsed years of manhood. This is the test which Burke endures—the test of fire. It has not often been judged so, I

[Woodrow Wilson, "Edmund Burke and the French Revolution," *The Century Magazine*, vol. 62 (September, 1901).]

know; but let any man of true insight take that extraordinary "Letter to a Noble Lord," which was written in 1796, and which is Burke's *apologia pro vita sua*, consider the circumstances under which it was written, its tone, its scope, its truth, its self-revelations, and the manner of man revealed, and say whether this be not the real Burke, undaunted, unstained, unchanged in purpose and in principle.

Some of Burke's biographers have turned their faces away from these last scenes and from the last writings of his life with a sort of sad reverence, as if loath to blame and yet unable to approve. They have bidden us draw the veil over these days of disturbed judgment and unbalanced passion, and think only of the great days when he was master of himself and the foremost political thinker in Europe. His vision had until now been so clear, his judgment so sane and sure-footed, his knowledge of the facts with which he dealt so comprehensive and unerring, that it is simple pity, they say, that he should have gone mad about the French Revolution. For that is the fact they are at a loss to account for and despair of justifying. Burke threw all his magnificent resources against the French Revolution, and with a sort of fury assisted to carry England into the war which monarchical Europe was waging to suppress or annul it. Yet that Revolution was the salvation of France, and perhaps of Europe too. How else could the fetters that bound men to an antiquated and intolerable system of tyranny have been shaken off? Certainly it would seem that France, at any rate, could not otherwise have been set in the way of a free life and a reformed and purified government. Frightful as were its excesses, her Revolution was but the violent purging of a wholesome and cleansing disease; and Burke, with his knowledge of France and of affairs, ought to have seen how inevitable and how tonic a thing it was. Burke, they will tell you, knew France better than any other Englishman living, except Arthur Young. He was not arguing for or against France, you suggest, but only crying out against the introduction of the French revolutionary ideas into England, whither the disease seemed likely to be carried by contagion, and where it would feed upon a healthy, not upon a distempered, society, and work death, it might be, instead of purification and a healing restoration. There was no such danger, they reply; and Burke of all men should have known that there was none. They will cite you that famous passage in which, in the days of his calm vision, Burke had described the placid self-possession and content of England, and had laughed at those who supposed that the noise of a few politicians could disturb it. "Because half a dozen grasshoppers under a fern make the field ring with their importunate chink," he had laughed, "while thousands of great cattle beneath the shadow of the British oak chew the cud and are silent, pray do not imagine that those who make the noise are the only inhabitants of the field, that of course they are many in number, or that, after all, they are other than the little, shriveled, meager, hopping, though loud and troublesome, insects of the hour." Had he now himself at last been betrayed into mistaking the insects of the field for the great cattle of the herd, and did he fear a stampede because these chirped with excited clamor?

The question is radical. Settle it, and you have analyzed Edmund Burke. You are easily able to prove that, at any rate in the late year 1791, the year after he wrote his great "Reflections on the Revolution in France," which was his first ordered attack, he was as clear-sighted as ever, and as poised in judgment. A correspondent in France, a member of the National Assembly, had asked him to suggest a course of action for those who were seeking to guide affairs at that critical juncture in the unhappy kingdom; but he had declined, and had given these luminous and statesmanlike reasons for declining. "Permit me to say," he wrote, "that if I were as confident as I ought to be diffident in my own loose general ideas, I never should venture to broach them, if but at twenty leagues' distance from the center of your affairs. I must see with my own eyes; I must in a manner touch with my own hands, not only the fixed, but momentary circumstances, before I could venture to suggest any political project whatsoever. I must know the power and disposition to accept, to execute, to persevere. I must see all the aids and all the obstacles. I must see the means of correcting the plan, where correctives would be wanted. I must see the things; I must see the men. Without a concurrence and adaptation of these to the design, the very best speculative projects might become not only mischievous but useless. Plans must be made for men. People at a distance must judge ill of men. They do not always answer to their reputation when you approach them. Nay, the perspective varies, and shows them quite other than you thought them. At a distance, if we judge uncertainly of men, we must judge worse of *opportunities*, which continually vary their shapes and colors, and pass away like clouds." Here, assuredly, was a lucid interval, if the man was mad. It is matter of common knowledge, too, that in the very midst of his excitement about French affairs he was able to give counsel with all his old-time wisdom and self-possession about the deeply disturbed and almost revolutionary affairs of Ireland—counsel which rang true to the sane and tolerant and liberal standards he had so courageously stood by while there was revolutionary war in America. He wrote, too, the while, calm "Thoughts and Details on Scarcity," from every line of which spoke the hopeful, the informed, the philosophical economist. His thought held steadily on its way, without excitement or serious error. His training held good, as in every previous effort of his mind. "I had earned my pension before I set my foot in St. Stephen's Chapel," he said, with a flash of pride. "The first session I sat in Parliament I found it necessary to analyze the whole commercial, financial, constitutional, and foreign interests of Great Britain and its empire." He keeps to the last the assured and confident step of the veteran. I take leave to say again that the real Burke may be found and admired in the "Letter to a Noble Lord," written in 1796, in the midst of the French frenzy, no less than in the noble utterances of twenty years before, in which he defended his opposition to the American war, and opened to the world the real principles of constitutional liberty.

The "Letter" was written in defense of the pension which had been granted him in 1794, and contains his own estimate of his public services. If a man can be petty, expect him to be so when he is defending a bounty bestowed upon himself; if ever an old man may be petulant, indulge him when the rewards of his old age are sneered at and condemned. But Burke is neither. There was everything to sting him in the circumstances of the attack. He had in these last days accepted a considerable pension from the government of William Pitt, his arch opponent in politics until now, when their common fear of the French Revolution had drawn them together and brought about an artificial coalition in affairs. It was possible for malicious men to make him out an apostate Whig and twit him cruelly with being a beneficiary of the court, though all his life he had championed a proud independence and talked against the extravagance of private grants. Pitt had not brought the matter of the pension before Parliament, but had arranged it by direct gift from the crown, and Burke had had the mortification of feeling that Pitt had taken this course because he feared the opposition the grant would excite in Parliament and the awkwardness of defending it. Outside Parliament it raised a storm of animadversion and abuse, as it was, and its discussion was not wholly avoided in the houses. The Duke of Bedford and the Earl of Lauderdale attacked the pension in the Lords, as part of their general indictment of the ministry; and it was to their attack that Burke replied. "Loose libels ought to be passed by in silence and contempt," he said, with his accustomed gravity. "By me they have been so always. I knew that, as long as I remained in public, I should live down the calumnies of malice and the judgments of ignorance. If I happened to be now and then in the wrong (as who is not?), like all other men, I must bear the consequence of my faults and my mistakes. The libels of the present day are just of the same stuff as the libels of the past. But they derive an importance from the rank of the persons they come from, and the gravity of the place where they were uttered. In some way or other I ought to take some notice of them. To assert myself thus traduced is not vanity or arrogance. It is a demand of justice; it is a demonstration of gratitude." And it must be said that the defense is made with singular moderation and dignity, considering the passions of the man and the times.

The year 1794, the year in which the pension was granted, had been the darkest of all Burke's strenuous career. The active work of his life was ended. The long trial of Hastings, begun in 1788, had that very year at length been concluded, and with it the last, as it was also the most arduous, public business he was to engage in. He had recognized this as the end of active duty, had withdrawn from the House of Commons, and had but just turned to Beaconsfield for the solace of a quiet old age, when the cruel blow fell upon him which was to poison the sources of happiness and snatch hope away. He had loved Richard Burke, his son and only child, with all the passion of his ardent nature; and the year had opened bright with the hope that Richard was to succeed him as member for Malton in the Commons. But death had come of a sudden and taken his son away. "The storm has gone over me," he cried, "and I lie like one of those old oaks which the late hurricane had scattered about me. I am stripped of all my honors, I am torn up by the roots, and lie prostrate on the earth. . . . I live in an inverted order. They who ought to have succeeded me have gone before me. They who should have been to me as posterity are in the place of ancestors."

There was nothing to break the force of the blow. Only absorbing labor can lighten such a man of a grief like this. Quiet Beaconsfield, lying remote from the business of the world, out upon the gentle plains of Buckinghamshire, was no place in which to seek forgetfulness. Here was leisure for every memory; here were days open to be possessed by any thoughts that might come; here was no business, but only a desolated home, with an old man for tenant. The very sympathy of his tender wife, bereaved like himself, was but a part of the same grief. Even the relish of old friendships was not vouchsafed him. His friends of the old days which had seen his life run strong, with the full sunlight on it,—the friends whose comradeship and sympathy and counsel had given to his days of labor their keenest zest and confidence,—now no longer sought him out or could bring him any succor. They had not cast him off; he had withdrawn himself from them, because they would not think as he did of the Revolution oversea, in France. He had feared and hated it from the first; they had been tolerant toward it, had even hailed its advent with a burst of hopeful ardor. "How much the greatest event it is that ever happened in the world," Fox had cried, "and how much the best!" It would render

France, he said, "a better neighbor, and less disposed to hostility, than
when she was subject to the cabal and intrigues of ambitious and interested statesmen"; and it would advance the cause of liberty throughout
the world, as the revolt of the colonies had done. From such sentiments
Burke turned relentlessly away, for he deemed them mad who uttered
them. He broke with Fox in the open House, though they had loved and
consorted like brothers. "Whatever the risk of enmity," he said, "and
however bitter the loss of friendship, he would never cease from the warning to flee from the French constitution." "But there is no loss of friends,"
exclaimed Fox, eagerly. "Yes," cried Burke, "there *is* a loss of friends. I
know the penalty of my conduct. I have done my duty at the price of my
friend; our friendship is at an end." It was the price, not of his conduct,
but of his nature. His passion for the principles he served was deeper
than his passion for his friend. A shallower man, for whom public questions were less like the very essences of life and thought and action, might
have kept his friend without giving up his opinions; but for Burke no
such divided comradeship and allegiance was possible, and he had found
himself among strangers and one-time foes for a little in the debates of
the hour. How it fared with his own feelings in these painful times we
have good evidence in the pathetic closing passage of his will. "If the
intimacy which I have had with others"—these are the sad words—"has
been broken off by political differences on great questions concerning the
state of things existing and impending, I hope they will forgive whatever
of general human infirmity or of my own particular infirmity has entered into that contention; I heartily entreat their forgiveness."

Many of his old associates had followed him at last, indeed,—the great
Duke of Portland, Lord Fitzwilliam, Windham, Grenville, and a great
company of the rank and file of the old Whigs, till men laughed and said
there were not enough members left in the minority that clung to Fox
to fill a hackney-coach,—for the atrocities of the revolutionists in France
had wrought a deep change in English opinion. But this was, after all, no
rehabilitation of former companionships; and Burke must have felt it,
though no humiliation or dishonor, yet a thing unpalatable and in need
of explanation, that he should be the pensioner of a Tory government
with which his old-time associates were acting only for a little, and because political necessity and the critical stress of affairs compelled them.
And so his apology was written, in answer to the taunts of Bedford and
Lauderdale, and we turn to it to learn his assessment of himself.

Here, if you look nowhere else, is a sufficient explanation of the critical
matter of his life's history: there need be no mystery about Burke's attitude toward the French Revolution after reading this luminous "Letter";

and there need no longer be any pitiful apologizing for it, either, or any whispering that the man was out of his mind. He had not mistaken the noisy insects of the hour for the great cattle of the pasture. Some of the first minds of the kingdom, whether for philosophy or for statesmanship, had hailed the doctrines of the French revolutionists as the true gospel of liberty; men of both parties in the state, and not a few of those who were most seriously studious in affairs, were looking to see the world liberalized by the gracious influences of "The Rights of Man." No doubt it was clear enough in the end that the mass of the steady English people were safe against the infection, and that Burke's fears were exaggerated: the "thousands of great cattle beneath the shadow of the British oak" continued to chew the cud and looked forth upon their quiet fields with unruffled philosophy. But who could foresee that they would thus keep the subtle breath of war and panic out of their nostrils? Who can say how much of their quiet they took from the voice of their herdsman, crying out the familiar words of government and control? This was no common or vulgar danger that Burke set himself first to expose and then to neutralize. It was no mere French spirit of disorder that he feared would cross the Channel, but a spirit of change that was without nationality or country, an abstract thing of dogma and belief, like the spirit of the Reformation, which had ignored all boundaries of states, and moved upon the kingdoms of the world, as if they had been but a single community.

"The present Revolution in France," he said, "seems to me to bear little resemblance or analogy to any of those which have been brought about in Europe upon principles merely political. *It is a revolution of doctrine and theoretic dogma.* It has a much greater resemblance to those changes which have been made upon religious grounds, in which a spirit of proselytism makes an essential part. The last revolution of doctrine and theory which has happened in Europe is the Reformation. It is not for my purpose to take any notice here of the merits of that revolution, but to state only one of its effects. That effect was, *to introduce other interests into all countries than those which arose from their locality and natural circumstances.* The principle of the Reformation was such as, by its essence, could not be local or confined to the country in which it had its origin. For instance, the doctrine of 'justification by faith or by works,' which was the original basis of the Reformation, could not have one of its alternatives true as to Germany and false as to every other country. Neither are questions of theoretic truth or falsehood governed by circumstances any more than by places. On that occasion, therefore, the spirit of proselytism expanded itself with great elasticity upon all sides; and great divisions were everywhere the result." Similarly, Burke saw, the new gospel of the rights of man might be counted on, if unchecked, to divide the nations of the world and unsettle every government of them all. "The political dogma," he said, "which, upon the new French system, is to unite the factions of different nations, is this: that the majority, told by the head, of the taxable people in every country, is the perpetual, natural, unceasing, indefeasible sovereign; that the majority is perfectly master of the form as well as the administration of the state, and that the magistrates, under whatever names they are called, are only functionaries to obey the orders which that majority may make; that this is the only natural government; that all others are tyranny and usurpation." He did not pretend to prescribe for France: but he saw her leaders engaged in a mad work of destruction; he knew that such doctrines as theirs logically and inevitably breed a corresponding practice; he believed that such a way of reform as they had produced in France would mar not only the institutions of England, but also the whole moral and political habit of the English people; and he meant to keep out the infection, if he could. He meant to keep England, if he might, from the "dreadful contagion" of revolutionary ideas—"to preserve, pure and untainted, the ancient, inbred integrity, piety, good nature, and good humor of the people of England," so he put it, "from the dreadful pestilence which, beginning in France, threatens to lay waste the whole moral, and in a great degree the whole physical world, having done both in the focus of its most intense malignity."

There is here the whole philosophy of his course with regard to the Revolution in France. If his excitement rose beyond measure in the struggle, who shall say that it was an unnatural excitement, or an unhallowed? If you would see him at his best, Miss Burney said, you must not mention politics. "His irritability is so terrible on that theme," she declared, "that it gives immediately to his face the expression of a man who is going to defend himself from murderers." We should not expect a man to be easy and affable when he deems himself in a death-grapple with the enemies of his country. If the French revolutionary doctrines *had* taken root in England, what then? They did not. Who shall say how much this vehement and eloquent Irishman did to keep them out?

At any rate, it turned out that he was speaking the real mind of England about the Revolution. When once they saw the monstrous progeny it brought forth in action, Englishmen flocked, rank and file, to the defense of authority and orderly government, and Burke found himself for the nonce a European power. Statesmen of every opinion sought his advice. He had in the first days of his new power sent his son to Koblenz to act as his representative in helping the exiled noblemen of France to form practicable plans of action. Richard Burke had neither the talents nor the nobleness of disposition with which his father credited him. The great-hearted man gave his love as his nature bade him; chose his intimates by rules of affection and duty, rather than by rules of interest; and had fewer connections to commend him to the great than any other public man of his generation, and yet ruled by sheer force of genius among those who sought and formed counsel. "Burke has now got such a train after him," wrote Gilbert Elliot in 1793, "as would sink anybody but himself: his son, who is quite *nauseated* by all mankind; his brother, who is liked better than his son, but is rather oppressive with animal spirits and brogue; and his cousin William Burke, who is just returned unexpectedly from India, as much ruined as when he went years ago, and who is a fresh charge on any prospects of power Burke may ever make. Mrs. Burke has in her train Miss French, the most perfect *She Paddy* that ever was caught. Notwithstanding these disadvantages, Burke is in himself a sort of power in the state." (It is noteworthy that this critical contemporary should have seen it.) "It is not too much to say that he is a sort of power in Europe, though totally without any of those means, or the smallest share in them, which give or maintain power in other men."

Sir James Mackintosh, who had written an earnest defense of the Revolution in answer to Burke's first and great pamphlet against it, himself surrendered at discretion when he saw what things the year brought forth in France; confessed that he had been the dupe of his enthusiasm; and sought Burke out in his retirement at Beaconsfield to win his friendship and render him homage in his closing days. There he saw Burke roll on the carpet, a gleeful participant in the sports of children, and heard such talk as no man else could utter, so full of life and power was it, so amazingly various, so free and unpremeditated in its copiousness and beauty. This was not the morbid and unbalanced man some have thought they saw, who now look back to the French Revolution as, after all, a wholesome, though terrible, catastrophe, and feel themselves repelled by Burke's savage onslaught upon it. These were the days in which Burke wrote his defense of his pension, and surely that masterly "Letter" is a wonderfully perfect mirror in which to see the man and the meaning of his life. We are first of all struck by the splendid pride of this once obscure attorney's son, with his queer following of discredited Irishmen, his own tongue, as we know, touched with the brogue of that volatile race which Englishmen half despised, half feared, and wholly distrusted. It was a sad indiscretion on the part of the Duke of Bedford, it turned out, to have ventured to attack this apparently broken old man. "Why will his Grace, by attacking me," cries the formidable Celt, "force me reluctantly to compare my little merit with that which obtained from the crown those prodigies of profuse donation by which he tramples on the mediocrity of humble and laborious individuals? I would willingly leave him to the Heralds' College. . . . The merit of the grantee he derives from was that of being a prompt and greedy instrument of a *leveling* tyrant, who oppressed all descriptions of his people, but who fell with particular fury on everything that was *great and noble*. Mine has been in endeavoring to screen every man, in every class, from oppression, and particularly in defending the high and eminent, who, in the bad times of confiscating princes, confiscating chief governors, or confiscating demagogues, are the most exposed to jealousy, avarice, and envy." Had the duke forgot that the first peer of his name was a Mr. Russell, "raised by being a minion of Henry VIII," or was he too young to know, that he should attack the pension of this man, who had, by his steadfast defense of the existing order, "strained every nerve to keep the Duke of Bedford in that situation" of power and property which alone gave him privilege and precedence? "Let him employ all the energy of his youth," exclaimed the indignant old statesman, "and all the resources of his wealth to crush rebellious principles which have no foundation in morals, and rebellious movements that have no provocation in tyranny. Then will be forgot the rebellions which, by a doubtful priority in crime, his ancestor had provoked and extinguished. . . . My merits, whatever they are, are original and personal. . . . I was not, like his Grace of Bedford, swaddled and rocked and dandled into a legislator: *Nitor in adversum* is the motto for a man like me. I possessed not one of the qualities, nor cultivated one of the arts, that recommend men to the favor and protection of the great. . . . At every step of my progress in life (for in every step was I traversed and opposed), and at every turnpike I met, I was obliged to show my passport, and again and again to prove my sole title to the honor of being useful to my country by a proof that I was not wholly unacquainted with its laws and the whole system of its interests both abroad and at home." As we read, how much greater does the recent house of Burke seem, in the person of this single man, than all the generations of the ancient house of Bedford, and how noble, without patent from the crown!

In this great "Letter" is set forth, too, Burke's own estimate of the services he had rendered. "If I were to call for a reward (which I have never done), it should be for those services in which for fourteen years without intermission I showed the most industry and had the least success: I mean in the affairs of India. They are those on which I value myself the most: most for the importance, most for the labor, most for the judgment, most for constancy and perseverance in the pursuit." There is here no egotism. It is a great mind's satisfaction in great tasks to which it justly feels itself equal. More than that, it is a great mind's satisfaction in great ideals. This "Letter" is, indeed, from first to last, a defense of his own life and motives, and, knowing it to be this, you can but wonder at its noble dignity, its largeness of spirit, its essential importance, as if it were a state paper. And yet, if you will analyze it, if you will look again at the quality that has struck you, you will find that you do not think of Burke's life as you read. First you think of the indiscretion the young Duke of Bedford has committed in attacking this veteran master of argument and retort. His young bones hardly so much as crack in the jaws of the lion, so soft are they, so swift and utter is their annihilation. There is a sense of over-whelming, if not of pitiless, power to be got from those terrible sentences in which the fame of the house of Bedford is to be seen engulfed and ruined. But there ensues upon this another impression. You feel that there is no personal passion, no anger, no spirit of retaliation or revenge. You have risen, imperceptibly, into a region of high principle. You begin to realize that the Duke of Bedford has not offended Burke (that is a mere detail) so much as he has outraged great principles of moral order and political wisdom. Burke is taking you straight to the uplands of the region of thought in which he finds himself,—not so much by deliberation, it would seem, as by instinct,—and is placing you at the point he knows and loves so well: the point from which you can see all the ancient kingdoms of government, their old landmarks and strong defenses.

He must always have a concrete object for his thought. It is the folly of Bedford that has brought him out of Beaconsfield into the familiar forum of public controversy again. This peer of the realm has shown himself ready to consort with those who justify the revolutionists oversea, and has found fellows in the Lords to cheer him while he questions the very principles of ancient privilege upon which that house and the peerage itself were founded. Burke runs upon the challenge to the defense of the realm and its immemorial constitution. It is there he feels his passions deeply engaged. He writes a manual of statesmanship for the rebuke of a heady young duke and the behoof of all England. A single, very celebrated passage from the "Letter" will illustrate the whole purpose and habit of this great mind.

As long [he says, with deep and solemn passion]—as long as the well-compacted structure of our Church and State, the sanctuary, the holy of holies of that ancient law, defended by reverence, defended by power, a fortress at once and a temple, shall stand inviolate on the brow of the British Sion,—as long as the British monarchy, not more limited than fenced by the orders of the state, shall, like the proud Keep of Windsor, rising in the majesty of proportion, and girt with the double belt of its kindred and coeval towers, as long as this awful structure shall oversee and guard the subjected land,—so long the mounds and dikes of the low, fat Bedford level will have nothing to fear from all the pickaxes of all the levelers of France. As long as our sovereign lord the king, and his faithful subjects, the lords and commons of this realm,—the triple cord which no man can break,—the solemn, sworn, constitutional frank-pledge of this nation,—the firm guaranties of each other's being and each other's rights,—the joint and several securities, each in its place and order, for every kind and every quality of property and dignity,—as long as these endure, so long the Duke of Bedford is safe, and we are all safe together,—the high from the blights of envy and the spoliations of rapacity, the low from the iron hand of oppression and the insolent spurn of contempt.

Here is to be had a key to the whole "Letter"—a key to Burke's thought when he spoke of government, a key to his method and to his style throughout all his writings.

He did not erect "the proud Keep of Windsor" there, in that famous passage, merely as a majestic ornament of style, nor in any way as an object of pleasure. It, in fact, stands not very far away from the "low, fat Bedford level." There is but Buckinghamshire and a slender arm of Hertford between; and Burke means you to see it as an actual bulwark of the land. But as his own eye turns southward to the majestic pile, his thought is quickened, as always, by the simile of power. It seems to him a type and image of the law, upon its walls "the awful hoar of innumerable ages," within it the title-deeds of a nation grown old in privilege and in ordered liberty. It is this that exhilarates the mind in Burke, this *reality* of great thought. You stand ever with your feet upon the earth, you are always in the midst of affairs, men and concrete powers round about you; and yet your vision is not of them, it is of the great verities in the midst of which they move. You are strengthened by a sense of the nearness, the immanence of great principles of action. They are seen to dwell at the very heart of affairs, and to form as it were an intrinsic part of circumstance. They are abroad and operative in the world. Burke's thought has, therefore, a certain *visible* quality. It does not seem wholly bred of the mind. It has always about it the scenery and atmosphere of action.

That you should be moved by such thinking is of course inevitable: it comes from a mind itself stirred and quick with practical effort. Never, while it keeps to its normal processes, is that mind betrayed into preferring the speech it uses to the meaning it would convey, and that meaning carries with a quite inevitable appropriateness the superb ornaments with which it is so often adorned. If images abound, it is because the mind that speaks conceives the world always thus in concrete and almost tangible shapes. It is because its eye is ever upon the object of its thought. It is not reflecting; it is observing: it *sees* the field of action. Men and nations are not still before it, but move always with the large variety and dramatic force of life itself. Its retina is crowded with images and deeply touched with color, like a little world.

It is this vivid realization of the world of fact and of spirit as it is that makes Burke's thought seem so conservative, and makes us wonder whether, after all, we should call him a liberal or not. There is no element of speculation in it. It keeps always to the slow pace of inevitable change, and invents nothing, content to point out the accepted ways and to use the old light of day to walk by. Nevertheless, there is one infallible test by which you know Burke's thought to have the power of life in it, and, if the power of life, the power of growth. You are exhilarated by it. It does not hold your powers back; it quickens them mightily. There are visions of the future in it, as well as of the past, and the future is bright with a reasonable hope of healing change. But he loved above all things, and very wisely loved, a sober, provident, and ordered progress in affairs; the balanced force of government seemed to him more likely to work out results that would last and could be lived by than the wilful and too hasty ardor of enthusiasm. "I have ever abhorred," he said in that memorable "Letter"—"I have ever abhorred, since the first dawn of my understanding to this its obscure twilight, all the operations of opinion, fancy, inclination, and will, in the affairs of government, where only a sovereign reason, paramount to all forms of legislation and administration, should dictate. Government is made for the very purpose of opposing that reason to will and to caprice, in the reformers or in the reformed, in the governors or in the governed, in kings, in senators, or in people."

This is our own doctrine. It is with a hope to have such moderation and restraint in affairs that we have made our written constitutions, that they may govern the course of law and of policy. "It was my aim," said Burke, "to give to the people the substance of what I knew they desired, and what I thought was right, whether they desired it or not; and this must ever be the best maxim of statesmanship among a free people."

It was this very genius for slow action and confident self-mastery that Tocqueville found and praised as the first and greatest of all political qualities in the conduct of our own affairs. He had seen France stagger from revolution to revolution like a tipsy lad, high-spirited, generous, full of an engaging dash and hope, but incapable of self-government or of sober effort, sustained and manful, and he knew how to appreciate the maturer powers of a self-governing race.

"The temperament of our nation," he said, speaking of his own France, "is so peculiar that the general study of mankind fails to embrace it. France is ever taking by surprise even those who have made her the special object of their researches: a nation more apt than any other to comprehend a great design and to embrace it, capable of all that can be achieved by a single effort of whatever magnitude, but unable to abide long at this high level, because she is ever swayed by sensations, and not by principles, and that her instincts are better than her morality; a people civilized among all civilized nations of the earth, yet, in some respects, still more akin to the savage state than any of them, for the characteristic of savages is to decide on the sudden impulse of the moment, unconscious of the past and careless of the future." Tocqueville knew, as Burke did, with his vivid insight, that it is a long drill in the moderate processes of an ordered liberty that makes a people conscious of the past and careful of the future; and it was under the influence of this thought that, with a half-envious admiration, Tocqueville paid us that incomparable compliment, the perfect phrases of which linger in the memory like the tones of verse. "It is a novelty in the history of society"—he is speaking of the self-possession and capable deliberateness of those critical days during which we exchanged the flimsy Confederation for our present firm and consistent frame of government—"it is a novelty in the history of society to see a great people turn a calm and scrutinizing eye upon itself, when apprised by the legislature that the wheels of government are stopped; to see it carefully examine the extent of the evil, and patiently wait for two years until a remedy was discovered, which it voluntarily adopted without having wrung a tear or a drop of blood from mankind."

It was this superlative gift of sobriety and good temper in affairs that Burke feared to see England lose, should she too weakly indulge herself in any feeling of partiality for the feverish reforms of France. Those who blame him dispraise the very qualities that made him great. Burke had the supreme literary gift of vision. He saw things steadily and saw them whole, and other men were daunted and in doubt about his trustworthiness because they could not see so much. But he had not the literary mind in affairs, and protested it should not be used in matters of government. "I have lived long and variously in the world," said he. "Without any considerable pretensions to literature myself, I have aspired to the love of letters. . . . I can form a tolerable estimate of what is likely to happen from a character chiefly dependent for fame and fortune on knowledge and talent. . . . Naturally men so formed and finished are the first gifts of Providence to the world. But when they have once thrown off the fear of God . . . and the fear of man, . . . nothing can be conceived more hard than the heart of a thoroughbred metaphysician. . . . It is like that of the Principle of Evil himself, incorporeal, pure, unmixed, dephlegmated, defecated evil. . . . Their imagination is not fatigued with the contemplation of human suffering through the wild waste of centuries added to centuries of misery and desolation, Their humanity is at their horizon—and, like the horizon, it always flies before them. . . . These philosophers consider men in their experiments no more than they do mice in an air-pump or in a recipient of mephitic gas." Only philosophers and philosophical historians—philosophical after the fact—blame Burke for his hot antipathy for the French Revolution. It is all very well for the literary mind to brood in air, high above the levels whereon men breathe the atmosphere of their own time and neighborhood, and from this aërial point of vantage look down with unruffled composure, cool tolerance, and a final reckoning of loss and gain upon the troubled affairs of generations gone, looking before and after, and saying all was well, like a minor Providence. But statesmen cannot afford thus to withdraw from affairs. Opportunities change from moment to moment, like the color and shape of summer clouds, as Burke said. After you have seen and done your duty, then philosophers may talk of it and assess it as they will. Burke was right, and was himself, when he sought to keep the French infection out of England.

18 | DEWEY

JEFFERSON

Thomas Jefferson (see page 3) magnificently combined in his life and thought the marriage between philosophy and government of which Plato dreamed, and which he thought possible only in an aristocracy of philosopher-kings; Jefferson's own life is a monument to the contrary belief that reason and government can best be merged in a society of free men. As long as the American nation lives, as long as the American ideals of human equality and liberty survive, Jefferson will always be revered as the greatest American. The projected edition of *The Papers of Thomas Jefferson* in fifty-two volumes by the Princeton University Press (1950–) will for the first time fully reveal the scope and range of Jefferson's interests and ideas, rarely matched in the whole history of Western thought. His position in American life and his place in Western thought are fittingly evaluated by John Dewey, the foremost American educator and philosopher of the twentieth century. Dewey (1859–1952) is in the long line of Anglo-American empiricism starting with John Locke, and his influence on American life, particularly in the field of education, has been second to none. In the Jeffersonian tradition, Dewey did not confine himself to pure philosophical speculation, but concerned himself with social, economic, and political issues of his time, urging that organized intelligence be applied to the solution of human problems as it has long been to the solution of problems of the physical sciences. Dewey's liberalism thus became one of the mainsprings of reform in the United States, based on the Jeffersonian faith that critical intelligence must remain sterile unless it can contribute to the liberation of man from injustice and inequality. His writings include *German Philosophy and Politics* (1915), *Democracy and Education* (1916), *Human Nature and Conduct* (1922), and *The Public and Its Problems* (1927).

Dewey on JEFFERSON

Thomas Jefferson was fortunate in his birth and early surroundings, being a product both of the aristocracy of the time and of the pioneer frontier. He was fortunate in his contacts and his experiences. The United States is fortunate that he had them. The fact that he occupied certain offices is of little account in itself; comparative nonentities have been foreign envoys and presidents. The use he made of these positions is what counts, and the use includes not only the political policies be urged and carried through, but even more the observations he made and the reflections they produced. His duties, for example, in Paris were few and not very important, "the receipt of our whale-oils, salted fish and salted meats on favourable terms." But the French Revolution began while he was there and he was its keen and intelligent observer. It is typical of him that the political offices he held are not mentioned in the epitaph he wrote for his tombstone. He wished to be remembered as "the author of the Declaration of Independence, the statute of Virginia for religious liberty, and father of the University of Virginia."

His activities in public life provided for him the opportunity for the experiences which inspired and matured his ideas. His republican convictions were formed early in his life; they were absorbed into his life upon what was then the western frontier; they seem to have been crystallized when he was only twenty-two years old by hearing a speech of Patrick Henry in opposition to the British Stamp Act. From that time on he was a leader in every movement for freedom and independence, usually somewhat in advance of other "rebels," finding what he said or wrote disapproved of at the time, only to win later assent. He developed with the experiences enlarged responsibilities gave him, but it was uninterruptedly in one direction. Political expediency may have caused him to deviate on special points, but there are few men in public life whose course has

[From John Dewey, *Thomas Jefferson* (The Living Thoughts Library, David McKay Company, Inc., 1941). By permission.]

been so straight. Natural sympathies, actual experiences, intellectual principles united to produce a character of singular consistency and charm.

Two days before he retired from the presidency, he wrote to his French friend, de Nemours, as follows: "Nature intended me for the tranquil pursuits of science by rendering them my supreme delight. But the enormities of the times in which I have lived have forced me to take part in resisting them." Later "the hermit of Monticello," as he sometimes called himself, remarked in a passage that comes nearer to tapping a poetical vein than almost anything he ever wrote: "The motion of my blood no longer keeps time with the tumult of the world. It leads me to seek for happiness in the lap and love of my family, in the society of my neighbours and my books, in the wholesome occupation of my farm and my affairs, in an interest or affection in every bud that opens, in every breath that blows around me, in an entire freedom of rest, of motion, of thought, owing account to myself alone of my hours and actions."

I do not quote these passages in order to make them the text for a defence of Jefferson's sincerity, which has been questioned on the ground that while he purported to live in the retirement of a country gentleman, he was in fact the focal point of all policies and movements that maintained the integrity of republican institutions against what seemed to him to invade them in any way. I quote them to illustrate what I believe to be the key to the work and character of America's first great democrat: the vital union of attitudes and convictions so spontaneous that they are of the kind called instinctive with fruits of a rich and varied experience: a union that was cemented by the ceaseless intellectual activity which was his "supreme delight." But in a more conventional way, he was that rare person in politics, an idealist whose native faith was developed, checked and confirmed by extremely extensive and varied practical experience. It is seldom, I imagine, that an unusually sincere and unified natural temperament has been so happily combined with rich opportunities for observation and reflection. If he left the stamp of his idealism upon the course of events, it is because this experience added realistic substance to the inherent bent of his natural disposition. If it is true, as he wrote to Adams, that "Whig and Tory are terms of natural as well as of civil history," the pages of the latter may be searched to find another man whose native constitution so properly destined him to espouse the liberal cause and whose career so happily furnished the conditions that gave that constitution opportunity for articulate expression in deed and word.

As long as there are different parties in the United States, there will be dispute as to the soundness of the respective political philosophies associated with the names of Hamilton and Jefferson. If Jefferson was right, the source of the difference lies deep in the varying attitudes of human nature. But it would be a great pity if partisan differences are allowed to identify the teachings of these two men with party strife so as to disable Americans from appreciating the greatness of their common heritage. They would do well to declare a truce in party controversy till they have congratulated themselves upon their great good fortune in having two extraordinarily able men formulate the fundamental principles upon which men divide.

Considering the small size of the American population a hundred and fifty, a hundred and twenty years ago, we may well be amazed, as well as grateful, at the spectacle of the intellect and moral calibre of the men who took a hand in shaping the American political tradition. The military and moral, although not especially the intellectual, repute of Washington has made him a part of a common heritage. There are also Jefferson, Hamilton, Madison, followed at some distance by Franklin and John Adams, and at a greater distance by Monroe. There were giants in those days. It is more than a pity if either partisan differences or a vague indiscriminate adulation of the Founding Fathers is allowed to produce and create indifference to what they contributed to American institutions and to what we still may learn from them. There still exists among us a kind of intellectual parochialism which induces us to turn to political philosophers of the old world who do not measure up to the stature of our own political thinkers—to say nothing of their remoteness from our own conditions.

Before speaking specifically of Jefferson's social and moral philosophy, something will be said about the range and depth of Jefferson's interests. Irrespective of any question of whose political ideas are sound, there is no doubt that Jefferson was the most universal as a human being of all of his American and perhaps European contemporaries also. We cannot pride ourselves that he was a typical or representative American. He is too far above the average for that. But we can say that he embodied in himself typical American characteristics that are usually dispersed. His curiosity was insatiable. The passage of Terence, accounting nothing human foreign, made trite by frequent usage, applies with peculiar force to him. His interest in every new and useful invention was at least equal to that of Franklin; his sayings are without that tinge of smugness that sometimes colours Franklin's reflections on life. He occupied practically every possible position of American public life, serving in each not only with distinction but marked power of adaptability to the new and unexpected.

The more one reads his letters and other records, the more surprised is one that a single person could find time and energy for such a range of diverse interests. As a farmer, he kept abreast with every advance in botanical and agricultural theory and practice. His notes of travel in France and Italy include the most detailed observations of soils, crops, domestic animals, farm implements and methods of culture. He is moved by what he sees to design a new mouldboard for a plough, having minimum mechanical resistance. Just before retiring from the presidency he notes with pleasure the invention in France of a plough which was proved by test with a dynamometer to have increased efficiency. He was busy in correspondence with European societies and individuals in exchange of seeds. Of his introduction of the olive tree into South Carolina and Georgia and of upland rice into the same states, he says, "The greatest service which can be rendered any country is to add a useful plant to its culture, especially a bread grain; next in value to bread is oil."

As far as I have discovered, his inclusion of a professorship of agriculture in the faculty of the University of Virginia marks the first recognition of the subject for study in higher education. He himself ranked it as of equal importance with the professorship in government that was provided. The plan he drew up for the institution of a system of agricultural societies includes most of the topics now forming the studies of our agricultural colleges, save the problem of marketing. His constant attention to the checking of theory by practical experience is seen in his desire for a report upon "the different practices of husbandry, including the bad as well as the good," with the statement that a selection of all the good ones for imitation and the bad ones for avoidance "would compose a course probably near perfection."

There is no discovery in natural science to the credit of Jefferson similar to that of Franklin in electricity. But his faith in scientific advance as a means of popular enlightenment and of social progress was backed by continual interest in discoveries made by others. When helping his grandson with his scholastic mathematical studies, he writes to a friend that he had resumed that study with great avidity, since it was ever his favourite one, there being no theories, no uncertainties, but all "demonstration and satisfaction." He notes in a letter the superiority of French mathematicians of the time, due to their development of analytic methods, and expresses his pleasure that English mathematicians are adopting them and are also abandoning the method of fluxions in calculus. His most active interest was in the natural sciences. The foundations of modern chemistry were laid during his life time. Priestley is one of the correspondents with whom Jefferson has closest intellectual sympathy. His "utilitarian" interest is manifested in an expression of regret that chemists had not followed Franklin in directing science to something "useful in private life"; with a hope that their science would be applied to "brewing, making cider, fermentation and distillation generally, making bread, butter, cheese, soap, incubating eggs, etc." He was also sceptical about theories not backed by evidence gained through observation, and thought the French *philosophes,* whose acquaintance he made, indulged in altogether too much unverifiable speculation. He says in one letter: "I am myself an empiric in natural philosophy, suffering my faith to go no further than my facts. I am pleased, however, to see the efforts of hypothetical speculation, because by the collisions of different hypotheses, truth may be elicited and science advanced in the end."

Because of the evidence it provides regarding Jefferson's belief in the union of theory and experience—or practice—it is worth while to quote a passage in which he expresses his opinion about medicine, the passage being taken from a letter to a physician in which he explains that he is sending a grandson to Philadelphia to study botany, natural history, anatomy, possibly surgery, but not medicine. "I have myself lived to see the disciples of Hoffmann, Boerhaave, Stahl, Cullen, Brown, succeed one another like the shifting figures of a magic lantern and their fancies, like the annual doll-babies from Paris, becoming, from their novelty, the vogue of the day, and yielding to the next novelty their ephemeral favour. . . . It is in this part of medicine that I wish to see a reform, an abandonment of hypothesis for sober facts, the first degree of value set on clinical observation, and the lowest on visionary theories. . . . The only sure foundations of medicine are an intimate knowledge of the human body, and observation of the effect of medicinal substances on that." It is characteristic of him to end his letter with the following statement: "At any rate the subject has permitted me for a moment to abstract myself from the dry and dreary waste of politics, into which I have been impressed by the times on which I happened, and to indulge in the rich fields of Nature where alone I should have served as a volunteer, if left to my natural inclinations and partialities."

It would be a mistake, however, to suppose that Jefferson's interest in science was confined to the field in which useful applications were favourable. He somehow found time to keep up with progress made in astronomy; he made personal observations in the case of a total eclipse of the sun, obtaining a specially accurate chronometer in order that his observations of times might be accurate; he recommended the use of platinum in mirrors of telescopes; he interested himself in the problem of a new method for determining longitude, which he wished to apply also to correction of maps made by ordinary methods of surveying. His letters on weights and measures are quite extensive; he favoured a decimal metric system but was opposed to the French selection of its basis. He expended a good deal of ingenuity in devising a standard pendulum swing as a more natural basis, and seems even to have entertained the hope that his project might—after Bonaparte was defeated in war—take the place of the French system. His geological interest was aroused by the existence of fossils, from bones of mammoths to sea-shells found thousands of feet above the sea—a subject on which he rejected all theories advanced at the time, holding that more evidence was required before an adequate theory could be framed. His interest in mineralogy was great but mainly practical, since he thought the controversies between "Vulcanists" and "Neptunians" futile. He regretted the backwardness of meteorology and in addition to keeping weather records himself, urged others to do so.

"Science" is used by Jefferson, in agreement with the habit of his day, as an equivalent of *knowledge*. It included what we now call scholarship as well as what we call science. Jefferson was interested in language theoretically as well as practically. He discussed the contemporary pronunciation of Greek—with which he became acquainted while in Paris—in relation to that of classic Greece. He made a collection of vocabularies of fifty different Indian tribes. He began the collection as part of a project for writing a history of the Indians—in whose fate he took a civilized interest not characteristic of the usual attitude. For thirty years he took every opportunity to obtain from correspondents a list of about two hundred and fifty words, covering such objects and acts as every tribe would have names for. He compared names common to these lists with vocabularies of races in Eastern Europe as they were published in Russia, for he was convinced that "filiation of languages was the best means of studying filiation of peoples." His great and abiding interest in Anglo-Saxon undoubtedly had a political bias. For he was convinced that the liberal element in the British constitution was derived from Anglo-Saxon sources while the Norman sources introduced the "Tory" element. As a reason for introducing Anglo-Saxon into the subjects taught in the University of Virginia, he said "the learners will imbibe with the language their free principles of government."

Finally, it is instructive, if not especially important, to note his attitude on the growth of the English language, his idea on this special point being completely consistent with his general philosophy. After saying he is a foe of purisms and a friend of neologisms, since language grows by their introduction and testing, he says: "Dictionaries are but the depositories of words already legitimated by usage. Society is the workshop in which new ones are elaborated. When an individual uses a new word, if ill formed it is rejected in society; if well formed, adopted, and after due time laid up in the depository of dictionaries. And if, in this process of sound neologisation, our trans-atlantic brethren shall not choose to accompany us, we may furnish, after the Ionians, a second example of a colonial dialect improving on its primitive." The principles here expressed are now generally accepted, but I doubt if a half-dozen men in the country were bold enough to assert them when Jefferson gave expression to them.

Jefferson's ideas about the fine arts suffer from his habit of subjecting things in which the old world was more advanced than the new to the test of utility as a measure of the value of their introduction here. Only in the case of architecture, gardens and music does he allow his own personal taste free manifestation—and in the former case, motives of utility also enter. It was, however, a lifelong concern of his, both in theory and practice. Of music, he says it is the one thing in France about which he is tempted to disobey the Biblical injunction against coveting. In literature (in the sense of belles-lettres), only the classics command his complete admiration. He regarded them as luxuries, but as "sublime" ones. "Homer in his own language" was his chief delight, and he goes so far as to say that he thanked God on his knees for directing his early education so as to put him in "possession of this rich source of delight." Of modern poetry, the following is, as far as I am aware, all he has to say: "Pope, Dryden, Thomson, Shakespeare, and of the French, Molière, Racine, the Corneilles, may be read with pleasure and improvement." The factor of "improvement" bulked rather large in his mind, since he seemed to have limited the scope of "luxury" to Greek and Latin authors. Novels he regarded as mostly a "mass of trash, fostering bloated imagination, sickly judgment and disgust toward all the real businesses of life." The exceptions he admitted were those which were "interesting and useful vehicles of a sound morality." However, while he ranked the writing of Miss Edgeworth among the latter, he gave the palm to Sterne. Nevertheless, external evidence bears out the truth of his statement (made in a letter to John Adams)—that he "could not live without books." While he was in France, he collected a library by spending "every afternoon in which I was disengaged in examining all the principal bookstores, turning over every book with my own hand, and putting by everything that related to America and indeed whatever was rare and valuable in every science." He attempted to have the duty on foreign books removed. He introduced bills for establishment of libraries at public expense, and hoped to see a circulating library in every county. It is doubtful if any public man to-day could quote as freely from the classics as he and John Adams did in their correspondence with each other.

While Jefferson's views on the arts, as on science, reflected the preferences of Franklin—and of Americans generally—for the useful and the practical, his standard of utility and of practical value was that of the benefit of the people as a whole, not that of individuals or of a class. I have quoted in the text a passage from a letter written to John Adams, in which he says that America has given the world "physical liberty"; contribution to "moral emancipation is a thing of the future." Just before leaving France, he wrote as follows in acknowledging the receipt of the degree of Doctorate of Laws from Harvard University: "We have spent the prime of our lives in procuring them [the youth of the country] the precious blessing of liberty. Let them spend theirs in showing that it is the great parent of *science* and of virtue." Jefferson, when at liberty to give his personal interests free range, was much less limited than some of the quotations given above might suggest. The quotations, taken in their full context, are not so much evidence of his personal taste as to what he thought was the immediate need of a new nation occupying a new and still physically unconquered country. If his *acting* principle had been expressed, it would have been: "Necessities first; luxuries in their due season."

Just as it was the "people" in whom he trusted as the foundation and ultimate security of self-governing institutions, so it was the enlightenment of the people as a whole which was his aim in promoting the advance of science. In a letter to a French friend, in which he says that his prayers are offered for the well-being of France, he adds that her future government depends not on "the state of science, no matter how exalted it may be in a select band of enlightened men, but on the condition of the general mind." What is hinted at in these remarks is openly stated in other letters. As the French Revolution went on from its beginnings, which aroused his deepest sympathies, until there followed the despotism and wars of Napoleon, he became increasingly sceptical of the social influence of a small band of enlightened men—like the French *philosophes*. His most extreme reaction is found in a letter to John Adams: "As for France and England, with all their pre-eminence in science, the one is a den of robbers, and the other of pirates. And if science produces no better fruits than tyranny, murder, rapine and destitution of national morality, I should wish our country to be ignorant, honest and estimable, as our neighbouring savages are." A more temperate statement of the response evoked in him is found in a letter written in 1811 in which he acknowledged the receipt of a history of the French Revolution. "Is reason to be forever amused with the *hochets* of physical science, in which she is indulged merely to divert her from solid speculations on the rights of man and wrongs of his oppressors—it is impossible." At the same time, in speaking of freedom, he throws in the phrase "the first born daughter of science." Jefferson's emphasis upon the relation of science and learning to practical serviceability had two sources. One of them was the newness of his own country, and his conviction that needs should be satisfied in the degree of their urgency. Political liberty—or, as he calls it in one place, physical liberty—came first. A certain measure of material security was needed to buttress this liberty. As these were achieved, he was confident that the spread of education and general enlightenment would add what was lacking in the refinements of culture, things very precious to him personally. Jefferson was a child of both the pioneer frontier and of the enlightenment of the eighteenth century—that century which he and John Adams regarded as the inauguration of a new era in human affairs.

The other cause of Jefferson's subordination of science and arts to social utility was his European experience. Science, no matter how "exalted," did not prevent wholesale misery and oppression if it was confined to a few. In spite if his very enjoyable personal relations with the leading intellectuals of Paris, his deepest sympathies went to the downtrodden masses whose huts he visited and whose food he ate. His affection for the "people" whose welfare was the real and final object of all social institutions, and his faith in the "will of the people" as the basis of all legitimate political arrangements, made him increasingly sceptical of advances in knowledge and the arts that left the mass of the people in a state of misery and degradation.

The balanced relation in Jefferson's ideas between the well-being of the masses and the higher cultivation of the arts and sciences is best expressed in his educational project. Elementary popular schooling educated the many. But it also served a selective purpose. It enabled the abler students to be picked out and to continue instruction in the middle grade. Through the agency of the latter the "natural aristocracy" of intellect and character would be selected who would go on to university education. State universities have carried forward Jefferson's idea of a continuous educational ladder, that of Michigan being directly influenced by him. But in some respects, the plan is still in advance of what has been accomplished.

Jefferson's stay in France gave rise to the notion that his political philosophy was framed under French intellectual influence. It is easy to understand why, after the reaction produced by the excesses of the Revolution, Jefferson's political enemies put forward the idea as an accusation, extremists calling him a participant in Gallic atheism, licentiousness and anarchy. Just why scholars have entertained the same idea, not as a charge against him, but as evidence of close intellectual relations between American social theory and the French enlightenment is not so clear. Every one of Jefferson's characteristic political ideas (with one possible exception) was definitely formulated by him before he went to France. It is probable that his inclination toward the moral ideas of Epicurus, among the classic writers, dates from acquaintance made in Paris, but that did not affect his political ideas or even his working ethical views. Rousseau is not even mentioned by him. The moderate French Charter of Rights—a practical not a theoretical document—receives fairly extensive notice; the Rights of Man the barest casual mention.

The fact is—as [many of his writings] show clearly—in Jefferson's opinion the movement, intellectual and practical, was from the United States to France and Europe, not from the latter to America. The possible exception, alluded to above, is found in Jefferson's emphasis upon the moral inability of one generation to bind a succeeding generation by imposing either a debt or an unalterable constitution upon it. His assertion that the "earth belongs in usufruct to the living; that the dead have neither powers nor rights over it" was general in scope. But his argument (in a letter written from Paris) closes with a statement of the importance of the matter "in every country and most especially in France." For, as he saw, if the new government could not abolish the laws regulating descent of land, recover lands previously given to the Church, abolish feudal and ecclesiastical special privileges, and all perpetual monopolies, reformation of government would be hamstrung before it got started.

The genuine and undeniable influence of France upon Jefferson is shown in a letter he wrote expressing his amazement upon finding the prevalence of monarchical ideas upon his return to New York, when, as he says, "fresh from France, while in its first and pure stage," he was "somewhat *whetted* up in my own republican principles." The real significance of the question of French influence upon him is found in a larger matter. The text which follows quotes at some length what Jefferson had to say about the sources of the ideas he expressed in the Declaration of Independence. I do not believe his remarks are intended, in their denial of indebtedness to this and to that writer, to set up a claim for originality. On the contrary, I believe his statement is to be taken literally that his purpose was simply to be "an expression of the American mind in words so firm and plain as to command assent." There was nothing that was novel in the idea that "governments derive their just powers from the consent of the governed," nor did it find its origin in Locke's writings— "nearly perfect" as were the latter in Jefferson's opinion. Even the right of the people "to alter or abolish" a government when it became destructive of the inherent moral rights of the governed had behind it a tradition that long antedated the writings of even Locke.

There was, nevertheless, something distinctive, something original, in the Declaration. It was not, however, in ideas at least, as old as Aristotle and Cicero; the civil law was expounded by Pufendorf and others, and the political philosophy by the Fathers of the Church. What was new and significant was that these ideas were now set forth as an expression of the "American mind" that the American will was prepared to *act* upon. Jefferson was as profoundly convinced of the novelty of the *action* as a practical "experiment"—favourite word of his in connection with the institution of self-government—as he was of the orthodox character of the ideas as mere theory. The novelty of the practical attempt was, indeed, only set out in higher relief by the lack of novelty in underlying principles.

Jefferson used the language of the time in his assertion of "natural rights" upon which governments are based and which they must observe if they are to have legitimate authority. What is not now so plain is that the word *moral* can be substituted for the word *natural* whenever Jefferson used the latter in connection with law and rights, not only without changing his meaning but making it clearer to a modern reader. Not only does he say: "I am convinced man has no natural right in opposition to his social duties," and that "man was destined for society," but also that "questions of natural right are triable by their conformity with the moral sense and reason of man." In his letter to his French friend de Nemours, Jefferson develops his moral and political philosophy at some length by making a distinction "between the structure of the government and the moral principles" on which its administration is based. It is here that he says, "We of the United States are constitutionally and conscientiously democrats," and then goes on to give the statement a moral interpretation. Man is created with a want for society and with the powers to satisfy that want in concurrence with others. When he has procured that satisfaction by institution of a society, the latter is a product which man has a right to regulate "jointly with all those who have concurred in its procurement." "There exists a right independent of force" and "Justice is the fundamental law of society."

So much for the moral foundation and aim of government. Its structure concerns the special way in which men jointly exercise their right of control. He knew too much history and had had a share in making too much history not to know that governments have to be accommodated to the manners and habits of the people who compose a given state. When a population is large and spread over considerable space, it is not possible for a society to govern itself directly. It does so indirectly by representatives of its own choosing; by those to whom it delegates its powers. "Governments are *more or less* republican as they have more or less of the element of popular election and control in their composition." Writing in 1816, he said that the United States measured by this criterion, were less republican than they should be, a lack he attributed to the fact that the lawmakers who came from large cities had learned to be afraid of the populace, and then unjustly extended their fears to the "independent, the happy and therefore orderly citizens of the United States." Anyone who starts from the just-mentioned moral principle of Jefferson as a premise and adds to it as another premise the principle that the only legitimate "object of the institution of government is to secure the greatest degree of happiness possible to the general mass of those associated under it" can, with little trouble, derive the further tenets of Jefferson's political creed.

The will of the people as the moral basis of government and the happiness of the people as its controlling aim were so firmly established with Jefferson that it was axiomatic that the only alternative to the republican position was fear, in lieu of trust, of the people. Given fear of them, it followed, as by mathematical necessity, not only that they must *not* be given a large share in the conduct of government, but that they must themselves be controlled by force, moral or physical or both, and by appeal to some special interest served by government—an appeal which, according to Jefferson, inevitably meant the use of means to corrupt the people. Jefferson's trust in the people was a faith in what he sometimes called their common sense and sometimes their reason. They might be fooled and misled for a time, but give them light and in the long run their oscillations this way and that will describe what in effect is a straight course ahead.

I am not underestimating Jefferson's abilities as a practical politician when I say that this deep-seated faith in the people and their responsiveness to enlightenment properly presented was a most important factor in enabling him to effect, against great odds, "the revolution of 1800." It is the cardinal element bequeathed by Jefferson to the American tradition.

Jefferson's belief in the necessity for strict limitation of the powers of officials had both a general and a special or historic source. As for the latter, had not the Revolution itself been fought because of the usurpation of power by the officers of a government? And were not the political opponents of Republicanism, in Jefferson's opinion, men so moved by admiration of the British Constitution that they wished to establish a "strong" government in this country, one not above the use of methods of corruption—not indeed as an end in itself but as a means of procuring the allegiance of the populace more effectively and in a less costly way than by use of direct coercion? On general principles, Jefferson knew that possession of unusual and irresponsible power corrupts those who wield it; that officials are, after all, human beings affected by ordinary weaknesses of human nature, "wares from the same workshop, made by the same materials." Hence they were to be continually watched, tested and checked, as well as constitutionally limited in their original grant of powers.

There are, however, two important points in which popular representations of Jeffersonian democracy are often at fault. One of them concerns the basic importance of the will of the people in relation to the law-making power, constitutional and ordinary. There is no doubt that Jefferson was strongly in favour of specifying in the constitution the powers that could be exercised by officials, executive, legislative and judicial, and then holding them, by strict construction, to the powers specified. But he also believed that "every people have their own particular habits, ways of thinking, manners, etc., which have grown up with them from their infancy, are become a part of their nature, and to which the regulations which are to make them happy must be accommodated." As he states the principle elsewhere: "The excellence of every government is its adaptation to the state of those to be governed by it." In this matter, especially, Jefferson's theories were tempered by practical experience.

His idealism was a moral idealism, not a dreamy Utopianism. He was aware that conclusions drawn from past history of mankind were against the success of the experiment that was being tried on American soil. He was quite sure that Latin American countries would succeed in throwing off the yoke of Spain and Portugal, but he was decidedly sceptical about their capacity for self-government, and feared their future was one of a succession of military despotisms for a long time to come. He was conscious that chances for greater success of the experiment in the United States were dependent upon events which might be regarded either as fortunate accidents or as providential dispensations: the wide ocean protecting the country from oppressive governments in Europe; the "Anglo-Saxon" tradition of liberties; even the jealousies of religious denominations that prevented the state establishment of any one Church, and hence worked for religious liberty; the immense amount of free land and available natural sources with consequent continual freedom of movement; the independence and vigour that were bred on the frontier, etc. Even so, he had fears for the future when the country should be urbanized and industrialized, though upon the whole, he says, he tended by temperament to take counsel of his hopes rather than his fears.

In direct line with his conviction on this point was his belief in the necessity of periodic revisions of the constitution, one to take place every twenty years, and his belief that the process of ordinary amendment had been made too difficult. His faith in the right of the people to govern themselves in their own way and in their ability to exercise the right wisely—provided they were enlightened by education and by free discussion—was stronger than his faith in any article of his own political creed—except this one. His own convictions as to the proper forms of government were strong, and he contended ably for their realization. But he was conciliatory by temperament and by practical policy. Students and historians have criticized him for not trying harder to put into effect after the "revolution of 1800" the reforms he had been urging before that time, especially as he based his opposition to Adams upon their absence. Doubtless he was moved by considerations of political expediency. But there is also no reason to doubt the sincerity of those expressions of his which set forth his willingness to subordinate his own political policies to the judgment of the people. Trust in the popular will was temperamental, constitutional with him.

In any case, he was no friend of what he called "sanctimonious reverence" for the Constitution. He adhered to the view, expressed in the Declaration of Independence, that people are more disposed to suffer evils than to right them by abolishing forms to which they are accustomed. It was the more important, accordingly, to recognize that "laws and institutions must go hand in hand with the progress of the human mind" and that institutions must change with change of circumstances brought about by "discoveries, new truths, change of opinions and manners." Were he alive he would note and scourge that lack of democratic faith which, in the professed name of democracy, asserts that the "ark of the covenant is too sacred to be touched." Jefferson saw that periodical overhauling of the fundamental law was the alternative to change effected only by violence and repetition of the old historic round "of oppressions, rebellions, reformations, oppressions. . . ." There was but one thing which was unchangeable, and that was the "inherent and inalienable rights of man."

The other point in which Jefferson's ideas have not been adequately represented has to do with his belief that state governments "are the true barriers of our liberty"; and his fear of centralized government at Washington: not that he did not have the belief and the fear, and hold them with strong conviction, but that the ideas with which he supplemented them have not received due attention. In [many of his writings there are passages], of considerable extent, which show the importance he attached to self-governing communities of much smaller size than the state or even the county. He was impressed, practically as well as theoretically, with the effectiveness of the New England town meeting, and wished to see something of the sort made an organic part of the governing process of the whole country. Division of every county into wards was first suggested by him in connection with organization of an elementary school system. But even from his early service in the legislature of Virginia to the latest years of his life he urged his plan and expressed the hope that while it had not been adopted, it would be at some time. In a letter written after he had reached the age of three score years and ten, he says: "As Cato concluded every speech with the words *'Carthago delenda est,'* so do I every opinion with the injunction 'Divide the counties into wards,'" referring in 1815 to a bill he had introduced forty years at least before, at the time when his other bills for abolition of entails in land and of primogeniture were adopted.

While the first aim of the division into small local units was the establishment and care of popular elementary schools, their purpose extended, in the mind of Jefferson, far beyond that function. The aim was to make the wards "little republics, with a warden at the head of each, for all those concerns, which being under their eye, they would better manage than the larger republics of the county or state." They were to have the "care of the poor, roads, police, elections, nomination of jurors, administration of justice in small cases, elementary exercises of militia." In short, they were to exercise directly with respect to their own affairs all the functions of government, civil and military. In addition, when any important wider matter came up for decision, all wards would be called into meetings on the same day, so that the collective sense of the whole people would be produced. The plan was not adopted. But it was an essential part of Jefferson's political philosophy. The significance of the doctrine of "states rights" as he held it, is incomplete both theoretically and practically until this plan is taken into the reckoning. "The elementary republics of the wards, the county republics, the state republics and the republic of the Union would form a gradation of authorities." Every man would then share in the government of affairs not merely on election day but every day. In a letter to John Adams, written in 1813, he says he still has great hope that the plan will be adopted, as it then will form "the keystone of the arch of our government." It is for this reason that I say this view of self-government is very inadequately represented in the usual form in which it is set forth—as a glorification of state against federal governments, and still more as a theoretical opposition to all governments save as a necessary evil. The heart of his philosophy of politics is found in his effort to institute these small administrative and legislative units as the keystone of the arch.

As was suggested earlier, the essentially moral nature of Jefferson's political philosophy is concealed from us at the present time because of the change that has taken place in the language in which moral ideas are expressed. The "self-evident truths" about the equality of all men by creation and the existence of "inherent and inalienable rights"[1] appear to-day to have a legal rather than a moral meaning; and in addition, the intellectual basis of the legal theory of natural law and natural rights has been undermined by historical and philosophical criticism. In Jefferson's own mind, the words had a definitely ethical import, intimately and vitally connected with his view of God and Nature. The latter connection comes out more clearly if possible in the Preamble, in which he refers to the necessity of the American people taking the "separate and equal station to which the laws of Nature and of Nature's God entitle them."

These phrases were not rhetorical flourishes nor were they accommodated for reasons of expediency to what Jefferson thought would be popular with the people of the country. Jefferson was a sincere theist. Although his rejection of supernaturalism and of the authority of Churches and their creeds caused him to be denounced as an atheist, he was convinced, beyond any peradventure, on *natural* and rational grounds of the existence of a divine righteous Creator who manifested his purpose in the structure of the world, especially in that of society and the human conscience. The natural equality of all human beings was not psychological nor legal. It was intrinsically moral, as a consequence of the equal *moral* relation all human beings sustain to their Creator—equality of moral claims and of moral responsibilities. Positive law—or municipal law, as Jefferson termed it—and political institutions thus have both a moral foundation and a moral criterion or measure.

The word "faith" is thus applied advisedly to the attitude of Jefferson towards the people's will, and its right to control political institutions and policies. The faith had a genuinely religious quality. The forms of government and law, even of the Constitution, might and should change. But the inherent and inalienable rights of man were unchangeable, because they express the will of the righteous Creator of man embodied in the very structure of society and conscience. Jefferson was not an "individualist" in the sense of the British *laissez-faire* liberal school. Individual human beings receive their right of self-government "with their being from the hand of Nature." As an eighteenth-century deist and believer in natural religion, Jefferson connected Nature and Nature's God inseparably in his thought. He writes that he had "no fear but that the result of our experiment will be that men may be trusted to govern themselves without

[1] "Certain" was substituted for "inherent" by the Congress. The first manuscript draft, later changed by Jefferson himself, read that "all men are created equal and independent; that from that equal creation they derive rights."

a master. Could the contrary of this be proved, I should conclude either that there is no God, or that he is a malevolent being." These words are to be taken literally, not rhetorically, if one wishes to understand Jefferson's democratic faith. He even engages in construction of the following syllogism: "Man was created for social intercourse; but social intercourse cannot be maintained without a sense of justice; then man must have been created with a sense of justice." The connection of justice—or equity—with equality of rights and duties was a commonplace of the moral tradition of Christendom. Jefferson took the tradition seriously. The statements of Jefferson about the origin of the Declaration of Independence, statements already quoted, are confirmed in what he wrote shortly before his death. "We had no occasion to search into musty records, to hunt up royal parchments, or to investigate the laws and institutions of a semi-barbarous ancestry. We appealed to those of Nature, and found them engraved on our hearts."

Other days bring other words and other opinions behind words that are used. The terms in which Jefferson expressed his belief in the moral criterion for judging all political arrangements and his belief that republican institutions are the only ones that are morally legitimate are not now current. It is doubtful, however, whether defence of democracy against the attacks to which it is subjected does not depend upon taking once more the position Jefferson took about its moral basis and purpose, even though we have to find another set of words in which to formulate the moral ideal served by democracy. A renewal of faith in common human nature, in its potentialities in general and in its power in particular to respond to reason and truth, is a surer bulwark against totalitarianism than is demonstration of material success or devout worship of special legal and political forms.

Jefferson wrote no set treatises. In reply to a suggestion that he write a history of his own times, he replied that "while in public life I had not the time, and now that I am retired I am past the time." He probably would have made a similar reply, couched in even more emphatic terms, to a suggestion that he write a book on the principles of government. He would have been content to point to the record of his activities. But he was an indefatigable letter writer. In a letter written after he was seventy years of age, he says he engages in correspondence till noon every day, some days from sunrise to one or two o'clock. In his eightieth year he reports that having counted the letters in his file of the previous year, he found they amounted to 1267, "many requiring answers of elaborate research."

*   *   *

Jefferson's life was peculiarly divided, almost split, between his public career and his private and domestic activities. It is probably owing to something pretty fundamental in his own character that for the most part he preferred to permit the former to speak for itself, and that, when questioned about the latter, he said they were substantially similar to those of any other American citizen of the time. Consequently, in spite of the autobiographical notes which he wrote, there is curiously little material available of a strictly personal kind. We know he was a cultivated gentleman of personal charm. That he was of handsome physique is proved by the portraits painted of him by Stuart, Peale, Desnoyers, Sully, and by the statues of Powers and D'Angers. Strongly opposed to extravagance and debt in public affairs, he was never out of debt himself. He must have spent several small fortunes in building, tearing down and rebuilding his home at Monticello and experimenting with the buildings for the University of Virginia, whose architect and supervisor he was, down to personally deciding by chemical experiment the composition of the cement used in laying the brick walls.

His father was a pioneer frontiersman, one of the first three or four to venture to what was at that time the western limit of settlement in the Virginia territory, a man with slight opportunity for schooling and yet so "eager after information" and so bent on improvement that he made of himself a skilled surveyor who, in company with a professor of mathematics, fixed the boundary line between Virginia and North Carolina, and who insisted upon giving his son the best classical education attainable at that time in America. Doubtless it was from him and from the pioneer environment in which men were compelled to be jacks-of-all-trades that Thomas Jefferson derived his lifelong interest in all mechanical inventions and gadgets, and his abiding respect for personal industry and handicraft. His respect for labour is expressed in a letter he wrote to a friend in France when, upon his return from that country, he found that the deranged state of his farms required him to find a new source of revenue: "My new trade of nailmaking is to me in this country what an additional title of nobility or the ensigns of a new order are in Europe." It is not unduly speculative to suppose that it was from his frontier experience that he also derived that sense of the inevitable continental expansion of the United States which seems to have marked him alone among the statesmen of the time, and which later expressed itself in the Louisiana purchase and in his attitude towards Florida and even Cuba.

We know that Jefferson married, when approaching the age of thirty, a widow twenty-three years old, the daughter of a successful local lawyer; that for ten years before her death they lived in great happiness, and that Jefferson never remarried. But again it seems characteristic of the sharp line drawn by Jefferson between his public career and his private life that he left little record of her and his life with her, save a statement in a letter to a French friend that having "rested all prospects of future happiness on domestic and literary objects, a single event wiped away my plans and left me a blank." This blank, caused by his wife's death, he intimates to be the main reason why he was willing to accept his appointment as Ambassador to France, to succeed, but *not*, as he always said, to "replace" Benjamin Franklin, "The greatest man and ornament of the age and country in which he lived." During the ten years of married life, five daughters and one son were born to them. The son lived less than a month; the husbands of two of his daughters were amongst the closest of Jefferson's correspondents, but even with them ideas and public affairs are discussed rather than intimate personal and family matters.

The combination in Jefferson of a kind of objective pride in his public career and a frequently expressed preference for a life of retirement devoted to management of his estate, to reading and writing, to making scientific observations and studies, and to domestic happiness, finds expression in his replies to correspondents who asked him for material for a biography. The uniform tenor of his response is that "The only exact testimony of a man is his actions" and of these others must be left to be the judges. Apart from his public activities there was nothing in his life worthy of special record. After his fame was firmly established he even refused to state the date of his birth, on the ground that the only birthday he wished to have recognized was "that of my country's liberties."

The combination of reserve and dislike for public office with extraordinary skill and success as a practical politician laid Jefferson open to the charge of inconsistency and even insincerity. Such charges are impossible either to support or to refute long after the events which occurred, and are unprofitable. That Jefferson disliked controversy and was disposed to be conciliatory and compromising there is, however, no reason to doubt. The exceptions made in the case of Hamilton and to a lesser degree in that of Chief Justice Marshall are of the kind that prove a rule. The latter is exemplified in the pain he felt at the break with John Adams and the great joy he experienced in the restoration of friendly relations. What he said about the conduct of Franklin at the French Court might almost be taken as defence of charges sometimes brought against himself: "His temper was so amiable and conciliatory, his conduct so rational, never urging impossibilities, so moderate and attentive to the difficulties of others, that what his enemies called subserviency, I saw was only a reasonable disposition"—not that he was charged with subserviency, but with inconsistency between professed principles and actual behaviour. In any case, if Jefferson is better known for his political ideas and his public acts than as a human being, it is just what he would have wished for himself. Considering his times and the difficult and important part he played in them, there remains the image of a magnanimous, high-spirited public gentleman who subordinated himself with complete devotion to what he conceived to be the welfare of the country he loved. I do not see how anyone can doubt that he was careless of his own future fame when that was put in comparison with the future of the democratic ideas he served, nor that, on the other hand, he felt sure of his own reputation as long as those ideas were safe.

19 | MILL

BENTHAM

Burke, like other statesmen and writers of his time, failed to see that the French Revolution was a symptom of something much more profound: the changing class structure of Western Europe caused by the Industrial Revolution. In Britain the rising middle classes developed a new social and political philosophy that was clearly distinct from Burke's adulation of landed aristocracy, as well as from Paine's radicalism and Godwin's anarchy. Burke was too conservative, pessimistic, and traditional, whereas Paine and Godwin were too radical, utopian, and revolutionary. What was needed was a political faith reflecting the outlook of the middle classes, which was essentially empirical, optimistic, willing to innovate, and eager to translate natural science into technology and industry, and political science into government and administration. The most characteristic expression of that outlook is to be found in the work of Jeremy Bentham (1748–1832), the founder of utilitarianism, or, as it is also called, philosophical radicalism. He spent most of his life under King George III, who reigned from 1760 to 1820—the last British monarch of autocratic leanings. Bentham died the day before the Reform Bill of 1832 became law. His life thus spanned a long period of transition in British history; while experiencing eighteenth-century autocracy at its worst, he also witnessed the birth of nineteenth-century democracy. His own life reflects the transformation of his country: Bentham was a Tory until 1808, and he became a radical democrat at the age of sixty, when he became convinced that "the people in power" were against reform, whereas earlier he had assumed that "they only wanted to know what was good in order to embrace it." His disinterestedness and sympathy were as much the cause of his world-wide influence as his intellectual zeal and liberality of outlook. Bentham's first book, which brought him immediate fame, was the *Fragment on Government* (1776), an attack against Blackstone, the oracle of English law. His most widely known book is his *Principles of Morals and Legislation* (1789), which developed in detail his concept of utility as the greatest happiness of the greatest number. He is the greatest single reformer in English history, particularly in the field of law. His main contribution to political science was not that he invented a new principle of political philosophy, but that he steadily applied an empirical and critical method of investigation to concrete problems of government and administration. He justly said of his own work that it was an attempt to "extend the experimental method of reasoning from the physical branch to the moral."

Bentham the man, the thinker, the reformer, is appraised below by John Stuart Mill, the son of James Mill, Bentham's closest disciple and collaborator, and the essay was fittingly published in the *Westminster Review* (1838), founded by Bentham as the organ of philosophical radicalism in 1824, and published until 1914 by a series of distinguished editors. Like Bentham, John Stuart Mill was a child prodigy, who began the study of Greek at the age of three, and Latin at the more advanced age of seven, supplemented by ancient philosophy and ancient and modern history. Like all philosophical radicals, Bentham and both Mills regarded the United States as the advance guard of democracy and the model of future development in their own country. Mill started his literary career in his teens, and in 1834 he published the *System of Logic*, his major work on philosophy. In 1848 he published his *Political Economy*, next to Adam Smith's *Wealth of Nations* (1776) the most authoritative work in its field for several generations, and for a long time the most popular textbook in economics in England and the United States. Yet Mill's claim to enduring fame derives from his essay *On Liberty* (1859), one of the finest and most moving defenses of liberty in English, and perhaps in any language. In his *Autobiography* (1873) Mill describes the stages which led him from Bentham's economic individualism to the position of a "qualified socialist," and shortly before his death Mill began a book on socialism, portions of which were published after his death under the title *Chapters on Socialism* (1879). Yet Bentham himself was prevented from becoming a doctrinaire adherent of laissez faire by his utilitarianism and his concern for human welfare, and Mill's acceptance of welfare as the primary consideration in economic analysis and policy merely carried Benthamism a step further, paving the way for Fabian socialism and the welfare state.

Mill on BENTHAM

A man of great knowledge of the world, and of the highest reputation for practical talent and sagacity among the official men of his time (himself no follower of Bentham, nor of any partial or exclusive school whatever) once said to us, as the result of his observation, that to Bentham more than to any other source might be traced the questioning spirit, the disposition to demand the *why* of everything, which had gained so much ground and was producing such important consequences in these times. The more this assertion is examined, the more true it will be found. Bentham has been in this age and country the great questioner of things established. It is by the influence of the modes of thought with which his writings inoculated a considerable number of thinking men, that the yoke of authority has been broken, and innumerable opinions, formerly received on tradition as incontestable, are put upon their defence, and required to give an account of themselves. Who, before Bentham, (whatever controversies might exist on points of detail,) dared to speak disrespectfully, in express terms, of the British Constitution, or the English Law? He did so; and his arguments and his example together encouraged others. We do not mean that his writings caused the Reform Bill, or that the Appropriation Clause owns him as its parent: the changes which have been made, and the greater changes which will be made, in our institutions, are not the work of philosophers, but of the interests and instincts of large portions of society recently grown into strength. But Bentham gave voice to those interests and instincts: until he spoke out, those who found our institutions unsuited to them did not dare to say so, did not dare consciously to think so; they had never heard the excellence of those institutions questioned by cultivated men, by men of acknowledged intellect; and it is not in the nature of uninstructed minds to resist the united authority of the instructed. Bentham broke the spell. It was not Bentham by his own writings; it was Bentham through the minds and pens which those writings fed—through the men in more direct contact with the world, into whom his spirit passed. If the superstition about ancestorial

[From J. S. Mill, "The Works of Jeremy Bentham," *The London and Westminster Review*, vol. 31 (August, 1838).]

wisdom has fallen into decay; if the public are grown familiar with the idea that their laws and institutions are in greater part not the product of intellect and virtue, but of modern corruption grafted upon ancient barbarism; if the hardiest innovation is no longer scouted *because* it is an innovation—establishments no longer considered sacred because they are establishments—it will be found that those who have accustomed the public mind to these ideas have learnt them in Bentham's school, and that the assault on ancient institutions has been, and is, carried on for the most part with his weapons. It matters not although these thinkers, or indeed thinkers of any description, have been but scantily found among the persons prominently and ostensibly at the head of the Reform movement. All movements, except directly revolutionary ones, are headed, not by those who originate them, but by those who know best how to compromise between the old opinions and the new. The father of English innovation, both in doctrines and in institutions, is Bentham: he is the great *subversive*, or, in the language of continental philosophers, the great *critical*, thinker of his age and country.

We consider this, however, to be not his highest title to fame. Were this all, he were only to be ranked among the lowest order of the potentates of mind—the negative, or destructive philosophers; those who can perceive what is false, but not what is true; who awaken the human mind to the inconsistencies and absurdities of time-sanctioned opinions and institutions, but substitute nothing in the place of what they take away. We have no desire to undervalue the services of such persons: mankind have been deeply indebted to them; nor will there ever be a lack of work for them, in a world in which so many false things are believed, in which so many which have been true, are believed long after they have ceased to be true. The qualities, however, which fit men for perceiving anomalies, without perceiving the truths which would rectify them, are not among the rarest of endowments. Courage, verbal acuteness, command over the forms of argumentation, and a popular style, will make, out of the shallowest man, with a sufficient lack of reverence, a considerable negative philosopher. Such men have never been wanting in periods of culture; and the period in which Bentham formed his early impressions was emphatically their reign, in proportion to its barrenness in the more noble products of the human mind. An age of formalism in the Church and corruption in the State, when the most valuable part of the meaning of traditional doctrines had faded from the minds even of those who retained from habit a mechanical belief in them, was the time to raise up all kinds of sceptical philosophy. Accordingly, France had Voltaire, and his school of negative thinkers, and England (or rather Scotland) had the

profoundest negative thinker on record, David Hume: a man, the pecu-
liarities of whose mind qualified him to detect failure of proof, and want
of logical consistency, at a depth which French sceptics, with their comparatively feeble powers of analysis and abstraction, stopt far short of, and
which German subtlety could alone thoroughly appreciate, or hope to
rival.

If Bentham had merely continued the work of Hume, he would
scarcely have been heard of in philosophy; for he was far inferior to
Hume in Hume's qualities, and was in no respect fitted to excel as a
metaphysician. We must not look for subtlety, or the power of recondite
analysis, among his intellectual characteristics. In the former quality, few
great thinkers have ever been so deficient; and to find the latter, in any
considerable measure, in a mind acknowledging any kindred with his, we
must have recourse to the late Mr. Mill—a man who united the great
qualities of the metaphysicians of the eighteenth century, with others of
a different complexion, admirably qualifying him to complete and correct
their work. Bentham had not these peculiar gifts; but he possessed others,
not inferior, which were not possessed by any of his precursors; which
have made him a source of light to a generation which has far outgrown
their influence, and, as we called him, the chief subversive thinker of an
age which has long lost all that they could subvert.

To speak of him first as a merely negative philosopher—as one who
refutes illogical arguments, exposes sophistry, detects contradiction and
absurdity; even in that capacity there was a wide field left vacant for
him by Hume, and which he has occupied to an unprecedented extent;
the field of practical abuses. This was Bentham's peculiar province: to
this he was called by the whole bent of his disposition: to carry the warfare against absurdity into things practical. His was an essentially practical
mind. It was by practical abuses that his mind was first turned to speculation—by the abuses of the profession which was chosen for him, that of
the law. He has himself stated what particular abuse first gave that shock
to his mind, the recoil of which has made the whole mountain of abuse
totter; it was the custom of making the client pay for three attendances in
the office of a Master in Chancery, when only one was given. The law, he
found, on examination, was full of such things. But were these discoveries
of his? No; they were known to every lawyer who practised, to every
judge who sat on the bench, and neither before nor for long after did
they cause any apparent uneasiness to the consciences of these learned
persons, nor hinder them from asserting, whenever occasion offered, in
books, in parliament, or on the bench, that the law was the perfection of
reason. During so many generations, in each of which thousands of well-

educated young men were successively placed in Bentham's position and
with Bentham's opportunities, he alone was found with sufficient moral
sensibility and self-reliance to say to himself that these things, however
profitable they might be, were frauds, and that between them and himself
there should be a gulf fixed. To this rare union of self-reliance and moral
sensibility we are indebted for all that Bentham has done. Sent to Oxford
by his father at the unusually early age of fifteen—required, on admission,
to declare his belief in the Thirty-nine Articles—he felt it necessary to
examine them; and the examination suggested scruples, which he sought
to get removed, but instead of the satisfaction he expected, was told that
it was not for boys like him to set up their judgment against the great men
of the Church. After a struggle, he signed; but the impression that he
had done an immoral act, never left him; he considered himself to have
committed a falsehood, and throughout life he never relaxed in his indignant denunciations of all laws which command such falsehoods, all
institutions which attach rewards to them.

By thus carrying the war of criticism and refutation, the conflict with
falsehood and absurdity, into the field of practical evils, Bentham, even if
he had done nothing else, would have earned an important place in the
history of intellect. He carried on the warfare without intermission. To
this, not only many of his most piquant chapters, but some of the most
finished of his entire works, are entirely devoted: the 'Defence of Usury';
the 'Book of Fallacies'; and the onslaught upon Blackstone, published
anonymously under the title of 'A Fragment on Government', which,
though a first production, and of a writer afterwards so much ridiculed
for his style, excited the highest admiration no less for its composition
than for its thoughts, and was attributed by turns to Lord Mansfield, to
Lord Camden, and (by Dr. Johnson) to Dunning, one of the greatest
masters of style among the lawyers of his day. These writings are altogether original; though of the negative school, they resemble nothing
previously produced by negative philosophers; and would have sufficed
to create for Bentham, among the subversive thinkers of modern Europe,
a place peculiarly his own. But it is not these writings that constitute the
real distinction between him and them. There was a deeper difference. It
was that they were purely negative thinkers, he was positive: they only
assailed error, he made it a point of conscience not to do so until he
thought he could plant instead the corresponding truth. Their character
was exclusively analytic, his was synthetic. They took for their starting-
point the received opinion on any subject, dug round it with their logical
implements, pronounced its foundations defective, and condemned it: he
began *de novo*, laid his own foundations deeply and firmly, built up his

own structure, and bade mankind compare the two; it was when he had solved the problem himself, or thought he had done so, that he declared all other solutions to be erroneous. Hence, what they produced will not last; it must perish, much of it has already perished, with the errors which it exploded: what he did has its own value, by which it must outlast all errors to which it is opposed. Though we may reject, as we often must, his practical conclusions, yet his premises, the collections of facts and observations from which his conclusions were drawn, remain for ever, a part of the materials of philosophy.

A place, therefore, must be assigned to Bentham among the masters of wisdom, the great teachers and permanent intellectual ornaments of the human race. He is among those who have enriched mankind with imperishable gifts; and although these do not transcend all other gifts, nor entitle him to those honours 'above all Greek, above all Roman fame', which by a natural reaction against the neglect and contempt of the world, many of his admirers were once disposed to accumulate upon him, yet to refuse an admiring recognition of what he was, on account of what he was not, is a much worse error, and one which, pardonable in the vulgar, is no longer permitted to any cultivated and instructed mind.

If we were asked to say, in the fewest possible words, what we conceive to be Bentham's place among these great intellectual benefactors of humanity; what he was, and what he was not; what kind of service he did and did not render to truth; we should say—he was not a great philosopher, but he was a great reformer in philosophy. He brought into philosophy something which it greatly needed, and for want of which it was at a stand. It was not his doctrines which did this, it was his mode of arriving at them. He introduced into morals and politics those habits of thought and modes of investigation, which are essential to the idea of science; and the absence of which made those departments of inquiry, as physics had been before Bacon, a field of interminable discussion, leading to no result. It was not his opinions, in short, but his method, that constituted the novelty and the value of what he did; a value beyond all price, even though we should reject the whole, as we unquestionably must a large part, of the opinions themselves.

Bentham's method may be shortly described as the method of detail; of treating wholes by separating them into their parts, abstractions by resolving them into Things,—classes and generalities by distinguishing them into the individuals of which they are made up; and breaking every question into pieces before attempting to solve it. The precise amount of originality of this process, considered as a logical conception—its degree of connexion with the methods of physical science, or with the previous

labours of Bacon, Hobbes, or Locke—is not an essential consideration in
this place. Whatever originality there was in the method—in the subjects
he applied it to, and in the rigidity with which he adhered to it, there was
the greatest. Hence his interminable classifications. Hence his elaborate
demonstrations of the most acknowledged truths. That murder, incen-
diarism, robbery, are mischievous actions, he will not take for granted
without proof; let the thing appear ever so self-evident, he will know the
why and the how of it with the last degree of precision; he will distinguish all the different mischiefs of a crime, whether of the *first*, the *second*, or the *third* order, namely, 1. the evil to the sufferer, and to his
personal connexions; 2. the *danger* from example, and the *alarm* or painful feeling of insecurity; and 3. the discouragement to industry and useful
pursuits arising from the *alarm*, and the trouble and resources which must
be expended in warding off the *danger*. After this enumeration, he will
prove from the laws of human feeling, that even the first of these evils,
the sufferings of the immediate victim, will on the average greatly out-
weigh the pleasure reaped by the offender; much more when all the other
evils are taken into account. Unless this could be proved, he would account the infliction of punishment unwarrantable; and for taking the
trouble to prove it formally, his defence is, 'there are truths which it is
necessary to prove, not for their own sakes, because they are acknowledged, but that an opening may be made for the reception of other truths
which depend upon them. It is in this manner we provide for the reception of first principles, which, once received, prepare the way for admission of all other truths.' To which may be added, that in this manner
also do we discipline the mind for practising the same sort of dissection
upon questions more complicated and of more doubtful issue.

It is a sound maxim, and one which all close thinkers have felt, but
which no one before Bentham ever so consistently applied, that error lurks
in generalities: that the human mind is not capable of embracing a complex whole, until it has surveyed and catalogued the parts of which that
whole is made up; that abstractions are not realities *per se*, but an
abridged mode of expressing facts, and that the only practical mode of
dealing with them is to trace them back to the facts (whether of experience or of consciousness) of which they are the expression. Proceeding on
this principle, Bentham makes short work with the ordinary modes of
moral and political reasoning. These, it appeared to him, when hunted to
their source, for the most part terminated in *phrases*. In politics, liberty,
social order, constitution, law of nature, social compact, &c. were the catch-
words: ethics had its analogous ones. Such were the arguments on which
the gravest questions of morality and policy were made to turn; not

reasons, but allusions to reasons; sacramental expressions, by which a summary appeal was made to some general sentiment of mankind, or to some maxim in familiar use, which might be true or not, but the limitations of which no one had ever critically examined. And this satisfied other people; but not Bentham. He required something more than opinion as a reason for opinion. Whenever he found a *phrase* used as an argument for or against anything, he insisted upon knowing what it meant; whether it appealed to any standard, or gave intimation of any matter of fact relevant to the question; and if he could not find that it did either, he treated it as an attempt on the part of the disputant to impose his own individual sentiment on other people, without giving them a reason for it; a 'contrivance for avoiding the obligation of appealing to any external standard, and for prevailing upon the reader to accept of the author's sentiment and opinion as a reason, and that a sufficient one, for itself.' Bentham shall speak for himself on this subject: the passage is from his first systematic work, 'Introduction to the Principles of Morals and Legislation,' and we could scarcely quote anything more strongly exemplifying both the strength and weakness of his mode of philosophizing.

It is curious enough to observe the variety of inventions men have hit upon, and the variety of phrases they have brought forward, in order to conceal from the world, and, if possible, from themselves, this very general and therefore very pardonable self-sufficiency.

1. One man says, he has a thing made on purpose to tell him what is right and what is wrong; and that is called a 'moral sense:' and then he goes to work at his ease, and says, such a thing is right, and such a thing is wrong—why? 'Because my moral sense tells me it is.'

2. Another man comes and alters the phrase: leaving out *moral*, and putting in *common* in the room of it. He then tells you that his common sense tells him what is right and wrong, as surely as the other's moral sense did: meaning by common sense a sense of some kind or other, which, he says, is possessed by all mankind: the sense of those whose sense is not the same as the author's being struck out as not worth taking. This contrivance does better than the other; for a moral sense being a new thing, a man may feel about him a good while without being able to find it out: but common sense is as old as the creation; and there is no man but would be ashamed to be thought not to have as much of it as his neighbours. It has another great advantage: by appearing to share power, it lessens envy; for when a man gets up upon this ground, in order to anathematize those who differ from him, it is not by a *sic volo sic jubeo*, but by a *velitis jubeatis*.

3. Another man comes, and says, that as to a moral sense indeed, he cannot find that he has any such thing: that, however, he has an *understanding*, which will do quite as well. This understanding, he says, is the standard of right and wrong: it tells him so and so. All good and wise men understand as he does: if other men's understandings differ in any part from his, so much the worse for them: it is a sure sign they are either defective or corrupt.

4. Another man says, that there is an eternal and immutable Rule of Right: that that rule of right dictates so and so: and then he begins giving you his sentiments upon anything that comes uppermost: and these sentiments (you are to take for granted) are so many branches of the eternal rule of right.

5. Another man, or perhaps the same man (it is no matter), says that there are certain practices conformable, and others repugnant, to the Fitness of Things; and then he tells you, at his leisure, what practices are conformable, and what repugnant: just as he happens to like a practice or dislike it.

6. A great multitude of people are continually talking of the Law of Nature; and then they go on giving you their sentiments about what is right and what is wrong; and these sentiments, you are to understand, are so many chapters and sections of the Law of Nature.

7. Instead of the phrase, Law of Nature, you have sometimes Law of Reason, Right Reason, Natural Justice, Natural Equity, Good Order. Any of them will do equally well. This latter is most used in politics. The three last are much more tolerable than the others, because they do not very explicitly claim to be anything more than phrases: they insist but feebly upon the being looked upon as so many positive standards of themselves, and seem content to be taken, upon occasion, for phrases expressive of the conformity of the thing in question to the proper standard, whatever that may be. On most occasions, however, it will be better to say *utility: utility* is clearer, as referring more explicitly to pain and pleasure.

8. We have one philosopher, who says, there is no harm in anything in the world but in telling a lie; and that if, for example, you were to murder your own father, this would only be a particular way of saying, he was not your father. Of course when this philosopher sees anything that he does not like, he says, it is a particular way of telling a lie. It is saying, that the act ought to be done, or may be done, when, *in truth*, it ought not to be done.

9. The fairest and openest of them all is that sort of man who speaks out, and says, I am of the number of the Elect: now God himself takes care to inform the Elect what is right: and that with so good

effect, that let them strive ever so, they cannot help not only knowing it but practising it. If therefore a man wants to know what is right and what is wrong, he has nothing to do but to come to me.

Few will contend that this is a perfectly fair representation of the *animus* of those who employ the various phrases so amusingly animadverted on; but that the phrases contain no argument, save what is grounded on the very feelings they are adduced to justify, is a truth which Bentham had the eminent merit of first pointing out.

It is the introduction into the philosophy of human conduct, of this method of detail—of this practice of never reasoning about wholes till they have been resolved into their parts, nor about abstractions till they have been translated into realities—that constitutes the originality of Bentham in philosophy, and makes him the great reformer of the moral and political branch of it. To what he terms the 'exhaustive method of classification,' which is but one branch of this more general method, he himself ascribes everything original in the systematic and elaborate work from which we have quoted. The generalities of his philosophy itself have little or no novelty: to ascribe any to the doctrine that general utility is the foundation of morality, would imply great ignorance of the history of philosophy, of general literature, and of Bentham's own writings. He derived the idea, as he says himself, from Helvetius; and it was the doctrine no less, of the religious philosophers of that age, prior to Reid and Beattie. We never saw an abler defence of the doctrine of utility than in a book written in refutation of Shaftesbury, and now little read—Brown's [1] 'Essays on the Characteristics'; and in Johnson's celebrated review of Soame Jenyns, the same doctrine is set forth as that both of the author and of the reviewer. In all ages of philosophy one of its schools has been utilitarian—not only from the time of Epicurus, but long before. It was by mere accident that this opinion became connected in Bentham with his peculiar method. The utilitarian philosophers antecedent to him had no more claims to the method than their antagonists. To refer, for instance, to the Epicurean philosophy, according to the most complete view we have of the moral part of it, by the most accomplished scholar of antiquity, Cicero; we ask any one who has read his philosophical writings, the 'De Finibus' for instance, whether the arguments of the Epicureans do not, just as much as those of the Stoics or Platonists, consist of mere rhetorical appeals to common notions, to ἐικότα and σημεῖα instead of τεκμήρια, notions picked up as it were casually, and when true at all, never so nar-

---

[1] Author of another book which made no little sensation when it first appeared, —'An Estimate of the Manners of the Times.'

rowly looked into as to ascertain in what sense and under what limitations they are true. The application of a real inductive philosophy to the problems of ethics, is as unknown to the Epicurean moralists as to any of the other schools; they never take a question to pieces, and join issue on a definite point. Bentham certainly did not learn his sifting and anatomizing method from them.

This method Bentham has finally installed in philosophy; has made it henceforth imperative on philosophers of all schools. By it he has formed the intellects of many thinkers, who either never adopted, or have abandoned many of his peculiar opinions. He has taught the method to men of the most opposite schools to his; he has made them perceive that if they do not test their doctrines by the method of detail, their adversaries will. He has thus, it is not too much to say, for the first time introduced precision of thought into moral and political philosophy. Instead of taking up their opinions by intuition, or by ratiocination from premises adopted on a mere rough view, and couched in language so vague that it is impossible to say exactly whether they are true or false, philosophers are now forced to understand one another, to break down the generality of their propositions, and join a precise issue in every dispute. This is nothing less than a revolution in philosophy. Its effect is gradually becoming evident in the writings of English thinkers of every variety of opinion, and will be felt more and more in proportion as Bentham's writings are diffused, and as the number of minds to whose formation they contribute is multiplied.

The first question in regard to any man of speculation is, what is his theory of human life? In the minds of many philosophers, whatever theory they have of this sort is latent, and it would be a revelation to themselves to have it pointed out to them in their writings as others can see it, unconsciously moulding everything to its own likeness. But Bentham always knew his own premises, and made his reader know them: it was not his custom to leave the theoretic grounds of his practical conclusions to conjecture. Few great thinkers have afforded the means of assigning with so much certainty the exact conception which they had formed of man and of man's life.

Man is conceived by Bentham as a being susceptible of pleasures and pains, and governed in all his conduct partly by the different modifications of self-interest, and the passions commonly classed as selfish, partly by sympathies, or occasionally antipathies, towards other beings. And here Bentham's conception of human nature stops. He does not exclude religion; the prospect of divine rewards and punishments he includes under the head of 'self-regarding interest,' and the devotional feeling under that of sympathy with God. But the whole of the impelling or restraining principles, whether of this or of another world, which he recognises, are either self-love, or love or hatred towards other sentient beings. That there might be no doubt of what he thought on the subject, he has not left us to the general evidence of his writings, but has drawn out a 'Table of the Springs of Action,' an express enumeration and classification of human motives, with their various names, laudatory, vituperative, and neutral: and this table, to be found in Part I. of his collected works, we recommend to the study of those who would understand his philosophy.

Man is never recognised by him as a being capable of pursuing spiritual perfection as an end; of desiring, for its own sake, the conformity of his own character to his standard of excellence, without hope of good or fear of evil from other source than his own inward consciousness. Even in the more limited form of Conscience, this great fact in human nature escapes him. Nothing is more curious than the absence of recognition in any of his writings of the existence of conscience, as a thing distinct from philanthropy, from affection for God or man, and from self-interest in this world or in the next. There is a studied abstinence from any of the phrases which, in the mouths of others, import the acknowledgment of such a fact.[2] If we find the words 'Conscience', 'Principle', 'Moral Rectitude', 'Moral Duty', in his Table of the Springs of Action, it is among the synonymes of the 'love of reputation'; with an intimation as to the two former phrases, that they are also sometimes synonymous with the *religious* motive, or the motive of *sympathy*. The feeling of moral approbation or disapprobation properly so called, either towards ourselves or our fellow-creatures, he seems unaware of the existence of; and neither the word *self-respect*, nor the idea to which that word is appropriated, occurs even once, so far as our recollection serves us, in his whole writings.

Nor is it only the moral part of man's nature, in the strict sense of the term—the desire of perfection, or the feeling of an approving or of an accusing conscience—that he overlooks; he but faintly recognises, as a fact in human nature, the pursuit of any other ideal end for its own sake. The sense of *honour*, and personal dignity—that feeling of personal exaltation and degradation which acts independently of other people's opinion, or even in defiance of it; the love of *beauty*, the passion of the artist; the

---

[2] In a passage in the last volume of his book on Evidence, and possibly in one or two other places, the 'love of justice' is spoken of as a feeling inherent in almost all mankind. It is impossible, without explanations now unattainable, to ascertain what sense is to be put upon casual expressions so inconsistent with the general tenor of his philosophy.

love of *order*, of congruity, of consistency in all things, and conformity
to their end; the love of *power*, not in the limited form of power over
other human beings, but abstract power, the power of making our voli-
tions effectual; the love of *action*, the thirst for movement and activity, a
principle scarcely of less influence in human life than its opposite, the
love of ease:—None of these powerful constituents of human nature are
thought worthy of a place among the 'Springs of Action;' and though
there is possibly no one of them of the existence of which an acknowledgment might not be found in some corner of Bentham's writings, no
conclusions are ever founded on the acknowledgment. Man, that most
complex being, is a very simple one in his eyes. Even under the head of
sympathy, his recognition does not extend to the more complex forms
of the feeling—the love of *loving*, the need of a sympathising support, or
of objects of admiration and reverence. If he thought at all of any of the
deeper feelings of human nature, it was but as idiosyncrasies of taste, with
which the moralist no more than the legislator had any concern, further
than to prohibit such as were mischievous among the actions to which
they might chance to lead. To say either that man should, or that he
should not, take pleasure in one thing, displeasure in another, appeared to
him as much an act of despotism in the moralist as in the political ruler.

It would be most unjust to Bentham to surmise (as narrow-minded
and passionate adversaries are apt in such cases to do) that this picture of
human nature was copied from himself; that all those constituents of humanity which he rejected from his table of motives, were wanting in his
own breast. The unusual strength of his early feelings of virtue, was, as
we have seen, the original cause of all his speculations; and a noble sense
of morality, and especially of justice, guides and pervades them all. But
having been early accustomed to keep before his mind's eye the happiness
of mankind (or rather of the whole sentient world), as the only thing
desirable in itself, or which rendered anything else desirable, he confounded all disinterested feelings which he found in himself, with the
desire of general happiness: just as some religious writers, who loved
virtue for its own sake as much perhaps as men could do, habitually confounded their love of virtue with their fear of hell. It would have required
greater subtlety than Bentham possessed, to distinguish from each other,
feelings which, from long habit, always acted in the same direction; and
his want of imagination prevented him from reading the distinction,
where it is legible enough, in the hearts of others.

Accordingly, he has not been followed in this grand oversight by any
of the able men who, from the extent of their intellectual obligations to
him, have been regarded as his disciples. They may have followed him in

his doctrine of utility, and in his rejection of a moral sense as the test of right and wrong: but while repudiating it as such, they have, with Hartley, acknowledged it as a fact in human nature; they have endeavoured to account for it, to assign its laws: nor are they justly chargeable either with undervaluing this part of our nature, or with any disposition to throw it into the background of their speculations. If any part of the influence of this cardinal error has extended itself to them, it is circuitously, and through the effect on their minds of other parts of Bentham's doctrines.

Sympathy, the only disinterested motive which Bentham recognised, he felt the inadequacy of, except in certain limited cases, as a security for virtuous action. Personal affection, he well knew, is as liable to operate to the injury of third parties, and requires as much to be kept under government, as any other feeling whatever: and general philanthropy, considered as a motive influencing mankind in general, he estimated at its true value when divorced from the feeling of duty—as the very weakest and most unsteady of all feelings. There remained, as a motive by which mankind are influenced, and by which they may be guided to their good, only personal interest. Accordingly, Bentham's idea of the world is that of a collection of persons pursuing each his separate interest or pleasure, and the prevention of whom from jostling one another more than is unavoidable, may be attempted by hopes and fears derived from three sources—the law, religion, and public opinion. To these three powers, considered as binding human conduct, he gave the name of *sanctions*: the *political* sanction, operating by the rewards and penalties of the law; the *religious* sanction, by those expected from the Ruler of the Universe; and the *popular*, which he characteristically calls also the *moral* sanction, operating through the pains and pleasures arising from the favour or disfavour of our fellow-creatures.

Such is Bentham's theory of the world. And now, in a spirit neither of apology nor of censure, but of calm appreciation, we are to inquire how far this view of human nature and life will carry any one:—how much it will accomplish in morals, and how much in political and social philosophy: what it will do for the individual, and what for society.

It will do nothing for the conduct of the individual, beyond prescribing some of the more obvious dictates of worldly prudence, and outward probity and beneficence. There is no need to expatiate on the deficiencies of a system of ethics which does not pretend to aid individuals in the formation of their own character; which recognises no such wish as that of self-culture, we may even say no such power, as existing in human nature; and if it did recognise, could furnish little assistance to that great duty, because it overlooks the existence of about half of the whole number of mental feelings which human beings are capable of, including all those of which the direct objects are states of their own mind.

Morality consists of two parts. One of these is self-education; the training, by the human being himself, of his affections and will. That department is a blank in Bentham's system. The other and co-equal part, the regulation of his outward actions, must be altogether halting and imperfect without the first: for how can we judge in what manner many an action will affect even the worldly interests of ourselves or others, unless we take in, as part of the question, its influence on the regulation of our, or their, affections and desires? A moralist on Bentham's principles may get as far as this, that he ought not to slay, burn, or steal; but what will be his qualifications for regulating the nicer shades of human behavior, or for laying down even the greater moralities as to those facts in human life which are liable to influence the depths of the character quite independently of any influence on worldly circumstances—such, for instance, as the sexual relations, or those of family in general, or any other social and sympathetic connexions of an intimate kind? The moralities of these questions depend essentially on considerations which Bentham never so much as took into the account; and when he happened to be in the right, it was always, and necessarily, on wrong or insufficient grounds.

It is fortunate for the world that Bentham's taste lay rather in the direction of jurisprudential than of properly ethical inquiry. Nothing expressly of the latter kind has been published under his name, except the 'Deontology'—a book scarcely ever, in our experience, alluded to by any admirer of Bentham without deep regret that it ever saw the light. We did not expect from Bentham correct systematic views of ethics, or a sound treatment of any question the moralities of which require a profound knowledge of the human heart; but we did anticipate that the greater moral questions would have been boldly plunged into, and at least a searching criticism produced of the received opinions; we did not expect that the *petite morale* almost alone would have been treated, and that with the most pedantic minuteness, and on the *quid pro quo* principles which regulate trade. The book has not even the value which would belong to an authentic exhibition of the legitimate consequences of an erroneous line of thought; for the style proves it to have been so entirely rewritten, that it is impossible to tell how much or how little of it is Bentham's. The collected edition, now in progress, will not, it is said, include Bentham's religious writings; these, although we think most of them of exceedingly small value, are at least his, and the world has a right to whatever light they throw upon the constitution of his mind. But the omission of the 'Deontology' would be an act of editorial discretion which we should deem entirely justifiable.

If Bentham's theory of life can do so little for the individual, what can it do for society?

It will enable a society which has attained a certain state of spiritual development, and the maintenance of which in that state is otherwise provided for, to prescribe the rules by which it may protect its material interests. It will do nothing (except sometimes as an instrument in the hands of a higher doctrine) for the spiritual interests of society; nor does it suffice of itself even for the material interests. That which alone causes any material interests to exist, which alone enables any body of human beings to exist as a society, is national character: *that* it is, which causes one nation to succeed in what it attempts, another to fail; one nation to understand and aspire to elevated things, another to grovel in mean ones; which makes the greatness of one nation lasting, and dooms another to early and rapid decay. The true teacher of the fitting social arrangements for England, France, or America, is the one who can point out how the English, French, or American character can be improved, and how it has been made what it is. A philosophy of laws and institutions, not founded on a philosophy of national character, is an absurdity. But what could Bentham's opinion be worth on national character? How could he, whose mind contained so few and so poor types of individual character, rise to that higher generalization? All he can do is but to indicate means by which, in any given state of the national mind, the material interests of society can be protected; saving the question, of which others must judge, whether the use of those means would have, on the national character, any injurious influence.

We have arrived, then, at a sort of estimate of what a philosophy like Bentham's can do. It can teach the means of organizing and regulating the merely *business* part of the social arrangements. Whatever can be understood or whatever done without reference to moral influences, his philosophy is equal to; where those influences require to be taken into account, it is at fault. He committed the mistake of supposing that the business part of human affairs was the whole of them; all at least that the legislator and the moralist had to do with. Not that he disregarded moral influences when he perceived them; but his want of imagination, small experience of human feelings, and ignorance of the filiation and connexion of feelings with one another, made this rarely the case.

The business part is accordingly the only province of human affairs which Bentham has cultivated with any success; into which he has introduced any considerable number of comprehensive and luminous practical

principles. That is the field of his greatness; and there he is indeed great.
He has swept away the accumulated cobwebs of centuries—he has untied
knots which the efforts of the ablest thinkers, age after age, had only
drawn tighter; and it is no exaggeration to say of him that over a great
part of the field he was the first to shed the light of reason.

We turn with pleasure from what Bentham could not do, to what he
did. It is an ungracious task to call a great benefactor of mankind to account for not being a greater—to insist upon the errors of a man who has
originated more new truths, has given to the world more sound practical
lessons, than it ever received, except in a few glorious instances, from any
other individual. The unpleasing part of our work is ended. We are now
to show the greatness of the man; the grasp which his intellect took of
the subjects with which it was fitted to deal; the giant's task which was
before him, and the hero's courage and strength with which he achieved
it. Nor let that which he did be deemed of small account because its
province was limited: man has but the choice to go a little way in many
paths, or a great way in only one. The field of Bentham's labours was like
the space between two parallel lines; narrow to excess in one direction, in
another it reached to infinity.

Bentham's speculations, as we are already aware, began with law; and
in that department he accomplished his greatest triumphs. He found the
philosophy of law a chaos, he left it a science: he found the practice of the
law an Augean stable, he turned the river into it which is mining and
sweeping away mound after mound of its rubbish.

Without joining in the exaggerated invectives against lawyers, which
Bentham sometimes permitted to himself, or making one portion of society alone accountable for the fault of all, we may say that circumstances
had made English lawyers in a peculiar degree liable to the reproach of
Voltaire, who defines lawyers the 'conservators of ancient barbarous
usages.' The basis of the English law was, and still is, the feudal system.
That system, like all those which existed as custom before they were established as law, possessed a certain degree of suitableness to the wants of
the society among whom it grew up—that is to say, of a tribe of rude
soldiers, holding a conquered people in subjection, and dividing its spoils
among themselves. Advancing civilization had, however, converted this
armed encampment of barbarous warriors in the midst of enemies reduced to slavery, into an industrious, commercial, rich, and free people.
The laws which were suitable to the first of these states of society, could
have no manner of relation to the circumstances of the second; which
could not even have come into existence unless something had been done

to adapt those laws to it. But the adaptation was not the result of thought and design; it arose not from any comprehensive consideration of the new state of society and its exigencies. What was done, was done by a struggle of centuries between the old barbarism and the new civilization; between the feudal aristocracy of conquerors, holding fast to the rude system they had established, and the conquered effecting their emancipation. The last was the growing power, but was never strong enough to break its bonds, though ever and anon some weak point gave away. Hence the law came to be like the costume of a full-grown man who had never put off the clothes made for him when he first went to school. Band after band had burst, and, as the rent widened, then, without removing anything except what might drop off of itself, the hole was darned, or patches of fresh law were brought from the nearest shop and stuck on. Hence all ages of English history have given one another rendezvous in English law; their several products may be seen all together, not interfused, but heaped one upon another, as many different ages of the earth may be read in some perpendicular section of its surface—the deposits of each succes-sive period not substituted but superimposed on those of the preceding. And in the world of law no less than in the physical world, every com-motion and conflict of the elements has left its mark behind in some break or irregularity of the strata: every struggle which ever rent the bosom of society is apparent in the disjointed condition of the part of the field of law which covers the spot: nay, the very traps and pitfalls which one contending party set for another are still standing, and the teeth not of hyenas only, but of foxes and all cunning animals, are imprinted on the curious remains found in these antediluvian caves.

In the English law, as in the Roman before it, the adaptations of barbarous laws to the growth of civilized society were made chiefly by stealth. They were generally made by the courts of justice, who could not help reading the new wants of mankind in the cases between man and man which came before them; but who, having no authority to make new laws for those new wants, were obliged to do the work covertly, and evade the jealousy and opposition of an ignorant, prejudiced, and for the most part brutal and tyrannical legislature. Some of the most necessary of these improvements, such as the giving force of law to trusts, and the breaking up of entails, were effected in actual opposition to the strongly-declared will of Parliament, whose clumsy hands, no match for the astute-ness of judges, could not, after repeated trials, manage to make any law which the judges could not find a trick for rendering inoperative. The whole history of the contest about trusts may still be read in the words of a conveyance, as could the contest about entails, till the abolition of fine and recovery by a bill of the present Attorney-General; but dearly did the client pay for the cabinet of historical curiosities which he was obliged to purchase every time that he made a settlement of his estate. The result of this mode of improving social institutions was, that whatever new things were done had to be done in consistency with old forms and names; and the laws were improved with much the same effect as if, in the improvement of agriculture, the plough could only have been introduced by making it look like a spade; or as if, when the primeval practice of ploughing by the horse's tail gave way to the innovation of harness, the tail, for form's sake, had still remained attached to the plough.

When the conflicts were over, and the mixed mass settled down into something like a fixed state, and that state a very profitable and therefore a very agreeable one to lawyers, they, following the natural tendency of the human mind, began to theorise upon it, and, in obedience to necessity, had to digest it and give it a systematic form. It was from this thing of shreds and patches, in which the only part that approached to order or system was the early barbarous part, already more than half superseded, that English lawyers had to construct, by induction and abstraction, their philosophy of law; and without the logical habits and general intellectual cultivation which the lawyers of the Roman empire brought to a similar task. Bentham found the philosophy of law what English practising lawyers had made it; a jumble, in which *real* and *personal* property, *law* and *equity, felony, premunire, misprision,* and *misdemeanour,* words without a vestige of meaning when detached from the history of English institutions—mere tide-marks to point out the line which the sea and the shore, in their secular struggles, had adjusted as their mutual boundary—all passed for distinctions inherent in the nature of things; in which every absurdity, every lucrative abuse, had a reason found for it—a reason which only now and then even pretended to be drawn from expediency; most commonly a technical reason, one of mere form, derived from the old barbarous system. While the theory of the law was in this state, to describe what the practice of it was would require the pen of a Swift, or of Bentham himself. The whole progress of a suit at law seemed like a series of contrivances for lawyers' profit, in which the suitors were regarded as the prey; and if the poor were not the helpless victims of every Sir Giles Overreach who could pay the price, they might thank opinion and manners for it, not the law.

It may be fancied by some people that Bentham did an easy thing in merely calling all this absurd, and proving it to be so. But he began the contest a young man, and he had grown old before he had any followers. History will one day refuse to give credit to the intensity of the superstition which, till very lately, protected this mischievous mess from examination or doubt—passed off the charming representations of Blackstone for a just estimate of the English law, and proclaimed the shame of human reason to be the perfection of it. Glory to Bentham that he has dealt to this superstition its deathblow—that he has been the Hercules of this hydra, the St. George of this pestilent dragon! The honour is all his—nothing but his peculiar qualities could have done it. There were wanted his indefatigable perseverance, his firm self-reliance, needing no support from other men's opinion; his intensely practical turn of mind, his synthetical habits—above all, his peculiar method. Metaphysicians, armed with vague generalities, had often tried their hands at the subject, and left it no more advanced than they found it. Law is a matter of business; means and ends are the things to be considered in it, not abstractions: vagueness was not to be met by vagueness, but by definiteness and precision: details were not to be encountered with generalities, but with details. Nor could any progress be made, on such a subject, by merely showing that existing things were bad; it was necessary also to show how they might be made better. No great man whom we read of was qualified to do this thing except Bentham. He has done it, once and for ever.

Into the particulars of what Bentham has done we cannot enter: many hundred pages would be required to give a tolerable abstract of it. To sum up our estimate under a few heads. First: he has expelled mysticism from the philosophy of law, and set the example of viewing laws in a practical light, as means to certain definite and precise ends. Secondly: he has cleared up the confusion and vagueness attaching to the idea of law in general, to the idea of a body of laws, and all the general ideas therein involved. Thirdly: he demonstrated the necessity and practicability of *codification*, or the conversion of all law into a written and systematically arranged code: not like the Code Napoleon, a code without a single definition, requiring a constant reference to anterior precedent for the meaning of its technical terms; but one containing within itself all that is necessary for its own interpretation, together with a perpetual provision for its own emendation and improvement. He has shown of what parts such a code would consist; the relation of those parts to one another; and by his distinctions and classifications has done very much towards showing what should be, or might be, its nomenclature and arrangement. What he has left undone, he has made it comparatively easy for others to do. Fourthly: he has taken a systematic view of the exigencies of society for which the civil code is intended to provide, and of the principles of human nature by which its provisions are to be tested: and this view, defective (as we have already intimated) wherever spiritual interests require to be taken into account, is excellent for that large portion of the laws of any country which are designed for the protection of material interests. Fifthly: (to say nothing of the subject of punishment, for which something considerable had been done before) he found the philosophy of judicial procedure, including that of judicial establishments and of evidence, in a more wretched state than even any other part of the philosophy of law; he carried it at once almost to perfection. He left it with every one of its principles established, and little remaining to be done even in the suggestion of practical arrangements.

These assertions in behalf of Bentham may be left, without fear for the result, in the hands of those who are competent to judge of them. There are now even in the highest seats of justice, men to whom the claims made for him will not appear extravagant. Principle after principle of those propounded by him is moreover making its way by infiltration into the understandings most shut against his influence, and driving nonsense and prejudice from one corner of them to another. The reform of the laws of any country according to his principles, can only be gradual, and may be long ere it is accomplished; but the work is in progress, and both parliament and the judges are every year doing something, and often something not inconsiderable, towards the forwarding of it.

It seems proper here to take notice of an accusation sometimes made both against Bentham and against the principle of codification—as if they required one uniform suit of ready-made laws for all times and all states of society. The doctrine of codification, as the word imports, relates to the form only of the laws, not their substance; it does not concern itself with what the laws should be, but declares that whatever they are, they ought to be systematically arranged, and fixed down to a determinate form of words. To the accusation, so far as it affects Bentham, one of the essays in the collection of his works (then for the first time published in English) is a complete answer: that 'On the Influence of Time and Place in Matters of Legislation.' It may there be seen that the different exigencies of different nations with respect to law, occupied his attention as systematically as any other portion of the wants which render laws necessary: with the limitations, it is true, which were set to all his speculations by the imperfections of his theory of human nature. For, taking, as we have seen, next to no account of national character and the causes which form and maintain it, he was precluded from considering, except to a very limited extent, the laws of a country as an instrument of national culture: one of their most important aspects, and in which they must of course vary according to the degree and kind of culture already attained; as a tutor gives his pupil different lessons according to the progress already made in his education. The same laws would not have suited our wild ancestors, accustomed to rude independence, and a people of Asiatics bowed down by military despotism: the slave needs to be trained to govern himself, the savage to submit to the government of others. The same laws will not suit the English, who distrust everything which emanates from general principles, and the French, who distrust whatever does not so emanate. Very different institutions are needed to train to the perfection of their nature, or to constitute into a united nation and social polity, an essentially *subjective* people like the Germans, and an essentially *objective* people like those of Northern and Central Italy; the one affectionate and dreamy, the other passionate and worldly; the one trustful and loyal, the other calculating and suspicious; the one not practical enough, the other overmuch; the one wanting individuality, the other fellow-feeling; the one failing for want of exacting enough for itself, the other for want of conceding enough to others. Bentham was little accustomed to look at institutions in their relation to these topics. The effects of this oversight must of course be perceptible throughout his speculations, but we do not think the errors into which it led him very material in the greater part of civil and penal law: it is in the department of constitutional legislation that they were fundamental.

The Benthamic theory of government has made so much noise in the world of late years; it has held such a conspicuous place among Radical philosophies, and Radical modes of thinking have participated so much more largely than any others in its spirit, that many worthy persons imagine there is no other Radical philosophy extant. Leaving such people to discover their mistake as they may, we shall expend a few words in attempting to discriminate between the truth and error of this celebrated theory.

There are three great questions in government. First, to what authority is it for the good of the people that they should be subject? Secondly, how are they to be induced to obey that authority? The answers to these two questions vary indefinitely, according to the degree and kind of civilization and cultivation already attained by a people, and their peculiar aptitudes for receiving more. Comes next a third question, not liable to so much variation, namely, by what means are the abuses of this authority to be checked? This third question is the only one of the three to which Bentham seriously applies himself, and he gives it the only answer it admits of—Responsibility: responsibility to persons whose interest, whose obvious and recognisable interest, accords with the end in view—good government. This being granted, it is next to be asked, in what body of persons this identity of interest with good government, that is, with the interest of the whole community, is to be found? In nothing less, says Bentham, than the numerical majority: nor, say we, even in the numerical majority itself; of no portion of the community less than all, will the interest coincide, at all times and in all respects, with the interest of all. But, since power given to all, by a representative government, is in fact given to a majority; we are obliged to fall back upon the first of our three questions, namely, under what authority is it for the good of the people that they be placed? And if to this the answer be, under that of a majority among themselves, Bentham's system cannot be questioned. This one assumption being made, his 'Constitutional Code' is admirable. That extraordinary power which he possessed, of at once seizing comprehensive principles, and scheming out minute details, is brought into play with surprising vigour in devising means for preventing rulers from escaping from the control of the majority; for enabling and inducing the majority to exercise that control unremittingly; and for providing them with servants of every desirable endowment, moral and intellectual, compatible with entire subservience to their will.

But *is* this fundamental doctrine of Bentham's political philosophy an universal truth? Is it, at all times and places, good for mankind to be under the absolute authority of the majority of themselves? We say the authority, not the political authority merely, because it is chimerical to suppose that whatever has absolute power over men's bodies will not arrogate it over their minds—will not seek to control (not perhaps by legal penalties, but by the persecutions of society) opinions and feelings which depart from its standard; will not attempt to shape the education of the young by its model, and to extinguish all books, all schools, all combinations of individuals for joint action upon society, which may be attempted for the purpose of keeping alive a spirit at variance with its own. Is it, we say, the proper condition of man, in all ages and nations, to be under the despotism of Public Opinion?

It is very conceivable that such a doctrine should find acceptance from some of the noblest spirits, in a time of reaction against the aristocratic governments of modern Europe; governments founded on the entire sacrifice (except so far as prudence, and sometimes humane feeling interfere) of the community generally, to the self-interest and ease of a few. European reformers have been accustomed to see the numerical majority everywhere unjustly depressed, everywhere trampled upon, or at the best overlooked, by governments; nowhere possessing power enough to extort redress of their most positive grievances, provision for their mental culture, or even to prevent themselves from being taxed avowedly for the pecuniary profit of the ruling classes. To see these things, and to seek to put an end to them, by means (among other things) of giving more political power to the majority, constitutes Radicalism; and it is because so many in this age have felt this wish, and have felt that the realization of it was an object worthy of men's devoting their lives to it, that such a theory of government as Bentham's has found favour with them. But, though to pass from one form of bad government to another be the ordinary fate of mankind, philosophers ought not to make themselves parties to it, by sacrificing one portion of important truth to another.

The numerical majority of any society whatever, must consist of persons all standing in the same social position, and having, in the main, the same pursuits, namely, unskilled manual labourers; and we mean no disparagement to them: whatever we say to their disadvantage, we say equally of a numerical majority of shopkeepers, or of squires. Where there is identity of position and pursuits, there also will be identity of partialities, passions and prejudices; and to give to any one set of partialities, passions, and prejudices, absolute power, without counter-balance from partialities, passions, and prejudices of a different sort, is the way to render the correction of any of those imperfections hopeless; to make one narrow, mean type of human nature universal and perpetual, and to crush every influence which tends to the further improvement of man's intellectual and moral nature. There must, we know, be some paramount power in society; and that the majority should be that power, is on the whole right, not as being just in itself, but as being less unjust than any other footing on which the matter can be placed. But it is necessary that the institutions of society should make provision for keeping up, in some form or other, as a corrective to partial views, and a shelter for freedom of thought and individuality of character, a perpetual and standing Opposition to the will of the majority. All countries which have long continued progressive, or been durably great, have been so because there has been an organized opposition to the ruling power, of whatever kind that power was: plebeians to patricians, clergy to kings, freethinkers to clergy, kings to barons, commons to king and aristocracy. Almost all the greatest men who ever lived have formed part of such an Opposition. Wherever some such quarrel has not been going on—wherever it has been terminated by the complete victory of one of the contending principles, and no new contest has taken the place of the old—society has either hardened into Chinese stationariness, or fallen into dissolution. A centre of resistance, round which all the moral and social elements which the ruling power views with disfavour may cluster themselves, and behind whose bulwarks they may find shelter from the attempts of that power to hunt them out of existence, is as necessary where the opinion of the majority is sovereign, as where the ruling power is a hierarchy or an aristocracy. Where no such *point d'appui* exists, there the human race will inevitably degenerate; and the question, whether the United States, for instance, will in time sink into another China (also a most commercial and industrious nation), resolves itself, to us, into the question, whether such a centre of resistance will gradually evolve itself or not.

These things being considered, we cannot think that Bentham made the most useful employment which might have been made of his great powers, when, not content with enthroning the majority as sovereign, by means of universal suffrage without king or house of lords, he exhausted all the resources of ingenuity in devising means for riveting the yoke of public opinion closer and closer round the necks of all public functionaries, and excluding every possibility of the exercise of the slightest or most temporary influence either by a minority, or by the functionary's own notions of right. Surely when any power has been made the strongest power, enough has been done for it; care is thenceforth wanted rather to prevent that strongest power from swallowing up all others. Wherever all the forces of society act in one single direction, the just claims of the individual human being are in extreme peril. The power of the majority is salutary so far as it is used defensively, not offensively—as its exertion is tempered by respect for the personality of the individual, and deference to superiority of cultivated intelligence. If Bentham had employed himself in pointing out the means by which institutions fundamentally democratic might be best adapted to the preservation and strengthening of those two sentiments, he would have done something more permanently valuable, and more worthy of his great intellect. Montesquieu, with the lights of the present age, would have done it; and we are possibly destined to receive this benefit from the Montesquieu of our own times, M. de Tocqueville.

Do we then consider Bentham's political speculations useless? Far from it. We consider them only one-sided. He has brought out into a strong light, has cleared from a thousand confusions and misconceptions, and pointed out with admirable skill the best means of promoting, one of the ideal qualities of a perfect government—identity of interest between the trustees and the community for whom they hold their power in trust. This quality is not attainable in its ideal perfection, and must moreover be striven for with a perpetual eye to all other requisites; but those other requisites must still more be striven for without losing sight of this: and when the slightest postponement is made of it to any other end, the sacrifice, often necessary, is never unattended with evil. Bentham has pointed out how complete this sacrifice is in modern European societies: how exclusively, partial and sinister interests are the ruling power there, with only such check as is imposed by public opinion—which being thus, in the existing order of things, perpetually apparent as a source of good, he was led by natural partiality to exaggerate its intrinsic excellence. This sinister interest of rulers Bentham hunted through all its disguises, and especially through those which hide it from the men themselves who are influenced by it. The greatest service rendered by him to the philosophy of universal human nature, is, perhaps, his illustration of what he terms 'interest-begotten prejudice'—the common tendency of man to make a duty and a virtue of following his self-interest. The idea, it is true, was far from being peculiarly Bentham's: the artifices by which we persuade ourselves that we are not yielding to our selfish inclinations when we are, had attracted the notice of all moralists, and had been probed by religious writers to a depth as much below Bentham's, as their knowledge of the profundities and windings of the human heart was superior to his. But it is selfish interest in the form of class-interest, and the class morality founded thereon, which Bentham has illustrated: the manner in which any set of persons who mix much together, and have a common interest, are apt to make that common interest their standard of virtue, and the social feelings of the members of the class are made to play into the hands of their selfish ones; whence the union so often exemplified in history, between the most heroic personal disinterestedness and the most odious class-selfishness. This was one of Bentham's leading ideas, and almost the only one by which he contributed to the elucidation of history: much of which, except so far as this explained it, must have been entirely inexplicable to him. The idea was given him by Helvetius, whose book, 'De l'Esprit', is one continued and most acute commentary on it; and, together with the other great ideas of Helvetius, the influence of circumstances on character, it will make his name live by the side of Rousseau, when most of the other French metaphysicians on the eighteenth century will be extant as such only in literary history.

In the brief view which we have been able to give of Bentham's philosophy, it may surprise the reader that we have said so little about the first principle of it, with which his name is more identified than with anything else; the 'principle of utility', or, as he afterwards named it, 'the greatest-happiness principle.' It is a topic on which much were to be said, if there were room, or if it were in reality necessary for the just estimation of Bentham. On an occasion more suitable for a discussion of the metaphysics of morality, or on which the elucidations necessary to make an opinion on so abstract a subject intelligible could be conveniently given, we should be fully prepared to state what we think on this subject. At present we shall only say, that while, under proper explanations, we entirely agree with Bentham in his principle, we do not hold with him that all right thinking on the details of morals depends on its express assertion. We think utility, or happiness, much too complex and indefinite an end to be sought except through the medium of various secondary ends, concerning which there may be, and often is, agreement among persons who differ in their ultimate standard; and about which there does in fact prevail a much greater unanimity among thinking persons, than might be supposed from their diametrical divergence on the great questions of moral metaphysics. As mankind are much more nearly of one nature, than of one opinion about their own nature, they are more easily brought to agree in their intermediate principles, *vera illa et media axiomata,* as Bacon says, than in their first principles: and the attempt to make the bearings of actions upon the ultimate end more evident than they can be made by referring them to the intermediate ends, and to estimate their value by a direct reference to human happiness, generally terminates in attaching most importance, not to those effects which are really the greatest, but to those which can most easily be pointed to and individually identified. Those who adopt utility as a standard can seldom apply it truly except through the secondary principles; those who reject it, generally do no more than erect those secondary principles into first principles. It is when two or more of the secondary principles conflict, that a direct appeal to some first principle becomes necessary; and then commences the practical importance of the utilitarian controversy; which is in other respects, a question of arrangement and logical subordination rather than of practice; important principally in a purely scientific point of view, for the sake of the systematic unity and coherency of ethical philosophy. It is probable, however, that to the principle of utility we owe all that Bentham did; that it was necessary to him to find a first principle which he could receive as self-evident, and to which he could attach all his other doctrines as logical consequences: that to him systematic unity was an indispensable condition of his confidence in his own intellect. And there is something further to be remarked. Whether happiness be or be not the end to which morality should be referred—that it be referred to an *end* of some sort, and not left in the dominion of vague feeling or inexplicable internal conviction, that it be made a matter of reason and calculation, and not merely of sentiment, is essential to the very idea of moral philosophy; is, in fact, what renders argument or discussion on moral questions possible. That the morality of actions depends on the consequences which they tend to produce, is the doctrine of rational persons of all schools; that the good or evil of those consequences is measured solely by pleasure or pain, is all of the doctrine of the school of utility, which is peculiar to it.

In so far as Bentham's adoption of the principle of utility induced him to fix his attention upon the consequences of actions as the consideration determining their morality, so far he was indisputably in the right path: though to go far in it without wandering, there was needed a greater knowledge of the formation of character, and of the consequences of actions upon the agent's own frame of mind, than Bentham possessed. His want of power to estimate this class of consequences, together with his want of the degree of modest deference which, from those who have not competent experience in their own, is due to the experience of others on that part of the subject, greatly limit the values of his speculations on questions of practical ethics.

He is chargeable also with another error, which it would be improper to pass over, because nothing has tended more to place him in opposition to the common feelings of mankind, and to give to his philosophy that cold, mechanical, and ungenial air which characterizes the popular idea of a Benthamite. This error, or rather one-sidedness, belongs to him not as a utilitarian, but as a moralist by profession, and in common with almost all professed moralists, whether religious or philosophical: it is that of treating the *moral* view of actions and characters, which is unquestionably the first and most important mode of looking at them, as if it were the sole one: whereas it is only one of three, by all of which our sentiments towards the human being may be, ought to be, and without entirely crushing our own nature cannot but be, materially influenced. Every human action has three aspects: its *moral* aspect, or that of its *right* and *wrong*; its *aesthetic* aspect, or that of its *beauty*; its *symphathetic* aspect, or that of its *loveableness*. The first addresses itself to our reason and conscience; the second to our imagination; the third to our human fellow-feeling. According to the first, we approve or disapprove; according to the second, we admire or despise; according to the third, we love, pity, or dislike. The morality of an action depends on its foreseeable consequences; its beauty, and its loveableness, or the reverse, depend on the qualities which it is evidence of. Thus, a lie is *wrong*, because its effect is to mislead, and because it tends to destroy the confidence of man in man; it is also *mean,* because it is cowardly—because it proceeds from not daring to face the consequences of telling the truth—or at best is evidence of want of that *power* to compass our ends by straightforward means, which is conceived as properly belonging to every person not deficient in energy or in understanding. The action of Brutus in sentenc-

ing his sons was *right,* because it was executing a law essential to the
freedom of his country, against persons of whose guilt there was no doubt:
it was *admirable,* because it evinced a rare degree of patriotism, courage,
and self-control; but there was nothing *loveable* in it; it affords either no
presumption in regard to loveable qualities, or a presumption of their
deficiency. If one of the sons had engaged in the conspiracy from affection for the other, his action would have been loveable, though neither
moral nor admirable. It is not possible for any sophistry to confound
these three modes of viewing an action; but it is very possible to adhere
to one of them exclusively, and lose sight of the rest. Sentimentality consists in setting the last two of the three above the first; the error of moralists in general, and of Bentham, is to sink the two latter entirely. This is
pre-eminently the case with Bentham: he both wrote and felt as if the
moral standard ought not only to be paramount (which it ought), but to
be alone; as if it ought to be the sole master of all our actions, and even
of all our sentiments; as if either to admire or like, or despise or dislike a
person for any action which neither does good nor harm, or which does
not do a good or a harm proportioned to the sentiment entertained, were
an injustice and a prejudice. He carried this so far, that there were certain
phrases which, being expressive of what he considered to be this groundless liking or aversion, he could not bear to hear pronounced in his
presence. Among these phrases were those of *good* and *bad taste.* He
thought it an insolent piece of dogmatism in one person to praise or condemn another in a matter of taste: as if men's likings and dislikings, on
things in themselves indifferent, were not full of the most important
inferences as to every point of their character; as if a person's tastes did
not show him to be wise or a fool, cultivated or ignorant, gentle or rough,
sensitive or callous, generous or sordid, benevolent or selfish, conscientious
or depraved.

HEGEL

Modern totalitarianism—both the communist and fascist varieties—traces some of its principal origins to Hegel (see page 2). Marx himself evolved from orthodox Hegelianism to a position of qualified and transformed Hegelianism, claiming that he had "put Hegel upside down," although it could be argued that Hegel upside down is still Hegel. Marx's loyal friend and collaborator, Friedrich Engels (1820–1895), critically examines the place of Hegel in German and European philosophy in his study of *Ludwig Feuerbach and the Outcome of Classical German Philosophy* (1888). Engels was the son of a wealthy German textile manufacturer with business interests in England. While passing through Paris in 1844, Engels met Karl Marx, and out of that meeting a life-long friendship developed, in which Engels served not only as an intellectual and political collaborator and adviser, but also as the main financial provider for Marx, enabling him to carry on his scholarly and political activities. In 1850 Engels returned to England for good and spent there the rest of his life. While overshadowed by Marx in intellect and personality, Engels made important contributions to Marxian communism, and his modesty, loyalty, and generosity made him one of the most revered figures in the international labor movement. His first important work was on *The Condition of the Working Class in England in 1844* (1845), an indictment of early capitalism, but still a classic in the historical study of working conditions in modern industrial civilization. He collaborated with Marx in the writing of the *Communist Manifesto* (1848) and later turned his main attention to the elaboration of dialectical materialism and other philosophical aspects of Marxism in *Landmarks of Scientific Socialism* (1878) and *The Origin of the Family, Private Property, and the State* (1884).

The relation of Hegelianism to German militarism and authoritarianism is examined by George Santayana (1863–1952), American philosopher, essayist, novelist, and poet, in his *Egotism in German Philosophy* (1916). Although published at the height of World War I, *Egotism in German Philosophy* was more than a "war book." Probing deeply into the issues of the war, Santayana was less interested in the immediate political, dynastic, economic, and colonial issues than in the underlying long-range intellectual and moral forces that had shaped modern Germany. The conflict between German philosophy and Western thought seemed to Santayana the real issue of the war, as was seen again in World War II. Santayana was born in Madrid, and came to the United States at the age of nine. After graduating from Harvard, he taught in its department of philosophy from 1889 until 1912, but later returned to Europe, where he finally settled in Rome. His major works include *The Life of Reason* (1905–1906), *The Realms of Being* (4 vols., 1927–1940), and *Dominations and Powers* (1951).

Engels on HEGEL

Just as in France in the eighteenth century, so in Germany in the nineteenth, a philosophical revolution ushered in the political collapse. But how different the two appeared! The French were in open combat against all official science, against the Church and often also against the state; their writings were printed across the frontier, in England or Holland, while they themselves were often in jeopardy of imprisonment in the Bastille. On the other hand, the Germans were professors, state-appointed instructors of youth; their writings were recognized textbooks, and the terminating system of the whole development—the Hegelian system—was even raised, in some degree, to the rank of a royal Prussian philosophy of state! Was it possible that a revolution could hide behind these professors, be-

[From Friedrich Engels, *Ludwig Feuerbach and the Outcome of Classical German Philosophy* (1888).]

hind their obscure, pedantic phrases, their wearisome, ponderous sentences? Were not precisely those people who were then regarded as the representatives of the revolution, the liberals, the bitterest opponents of this brain-confusing philosophy? But what neither the government nor the liberals were able to see was seen at least by one man as early as 1833, and this man was indeed none other than Heinrich Heine.

Let us take an example. No philosophical proposition has earned more gratitude from narrow-minded governments and wrath from equally narrow-minded liberals than Hegel's famous statement: "All that is real is rational; and all that is rational is real." That was tangibly a sanctification of things that be, a philosophical benediction bestowed upon despotism, police-government, Star Chamber proceedings and censorship. That is how Frederick William III and his subjects understood it. But according to Hegel certainly not everything that exists is also real, without further qualification. For Hegel the attitude of reality belongs only to that which at the same time is necessary: "In the course of its development reality proves to be necessity." A particular governmental act—Hegel himself cites the example of "a certain tax regulation"—is therefore for him by no means real without qualification. That which is necessary, however, proves itself in the last resort to be also rational; and, applied to the Prussian state of that time, the Hegelian proposition therefore merely means: this state is rational, corresponds to reason, in so far as it is necessary; and if it nevertheless appears to us to be evil, but still, in spite of its evil character, continues to exist, then the evil character of the government is justified and explained by the corresponding evil character of its subjects. The Prussians of that day had the government that they deserved.

Now, according to Hegel, reality is, however, in no way an attribute predicable of any given state of affairs, social or political, in all circumstances and at all times. On the contrary. The Roman Republic was real, but so was the Roman Empire, which superseded it. In 1789 the French monarchy had become so unreal, that is to say, so robbed of all necessity, so irrational, that it had to be destroyed by the Great Revolution—of which Hegel always speaks with the greatest enthusiasm. In this case the monarchy was the unreal and the revolution was the real. And so, in the course of development, all that was previously real becomes unreal, loses its necessity, its right of existence, its rationality. And in the place of moribund reality comes a new, viable reality—peacefully if the old has enough intelligence to go to its death without a struggle; forcibly if it resists this necessity. Thus the Hegelian proposition turns into its opposite through Hegelian dialectics itself: All that is real in the sphere of human history becomes irrational in the process of time, is therefore irrational already by its destination, is tainted beforehand with irrationality; and everything which is rational in the minds of men is destined to become real, however much it may contradict the apparent reality of existing conditions. In accordance with all the rules of the Hegelian method of thought, the proposition of the rationality of everything which is real resolves itself into the other proposition: All that exists deserves to perish.

But precisely here lay the true significance and the revolutionary character of the Hegelian philosophy (to which, as the close of the whole movement since Kant, we must here confine ourselves), that it once and for all dealt the deathblow to the finality of all products of human thought and action. Truth, the cognition of which is the business of philosophy, became in the hands of Hegel no longer an aggregate of finished dogmatic statements, which, once discovered, had merely to be learned by heart. Truth lay now in the process of cognition itself, in the long historical development of science, which mounts from lower to ever higher levels of knowledge without ever reaching, by discovering so-called absolute truth, a point at which it can proceed no further and where it would have nothing more to do than to fold its hands and admire the absolute truth to which it had attained. And what holds good for the realm of philosophic knowledge holds good also for that of every other kind of knowledge and also for practical affairs. Just as knowledge is unable to reach a perfected termination in a perfect, ideal condition of humanity, so is history unable to do so; a perfect society, a perfect "state," are things which can only exist in imagination. On the contrary, all successive historical situations are only transitory stages in the endless course of development of human society from the lower to the higher. Each stage is necessary, and therefore justified for the time and conditions to which it owes its origin. But in the newer and higher conditions which gradually develop in its own bosom, each loses its validity and justification. It must give way to a higher stage which will also in its turn decay and perish. Just as the bourgeoisie by large-scale industry, competition and the world market dissolves in practice all stable, time-honoured institutions, so this dialectical philosophy dissolves all conceptions of final, absolute truth and of absolute states of humanity corresponding to it. For it [dialectical philosophy] nothing is final, absolute, sacred. It reveals the transitory character of everything and in everything; nothing can endure before it except the uninterrupted process of becoming and of passing away, of endless ascendency from the lower to the higher. And dialectical philosophy itself is nothing more than the mere reflection of this process in the thinking brain. It has, of course, also a conservative side: it recognizes that definite stages of knowledge and society are justified for their time and circumstances; but only so far. The conservatism of this mode of outlook is relative; its revolutionary character is absolute—the only absolute dialectical philosophy admits.

It is not necessary, here, to go into the question of whether this mode of outlook is thoroughly in accord with the present position of natural science, which predicts a possible end for the earth, and for its habitability a fairly certain one; which therefore recognizes that for the history of humanity also there is not only an ascending but also a descending branch. At any rate we still find ourselves a considerable distance from the turning point at which the historical course of society becomes one of descent, and we cannot expect Hegelian philosophy to be concerned with a subject which natural science, in its time, had not at all placed upon the agenda as yet!

But what must, in fact, be said here is this: that in Hegel the views developed above are not so sharply delineated. It is a necessary conclusion from this method, but one which he himself never drew with such explicitness. And this, indeed, for the simple reason that he was compelled to make a system and, in accordance with all the traditional requirements, a system of philosophy must conclude with some sort of absolute truth. Therefore, however much Hegel, especially in his *Logic*, emphasized that this eternal truth is nothing but the logical, *i.e.*, the historical, process itself, he nevertheless finds himself compelled to supply this process with an end, just because he has to bring his system to a termination at some point or other. In his *Logic* he can make this end a beginning again, since here the point of conclusion, the absolute idea—which is only absolute in so far as he has absolutely nothing to say about it—"alienates," *i.e.*, transforms, itself into nature and comes to itself again later in the mind, *i.e.*, in thought and in history. But at the end of the whole philosophy a similar return to the beginning is possible only in one way, namely, by putting as the end of all history the arrival of mankind at the cognition of this self-same absolute idea, and by explaining that this cognition of the absolute idea is reached in Hegelian philosophy. In this way, however, the whole dogmatic content of the Hegelian system is declared to be absolute truth, in contradiction to his dialectical method, which dissolves all dogmatism. Thus the revolutionary side becomes smothered beneath the overgrowth of the conservative side. And what applies to philosophical cognition applies also to historical practice. Mankind, which, in the person of Hegel, has reached the point of working out the absolute idea, must also in practice have gotten so far that it can carry out this absolute idea in reality. Hence the practical political demands of the absolute idea on contemporaries may not be stretched too far. And so we find at the conclusion of the *Philosophy of Law* that the absolute idea is to be realized in that monarchy based on estates which Frederick William III so persistently but vainly promised to his subjects, *i.e.*, in a limited, moderate, indirect rule of the possessing classes suited to the petty-bourgeois German conditions of that time. Herewith also the necessity of the nobility is demonstrated to us in a speculative fashion.

The inner necessities of the system are therefore of themselves sufficient to explain why a thoroughly revolutionary method of thinking produced an extremely tame political conclusion. As a matter of fact the specific form of this conclusion springs from this, that Hegel was a German, and like his contemporary Goethe had a bit of the philistine's queue dangling behind. Each of them was an Olympian Zeus in his own sphere, yet neither of them ever quite freed himself from German philistinism.

But all this did not prevent the Hegelian system from covering an incomparably greater domain than any earlier system, nor from developing in this domain a wealth of thought which is astounding even today. The phenomenology of mind (which one may call a parallel of the embryology and palaeontology of the mind, a development of individual consciousness through its different stages, couched in the form of an abbreviated recapitulation of the stages through which the consciousness of man has passed in the course of history), logic, natural philosophy, philosophy of mind, and the latter worked out in its separate, historical sub-divisions: philosophy of history, of law, of religion, history of philosophy, aesthetics, etc.—in all these different historical fields Hegel laboured to discover and demonstrate the pervading thread of development. And as he was not only a creative genius but also a man of encyclopaedic erudition, he played an epoch-making role in every sphere. It is self-evident that owing to the needs of the "system" he very often had to resort to those forced constructions about which his pigmy opponents make such a terrible fuss even today. But these constructions are only the frame and scaffolding of his work. If one does not loiter here needlessly, but presses on farther into the immense building, one finds innumerable treasures which today still possess undiminished value. With all philosophers it is precisely the "system" which is perishable; and for the simple reason that it springs from an imperishable need of the human mind—the need to overcome all contradictions. But if all contradictions are once and for all disposed of, we shall have arrived at so-called absolute truth: world history will be at an end. And yet it has to continue, although there is nothing left for it to do—a new, insoluble contradiction. As soon as we have once realized—

and in the long run no one has helped us to realize it more than Hegel himself—that the task of philosophy thus stated means nothing but the task that a single philosopher should accomplish that which can only be accomplished by the entire human race in its progressive development— as soon as we realize that, there is an end of all philosophy in the hitherto accepted sense of the word. One leaves alone "absolute truth," which is unattainable along this path or by any single individual; instead, one pursues attainable relative truths along the path of the positive sciences, and the summation of their results by means of dialectical thinking. At any rate, with Hegel philosophy comes to an end: on the one hand, because in his system he comprehended its whole development in the most splendid fashion; and on the other hand, because, even if unconsciously, he showed us the way out of the labyrinth of systems to real positive knowledge of the world.

One can imagine what a tremendous effect this Hegelian system must have produced in the philosophy-tinged atmosphere of Germany. It was a triumphal procession which lasted for decades and which by no means came to a standstill on the death of Hegel. On the contrary, it was precisely from 1830 to 1840 that Hegelianism reigned most exclusively, and to a greater or lesser extent infected even its opponents. It was precisely in this period that Hegelian views, consciously or unconsciously, most extensively permeated the most diversified sciences and leavened even popular literature and the daily press, from which the average "educated consciousness" derived its mental pabulum. But this victory along the whole front was only the prelude to an internal struggle.

As we have seen, the doctrine of Hegel, taken as a whole, left plenty of room for giving shelter to the most diverse practical party views. And in the theoretical Germany of that time, two things above all were practical: religion and politics. Whoever placed the chief emphasis on the Hegelian *system* could be fairly conservative in both spheres; whoever regarded the dialectical *method* as the main thing could belong to the most extreme opposition, both in politics and religion. Hegel himself, despite the fairly frequent outbursts of revolutionary wrath in his works, seemed on the whole to be more inclined to the conservative side. Indeed, his system had cost him much more "hard mental plugging" than his method. Towards the end of the 'thirties, the cleavage in the school became more and more apparent. The Left wing, the so-called Young Hegelians, in their fight with the pietist orthodox and the feudal reactionaries, abandoned bit by bit that philosophical-aristocratic reserve in regard to the burning questions of the day which up to that time had secured state toleration and even protection for their teachings. And when, in 1840, orthodox pietism and absolutist feudal reaction ascended the throne with Frederick William IV, open partisanship became unavoidable. The fight was still carried on with philosophical weapons, but no longer for abstract philosophical aims. It turned directly on the destruction of traditional religion and of the existing state. And while in the *Deutsche Jahrbücher* the practical ends were still predominantly put forward in philosophical disguise, in the *Rheinische Zeitung* of 1842 the Young Hegelian school revealed itself directly as the philosophy of the aspiring radical bourgeoisie and still used the meagre cloak of philosophy only to deceive the censorship.

At that time, however, politics was a very thorny field, and hence the main fight came to be directed against religion; this fight, particularly since 1840, was indirectly also political. Strauss' *Life of Jesus*, published in 1835, had provided the first impulse. The theory therein developed of the formation of the gospel myths was combated later by Bruno Bauer with proof that a whole series of evangelical stories had been fabricated by the authors themselves. The controversy between these two was carried out in the philosophical disguise of a battle between "self-consciousness" and "substance." The question whether the miracle stories of the gospels came into being through an unconscious-traditional myth-creation, within the bosom of the community or whether they were fabricated by the evangelists themselves was magnified into the question whether, in world history, "substance" or "self-consciousness" was the decisive operative force. Finally came Stirner, the prophet of contemporary anarchism—Bakunin has taken a great deal from him—and capped the sovereign "self-consciousness" by his sovereign "ego."

We will not go further into this side of the decomposition process of the Hegelian school. More important for us is the following: the main body of the most determined Young Hegelians was, by the practical necessities of its fight against positive religion, driven back to Anglo-French materialism. This brought them into conflict with their school system. While materialism conceives nature as the sole reality, nature in the Hegelian system represents merely the "alienation" of the absolute idea, so to say, a degradation of the idea. At all events, thinking and its thought-product, the idea, is here the primary, nature the derived element, which only exists at all by the condescension of the idea. And in this contradiction they floundered as well or as ill as they could.

Then came Feuerbach's *Essence of Christianity*. With one blow it pulverized the contradiction, in that without circumlocutions it placed materialism on the throne again. Nature exists independently of all philosophy. It is the foundation upon which we human beings, ourselves products of nature, have grown up. Nothing exists outside nature and man, and the higher beings our religious fantasies have created are only the fantastic reflection of our own essence. The spell was broken; the "system" was exploded and cast aside, and the contradiction, shown to exist only in our imagination, was dissolved. One must himself have experienced the liberating effect of this book to get an idea of it. Enthusiasm was general; we all became at once Feuerbachians. How enthusiastically Marx greeted the new conception and how much—in spite of all critical reservations—he was influenced by it, one may read in *The Holy Family*.

Even the shortcomings of the book contributed to its immediate effect. Its literary, sometimes even highflown, style secured for it a large public and was at any rate refreshing after long years of abstract and abstruse Hegelianizing. The same is true of its extravagant deification of love, which, coming after the now intolerable sovereign rule of "pure reason," had its excuse, if not justification. But what we must not forget is that it was precisely these two weaknesses of Feuerbach that "true socialism," which had been spreading like a plague in "educated" Germany since 1844, took as its starting point, putting literary phrases in the place of scientific knowledge, the liberation of mankind by means of "love" in place of the emancipation of the proletariat through the economic transformation of production—in short, losing itself in the nauseous fine writing and ecstasies of love typified by Herr Karl Grün.

Another thing we must not forget is this: the Hegelian school was broken up, but Hegelian philosophy was not overcome through criticism; Strauss and Bauer each took one of its sides and set it polemically against the other. Feuerbach broke through the system and simply discarded it. But a philosophy is not disposed of by the mere assertion that it is false. And so powerful a work as Hegelian philosophy—which had exercised so enormous an influence on the intellectual development of the nation— could not be disposed of by simply being ignored. It had to be "sublated" in its own sense, that is, in the sense that while its form had to be annihilated through criticism, the new content which had been won through it had to be saved.

But in the meantime the Revolution of 1848 thrust the whole of philosophy aside as unceremoniously as Feuerbach had himself thrust aside Hegel. And in the process Feuerbach himself was also pushed into the background.

Santayana on HEGEL

When we are discussing egotism need we speak of Hegel? The tone of this philosopher, especially in his later writings, was full of contempt for everything subjective: the point of view of the individual, his opinions and wishes, were treated as of no account unless they had been brought into line with the providential march of events and ideas in the great world. This realism, pronounced and even acrid as it was, was still idealistic in the sense that the substance of the world was conceived to be not material but conceptual—a law or logic which animated phenomena and was the secret of their movement. The world was like a riddle or confused oracle; and the solution to the puzzle lay in the romantic instability or self-contradiction inherent in every finite form of being, which compelled it to pass into something different. The direction of this movement we might understand sympathetically in virtue of a sort of vital dialectic or dramatic necessity in our own reflection. Hegel was a solemn sophist: he made discourse the key to reality.

This technical realism in Hegel was reinforced by his historical imagination, which continually produces an impression of detachment, objectivity, and impersonal intelligence; he often seems to be lost in the events of his story and to be plucking the very heart out of the world. Again, he adored the State, by which in his view the individual should be entirely subjugated, not for the benefit of other individuals (that would be a sort of vicarious selfishness no less barren than private profit), but in the rapt service of common impersonal ends.

The family was a first natural group in which the individual should be happy to lose himself, the trade-guild was another, and the State was the highest and most comprehensive of all; there was nothing worthy or real in a man except his functions in society.

Nevertheless this denial of egotism is apparent only. It is a play within the play. On the smaller stage the individual—save for his lapses and stammerings—is nothing but the instrument and vehicle of divine decrees; in fact he is a puppet, and the only reality of him is the space he fills in the total spectacle. But that little stage is framed in by another, often overlooked, but ever present; and on this larger and nearer stage the ego struts alone. It is I that pull the strings, enjoy the drama, supply its plot

[From George Santayana, *Egotism in German Philosophy* (Charles Scribner's Sons, 1916). By permission.]

and moral, and possess the freedom and actuality which my puppets lack. On the little stage the soul of a man is only one of God's ideas, and his whole worth lies in helping out the pantomime; on the big stage, God is simply my idea of God and the purpose of the play is to express my mind. The spectacle in which every individual dances automatically to the divine tune is only my dream.

The philosophy of Hegel is accordingly subjective and all its realism is but a pose and a tone wilfully assumed. That this is the truth of the matter might be inferred, apart from many continual hints and implications, from the fact that the system is transcendental and founded on Kant. Objectivity can, therefore, be only a show, a matter of make-believe, something imputed to things and persons by the mind, whose poetic energies it manifests. Everything must be set down as a creation of mind, simply because it is an object of thought or knowledge.

This underlying subjectivism also explains the singular satisfaction of Hegel, whose glance was comprehensive enough, with so strangely limited a world as he describes to us. He described what he knew best or had heard of most, and felt he had described the universe. This illusion was inevitable, because his principle was that the universe was created by description and resided in it. The mission of Hegel, as he himself conceived it, was not to discover the real world or any part of it: in theory he retracted all belief in a real world and set in its place his conception or knowledge of it—therefore quite adequate to its object. If China was the oldest country he had heard of, the world began with China, and if Prussia was the youngest and he (as he had to be) its latest philosopher, the world ended with Prussia and with himself. This seems a monstrous egotism, but it is not arbitrary; in one sense it was the least pretentious of attitudes, since it was limited to the description of a current view, not of a separate or prior object. The value of a philosophy could lie only in the fullness and fidelity with which it might focus the conceptions of the age in which it arose. Hegel hoped to do this for his own times; he did not covet truth to anything further.

The same attitude explains the servility of his moral philosophy, which is simply an apology for the established order of things and for the prejudices of his time and country. His deepest conviction was that no system of ethics could be more, and if it tried to be more would be less, because it would be merely personal. When, for instance, he condemned harshly the Roman *patria potestas* it was because it offended the individualism of the Protestant and modern conscience; and if in the next breath he condemned even more harshly the sentimentalists who made tender feeling and good intentions the test of virtue, it was because these individual consciences absolved themselves from conformity to the established Church and State. To inquire whether in itself or in respect to human economy generally, the morality of Buddha, or Socrates, or Rousseau was the best would have seemed to him absurd: the question could only be what approaches or contributions each of these made to the morality approved by the Lutheran community and by the Prussian ministry of education and public worship. The truth, then as now, was whatever every good German believed. This pious wish of Hegel's to interpret the orthodoxy of his generation was successful, and the modest hopes of his philosophy were fulfilled. Never perhaps was a system so true to its date and so false to its subject.

The egotism of Hegel appears also in his treatment of mathematical and physical questions. The infinite he called the false infinite, so as to avoid the dilemmas which it placed him in, such as why the evolution of the Idea began six thousand years ago, or less; what more could happen now that in his self-consciousness that evolution was complete; why it should have gone on in this planet only, or if it had gone on elsewhere also, why the Idea evolving there might not have been a different Idea. But all such questions are excluded when one understands that this philosophy is only a point of view: the world it describes is a vista not separable from the egotistical perspectives that frame it in. The extent of the world need not be discussed, because that extent is an appearance only; in reality the world has no extent, because it is only my present idea.

The infinite thus lost its application; but the word was too idealistic to be discarded. Accordingly the title of true infinite was bestowed on the eventual illusion of completeness, on an alleged system of relations out of relation to anything beyond. That nothing existent, unless it was the bad infinite, could be absolute in this manner did not ruffle Hegel, for the existent did not really concern him but only 'knowledge,' that is, a circle of present and objectless ideas. Knowledge, however limited in fact, always has the completeness in question for the egotist, whose objects are not credited with existing beyond himself. Egotism could hardly receive a more radical expression than this: to declare the ego infinite because it can never find anything that is beyond its range.

The favourite tenet of Hegel that everything involves its opposite is also a piece of egotism; for it is equivalent to making things conform to words, not words to things; and the ego, particularly in philosophers, is a nebula of words. In defining things, if you insist on defining them, you are constrained to define them by their relation to other things, or even exclusion of them. If, therefore, things are formed by your definitions of them, these relations and exclusions will be the essence of things. The notion of such intrinsic relativity in things is a sophism even in logic, since elementary terms can never be defined yet may be perfectly well understood and arrested in intuition; but what here concerns us is rather the egotistical motive behind that sophism: namely, that the most verbal and subjective accidents to which the names of things are subject in human discourse should be deputed to be the groundwork of the things and their inmost being.

Egotistical, too, was Hegel's tireless hatred of what he called the abstract understanding. In his criticisms of this faculty and the opinions it forms there is much keenness and some justice. People often reason in the abstract, floating on words as on bladders: in their knowingness they miss the complexity and volume of real things. But the errors or abuses into which verbal intelligence may fall would never produce that implacable zeal with which Hegel persecutes it. What obsesses him is the fear that, in spite of its frivolity, the understanding may some day understand; that it may correct its inadequacies, trace the real movement of things, and seeing their mechanism lose that *effet d'ensemble*, that dramatic illusion, which he calls reason.

Imagine a landscape-painter condemned to have a naturalist always at his elbow: soon it would not be merely the errors of the naturalist that would irritate him, but the naturalist himself. The artist intent on panoramic effects does not wish to be forced to look through a microscope; in changing his focus he loses his subjective object: not reality but appearance is the reality for him. Hegel, since it was his mission to substitute so-called knowledge for being, had to go further; he had to convince himself, not only that the structure of nature discovered by the understanding was irrelevant to his own conceptual mythology, but that such a structure did not exist. He was not willing to confess (as the landscape-painter might) that he *was* an egotist; that it was the subjective that interested him, and that in so great a world the subjective too has its place. No! he must pretend that his egotism was not egotism, but identity with the absolute, and that those who dared to maintain that the world wagged in its own way, apart from the viewing mind, were devils, because they suggested that the viewing mind was not God.

It is this latent but colossal egotism that makes plausible the strange use which Hegel sometimes makes of the word substance. His substance is but his grammar of discourse; for he was not looking for substance, in which he could not consistently believe, but only for the ultimate synthetic impression which he might gather from appearances. For the theatre-goer, the function of scenery and actors is that they should please and impress him: but what, in the end, impresses and pleases him? The cumulative burden and force of the play; the enhanced life which it has stimulated in himself. This, for that ruthless egotist, the aesthete, is the *substance* of all things theatrical. Of course, in fact, nothing could be falser, for the author and actors are real people, with lives far outrunning their function in the theatre and truly grounding it. Even the stage machinery has its natural history, and the artisans who made it have theirs, both full of mute inglorious tragedies. These real substances behind his entertainment the spectator, in his aesthetic egotism, laughs at as irrelevant; for him, as for Hamlet, the play's the thing. What is most his own, his imaginative reaction on the spectacle, the terms in which he finds it easiest and most exciting to describe it, he calls the substance of it: a term which betrays the profound impudence of the deliberate egotist; the deepest reality he will recognize is merely specious, existing only for the mind that imagines it. What is supposed to rescue the system of Hegel from subjectivism is the most subjective of things—a dialectic which obeys the impulses of a theoretical *parti pris*, and glorifies a fixed idea.

When we have understood all this, those traits of Hegel's which at first sight seem least egotistical—his historical insight and his enthusiasm for organized society—take on a new colour. That historical insight is not really sympathetic; it is imperious, external, contemptuous, feigned. If you are a modern reading the Greeks, especially if you read them in the romantic spirit of Goethe's classicism, and know of them just what Hegel knew, you will think his description wonderfully penetrating, masterly, and complete: but would Aeschylus or Plato have thought it so? They would have laughed, or rather they would not have understood that such a description referred to them at all. It is the legend of the Greeks, not the life of the Greeks, that is analysed by him. So his account of medieval religion represents the Protestant legend, not the Catholic experience. What we know little or nothing about seems to us in Hegel admirably characterized: what we know intimately seems to us painted with the eye of a pedantic, remote, and insolent foreigner. It is but an idea of his own that he is foisting upon us, calling it our soul. He is creating a world in his head which might be admirable, if God had made it.

Every one is subject to such illusions of perspective and to the pathos of distance, now favourable, now unfavourable to what he studies; but Hegel, thinking he had the key to the divine design, fancied himself deeply sympathetic because he saw in everything some fragment of himself. But no part of the world was that; every part had its own inalienable superiority, which to transcend was to lose for ever. To the omniscient egotist every heart is closed. The past will never give away its secret except to some self-forgetful and humble lover who by nature has a kindred destiny. The egotist who thinks to grasp it, so as to serve it up at his philosophic banquet, or exhibit it in his museum of antiquities, grasps only himself; and in that sense, to his confusion, his egotism turns out true.

The egotism that appears in this lordly way of treating the past is egotism of the imagination, the same that was expressed in the romantic love of nature, which was really a very subtle, very studious, very obstinate love of self, intent on finding some reference and deference to oneself in everything. But there is also an egotism of passion, which in Hegel appears in his worship of the state. 'The passions' is the old and fit name for what the Germans call ideals. The passions are not selfish in the sense in which the German moralists denounce selfishness; they are not contrived by him who harbours them for his ulterior profit. They are ideal, dangerous, often fatal. Even carnal passions are not selfish, if by the self we understand the whole man: they are an obsession to which he sacrifices himself. But the transcendental philosophy with its migratory ego can turn any single passion, or any complex of passions, into a reputed centre of will, into a moral personage. As the passion usurps more and more of the man's nature it becomes a fierce egotist in his place; it becomes fanaticism or even madness.

This substitution of a passion for a man, when nobody thought the ego migratory, seemed a disease. What folly, we said to the human soul, to sacrifice your natural life to this partial, transitory, visionary passion! But the German idealist recognises no natural life, no natural individual. His ego can migrate into any political body or any synthetic idea. Therefore, his passions, far from seeming follies to him, seem divine inspirations, calls to sacrifice, fidelities to the ideal.

I am far from wishing to say that a German idealist is commonly just to all the passions and raises them in turn to be his highest and absolute will. His passions are generally few and mental. Accidents of training or limitations of temperament keep him respectable; but he is never safe. Dazzle him with a sophism, such, for instance, as that 'the more evil the more good,' or hypnotize him with a superstition, such as that 'organization is an end in itself,' and nothing more is needed to turn him into a romantic criminal.

Even the absolute requires an enemy to whet its edge upon, and the State, which according to Hegel is morally absolute, requires rival states in order that its separate individuality may not seem to vanish, and with it the occasion for blessed and wholesome wars. Hegel rejects the notion that nations have any duties to one another because, as he asserts, there is no moral authority or tribunal higher than the State, to which its government could be subject. This assertion is evidently false, since in the first place there is God or, if the phrase be preferred, there is the highest good of mankind, hedging in very narrowly the path that states should follow between opposite vices; and in the second place there is the individual, whose natural allegiance to his family, friends, and religion, to truth and to art, is deeper and holier than his allegiance to the State, which for the soul of man is an historical and geographical accident. No doubt at the present stage of civilization there is more to be gained than lost by co-operating loyally with the governments under which we happen to live, not because any state is divine, but because as yet no less cumbrous machinery is available for carrying on the economy of life with some approach to decency and security. For Hegel, however, the life of the State was the moral substance, and the souls of men but the accidents; and as to the judgment of God, he asserted that it was none other than the course of history. This is a characteristic saying, in which he seems to proclaim the moral government of the world, when in truth he is sanctifying a brutal law of success and succession. The best government, of course, succumbs in time like the worst, and sooner; the dark ages followed upon the Roman Empire and lasted twice as long. But Hegel's God was simply the world, or a formula supposed to describe the world. He despised every ideal not destined to be realized on earth, he respected legality more than justice, and extant institutions more than moral ideals; and he wished to flatter a government in whose policy war and even crime were recognized weapons.

This reign of official passion is not, let me repeat, egotism in the natural man who is subject to it; it is the sacrifice of the natural man and of all men to an abstract obsession, called an ideal. The vice of absoluteness and egotism is transferred to that visionary agent. The man may be docile and gentle enough, but the demon he listens to is ruthless and deaf. It forbids him to ask, 'At what price do I pursue this ideal? How much harm must I do to attain this good?' No; this imperative is categorical. The die is cast, the war against human nature and happiness is declared, and an idol that feeds on blood, the Absolute State, is set up in the heart and over the city.

21 | COLE

OWEN

The filial link between socialism and capitalism can be illustrated by the fact that the first modern socialist was a wealthy and successful capitalist, Robert Owen (1771–1858). Generally regarded as the founder of British socialism, Owen was also the first to use the word "socialism." A self-made capitalist, he had made a fortune by the age of forty. His views were the result, not (like Marx's) of study in the British Museum, but of experience in his own industrial enterprises. He was no refugee from his own society, as were Marx and Lenin later, but a respectable, wealthy man, who dedicated his best-known book, *A New View of Society* (1813), to His Royal Highness, the Prince Regent of the British Empire. Far from looking upon capitalist Britain as a dungeon of inhumanity, he described the British constitution as being "among the best devised and most enlightened that have hitherto been established," and, strongly rejecting change by revolution, he thought that the British constitution was "admirably adapted" to gradual and progressive reform of unjust social and economic conditions. Realizing that love and fellowship cannot be conceived in hatred and born in strife, Owen hoped for cordial cooperation and unity of action between the Government, Parliament, the Church, and the People. A believer in the individualist principle of self-help, Owen started the cooperative movement and supported the incipient trade unions springing up throughout England and Scotland. In his search for a socialist cooperative commonwealth, he never faltered in his conviction, central also in the liberal-capitalist tradition, that important change must originate in society rather than in the state.

The antistatist conception of Owenite socialism was revived in this century—albeit along different lines—by the foremost biographer of Owen, G. D. H. Cole (1889–   ), in *Social Theory* (1920) and *Guild Socialism Restated* (1920). Cole started out as a philosopher and then moved on to economics, history, and political theory. One of the most prolific writers of his age (his books include numerous novels of mystery and detection), Cole exercised considerable influence on the generation that grew up between World Wars I and II. He also took part in public affairs and served as the chairman of the Fabian Society from 1939 to 1946. His book on *Robert Owen* (1925) is the standard work on the subject, and he deals again with Robert Owen in *Persons and Periods* (1938), which appraisal is reproduced below. In the nineteen-thirties and forties Cole seemed to adopt a more statist conception of socialism, but after the experiences of nationalization under Labor governments (1945–1951), he became aware of the dangers of statism and gradually returned to a philosophy of socialism which was clearly indebted to Owen.

Cole on OWEN

Robert Owen, shop-boy and manufacturer, factory reformer and educationist, Socialist and Co-operative pioneer, Trade Union leader and secularist, founder of ideal communities and practical man of business, was something of a puzzle to his own generation, and is no less a puzzle to posterity. Surely no man ever founded so many movements, and yet had so simple and unvarying a body of ideas. Surely no man was ever at once so practical and so visionary, so lovable and so impossible to work with, so laughed at and yet so influential. And there are few men who are so much talked about, and whose works are so little read.

There is a reason for this. Owen wrote voluminously, and often ill. He lived to be eighty-seven, and he was writing steadily up to the last weeks of his life. But of his later works, which make up the great bulk of his writings, by far the larger part is valueless. Owen said what he had to say in his earlier books; his later works are merely more and more elaborate and prosy repetitions of his better writings. There is but one

[From G. D. H. Cole, *Persons and Periods* (The Macmillan Company, 1938). By permission.]

exception: his Life of himself, of which he completed only a first volume, is delightfully fresh and attractive—the best and most readable of all his books, though it was published in his eighty-sixth year. It can best be read as a companion volume to his expository writings; for it gives Owen's own version of the circumstances which attended their issue.

With this one exception, all Owen's later works can be disregarded, except by the specialist. Indeed, one volume, even one slender volume, is enough to contain all the best of Owen's writings with the exception of his unfinished Autobiography. And all that need be included in such a volume was issued within a space of eight years. The opening essay of the *New View of Society* appeared in 1813, and the *Report to the County of Lanark* in 1821. In these eight years Robert Owen made his essential contribution to human knowledge. And, incidentally out of his work during these years arose in Great Britain the two great movements of Socialism and Co-operation.

In order to understand Owen's doctrines aright, it is necessary to know something both of the man himself and of the circumstances in which his ideas were developed. Owen was born in 1771, and the years of his manhood coincided with the most critical years of the great social change which we call the "Industrial Revolution." And his doctrines were above all designed as answers to the vast social and economic problems which the Industrial Revolution had raised up.

Let us begin with the man himself. Robert Owen was born in Newtown, Montgomeryshire, in Central Wales, on the Upper Severn. His father was a saddler and ironmonger, and also the local postmaster. Owen was a weakly boy, much given to introspection, but intelligent beyond his fellows. He was only seven years old when he became a sort of pupil-teacher in the local school. At nine, he left school and began work as shop-boy in a neighbour's shop. At ten, after a brief visit to London, he was apprenticed to a draper in good business at Stamford in Lincolnshire. There he remained three years, and then became assistant at a draper's in London. A year later he migrated to Manchester, and for four years was assistant there in a good drapery house. Then, at eighteen, his chance came, and the boy set up in business for himself.

Manchester, which was to be the scene of Owen's first considerable successes, was then at the height of a great and rapid industrial transformation. The great inventions of Hargreaves, Arkwright, and Crompton were in process of revolutionising the methods of cotton manufacture, and new factories for preparing, roving and spinning the cotton were springing up right and left. It was a time when great fortunes were to be made by the fortunate and the adventurous; and young Owen seized his chance.

He began business for himself, with a borrowed hundred pounds, in partnership with a mechanic who knew how to make certain of the new machines. Before long his partner left him, in search of a better-equipped colleague, and Owen was left on his own. No longer able to make machines, he set out to use those which remained in his hands. He succeeded; but within a few months a better chance came his way. The position of manager to one of the largest and best-equipped spinning mills in Lancashire fell vacant, and Owen, still under twenty, was appointed, at a salary of three hundred a year—a handsome remuneration in those days. At twenty he found himself in full charge of a factory in which five hundred workers were employed.

Again Owen made good. The products of his factory became well known for excellence in the trade, not only in Manchester but as far away as Glasgow. His employer, a Mr. Drinkwater, offered him a partnership; but difficulties arose, and instead Owen entered into partnership with two younger men who were starting a new company for the manufacture of yarn. He remained for some years in sole control of the new mill, and then on behalf of his company acquired from David Dale, whose daughter he soon afterwards married, the famous New Lanark Mills, the largest and best equipped spinning mills in Scotland.

This bald summary does far less than justice to the romance of Owen's early career. Every episode in it was an adventure, through which he climbed steadily to a further success. At twenty-eight, when he became managing partner in the New Lanark establishment, Owen was already a wealthy manufacturer according to the standards of the times, and bade fair to be before long very wealthy indeed.

Owen was by now well known as a successful business man; but, beyond a small circle of friends, that was his only claim to distinction. He had, indeed, as a leading member of the Manchester Literary and Philosophic Society, given utterance to some peculiar opinions on the subject of religion and the formation of character; but these did not appear to possess any special significance in relation to his business. Only when he was established at New Lanark did it appear that he was aiming at something very much bigger than mere money-making or business success.

Owen remained at New Lanark for more than a quarter of a century. He made of it not only a most successful commercial establishment, but a show place which visitors came from all over the world to see. Through all the successive partnerships in which he was associated—and he quarrelled with each group of partners in turn because they would not give him full freedom to follow out his ideas—he aimed at making New Lanark, not merely an efficient factory, but a well-governed human community based on his ideals. The manufacturer of those days—especially when his factory stood in an isolated place—had a tremendous hold over his employees. The houses in which they lived, the shops at which they bought their provisions, the entire village as well as the factory belonged to the employer, who gathered together his force of labourers from far and near, and could rule over them as a benevolent or malevolent despot. Owen had a high idea of the duties which this vast power entailed. In his view, the employer had no right merely to treat his employees as a means to profit. It was his duty to ensure to them all the means of good living—to pay good wages, to avoid unreasonably long hours of work, to provide good houses and good food and clothing at reasonable prices, to make the factory village a sanitary and a pleasant place, and, above all, to ensure to the children, whether employed in the factory or not, the best education that sympathy and knowledge could place at their command. In his later partnerships, when he was in a position to make his own terms, Owen strictly limited the reward of capital to a fixed amount, and insisted that all surplus profits should be applied to the provision of communal services on the employees' behalf.

At New Lanark, Owen paid better wages, worked shorter hours, and gave infinitely better conditions than most of his competitors. He abolished all "pauper apprentice" labour immediately on assuming control, and refused to employ children at less than ten years of age when others were freely working them intolerably long hours at less than six years old. And yet he had no difficulty in making the factory pay, despite the large sums he was constantly spending on all manner of improvements and amenities. In short, he gave an astonishingly convincing demonstration of what later generations have called the "economy of high wages," at a time when appalling under-payment and over-work were almost everywhere regarded as the indispensable conditions of commercial success.

Owen's earlier writings, such as the *New View of Society* and the *Address to the Inhabitants of New Lanark*, reflect this phase of his career. And they make it clear that there was already a quite definite theory behind his activities. He did what he did because he believed that in no other way could the foundations of a reasonable social order be truly laid. His main purpose, he insisted throughout, was educational. There was no way of making good citizens except by educating men and women so as to make them such. And there was no way of so educating them save by providing an environment in which their better natures would be encouraged to grow, and body and mind together be well cared for and trained in right habits and ways of living.

"Man's character is made for, and not by, him," Owen was never weary of proclaiming; and his whole system at New Lanark was based on this belief. What appalled him about the new "manufacturing system" was not only its inhumanity, but also that it seemed to him to result in a perversion of the characters of those who were subjected to its rule. What chance had the child, forced into the factory at a tender age and there remorselessly compelled to labour under rigid discipline for the profits of others, of becoming a good citizen? What sort of civic virtues was the rule of unlimited competition and "devil take the hindmost" likely to breed up in both master and man? The child should not labour at all until it had been thoroughly grounded by education in right social principles. When it did go to work, the labour must be suited to its years, and animated by a social, instead of a competitive, motive. And education, while it must begin with the child, must not stop with the child; it must continue throughout life. Above all, a man's occupation has so strong an influence on his character that, if the factory is wrongly organised so as to appeal to the wrong motives in men, the whole of society will be poisoned by it.

It is important to understand exactly what Owen meant by his view of human character. He did not mean, as some people have supposed, that man's individuality has no real existence, or that the individual is merely the result of the circumstances in which he has been placed. On the contrary, he insisted strongly on the importance of individuality and on the large differences between one man and another, and made these differences in individuality an essential foundation of the system of education which he established at New Lanark. He held, however, that each individual would react in a different way according to the environment in which he was placed, and that, in particular, men's social and ethical ideas—what, in effect, he meant by their "character"—were taken by them from the environment and the social and economic institutions under which they lived. Accordingly, he held that the evils which existed in the world of his own day, the competition between man and man which he regarded as the root of social antagonisms, and the competition between country and country which prevented concerted effort to develop the resources of the whole world in the common interests of its inhabitants, were the result of evil social institutions, including wrong traditional doctrines, and could be eradicated by a change in these institutions, including a change in men's beliefs. In particular he thought that the doctrine of individual responsibility, preached by the Churches, was a powerful influence in perpetuating social evils, because it led men to impute social misfortunes to individual sinfulness rather than to faulty social arrangements. This was the basis of his famous denunciation of all existing religions and of his attempt to create a new rational religion based on the denial of man's individual responsibility and the recognition that men's characters are formed for them and not by them. On this foundation too, he built up his system of education at New Lanark, and on the same principle the Owenites founded at a later period the numerous educational experiments which they carried on throughout the country in their Halls of Science.

Owen, then, set out to find a new basis for society in place of the existing competitive system, with the idea of establishing a set of social institutions on the basis of which men and nations would be brought to live in harmony one with another, and taught from infancy the moral doctrine of social co-operation. This was for him the significance of the Villages of Co-operation which, largely on the model of his own experiment at New Lanark, he proposed everywhere to establish. For he held that, if the basic unit of society came to be a small co-operative group working not for individual profit but for common service, this would effect a fundamental change in men's character and remove all danger of class rivalries within communities, or of war and competition between one community and another.

Although Owen ranks as the pioneer of the Co-operative Movement, he had little interest in consumers' co-operation as such. Indeed, at the outset the consumers' co-operative stores which grew up under the influence of his ideas, such as the famous Toad Lane Store of the Rochdale Pioneers of 1844, did not regard the retailing of goods on a non-profit-making basis as an end in itself, but only as a preparatory step towards the building-up among the members of a system of co-operative production and self-employment which would get rid of competition and the need for a separate employing class. The declared object, for example, of the Rochdale Pioneers, when they founded their store, was not shopkeeping on a mutual basis, but the building-up of a collective fund which could be subsequently used for co-operative production and ultimately for the establishment of an Owenite Co-operative Community.

These ideas of Owen's bear certain marked resemblances to the theory on which the Communists of the Soviet Union have been working of late in their plans of industrialisation, and above all in their intensive efforts to bring about the socialisation of agriculture. For the Russian experiment is not only, or even at bottom mainly, an attempt to raise the material standard of living of the Russian people, but far more an attempt to change the basis of men's thought by bringing them under the influence of a different social and economic environment. The Russians want, as Owen wanted, gradually to abolish the difference between town and country and the difference between industrial and agricultural conditions. They want to industrialise and collectivise agriculture because they believe that only by causing the peasants, as well as the industrial workers, to live in an environment of collective institutions based on co-operative rather than competitive principles can they hope to bring into existence a mental condition consistent with the successful functioning of a Communist community. In other words, they, like Owen, believe that man's "character," in the Owenite sense, is made for him and not by him, as the product of his social and economic environment. This doctrine, commonly regarded as distinctively Marxian, is in effect Owenite, and it is impossible to doubt that Marx, though he regarded Owen as a "Utopian" Socialist, owed far more to him in the formulation of the Materialist Conception of History than has generally been admitted. Owen, in this as in other respects, deserves much more credit than he has ever received as the true progenitor of modern Socialist ideas.

It can, no doubt, be urged that this root idea of Owenism concerning the influence of environment upon character was not original, and that Owen himself may have derived it largely from Godwin, who in turn was influenced by such eighteenth-century rationalists as d'Holbach and Helvetius. This is doubtless true, but the fact remains that Owen was the first person definitely to link up this doctrine of social determinism with economic conditions, and particularly with the new industrial system which was coming into existence in his day, and that he anticipated Marx in urging that the problems of the new industrialism demanded a co-operative rather than a competitive solution and accordingly a radical change from competition to co-operation as the basis of social institutions.

Owen lived on until 1858, and in his last years when his powers were failing became involved in spiritualist experiments. He had in fact finished his constructive work long before these later mental meanderings set in. His real importance to history is that, as an employer, he was the first man to demonstrate clearly the advantages of good wages and conditions and a pleasant hygienic factory environment; that, as an educationist, he was in many respects a pioneer of new methods which are only now beginning to find substantial recognition, especially in his insistence on the inadequacy of mere book teaching and the necessity of an appeal to the eye and ear of the child and on the immense formative importance of the earliest years of life; and, finally, that, as a Socialist and Co-operative thinker, he was the first person to formulate in the light of the new industrialism a doctrine plainly relating the possibilities of social and economic improvement to the material and mental environment in which men had to live, and to urge the necessity of a complete transformation of the social system based on the essentially co-operative character of modern large-scale processes of production.

We may think that, in the *New View of Society*, Owen pushed his view of the effect of environment on character too far. But it can hardly be disputed that, in the circumstances of his own time, his insistence on it was wholly salutary. Owen's contemporaries were for the most part acting on very different principles—treating the acquisition of wealth as the highest good, and justifying the most ruthless exploitation of labour by an appeal to that standard. By insisting that the acquisition of wealth on such terms might mean the destruction of men, Owen put forward a different ideal, and became the pioneer of new views both of education and of factory management. By common consent, the schools at New Lanark were pronounced the outstanding success of that astonishing factory. Both in ideas of education and in their practical working out Owen was far ahead of his time. He saw at once the inadequacy of Lancaster's monitorial system, and insisted that the first aim of education must be not to cram the memory but to equip the mind. He realised the limitations of books, especially in their appeal to the younger children, and the place of dancing, of physical exercises, of appeals to eye and ear in any sensible system of education. He trained his own teachers in his own methods, and raised up a host of disciples in his faith. And, above all, he realised that a tired mind cannot learn, and that long hours of toil are incompatible with the making of good citizens.

In all his work at New Lanark, Owen was doubtless very much the benevolent autocrat, whose word all men in his village were bound to obey. And, as he came to wish to apply his doctrines over a sphere wider than his own factory, he began to visualise a world made in the image of New Lanark. He had done wonders. Why should not others do as much? His employees were orderly, prosperous and happy. Why should other employers complain of the turbulence, laziness, drunkenness of their workers? Why should there be so much misery in the world? Need there be any misery at all, if the world would but follow his example?

So Owen became gradually the leader of a crusade. For more than twelve years after his coming to New Lanark he worked away quietly, testing his theories and gradually proving their soundness. Then he set to work to convert others. His *New View of Society* was his first effort at propaganda of his views. For it seemed to him that if he could but convince the world of his doctrine concerning the formation of character, everything else would follow as a matter of course. If the world knew that "man's character is formed for, and not by, him," it would cease to blame the poor for being what they were, and would set out to provide an en-

vironment in which they would speedily become, as the workers at New
Lanark were becoming under his guidance, industrious, prosperous, good
and happy. It would cease to blame the poor for their condition, and
would take the obvious steps necessary to improve it.

Side by side with this wider crusade, Owen set on foot another. He
began to work hard for a Factory Act which would prohibit the labour
of young children, regulate hours of work, and set up a State system of
factory inspection. Owen was the great pioneer of the movement for factory reform. Principally to his initiative the first Factory Act—that of
1819—was due, though he repudiated it as falling far short of what he
held to be both just and expedient.

Owen was engaged in this double crusade when the ending of the
Napoleonic wars ushered in a period of intense unemployment and economic crisis. "On the day the peace was signed," he wrote, "the great cus-
tomer of the producers died." Everywhere trade stagnated, thousands were
flung out of work, wages came tumbling down. Soon there were throughout the country mutterings of discontent from the starving operatives;
and before long the mutterings swelled to a mighty clamour. The workers
were driven in masses to the Poor Law for support; and the parishes, appalled at the heavy rates, barely kept them from sheer mass starvation.
The workers cried out for the Reform of Parliament as a means to the
redress of their grievances; the Government, fearing revolution, retaliated
with the "Peterloo" massacre, the Six Acts of 1819, and a general campaign of repression.

To Owen, meanwhile, it seemed as if the world had gone mad. He
had no belief in political reform as a means to the remedying of economic grievances; but the repression of the workers seemed to him utterly
beside the point. The thing to do was to remove the causes of distress,
instead of tinkering with its effects. As early as 1816 he developed, with
this end in view, the first outline of his famous "Plan," the germ of Socialism and of Co-operation, but in its first inception essentially a practical
scheme for relieving the economic distress of the years immediately after
the war.

The gist of Owen's plan can be very shortly stated. He proposed that,
instead of paying out doles, the Government should employ the poor in
"Villages of Co-operation" modelled on his own establishment at New
Lanark and, like it, essentially centres of social life and rational education
as well as of productive activity. These "Villages," Owen suggested, should
be in the main self-supporting. They should be agricultural as well as industrial, and should raise the produce needed for their own consumption,
exchanging their surplus products of different kinds one with another. As

they would be based on rational principles of education, they would not compete but co-operate one with another, and their aim would be as much to train good citizens as to relieve the necessities of the poor. If this were done, Owen argued, the need for poor rates would speedily disappear, and, by the same token, the foundations of a new and better social order for the whole community would speedily be laid.

This is the "Plan" which, with minor variations, is expounded in many of Owen's writings, but most fully and maturely in the *Report to the County of Lanark*. As Owen expounded it, the conception of it broadened out in his mind. He began by preaching it as a cure for unemployment; but soon he was putting it forward as a complete and immediately practicable social Utopia, destined speedily to sweep away capitalism and the competitive system, and to inaugurate for all the world a new era of peace and brotherhood based on a rational idea of the formation and development of human character under the influence of environment. "Any character from the best to the worst, from the most ignorant to the most enlightened, may be given to any community, even to the world at large, by applying certain means, which are to a great extent at the command, and under the control, or easily made so, of those who possess the government of nations." So Owen had written in his *New View of Society*; and in his "Plan" he was proposing the actual means by which the great change might be brought about.

There was, at the outset, nothing "Radical" or democratic in Owen's conception. He appealed for its execution to the Tory Government and the Unreformed Parliament. He enlisted for a time the respectful interest of Lord Sidmouth, the Tory Home Secretary and noted persecutor of Radicals. His projects were blessed by the Archbishop of Canterbury, and supported by the Duke of Kent. David Ricardo and other noted economists sat on a committee pledged to further his "Plan." As the famous and successful manufacturer of New Lanark, he received a respectful hearing in high quarters. But it was one thing to listen, and another to act; and, as the cries of distress and anger among the poor grew louder, the Government and the Parliament turned more and more from considering ways of relieving distress to taking measures for the suppression of disturbance and riot. Owen found himself less and less respectfully received; he made up his mind to appeal from the Government to the general public.

This wider appeal is embodied in the Addresses and Manifestos which Owen poured out one after another during the troublous years after 1815. In one of them occurs Owen's famous denunciation of all established religions as inveterate foes to the progress of mankind. There was nothing particularly novel in this declaration, save its outspokenness. All the religions, Owen held, treated man as a responsible agent—responsible for his own misdoings, whereas his faults of character and his sins were really the products of his environment, and could be washed away by a better moral and physical education. Owen had been preaching this doctrine for years, though he had never before declared so plainly his hostility to the Churches. But it was largely as a stick wherewith to beat his growingly unpopular social doctrines that the remark was seized upon, and quoted against him in every accent of horrified surprise. Owen suddenly ceased to be respectable; and, though some of his highly placed friends stood by him for a time, yet from the date of this declaration his main appeal was made in effect to the working class.

Indeed, it became clear within a few years that a section of the workers was almost alone in taking Owen seriously. For a time he had still a following among the middle and professional classes, and produced for their consumption successive elaborations of his "Plan," culminating in the famous *Report to the County of Lanark*. But gradually, in despair of seeing any practical outcome of his labours in Great Britain, he conceived the idea of trying out his schemes in the more congenial, because less contaminated, air of the New World. In 1824 Owen left for the United States, and there, the following year, he founded the Co-operative Community of New Harmony.

The story of that failure has been often told. How the settlers, a motley band of enthusiasts and adventurers of every sort, fell out among themselves, how the parent community broke into several lesser communities, how finally the communal basis of settlement was given up, and New Harmony relapsed into a successful pioneer town based on individual tenure, and how Owen, having sunk his whole fortune in the venture, emerged poor but not discouraged from its collapse, cannot here be described. It is enough to say that in 1829 Owen returned to Great Britain to find that the face of the world had greatly changed in his absence.

For now Owenism had attracted a new body of disciples, and these were chiefly found among the most intelligent leaders of the working class. The Combination Acts had been repealed in 1824, and a rapid growth of Trade Unionism had immediately followed. The great political uprising which culminated in the Reform Act of 1832 was nearing its height; but the workers were organising for industrial protection as well as for political agitation. There had begun too among the workers a growth of little Co-operative Societies and stores for mutual trading, explicitly based on Owen's teaching, and regarding themselves as forerunners of purely working-class "Villages of Co-operation" to be founded when the surplus funds accumulated through mutual trade grew large enough for so ambitious a venture.

After a momentary hesitation, Owen, who had by this time severed his connection with New Lanark and ceased to be an employer of labour, put himself at the head of the movement. All over the country his disciples set to work to bring the Trade Unions and other working-class bodies over to their way of thinking. John Doherty, the great Trade Union leader of the North and secretary of the Spinners, was a convinced Owenite. One after another, the Unions were converted: there was a rapid growth of Co-operative Stores, and many Unions set on foot Producers' Co-operative Societies of their own.

The Operative Builders' Union, the most powerful of the new Trade Unions which had sprung up during the excitements of the preceding years, went over completely to Owenism after Owen himself had addressed its national conference, ambitiously styled the "Builders' Parliament." Plans were made for basing on the Union a Grand National Guild of Builders, which was to dispense altogether with employers and new-fangled "building contractors," and to take the entire industry into its own hands. Moreover, in order to provide a market for the rapidly growing number of Producers' Co-operative Societies, or "Union Shops," Owen founded in 1832 his National Equitable Labour Exchange, of which branches were speedily opened in Birmingham, Liverpool, and Glasgow, as well as London. In these Exchanges, Owen's principle of "labour value," as expounded in his *Report to the County of Lanark*, was to be put into practice, and goods were to be exchanged for goods between the various groups of producers by means of "labour notes" standing for definite amounts of "labour time" embodied in each commodity.

Till the end of 1832 the preoccupation of the main body of the workers with the Reform struggle had delayed the growth of the movement. But thereafter disillusionment with the fruits of the political agitation, which had enfranchised the middle classes and left the workers voteless, had brought fresh recruits thronging into the Trade Unions and Owenite Societies. Political means having failed, the workers were minded to try Trade Unionism and Co-operation as the roads to social emancipation. By 1833 Owen found himself at the head of a huge working-class movement eagerly demanding a lead.

It was at this stage that most of the numerous Trade Unions which had come into being were organised under Owen's leadership into a Grand National Consolidated Trades Union with an Owenite programme. A little later, in the North, the Owenites, through the National

Regeneration Society, placed themselves at the head of a movement for factory reform and the eight-hour day, which they set out to secure not by legislation but by industrial action. The Grand National Consolidated Trades Union at the height of its influence in 1834 is said to have had over half a million members, and another half million are said to have been enrolled in Unions, such as the Builders' Union, which were working in association with it.

The Grand National Consolidated Trades Union, known to its contemporaries as *the Trades Union*, speedily came to be feared as a vast and potentially revolutionary uprising of the working class. For a while Owen dreamed great dreams. In 1816 it had seemed to him that, if only his "Plan" were adopted, the whole face of the world could be at once changed. The failure of New Harmony had not taught him to moderate his hopes; he had become steadily more Utopian and millennial as he grew older. Now, he proclaimed to the workers that by their might and rationality there should come speedily a great change by which all misery and poverty would at once be swept away.

How rapidly this great movement crumbled students of the history of the Trade Union movement are well aware. The Owenites had projected a General Strike, to be followed by the sudden and complete institution of the new Co-operative system which Owen had preached. But in fact the "Trades Union," as it was commonly called, soon found itself involved in a large number of sectional disputes, mostly lock-outs declared by employers who refused to employ anyone who admitted membership of the "Trades Union." Moreover, the trial and transportation for the administration of unlawful oaths of the Dorchester labourers who had formed a branch of the "Trades Union" indicated the readiness of the Government to go to all lengths in repressing the new movement. Under these blows the "Trades Union" rapidly crumbled away, and in the summer of 1834 Owen, realising its failure, decreed its dissolution. Thereafter Owen played little direct part in the fortunes of the organised working-class movement. For the rest of his life he devoted the whole of his energies to a social propaganda which became more and more ethical and rationalistic rather than directly political and industrial.

Within a year of its formation, the great Trades Union was shattered into a thousand fragments, and Owen had ceased to be the leader of the British working class. Within two years more, a new political agitation— the Chartist Movement—was arising, and the great Trade Union struggle of 1834 was no more than a memory.

Owenism, however, did not die. From one stream of Owenite influence sprang the modern Co-operative Movement; another went on to give birth to the Secularist agitation. Owen himself, turning more and more from reformer to prophet, became the apostle of a "Rational Religion" which was the forerunner of the modern Ethical movement. For more than twenty years longer he poured out books, pamphlets and magazines in an endless stream, and a body of faithful disciples continued to spread his gospel. But he was already an old man when the great Trades Union collapsed; and his later work was no more than a repetition of his earlier writings. The new Co-operative Colony, Queenwood, or Harmony Hall, which he founded in Hampshire in 1839, only repeated the failure of New Harmony in the 'twenties. Owen's real work was over in 1834.

I began by calling Robert Owen something of a puzzle. Leslie Stephen called him "one of those bores who are the salt of the earth." He was essentially a man of one idea, which he preached tirelessly, in and out of season, through the whole of his public life. In pursuit of this idea, practical business man though he had been, he lost all sense of the difference between conception and accomplishment. The millennium seemed to him always just round the next corner; he was endlessly and fatuously hopeful and sure of success. He aimed constantly at the impossible, and was never in the least deterred by failure from aiming at it again. Consequently he became, despite his early and outstanding successes, an exceedingly bad leader of men. He was, moreover, more than a little autocratic in his ways—a habit bred in him by his position of unquestioned command at New Lanark, and confirmed by his unswerving and absolute assurance of being on all occasions perfectly right.

This sounds an unlovable picture; and yet, by the general testimony of those who knew him, Owen was a most lovable man. He was utterly without taint of self-seeking, a real and feeling lover of his fellow men, an unfailing favourite with children. His own children loved him very dearly, and were ardent disciples of his doctrine. Perhaps the easiest answer to the riddle of his personality is that he was a little mad.

If there are grave faults to be found with Owen's practical qualities of leadership, and many failures to his record, few men of the nineteenth century have more solid achievements to their credit. It was a very great thing to have demonstrated, as he did in the worst days of the Industrial Revolution, that low wages, long hours, and bad conditions of labour were not the indispensable foundations of Britain's greatness. It was a fine thing to have realised the need for a liberalising education as the basis of a rational citizenship at a time when the Lancasterian monitorial system was regarded as the last word in progressive education for the poor. And it was a fine thing to have spoken, even for the time in vain, a word of hope and promise to the unfortunate victims of the Industrial Revolution, and to have set them building up their Trade Unions and their Co-operative Societies with a new vision of self-government and freedom before their eyes. Long before Carlyle or Ruskin, Owen looked upon the new world which the "Manchester School" was making, and called it "evil"; and his calling it so was the more remarkable because he was himself one of the most successful learners in that school. But Owen was greatest because he not only revolted against the horrors of the Industrial Revolution, but also sought a constructive way of escape. His Co-operative Colonies and his great Trades Union alike failed; but he laid the foundations on which a later generation was better able to build. Few men have exerted a wider or more beneficent influence; and none has been more whole-hearted in the service of his faith.

22 | **BRYCE**
LEROY

TOCQUEVILLE

The first major democracy in the modern world is that of the United States; only after its establishment and success could the issue of democracy be brought down from speculation to observation. The political writer in the nineteenth century first to perceive that democracy was the "irresistible" new form of society and government and that the United States was the world's key laboratory of democracy was an aristocratic Frenchman, Alexis de Tocqueville (1805–1859). His *Democracy in America* (1835) is generally conceded to be the greatest work on the United States written by a foreign observer, and it would be difficult to find a work of similar depth and penetration written by an American on his own country. The main theme of *Democracy in America* is the relation, and frequent antagonism, between liberty and equality in a democratic society; whereas enthusiastic democrats assumed that liberty would cease to be a serious issue in democracy, Tocqueville pointed out that democracy, by the very fact of solving the issue of equality, created new problems of liberty that had not hitherto existed. The despotism of monarchy and aristocracy may be replaced in democracy by the power of public opinion to suppress unpopular views, and much that Tocqueville said over a century ago about the "tyranny of the majority" as an inherent tendency in democracy has been validated by subsequent events on many an occasion. Yet Tocqueville was by no means pessimistc about the future of democracy: he felt that there was no going back, and that the process of democratic world revolution would eventually also embrace the economic sphere. Moreover, he prophetically predicted that by the middle of the twentieth century the United States and Russia would each "sway the destinies of half the globe," liberty being the principle of expanding American influence, whereas servitude would be the Russian means of expansion.

The traditional interpretation of Tocqueville as one of the great liberal thinkers of the nineteenth century is to be found in the appraisal of Tocqueville by James Bryce (1838–1922) in an essay on "The Predictions of Hamilton and De Tocqueville" (1887). Like Tocqueville, Bryce took an active part in politics and was one of the leaders of the Liberal party in England, eventually becoming a member of the British Cabinet and serving as British Ambassador to the United States. His numerous writings include the *History of the Holy Roman Empire* (1888), *Studies in History and Jurisprudence* (1901), *Modern Democracies* (2 vols., 1921), and *The American Commonwealth* (2 vols., 1888), still a landmark in the study of American government and politics and, next to Tocqueville's *Democracy in America*, the outstanding work on the United States by a foreign scholar and statesman.

A more critical interpretation of Tocqueville as an essentially conservative political thinker will be found in a French appraisal by Maxime Leroy of "Alexis de Tocqueville" (1935). Leroy (1873–   ), perhaps not unnaturally for a French critic, argues to a considerable extent on the basis of Tocqueville's position in French politics and his immediate influence on French political thought, whereas foreign students of Tocqueville have tended to emphasize the more universal and philosophical message of his ideas. A leading French student of labor and syndicalism, Leroy has made his greatest contribution to the history of political ideas, and his numerous books include studies of *Descartes* (1929), *The French Precursors of Socialism* (1948), and *History of Social Ideas in France* (3 vols., 1946–1954).

Bryce on TOCQUEVILLE

Fifty-one years after the recognition of the independence of the United States, fifty-three years before the present year, Alexis de Tocqueville published his *Democracy in America*, one of the few treatises on the philoso-

[From James Bryce, *The Predictions of Hamilton and De Tocqueville*, Johns Hopkins University Studies in Historical and Political Science (Fifth Series, IX, September, 1887).]

phy of politics which has risen to the rank of a classic. His book, therefore, stands half way between our own days and those first days of the Republic which we know from the writings of the Fathers, of Washington, Hamilton, Jefferson, Adams, Madison. It offers a means of measuring the changes that had passed on the country during the half century from the birth of the Union to the visit of its most famous European critic, and again from the days of that critic to our own.

It is a classic, and because it is a classic one may venture to canvas it freely, without the fear of seeming to detract from the fame of its author. The more one reads De Tocqueville, the more admiration does one feel for his acuteness, for the delicacy of his analysis, for the elegant precision of his reasonings, for the limpid purity of his style; above all for his love of truth and the elevation of his views. He is not only urbane, but judicial; not only noble, but edifying. There is perhaps no book of the generation to which he belonged which contains more solid wisdom in a more attractive dress.

We have here, however, to regard the treatise not merely as a model of art and a storehouse of ethical maxims, but as a picture and criticism of the government and people of the United States. And before using it as evidence of their condition fifty years ago, some observations must be made as to the reliance we may place upon it.

The first observation is that not only are its descriptions of democracy as displayed in America no longer true in many points, but that in certain points they were never true. That is to say, some were true of America, but not of democracy in general, while others were true of democracy in general but not true of America. It is worth while to attempt to indicate the causes of such errors as may be discovered in his picture, because they are errors which every one who approaches a similar task has to guard against. De Tocqueville is not much read in the United States, where the scientific, historical and philosophical study of the institutions of the country, apart from the legal study of the Constitution, is of quite recent growth. He is less read than formerly in England and even in France. But his views of the American government and people have so passed into the texture of our thoughts that we cannot shake off his influence, and in order to profit by it are bound to submit his conclusions and predictions to a searching though respectful examination.

The defects of the book are due to three causes. He had a strong and penetrating intellect, but it moved by preference in the *a priori* or deductive path, and his power of observation, quick and active as it was, did not lead but followed the march of his reasonings. It will be found, when his method is closely observed, that the facts he cites are rather the illustrations than the sources of his conclusions. He had studied America carefully and thoroughly. But he wanted the necessary preparation for that study. His knowledge of England, while remarkable in a foreigner, was not sufficient to show him how much in American institutions is really English, and explainable only from English sources.

He wrote about America, and meant to describe it fully and faithfully. But his heart was in France, and the thought of France, never absent from him, unconsciously colored every picture he drew. It made him think things abnormal which are merely un-French; it made him attach undue importance to phenomena which seemed to explain French events or supply a warning against French dangers.

He reveals his method in the introduction to his book. He draws a fancy sketch of a Democratic people, based on a few general principles, passes to the condition of France, and then proceeds to tell us that in America he went to seek the Type of Democracy—Democracy pure and simple—in its normal shape. *"J'avoue que dans l'Amérique, j'ai vu plus que l'Amérique: j'y ai cherché une image de la démocratie elle-même, de ses penchants, de son caractère, de ses préjugés, de ses passions."*

Like Plato in the *Republic*, he begins by imagining that there exists somewhere a Type or Pattern of Democracy, and as the American Republic comes nearest to this pattern, he selects it for examination. He is aware, of course, that there must be in every country and people many features peculiar to the country which reappear in its government, and repeatedly observes that this or that is peculiar to America, and must not be taken as necessarily or generally true of other Democracies. But in practice he underrates the purely local and special features of America, and often, forgetting his own scientific cautions, treats it as a norm for Democracy in general. Nor does he, after finding his norm, proceed simply to examine its facts and draw inferences from them. In many chapters he begins by laying down one or two large principles, he develops conclusions from them, and then he points out that the phenomena of America conform to these conclusions. Instead of drawing the character of Democracy from the aspects it presents in America, he arrives at its character *a priori*, and uses those aspects only to point and enforce propositions he has already reached. It is not Democracy in America he describes, but Democracy illustrated from America. He is admirably honest, never conceding or consciously evading a fact which he perceives might tell against his theories. But being already prepossessed by certain abstract principles, facts do not fall on his mind like seeds on virgin soil. He is struck by those which accord with, he is apt to ignore those which diverge from his preconceptions. Like all *a priori* reasoners, he is peculiarly exposed to the

danger of pressing a principle too far, of seeking to explain a phenomenon by one principle only when it is perhaps the result of an accidental
concurrence of several minor causes. The scholasticism we observe in him
is due partly to this deductive habit, partly to his want of familiarity with
the actualities of politics. An instance of it appears in his tendency to over-
estimate the value of constitutional powers and devices, and to forget how
often they are modified, almost reversed in practice by the habits of those
who use them. Though no one has more judiciously warned us to look to
the actual working of institutions and the ideas of the men who work
them rather than to their letter, he has himself failed to observe that the
American Constitution tends to vary in working from its legal theory,
and the name Legislature has prevented him, like so many other foreign
observers, from seeing in the English Parliament an executive as well as
a law-making body.

In saying that he did not know England, I fully admit that his knowledge of that great free government was far beyond the knowledge of most
cultivated foreigners. He had studied its history, had lived among and
learnt the sentiments of its aristocracy. But he had little experience of the
ideas and habits of the middle class, whom the Americans then more resembled, and he was not familiar—as how could a stranger be?—with the
details of English politics and the working of the English Courts. Hence
he has failed to grasp the substantial identity of the American people with
the English. He perceives that there are many and close resemblances, and
traces much that is American to an English source. He has seen and described with perfect justness and clearness the mental habits of the English
and American lawyer as contrasted with those of the French lawyer. But
he has not grasped, as perhaps no one but an Englishman or an American
can grasp, the truth that the American people is the English people, modified in some directions by the circumstances of its colonial life and its
more popular government, but in essentials the same. Hence much which
is merely English appears to De Tocqueville to be American or Democratic. The functions of the judges, for instance, in expounding the Constitution (whether of the Federation or of a State) and disregarding a
statute which conflicts therewith, the responsibility of an official to the
ordinary courts of the land, the co-existence of laws of a higher and lower
degree of authority, seem to him to be novel and brilliant inventions instead of mere instances of general doctrines of English law, adapted to the
circumstances of a colony, dependent on a Home Government or a State
partially subordinated to a Federal Government. The absence of what the
French call "Administration" and the disposition to leave people to themselves which strike him, would not surprise an Englishman accustomed to

the like freedom. Much that he remarks in the mental habits of the ordinary American, his latent conservatism for instance, his indifference to amusement as compared with material comfort, his commercial eagerness and tendency to take a commercial view of all things, might have been just as well remarked of the ordinary middle-class Englishman, and has nothing to do with a Democratic Government. Other features which he ascribes to this last named cause, such as habits of easy social intercourse, the disposition to prize certain particular virtues, the readiness to give mutual help, are equally attributable to the conditions of life that existed among settlers in a wild country where few persons were raised by birth or wealth above their fellows, and everyone had need of the aid of others —conditions whose results remain in the temper of the people even when the community has passed into another phase, a phase in which inequalities of wealth have already begun to be marked, and temptations have appeared which did not beset the Puritans of the seventeenth century.

It is no reproach to De Tocqueville that France formed to him the background of every picture whose foreground was the New World. He tells us frankly in the Introduction that the phenomena of social equality, as they existed in France, and the political consequences to be expected from them, filled his mind when he examined the institutions of America; he hoped to find there lessons by which France might profit: "J'ai voulu y trouver des enseignements dont nous puissions profiter." But with this purpose before him, he could hardly avoid laying too much stress on points which seemed to have instruction for his own countrymen, and from fancying those things to be peculiar and abnormal which stood contrasted with the circumstances of France. De Tocqueville is, perhaps of all eminent French writers, the least prone to assume the ways and ideas of his own country to be the rule, and those of another country the exception; yet even in him the tendency lurks. There is more than a trace of it in his surprise at the American habit of using without abusing political associations, and at the disposition of Legislatures to try experiments in legislation, a disposition which struck him chiefly by its contrast with the immutability which the Code of the First Empire seemed to have stamped upon the private law of France.

But this constant great reference to France goes deeper than the political philosophy of the book. It determines its scope and aim. The *Democracy in America* is not so much a political study as a work of edification. It is a warning to France of the need to adjust her political institutions to her social condition, and above all to improve the tone of her politics, to create a moral and religious basis for her national life, to erect a new fabric of social doctrine, in the place of that which, already crumbling, the Revolution had overthrown. We must not, therefore, expect to find in him a complete description and criticism such as a German would have given of the government of America in all its details and aspects. To observe this is not to complain of the book. What he has produced is more artistic, and possibly more impressive than such a description would have been, as a landscape gives a juster notion of scenery than a map. His book is permanently valuable, because its reflections and exhortations are applicable, not merely to the Frenchmen of fifty years ago, but to mankind generally, since they touch upon failings and dangers permanently inherent to political society. Let it only be remembered that in spite of its scientific form, it is really a work of art rather than a work of science, and a work suffused with strong, though carefully repressed emotion.

The best illustration I can give of these tendencies of De Tocqueville will be found in a comparison of the first part of his work, published in 1834, and now included in the first and second volumes of recent editions with the second part published in 1840, and now forming the third volume. In the first part the author keeps close to his facts. Even when he has set out on the *a priori* road, he speedily brings his theory to the test of American phenomena: they give substance to, and (so to speak) steady the theory, while the theory connects and illumines them. But in the second part (third volume) he soars far from the ground and is often lost in the clouds of his own sombre meditation. When this part was written, the direct impressions of his transatlantic visit had begun to fade from his mind. With all his finesse and fertility, he had neither sufficient profundity of thought nor a sufficient ample store of facts gathered from history at large to enable him to give body and substance to his reflections on the obscure problems wherewith he attempts to deal. Hence, this part of the book is not so much a study of American democracy as a series of ingenious and fine-spun abstract speculations on the features and results of equality on modern society and thought, speculations which, though they have been singled out for admiration by some high judges, such as Ampère and Laboulaye, will appear to most readers over fanciful, over confident in their effort to construct a general theory applicable to the infinitely diversified facts of human society, and occasionally monotonous in their repetition of distinctions without differences and generalities too vague, perhaps too hollow, for practical use.

How far do these defects of De Tocqueville's work affect its value for our present purpose, that of discovering from it what was the condition, political, social, intellectual, of the United States in 1833 and what the forces that were then at work in determining the march of the nation and the development of its institutions?

It is but slightly that they impair its worth as a record of facts. De Tocqueville is so careful and so unprejudiced an observer that I doubt if there be a single remark of his which can be dismissed as simply erroneous. There is always some basis for every statement he makes. But the basis is occasionally too small for the superstructure of inference, speculation and prediction which he rears upon it. To borrow an illustration from chemistry, his analysis is always right so far as it is qualitative, often wrong where it attempts to be quantitative. The fact is there, but it is perhaps a smaller fact than he thinks, or a transient fact, or a fact whose importance is, or shortly will be, diminished by other facts which he has not adequately recognized.

When we pass from description to argument he is a less safe guide. By the light of subsequent experience we can perceive that he mistook transitory for permanent causes. Many of the phenomena which he ascribes to democracy were due only to the fact that large fortunes had not yet grown up in America, others to the absence, in most parts of the country, of that higher education and culture which comes with wealth, leisure and the settlement of society. I have already observed that he sometimes supposes features of American politics to be novel and democratic which are really old and English, that he does not allow sufficiently for the imprint which colonial life had left on the habits and ideas of the people, an imprint which though it partly wears off with time, partly becomes transformed into something which, while you may call it democratic, remains different from the democracy of an old, European country, and is not an index to the character of democracy in general.

It need hardly be said that the worth of a book like his is not to be measured by the number of flaws which a minute criticism can discover in it. Even a sovereign genius like Aristotle cannot be expected to foresee which of the influences he discerns will retain their potency: it is enough if his view is more piercing and more comprehensive than that of his greatest contemporaries; if his record shows the high water mark of the learning and philosophy of the time. Had history falsified far more of De Tocqueville's predictions than she has done, his work would still remain eminently suggestive and stimulating. And it is edificatory not merely because it contains precepts instinct with the loftiest morality. It is a model of that spirit of fairness and justice, that love of pure truth which is conspicuously necessary and not less conspicuously difficult in the discussion, even the abstract discussion, of the problems of political philosophy.

Leroy on TOCQUEVILLE

When one reopens *De la Démocratie en Amérique*, one is drawn, almost despite oneself, by the turn of its thought, by the presentation of the chapters with their sententious titles, sometimes short, sometimes long, to return to *L'Esprit des lois* and to suggest comparisons. On the appearance of this famous book, Royer-Collard and Stuart Mill a century ago, and later Sainte-Beuve and Scherer in particular, have compared Tocqueville with Montesquieu; and he himself avowed that *L'Esprit* and *Les Considérations sur la grandeur des Romains et leur décadence* were two of his favourite books. In our day, when discussing the first part of *La Démocratie*, A. Redier has written that Tocqueville is the Montesquieu of the United States.[1]

Certainly in both one finds a taste for and a sense of history, one admires in each the same genius for deduction and generalisation; but should not one discern in the author of the *Lettres persanes* an irony and a scepticism which Tocqueville never knew? Sainte-Beuve reproached this Norman with his seriousness. But if Montesquieu and Tocqueville were alike the historians of institutions, hardly anything unites them when the foundation of their method is examined; Tocqueville had not the least belief in climatic conditions which the author of *L'Esprit des lois* possessed and which he put forward as the essential explanation of the progress of civilisation and of the destiny of empires. It should even be said that this determinism, an anticipation of contemporary sociology, irritated him. "These are," he said, "false and cowardly doctrines, which can only produce feeble men and pusillanimous nations." [2]

On the other hand, a similar moderation of spirit unites the two philosopher-historians: it is the political approach of Montesquieu, theorist of the balance of the three powers, that Tocqueville, constitutional monarchist, adopted in his thought, criticism and active politics. If we group thinkers in families—aristocrats, liberals, emotionalists—Montesquieu and

[1] *Comme disait M. de Tocqueville*, Paris, 1925, p. 108.
[2] Last page of *La Démocratie*. One should note, however, that Tocqueville gave a large place to the study of environment in the first chapters. (I quote from the 13th edition, Vol. 2, Pagnère, éd. Paris, 1890.)

[Maxime Leroy, "Alexis de Tocqueville," *Politica*, vol. I (August, 1935). By permission.]

Tocqueville belong to the same family. An identical, rather grey tint, colours their systems, of which the original colours are so different. The one prepared for a constitutional royalty, the other longed for a democratic constitution with monarchical tendencies, less as practical men of the world than as doctrinaires and intellectuals.

In *L'Esprit* we find: "The good sense and the happiness of individuals consists largely in the mediocrity of their talents and their fortunes. A republic where the laws have created many mediocre people, containing wise people among them, will govern itself wisely, and being composed of happy people it will itself be happy." [3] When one thinks of the similarities of Tocqueville and Montesquieu, it is to such texts as this, pessimistic enough in their view of the human species, that it is necessary to refer, because it is they which reveal a true, direct thought underlying the assurances, more or less pompous, about virtue in one, and about liberty in the other.

Here is a further statement of Montesquieu: "The spirit of moderation is what one calls virtue in an aristocracy; it takes the place of the spirit of equality in a popular state." [4] We can see the type of moderation understood by these liberals. It is synonymous with politeness, deference, in a given environment.

As for the moderates! Tocqueville, more even than Montesquieu, is illumed by this word, of which the sense, we must admit, escapes us a little in France since the disappearance in our political assemblies of that "Centre" where the last descendants and disciples of these great liberals fought their battles. Temperate spirits, measured spirits, we need to use all these epithets which picture them and define them in order to give significance to their actions as well as to their doctrines.

I do not believe that we can understand an intelligence without having penetrated the character which surrounds it: it is only a metaphysician who can imagine that his own temper does not play an important part in the expression and even the formation of his ideas. Let us enquire then, if this moderation does not reveal in general some uncertainty in ideas; does it not correspond often enough to a certain incapacity to choose, to a certain emotional coldness? La Bruyère, three centuries ago, believed in this correlation, giving it a rather clever and cruel twist. When one observes that Tocqueville did not arrive at conclusions easily, or arrived at them in a confused manner, even when he might have been expected to be sure of himself, one is led to think that this defect of mind arose from a defect of character in the man who was ready successively (I hasten to add, with much dignity and disinterestedness) to collaborate

[3] *L'Esprit des lois*, V, p. 3.   [4] *Ibid.*, V, p. 8.

with legitimism, the citizen king, the republic of 1848, with Charles X, with Louis-Philippe, with the Prince-President, and with the Comte de Chambord, without tying himself down to a single system or assuming a permanent attitude. Undoubtedly he wished to consider in these governments less their principle than the means they offered for assuring the triumph of his liberal conceptions. The manner in which he practised this pragmatism shows him to be in fact more intellectually indecisive than healthily sceptical about the possible question of political dogmatism. He was more bitter than sceptical; it was never otherwise than superficially that his fits of bitterness assumed the aspect of considered and definite doubt. The seriousness of his mind disguised its hesitancy.

There is something of Fénélon in this Tocqueville, liberal, courteous, moderate. Some of his writings make one forget *L'Esprit* and think of *Télémaque*. I allude to those charming phrases in the Introduction of *La Démocratie en Amérique* which, written in the years following 1830—the first volume appeared in 1835—cause that flute-like air, of which the cymbals of Marx have not yet completely stifled the gentle melody, to echo again in our ears. These phrases must be quoted in order to understand Tocqueville better; and in order to show, too, in its most gracious moments, the liberal thought of the French aristocracy and upper middle classes in the middle of the nineteenth century. A flute-like air, we say: we shall see later that Tocqueville, seeing the first shadow of historic materialism, knew too, on occasion, how to shout resounding words.

"I conceive a society where all, regarding the law as their work, will love it and submit to it without hardship; where the authority of government being respected as necessary and not as divine, the love borne for the head of the State will be not a passion but a reasoned and tranquil sentiment. Each having his rights, and being assured of preserving his rights, there will be established among all classes a manly confidence, and a sort of reciprocal tolerance as far removed from pride as from obsequiousness.

"Instructed in its real interests, the people will understand that, in order to profit from the advantages of society, it is necessary to submit to its obligations. The free association of citizens can then replace the individual power of noblemen, and the State will be protected from tyranny and from licence.

"I understand that in a democratic State, constituted in this way, society will be by no means without fluctuation; but the movements of social groups in it will be regulated and progressive; if we meet in it less culture than in an aristocracy we shall find in it less misery; enjoyment in it will be less extreme and well-being more general; science less profound and ignorance more rare; feelings less violent and customs more friendly; we shall find in it more defects and less crime.

"The people taken as a body will be less brilliant, less glorious, less strong in character, perhaps; but the majority of citizens will enjoy in it a lot more prosperous, and the population will show themselves peaceful, not because they despair of being better, but because their condition is good."

This picture in the manner of Fénélon has the soft elegance, a little cold, of a canvas of Delaroche or Scheffer, the contemporaries of Tocqueville; how little the softened colour corresponds to the truth, already alarming and cruel, of the social circumstances of the '30's! Obviously: but whatever liberalism possessed that was better and more benevolent, Tocqueville gave it. This belief in a progressive, poetic evolution had reality only in the mind of this well-intentioned, distinguished man, for, as we know from experience, nothing is more Utopian than to found a State upon collective reason, upon the reciprocal good intentions of citizens, upon their courtesy, upon that collection of amiable and conciliatory sentiments which inspired Fénélon, that refined nobleman, to write his chimerical pastorals. And, in fact, what are the "true interests of the people"? He does not know them himself. Corbon, who was a representative of the people in 1848, notices it already: "It is to himself above all that the people is a mystery." [5] The heads of the State know it no better than he, Tocqueville having taken care to prove to us in his *Ancien régime* the lack of curiosity with regard to the growing democracy on the eve of '89, the surprise of both governors and governed in February '48, of both the men in power and the men in the street. And what does he know of it, this great nobleman, whose mind was formed in rustic surroundings in the heart of a peaceful province? This generous, anxious, disenchanted Tocqueville, did he know any better, even at the end of his career, he of whom it has so often been remarked how hesitant he was as soon as it became a question of facing the concrete and the immediate?

"I conceive," wrote Tocqueville; there is the word which reveals the philosopher, the dreamer, the man who would like to overcome reality with generous ideas; the word of a man who preferred country life in his Norman château to the activities of the town. It is not the word of the politician in battle, of the man of action. He said: reason, tranquil, peaceful, regulated, progressive—so many expressions which reveal the character and the tendency of this well-intentioned and reflective mind. What he hopes for is a State in which there will be only wise men. If this hope, which is not platonic with him, proves his nobility, we must add that it

[5] *Le Secret du peuple*, Paris, 1863, p. 3.

shows his weakness, the weakness indeed of his political idealism. Who
has not hoped in a moment of optimism for a State equilibrated by the
goodwill of equal and free men! But who has not quickly reprimanded
himself for abandoning himself to this too facile phantasm! Tocqueville
sincerely admits his fault and then condones it. I fear that he remained
right up to the end of his life dominated by this dream, which made him
lovable, but which explains his failure in practice as soon as he thought
of entering into active politics.

At the time when Tocqueville begins to think, that is to say, on the
eve of 1830, two powerful currents are flowing within the monarchy of
Louis XVIII and Charles X; soon they will overflow into the monarchy
of the *juste milieu*, which Guizot and Thiers govern while Louis-Philippe
reigns. The first current is that liberalism to which belong, according to
their separate fashions, Guizot and Thiers, and which was expressed too
by Royer-Collard, the dogmatist, and Benjamin Constant, the versatile.
The second current is the nascent socialism summoned to life at the call
of Saint-Simon and of his followers, already illustrious themselves. These
two currents, if they oppose one another, come none the less, both of
them, from the Revolution, from the same words, the one taking them
direct from the Declaration of 1789, the other from the Montagnards and
those who continue to demand a "supplementary revolution" as the corollary of this Declaration, a corollary formulated by Robespierre during the
discussion of the Constitution of 1793 when he affirmed the right to live
and the right to work. As Aulard has said, the Declaration of this Constitution became the "charter of French Socialists" under Louis-Philippe
and the Republic of 1848, and from it Babeuf drew his agrarian thesis
which so terrified his contemporaries.[6]

Tocqueville, as we shall see, refusing to restrict himself to wishing for
a better political constitution, touched in certain places upon those projects
of Robespierre which looked towards an improvement of social conditions.
One name brings together those liberals and those socialists of 1830, in
conflict and in rivalry though they be: that of Condorcet, in whose pen
one discovers much of the Declaration of 1793, which, as Aulard has also
noted, was to be in many ways more liberal than that of '89. There are,
that is to say, two currents but with points of union. It is not at the moments at which the two doctrines confront one another that their divergences appear irreconcilable; from the distance, the similarities appear
so clearly that Aulard—criticised, it is true, by Albert Mathiez—was unable to define doctrinally the contrasts which separated, to the point of
crime, Girondins and Montagnards, during so many furious and pas-

[6] *Histoire politique de la Révolution*, Paris, 1901, pp. 290, 291.

sionate discussions. We must distinguish, but we must not press the distinctions too far.

What is the place of Tocqueville among these parties, in the midst of these tendencies? In a parliamentary sense he belonged to the Left, namely to the Left Centre at the side of Odilon-Barrot, Lanjuinais, Gustave de Beaumont. Born a nobleman, Tocqueville delighted in the qualification of liberal; he rejected the epithet of "reactionary"; he detested the word, which he called jargon. He rejected with no less vigour the epithet of conservative. "I am not," he wrote himself, "either of the revolutionary party or of the conservative party." [7] He was a man who remained at the beginning constitutionalist of the Revolution, not through hatred of political and social novelties, but because he believed that political and social progress could not come about except through a development of the liberal principles of the Constituent Assembly. Let us take away from him, therefore, the epithet, current in his time, of "satisfied." Under Louis-Philippe the middle classes who were the "satisfied" were often denounced with the most bitter violence by the democrats and socialists. In order to resuscitate the term among us, let us think of an Albert de Mun, Catholic Liberal, or of a Ribot, Liberal Republican, or of those neutral politicians who in our time say neither "reaction" nor "revolution." Although Tocqueville was partisan of a certain "supplementary revolution" we must say, none the less, that the way in which he understood the perfecting of institutions placed him to the right of the constituents of 1789, in a line which, if it had been followed by the Constituent Assembly itself, would not have given to the revolutionary legislation that character of dramatic novelty which it had: the principles of '89 he understood only as allied to the Catholic Church. Undoubtedly the Constituent Assembly was anti-Catholic; undoubtedly the Declaration laid down as a political principle tolerance and not full religious liberty; but that does not matter, for, in its essence, that Declaration led already to the provision of civil status for the clergy at a time when Mirabeau, the most symbolic champion of the Revolution in action, never stopped proclaiming that "it is necessary to de-catholicise France." That is an extension which he would not have admitted if he had sat on the benches of the Constituent Assembly. As Père Lanfrey has observed, not without profundity, this whole movement of political and religious liberation, which began under the direction of a pure enough constitutional liberalism, manifested already the forces of intolerance and violence which would destroy it: "it began with Dupont and finished with Babeuf." [8] Tocqueville might have been perhaps a

[7] A. Redier, *op. cit.*, p. 48.   [8] *Essai sur la Révolution française,*
Paris, 1879, pp. 178, 203.

Noailles, a Lamette, or a Montmorency in these beginnings of '89 which were so generous and so clear. Certainly he would have fought La Fayette.

In the social sense he wished to go farther than his liberal friends, but with the avowed hope that Catholicism would slow down the development of democracy of which the demagogic excesses horrified him. If he touches at certain points upon socialism, at others, more numerous, stronger, he is in contact with the traditions of the great liberal aristocrats of the Constituent Assembly, who were far from dreaming of an overthrow of property and dogma.

Tocqueville is a man of '89, that '89 which he himself qualified as liberal; [9] one can see how. Here is a quotation from him which gives the tone of his ardent adherence with more generality than is desirable; the reservations will follow.

"Do not let us give to the legitimists the joy and to those who have remained faithful to the cult of 1789 the sorrow of believing that the immense fact of the French Revolution, which has moved almost the entire human race, has only resulted after all in satisfying new interests and not in bringing to triumph in the world new rights and new guarantees." [10]

What remains in our day of the state of mind symbolised by the Declaration of '89? In the time of Tocqueville, and right up to the end of the second Empire, the Declaration of Rights is spoken of as holy; Tocqueville himself invoked a holy liberty. By the language which we use to-day, dry, indifferent, may be measured our removal at the same time chronologically and politically from this enthusiastic terminology. For Tocqueville and his friends it is more than a memory: throughout their lifetime '89 remains a hope, an example, a method, in fact, a magnificent truth to which it is necessary to attach oneself firmly as to a supreme political lesson. '89 is an event which continues to live, however great may be the abyss between it and the dictatorships which followed. As it has often been remarked, "that great stretch of time which lasted from 1789 until our day . . . which, as Tocqueville said, I continue to call the French Revolution. . . ." [11]

There are Montagnard and Girondin disciples of '89: these brother enemies claimed their authority from this same source. Tocqueville is a liberal disciple of '89; he is even the type of this liberalism. "Liberty is the first of my passions," [12] one reads in one of his confidential notes. Should we note here, in passing, something of romanticism in this steadfast

[9] *Oeuvres complètes, Mélanges*, p. 182.
[10] A. Redier, *op. cit.*, p. 151.

[11] Sainte-Beuve, *Nouveaux lundis*, X, p. 32.
[12] A. Redier, *op. cit.*, p. 48.

Tocqueville? Of passions he wrote: "I love them when they are good and I are not sure that I detest them when they are bad. They are strength." [13] In the same manner Saint-Simon, on his death-bed in 1825, said to his disciples: "Be passionate!"

Tocqueville believed in liberty with a religious passion; of no one more than of him may it be said that he had the religion of liberty: he admitted no joking on this subject. If this serious man admitted joking on no point, this it was, in any case, which inspired in him the most unshakable gravity of all. This belief in liberty animates his texts, gives its reason to his doctrinal and political attitude, explains their fervour and supports their eloquence. Never did he abandon it. To his last breath he was an impenitent liberal. [14]

What kind of liberal was he? He regarded himself as being one according to a particular and original fashion. He was mistaken in this point; for he was one in the conservative spirit as were a number of his liberal friends.

Tocqueville does not say liberty without understanding by it liberty and property. "Peoples," he argued, "are less disposed to revolution in measure as personal belongings are multiplied and spread and the number of those who possess them increases." [15] "If you can create a society in which each will have something to keep and little to take, you will have done much for the peace of the world." [16]

Like Guizot, he is ready to declare that the "owning classes" must be the foundations of the new society; [17] and this was the thesis of Dupont de Nemours, the follower of the physiocrats during the Revolution.

If this is the doctrine of Tocqueville and Guizot, it is also that of Mme de Staël and Benjamin Constant, in face of the Saint-Simoniens, who even before 1830 rejected these owning classes because they were "idle."

Tocqueville spoke of liberty and religion; "One of my dreams, the principal, on entering political life, was to work for the reconciliation of the liberal and the religious spirit, the new society and the Church." To his brother he confesses that this was his "greatest dream." He wrote further: "The true grandeur of man is only in the harmony between the liberal and the religious sentiment working both to animate and to satisfy the soul." [18]

Here is another statement in which Tocqueville shows that he understood by liberty less an impartial regulator of society than a means

[13] *Oeuvres complètes*, VI, p. 115.
[14] *Oeuvres complètes*, VI, p. 395.
[15] *La Démocratie*, II, p. 287.

[16] *Ibid.*, p. 284.
[17] Guizot, *Mémoires*, I, p. 294.
[18] *Oeuvres complètes*, VI, pp. 119, 232.

destined to favour catholicism: "I have never been more convinced than I am to-day that there is only liberty (I mean the moderate and the regulated) and religion, which, by a combined effort, can raise man above the slough in which democratic equality plunges him as soon as one or other of these supports is lacking."

He believed that catholicism was of all religions that most appropriate to the development of liberty. He pretended paradoxically enough to prove this assertion from the Protestants of the United States.[19] This optimism the failure of *L'Avenir*,[20] the newspaper of the Liberal Catholics grouped around Lamennais, in 1830, then the adherence of the clergy to Napoleon III, which he scorned as perjury, did not appear to justify; and, to tell the truth, Tocqueville was profoundly grieved by this adherence of the Catholic Church to a liberticide Caesarism: he saw in it an error of the spirit and a fault of the heart; he reproaches it with allowing itself to be "so fatally won over by rich pastures."[21] At the end of his life he considered the alliance between religion and liberty, such as it then was, with a bitterness which he never dissimulated, remembering the hopes of his youth.[22]

One of the liberal philosophers of this period, Vacherot, who, two years after the appearance of Tocqueville's book, was to become Director of Studies at the École Normale, submitted the principle of this liberal catholicism to a meticulous criticism in his book, *La Démocratie*, in 1859. Later, Eugène d'Eichthal noted, in his penetrating study of Tocqueville, that it was a fantasy to imagine that religion would remain by its permanence the immovable regulator of the moving spirit of democratic liberty; that religion would escape no more than democracy, which Tocqueville claimed to master and direct with its aid, from the crisis which overthrew even in his time political institutions and ideas, as well as doctrines of morality. "The Churches," wrote the political philosopher who was later to become the authoritative Director of the École des Sciences Politiques, "have they not been undermined by the same revolution as monarchies? To exhort a people to believe, is that not to suppose that they will believe what they wish?"[23]

Struck by the English example, so dear to Montesquieu, Tocqueville

[19] *Oeuvres complètes*, V, Ch. xvii, first volume.

[20] The motto of *L'Avenir* was: God and Liberty. It defended the separation of Church and State, the liberty of the press, and of teaching.

[21] A. Redier, *op. cit.*, p. 230.

[22] *Oeuvres complètes*, Correspondance, II, p. 312.

[23] Eugène d'Eichthal, *Alexis de Tocqueville et la démocratie libérale*, Paris, 1897, p. 46 *et seq.*, in particular p. 50.

and his liberal friends, who, moreover, interpreted that country not without certain fantasies, wished to create a progressive State where liberty would adopt the mission of strengthening liberty and religion, at a time when—under the Restoration—the Catholic religion and Bourbon legitimism were identical. This was an original point of view, and a bold one, since this thesis took Tocqueville and his friends out of their environment. As a reliable witness wrote, "One was Catholic and one was Royalist by the same argument, almost in virtue of the same ideas and the same opinions." And the same Sainte-Beuve, from whom we borrow this line, written during his short hour of liberal catholicism, wrote about Père Lacordaire what he might have said of Tocqueville: "Such a confusion seemed most regrettable to the Abbé Lacordaire; it appeared to him as a diminution and a degradation of Christianity; and he believed that it was good to show, at least to France, that it was possible to be faithful to Christ without being enslaved by a vanished throne, even though that throne might belong to the descendants of Saint Louis." [24] That is, indeed, what Tocqueville thought. Those Liberals, men of compromise, dreamed of a reconciliation, but within limits which they hoped to maintain both narrow and firm, and, it must be admitted, a larger part was given to the past than to the future. They were greater friends of religion than of liberty, despite so many invocations of '89.

We have written "liberty" without defining it. What then is this liberty which Tocqueville defended, this liberty longed for by a society of wise men—this cherished liberty, as the Marseillaise sang? "Man is born free," said Rousseau, "and everywhere he is in chains."

Liberty is defined in Montesquieu and Tocqueville by the institutions upon which it is founded and which protect it rather than by considerations of a moral order. Both are terminologically sober enough, Tocqueville more even than Montesquieu, in distinction from Rousseau, who analysed at great length these moral arguments. The free man, according to Montesquieu, is he who only has to obey laws, the laws of a temperate monarch. The free man may do anything which the laws do not forbid; and it is in the measure that the author of these laws is independent of the judiciary and of the executive that these laws are good, deserving the epithet of liberal.

Founded upon liberty, it is to the development of individual self-control that laws must tend, at least if one wishes to stay in line with the Declaration of the Rights of Man of '89. "The aim of every political association is the preservation of the natural and imprescriptible rights of man." The Declaration of 1793 affirms imperatively: "There is oppression

[24] *Causeries du lundi*, I, p. 225.

against the whole social body when a single one of its members is oppressed." There is the theory. And the fact?

An aristocrat himself, Tocqueville defended liberty as an aristocrat; and I fear that he did not realise that the kind of liberty for which he wished with so much ardour in democratic society was founded in his mind and those of his friends, less on reason, of which he thought it was the child, than on the very aristocratic institutions to which he belonged. It was a restricted liberty, protecting a small group of privileged people who were really independent so far as economic circumstances went, and quite in a position to lead a life full of pleasantness and a truly liberal existence. It is a liberty for believers, liberty for owners, that he foreshadowed, by no means liberty abandoned to itself, rude, savage, leading societies towards irreligion, towards socialism, nor even towards a rigorous state of industrial development. This liberalism of 1830 has the colour of the place in which it is born, expressing a category, a moment of French political thought, while Tocqueville imagined that he was formulating and defending a timeless idea, remaining valid for all conditions and all continents. There is an aristocratic liberalism—it is this: does there exist a proletarian liberalism? I doubt it, unless we take the anarchism of Proudhon as the liberal effort of the working classes.

We have just said that the liberalism of Tocqueville is defined by the institutions which in his thought must support and defend liberty. By what institutions did he demand protection? It is as liberals that Tocqueville and his friends were ardent decentralisers. This had led Eugène d'Eichthal to write, "In Tocqueville liberty is the equivalent of decentralisation or rather the absence of centralisation." [25] In his eyes it is in the commune that the strength of free peoples resides. "Without the institutions of the commune, the nation can find itself with free government, but it has not the spirit of liberty. . . . Despotism pushed back into the interior of the social body reappears sooner or later at the surface." [26]

What is the value of such an affirmation supported by no contemporary fact, which the American system of government supported only at its beginning and then less through liberalism than through the absence of a civilisation? It is not only the commune which is then little regulated, but the central power also. The inhabitants of the United States had still few needs at the time at which Tocqueville observed them; and those few needs accommodated themselves to a political system of the greatest simplicity. In any case, Tocqueville remarked himself that no European nation understood municipal liberalism.

The ample development of municipal institutions in the nineteenth

[25] Eugène d'Eichthal, *op. cit.*, p. 57.   [26] *Démocratie*, I, p. 102.

century renders the decentralising idea of Tocqueville less and less clear.
While developing, the modern commune has not undergone that emancipating liberalism for which he wished, and which he thought would limit
central despotism and might perhaps transform France into a half-
Girondin federation of free municipalities. In fact, we have seen the
charges upon citizens multiplied in conditions which have rendered our
communes increasingly dependent upon the State, for in order to meet
these charges the municipal councils, on the demand of the ratepayers,
have had more and more to appeal for the financial help of the State. We
know in this way a municipal socialism to which we owe numerous services of a collective interest which, increasingly regulated by a suspicious
central power, remove us more and more from this political individualism
which Tocqueville wished to make the inspiration and the means of regulating 36,000 little communal republics.

Communal decentralisation was understood with too much simplicity
and optimism by Tocqueville and his friends, and, moreover, as appeared
from their writings, especially from the book of the Baron de Barante,
Des Communes et de l'aristocratie (1821), it is less a development of
democracy on a genuinely liberal plan that they wish than a "return of
power to its ancient beneficiaries who had been more or less dispossessed
since '89." What they demanded was a reform for the benefit of "citizens
whom their position raised above their equals." Thus would have been
created, as the basis of national institutions, small governments of notables.
Thus, as Barante says, "a progressive hierarchy would establish an uninterrupted chain between the monarch and his subjects." Reformers think
in time, and the understanding of their time alone permits an understanding of projects which we have too often the inclination to consider in the
abstract. Tocqueville spoke of liberty; we must read for it liberty through
the intermediary of the notables; we must read: liberty controlled by religion. Tocqueville ought to have realised this, he who wrote the significant
lines: "One can say in a general way that there is nothing more propitious
for the establishment and the continuance of a system of local administration than an aristocracy." [27]

In truth, we must recognise that legislation has, little by little, if not
undone, at least lessened the administrative link which in Tocqueville's
time attached the commune to the central power. In his day, the administration of the communes was in strict dependence upon the central power;
mayors were not elected but appointed, were veritable officials of the executive, a kind of sub-prefect without initiative, removable.

These municipal officers were chosen from among the notables, it is

[27] *Mélanges,* p. 32. (Extract from an article which appeared in 1836.)

hardly necessary to say; but why, Tocqueville demanded, should not the collectivities be left the right to nominate them freely themselves?

It was only in 1882 that the communes reconquered the fullness of electoral rights which they had lost in the year VIII. What would Tocqueville and Barante say if they saw municipal liberty create socialist municipalities instead of centres of aristocratic resistance under the flag of liberalism? There has been municipal reform but not in the political line of Tocqueville; it is only in abstract doctrine that it connects with the liberal idea of 1830.[28]

Tocqueville urges that decentralisation is necessary, but if the deepest tendencies of democracies, as he says, incline modern societies to place all power at the centre of the State, is it not unrealistic to advise us to struggle for decentralisation, all the more since democracies are, if we are to believe him, apathetic by nature.[29]

Tocqueville wrote: "I believe that in the democratic centuries which are about to open, individual independence and local liberties will always be a product of art." [30]

A product of art, we can understand what the philosopher means by that: the fate of these local liberties so ardently defended is dependent upon an effort which must go constantly against the natural movement of democratic societies. Will a democratic society be able, admitting the rightness of Tocqueville's point of view, to struggle continuously against its own nature? To confide the fate of liberty to the communes in such conditions, is that not to forget fact too much? In trusting to political art for the success of such an enterprise are we not, from Tocqueville's own point of view, endeavouring to destroy this same nature of things and to substitute for it a purely artificial work?

The liberal Tocqueville wished to create another counterweight to the central power: he had faith in associations. That is an idea which was beginning to spread in his time, thanks to the followers of Fourier and Saint-Simon; it was defended in *L'Avenir*. On this point, as on the other, the future was to realise only in a formal way Tocqueville's hopes. If municipal liberty created a socialism which would have horrified him, the liberty to associate has created economic groups of which the anti-liberal character is suggested by the name of "congrégations économiques" given to them. Financial and industrial companies have grown up everywhere, trade unions also, in conditions which were by no means liberal. Proud-

[28] I take the liberty of making reference (in an English review) to my book, *La Ville française, Institutions et Libertés locales*, Paris, 1927.

[29] *Démocratie*, II, p. 432.
[30] *Ibid.*, p. 334.

hon often made this assertion. Born of individualism, these groupings of interest and of creeds have developed a method of concentration in which nothing can be found of the individualism so dear to Tocqueville. There has been a concentration of interests on other points than those accepted by the State. The unions of civil servants, in particular, have created a power at the margin of regular power, while economic groups have hastened the end of liberalism in a domain where the orthodox economists, to whom Tocqueville was friendly enough, had hoped to establish it for ever, as the most precious result of the system of law which grew out of '89.

These groupings would have surprised Tocqueville, but perhaps they would have annoyed him more even than they surprised him. This pessimist wrote in the '30's those lines which echo in our day as though they had been the consequence of its conditions: "Man has need of much intelligence, science, and art, in order to organise and to maintain secondary powers, and in order to create amid the independence and individual weakness of citizens, free associations which will be in a condition to fight against tyranny without destroying order."

How bitter! Above all, what distrust! Should we not emphasise this absence of confidence which Tocqueville shows through such words in that political art upon which he rested, as we have just seen, the fate of political liberty!

It is not in order to fortify liberty such as it was believed to be in '89 that groups have been created during the nineteenth century; but in order to allow the members, the democratic force, properly so-called, to influence either the State, the consumers, or the producers in order to replace the struggle of isolated individuals by the struggle of disciplined groups. It is no longer the isolated individual, thinking in isolation, according to Tocqueville's wish, who affects society, but coalitions born of democracy. But do not these groups destroy it?

This movement of concentration was unforeseen by Tocqueville a century ago. On all sides it is through compact masses that men group themselves according to their ideas or their interests; and we hardly think to-day of anything more than increasing the prerogatives of the State in order to make more valuable the efforts of these masses, so bitterly insisting on their claims.

The liberals, partisans of a progressive State, under the direction of leaders, wished to have beside the municipal institutions and more or less powerful associations, a judiciary power which should be strong, independent, and respected. "Let us take good care; an elective power which is not submitted to a judiciary power escapes sooner or later from control.

. . . The extension of judiciary power in the State must, then, be related to the extension of elective power, and if the two do not come together the State will finish by falling into anarchy or servitude."

"In the United States, this power was placed above the legislative and executive; there is another institution which serves the purpose of defining liberty. The American judge perfectly resembles the magistrates of other countries. However, he is clothed in an immense political power. From what does this come? . . . The cause of it is in this single fact, that Americans have allowed their judges to refuse to apply the laws which seem to them to be unconstitutional. . . . From the moment when the judge refuses to apply a law in a given case it loses at that instant a part of its moral force. Those whom it had restricted are then made aware that there exists a means of evading their obligations: litigation multiplies and the law falls into impotence. There then follows one of two things: the people changes its constitution or the legislature takes back its law. The power given to the courts forms one of the most powerful barriers which have ever been erected against the tyranny of political assemblies." [31]

And should we not add: against democracy itself, or at least, democracy as it is understood in France?

Are we ready in France to adopt this government by judges? Among radicals and socialists, even the collaboration of the Conseil d'État with the Chambers for the drafting of law is considered as an inadmissible encroachment upon the national sovereignty, as an insupportable reminder of the First and Second Empires. Again, in the present state of ideas we cannot hope for the introduction of the American system, even during a distant future. When the legislature has absorbed the executive, according to the centralising tendency calculated by Tocqueville, it cannot be feasible to take away from Parliament its independence, its supremacy, its absolute sovereign will in order to confide a part of it even in the highest judiciary, in elected judges. Moreover, who, in France, thinks of instituting elected judges?

But at bottom, did Tocqueville wish to see created in France a supreme court charged with the function of deciding upon the constitutionality of law?

It is not certain that Tocqueville believed that the courts of justice worked perfectly in the United States. What then could be the value of its example for Europe and for France? "In America the people appoint the man who makes the law and the man who executes it; it forms the jury and punishes the breach of law. . . . It is, therefore, the people who direct, and although the form of government may be representative, it is

[31] *Démocratie*, I, p. 120.

clear that the opinions, the prejudices, the interests and even the passions of the people can find no durable obstacles to prevent them from going in the direction in which at the moment they may wish to go." One cannot be more pessimistic than that. What is the value of this representative democracy upon which liberty breaks, this régime which no institution appears capable of maintaining in a lawful channel of political equity?

Democracy is equality of conditions, that is to say, in Tocqueville's language, equality of rights, in conformity with the definition of the Constitution in the year III: "Equality consists in that the law is the same for all, whether it protects or punishes." There we have the centre of Tocqueville's thought, of his work, his great study of equality, his book, *De la Démocratie en Amérique*, of which we shall note what it contains of European, and, more particularly, of French, significance.

The first part of *De la Démocratie en Amérique* was published in 1835, the second in 1840. In it Tocqueville took the title of barrister at the Paris courts. It is a book the prophetic nature of which renders it singular, since, contrary to the general rule, some of his prognostications were realised in practice in the '40's. As we know, prophecy of this kind is only an especially keen vision of the present; a "good" prophet is a man who well understands the present. This ability Tocqueville had acquired studiously, and he gave expression to it with talent. It is a book which the "religious terror" which inspired him (these are the author's own terms) renders in another way no less singular; singular in fact through its mixture of objectivity and mysticism. It is a unique book in which the most diverse and rare tendencies neither neutralise nor exclude one another.

These few lines taken from the Introduction—that wonderful literary storehouse—illuminate the direction and philosophy of this book which is so full of intelligence, but which is, it must be admitted, rather long and rather boring.

"The gradual development of equality of conditions is a providential fact, having the principal characteristics of a providential fact: it is universal, it is lasting, it escapes daily from human control; all events, like all men, have served for its development. Would it be wise to believe that a social movement which comes from so far could be held up by the efforts of a generation? Can we believe that after having destroyed feudalism and conquered kings, democracy will recoil before the bourgeois and the rich? Will it stop now that it has become so strong and its enemies so weak?" Democracy is irresistible: "A great democratic revolution is in operation among us; all see it, but all do not judge it in the same way. Some consider it as something new, and, taking it for an accident, they hope to be able to stop it still; while others regard it as irresistible because it seems to them to be the most continuous, the oldest, and the most permanent fact which we know in history. When we scan the pages of our history we do not meet any great events which during 700 years have not turned to the profit of equality."

Equality of conditions—there for Tocqueville is the underlying fact of contemporary civilisation. By it everything is explained, political rules, moral rules, literary rules, manners as much as philosophy, the forms of enquiry as much as the needs of welfare. It impresses itself upon the spirit of public opinion, gives their tendency to laws, provides governments with their maxims, and the governed with their customs.

Democracy is the "underlying fact," says Tocqueville. Thus Taine, his disciple, some forty years later was to discover, using analogous formulae, in a single underlying fact, the classical spirit, the explanation from which as from a central point he was to make his explanations of the Revolution, the Consulate and the Empire radiate, after having made all his particular observations verge upon the *ancien régime*. If that is the same method it is also open to the same criticism, for if history teaches one rule it is that facts can never be moulded to such simplified explanations, to this sort of centralisation of human psychology. Where Tocqueville, on the other hand, showed himself fully faithful to historical experience is in the three fine passages in which he traces to the *ancien régime* the origins of this "historical levelling" of conditions.

We know these two famous phrases which deserve to survive, in which he has summarised this evolution; "In France kings have shown themselves the most active and the most constant of levellers. When they were ambitious and strong they worked to raise the people to the level of the nobles; and when they were moderate and feeble they allowed the people to place themselves above them. The first aided democracy by their talent, the second by their defects."

Tocqueville perhaps showed himself even more profound, when, forestalling then as in so many other places certain historical methods of analysis which we believe contemporary, he explained the advance of political democracy by the progress of technique and by the transformation of landed property. It is not by any ideological process that he describes, but through facts, a movement of facts in the most definite and suggestive terms: "As soon as citizens began to own the land otherwise than by feudal tenure, and as movable wealth could in its turn create influence and give power, discoveries were not made in art, improvements were not introduced in commerce and industry, without creating as many new elements of equality among men. From this moment all the processes which are discovered, all the needs which are born, all the desires which demand satisfaction, are steps towards the universal levelling. The taste for luxury, the love of war, the rule of fashion, the most superficial cravings of the human heart, as indeed the most profound, appear to work together to impoverish the rich and enrich the poor."

Tocqueville described also the new sentiments aroused by these facts. "Industry collects together ordinarily a multitude of men in the same place; it establishes between them new and complicated relationships. It exposes them to great and sudden alternations of abundance and misery, during which public tranquillity is endangered. It may be then that these undermine the health and even the life of those who profit from them or those who are abandoned to them. Thus the industrial class has more need of being ruled, supervised and restricted than the other classes; it is natural that the functions of government grow with this." [32]

In these lines do we not find something of a socialist accent? They date from 1836. And in these, too?

"Those who believe that complete equality can be established in a permanent way in the political world without introducing at the same time a certain equality in civil society—these seem to me to commit a dangerous error." [33]

We must agree with Professor Harold J. Laski,[34] to whom we owe a remarkable study of Tocqueville, in finding here, as we might find also in Saint-Simon, his followers, or Sismondi, about at the same time, a first sketch of the views of Marx upon the influence of economic determinism.

But Tocqueville does not like this democracy which he declares so irresistible. If he announces its reign it is as a king's herald discontented with his sovereign. It has been said that he resigned himself to its coming, but I do not believe that to be very exact, for his criticisms of the system carry the reader to the point of wishing for its destruction; they tend to prove that modern society, far from being the victim of a light and durable malady, suffers from a constitution congenitally bad. That his mind

[32] *Démocratie*, II, p. 348. At the time at which Tocqueville wrote, the contract of labour was summarily regulated by seven articles of the Code Civil and by numerous police regulations. There was no social legislation. The oldest laws concerning the person of the worker in the sense desired by Tocqueville go back to 1836, the year of the foundation of the *Presse*, to Emile de Girardin. It is not without interest to recall here that Royer-Collard, who exercised a great influence

on the mind of Tocqueville, already in 1822 reproached law-makers with having "reduced society to the state of dust because they are not occupied with social problems" (cf. Maxime Leroy, *Le Code Civil et le droit nouveau*, Paris, 1904, p. 40).

[33] *Mélanges*, p. 29.

[34] *The Social and Political Ideas of Some Representative Thinkers of the Victorian Age*, ed. F. J. C. Hearnshaw, London, 1933.

as well as his heart remained hostile to it can hardly be doubted when we remember that he said: "I am aristocratic by instinct." [35]

Undoubtedly, he said that it was necessary to improve democracy, but it was with his tongue in his cheek, for how can we hope that the people will transform itself, renew itself to the point of becoming unrecognisable? If mistakes have frequently been made as to the true thought of Tocqueville it is because his pen is not always precise.

Nothing is more important than the choice of the delegates of the people since the people cannot govern directly. From this choice depends, therefore, the proper movement of affairs. Tocqueville asserts that this choice, contrary to the opinion of Montesquieu, is always bad, with a tendency to go from bad to worse: this choice can only be bad.

He writes: "I will admit without any difficulty that the mass of citizens are sincere in their wish for the good of the country, I say even that the lower classes of society seem to me to mix with this desire, in general, fewer combinations of personal interest than the upper classes: but what they always lack, more or less, is the art of judging the means, even while they sincerely will the end. What a long study, what divergent ideas are necessary in order to form a clear idea of the character of a single man! The greatest genius fails and yet the crowd are to succeed! The people never finds the time and the means to devote itself to this work. It must always judge hastily. From that comes the fact that charlatans of all kinds know so well the secret of pleasing it, while so often its real friends fail to do so."

He adds: "Absolute monarchies have dishonoured despotism; let us be careful lest the democratic republics rehabilitate it, and that by making its yoke heavier for a few they deprive it for the greater number of its odious aspect and degrading character."

If the level of reason is increasing, will not the choice become better in the long run? Tocqueville refuses us this hope. The people has not the time to learn and, moreover, if it learned too much, democracy would perish none the less from the inequality which this enlightenment arouses: "Men become more unequal in property in measure as their knowledge widens," and further, "it is impossible, whatever we may do, to enlighten the people above a certain level." [36]

Envy blinds the people. "Democratic institutions develop to a high degree the sentiment of envy in the human heart. . . . They awaken and flatter the passion for equality without ever being able to satisfy it completely. . . . The people warms itself in the search for this good which is

[35] Phrases inédites citées par A. Redier, *op. cit.*, p. 48.   [36] *Démocratie*, I, p. 237.

all the more precious for being near enough to be understood and far enough never to be tasted. . . . Everything which excels appears to the people to be an obstacle to its desires and there is no superiority legitimate enough for the sight of it not to tire the people's eyes. Many people imagine that this secret instinct which leads the lower classes with us to remove as far as they can the higher from the control of affairs is only to be found in France; that is a mistake: the instinct of which I speak is not French, it is democratic. . . ."

Could an improvement of the electoral system improve the quality of popular choice? He believes that indirect election must be "the only means of bringing the enjoyment of political liberty within the reach of all classes of the people." A vain hope, for experience of politics, even in Tocqueville's time, furnished no facts as evidence in its favour!

And the democratic basis? "What I dislike most in America is not the extreme liberty which reigns there, but the few guarantees against tyranny."

Democracies are, Tocqueville declares, despotic, spendthrift, unstable, corrupt, incapable of directing diplomatic negotiations to a satisfactory conclusion. What remains to be said in their favour? Here are some lines in which Tocqueville tries to lighten this sombre picture of popular ills, but these repentant touches, added to a finished canvas, hardly relieve the tone of this lugubrious and desolating criticism as much as has been said or as he himself perhaps thought.

"The methods of democracy are more imperfect than those of aristocracy: often it works without wishing to do so against itself, but its purpose is more useful. In general the laws of democracy make for the good of the largest number, for they spring from the majority of all citizens. . . . Those of aristocracy, on the contrary, tend to give to a small number the monopoly of riches and of power."

He writes further: "In a general way, the object of democracy in its legislation is more to the advantage of humanity than is the case with aristocracy." And he concludes, "but there finish its advantages." [37]

Does democracy offer only these advantages? They are very quickly enumerated. He adds, further: "Democratic government causes the idea of political rights to descend right down to the lowest of citizens, just as the division of goods brings the idea of the right of property in general within the reach of all men."

The rightness of this view can be admitted; but to what extent does it correspond with the facts in Tocqueville's mind? It corresponds with no practical possibilities if I have well understood the following lines of

[37] *Démocratie*, I, p. 279.

this categorical assertion: "There is nothing more productive of marvels than the art of being free; but there is nothing harder than the apprenticeship of freedom; it is born amid storms, it is established with difficulty in the midst of civil strife, and it is only when freedom is already old that its benefits can be known."

Already old! But it is not yet born!

If American democracy succeeded to a certain extent, if a great future is reserved to it, that is, Tocqueville suggests, owing to the fact that it has grown up without warlike and powerful neighbours, that it was established on a fertile soil, rich in minerals, watered by large rivers and inland seas. And even more than to these circumstances of place, does it not owe its success to the race of men who peopled its vast expanse? Tocqueville replies: "Bad laws, revolutions and anarchy cannot destroy among them the taste for well-being and the spirit of enterprise which seem to be the distinctive characteristics of their race." [38]

Racial advantages? [39] What remains here of democracy which Tocqueville makes synonymous, almost without realizing it, with bad laws, revolutions and anarchy? This statement, extracted from his *Notes de voyage*, stresses the pessimism with which democracy inspires Tocqueville. "What I see so far gives me little enthusiasm because I have more belief in the nature of things than in man's will. Never have such happy and powerful conditions of existence been found together. . . . the fact is that this society develops automatically."

In his *Souvenirs* Tocqueville reports with some disgust that on May 15th, 1848, the day when the Assembly was invited by the friends of Barbès and of Blanqui, the representatives were treated as "clerks." And this word he remembered as an injury: "I saw people who showed us their fists calling us their clerks. They repeated this expression many times; for many days the older democratic papers called the representatives only clerks of the people, and these lackeys were pleased with the idea."

On that day Tocqueville saw Blanqui at the tribune. He drew a portrait of him extraordinarily lifelike but with no sympathy. "That is when I saw appear at the tribune in his turn a man whom I only saw on that day, but the memory of whom has always filled me with disgust and horror; he had pale, thin cheeks, white lips, an unhealthy and evil air,

[38] He writes further: "In New England, where education and liberty are the daughters of morality and religion." *Démocratie*, I, p. 240.

[39] The Comte du Gobineau was Tocqueville's *Chef de Cabinet* when the latter was Minister of Foreign Affairs in 1849. It is hardly necessary to point out that dates remove the possibility of the hypothesis that Gobineau had an influence upon Tocqueville.

an unclean pallor, the appearance of a rotting corpse; he had no linen visible, an old black coat covering a thin and puny body; he seemed to have lived in a drain and to have just come out of it; I was told that this was Blanqui."

Tocqueville does not love the democratic crowd: he loves its leaders no more. Is it necessary to add here that he spoke with much scorn of Victor Considérant?

With these lines written about 1840 must be compared his admirable speech of January 29th, 1848,[40] in which, inspired by "a curiosity mixed with fear," he sketched the revolution which was coming with a rushing tide amid universal blindness. He feared this revolution because property was no longer considered by an important fraction of public opinion as the necessary foundation of society. "Do you not see that there are spreading little by little works and ideas which do not aim only at overthrowing such and such laws, ministries, governments even, but society itself, at destroying the foundations upon which it rests to-day? Do you not understand that the division of wealth made in the world up to the present day is unjust, that property rests upon foundations which are not equitable foundations?"

Democracies are based in the practice of all peoples upon the rights of the majority: how can we assure the reconciliation of democracy with liberty? By liberty is meant here the liberty of minorities. As Tocqueville observed, there is equality in servitude as well as in liberty.

It is only superficially that Tocqueville appears to reject democracy solely when it partakes of Caesarism or Jacobinism. In reality, it is all democracy that he rejects, for he does not admit the right of the majority which is traditionally the essence of democracy. He rejects it as an abuse. "I regard as both impious and detestable the maxim that in matters of government the majority of a people has the right to do anything. . . . For me it is impossible to give to several of my fellow creatures the power of empire which I refuse to a single one." [41]

As soon as the right of the majority enters into discussion, is it not the right of democracy to govern itself which is really in question? And if one denies this right can one claim to be a democrat? Should we not here charge Tocqueville, who spoke of the providential nature of democracy, with rebellion against Providence, the animator of this experience and of this ideology?

If we contest the sovereignty of the majority, at what result will the

[40] To be found in the *Moniteur* of the 30th and, reproduced by Tocqueville, in his *Souvenirs*, p. 15.

[41] *Démocratie*, I, pp. 303 and 305.

philosopher and the partisan arrive? Republicans will reply to the plebis-
citary *coup d'état* of the Prince-President: "The Republic is above universal suffrage," while Proudhon gave as the conclusion to his *Idée générale
de la Révolution* at the same moment this other formula: "The Revolution
is above the Republic," a formula no less anti-electoral, no less anti-
democratic.

Is not the democrat bound essentially to cling to the principle of
Rousseau—but to his crude principle, for he included the minority in the
general will—the people cannot do wrong? That was also one of the favourite formulas of Marat, an alliance which will perhaps rejoice the
ghost of Tocqueville. It is a formula which means that the popular vote
must, whatever happens, have the last word.[42]

I believe that we can avoid all controversy on this point if we are determined to consider democracy simply as a balance, a thermometer, a
method of weighing opinions, of measuring their heat. By itself it is
neither Caesarian nor Liberal. It serves to count opinions; it is not an instrument destined to arouse the wisest judgment; number is no more
than number. The democratic electorate is a fact independent of systems
and government, leading to any one of them, without any one of them,
as Tocqueville believed of his own, having the right to invoke any other
justification than a purely statistical lawfulness. Those who have identified
democracy and liberty, or democracy and Caesarism, have confounded the
object weighed with the scales; they have forgotten that the scales support
everything which is put upon them. The universal practice of peoples
since '89 has shown constantly that the sovereignty of the people has
represented every principle which it was necessary for it to express. He is
a bold philosopher or politician who, in the face of so clear an experience,
will dare to affirm that there is a lawfulness peculiar to liberal democracy.

Tocqueville demanded that above the majority there should be placed
a disinterested power.

"I believe that it is always necessary to place somewhere a power superior to all these; but I find liberty in peril when this power sees before
it no obstacle which can hinder its march and give it time to moderate
itself." [43]

One chapter of *La Démocratie* is entitled: Why democratic peoples
show a more ardent and lasting love for equality than for liberty.[44]

He replies: because equality is an older and more easily comprehen-

---

[42] Tocqueville well knew the principle:
"It is as the very essence of democratic
government that the empire of the majority is absolute, for, without the majority, there is nothing which is solid."
Démocratie, I, p. 297.

[43] *Démocratie*, I, p. 304.

[44] *Ibid.*, II, p. 105.

sible fact. Liberty demands more effort in order to be conquered and to be maintained. "It is more recent than equality; it has not yet entered into custom: the one has already created opinion, habits, laws, which belong to it, the other is appearing alone and for the first time in daylight. Thus the second is not yet to be found among common ideas and groups of men, while the first has already penetrated our habits and customs, and had a specific influence on the least actions of life."

Tocqueville concludes: "Why should we be surprised if men of to-day prefer the one to the other . . . they will suffer poverty, enslavement, barbarism, but they will not suffer aristocracy."

Always the same pessimistic note! Is it not here that we should reproduce those other lines of Tocqueville? "Democracy abandoned to its own savage instincts has grown up like those children deprived of paternal care who educate themselves and know nothing of society but its vices and its miseries."

The same is true of the liberalism of Tocqueville as of the democracy "without limits" of Barbès and Blanqui: as soon as liberty reaches a certain point doctrinaires retire invoking, themselves also, a superior authority to free criticism. Thus Tocqueville had no conception of a liberty which did not respect the Christian religion, was not limited by a moderating system, was forbidden by an independent judicial power proper to the maintenance of a strong tradition. Far from recognising in liberty a power of infinite expansion, he restricted its movement by reason of facts which, in his opinion, ought to escape it in principle. And thus, instead of the formula of Proudhon, *Revolution is above the Republic*, could not Tocqueville, following out his own logic, but stronger in logic than in observation, have written—Catholic religion and municipal decentralisation are above individual liberty? Political doctrines, we must continually repeat, always define states of fact, actual situations, and it is because they sometimes forget this that so many writers and historians have allowed themselves to accept the absolute declarations true for all time made by so many doctrinaires of liberalism and democracy.

Tocqueville drew the most sombre picture of the future of democratic society. Let us see what he says.

"I imagine with what new features despotism may reproduce itself in the world. I see an innumerable crowd of men, equal and alike, who turn ceaselessly to themselves in order to procure small and vulgar pleasures, with which they fill their being. Each, retired into himself, is a stranger to the fate of all the others; his children and his friends are for him the human race. As for the life of his fellow citizens, he is beside them but he does not see them; he touches them but is unaware of them. He exists only in himself and for himself; and if he has a family, we may say that he has no country.

"Above such people there is an immense paternal power which takes care only to ensure their pleasures and to control their fate. It is absolute, meticulous, regular, foreseeing and kind. It would be like a father's power if, as that does, it had for its object to prepare men for manhood; but it seeks on the contrary to keep them irrevocably in a state of infancy. It is happy that citizens enjoy themselves provided that they think only of enjoying themselves. It works willingly for their happiness but it desires to be the sole agent and the sole arbiter of that happiness; it provides for their security, foresees and satisfies their needs, facilitates their pleasure, conducts their chief business, directs their industry, regulates and divides their inheritance. Cannot it entirely save them the trouble of thinking and the hardship of living?

"It is thus that every day it makes the use of free will less valuable and more rare, that it encloses the action of decision in a more confined space and takes away from the citizen little by little the control of his own actions. Equality has prepared men for everything, it has disposed them to suffer everything and often even to regard suffering as a benefit.

"After having thus bit by bit taken each citizen into its powerful hands, and after having formed him in its fashion, the sovereign stretches out its arms to the whole society; it covers the surface with a network of small and complicated rules through which the most original and vigorous minds can find no freedom to surpass the crowd; it does not break the will . . . but it softens it, bends it and directs it; it rarely forces men to act, but it opposes unceasingly the taking of action; it does not destroy, but prevents from being born; it does not tyrannise, it hinders, it oppresses, it enervates, it extinguishes, it renders stupid, and finally it reduces every nation to a herd of timid and industrious animals whose shepherd is the government.

"I have always believed that this sort of servitude, regulated, kindly, and peaceful, whose picture I have just drawn, may be combined more easily than one fancies with certain of the external forms of liberty, and that it would not be impossible for it to be established under the very shadow of the sovereignty of the people."

Can we regard this picture of Tocqueville as the prophetic announcement of contemporary dictatorship in Italy, in Germany, in Russia, which, despotic though they may be, claim to base themselves none the less upon the legitimacy of a national idea and of a popular will?

Tocqueville criticises democracy from a political point of view. Proudhon, who read *La Démocratie* and was influenced by it, criticised it chiefly from an economic point of view; he spoke of the prevalent democracy as "a patrician mediocrity." Why? Because economic inequality limits political liberty. He summarised his opinion in that insolent formula: "With the electoral vote democracy eliminates men; with the legislative vote it eliminates ideas." [45]

Proudhon defined democracy as "a disguised aristocracy," [46] because working-men electors chose their representatives from outside their ranks and, by reason of this, ceased to be represented in all their opinions and in all their interests.

What is this elective democracy which is not the exact image of electoral democracy? Whom should these workmen choose to represent them if it is not their bourgeois?

Breaking with this democratic thesis the militant workers of the end of the Second Empire organise working-men candidates with a view to making universal a democracy which, until then, had only been a democracy of notabilities. It was in 1863 and in 1864 that the workers of Paris, for the first time, made this attempt; and on this occasion Proudhon wrote the most original of his books: *De la Capacité Politique des Classes Ouvrières*. Thus was born in an electoral sense a Liberal Party. The first workers' congress, held in Paris in 1876, discussed at length "the direct representation of the proletariat in Parliament" and the opportunities of working-men candidates.

At the same time, emphasising this movement, which was anti-democratic in its tendency, there developed an anti-democratic "custom" in trade union groups. We may see that it is not only in countries of dictatorships that we are witnessing a retreat of democracy. The classical ground of popular democracy knew it and knows it still among the descendants of those anti-parliamentary storm troops who invaded the Legislative Assembly of '48.

Tocqueville is right. The working classes think more of equality than of liberty; and, at bottom, they love authority. The Soviet experience has supplied us with a factual proof which Marx had already furnished in the realm of ideas. If the liberals look to an extension of liberty for the reform of abuses, the working classes look only for the coming of a better distribution of commodities through a strengthening of authority. Authority of the traditional State for the one; revolutionary dictatorship substituting itself for this State, for the others. Both limit their dream by a class view, using words which suggest that both systems are capable of universalising happiness.

[45] *Solution du problème social*, pp. 59   [46] *Ibid.*, p. 48.
and 55, Paris, 1868. (New edition.)

In the Introduction to *La Démocratie* Tocqueville wrote: "A new political science is needed for an entirely new world."

Was it of a purely objective science that Tocqueville thought? The following text, taken also from the Introduction, suggests that Tocqueville thought less of a true science than of an art destined to apply his doctrines: "To instruct democracy, to revivify, if possible, its beliefs, to purify its manners, to regulate its movement, to substitute little by little science for inexperience, the knowledge of its true interests for blind instinct, to adapt its government to time and place, to modify it according to circumstances and men: such is the first of the duties imposed in our day upon those who direct society."

Philosophers did not cease, in the eighteenth century with Sieyès, and in the nineteenth with the followers of Saint-Simon, to seek among facts for rules susceptible of elucidating the present, and, it must be admitted, we only begin to see certain glimmerings of light from this direction since sociologists decided to study social facts coldly, as though they were phenomena of the physical world, acting upon the advice of Durkheim and his emulators.

There can be no doubt that Tocqueville is one of the first, thanks rather to his pessimism than to his method, who was able to point the thought of historians and philosophers towards this happy scepticism of sociologists. His *Ancien régime* and his *Souvenirs*, in particular, are full of notes which are truly impartial and of the clearest political utility. He showed notably to what a degree the past remains a determining factor in the present, at the very moment when we imagine that it has been entirely destroyed. A precious observation, the implacable reality of which has been obscured by so many categorical formulae born of revolutionary phraseology.

Tocqueville is a dogmatist, but a dogmatist who had the sense of the evolution of ideas and institutions. He had that sense clearly enough to be led to believe that this evolution ought to be understood and studied as an experience, and not accepted as a sort of necessary and transcending revolution.

He gave certain restrictions to political liberty without disguising, however, the solid character of its experience and of the distant factors which determine it. He spoke of the movement of "the mass of human societies." [47]

He lived in a time which was able to advance the science of nature remarkably far; he himself, much like Balzac or Taine, invoked Cuvier to explain the connection between facts and the regularity of the laws by

[47] *Mélanges,* I, p. 37.

which they are governed.[48] The attempt at conciliation between royalty and the parliamentary system under Louis-Philippe he calls, in a note of 1847, "an experience."

He adds: "There is the greatest problem of the time; it is posed, but not solved." It has not been solved since and there are other problems which have been set because societies are in perpetual revolution, "a single revolution, always the same despite fluctuating fortunes, which our fathers saw begin and which, in all probability, we shall not see end." [49]

Who will be optimist enough to hope that we shall see it end, we or our children?

Let us reproduce these few further lines in order to underline this attitude: "I am tempted to believe that what are called necessary institutions are often only those institutions to which we are accustomed, and that in matters of social constitution, the field of the possible is very much vaster than the men who live in any society imagine." [50]

I like, I must admit, this attitude of frank scepticism before the present and the future; for he is without fanaticism the observer who thinks that evolution continues. Many are the minds who predict the end of experience, I mean the coming of a Golden Age: they swarm in the '40's and Tocqueville mocked those ignorant makers of "plans." We know to what extent these hopes imply blindness and taste for violence. It is only by patient study that we know the tendencies of our day, and by experiment that we can usefully try to create a better justice among us.

Tocqueville was not among those inspired and those fanatics, partly because he was of a bitter turn of mind, but also because he was a good historian, a good observer of the facts among which he lived, because he was human and genuine. He calls himself "an observer"; and this title which he takes with pride suits him perfectly. He writes that in 1830 he took "The end of the act for the end of the play." [51] He had the wisdom to learn by his mistake in order to avoid falling a prey to that vain optimism which the liberal victory had inspired in him.

There, perhaps, in those few words, is the expression of the highest wisdom of Tocqueville, increased by the spectacle of '48, that singular mixture of governmental stupidity and popular sedition: "One must have lived for a long time in the midst of parties and in the storm itself in which they move in order to understand to what point men travel away from their own purposes, and how the destiny of this world works as the effect of, but often in reaction to, the wills which produce it: like a kite

[48] *Ibid.*, p. 39 (in an article which appeared in 1836).
[49] *Souvenirs*, p. 5.
[50] *Ibid.*, p. 111.
[51] *Ibid.*, p. 13.

which is moved by the opposite actions of the wind which blows and the string which holds it." [52]

It is with these words that are so wise that we take leave of this intelligent and generous Tocqueville, adding, alas!—a too solemn Tocqueville.

[52] *Souvenirs,* p. 36.

23

ACTON
SPENCER

MILL

Just as John Stuart Mill (see page 403) was strongly influenced by Tocqueville, the third great European liberal thinker of the nineteenth century, Lord Acton, was strongly influenced by Mill. Acton (1834–1902), also like Tocqueville and Mill, combined statesmanship with scholarship, and, like his two illustrious liberal compères, he was for some time a Member of Parliament. A devout Catholic, Acton frequently found himself in conflict with official Roman Catholic policy and belief, and he particularly opposed the doctrine of papal infallibility before it became church law. He was editor of *The Rambler*, a Catholic review, to which he contributed in 1859 and 1860 a searching examination of Mill's *On Liberty*, trying to reconcile his liberal views with his Catholic faith. A brilliant historical scholar and lecturer, Acton never completed a book in his lifetime; after his death his essays and lectures were published in book form, the most notable among them being his *Lectures on Modern History* (1906), *The History of Freedom and Other Essays* (1907), and *Lectures on the French Revolution* (1910).

One of John Stuart Mill's outstanding personal qualities was his generosity, and this trait is emphasized by Herbert Spencer in an essay on "John Stuart Mill: His Moral Character" (1873), contributed to a memorial volume on Mill shortly after his death. Spencer (1820–1903) was the most consistent and influential apostle of laissez faire in the nineteenth century, and his impact on American thinking was even greater than on

British political and social thought. From early manhood he adhered to the most rigid concepts of laissez faire and, while most liberals of his generation gradually underwent a change—as could be seen particularly in the case of John Stuart Mill—Spencer never abandoned the creed of his youth. He wrote voluminously in the fields of history, ethics, biology, psychology, and sociology, of which latter discipline he was one of the founders. The application of the concept of evolution to social problems and processes is probably the key concept of his thought, and he tried to do for the world of human relations what Darwin had done for the systematic understanding of biology and zoology. His *Social Statics* (1851) and *The Man versus the State* (1884) most clearly and succinctly synthesize his social and political philosophy, and are still looked upon as landmarks of laissez-faire doctrine by its unreconstructed followers.

Acton on MILL

Any book of Mr. Mill's which professes to lay down fixed principles, applicable to important questions of social and individual ethics, deserves to be as carefully studied by those who possess known landmarks and unalterable methods for the guidance of life and the discipline of the soul, as by those to whom all questions of the kind are still open. The Catholic faith places a man in the best position for forming a sound ethical code, and extending it to new cases and exigencies as they arise; but it does not itself explicitly include such a code. The leading rules and distinctions of ethics form no part of divine revelation: no one ever laid them down so clearly as Aristotle; and from him, in the middle ages, saints received them, to blend them into one harmonious whole with the truths of revelation. Even now all the work is not done to our hand, for the ethical philosophy of Catholics is not unprogressive; and therefore a work like the *Essay on Liberty*, though chiefly interesting to Protestants, concerns us also. A denial of this would go far to justify the imputations of mental torpor which are so freely made against us. Although ethical *principles* do not change, the *applications* of those principles may vary with changing circumstances and relations. The moral relation between a child and a father changes as the child grows to be fifteen. Slavery may be, under one set of circumstances, justifiable; or, under another set, abominable. So with

[Lord Acton, "Mill on Liberty," *The Rambler*, vol. 2 (New Series, November, 1859 and March, 1860).]

liberty of thought and of action. It may be that, under the social conditions of former ages, a degree and kind of repression of error might advisably, because successfully, be employed; which under modern conditions would, if attempted, cause more evil than it would cure.

Perhaps there is no single moral question upon which a greater medley of opinions is afloat among Catholics than that of individual liberty. This by itself shows the disputable nature of the whole subject; for upon articles of faith it is notorious that there is no such discordance. Yet the *data* possessed by a Catholic places him in a peculiarly favourable position for solving difficulties. But to recommend his views to others, he must neither spare the labour of thought nor shrink from the arena of discussion.

The occasion of Mr. Mill's Essay is to be found in the relation of the rationalist party in England to the prevailing state of opinion. As far as external indications go, rationalism in England is less influential, less progressive, than it was twenty years ago. In these last years, such wild outbursts of spiritual rebellion as the *Nemesis of Faith* no longer rise to startle the religious world from its propriety. Fifteen years back, the popular book on cosmogony and geology was the *Vestiges of the Natural History of the Creation*; now it is the *Testimony of the Rocks*. Among the Reviews of that school, some, like the *Prospective*, have vanished altogether; others, like the *Westminster*, contrive to exist, but with a stationary circulation, and less than the old pugnacity. The *Examiner* has dropped its racy diatribes upon Anglican Bishops, finding probably that they would not suit the soberer tastes of its present public. In 1834 the Church Establishment appeared to be tottering under the blows of a legion of enemies; in 1859 it seems to be as secure against a crash as the Bank; and yet, in spite of these appearances, it is certain that rationalism is not less, but probably more widely spread. The thinking, reasoning persons in a nation must always form a small minority; and when the mediocre majority are attached to orthodox opinions, or what they deem such, while the social fabric is steady and the social bond strong, the dissenting or rationalist opinions can only find favour among the thinking minority. Now in England it is probable that a considerably larger proportion of this small class belongs to the rationalist camp at the present day than twenty years ago. On the Continent, at least in France, the course of things I believe has been the reverse. Meantime the majority, little suspecting the true movement of the currents of thought, are so well pleased with themselves, and their national character and religion, that, with the usual insolence of ascendency, they are gradually becoming more intolerant of marked divergence on either side from the popular standards. For the system of the Catholic is no less offensive in their eyes than that of the rationalist. Strange to say, English Protestantism is tending to a sort of unity, which may be described as a common national sentiment, strong enough to cause the special differences between sects to be felt as very small matters. In vain do a few hundred clergymen, and a few rural coteries, point to the language of the Liturgy, insist on the value of the old fringe which Martin still bears upon his coat, and utter solemn warnings against the sin of schism. In Mr. Carlyle's language, "the Puseyite logic runs off John Bull like water;" and he answers, in no gentle tone, "In spite of all your formularies, Protestant I am, and Protestant I will remain."

Against this disposition of the majority to encroach upon the freedom of thought and action of dissenting minorities, Mr. Mill, on the side of the rationalists, has skilfully chosen his ground. In some ways, the yoke of the dominant system is more oppressive to rationalists than to Catholics. We are, indeed, liable to be treated with unjust suspicion, to have our children proselytised, and to experience in the court of law and in the board-room the intolerance of the half-educated masses; but, at any rate, we are not now persecuted into conformity. But rationalists, having no external organisation, are left under the full pressure of the popular system in many things where it is most irksome. They may think that marriage should be a revocable contract; yet public opinion renders a marriage before a registrar ordinarily inadmissible. They may consider baptism an idle ceremony; yet few of them will brave social opinion so far as to deprive their children of it. Thus opinion exacts a conformity to the usages of the popular religion, which rationalists cannot but feel to be humiliating. In order to mitigate this rigour of opinion, Mr. Mill correctly judged that a direct attack upon the received system would not advance his object. But he took up the cry which the received system loudly utters, and prefixing the name of Liberty to his essay, he claimed for the thing its full application in the domain of law and of opinion.

In his introductory chapter, Mr. Mill traces the gradual development of the idea of human liberty. The first epoch of the struggle between liberty and authority is marked by the establishment of definite rights and immunities, wrung by the subjects from the governing few with the view of protecting themselves against abuses of power. Such was the law erecting the tribuneship of the commons at Rome; such the Magna Charta of our ancestors. A further step in the same direction consisted in the establishment of constitutional checks, mainly through the contrivance of a system of representation, and by committing to the representatives a control over the public expenditure. When power was so limited by checks that it ceased to be formidable, it was perceived that antagonism between the governors and the governed was, after all, no necessity of nature; that when the idea of representation is completely carried out, the distinction would be obliterated by the people coming to be their own governors. Since, then, the powers of the government had come to emanate solely from the governed, the necessity for multiplying checks on its exercise seemed to be superseded; for why should the people require to be protected against itself? But experiments have made it evident that new dangers to liberty have emerged. "The 'people' who exercise the power, are not always the same people with those over whom it is exercised; and the 'self-government' spoken of is not the government of each by himself, but of each by all the rest. The will of the people, moreover, practically means the will of the most numerous, or the most active, *part* of the people." Hence arose a new species of tyranny, the 'tyranny of the majority'—as manifested either in the acts of the public authorities, or in the *social* intolerance habitual to a majority. "Protection, therefore, against the tyranny of the magistrate is not enough; there needs protection also against the tyranny of the prevailing opinion and feeling, against the tendency of society to impose, by other means than civil penalties, its own ideas and practices as rules of conduct on those who dissent from them; to fetter the development, and, if possible, prevent the formation, of any individuality not in harmony with its ways; and to compel all characters to fashion themselves upon the model of its own." The object of the Essay, therefore, is, "to assert one very simple principle,—that the sole end for which mankind are warranted, individually or collectively, in interfering with the liberty of action of any of their number, is self-protection." Our ideas of our neighbour's good may justify our remonstrating with, or counselling him; "but not our compelling him, or visiting him with any evil, in case he do otherwise."

In the second chapter Mr. Mill states four grounds on which he infers that it is necessary to the welfare of society to allow the liberty of thought and discussion in the fullest extent. First, the opinions prevailing in society may be false; but unless a free examination and public discussion of their grounds be permitted, they cannot be disproved. Secondly, the received opinion may be partly true, partly false; while the dissenting opinion, though also partly false, may contain the truth which is wanted to complete the popular half-truth. Thirdly, though the received opinion is wholly true, yet, unless it be vigorously attacked from time to time, so as to elicit equal vigour in its defence, it may become a mere prejudice, a matter of habit, not of understanding. And lastly, the meaning of the received doctrine itself may be lost or enfeebled: it may become a mere lip profession, ineffectual for good, only obstructing the growth of other truths which might be held with real conviction.

Mr. Mill, in the third chapter, inquires whether the same considerations do not require that men should be free to *act* on their opinions, provided it be at their own risk. Here the chief difficulty is, that the end to be attained—individual spontaneity of conduct—is so little valued; that few even comprehend William Humboldt's dictum, "the end of man, or that which is prescribed by the eternal immutable dictates of reason, and not suggested by vague and transient desires, is the highest and most harmonious development of his powers to a complete and consistent whole." Not that each man is to aim at independence of self-development, so as to undervalue the teachings of experience; on the contrary, education is unceasingly to communicate them to us. But afterwards the individual should be free to use and interpret experience in his own way, instead of having some customary rendering imposed upon him. Conformity to custom, merely *as* custom, even though it may happen to be good, involves no practice of the faculties, no moral choice. "It really is of importance, not only what men do, but also what manner of men they are that do it." To choose his plan of life, and follow it, demands the employment of all a man's faculties, judgment, observation, activity, discrimination, decision, and firmness. This makes him more of a man, and his life ampler, more eventful, and more richly stored, than the life of the slaves of custom. His desires and impulses, "the raw material of human nature," are strengthened; and their possessor is made capable, perhaps of more evil, but certainly of more good.

In early stages of society individuality was in excess, and the difficulty was to keep the passions of individuals within the bounds of the general interests of society. But in our own day "society has got fairly the better of individuality." The danger lies now in the uniform mediocrity which threatens to become the almost universal type of character; even in amusements men "like in crowds;" "until, by dint of not following their own nature, they have no nature to follow, their human capacities are withered and starved."

Is such a state, he asks, desirable for a human being? It is so according to the Calvinistic theory, which makes obedience the one duty of man, and self-will his one offence. Yet surely, he argues, it is more religious to believe that a good Creator gave all human faculties that they might be cultivated and unfolded, not rooted out and consumed. In what follows, the author confounds Calvinism with Christianity; but a nobler passage succeeds:

It is not by wearing down into uniformity all that is individual in themselves, but by cultivating it and calling it forth within the limits imposed by the rights and interests of others, that human beings become a noble and beautiful object of contemplation; and as the works partake the character of those who do them, by the same process human life also becomes rich, diversified, and animating; furnishing more abundant aliment to high thoughts and elevating feelings, and strengthening the tie which binds every individual to the race, by making the race infinitely better worth belonging to. In proportion to the development of his individuality, each person becomes more valuable to himself; and is therefore capable of being more valuable to others. There is a greater fullness of life about his own existence; and when there is more life in the units, there is more in the mass which is composed of them [p. 113].

If genius is necessary to mankind, the soil in which it grows must be preserved. "Genius can only breathe freely in an atmosphere of freedom." The present ascendency of society, and the power of the masses, was perhaps inevitable; but still, "the government of mediocrity is mediocre government." "The initiation of all wise or noble things comes, and must come, from individuals; . . . . the honour and glory of the average man is, that he is capable of following that initiative." The increasing tendency of European society is to frown down individual diversities of character and practice, and to gravitate towards the state of things which prevails in China and all oriental countries, which, though once progressive, have for many ages been, properly speaking, without a history, because they have become stationary and inanimate under the numbing despotism of custom. This tendency must, it is argued, be resisted before it is too late, by asserting the claims of individuality.

Having now stated the doctrine of individual freedom, Mr. Mill considers what restraints on that freedom are permissible, and where the line is to be drawn between the authority of society and the liberty of its individual members. His principle is simple: "To individuality should belong that part of life in which it is chiefly the individual that is interested; to society, that part which chiefly interests society." The individual (supposing him of legal age and of sound mind) should be free to act in any manner that pleases him, so long as the interests of others are not directly injured. But how to apply this principle? Is a person who is grossly deficient in the "self-regarding" as distinct from the social virtues,—in industry, sobriety, frugality, and the like,—yet who directly injures no one else by his conduct,—to be in no way amenable to society? Such a person is amenable to society in respect of the *spontaneous* and *natural* consequences which flow from his conduct, viz. the displeasure, contempt, and avoidance of his neighbours; but not in respect of positive penalties. If, indeed, he is so deficient in his duty to himself as to become disabled from discharging some definite duty to others, he may become the fitting subject of moral reprobation and punishment. But for the merely contingent or *constructive* injury which his conduct may cause to society, it is better that society should bear the inconvenience than that the principle of liberty should be infringed; especially as it will generally happen that society itself is partly to blame, in having neglected to provide for the education of the offender to a right understanding of his duties and opportunities as a human being. Ill-judged attempts at the coercion of conduct generally end, as in the case of the Puritan government before the Restoration, in a strong rebound in the contrary direction. With reference to certain cases, in which the free action of the individual or the minority might appear disputable, as in the abhorrence felt by a Mohammedan society for the practice of eating pork, the disgust with which a Catholic population regard a married clergy and a heretical worship, the horror with which Sabbatarians are inspired by Sunday amusements, or teetotalers by dram-drinking,—the author argues that the only principle which will apply to all these cases, and defend the weaker body against coercion into conformity to the tastes of the stronger, is this, "that with the personal tastes and self-regarding concerns of individuals the public has no business to interfere."

To the doctrine of human freedom, thus explained, I am disposed to give a decided general adherence. That doctrine is, that the liberty of thought and of its expression should be entire; and that the liberty of tastes and modes of living should be only limited by the single condition, that the rights and interests of others be respected. By liberty, I mean absence of accountability to any *temporal* authority; and, with Mr. Mill, I understand by the subjects of this liberty persons of full age and of sound mind. And my thesis is this, that although, in bygone states of society, the employment of coercion in order to bring recusants to conformity may have been occasionally defensible, as producing, on the whole, more good than evil, the circumstances of modern society are such as to render the use of such coercion inexpedient and reprehensible, because certain to produce more evil than good.

It is objected that such a doctrine is suitable enough to the circumstances of a Catholic minority in England, but that no English Catholic would advocate is application to the case of the Catholic majority in Austria, or France, or Spain, or adapt to the latitude of Vienna the rule which he approves for the latitude of London. I answer, that I make no mental reservations. Having faith in my thesis, I am prepared beforehand for the extension of the principle laid down to every variety of circumstances.

Mr. Mill himself, in defining the range of his doctrine,

> leaves out of consideration those backward states of society in which the race itself may be considered as in its "nonage" [p. 23]. Liberty, [he says], as a principle, has no application to any state of things anterior to the time when mankind have become capable of being improved by free and equal discussion. When the wisdom of the governors is far in advance of the wisdom of the governed, and the means do not exist, by the communication and comparison of ideas, of equalising the two, it is desirable and right that the subjects should be coerced, if necessary, to their own good.

In the employment of coercion, whether directly or by penalties attached to non-compliance, to bring men to the true faith, I believe that the test of lawfulness is success. To exact the hollow profession of the truth, while the heart internally rebels, so far from being a success, is a more disastrous failure than acquiescence in open recusancy. Coercion *succeeds* only when it produces higher moral results to the persons coerced than were attained under toleration; only when they, or at least the majority of them, are brought to admit the expediency of the coercion, and are visibly benefited in their moral nature by having embraced the true and discarded the false opinion. To such success I conceive three concurrent conditions are requisite:

First, that the persons coerced should not be persons of fully-developed intellect, but in that immature mental state, akin to the case of children, which justifies, in Mr. Mill's own opinion, the use of despotic means to effect their improvement.

Secondly, that there should exist a body of teachers on the side of that true faith to which men are to be coerced, sufficiently wise, zealous, and virtuous, and also sufficiently numerous, to ensure that the true doctrine shall be exhibited in its proper light to the persons coerced; that they shall be led to see its intrinsic superiority to the falsehood which they had formerly embraced, and, partly through that insight, partly through the moral elevation caused by contact with the wise and good, attain to a higher and more developed state of being than they had formerly known.

Thirdly, that there should not exist, in the neigbourhood of the scene of coercion, a civilised community or communities of persons, who, having themselves repudiated the true doctrine, will sympathise with those who are being coerced to accept it—will encourage them to make resistance, active or passive, to the coercive measures employed, and will nourish in them a feeling of ill-usage, and of suffering unjustly in a good cause, if the resistance is unsuccessful.

Only when these three conditions meet can coercion be really successful, and therefore legitimate. It is not difficult to show that, at various times in the history of the Church, all three conditions have concurred. For three hundred years Christianity suffered from coercion, but could not inflict it. The laws and administration of Theodosius were the first attempt on a large scale to employ on the side of the true faith the weapons which had so often been turned against it. Heresy was made a crime punishable by the civil tribunals; the pagan worship was prohibited, and its temples transferred to the use of the Church. On the whole, this coercion was successful; its partial failure was owing to the imperfect fulfilment of one or other of the first two conditions. There were many individual cases in which the objects of coercion, being persons of fully-developed faculties, were irritated, not rendered submissive, by the treatment they received; and there was in many parts of the empire a dearth of good and wise Christian teachers to make the faith a living reality to the pagan multitude who were forced to profess it. Hence we read of individual Donatists and Priscillianists filled with a bitter and burning sense of wrong at the operation of the imperial laws; and also of numbers of the poorer classes relapsing secretly into paganism in remote districts, doubtless to their own grievous moral degradation,—because the truth had come to them in name only, and not in power.

St. Augustine's letter to Count Boniface (Epist. 185) on the complaints of the Donatists, to whom the severe laws of Theodosius had been applied to compel them into submission to the Church, is an exceedingly remarkable production. Defending the employment of coercion towards the Donatists, the saint makes use of language which has been on the lips of persecutors ever since; citing, for instance, the text, "compel them to come in," and the prophecy that "the kingdoms of the world are become the kingdoms of the Lord and of His Christ;" and referring to the conversion of St. Paul as a case of compulsion exercised by the Lord Himself. Yet, if we read this letter attentively, and note the heavenly and loving earnestness which it breathes, as of one bent to win souls to God and truth, we shall see in it not the narrow intellect and flinty heart of the

persecutor, but the earnest love of a father, rejoicing that even by chastise-
ment his erring children are brought back to the paths of duty. To restore
to the wanderer the priceless treasure of the truth is his one thought; and
if the severity of law will effect this, where persuasion would have failed,
he welcomes that severity. Moreover, he distinctly testifies that the coercion used *has* been successful; that crowds of schismatics, humbled and
penitent, have been received back into the Church, to their immense
moral gain: "Multis profuit (quod experimento probavimus et probamur)
prius dolore vel timore cogi, ut postea possent doceri." On the whole,
therefore, this experiment with the Donatists seems to have succeeded. Yet
there were individuals among them whom it was useless to treat like
children, and who maintained the right of the human mind to liberty;
they said (I quote from the same letter), "Liberum est credere vel non
credere; cui vim Christus intulit? quem coegit?" and I cannot feel the
answer of St. Augustine to be satisfactory.

Again, in the case of our Saxon forefathers, and other Teutonic tribes,
whom the authority of their princes compelled to relinquish heathenism
and embrace the truth faith, as all the three conditions were indubitably
present, so the act of coercion was eminently successful, and therefore
legitimate. So far as it failed, it was in consequence of the inadequate
fulfilment of the second condition; teachers could not be found in sufficient numbers to instruct in the Christian doctrine the obedient crowds
who came to receive baptism.

The coercion of the Albigenses is too mixed and difficult a question
for me now to discuss. That of the Lollards, though perhaps in the main
successful, is yet a doubtful case; partly because, through the prevalence
of ecclesiastical corruptions, the second condition was imperfectly fulfilled,
partly owing to the extravagant nature of the coercion itself. The statute
De haeretico comburendo, made for the use and behoof of the Lollards,
indicates an increased degree of severity in coercion, at the very time when
advancing civilisation was making even the minor degrees of questionable
utility. The cases, under the early Christian emperors, of the capital punishment of heretics are exceedingly rare. One memorable instance is that
of Priscillian, executed under the sentence of a civil court in 384. On this
occasion the great St. Martin (I quote from Fleury) "implored the Emperor Maximus to spare the blood of the guilty ones; saying that it was
quite enough that, having been declared heretics by the judgment of the
Bishops, they should be excluded from the churches: finally, that there
was no precedent for bringing an ecclesiastical cause before a secular
judge." The notion that it can be either right or advisable to kill one man,

in order to convince others that he and they are in the wrong, seems to me one of the most singular hallucinations which ever had a firm hold on the imagination of mankind.

An examination of the various conditions presented by the chief cases of religious coercion which have occurred since the time of Constantine would fill a volume. I will refer to one more instance, that of the coercion of the French Protestants under Louis XIV., culminating in the revocation of the Edict of Nantes. If ever, in modern times, coercion to the true faith stood a chance of success, it was now. And, in truth, it was very *nearly* successful. The mass of the Huguenot population held their opinions traditionally, and certainly did not stand on so high a grade of intellectual cultivation as the French Catholics. Many even of their ministers, so long as the coercion to which they were subjected did not proceed to extravagant lengths, and no extraneous sympathy came to their support, were led to enter into themselves, to meditate calmly, and either embrace, or approach very nearly to Catholic communion. Thus the first condition was tolerably well fulfilled. The second was fully carried out in some parts of France. What Protestant could feel any humiliation in yielding to the massive intellect, the glorious eloquence, the apostolic charity, of the great Bossuet? Accordingly, through all the coercive measures of the government, until they reached an extravagant height, the diocese of Meaux under Bossuet, like that of Hippo under St. Augustine, was the scene of innumerable *real* conversions, placing the converts in a higher state, morally and intellectually, than they were before.[1] In other parts of France, which then could boast of an unusually large number of holy and enlightened Bishops, things took, though less strikingly, the same course. But there were districts where instruction was wanting, or grossly defective; and here coercion produced lamentable results. However, its average operation had tended to produce good rather than evil, until the time when, overstraining the bent bow, it endeavoured, by one grand *coup*, to extirpate the remaining recusancy of France. The third, negative, condition, which had hitherto been fulfilled, immediately broke down. All the neighbouring Protestant communities took the alarm, and expressed by every means in their power their sympathy with the sufferers, and their indignation at the treatment they were receiving. England received them with open arms, subscribed for them, wrote for them, fought for them. Thenceforward the coercion employed could obtain at most a political success.

Ever since the revocation of the Edict of Nantes, the party of liter-

[1] For particulars I refer to the admirable Life of Bossuet by the Cardinal de Bausset.

ature, and the non-Catholic communities of Europe, have been incessantly
on the watch to detect any attempt at coercion to the true faith which may
be made in any part of Western Europe, and to encourage the objects of
this "persecution" to every species of resistance, material and moral. Evidently, therefore, the third condition of success does not and cannot exist
in Europe; whence I conclude that, in our times, coercion to the true faith
is impossible.

Again, every year that passes renders the first condition less easy of
fulfilment; because advancing civilisation develops the general intellect,
and alters that childlike condition of the human mind to which alone
compulsion can be applied with moral benefit. In Asia and Africa it is
still possible that occasions may arise when coercion may be employed
with profit; in Europe, that period seems past for ever.

The whole case may be illustrated by the laws of parental discipline.
It is obvious, that although in the early years of boyhood punishment is
often the best means of effecting moral improvement, it becomes ever less
and less expedient as the boy is passing into the youth; until a time arrives
when the attempt to inflict it, so far from tending to good, is attended
with the worst moral consequences to both parties. The early stage of the
boy's education answers to my first condition. But there may be cases in
which a father may find punishment inexpedient, even before the arrival
of the time when it would become so in the course of nature. Suppose that
a son, whom his father had just chastised, instead of being left to himself
to reflect in loneliness upon his fault and upon the means of regaining
his father's favour, were to be immediately surrounded by a number of
his playmates, assuring him that he had done nothing wrong, condoling
with him for what he had suffered, inveighing against the unjust severity
of the father, and suggesting to him measures of resistance for the future.
The case is not imaginary; a similar occurrence is related in Johnson's
Travels in New Brunswick, of a family that removed from Canada into
the United States. The consequence will be, that unless the boy is endowed with more than ordinary firmness and humility, he will adopt the
view of the case suggested to him;—he will mutiny internally, if not
openly rebel, against any future attempt on the part of his father to coerce
him by punishment; and any such attempt, if made, will have a hardening and lowering effect on his moral nature. This is an exact illustration
of the present state of European society. Any attempt to spread what is
deemed the truth by coercive means, raises up at once a swarm of sym-
pathisers, who denounce the employment of these means as persecution,
and encourage and assist the sufferers. I do not pretend to decide whether
this state of things is desirable or undesirable, but only to state the fact.

If it tells against coercion used *by* Catholics in one place, it checks coercion used *against* them in another. If it helps Protestants in Tuscany and Austria, it helps Catholics in Sweden, Denmark, and Poland. But from these facts the inference is inevitable, that coercion cannot succeed in Europe at the present day, and is therefore illegitimate.

I do not shrink from any consequences of this doctrine, however apparently startling. It may be said, "Would you, then, abolish the censorship of books by the civil power in Catholic countries, and allow not only foreign heterodox works to be imported, but those of home growth to be published? Would a Christian government which so acted, consult as it ought for the faith and morals of the people committed to its care?" I answer—not, with Mr. Mill, that restraints on reading and publishing such works may possibly keep out the truth; not, with Protestant divines, that every individual has a moral right to construct his religious creed for himself, and therefore ought to have an unshackled freedom, whether of choice for himself, or of suggestion for others;—but simply this, that experience shows that, at the present stage of European civilisation, these restraints do more harm than good. In spite of prohibition, works of this class are sure to make their way into any country where there is a demand for them; and the difficulty and secrecy which surround their perusal, lend additional zest to the doctrines which they contain. Under such circumstances, a writer inclined to heterodoxy will spread a film of orthodoxy over every page; but the practice which the Germans call "Zwischen den Zeilen lesen" then arises, and sympathising readers see in his guarded statements all the audacious things which the author would have said if he dared, and often a great many more. Nor is the practical difficulty of finding proper censors a slight one, as Milton pointed out long ago in his *Areopagitica*. A dull man will imagine that to be dangerous which is only novel; and will prevent new thoughts from coming into the world, because to his own torpid intellect they seem unsettling. Hence a twofold mischief; the suppression of a—perhaps important—truth, and the discouragement of an ardent soul from the pursuits for which God and nature designed it. An unfair man will have one rule for this writer, another for that. But even if it could be ensured that all censors should be saints and men of genius, the evils inseparable from restraint would remain.

Once for all, coercion is an educational instrument which Western Europe has outgrown; and the citizens of her commonwealth of states are all bound to assume,—and must be permitted to assume,—the burdens and the dangers of freedom.

All this reasoning applies, it must be observed, only to coercion by *temporal* authority. Coercion by ecclesiastical censures, proceeding in the last resort to excommunication, is inseparable from the idea of the Christian Church; all that my principle requires is, that such coercion should not be enforced by penalties inflicted by the temporal authority.

The line of argument followed in the first part of this article tends, though by a different road, to the same general conclusion with that of the Essay, namely, that the *liberty* of thought and discussion should be entire. For it need hardly be said that if the lawfulness, at the present day, of coercion *to* the true faith be denied, the lawfulness of any coercion from it is denied *a fortiori*. That, indeed, could not at any time have been legitimate, according to the premises laid down, since the third condition of success could by no possibility be fulfilled in the case of the coercion of Catholics by Protestants. No Lutheran or Anglican, however convinced he might be of the truth of his own opinions, could deny the existence of a large external body, ready to extend its sympathy to any Catholics whom he might attempt to coerce, and to encourage them in at least moral resistance. Protestant coercion cannot, therefore, by the nature of things, attain to more than *political success*. But to maintain that discussion ought to be perfectly *free*, is quite a different proposition from maintaining, as Mr. Mill does, that it is essentially necessary to the profitable holding of any truth. Mr. Mill speaks as if human improvement were entirely dependent on the culture of the ratiocinative faculties. In his view, an opinion is profitless to the holder if believed merely because others believe it; unless we know the adversary's case, we do not properly and efficaciously know our own. This would be true, if it were granted that whatever opinions a person may hold are either false or but partially true; for then discussion would either bring out the falsehood, so inducing us to renounce it,—a decided gain,—or it would make us appreciate and mentally appropriate the complemental truth, which would be also a gain. But assume that the opinion is entirely true, and also that it relates to matters in which the deepest and most vital interests of the soul of man are concerned. The utmost that the exercise of the ratiocinative faculties can now effect, will be to induce the conviction that the balance of probability lies on the side of the opinion. For, from the nature of the case, since the opinion relates to matters removed from the criticism of the senses, or of any faculty judging according to sense, physical or scientific certainty of the truth of the opinion is unattainable. Take as an obvious instance the opinion of the immortality of the soul. But now, if the ratiocinative faculties be not appealed to, is the opinion therefore necessarily a sterile encumbrance on the mind, and a clog on its free working?

Evidently not. There are other faculties,—the contemplative, the illustrative, the imaginative faculties, to say nothing of the sentiments and emotions,—which may be freely and largely exercised, while all the while the absolute truth of the opinion is assumed; and it cannot be denied that the exercise of these, no less than of the ratiocinative faculty, is calculated to deepen and enlarge the mind. Any one who understands what is meant by religious meditation will see at a glance the truth of what is here asserted, that a man's belief, though its grounds be not questioned, may be to him a vital and invaluable possession. He who, without questioning, has *realised* his opinion, holds it at last, not because it is the custom, not because others hold it, but because he has made it his own, and feels it by the testimony of his own consciousness to be true. Meditation upon it has brought out relations, before unperceived, with other truths; has presented it under various images, and illustrated it by various analogies; has seen it hold water under a wide range of circumstances, and tested its purifying and elevating influence upon many various natures.

The question of the abstract reasonableness of assuming the truth of any proposition prior to proof cannot be here entered upon; that would involve a long discussion having little bearing on the immediate subject of this article. It is here assumed that it *is* reasonable to take certain propositions on faith antecedently to proof; and if that be granted, it has been shown, that the propositions *being* true, they are capable of being of incalculable value to the mind, although no discussion of their grounds be engaged in.

The illustration used by Mr. Mill, when treating of this supposed *necessity* of discussion, does not appear, when examined, to be strictly relevant. "The greatest orator, save one, of antiquity," he says (p. 66), "has left it on record that he always studied his adversary's case with as great, if not with still greater, intensity than even his own." A mere advocate, in whom there existed no internal connection between the side of the case he supported and his own inner life, might reasonably do so; or again, if such connection did exist, the mastering of his adversary's case might be necessary, not for *his own* benefit, which is what Mr. Mill's argument requires, but to enable him to make a successful counter-impression on his hearers. An apter illustration may perhaps be found in the case of the possessor of a property whose title is impugned by a rival claimant. If perfectly satisfied of the soundness of his own title, he will give himself no trouble about the nature of his adversary's claim; nor will his *enjoyment* of the property be at all impaired by such neglect, but rather the contrary. This seems exactly a parallel case to that of the holder of some great religious truth, upon whom there rests no obligation to controversy; he enjoys and is nourished by that truth not one whit the less because there are many disputants abroad who suppose themselves to have demonstrated its untenableness. Mr. Mill must be well aware of all this; and when he speaks of the necessity of perpetually discussing all received opinions, it is evident that his secret meaning is, that those opinions are in a great measure *false*, and that unembarrassed and fearless discussion would disclose their falsehood. For if they were wholly or mainly *true*, he could not but allow that constant meditation upon them, rather than constant discussion of their grounds, should be recommended as the best means of again penetrating life and character with their spirit.

Again, to maintain that in the present state of society it is desirable that every man should be free to form and express what opinions he pleases, is a totally different thing from maintaining that opinions have no moral colour,—that whatever a man *has a right* to think and express (relatively to society) he *is right* in thinking and expressing relatively to God and conscience. Mr. Mill seems to imply this doctrine of the moral neutrality of opinions in several passages of the Essay; nor, indeed, is he inconsistent in so doing, since he is an avowed upholder of the doctrine of philosophical necessity. In the second volume of his *System of Logic* (p. 480) he says:

> The doctrine called philosophical necessity is simply this: given the motives present to an individual's mind, and given likewise the character and disposition of the individual, the manner in which he will act may be unerringly inferred; that if we knew the person thoroughly, and knew all the inducements which are acting on him, we could foretell his conduct with as much certainty as we can predict any physical event.

To this doctrine Mr. Mill expresses his adherence. But if it be assented to, it is evident that there is no place for culpability to come in, either in character, action, or opinion. For "character and disposition" are partly born with us, partly formed by the mutual action and reaction between ourselves and the external world; "motives" are mainly supplied to us by our passions and desires. At the beginning of action, therefore, the contact of motive (which is of physical origin, and therefore not culpable) with the character (for which, as it was born with us, we are not then morally responsible) produces, according to this doctrine, inevitable results in conduct. This inevitable conduct inevitably tends to mould the character into a certain form; and so the process goes on; and as this doctrine of necessity denies the self-determining power of the will, there is no place, from the beginning to the end of a life's actions, in which to insinuate any thing like culpability or moral turpitude. Opinions will of course follow the same rule. But those who believe in free-will in the sense in which the Church teaches it, in the sense in which Coleridge explains it in the *Aids to Reflection*, as a spiritual super-sensuous force in man, as a self-determining power, the existence of which justifies the solemn ceremonial of human justice, and authenticates the doctrine of a final judgment,—can never admit that man is not responsible for the regulation of his passions, and for the course which the formation of his character may take. And since our opinions are notoriously influenced in a high degree by our passions and our character, it follows that we are morally responsible for our opinions also. Let it not therefore be supposed that he who maintains the non-amenability of the individual to *society* for his opinions—provided their expression does not directly tend to injure others—is in any way restricted from maintaining most emphatically his amenability for them to a higher tribunal.

The last and most vital question, upon which I should desire to express a wide divergence from the views of Mr. Mill, regards the estimate which he has formed of the Christian, or, as he would prefer to term it, theological morality. Mr. Mill considers (p. 92) that "the Christian system is no exception to the rule, that in an imperfect state of the human mind the interests of truth require a diversity of opinions." It too, he thinks, is a half-truth, and requires to be supplemented by a morality derived from quite other sources than the New Testament. "Pagan self-assertion," he says elsewhere, quoting from Sterling, "is one of the elements of human worth as well as Christian self-denial." "Its ideal" (that of the Christian morality) "is negative rather than positive, passive rather than active, innocence rather than nobleness, abstinence from evil rather than energetic pursuit of good."

There are few Christians of any denomination who would not dispute the accuracy of this description. If Mr. Mill had said, "*holiness* rather than nobleness," he would have stated the Christian ideal correctly; but holiness is not a negative conception, and therefore the word would not suit his purpose. It is enough to refer to the parable of the talents, and to that of the barren fig-tree, for proof that the Founder of Christianity enforced the necessity of *active* goodness at least as strongly as any moral teacher whom the world has ever seen. But if by the expression "half-truth" it be meant that Christianity does not embrace within its scope a moral code adapted to all the various conditions and circumstances of human life, the proposition may be granted without the slightest prejudice to our maintaining that the Christian morality is divinely revealed. Be it remembered that morality is *natural* to man; its leading principles are impressed by the Creator, independently of a direct revelation, upon the conscience; and the natural reason is able to deduce from these original principles rules of conduct fitted to guide the individual in the emergencies which the conditions of life present. God does not *reveal* to His creatures that which the constitution with which He has endowed them enables them to discover for themselves; and hence it is no disparagement to the revealed morality of the Gospel to say that it is not a complete ethical code. Christianity reveals to us the true relation between man and God, and man's destiny beyond the grave; the Christian morality accordingly is simply that part of morals which teaches man so to pass through this life as to attain his true destiny in the next. In every moral principle which the Gospel proclaims there is a constant reference to a life to come,—to a scene where all partial or apparent wrong will be set right, and compared to which the concerns of the present life are mere vanity and futility. The distinguishing device of the Christian among other men is, *Credo vitam aeternam*. He cannot prize this life and its so-called realities at a very high rate, who, taught by religion, steadily fixes his eyes on the one fact, that in a few short years his puny being will be swallowed up in the immensities and splendours of God. The Christian ethics, therefore, are designed for a being placed at the Christian stand-point. Their main principles are:

1. The deliberate preference of the heavenly to the earthly life, of the future to the present.

2. The principle of love or charity, prescribing a heavenly temper, the exact opposite of the selfishness which Mr. Mill charges upon Christian morality.

3. The regulation of the passions, by the aid of the light afforded by the first principle, and of the example of Christ.

4. Entire purity of thought and act, of mind and body.

5. Humility, consisting partly in a child-like reception of the revelation of God, partly in the imitation of the lowly and suffering life of Jesus.

This is the morality of the Christian as such: he can dispense with any other while thoroughly in his life realising this. One thing is *necessary*; and multitudes of persons of either sex, in every age, have deliberately given up the world as an object of pursuit, in order that they might pursue the life eternal; and have gone through life guided by this morality alone, without ever finding the want of any other, or repenting of the choice which they had made. The practical inconsistency which prevails among Christians, and which furnishes the ground for Mr. Mill's strictures, arises from this,—that many, who are thoroughly addicted to the pursuit of temporal good, *pretend* nevertheless to walk in conformity to this Christian morality, and to need no other ethical rules than those which the Gospel furnishes. It is as if Dives, in the midst of his money-getting, were to affect the detachment and mortification of Lazarus. It is indisputably true, as Mr. Mill says, that the Koran contains excellent moral precepts which are not found in the New Testament; he might have added that Aristotle has yet more excellent maxims than the Koran. But what is the reason? These maxims are all fitted to aid man in arriving at his *natural* ideal, namely, "the harmonious development of all his powers to a complete and consistent whole." As reason is capable of discovering this ideal, so it is capable of ascertaining the ethical principles which subserve to its attainment. The morality of the temporal life, in all its parts,—that of the public assembly, that of the bar, that of the counter, or that of the farm,—is capable of being ascertained by human reason unaided by revelation, and a large part of it has been so ascertained. So far, then, as an individual is bound, or inclined, to bear a part in the world's work,—so far as he cannot, or will not, give himself up wholly to God,—so far it is his duty to guide himself by the best and wisest ethical rules which he can find, from whatever source derived, applicable to that particular department of the temporal life in which his station is. The higher Christian morality which he possesses will often enable, nay compel, him to *revise* ethical judgments which have been arrived at independently of religion; but it will not serve him, in these worldly matters, as an exclusive code.

But when Mr. Mill speaks (pp. 88, 89) of the Christian morality as being, "not the work of Christ or the Apostles, but gradually built up by the Catholic Church of the first five centuries,"—when, again, he speaks of its having "received additions in the middle ages," which the Protestant sects merely cut off, substituting fresh additions of their own, —one cannot but wonder at so strange a distortion of the facts. That the leading principles of the Christian morality, as above defined, were taught by our Lord and His apostles, is so palpably true, is so easily established by a multitude of texts, that it were waste of words to go about to prove it; that the same principles were taught by the Catholic Church of the first five centuries is also notorious; it is equally certain that these are the main principles of Catholic morality at the present day. Mr. Mill ought to

inform us what were the additional principles invented in the middle
ages. Some such might be found, perhaps, by culling extracts from mediaeval writers, after the fashion of Mosheim's citations from St. Eligius
(see Newman on *Popular Protestantism*), but certainly in no other way.
The separated bodies have, indeed, either impaired these original principles, or joined to them, as Mr. Mill says, "additions adapted to the character and tendencies" of each. By setting up the State as the supreme
power in the Church, the Anglican body has impaired the testimony of
its members to the first principle; many of them have had already, and
will have again, to choose between the edict of Caesar and the command
of God; while their position as a separate body disposes them, in case of
collision, to prefer the former to the latter. The Methodists have added to
the morality of Christ a kind of morbid self-inspection, which is perpetually asking itself the questions, "Am I right with God or not? is my
inward state satisfactory? shall I be saved, or shall I be lost?" The Antinomian sects have, to say nothing of what they have added, abandoned the
second and third principles,—purity and the regulation of the passions.
Lastly, all have, in different ways and degrees, abandoned the principle of
humility, and added various kinds and forms of pride. Dryden, it will be
remembered, challenged Stillingfleet to name a single Protestant work on
humility; and when his adversary produced one, it proved to be in the
main a translation from a Catholic treatise.

The last chapter consists of "applications" of the general doctrine of
the Essay, one of which only can here be noticed. Although not strictly
belonging to the subject of the Essay, which is social liberty, not political
enfranchisement, Mr. Mill has handled in this chapter the question as to
the limits of the interference of government in the business of society.
There is often a misuse of words here which leads to confusion of thought.
English popular writers, when they hold up England as a pattern of
political liberty to foreign nations, generally mean that we have a right
to vote for a member of parliament, which they have not; a right to tax
ourselves for local purposes, which they have not; together with many
other privileges of the same kind. On the other hand, there are those who,
revolted by the self-satisfied air with which these privileges are paraded,
and detecting an ambiguity in the terms used, are apt to speak slightingly
of these supposed advantages. These persons say, "Why attach the name
of liberty to functions which we are by no means impatient to exercise?
If government officials will undertake the laying of our water-pipes, and
the cleaning and lighting of our streets, we shall thank them for relieving
us of a task which the wider knowledge and experience they can com-

mand enables them probably to execute better than ourselves. Certainly we shall not regard their interference as an invasion of our *liberty*. Nor, again, do we think it essential to our liberty that we should have a voice *valeat quantum* in the election of the members of the Legislature, in preference to any other mode of appointment. Continental experience proves that towns can be made beautiful and healthy as well, perhaps better, by a centralised than a localised administration. Nor does our vaunted parliamentary machine always work smoothly or profitably; it economises neither time nor money. What we understand by liberty is exactly what Mr. Mill understands by it, namely, the power of managing our own life as we please; of reading what books we like; of unhampered locomotion; of cultivating and developing our own and our children's minds by the methods we think best, provided we do not trench upon the rights of others. If we think an institution wrong,—slavery, for in-stance,—we desire the liberty of publishing our thoughts without being tarred and feathered; if we prefer one style of religious worship to an-other, we would prefer to be free to practise it without constraint either from a government or from a mob. The charter of our civic rights may include all the fine openings for fussy self-importance that you describe, and perhaps many more; yet without the species of liberty we have in-sisted upon, we shall not be free in any sense that seems to us worth caring for."

A tendency to such reasoning as this is often perceivable on the part of the Catholic minority in England, and not unnaturally so. Local self-government and the representative system do not work favourably for English Catholics. Although they form more than one-twentieth of the population, they can command only one six hundred and fifty-fourth part of the parliamentary representation, and even that happens through a fortunate accident. The same is the case, as a general rule, with all mu-nicipal offices. Everywhere in England Catholics are in a minority; and minorities, being unrepresented under the present *régime,* cannot get their man elected, nor cause their voice to be more than imperfectly heard. The positive prejudice also which disqualifies Catholics, as such, in the general English mind for posts of honour and trust is still, though with diminished intensity, powerfully operative. It might seem, therefore, at first sight, to be our policy rather to aid in accumulating power in the hands of the government than in the maintenance and extension of the system of local management. Government officials, it may be said, are more or less accessible to reason; they are mostly raised by education above the sway of mere blind prejudice; if we can make out a clear case of hardship to them, they will redress it. But the blind unreasoning bigotry of the bulk of the English middle class is unimpressible and unassailable; to attempt to extract fair concessions from them, when the Pope is in the case, is, as Sir John Fortescue would say, to go "scheryng of hogges," with the old result of "moche cry and little wole."

All this is true; yet still Mr. Mill is probably right when he says, that the more narrowly government interference in local concerns can be circumscribed, the better. First, for the sake of the great principle, that "though individuals may not do the particular thing so well, on the average, as the officers of government, it is nevertheless desirable that it should be done by them rather than by the government, as a means to their own mental education,—a mode of strengthening their active faculties, exercising their judgment, and giving them a familiar knowledge of the subjects with which they are thus left to deal" (Essay, p. 196). Secondly, because Catholics have no cause to despair of being able ultimately to work round free institutions more to their advantage than they seem to be at present. Let them show themselves the equals of their Protestant fellow-citizens in public spirit, in intelligence sharpened by education, and in acquired knowledge,—in short, in the whole circle of the civic virtues and qualifications, and they may reckon on not being always excluded from posts of trust. This book itself, the weighty maxims of which are destined to leaven very extensively, if we mistake not, the general sentiments of society, will contribute to dissipate the intolerance which defeats their just claims. Thirdly, the precariousness of favours obtained by a minority from a government has to be considered. When we deal with our countrymen man to man, we know where we stand. We may be disliked and suspected at first; but if we can once get a footing, and satisfy them that we personally are a decent sort of people, and that our claims are just, we shall have gained a success which can never afterwards, unless through our own fault, be wrested from us. For all experience shows that rights thus gained are progressive, and that their expansion can only be arrested by external constraint; on the other hand, the concessions which a government has made to a minority in a time of quietness may be revoked in a time of excitement. Are examples needed? Look at the seeming prosperity of English Catholicity under the government of Charles I. before the year 1640, and again under James II. In each case the relief afforded by the government was given in defiance and in advance of the general sentiment of the nation, and was soon swept away beneath a torrent of penal inflictions; but to take advantage of more equal laws, and to disarm by sensible and spirited conduct the inveterate prejudices of individuals and of local coteries, is, *pro tanto*, to alter the general sentiment itself.

Spencer on MILL

To dilate upon Mr. Mill's achievements, and to insist upon the wideness of his influence over the thought of his time, and consequently over the actions of his time, seems to me scarcely needful. The facts are sufficiently obvious, and are recognized by all who know any thing about the progress of opinion during the last half-century. My own estimate of him, intellectually considered, has been emphatically though briefly given on an occasion of controversy between us, by expressing my regret at "having to contend against the doctrine of one whose agreement I should value more than that of any other thinker."

While, however, it is almost superfluous to assert of him that intellectual height so generally admitted, there is more occasion for drawing attention to a moral elevation that is less recognized, partly because his activities in many directions afforded no occasion for exhibiting it, and partly because some of its most remarkable manifestations in conduct are known only to those whose personal relations with him have called them forth. I feel especially prompted to say something on this point, because, where better things might have been expected, there has been, not only a grudging recognition of intellectual rank, but a marked blindness to those fine traits of character, which, in the valuation of men, must go for more than superiority of intelligence.

It might indeed have been supposed, that even those who never enjoyed the pleasure of personal acquaintance with Mr. Mill would have been impressed with the nobility of his nature as indicated in his opinions and deeds. How entirely his public career has been determined by a pure and strong sympathy for his fellow-men; how entirely this sympathy has subordinated all desires for personal advantage; how little even the fear of being injured in reputation or position has deterred him from taking the course which he thought equitable or generous,—ought to be manifest to every antagonist, however bitter. A generosity that might almost be called romantic was obviously the feeling prompting sundry of those courses of action which have been commented upon as errors. And nothing like a true conception of him can be formed, unless, along with dissent from

[Herbert Spencer, "John Stuart Mill: His Moral Character," in Herbert Spencer and others, *John Stuart Mill: His Life and Works* (James R. Osgood and Co., Boston, 1873).]

them, there goes recognition of the fact that they resulted from the eagerness of a noble nature impatient to rectify injustice and to further human welfare.

It may perhaps be that my own perception of this pervading warmth of feeling has been sharpened by seeing it exemplified, not in the form of expressed opinions only, but in the form of private actions; for Mr. Mill was not one of those, who, to sympathy with their fellowmen in the abstract, join indifference to them in the concrete. There came from him generous acts that corresponded with his generous sentiments. I say this, not from second-hand knowledge, but having in mind a remarkable example known only to myself and a few friends. I have hesitated whether to give this example, seeing that it has personal implications. But it affords so clear an insight into Mr. Mill's character, and shows so much more vividly than any description could do how fine were the motives swaying his conduct, that I think the occasion justifies disclosure of it.

Some seven years ago, after bearing as long as was possible the continued losses entailed on me by the publication of the "System of Philosophy," I notified to the subscribers that I should be obliged to cease at the close of the volume then in progress. Shortly after the issue of this announcement I received from Mr. Mill a letter, in which, after expressions of regret, and after naming a plan which he wished to prosecute for reimbursing me, he went on to say, "In the next place . . . what I propose is, that you should write the next of your treatises, and that I should guarantee the publisher against loss; i.e., should engage, after such length of time as may be agreed on, to make good any deficiency that may occur, not exceeding a given sum,—that sum being such as the publisher may think sufficient to secure him." Now, though these arrangements were of kinds that I could not bring myself to yield to, they none the less profoundly impressed me with Mr. Mill's nobility of feeling, and his anxiety to further what he regarded as a beneficial end. Such proposals would have been remarkable even had there been entire agreement of opinion; but they were the more remarkable as being made by him under the consciousness that there existed between us certain fundamental differences, openly avowed. I had, both directly and by implication, combated that form of the experiential theory of human knowledge which characterizes Mr. Mill's philosophy: in upholding Realism, I had opposed in decided ways those metaphysical systems to which his own Idealism was closely allied; and we had long carried on a controversy respecting the test of truth, in which I had similarly attacked Mr. Mill's positions in an outspoken manner. That, under such circumstances, he should have volunteered his aid, and urged it upon me, as he did, on the ground that it would not imply any personal obligation, proved in him a very exceptional generosity.

Quite recently I have seen afresh illustrated this fine trait,—this ability to bear with unruffled temper, and without any diminution of kindly feeling, the publicly-expressed antagonism of a friend. The last evening I spent at his house was in the company of another invited guest, who, originally agreeing with him entirely on certain disputed questions, had some fortnight previously displayed his change of view,—nay, had publicly criticised some of Mr. Mill's positions in a very undisguised manner. Evidently, along with his own unswerving allegiance to truth, there was in Mr. Mill an unusual power of appreciating in others a like conscientiousness, and so of suppressing any feeling of irritation produced by difference,—suppressing it, not in appearance only, but in reality, and that, too, under the most trying circumstances.

I should say indeed, that Mr. Mill's general characteristic, emotionally considered, was an unusual predominance of the higher sentiments,—a predominance which tended, perhaps, both in theory and practice, to subordinate the lower nature unduly. That rapid advance of age which has been conspicuous for some years past, and which doubtless prepared the way for his own somewhat premature death, may, I think, be regarded as the outcome of a theory of life which made learning and working the occupations too exclusively considered. But when we ask to what ends he acted out his theory, and in so doing too little regarded his bodily welfare, we see that even here the excess, if such we call it, was a noble one. Extreme desire to further human welfare was that to which he sacrificed himself.

24

LENIN
MASARYK
NEHRU

MARX

The two major European countries in which the ideas of Karl Marx (see page 285) were widely accepted were Germany and Russia—the two European empires most backward in the theory and practice of self-government. In czarist Russia the conditions for the acceptance of Marxism were even more favorable than in imperial Germany. Whereas Germany made the pretense of bowing to democracy and parliamentary government, czarism long recoiled from committing itself even to the formalities of liberalism and democracy, on the ground that pretenses, if practiced long enough, might too easily develop into reality. Of all major European states, czarist Russia was first in illiteracy, economic backwardness, religious obscurantism, oppression of minorities, political despotism, and social inequality. Marx's ideas, particularly the prospect of inevitable liberation of the working classes from bondage and oppression through revolutionary action, made a strong impression on Russian radicals, and Russian was the language into which *Das Kapital* was first translated. The man who, more than any other Russian, made of Marxism a political reality was Vladimir Ilyich Ulyanov, or Lenin, as he later called himself (1870–1924). Lenin came (as did Marx and Engels) from a middle-class family; he prepared himself for a legal career, but his university studies were prematurely terminated on account of his early revolutionary activities that brought him imprisonment and exile to Siberia. After his release from Siberia in 1900, Lenin went abroad and spent the next seventeen years, with but few interruptions, in various European countries, organizing from abroad the illegal revolutionary movement in Russia that was to culminate in the seizure of power in 1917. During World War I Lenin was in Switzerland, and in the spring of 1917 the German Government helped him to return to Russia, hoping to benefit from Lenin's defeatist propaganda, since Lenin urged the Russian proletariat to turn the international war into a civil war and seize power even at the expense of national defeat. In November 1917 Lenin led the Bolshevik uprising which established the first communist regime in history. He remained the head of the Bolshevik regime until his death in 1924, and he is still considered, next to Marx and Engels, the most important theorist of world communism. He wrote voluminously during his years of exile, as well as after his return to Russia in 1917, most of his writings consisting of scathing attacks on fellow Marxists who disagreed with Lenin. His most original contribution to the theory of communism is his pamphlet *What Is to Be Done?* (1902), in which he developed the concept of the professional revolutionary as the key figure in the strategy of communist conquest of power. Lenin's best-known pamphlet is *State and Revolution* (1918); written shortly before the Bolshevik seizure of power in November, 1917, the pamphlet contains both a critique of democracy from the communist viewpoint and a guide to successful communist strategy in seizing power. Lenin's essay on "The Three Sources and Three Component Parts of Marxism" was written in 1913; contrary to those who view Marxism as a new "irruption of Asian hordes" into Western civilization, Lenin points to the fact that Marx learned his philosophy from Germany, his economics from Britain, and his revolutionary politics from France. On this analysis, it may be argued that Marxism distorts Western ideas, rather than negates them *in toto*. Much of the later communist propaganda, particularly in the underdeveloped areas of Asia and Africa, has been based on this Leninist conception that Marxism is the true heir to the Western traditions of equality, fraternity, and justice, and it is doubtful whether such propaganda can be counteracted solely by military means.

 A more critical view of Marx is taken by Thomas Garrigue Masaryk, the founder and first President of Czechoslovakia from 1918 to 1935. Masaryk (1850–1937) was one of the few philosopher-rulers of history who never abandoned his high ideals of humanitarian liberalism. Married to an American woman, he was professor of philosophy at the Czech University of Prague from 1882 to 1911; yet his dominant aim in life was to see his people free and independent again, and during World War I he traveled widely in the Allied countries, including the United States, to which he was deeply attached, in order to bring about the political independence of the Czech nation. When Austria-Hungary collapsed in World War I, Masaryk was elected the first President of Czechoslovakia in 1918 and reelected three times before he retired from public life in 1935. His massive work on *The Spirit of Russia* (2 vols., 1913, English translation, 1919) is still a classic in the field of Russian studies, and his detailed examination of Marx and his influence in modern Russia is still indispensable to an understanding of the background of Communist Russia. As a liberal democrat throughout his whole life, Masaryk could not but reject Marxism and its inherent tendencies toward violence and totalitarianism. Masaryk's writings also include *The Making of a State* (1927) and *The Ideals of Humanity* (1938).

Jawaharlal Nehru (1889–   ) views Marx much more sympathetically in his *Glimpses of World History* (1942) than does Masaryk. The son of a well-known Indian nationalist, Nehru was educated at Harrow and Cambridge, and from early youth he worked for Indian freedom. Before India gained independence in 1947, Nehru spent much of his political career in prison, where he found the leisure to do most of his writing. Thus *Glimpses of World History* was written in prison as a series of letters to his young daughter. The first Prime Minister of free India since 1947, Nehru quickly acquired world fame as a statesman and publicist. A democratic socialist spending most of his life in a colony, he sympathizes with much of the anti-imperialist doctrine of Marxism, and he has become the world's leading spokesman of neutralism or, as the Indians prefer to call it, nonalignment, in the struggle between communism and the free world. His views on Marx are significant, not only on account of Nehru's stature as a world statesman, but also because they may reveal some of the deeper layers of Marxian influence in the underdeveloped countries in general. Nehru's other writings reflecting his political philosophy include, in addition to *Glimpses of World History*, his autobiography *Toward Freedom* (1941), and *The Discovery of India* (1946).

Lenin on MARX

The teaching of Marx evokes throughout the civilized world the greatest hostility and hatred on the part of all bourgeois science (both official and

[V. I. Lenin, "The Three Sources and Three Component Parts of Marxism" (1913).]

liberal) which regards Marxism as something in the nature of a "pernicious sect." No other attitude is to be expected, since there can be no "impartial" social science in a society which is built up on the class struggle. *All* official and liberal science *defends* wage-slavery in one way or another, whereas Marxism has declared relentless war on that slavery. To expect science to be impartial in a society of wage-slavery is as silly and naive as to expect impartiality from employers on the question as to whether the workers' wages should be increased by decreasing the profits of capital.

However, this is not all. The history of philosophy and that of social science shows with perfect clearness that there is nothing in Marxism resembling "sectarianism" in the sense of a secluded, fossilized doctrine originating somewhere away from the high road of development of world civilization. On the contrary, the genius of Marx manifested itself in that he provided the answers to questions which had already been put by the advanced brains of humanity.

His teaching came as a direct and immediate *continuation* of the teaching of the greatest representatives of philosophy, political economy, and socialism.

The teaching of Marx is all-powerful because it is true. It is complete and harmonious, providing men with a consistent view of the universe, which cannot be reconciled with any superstition, any reaction, any defense of bourgeois oppression. It is the lawful successor of the best that has been created by humanity in the nineteenth century—German philosophy, English political economy, and French socialism.

It is these three sources, which are also the three component parts of Marxism, that we will briefly dwell upon.

I

The philosophy of Marxism is *materialism*. Throughout the recent history of Europe, and particularly at the end of the eighteenth century in France, which was the scene of the decisive battle against every kind of medieval rubbish, against serfdom in institutions and ideas, materialism proved to be the only consistent philosophy, true to all the teachings of natural science, hostile to superstitions, cant, etc. The enemies of democracy tried, therefore, with all their energy, to "overthrow," undermine and defame materialism, and defended various forms of philosophic idealism, which always leads, in one way or another, to the defense and support of religion.

Marx and Engels always defended philosophic materialism in the most determined manner, and repeatedly explained the profound error of

every deviation from this basis. Their views are more clearly and fully
expounded in the works of Engels, *Ludwig Feuerbach* and *Anti-Dühring*,
which, like the *Communist Manifesto*, are household books for every conscious worker.

However, Marx did not stop at the materialism of the eighteenth century but moved philosophy forward. He enriched it by the achievements
of German classical philosophy, especially by Hegel's system, which in its
turn had led to the materialism of Feuerbach. Of these the main achievement is *dialectics, i.e.,* the doctrine of development in its fuller, deeper
form, free from one-sidedness—the doctrine, also, of the relativity of human knowledge that provides us with a reflection of eternally developing
matter. The latest discoveries of natural science—radium, electrons, the
transmutation of elements—are a remarkable confirmation of the dialectical materialism of Marx, despite the doctrines of bourgeois philosophers
with their "new" returns to old and rotten idealism.

While deepening and developing philosophic materialism, Marx carried it to its conclusion; he extended its perception of nature to the perception of *human society*. The *historical materialism* of Marx represented
the greatest conquest of scientific thought. Chaos and arbitrariness, which
reigned until then in the views on history and politics, were replaced by
a strikingly consistent and harmonious scientific theory, which shows how
out of one order of social life another and higher order develops, in consequence of the growth of the productive forces—how capitalism, for
instance, grows out of serfdom.

Just as the cognition of man reflects nature (*i.e.,* developing matter)
which exists independently of him, so also the *social cognition* of man
(*i.e.,* the various views and doctrines—philosophic, religious, political, etc.)
reflects the *economic order* of society. Political institutions are a superstructure on the economic foundation. We see, for example, that the various political forms of modern European states serve the purpose of
strengthening the domination of the bourgeoisie over the proletariat.

The philosophy of Marx completes in itself philosophic materialism
which has provided humanity, and especially the working class, with a
powerful instrument of knowledge.

II

Having recognized that the economic order is the foundation upon
which the political superstructure is erected, Marx devoted all the greater
attention to the study of that economic order. The principal work of
Marx, *Capital*, is devoted to a study of the economic order of modern, *i.e.,*
capitalist society.

Classical political economy, before Marx, was built up in England, the most developed capitalist country. Adam Smith and David Ricardo, in their investigations of the economic order, laid the foundations of the *labor theory of value*. Marx continued their work. He strictly proved and consistently developed this theory. He showed that the value of every commodity is determined by the quantity of socially necessary labor time spent in its production.

Where the bourgeois economists saw a relation of things (the exchange of one commodity for another) Marx revealed a *relation between men*. The exchange of commodities expresses the connection between individual producers by means of the market. *Money* signifies that this connection is becoming closer and closer, inseparably combining the entire economic life of the individual producers into one whole. *Capital* signifies a further development of this connection: the labor power of man becomes a commodity. The wage laborer sells his labor power to the owner of land, of factories and instruments of labor. The worker uses one part of the labor day to cover the expenditure for the maintenance of himself and his family (wages), and the other part of the day he toils without remuneration and creates *surplus value* for the capitalist, which is the source of profit, the source of wealth of the capitalist class.

The doctrine of surplus value is the cornerstone of the economic theory of Marx.

Capital, created by the labor of the worker, presses upon the workers, ruins the petty owners and creates an army of unemployment. In industry the victory of large-scale production may be seen at once, but we also see the same phenomenon in agriculture: the superiority of big capitalist agriculture becomes greater, the application of machinery grows, peasant economy is caught in the noose of money-capital, it declines and becomes ruined under the burden of a backward technique. In agriculture, the forms of decline of petty production are different, but the decline itself is an indisputable fact.

By beating petty production, capital leads to the increase of the productivity of labor and to the establishment of a monopoly position for associations of the biggest capitalists. Production itself becomes more and more social; hundreds of thousands and millions of workers are linked up in a systematic economic organism, but the product of the collective labor is appropriated by a handful of capitalists. Anarchy of production, crises, a furious hunt after markets, and the insecurity of existence for the masses of population are on the increase.

While increasing the dependence of the workers upon capital, the capitalist system creates the great power of combined labor.

Marx traced the development of capitalism from the first germs of commodity economy and simple exchange, to its highest forms, to large-scale production.

And the experience of all countries, whether old or new, clearly shows year after year, to an even greater number of workers, the truth of Marx's teaching.

Capitalism has been victorious all over the world, but this victory is only the eve of the victory of labor over capital.

III

After the overthrow of serfdom, when a *"free"* capitalist society appeared, it was at once discovered that this freedom signified a new system of oppression and exploitation of the toilers. Various socialist doctrines immediately began to arise as a reflection of this oppression and protest against it. But socialism in its first origin was *utopian*. It criticized the capitalist society, it condemned it and damned it, it dreamed of its destruction, it drew fantastic pictures of a better order and endeavored to convince the rich of the wickedness of exploitation.

But utopian socialism was unable to show a real way out. It could not explain either the essence of wage-slavery under capitalism, or discover the laws of its development, or find the *social force* which was capable of becoming the creator of a new society.

In the meantime, the stormy revolution which accompanied the fall of feudalism and serfdom everywhere in Europe, and especially in France, revealed ever more clearly the *struggle of classes* as the basis of the whole development and its motive force.

Not a single victory of political freedom over the class of feudal lords was won without desperate resistance. Not a single capitalist country was established on a more or less free and democratic basis without a life and death struggle between the different classes of capitalist society.

Marx was a genius because he was able before anyone else to draw from these facts and consistently elaborate the conclusion which world history teaches. This conclusion is the doctrine of the *class struggle*.

People always were and always will be the stupid victims of deceit and self-deceit in politics, as long as they have not learned to discover the *interests* of one or another of the classes behind any moral, religious, political and social phrases, declarations and promises. The supporters of reforms and improvements will always be fooled by the defenders of the old, as long as they will not realize that every old institution, however absurd and rotten it may appear, is kept in being by the forces of one or the other of the ruling classes. And there is *only one* way of breaking the resistance of these classes, and that is to find, in the very society which surrounds us, and to enlighten and organize for the struggle, the forces which can and, by their social position, *must* form the power capable of sweeping away the old and of establishing the new.

Only the philosophic materialism of Marx showed the proletariat the way out of the spiritual slavery in which all oppressed classes have languished up to the present. Only the economic theory of Marx explained the real position of the proletariat in the general system of capitalism.

The independent organizations of the proletariat are multiplying throughout the world from America to Japan and from Sweden to South Africa. The proletariat is being enlightened and educated in waging the class struggle, it is ridding itself of the prejudices of bourgeois society, consolidating itself ever more closely and learning to take the measure of its successes; it is hardening its forces and growing irresistibly.

Masaryk on MARX

According to Marx, the organisation of society in the epoch of civilisation, beginning in Greece with the dominance of Athens, and in Italy with the rise of Rome, fundamentally consists in the continual opposition and struggle between two classes; this struggle, he contends, makes up the essence and comprises the content of history; the mass of the working population is kept in subjection by the idle but dominant class, is kept in one form or another of social or political servitude. The state is the political expression of the dominant and oppressing class. In the modern era, class contrasts have become accentuated in the struggle between the proletarian masses and the capitalists. The proletarian masses undergo increasing impoverishment owing to the way in which the product of their labour, value and surplus value, is continuously absorbed by the capitalist entrepreneur; this process will continue until possessions become concentrated in the hands of a very small number of capitalists, and then will come the cataclysm, the definitive revolution, whereby the proletarians will reestablish communism. For in Marx's view, society in its most primitive stage was communistically organised, and primitive communism was swept away when the era of private property began. Extant capitalism is the terminal phase of private property, and in the comparatively near

[From Thomas Garrigue Masaryk, *The Spirit of Russia* (1913, trans. Eden and Cedar Paul, George Allen and Unwin, 1919). By permission.]

future will yield place to communism. This already imminent communism will doubtless differ in certain respects from primitive communism; it will be a complicated but deliberately thought-out system of social organisation. The coming of the communistic era can be foreseen by the scientific historian; and communism itself, therefore, is in part rooted in the historical process. Practically, socio-politically, the transformation inalterably determined by the objective dialectical process of historical evolution will be brought about in the following manner. In the very last phase of the capitalistic epoch the workers will gain control of the state (the dictatorship of the proletariat), will abolish the state, and will conduct society to the higher communistic stage of evolution. This stage will close the era of historical evolution.

Marx did not furnish a detailed account of the history of this evolution, but in his analysis of capitalist production and of the circulation of goods and commodities he endeavoured to elucidate the application of the dialectical process of evolution to the present day, to the most recent phase of history. It was left for Engels to undertake a detailed application of the Marxist scheme to history at large.

Marx and Engels were so exclusively historians, so exclusively dialecticians in Hegel's sense, that they were not concerned to undertake an exposition of social organisation (to deal with what Comte termed social statics in contrast with social dynamics). The concept of this organisation can, however, be abstracted from history, and we have moreover for this purpose the Marxist formula known as the doctrine of historical materialism.

Marx contends that the totality of the relationships of production, the economic structure of society, constitutes the real basis upon which the legal and political superstructure is built and to which definite forms of social consciousness correspond. These relationships of production are, in fact, independent of the human will; they have originated historically, in correspondence with a definite stage of the evolution of the material forces of production. In a certain phase of development the material productive forces of society come into conflict with the preexistent relationships of production (i.e. conditions of ownership) within which they have hitherto had their being. These earlier relationships, which were at first evolutionary forms of the productive energies, now manifest themselves as shackles to those energies, and an epoch of social revolution ensues. With the transformation of the economic basis, the whole colossal superstructure is more or less rapidly overthrown. When we are contemplating such transformations we must ever be careful to distinguish between the material transformation in the economic conditions of production, which is effected in strict conformity with the reign of natural law, and the legal, political, religious, artistic, or philosophical (in a word, ideological) forms wherein human beings become aware of this conflict and carry on the struggle. In broad outline Marx depicts the Asiatic, classical, feudal, and modern capitalist modes of production, respectively, as progressive epochs in the economic formation of society. The capitalist method of production has created the antagonism between the productive forces of society and the relationships of ownerships, an antagonism which will be solved by the material conditions which this same capitalist structure of society has already prepared; for humanity never sets itself problems which it is incompetent to solve, and indeed these problems can only become intelligible when the material conditions rendering their solution possible already exist, at least in the germ.

Such is the celebrated formula of historical or economic materialism whereby history is represented as a dialectical and objective mass process independent of the individual will. The formula will be found in the preface to Marx's *Critique of Political Economy*, published in the year 1859. The first sketches of this formulation exist in earlier works, but Marx himself, and to a still greater extent Engels and his younger disciples, were subsequently responsible for such extensive variations in the formula that the "real basis" of productive relationships has been supplemented or replaced by technical advances (including the fundamental sciences of mathematics, physics, chemistry, etc.), racial qualities, the geographical environment, the energies that determine the relationships of population, etc. At the same time, historical materialism, in view of the criticism it encountered, was reduced to a method, a heuristic method.

It would be quite incredible that so obscure and inaccurate a formula should have had so powerful an influence, had it not become the scientific basic formula of revolutionary socialism, which in Germany and other countries has effected the national and international organization of the working masses to constitute the social democracy.

Marxist historical materialism has been philosophically and sociologically superseded. The history of mankind has a significance different from that which Marx impressed upon it with his doctrine of historical materialism based upon the materialism of Feuerbach.

Practically and socio-politically, just as much as theoretically, Marxism abandons its positions, or at least modifies them to a great extent. In especial it is necessary to insist on the fact that Marxist social democracy, above all in Germany and Austria, has had the revision of its doctrines forced upon it by participation in political and parliamentary work. Revisionism has never possessed any theorist whose ability and force rivalled those of Marx. It was the work of practical politics which necessitated revisionism.

In Germany, Austria, Italy, Belgium, France, and England, the Marxists, during their political activities within their own party, during their work in parliaments, local governments, trade unions, etc., had forced upon them the conclusion that state and church are no mere superstructure, as Marx contended (Marx's own thought was obscure, since he conceived the superstructure, now as the state, now as political ideals, and now again as law). Moreover, in the work of practical politics the Marxist learned to prize nationality as an independent social organisation side by side with the organisation of state and church—in a word, he came to recognise that the complicated organisation of society cannot be accurately conceived in accordance with the simplifying formula of historical materialism. At the same time the practical Marxist learned that the social democracy and its program were less radically distinct from the other democratic parties and their programs than the founder of the social democracy had assumed and than many of its leaders still assume. Bernstein's phrase "from sect to party" affords a summary watchword of the new view which through the discussion of tactics has come to prevail widely among the Marxists of all lands.

This discussion of tactics relates in especial to the possible participation of the social democrats in the government. If the discussion laid especial stress upon the question of the acceptance of office by socialists and upon the question of voting for the state budget, the restriction of outlook, though comprehensible enough, is uncritical, for participation in local government is essentially of the same nature as participation in the government of the state—quite apart from the consideration that a Berlin town councillor may have more important functions than a minister in Baden.

In the last resort, the discussion of tactics must lead to a revision of the concept of social revolution; the terms revolution, reform, and evolution, must be accurately defined. The social democrat who enters parliament as a deputy, who enters a bourgeois institution, participates in the working of the state which in theory he boycotts and negates. In practice, therefore, he has decided in favour of the tactics of reform, for history has taught him that the time for the definitive social revolution anticipated by Engels and Marx has not yet arrived. In truth the people who expect too much are of as little practical use as were their forerunners the millenarians. In practice, the Marxist who is dominated by the revolutionary mood and aspires to the (definitive) social revolution is faced with a dilemma. According to his program, extant society is wholly bad; but he must either recognise it inasmuch as he makes no attempt to improve it, or else he must attempt to improve it and must thereby recognise it—and either course will conflict with the letter of the Marxist doctrine.

But theory, too, confutes Marxism. It is an old story that the materialism of Marx and Engels is untenable; the entire doctrine of historical or economic materialism is simply unscientific as a form of psychological and metaphysical materialism; and the whole conception of the "superstructure" is obscure and devoid of meaning.

The positivism of Marx and Engels, no less than their materialism, is epistemologically untenable and incapable of being carried out in practice.

With positivism, there falls likewise historism in its extreme form, the attempt to base socialism as communism in a purely objective manner and by a law of evolution. If Marx and Engels conceive the notion of science and conceive their scientific socialism in this sense of positivist historism, it is because they start from the entirely false assumption that for the masses, for society, for humanity (this concept is not accurately defined by Marx and Engels) and its history, the individual consciousness is a negligible quantity. The theory is in conformity with the teaching of Comte and with his contempt for psychology, but it is fundamentally erroneous. When Marx says, It is not the consciousness of human beings which determines their existence, but conversely it is their social existence which determines their consciousness, this is to say nothing at all, and is moreover to beg the question (by the use of "existence" and "social existence" as convertible terms). There is simply no such thing as a mass consciousness or a class consciousness; when Engels sacrifices the "beggarly individual" to the mass, and eliminates the individual consciousness as a negligible quantity, he is altogether wrong-headed. Everything which Engels and the Marxists adduce for the elucidation of their conception of ideology as a reflex, an indication, a sign, and so on, lacks clearness, and is erroneous, precisely for the reason that the individual consciousness is not falsified in the sense in which Engels declared it to be falsified when he explained individual motive as appearance, imagination, and illusion.

Postkantian philosophy has made so thorough a study of psychology and sociology, and above all of the philosophy of history, that, despite certain new attempts à la Durkheim, we can quietly ignore the mass consciousness talked of by Marx and Engels. The discussion concerning the nature of history has been so diligently and so persistently conducted that we are further in a position to discard Marx's conception of history and his purely would-be-objective historism. The historical dialectic which was

transferred from the Hegelian system into the Marxist system as an objective "material dialectic," has no real existence.

Marx and Engels developed historism into an ultra-positivist amoralism which is untenable precisely because the individual consciousness cannot be absorbed by the mythical mass consciousness. (The concept of mass
is vaguely employed by Marx and Engels, now as party, and now as humanity.) From the notion of the determinism of nature and of history,
Marx deduced the unfreedom of the individual will, instead of empirically
approaching the problem of the so-called freedom of the will through a
psychological analysis of facts. Thus determinism was transformed into
fatalism.

In practice, none the less, Marx and Engels made a predominant
appeal to the ethical decision of the individual; they continually appealed
against capitalism to the revolutionary sentiment; every speech in a social
democratic meeting, the entire social democratic party education, is a
flagrant disavowal of objectivist amoralism; theoretical amoralism is overthrown by practical moralism. To Marx and Engels, moral preachments
are tedious and appear ineffective—but they are themselves preachers, and
expect their sermons to change the bourgeois outlook. Marxism as a philosophical and sociological system is, after all, itself nothing but ideology,
and this ideology has been conceived prior to the practical realisation of
communism. Marxist ideology is not a superstructure but a substructure
and an anteroom!

Socialism can have no other than an ethical foundation. The European and Russian predecessors of Marx are perfectly right here. Criticism,
science, does not do away with the motivation of actions or with the formulation of aims; utopianism is not rooted in morality, but in inadequate
criticism and in the lack of scientific grasp. Consequently Marx's amoralism is itself utopian. Unquestionably it is far from easy to grasp and to
decide how the course of history exercises a codeterminative influence
upon the individual, or to what extent individual consciousness and will
find expression in the mass and in the course of evolution, but this is not
to admit that the individual is "beggarly" and of no account. There are
differences between individuals; historiographers speak of great men, and
associate historical happenings with the personalities of these; to what extent they are right in doing so is a question to be decided on its merits in
each case, but anyhow the so-called great men are themselves individuals.
Bernstein does no more than give expression to an admitted truth when
he desires to establish socialism subjectively not objectively, ethically not
historically. Socialism is an ethical problem.

Are we then to return to Kant? That is a different question. It is true that Engels discovered his philosophical mentors in Kant and Fichte as well as in Hegel, and reasons can be adduced for a synthesis of Marxism with Kantianism. Vorländer and others made such an attempt; Tugan-Baranovskii and men of similar views have written on the other side. The cry, Return to Kant, may signify that the Marxists wish to devote themselves to epistemological criticism, and to this extent there is good reason for the adoption of such a watchword. But Kant's philosophy is essentially ethical, and we are compelled to ask how the amoralist and positivist historism of Marx and Engels can be practically united (I mean of course organically united) with the teaching of Kant.

The orthodox Marxists, as contrasted with the younger socialists and the revisionists, raise the cry, Return to Marx. In many cases, especially in the field of political economy, there may be good reason for the demand. As a philosopher, Marx has been superseded, and revisionism has made no new contribution in this domain.

The Marxists, the orthodox Marxists that is to say, are accustomed to conduct their apologetics in a purely scholastic manner. Scholasticism arises everywhere and always when reputedly absolute concepts and absolute truths have to be maintained and restated in opposition to the progress of thought. For the orthodox Marxists, however, it remains a scandal that the so-called unorthodox revisionism should continue to find a place within the party, should be tolerated there, and should be enabled to maintain its place with the assistance of scholastic and ambiguous resolutions passed at party congresses.

Socialism is not identical with Marxism, but Marxism is an extremely important and significant socialistic system.

Marx and Engels had no clear and unambiguous formula of revolution. Although in the Marxist system the idea of revolution is of decisive importance, neither he nor Engels attempted to define the precise significance of the concept. Adopting the radical revolutionary trend in the mood that prevailed before and during the year 1848, Marx and Engels declared themselves and declared socialism to be preeminently revolutionary, and yet they offered no exact analysis of this most important element in their system. We cannot attribute the neglect solely to regard for the censorship of absolutism, for they were manifestly disinclined to say much about this serious theme. "A revolution is something to effect and not to talk about; for resolute practical men, the details are a matter of course; the prospects of success must be clear, or the attempt at revolution will not be made—this is the main point." Summarily expressed, this seems to be the attitude of these writers towards the revolution, as far as

I can ascertain it from the scanty, casual, and unsystematic utterances of Marx and Engels upon the subject.

An attempt at a philosophy of revolution is found in the writings on Feuerbach compiled in the year 1845, but the results are meagre.

Starting from the theoretic revolution of Feuerbach, Marx accepted Feuerbach's views by recognising that religion was anthropomorphism and by considering the religious world to be a mere reflex of the mundane world. But Marx considered that after Feuerbach had demonstrated these facts, the chief task was still left undone, for it was necessary to put an end to the contradiction inherent in the mundane world itself. Men, he said, had constructed for themselves a religious world in the clouds because their earthly basis did not suffice them. The contradiction between the religious world and the mundane world was, in fact, the contradiction within the mundane world. The disintegration of the mundane world must be understood and transcended, and this could only be effected by the political revolution. Marx censured the philosophical materialists because they had hitherto conceived reality solely as object or as perception, but had not conceived it subjectively as practical, human, sensuous activity. The idealists had developed the active side, but only on the abstract plane, because they would not recognise real sensuous activity. "Philosophers have done no more than give different *interpretations* of the world; but what we have to do is to *change* it." This change could not be effected in accordance with Owen's recipe that men are the products of circumstances and education, for this would imply the division of society into two parts, one of these superior to society. Owen had forgotten that circumstances are modified by men and that the educator must himself be educated. The modification of circumstances, and the alterative activities, can be conceived and rationally explained in no other way than as revolutionary practice.

Marx's terminology is obscure; there is no sociological precision about the way in which he speaks of "circumstances" and of the "world" which is to be "changed"; without further ado the change is identified with a "revolutionary transformation" and with the "practical and critical" activity of revolution. At this early stage he is already conceiving historical evolution in too objective a manner. He represents the individual and the subject as "an abstract individual," who, however, in reality belongs to a specific social form. For Feuerbach and the older materialists, this social form had been "bourgeois" society; the newer materialism of Marx recognised only human society or socialised humanity.

The defects of extreme objectivism are conspicuous in this theory of revolution. Engels extols Marx on the ground that he did not simply brush aside Hegel, but adopted the revolutionary side of the dialectical method, transforming the Hegelian conceptual dialectic into a materialist dialectic. Here, however, our sole concern is with the concept of revolution, which Engels and Marx attempted to deduce in a purely objectivist manner from the alleged dialectic of the world process. As an answer to this attempt it suffices to insist that there is no objective dialectic, that nature does not exhibit dualism or dialectical trialism, that the evolution of the world cannot be conceived either dualistically or trialistically. Marx and Engels merely foisted the subjective on the objective, projecting into the outer world the conceptual and psychological oppositions and contrasts and the solution of these, and then quite uncritically formulating the result as a sort of metaphysical law of the universe.

In the development of the individual there occur conflicts and crises which manifest themselves in the form of oppositions, but these are purely individual oppositions. In like manner there are logical, conceptual contrasts of different degrees and kinds. But it is necessary to determine precisely how far and in what sense it is permissible to speak of oppositions in social life and in history; we must not uncritically introduce psychological and logical contrasts into the sphere of sociology. Still less is it legitimate, in anthropomorphic fashion, to introduce psychological and logical oppositions into nature and the universe.

Marx makes an improper use of logical and psychological analogy when he bases his catastrophic theory upon the reputed opposition between two classes. Marx himself occasionally advocated a sounder view.[1]

As time passed, the views of Marx and Engels upon revolution underwent modification, for they came to conceive the social struggle in the spirit of the modern doctrine of evolution. They no longer represented this struggle solely in political and strategical terms as a violent physical struggle, for they looked upon it also as a bloodless economic struggle, thinking here of strikes and above all of the general strike—the struggle in this form being likewise conceived as revolutionary. To put the matter in general terms, they now conceived revolution rather as the gradual evolution of the definitive social state. In this double sense Engels frequently spoke of his party as "the most revolutionary party known to

[1] For example, in the criticism of the Gotha program the bourgeoisie is not described as a unified class, nor was the existence of such a unification suggested even in the Communist Manifesto. Kautsky, too, in his writing published in 1889, the Class Oppositions of 1789, attacked the views of those who hold that in accordance with the theory of historical evolution by class struggles there can be no more than two camps within society.

history"; in this sense it was asserted that capitalism was "revolutionising society"; and so on.

Eventually Marx and Engels accepted Darwinism, and were thereby led to modify their Hegelianism and their use of the Hegelian dialectic, although they failed to take clear note of their change of outlook. The modern cosmologist no longer regards the developmental process as revolutionary or catastrophic, but looks upon it as an evolution effected by infinitesimal and innumerable quantitative and qualitative modifications. Geological and cosmical catastrophe is looked upon as the terminal outcome of numerous gradational changes.

Many historians conceive historical evolution in like manner, and in the name of evolution such writers oppose the idea of political revolution. Such is the outlook of the revisionist reformists, of those who tell us that our aim must be to promote reform, not revolution.

The evolutionist argument against political revolution is not self-evident and is not entirely valid. Revolutions may well be a part of evolution; in actual fact, revolutions have occurred and do occur; but, despite this, evolutionists and historians espouse the theory of gradual evolution. Moreover, modern evolutionists incline to recognise the existence of an evolutionary process wherein progress is effected by leaps, and from this outlook the idea of revolution may likewise be defended in the domains of history and politics, although it is true that evolution by leaps may also be interpreted in the reformist sense.

As a matter of methodology it is necessary to point out that cosmological and botanical analogies cannot be taken as proof by the sociologist. Political revolution must be sociologically explained as a social and historical fact.

After 1848, during the first years of reaction, Marx had frequent occasion, in his political articles, to speak of the revolution of 1848 and of revolution in general, but he failed to define the term more precisely. For example, in articles upon the eastern question (1853 to 1856) he spoke of the explosive energy of democratic ideas, of man's natural thirst for freedom, and the like. Revolution and democracy in Europe were contrasted with absolutist Russia. In the *Communist Manifesto*, in the attack on Proudhon, in the series of articles entitled *Revolution and Counter-Revolution*, the definitive social revolution was assumed to be close at hand.

Marx's outlook was ever purely practical. He deprecated the "capricious attempts to foment revolution" made by many socialists and even by some of his own followers. In his essay upon the trial of the Cologne communists he showed that the overthrow of a government could be no more than an episode in the great struggle that was imminent, and that the matter of real importance was to make ready for this last and decisive contest. Capitalism, he said, was a mightier and more terrible power than political despotism. In like manner Engels distinguished in 1890 between the "fundamental transformation of society" and a "mere political revolution"; whilst shortly before his death (1895) he questioned the very possibility and need for revolution.

In Marx, therefore, and also in Engels, we have to note that a clear distinction is made. For Marx the definitive, terminal, "ultimate and decisive" revolution, the total transformation of the conditions of production and ownership, the negation of negation (in the Hegelian formula), was entirely different from lesser and indecisive revolutions. He did not clearly explain how far these lesser revolutions would be advantageous to the great revolution, but in accordance with the *Communist Manifesto* we may assume that such revolutions, too, were to be regarded as valuable. Granting this distinction, it is obvious that the critical question, the one that is decisive for the revolutionist, remains to be answered. When will the terminal revolution begin? How are we to recognise the decisive hour? Who shall determine that the decisive hour has struck?

To Marx it seemed self-evident that the terminal revolution must be unified, must be a mass revolution. In his literary and political contest with Stirner and Bakunin, Marx, from this outlook, sharply contrasted socialism with anarchism alike tactically and as a system. The Marxist conception of the mass movement eliminated the individual and individual consciousness, and at the same time an amoral estimate was formed of the purely objective historical process.

At Amsterdam in 1872 Marx declared that in the United States of America and in England a social revolution could be effected by legal means. For England, in particular, Marx subsequently mooted the buying out of the landlords as a possibility in lieu of forcible expropriation. The catastrophic theory was thus modified in the evolutionary sense, and simultaneously a high value was placed upon a political constitution—in the case of America, upon a republic.

In the frequently quoted preface to Marx's *Class Struggles*, Engels showed in 1895 that the revolutionist was not concerned solely with the question of revolution, but must also be a politician and tactician. Parliamentary activity, everyday political work upon the basis of universal suffrage, were proclaimed to be the "sharpest weapon," whilst street fighting was declared practically impossible. "The revolutionist would be insane who should select for the erection of barricades the new working-class districts of the north and east of Berlin." The immediate task of the party, said Engels, was to be found in "the slow work of propaganda and in parliamentary activity." The right to revolution might be left to foreign comrades. "We, 'the revolutionaries,' can advance far more rapidly by legal means than by extra-legal and revolutionary tactics."

These explanations of Engels were interpreted at the time, and are still interpreted, in various senses by orthodox scholastics of Marxist trend; but even the ultra-orthodox Kautsky and Mehring wrote contemptuously in the "Neue Zeit" of "revolutionary romanticism" and of "revolutionary philistinism," whilst the revisionists unhesitatingly advocated reformism and rejected revolutionism.

Concomitantly with their recognition of parliamentarism, the Marxists came more and more to advocate the economic organisation of the workers, to promote trade union and cooperative organisation, and to encourage self-help among the working classes. The dictatorship of the proletariat, the seizure of political power, politism in general, receded into the background as the new economism came to occupy the stage.

Connected with the discarding of revolutionism is the remarkable silence of orthodox Marxists concerning communism. Communism is the most essential, or at least the most important, social demand of Marxism, but to-day this demand is hardly voiced, or at any rate finds no place in the foreground of the program.

Within the social democracy there is an opposition movement against revisionist reformism, and the question of revolution is elaborately discussed in the party organs. The discussion is still far from its close.

To-day, in point of tactics, three trends may be distinguished in Marxist social democracy, for the radical opponents of reformism have split into two camps.

Kautsky, the literary opponent of revisionism, rejects reformism, and is able to appeal to Marx and Engels (first phase) on behalf of radical revolutionary tactics. Kautsky maintains the thesis that the party can for the nonce do no more than make ready for the definitive mass revolution, in order that, when the fitting moment arrives, it may be prepared to establish dictatorship and to inaugurate the social revolution.

But other representatives of a more radical tendency, other opponents of revisionist reformism, object to this outlook on the revolution (an outlook which is in the main that of orthodox Marxism), that this quiet preparation for the terminal revolution necessarily involves passivism, and that however radical it may be in theory it must inevitably in practice culminate in reformism. The representatives of the adverse conception of revolutionism demand that the need for direct action shall be continually inculcated upon the masses; they insist that the party executive must itself assume the revolutionary initiative, and must not content itself with the mere administration of the party organisation. In conformity with the revolutionary program of French syndicalism, mass action is advocated as the supplement and corrective to parliamentarism; in the trade unions and the cooperative societies and in all the democratic organisations, the revolutionary sentiment must not merely be sustained and fortified, but must be given practical expression whenever opportunity arises; in default of this radicalism, the spirit of those who advocate the terminal aim and the definitive revolution, tends to degenerate into a mere parliamentary opposition, and in the economic field into the advocacy of economic reform within the existing order.

When we talk of "from Marxism to idealism," we have to understand by idealism religion as the definite opposite of materialism. In Russia, materialism signifies, irreligion or antireligion, and in the narrower sense, atheism.

The return to religion effected by the revisionists was partly determined by the example of the German revisionists. For the most part, however, the Russian revisionists followed the current represented by Solov'ev and Dostoevskii. To-day, as I have said, it is no longer possible to speak of Struve, Bulgakov, and similar writers, as revisionists. But there do exist Marxists friendly to religion, of whom Lunačarskii is the best known—not to speak of Gor'kii, who has coined the term "creator of God" (not "seeker after God!"), a term used by opponents to designate the trend. At the head of the Marxists hostile to religion stands Plehanov, and Plehanov tilts with especial vigour against Lunačarskii, who has defended his position in a two-volume treatise.

The discussion has been somewhat unedifying and discursive, but may be briefly summarised as follows.

The question is frequently asked, what is the relationship between socialism and religion, and it is necessary to point out how the history of socialism shows that socialism and religion are not mutually incompatible. With regard to the special question whether socialism can or cannot be reconciled with Christianity, we have to ask what is meant by Christianity, the teaching of Jesus or the extant ecclesiastical forms, and further we have to ask which system of socialism is meant. Some desire to prove that materialism is essentially incompatible with Christianity and religion, whilst others believe that Marxism can be reconciled with religion in general and with Christianity in particular.

Another formulation of the problem occurs when socialism itself, or the social democratic movement, is spoken of as a religion, as the new religion. This line has been taken by Dietzgen, to whom others besides

Marxists and declared socialists appeal as an authority upon the matter. In the works of Filosofov, for example, I find such an appeal to Dietzgen, and a reminder that Dietzgen had lived in Russia for several years. Filosofov is one of those who recognise the great importance of socialism, and for that reason are loath to admit that religion and socialism are antagonistic.

Again, it often happens that socialism (or social democracy) is represented as a new stage in the development of the religious consciousness, a stage to which ecclesiastical religion will have to adapt itself.

In connection with all these formulations, it is necessary to insist upon a more precise definition of the concept religion, and above all it is essential to distinguish the principal elements of religion in general from extant ecclesiastical religion.

Frequently when people speak of the religious factor in socialism, they mean the faith, the believing energy, the conviction, and the hope, of the socialists. Plehanov extols this believing energy of socialism as contrasted with the scepticism of the bourgeoisie, and declares that the proletarian is peculiarly unsceptical. Before Plehanov, nearly all the socialists, and in particular the revolutionary socialists, valued and demanded this energy of belief. In such a sense, for example, the nihilists were "religious," were persons animated with faith. We recall, too, how the earlier writers, beginning with Bělinskii and Herzen, demanded faith and condemned scepticism. But it is necessary to distinguish between faith and religious faith, between belief and religion.

Intimately related with this mood of faith is the enthusiasm of the socialists, admired even by their adversaries—an enthusiasm which may on occasion pass into fanaticism.

Another notable trait is the self-sacrificingness and the active fraternity of the socialists. Those to whom the essence of religion lies in morality will gladly term socialists "religious persons."

We have further to consider the mystical tendency and the belief in miracle, factors which play a notable part in Russia in constituting the idea of religion. Whilst the orthodox Marxists cling to Marxist rationalism and its associations with the enlightenment, the Marxists with religious inclinations (to whom Plehanov, of course, refuses the name of Marxists) turn towards mysticism which is, they insist, a necessary supplement to purely scientific, one-sidedly scientific, Marxism. From this outlook, ceremonial and symbolism are recognised as important. (For Lunačarskii, for example, productive energies are the Father, the proletariat is the Son, and scientific socialism is the Holy Ghost.)

Finally an appeal is made (as by V. Bazarov, whose philosophic starting-point is Engel's empiricism) to religion as an authority which will be competent, in virtue of its higher religious power, to maintain order in a disintegrated society that is breaking up into separate classes and castes.

In this study of the relationships between Russian socialism and religion, it is interesting to note that Christian socialism is practically unknown in Russia. A certain number of priests have joined the liberal movement, and a few even have entered the Social Democratic Party; this party carries on an agitation among the sectaries and old believers, but there are few traces of Christian socialism. Whereas in France, England, Germany, and everywhere throughout the west, socialism first manifested itself as Christian or religious socialism, Russian socialism was from the outset a philosophic movement, influenced by western philosophic doctrines.

Nehru on MARX

Karl Marx and the Growth of Workers' Organizations

February 14, 1933

About the middle of the nineteenth century there appeared in the world of European labour and socialism a new and arresting personality. His name was Karl Marx. He was born in 1818, and became a student of law and history and philosophy. He came into conflict with the German authorities because of a newspaper he brought out. He went to Paris, where he came into touch with new people and read the new books on socialism and anarchism, and became a convert to the socialistic idea. Here he met another German, Friedrich Engels, who had settled in England and had become a rich factory-owner in the growing cotton industry. Engels was also unhappy and dissatisfied with existing social conditions, and his mind was seeking remedies for the poverty and exploitation he saw around him. Robert Owen's ideas and attempts at reform appealed to him, and he became an Owenite, as Owen's followers were called. The visit to Paris, which led to the first meeting with Karl Marx, changed him also. Marx and Engels henceforward became close friends and colleagues, holding the same views, and working whole-heartedly together for the same cause.

[From Jawaharlal Nehru, *Glimpses of World History* (The John Day Company, Inc., 1942). By permission.]

They were about the same age. So close was their co-operation that most of the books that they issued were joint books.

The French Government of the day—it was the time of Louis Philippe —expelled Marx from Paris. He went to London, and there he lived for many years, burying himself in the books of the British Museum, He worked hard and perfected his theories and wrote about them. And yet he was by no means a mere professor or philosopher spinning theories and cut off from ordinary affairs. Whilst he developed and clarified the rather vague ideology of the socialist movement, and placed definite and clear-cut ideas and objectives before it, he also took an active and leading part in the organization of the movement and of the workers. The events that took place in 1848, the year of revolution in Europe, naturally moved him greatly. In that very year he and Engels jointly issued a manifesto which has become very famous. This was the *Communist Manifesto*, in which they discussed the ideas which lay behind the great French Revolution as well as the subsequent revolts in 1830 and 1848, and pointed out how inadequate and inconsistent they were with actual conditions. They criticized the then prevailing democratic cries of liberty, equality and fraternity, and pointed out that they meant little to the people, and merely gave a pious covering to the *bourgeois* State. They then briefly developed their own theory of socialism, and ended the manifesto by an appeal to all workers: "Workers of the World, unite. You have nothing to lose but your chains, and have a world to win!"

This appeal was a call to action. Marx followed it up by ceaseless propaganda in newspapers and pamphlets and by efforts to bring the workers' organizations together. He seems to have felt that a great crisis was coming in Europe, and he wanted the workers to be ready for it so that they might take full advantage of it. According to his socialistic theory, the crisis was indeed bound to occur under the capitalistic system. Writing in a New York newspaper in 1854 Marx said:

> Yet, we must not forget that a sixth power exists in Europe, maintaining at certain moments its domination over all five so-called 'great powers', and causing them all to tremble. This power is revolution. After having long dwelt in quiet retirement, it is now again summoned to the field of battle by crisis and starvation. . . . There is needed only a signal, and the sixth and greatest European power will step forth in shining armour, sword in hand, like Minerva from the brow of the Olympian. The impending European war will give the signal.

Marx did not prove a correct prophet about the impending revolution in Europe. It took more than sixty years, after he wrote this, and a World War, to bring about the revolution in one part of Europe. An attempt in 1871, the Paris Commune, was, as we have seen, mercilessly crushed.

In 1864 Marx succeeded in gathering a motley assembly in London. There were many groups calling themselves, rather vaguely, socialists. On the one side, there were democrats and patriots from several European countries under foreign rule whose belief in socialism was in something very distant and who were immediately more interested in national independence; on the other, there were the anarchists out for immediate battle. Besides Marx, the outstanding personality was that of Bakunin, the anarchist leader, who had managed to escape from Siberia three years before after many years of imprisonment. Bakunin's followers came chiefly from south Europe, the Latin countries like Italy and Spain, which were industrially backward and undeveloped. They were unemployed intellectuals and other odd revolutionary elements who found no place in the existing social order. Marx's followers came from the industrial countries, especially Germany, where the workers' conditions were better. Marx thus represented the growing and organized and relatively well-to-do working class, Bakunin the poorer, unorganized workers and intellectuals and malcontents. Marx was for patient organization and education of the workers in his socialistic theories till the hour came for action, which he expected soon enough. Bakunin and his followers were for immediate action. On the whole Marx won. An "International Working-Men's Association" was established. This was the first of the Workers' "Internationals", as they were called.

Three years later, in 1867, Marx's great book, *Das Kapital* or "Capital", was published in German. This was the product of his long years of labour in London, and in this he analysed and criticized existing theories of economics and explained at length his own socialistic theory. It was a purely scientific work. He dealt with the development of history and economics dispassionately and scientifically, avoiding all vagueness and idealism. He discussed especially the growth of the industrial civilization of the big machine, and he drew certain far-reaching conclusions about evolution and history and the conflict of classes in human society. This new clear-cut and cogently argued socialism of Marx was therefore called "scientific socialism", as opposed to the vague "utopian" or "idealistic" socialism which had so far prevailed. Marx's *Capital* is not an easy book to read; indeed, it is about as far removed from light reading as one can imagine. But none the less it is of the select company of those few books which have affected the way of thinking of large numbers of people, changed their whole ideology, and thus influenced human development.

In 1871 came the tragedy of the Paris Commune, perhaps the first conscious socialistic revolt. This frightened European governments and made them harsher to the workers' movement. The next year there was a meeting of the Workers' "International", founded by Marx, and he succeeded in transferring the headquarters of this to New York. Marx did this apparently to get rid of the anarchist followers of Bakunin, and also perhaps because he thought that it would have a safer lodging there than under the European governments, which were angry because of the Paris Commune. But it was not possible for the International to exist so far away from its nerve centres. All its strength lay in Europe, and even in Europe the workers' movement was having a hard time. So the First International gradually expired.

Marxism or Marxian socialism spread among European socialists, especially in Germany and Austria, where it was generally known as "social democracy". England, however, did not take to it kindly. It was too prosperous at the time for any advanced social creed. The British brand of socialism was represented by the Fabian Society with a very mild programme of distant change. The Fabians had nothing to do with the workers. They were advanced liberal intellectuals. George Bernard Shaw was one of the early Fabians. Their policy may be gathered from the famous phrase of another noted Fabian, Sidney Webb: "the inevitability of gradualness".

In France it took a dozen years' slow recovery after the Commune for socialism to become an active force again. But it took a new form there, a cross between anarchism and socialism. This was called "syndicalism" from the French *syndicat*, a working-men's organization or trade union. The socialistic theory was that the State, representing society as a whole, should own and control the means of production—that is, land and factories, etc. There was some difference of opinion as to how far this socialization should go. There are obviously many personal things like tools and domestic machines which it might be absurd to socialize. But socialists were agreed that anything which could be used for making private profit out of other people's work should be socialized, that is, made the property of the State. Syndicalists, like anarchists, did not like the State, and tried to limit its power. They wanted each industry to be controlled by the workers in that industry, by its *syndicat*. The idea was that the various syndicates would elect representatives to a general council. This council would look after the affairs of the whole country, and act as a kind of parliament for general affairs, without the power to interfere with the inner arrangements of the industry. To bring about this state of affairs syndicalists advocated the general strike, to bring the life of the country to a standstill, and thus gain their objective. The Marxists did not approve of syndicalism at all, but, curiously enough, the syndicalists considered Marx (this was after his death) as one of themselves.

Karl Marx died in 1883, just fifty years ago. By that time powerful trade unions had grown up in England and Germany and other industrial countries. British industry had seen its best days and was declining in face of the growing competition of Germany and America. America of course had great natural advantages, which helped in rapid industrial growth. Germany was a curious mixture of political autocracy (tempered by a weak and powerless parliament) and industrial advance. The German Government under Bismarck, and even later, helped industry in many ways and tried to win over the working class by social reform which bettered their conditions. In the same way the English Liberals also passed some measures of social reform, lessening hours of work and improving the workers' lot to some extent. So long as prosperity lasted this method worked, and the English workers remained moderate and subdued and faithfully voted for the Liberals. But in the 'eighties the competition of other countries brought about an end to the long prosperous period, and a trade depression set in in England, and the wages of workers fell. So again there was an awakening of the working class, and a revolutionary spirit was in the air. Many people in England began to look at Marxism.

In 1889 another attempt was made to form a Workers' International. Many trade unions and labour parties were strong and wealthy now, with large numbers of paid officials. This International formed in 1889 (I think it was called the "Labour and Socialist International") is called the "Second International". It lasted for a quarter of a century, till the Great War came to test it and found it wanting. This International had many people in its ranks who later took high office in their countries. Some used the labour movement for their own advancement and then deserted it. They became prime ministers and presidents and the like; they had succeeded in life; but the millions who had helped them on and had faith in them were deserted and left where they were. These leaders, even those who swore by the name of Marx or were fiery syndicalists, went into parliaments, or became well-paid trade-union chiefs, and it became more and more difficult for them to risk their comfortable positions in rash undertakings. So they quietened down, and even when the masses of the workers, forced by desperation, became revolutionary and demanded action, they tried to keep them down. Social democrats of Germany became (after the War) president and chancellor of the Republic; in France, Briand, fiery syndicalist preaching the General Strike, became prime minister eleven times and crushed a strike of his old comrades; in England,

Ramsay MacDonald became prime minister, and deserted his own Labour Party which had made him; so also in Sweden, Denmark, Belgium, Austria. Western Europe to-day is full of dictators and people in authority who were socialists in their earlier days, but, as they aged, they mellowed down and forgot their old enthusiasm for the cause, and sometimes even turned against their old-time colleagues. Mussolini, the Duce of Italy, is an old socialist; so also is Pilsudski, the Dictator of Poland,

The labour movement and almost every national movement for independence has often suffered by such defections of its leaders and prominent workers. They grow tired after a while, weary of non-success, and the empty crown of a martyr does not appeal for long. They quieten down and the fire of their enthusiasm takes a duller hue. Some, who are more ambitious or more unscrupulous, walk across to the other side and make individual truce with those they had so far opposed and combated. It is easy enough to reconcile one's conscience to any step that one desires to take. The movement suffers and has a little setback by this defection, and because those who fight labour and suppress nationalities know this well, they try to win over individuals to their side by all manner of inducements and fair words. But individual preferment or fair words bring no relief to the mass of the workers or to a suppressed nation striving to be free. So despite desertions and setbacks the struggle inevitably goes on to its appointed end.

The Second International, started in 1889, grew in numbers and respectability. A few years later they turned out the anarchists under Malatesta on the ground that they refused to take advantage of the vote for parliaments. The socialists of the International showed that they preferred parliaments to association with their old comrades in a common struggle. Brave declarations were made by them as to the duty of socialists in the event of war in Europe. Socialists recognized no national boundaries so far as their work was concerned. They were not nationalists in the ordinary sense of the word. They said they would oppose war. But when war did come in 1914 the whole structure of the Second International broke up, and socialists and labour parties in each country, and even anarchists like Kropotkin, became rabid nationalists and haters of the other country, as much as any one else. Only a minority resisted, and as a consequence were made to suffer greatly in many ways, including long terms of imprisonment.

After the war was over, Lenin started a new Workers' International in Moscow in 1919. This was a purely communist organization, and only declared communists could join it. This exists now, and is called the Third International. The relics of the old Second International also gradually collected themselves together after the war. A few allied themselves to the new Moscow Third International, but most of them disliked Moscow and its creed intensely and refused to come anywhere near it. They revived the Second International. This also exists now. So that at present there are two International Workers' organizations, briefly known as the Second and Third Internationals. Strangely enough, they both swear by Marxism, but each has its own interpretation, and yet they hate each other even more than they do their common enemy, capitalism.

These Internationals do not include all the trade unions and working men's organizations in the world. Many of them do not belong to either. The American trade unions stand apart because most of them are very conservative. The Indian trade unions also do not belong to either International.

Perhaps you know the song *Internationale*. This is the accepted workers' and socialists' song all the world over.

Marxism

February 16, 1933

I had intended telling you something in my last letter of the ideas of Marx which created so much commotion in the world of European socialism. But that letter had grown long enough, and I had to hold this over. It is not an easy subject for me to write about, as I am no expert in it, and, as it happens, even the experts and the pundits differ. I shall only give you some leading characteristics of Marxism, and avoid the difficult parts of it. This will give you rather a patchy picture, but, then, it is not my aim in these letters to provide full and detailed pictures of anything.

Socialism, I have told you, is of many kinds. There is general agreement, however, that it aims at the control by the State of the means of production—that is, land and mines and factories and the like—and the means of distribution, like railways, etc., and also banks and similar institutions. The idea is that individuals should not be allowed to exploit any of these methods or institutions, or the labour of others, to their own personal advantage. To-day most of these are privately owned and exploited, with the result that some people prosper and grow rich, while society as a whole suffers greatly and the masses remain poor. Also a great deal of the energy of even the owners and controllers of these means of production goes at present in fighting each other in cut-throat competition. If instead of this private war there was a sensible arranging of production and a well-thought-out distribution, waste and useless competition would be avoided, and the present great inequalities in wealth between different classes and peoples would disappear. Therefore production and distribution and other important activities should be largely socialized or controlled by the State—that is, by the people as a whole. That is the basic idea of socialism.

What the State or form of government should be like under socialism is a different question into which we need not go for the moment, although it is a very important matter.

Having agreed as to the ideal of socialism, the next thing to decide is how one is to achieve it. Here socialists part company with each other, and there are many groups pointing different ways. Roughly they may be divided into two classes: (1) the slow-change, evolutionary groups, which believe in going ahead step by step and working through parliaments, like the British Labour Party and the Fabians; and (2) the revolutionary groups, which do not believe in achieving results through parliaments. These latter groups are mostly Marxist.

The former evolutionary groups are now very small in number, and even those in England are weakening and the line dividing them from the Liberals and other non-socialist groups is thinning away. So Marxism might now be considered the general socialist creed. But among Marxists also there are two main divisions in Europe—there are the Russian communists on the one hand, and the old social democrats of Germany, Austria and elsewhere on the other—and between the two there is no love lost. These social democrats lost much of their old prestige by their failure to live up to their professions during the World War and afterwards. Many of their more ardent spirits have gone over to the communists, but they still control the great trade-union machines in western Europe. Communism, because of its success in Russia, is an advancing creed. In Europe and all over the world to-day it is the chief opponent of capitalism.

What, then, is this Marxism? It is a way of interpreting history and politics and economics and human life and human desires. It is a theory as well as a call to action. It is a philosophy which has something to say about most of the activities of man's life. It is an attempt at reducing human history, past, present and future, to a rigid logical system with something of the inevitability of fate or *kismet* about it. Whether life is so very logical, after all, and so dependent on hard-and-fast rules and systems does not seem very obvious, and many have doubted this. But Marx surveyed past history as a scientist and drew certain conclusions from it. He saw from the earliest days man struggling for a living; it was a struggle against Nature as well as against brother-man. Man worked to get food and the other necessities of life, and his methods of doing so gradually changed as time went on, and became more complex and advanced. These methods to produce the means of living were, according to Marx, the most important thing in man's life and society's life in every age. They dominated each period of history and influenced all activities and social relations of that period, and as they changed great historical and social changes followed them. To some extent we have traced the great effects of these changes in the course of these letters. For instance, when first agriculture was introduced, it made a vast difference. The wandering nomads settled down and villages and cities grew, and because of the greater yield of agriculture, there was a surplus left over, and population grew, and wealth and leisure, which gave rise to arts and handicrafts. Another obvious instance is the Industrial Revolution, when the introduction of big machinery for production made another tremendous difference. And there are many other instances.

The methods of production at a certain period of history correspond to a definite stage in the growth of the people. In the course of this work of production, and as a consequence of it, men enter into definite relations with each other (such as barter, buying, selling, exchange and so on), which are conditioned by, and which correspond to their methods of production. These relations taken as a whole constitute the economic structure of society. And on this economic basis are built up the laws, politics, social customs, ideas and everything else. Therefore, according to this view of Marx, as the methods of production change, the economic structure changes, and this is followed by a change in people's ideas, laws, politics, etc.

Marx also looked upon history as a record of struggles between different classes. "The history of all human society, past and present, has been the history of class struggles." The class which controls the means of production is dominant. It exploits the labour of other classes and profits by it. Those who labour do not get the full value of their labour. They get just a part of it for bare necessaries, the rest, the surplus, goes to the exploiting class. So the exploiting class gets wealthier from this surplus value. The State and government are controlled by this class which controls production, and the first object of the State thus becomes one of protecting this governing class. "The State is an executive committee for managing the affairs of the governing class as a whole", says Marx. Laws are made for this purpose, and people are led to believe by means of education, religion, and other methods, that the dominance of this class is just and natural. Every attempt is made to cover the class character of the government and the laws by these methods, so that the other classes that are being exploited may not find out the true state of affairs, and thus get dissatisfied. If any person does get dissatisfied and challenges this system, he is called an enemy of society and morality, and a subverter of old-established customs, and is crushed by the State.

But in spite of all efforts, one class cannot remain permanently dominant. The very factors that gave it dominance now work against it. It had become the ruling and exploiting class because it controlled the then existing means of production. Now, as new methods of production arise, the new classes which control these come into prominence, and they refuse to be exploited. New ideas stir men; there is what might be called an ideological revolution which breaks the fetters of the old ideas and dogmas. And then there is a struggle between this rising class and the old class which clings hard to power. The new class inevitably wins, because it controls the economic power now, and the old class, having played its part in history, fades away.

The victory of this new class is both political and economic; it symbolizes the triumph of the new methods of production. And from this follow changes in the whole fabric of society—new ideas, a new political structure, laws, customs, everything is affected. This new class becomes now the exploiting class to the classes under it, till in its turn it is displaced by one of them. So the struggle goes on, and must go on till there is no one class exploiting another. Only when classes disappear and there is only one class left will the struggle end, for then there will be no further opportunity for exploitation. This one class cannot exploit itself. Only then will there be equilibrium in society and full co-operation, instead of ceaseless struggle and competition, as at present. And the State's chief business of coercion will no longer be required, for there will be no class to coerce, and so gradually the State itself will "wither away", and thus the anarchist ideal will also be approached.

So Marx looked upon history as a grand process of evolution by inevitable class struggles. With a wealth of detail and example he showed how this had taken place in the past, how the feudal times had changed to the capitalist period with the coming of the big machine, and the feudal classes given place to the *bourgeoisie*. According to him, the last class struggle was taking place in our times between the *bourgeoisie* and the working class. Capitalism was itself producing and increasing the numbers and strength of this class, which would ultimately overwhelm it and establish the classless society and socialism.

This view of looking at history which Marx explained was called the "materialist conception of history". It was called "materialist" because it was not "idealist", a word which was used a great deal in a special sense by philosophers in Marx's day. The idea of evolution was becoming popular at the time. Darwin, as I have told you, established it in the popular mind so far as the origin and development of species were concerned. But this did not explain in any way human social relations. Some philosophers had tried to explain human progress by vague idealistic notions of the progress of the mind. Marx said that this was a wrong approach. Vague speculation in the air and idealism were, according to him, dangerous, as in this way people were likely to imagine all manner of things which had no real basis in fact. He proceeded therefore in a scientific way, examining facts. Hence the word "materialist".

Marx constantly talks of exploitation and class struggles. Many of us become angry and excited at the injustice which we see around us. But, according to Marx, this is not a matter for anger or good virtuous advice. The exploitation is not the fault of the person exploiting. The dominance of one class over another has been the natural result of historical progress, and in due time gives place to another arrangement. If a person belonged to the dominant class, and as such exploited others, this was not a terrible sin for him. He was a part of a system, and it was absurd to call him unkind names. We are much too apt to forget this distinction between individuals and systems. India is under British imperialism, and we fight this imperialism with all our might. But the Englishmen who happen to support this system in India are not to blame. They are just little cogs in a huge machine, powerless to make any difference to its movement. In the same way, some of us may consider the *zamindāri* system out of date and most harmful to the tenantry which is exploited terribly under it. But that again does not mean that the individual *zamindar* is to blame; so also the capitalists who are often blamed as exploiters. The fault always lies with the system, not with individuals.

Marx did not preach class conflict. He showed that in fact it existed, and had always existed in some form or other. His object in writing *Capital* was "to lay bare the economic law of motion of modern society", and this uncovering disclosed these fierce conflicts between different classes in society. These conflicts are not always obvious as class struggles, because the dominant class always tries to hide its own class character. But when the existing order is threatened, then it throws away all pretence and its real character appears, and there is open warfare between the classes. Forms of democracy and ordinary laws and procedure all disappear when this happens. Instead of these class struggles being due to misunderstanding or the villainy of agitators, as some people say, they are inherent in society, and they actually increase with a better understanding of the conflict of interests.

Let us compare this theory of Marx's with existing conditions in India. The British Government has long claimed that its rule in India was based on justice and the good of the people of India, and there is no doubt that in the past many of our countrymen believed that there was some little truth in this claim. But now that this rule is seriously challenged by a great popular movement, its real character appears in all its crudity and nakedness, and any one can see the reality of this imperialist exploitation resting on the bayonet. All the covering of gilded forms and soft words has been removed. Special ordinances and the suppression of the most ordinary rights of speech, meeting, the Press, become the ordinary laws and procedure of the country. The greater the challenge to existing authority, the more will this happen. So also when one class seriously threatens another. We can see this happening in our country to-day in the savage sentences given to the peasants and workers and those who work for them.

Marx's theory of history was thus of an ever-changing and advancing society. There was no fixity in it. It was a dynamic conception. And it marched on inevitably whatever might happen, one social order being replaced by another. But a social order only disappeared after it had run its course and grown to its fullest extent. When society grew beyond this, then it simply tore the clothes of the old order, which it had outgrown and which fettered it, and put on new and bigger garments.

It was man's destiny, according to Marx, to help in this grand historical process of development. All the previous stages had been passed. The last class struggle between the capitalist *bourgeois* society and the working class was now taking place. (This was, of course, in the advanced industrial countries where capitalism was fully developed. Other countries where capitalism was not developed were backward, and their struggles were therefore of a somewhat mixed and different character. But essentially even there some aspect of this struggle was taking place, as the world was becoming more and more inter-related.) Marx said that capitalism would have to face difficulty after difficulty, crisis after crisis, till it toppled over, because of its inherent want of equilibrium. It is more than sixty years since Marx wrote, and capitalism has had many a crisis since then. But far from ending, it has survived them, and has grown more powerful, except in Russia, where it exists no longer. But now, as I write, it seems to be grievously sick all over the world, and doctors shake their heads about its chances of recovery.

It is said that capitalism managed to prolong its life to our day because of a factor which perhaps Marx did not fully consider. This was the exploitation of colonial empires by the industrial countries of the West. This gave fresh life and prosperity to it, at the expense, of course, of the poor countries so exploited.

We condemn often enough the exploitation of the poor by the rich, of the worker by the capitalist, under present-day capitalism. This is no doubt a fact, not because of the fault of the capitalist, but because the system itself is based on such exploitation. At the same time let us not imagine that this is a new thing under capitalism. Exploitation has been the hard and invariable lot of the workers and the poor in past ages under all systems. Indeed, it can be said that, in spite of capitalist exploitation, they are better off to-day than during any past period. But that is not saying very much.

The greatest modern exponent of Marxism has been Lenin. Not only did he expound it and explain it, but he lived up to it. And yet he has warned us not to consider Marxism as a dogma which cannot be varied. Convinced of the truth of its essence, he was not prepared to accept or apply its details everywhere unthinkingly. He tells us:

"In no sense do we regard the Marxist theory as something complete and unassailable. On the contrary, we are convinced that that theory is only the corner-stone of that science which socialists must advance in all directions if they do not wish to fall behind life. We think that it is especially necessary for Russian Socialists to undertake an independent study of the Marxist theory, for that theory gives only general guiding ideas, which can be applied differently in England, for instance, than in France, differently in France than in Germany, differently in Germany than in Russia."

I have tried to tell you in this letter something about Marx's theories, but I do not know if you can make much of this patchwork of mine, and whether it will convey any clear idea to you. It is well to know these theories, because they are moving vast masses of men and women to-day and they may be of help to us in our own country. A great nation, Russia, as well as the other parts of the Soviet Union, have made Marx their major prophet, and in the world's great distress to-day many people in search of remedies look to him for possible inspiration.

I shall finish up this letter by quoting some lines from the English poet Tennyson:

> The old order changeth yielding place to new,
> And God fulfils himself in many ways,
> Lest one good custom should corrupt the world.

25

TROTSKY
KAUTSKY
CHURCHILL

LENIN

Since the downgrading of Stalin by the authoritative Communist hierarchy in 1956, there has been a renewed interest in Lenin (see page 527) as the architect of the first communist state. One of Lenin's closest collaborators was Leon Trotsky (1879–1940), a convinced Marxist since his early youth. Like Lenin, Trotsky spent many years in exile, staying also for a short time in the United States in early 1917, before his return to Russia. During the civil war which followed the Russian Revolution of 1917, Trotsky was the principal organizer of the Red Army, which finally emerged victorious. His analysis of Lenin in his collection of memoirs under the same title (1925) is full of warmth and unqualified admiration, although differences between the two had developed after 1919, just as such differences had existed earlier during the years of exile for both. Because he sharply disagreed with Stalin, Trotsky was expelled from the Communist Party in 1927 and exiled to Siberia. In 1929 he was forced to leave the Soviet Union; after years of exile in Turkey, France, and Norway, he finally settled in 1937 in Mexico City. He was murdered there in 1940 by an alleged Stalinist agent. One of the leaders of the Russian Revolution, Trotsky acquired lasting literary fame by also being its foremost historian; while written from a strictly Bolshevik viewpoint, his *History of the Russian Revolution* (3 vols., 1932) is still a great literary document and likely to remain one of the key sources in the study of the

Russian Revolution. His theoretical contributions to communism are more fully elaborated in his *Defense of Terrorism* (1921), *The Permanent Revolution* (1931), and *The Revolution Betrayed* (1937).

The reality of communism, right after the seizure of power by Lenin in 1917, immediately challenged and divided socialists of all persuasions throughout the world. Before 1917 much of the discussion of socialism, both favorable and hostile, had dealt with the aims of socialism. After the Russian Revolution the question of means became for many socialists the primary one. In particular, the use of violence to seize power and the continued use of terror to maintain power brought about a reappraisal of Marxism. One of the foremost early attacks against the theory and practice of Leninist communism is to be found in Karl Kautsky's *Terrorism and Communism* (1920). Kautsky (1854–1938) was the leading Marxist theoretician on the European Continent since Marx and Engels, both of whom Kautsky knew personally. In his younger years Kautsky supported the more radical, orthodox Marxist tendency in German socialism and rejected the reformist ideas of Eduard Bernstein and others, who sought to follow the British pattern of gradual change by peaceful methods. Yet as time went by, and particularly after the practical lessons of totalitarian bolshevism, Kautsky became an uncompromising opponent of Lenin and his communist theories and practices. His large number of writings on socialism and communism include *Ethics and the Materialist Conception of History* (1907), *The Class Struggle* (1909), *The Economic Doctrines of Karl Marx* (1925), *Bolshevism at a Deadlock* (1931), and *Social Democracy versus Communism* (1946).

The final appraisal of Lenin is by Sir Winston Churchill (1874–   ), taken from *The Aftermath* (1929). No statesman in the free world saw the danger of communism as early and as clearly as did Churchill. After World War I, he unsuccessfully urged drastic action against Russian Bolshevism; the reason for his failure was not only fatigue and exhaustion on the part of the victorious Allies, but also the feeling (so widespread twenty years later in relation to Chinese communism) among many well-meaning persons in the democratic West that Communists were essentially agrarian reformers—who perhaps went a little too far. Again after World War II, Churchill was the first democratic statesman to warn the free world in 1946 (in his address in Fulton, Missouri) that communism had set up an Iron Curtain behind which it planned the domination of the whole world by means of aggressive expansion. Churchill's decisive contribution to victory over the fascist Axis in World War II has already given him immortality, and his name will be remembered as long as men cherish freedom won through courage and sacrifice. His many writings include *The World Crisis* (5 vols., 1923–1929), a history of World War I, and *The Second World War* (6 vols., 1948–1953).

Trotsky on LENIN

Lenin's internationalism needs no recommendation. Its distinguishing mark is the irreconcilable break, in the first days of the world war, with that falsification of internationalism that prevailed in the Second International. The official leaders of "Socialism," from the parliamentary tribune, by abstract arguments in the spirit of the old Cosmopolites, brought the interests of the fatherland into harmony with the interests of humanity. In practice this led, as we know, to the support of the rapacious fatherland through the proletariat.

Lenin's internationalism is by no means a form of reconciliation of Nationalism and Internationalism in words but a form of international revolutionary action. The territory of the earth inhabited by so-called civilized man is looked upon as a coherent field of combat on which the separate peoples and classes wage gigantic warfare against each other. No single question of importance can be forced into a national frame. Visible and invisible threads connect this question with dozens of phenomena at all ends of the world. In his appreciation of international factors and powers Lenin is freer than most people from national prejudices.

Marx was of the opinion that the philosophers had declared the world satisfactory and believed it to be his task to transform it. But he, the prophet of genius, had not lived to see it. The transformation of the old world is now in full swing and Lenin is its first worker. His internationalism is a practical appreciation of historical events and a practical adaptation to their course on an international scale and for international aims. Russia and her fate are only one element in this great historical struggle upon whose outcome the fate of humanity depends.

Lenin's internationalism needs no recommendation. Withal Lenin himself is national to a high degree. He is deeply rooted in the new Russian history, makes it his own, gives it its most pregnant expression, and thereby reaches the height of international action and international influence.

[From Leon Trotsky, *Lenin* (Minton, Balch and Company, 1925). By permission.]

At first the characterization of Lenin as "national" may seem surprising, and yet it is, fundamentally considered, a matter of course. To be able to direct such a revolution, without precedent in the history of peoples, as is now taking place in Russia, it is most evidently necessary to have an indissoluble organic connection with the main strength of popular life, a connection which springs from the deepest roots.

Lenin embodies in himself the Russian proletariat, a youthful class, that politically is scarcely older than Lenin himself, withal a deeply national class, for the whole past development of Russia is bound up with it, in it lies Russia's entire future, with it lives and dies the Russian nation. Lack of routine and example, of falseness and convention, moreover, firmness of thought and boldness of action, a boldness that never degenerates into want of understanding, characterize the Russian proletariat and also Lenin.

The nature of the Russian proletariat, that has actually made it the most important power in the international revolution, had been prepared beforehand by the course of Russian national history, by the barbaric cruelty of the most absolute of states, the insignificance of the privileged classes, the feverish development of capitalism in the dregs of exchange, the deterioration of the Russian bourgeoisie and their ideology, the degeneration of their politics. Our "Third Estate" knew neither a reformation nor a great revolution and could not know them. So the revolutionary problems of the proletariat assumed a more comprehensive character. Our historical past knows neither a Luther, nor a Thomas Münzer, neither a Mirabeau nor a Danton, nor a Robespierre. For that very reason the Russian proletariat has its Lenin. What was lacking in tradition was gained in revolutionary energy.

Lenin reflects in himself the Russian workman's class, not only in its political present but also in its rustic past which is so recent. This man, who is indisputably the leader of the proletariat, not only outwardly resembles a peasant, but has also something about him which is strongly suggestive of a peasant. Facing Smolny stands the statue of the other hero of the proletariat of the world: Marx on a pedestal in a black frock coat. To be sure, this is a trifle, but it is quite impossible to imagine Lenin in a black frock coat. In some pictures Marx is represented in a broad shirt front on which a monocle dangles.

That Marx was not inclined to coquetry is clear to all who have an idea of the Marxian spirit. But Marx grew up on a different basis of national culture, lived in a different atmosphere, as did also the leading personalities of the German workman's class, with their roots reaching back, not to the village, but to the corporation guilds and the complicated city culture of the middle ages.

Marx's style also, which is rich and beautiful, in which strength and flexibility, anger and irony, harshness and elegance are combined, betrays the literary and ethical strata of all the past German socialistic literature since the reformation and even before. Lenin's literary and oratorical style is extremely simple, ascetic, as is his whole nature. But this strong asceticism has not a share of moral preaching about it. This is not a principle, no thought-out system and assuredly no affectation, but is simply the outward expression of inward concentration of strength for action. It is an economic peasant-like reality on a very large scale.

The entire Marx is contained in the "Communist Manifesto," in the foreword to his "Critique," in "Capital." Even if he had not been the founder of the First International he would always remain what he is. Lenin, on the other hand, expands at once into revolutionary action. His works as a scholar mean only a preparation for action. If he had never published a single book in the past he would still appear in history what he now is: the leader of the proletarian revolution, the founder of the Third International.

A clear, scholarly system—materialistic dialectics—was necessary, to be able to renounce deeds of this kind that devolved upon Lenin; it was necessary but not sufficient. Here was needed that mysterious creative power that we call intuition: the ability to grasp appearances correctly at once, to distinguish the essential and important from the unessential and insignificant, to imagine the missing parts of a picture, to weigh well the thoughts of others and above all of the enemy, to put all this into a united whole and the moment the "formula" for it comes to his mind, to deal the blow. This is intuition to action. On the one side it corresponds with what we call penetration.

When Lenin, his left eye closed, receives by radio the parliamentary speech of a leader of imperialistic history of the expected diplomatic note, a web of bloodthirsty reserve and political cant, he resembles a damnably proud moujik who won't be imposed upon. This is the high-powered peasant cunning, which amounts almost to genius, equipped with the latest acquisitions of a scholarly mind.

The young Russian proletariat is able to accomplish what only he accomplishes who has plowed up the heavy sod of the peasantry to its depths. Our whole national past has prepared this fact. But just because the proletariat came into power through the course of events has our revolution suddenly and radically been able to overcome the national narrowness and provincial backwardness; Soviet Russia became not only the place of refuge of the Communist International, but also the living embodiment of its program and methods.

By unknown paths, not yet explored by science, on which the personality of man acquires its form, Lenin has taken from nationalism all that he needed for the greatest revolutionary action in the history of humanity. Just because the social revolution, that has long had its international theoretical expression, found for the first time in Lenin its national embodiment, he became, in the true sense of the word, the revolutionary leader of the proletariat of the world.

Kautsky on LENIN

After the Bolsheviks had expropriated the bourgeois class, and declared them "free as the air," and had made the proletariat into a "sacred entity," they attempted to inculcate some necessary improvements in this "sacred entity," which really should have been the pre-conditions of all socialisation and expropriation.

"We have known for some time past," said Trotsky, "that we lack the necessary organisation, the necessary discipline, and the necessary historical education. We knew all this, but it did not prevent us in any way from endeavouring, with open eyes, to acquire power for ourselves. We were convinced that we could in time learn and arrange everything." ("Work, Discipline, etc.," page 16.)

But would Trotsky undertake to get on a locomotive and set it going, in the conviction that he would, during the journey, "learn and arrange everything"? There is no doubt that he would be quite capable of doing this, but would he have the necessary time? Would not the train be very likely soon to become derailed or explode? One must have acquired something of the qualities necessary to drive an engine, before one attempts to set it going. In like manner the proletariat should have acquired those qualities, which are indispensable for organisation and production, if it wishes to undertake this task. For such organisation endures no vacuum, no condition of void, no standing still; and least of all a condition such as that created by the war, which has deprived us of all means of equipment, so that we have to live from hand to mouth, and are threatened with death from starvation, as a result of the cessation of production.

[From Karl Kautsky, *Terrorism and Communism* (George Allen and Unwin, 1920). By permission.]

Lenin himself already regards it as necessary to put a check on the process of expropriation.

"If we should now endeavour to continue any further expropriation of capital at the rate we did formerly, we should certainly suffer defeat. It is perfectly clear and obvious to every thinking man, that the task of organising the proletarian finance has remained subordinate to our work of the immediate expropriation of the expropriators." ("The Immediate Duties of the Soviet Power," page 14.)

But Lenin is in no spirit of renunciation. On the contrary, he still declares that, despite all, the Soviets would win in "the campaign against capital"; for the process of the development of the Russian proletariat is proceeding in giant strides. He says:

"As a condition of the increase of the productivity of labour, there appears an increase in the culture and education of the masses of the population. This increase is proceeding at a remarkable rate, thanks to the 'impetus' to life and initiative, which has begun to show itself deep in the souls of the people." (page 33.)

The rise in higher education of the masses of the people can take a double form. It may proceed in an orderly and systematic way through the schools. In this respect there is an enormous amount still to accomplish in Russia. An adequate system of popular education demands enormous means and a flourishing state of production, which provides a great surplus for such services. But the state of production in Russia brings such wretched results that the school system has had to suffer most grievously. Certainly the Bolsheviks have been striving all they can to spread knowledge of art and science among the masses; but all their endeavours have been frightfully hampered by the changed economic conditions in which they find themselves. From this it is clear that a speedy rise in education, which would make possible a rapid and satisfactory increase in production, cannot be expected. On the contrary, this increase in production is a pre-condition of the rise in education. Grown men, however, for the most part, do not learn any more in the schools that the State or the community sets up, but much more in the school of life. The best means of education are provided for them in a democracy, in which absolute freedom of discussion and publicity are essential. But this imposes on every party the obligation to strive for the emancipation of the souls of the people; and to put every member of the community in a position to examine the arguments of all sides, so that, by such means, each may arrive at some independent judgment.

Finally, class struggle takes over from democracy its best features; for in democracy each party addresses itself to the whole social community.

Each party certainly defends definite class interests; but it is compelled to show every side of these interests, which are intimately connected with the general interest of the whole social community. In this way modern State democracy is superior to the narrowness of village church policy, as also to the cliquish nature of professional politics. In democracy the horizon of the masses becomes enormously extended by participation in politics. All these possibilities of education of the people become simply shattered if, as the Soviet Republic has done, democracy is set aside in favour of an autocracy of the working-men's council, which deprives every "bourgeois" of his rights, and abolishes the freedom of the press. The particular interests of the wage-earners in this way become detached from general social interests, and the working man himself is, at the same time, denied an independent examination of the arguments that arise in the struggle of the various classes and parties. For this examination is already settled for him by a patronising authority, which anxiously tries to keep from him every thought and every feeling, which might cause doubts to arise in his heart as to the divine nature of the Soviet system. Naturally enough, this is exactly what should happen in the interests of truth. The poor ignorant people should be prevented from being deceived and poisoned by a bourgeois Press, with all its enormous and powerful machinery. But where in present-day Russia is this powerful machinery to be found, which grants to the bourgeois newspapers a superiority over the Bolshevik papers? Apart from all this, the bitterness of the Bolshevik enslaving of the press is employed not merely against the bourgeois papers alone, but against the whole of the press that does not swear allegiance to the existing system of government.

The justification of this system simply proceeds on the naive assumption that there really exists an absolute truth, and that the Communists alone are in possession of that truth. It also proceeds on another assumption, namely, that all journalists are, by their very nature, liars; whereas only the Communists are the fanatics of truth. Everywhere there are to be found liars as well as fanatics, who accept as true everything that they see. But the lie flourishes best in those places where it has no control to fear, and where, moreover, the press of a certain tendency alone has the right to speak. In this way it simply has *carte blanche* to lie, and this encourages those elements that tend to deception. Therefore it is turned to account the more desperate the position of those in power, and the more they fear the truth. The truth in regard to information is in no way strengthened by the abolition of the freedom of the press. On the contrary, it is most adversely affected thereby. As to the truth of conceptions and ideas, we must say with Pilate: "What is truth?" There is no such thing as absolute truth. There is merely a process of knowledge, and this process is in every way impaired, and with it also men's possibilities of acquiring knowledge, if one party uses its power to monopolise its own conceptions as the one blessed truth, and seeks to suppress every other opinion. It is not to be doubted that the idealists among the Bolsheviks have acted in perfect good faith, in believing that they were in complete possession of the truth, and that only sheer perverseness could make others think differently from them. But we must equally attribute good faith to the men of the Holy Inquisition of Spain. The rise in culture and education among the masses of the people certainly received an impetus under its regime.

There is certainly a difference between the Inquisitors and the leaders of the Soviet Republic. The former did not in any way desire the material and spiritual improvement of the masses on this earthly sphere. They wished merely to ensure their souls for the future life. The Soviet people believed they could, by means of the methods of the Inquisition, raise the masses of the people in every way. They do not at all see how very much they are degrading them. Besides, a high standard of popular education, a high "morale" among the masses is a pre-condition of Socialism, a morale which shows itself not merely in strong social instincts and feelings of solidarity, of sympathy and of self-sacrifice, but also in the extension of these feelings beyond the narrow circles of one's comrades to the generality of mankind. We found such a morale strongly developed among the proletarians of the Paris Commune. It is utterly failing in the masses of the people who mostly constitute the Bolshevik proletariat.

But this "morale" must be created at all costs, so says Trotsky. "This communist morale, my comrades, we are in duty bound to preach, to support, to develop and to establish. That is the finest and highest task of our party, in all departments of its activity." (Work, Discipline," etc., page 21).

Yes, but does Trotsky really believe that you can create morale overnight? That can develop but slowly. On the other hand, the encouragement to production suffers no delay. If the morale of the communists has not formed itself before the beginning of socialisation, it will be too late to develop it after expropriation has taken place. And how is it to be developed? It shall be preached. As if ever in this world anything had come from moral sermons. Whenever Marxists base their hopes on moral sermons, they merely show into how deep a blind alley they have fallen. But indeed this new morale is not to be merely preached, but supported. But again, how? "Morale" is the product of our lives and activities. From these it derives its nourishment and its form. The higher morale which the struggling proletariat develops depends on two factors. Being the poorest and weakest members of society, the proletariat can only assert itself by the most intimate co-operation. Sympathy and self-sacrifice of the individual are regarded in its ranks as the highest quality, in opposition to the capitalist class, in which the individual makes his wealth at the expense of the masses, without any consideration as to how he gains it. But even the strong feelings of solidarity can have a directly anti-social effect, if they are confined to a narrow circle, which seeks to gain its advantage at the cost of the rest of society, like the nobility, or the bureaucracy, or an officers' corps. What, however, does raise the solidarity of the modern proletariat to the height of social morale is its extension to the whole of humanity. The extension of such solidarity springs from the consciousness that the proletariat cannot emancipate itself without emancipating the whole of the human race. Long ago the youthful Engels hoped to derive from a knowledge of this fact the greatest aids to an improvement of the proletarian morale. He declares in his "Condition of the Working Classes in England," (2nd edition, page 299) :—

"In proportion as the proletariat assimilates socialist and communist elements, the revolution abates in bloodshed and rage. In its very principles Communism stands over and above the division of the bourgeois and the proletariat. It recognises this division in its historical significance for the present day, but does not regard it as justified for the future. Communism wishes to remove this division. So long as this division is maintained, it recognises the bitterness of the proletarian against his oppressor as a necessary evil, as the most forceful lever to be employed in the labour agitation that is just taking place; but it seeks to rise above this bitterness, because it represents the cause of humanity, and not merely the cause of the working-class alone. Nevertheless, no communist ever wishes to wreak vengeance on the individual, nor does he really believe that the individual bourgeois can act differently in the existing circumstances than he actually does. The more, therefore, the English working man adopts Socialist ideas, the more will his present bitterness, which if it remains as it does can achieve nothing, become superfluous; and the more will all action against the bourgeois lose in brutality and cruelty. If it were in any way possible to make the whole proletariat communist before the struggle began, the struggle itself would proceed on most peaceful lines. But that is no longer possible. It is already too late. (Engels expected, in 1845, the imminent outbreak of the Revolution which, however, came in 1848, but on the Continent and not in England, and the Revolution itself was not proletarian.—Editor.) I believe meanwhile that until the outbreak of the quite open and direct war of the poor against the rich, which has become inevitable in England, takes place, at least sufficient clearness over the social question will have spread among the proletariat; and that, with the help of coming events, the communist party will be in a position to overcome in time the brutal elements of the Revolution, and to yield to a Ninth Thermidor."

(9th Thermidor was the day on which Robespierre was overthrown, and the Paris Regiment of Terror collapsed.) Such a similar collapse Engels wished to prevent; and for this purpose he urged that all the communists should set to work, by eliminating from the proletarian class-struggle its coarseness and brutality against the bourgeois, and by placing in the forefront the general interests of humanity. It is obvious that Engels understood communism in an utterly different sense from the Bolsheviks of the present day. What Engels wanted, those Russian Socialists who are in opposition to the Bolsheviks are now fighting for. Bolshevism triumphed over its social opponents, by making the ferocity and brutality of the coming labour agitation "the motive force of the Revolution." This Bolshevism did, by degrading the social movement, by turning the cause of humanity into a mere cause of the working-men, and by announcing that to the wage earners alone belonged power (alongside of the poorest peasants in the country); further, by condemning all men to be deprived of their rights, if they did not blow the same trumpet as they did, and reducing them to the deepest misery; and further, by abolishing the different classes and virtually creating a new class of helots out of the existing bourgeois. Hence, by transforming what should have been the social struggle for liberty, and for the raising of the whole of humanity on a higher plane, into an outbreak of bitterness and revenge, which led to the worst abuses and tortures, Bolshevism has demoralised the proletariat, instead of raising it to a higher level of morale. It has further increased the demoralisation, by separating the "expropriating of the expropriators" from the intimate connection with the creation of a new social organisation, with which alone it can form a social element. This procedure soon extended in application from the means of production to the means of consumption. From this it was an easy step to brigandage, such as has been idealised in Stenka Razin.

"The masses had without any difficulty understood the negative programme of Bolshevism, which was that one need not fight. It did not recognise any more obligations. One had only to take, to seize, and to appropriate what one could get; or as Lenin so wonderfully puts it, one should steal what has been stolen." (D. Gavronski, "The Balance of Russian Bolshevism," Berlin, 1919, page 39.)

It is in keeping with this conception that the robber captain has already received his memorial in the Soviet Republic. In this manner Bolshevism "supported" and preached the new communist morale, without which socialistic construction is impossible. It meant nothing other than the increasing demoralisation of further sections of the Russian proletariat. This was a feature over which the idealists among the Bolsheviks themselves were horrified; but they could only see the appearance without recognising its cause, for that would have meant upsetting their whole system of government. In desperation they looked round for a means that should give the communist morale to the masses. They could discover nothing, these Marxists, these bold revolutionaries and innovators, except the miserable expedient with which the old society endeavoured to absolve itself from the results of its own sins, namely, the *tribunal, prison and execution,* in other words, Terrorism. Lenin writes in his book (already several times quoted) on the "Immediate Work of the Soviet Republic" (page 47):

"The tribunal is the instrument in education to discipline. There is not enough recognition of the very simple and obvious fact that, if all the misery that has befallen Russia, hunger, and unemployment have made their appearance, this misfortune cannot be overcome by mere force and energy, but by a general all-embracing organisation and discipline; that everyone, therefore, is responsible for misery, hunger, and unemployment who overrides the discipline determined by labour in any particular business concerned or in any particular affair; and that it is one's duty to find the culprits, bring them before the tribunal, and punish them mercilessly."

Thus, with merciless punishment, the Russian proletariat is to have pummelled into it the communist morale it lacks, in order to make it ripe for Socialism. But never was morale raised by merciless punishment. On the contrary, all that remained of it has always gone under. Merciless punishment was a necessary evil of the old order of things, when people did not know how to act differently, since the way towards a better morale and a better condition of life was barred to them. A Socialist regime, which could find no other way to awaken the proletariat to a higher morale than by means of merciless court proceedings proves its own state of bankruptcy.

The Dictatorship

It seems as if Lenin himself does not expect any particular incentive to morale from his own tribunals; for immediately after his demand for such tribunals he makes another claim for "dictatorial and unlimited powers for the individual leaders of all concerns" (page 49). "Every great industry, which represents the origin and foundation of Socialism, demands the unconditional and the strictest unity of purpose. How can the strictest unity of will and purpose be assured? By the subordination of the will of thousands to the will of an individual. This subordination, which embodies an ideal understanding and sense of discipline on the part of those occupied in combined labour, bears some resemblance to the subtle direction of an orchestra conductor. It can claim dictatorial powers in their severest form, if no ideal sense of discipline and understanding exists" (page 51).

Hitherto we have always assumed that understanding and discipline on the part of the working-classes were to be the necessary conditions for the development and growth of the proletariat, without which real Socialism could not be possible. Lenin himself says at the beginning of this book from which we have just quoted:

"Such revolution can only be realised with success, if it has the co-operation of the majority of the population, especially of the majority of the working-classes." After he has shown that Socialism cannot be the work of a minority, nor even of the majority of the population, but only "especially" and not exclusively of the working-classes; and after he has, by these admissions, justified democracy against his own will, he continues:—"Only when the proletariat and the poorest sections of the peasantry have acquired for themselves sufficient self-consciousness, strength of ideas, self-sacrifice and determination, can the triumph of the Socialist Revolution be assured." Nevertheless, its triumph is to be assured, it would seem, through the dictatorship of the tribunals and of the heads of factories.

"The Revolution has just destroyed the oldest, the strongest, and the heaviest chains, by which the masses were held in bondage under threat of the knout. Such was true of yesterday. To-day, however, this same revolution indeed in the interests of Socialism (page 52), demands the absolute subordination of the masses to the single will of the leaders of labour."

The freedom which they gained yesterday for themselves is to-day to be taken from them, since the masses apparently have not acquired sufficient "self-consciousness, strength of ideas, self-sacrifice and determination." But on page 7 the impracticability of Socialism as the result of the lack of these qualities has been shown, whereas on page 52, in the interests of Socialism, "the absolute subordination" of the immature masses to dictatorial leaders is demanded. By this means their position will sink below the level of that which they had on the old capitalist system. For in that system they were subordinated to capital, but, nevertheless, not absolutely subordinate. Lenin certainly comforts himself and the public by asserting that, in distinction from the old capitalist system of management, this dictatorship will become possible as the result of the co-operation of the masses of the workers, and of those who were formerly exploited; and, further, through the organisations, which will be so constructed that through them the masses will be roused, and will, by their active efforts, ultimately achieve something of historical importance. The Soviet organisations belong to this kind of organisation (page 51). In what way the exclusion and suppression of any kind of criticism is to help forward the awakening of the masses and their encouragement to creative activity has already been shown. The Soviet organisation alters nothing in this respect. How can this iron form of dictatorship of individuals, "with the absolute subordination of the masses," be realised through the organisation of the masses into individual activity? Whoever is to be elected by the masses or deposed by them, or whoever is to be re-elected will always remain dependent on them, for he cannot carry anything through which does not meet with their approval. He can certainly attempt to break the obstinacy of individual members of the organisation which elects him, if they should be in opposition to the majority; but he would very soon be at the end of his tether if he should wish to impose on the majority, against their will, his own ideas and orders. For this reason a personal dictatorship and democracy are incompatible. Such is also true for the Soviet democracy. Lenin does indeed declare that these remarks are liable to criticism, but vehemence is substituted for strength in his arguments, for he can give no other answer than:—

"If we are not anarchists we accept the fact that the State as such is necessary, that is, we accept the need for *compulsion* in the period of transition from Capitalism to Socialism" (page 50).

With this we are in complete agreement. Even democracy itself does not exclude a certain kind of compulsion; but the only kind of compulsion it concedes is that of the majority over the minority. The compulsion necessary for the transition from Capitalism to Socialism is the compulsion of the majority of the workers over the minority of the capitalists; but this is not the case in the second stage of the Revolution, of which Lenin himself speaks, and in which the proletariat has already broken its chains. Here it is a question of the compulsion exercised by single individuals over the masses of the workers. That this form of compulsion is incompatible with democracy Lenin does not attempt to show. He seeks rather to make it compatible, by a sort of conjuror's trick, by attempting to show that, since compulsion must be exercised by the great masses upon individual capitalists in order to bring about Socialism, and since such Socialism is perfectly well compatible with democracy, every form of compulsion which might be applied with a view to introducing Socialism is compatible with democracy, even if it should represent the absolute power of single individuals over the masses. He says:—

"Hence there is no fundamental opposition between the Soviet (i.e., Socialist) democracy and the delegation of the dictatorial powers to certain individuals."

That may be; but it would only show that the Soviet democracy is a very peculiar structure, which one could employ to uphold any form of arbitrary domination, provided one merely gave it the name of Socialism. If an absolute subordination of the workers in a business concern to their chief is to be brought about, he ought not to be elected by them, but should be put in command by some power superior to them. In such a case the business council in the concern should have nothing to say. Moreover, the Central Executive Committee, which appoints these dictators, would itself have acquired dictatorial power; and so the Soviets would be reduced to mere shadows, and the masses represented by them would lose all real power. A working-class which lacked "self-consciousness, strength of ideas, self-sacrifice and determination" is incapable itself of choosing its own dictator, through whom it is to be raised to a higher level, and to whom it must bend its will, if he should demand of them deeds which required "self-consciousness, strength of ideas, self-sacrifice and determination." It is as far from doing this as was Münchausen from extricating himself from the bog by means of his own hair. And where are these dictators with the necessary moral force, as well as the intellectual qualities and superiority, to be found? Every form of arbitrary rule carries with it the seed of corruption of the authority itself, be this a single individual or a small coterie. Only exceptional characters can remain exempt from pernicious consequences. Are we to assume that the Russian dictators are through and through all characters like this? Lenin promises that they are to be very carefully sifted.

"We wish to pursue our path by seeking, with all caution and patience, to examine the right organisations, and to take account of the men with clear intelligence and practical sense—men who combine enthusiasm for Socialism with the gift of being able, without undue bluster (and uninfluenced by the noise and bewilderment) to hold together a large number of men, and make them combine in determined, unified, and concerted labour within the framework of the Soviet organisations. Only such men, after the tenfold examination through which they go by passing from the most simple to the most difficult tasks, are to be placed in responsible positions as heads of administration. *We have not yet learned to do this. We shall learn"* (pages 41 and 42).

He does not say who is to be understood under this "we." Obviously not the ignorant, undisciplined, bewildered masses; more likely the higher authority, the Central Executive Committee. But even this body has not yet learnt the art of selecting aright leaders of massed labour. It promises to learn this difficult art. No time limit is given. Only this is certain, that at the present moment the selection of these leaders is proceeding in a highly unsatisfactory manner. The necessary capacity of the men at the head is lacking, just as much as the necessary maturity of the masses.

After they have been expropriating and are now proceeding to organisation, they find that they have first to set about learning—even learning how to choose aright the higher administrators of State economy.

If the Communists assert that democracy is none other than the method of *bourgeois* domination, the answer to that would be, that the alternative to democracy, namely, the dictatorship itself, could lead to nothing else but a revolution, and to methods of violence characteristic of bygone days. Democracy, with its universal equal suffrage, does not represent the domination of the bourgeoisie; for the bourgeoisie in its period of revolution did not introduce equal suffrage, but only suffrage according to census, which was introduced into France, England, Belgium and elsewhere. It was only after long and bitter struggle that the proletariat succeeded in acquiring universal and equal suffrage—a perfectly well-known fact, which, however, all Communists and their friends seem to have completely forgotten. Democracy, with its universal equal suffrage, is the method to transform the class-struggle out of a hand-to-hand fight into a battle of intelligence, in which one particular class can triumph only if it is intellectually and morally on a level with its opponent. Democracy is the one and only method through which the higher form of life can be realised, and which Socialism declares is the right of civilised men. Dictatorship leads only to that form of Socialism which has been called Asiatic; but unjustly, for Asia has given birth to a Confucius and a Buddha. It would be more exact to call it *Tartar* Socialism.

Quite apart from the terrible consequences of the world-war, which naturally bear the greater responsibility, it is due in a great measure to the subversive and destructive activity of the Communists, to their dissipation of the strength of the proletariat by fruitless adventures, that the working-classes of Germany have gained little from their own victory, and have not understood how to make democracy an adequate instrument for their own emancipation.

Democracy offers far better prospects for Socialism in West Europe and America. These regions, especially the Anglo-Saxon countries, have issued from the world-war less weakened economically than the others. Every form of progress, and every gain of power on the part of the proletariat, must immediately bring with it an improvement in the conditions of life.

But at the same time the struggle of the proletariat against the bourgeois world must assume more intensive forms than ever it did before the war.

The period of patriotic exuberance, which war and, after it, victory, had given rise to, is rapidly passing. The change has already begun, and will proceed at an increasing rate, when once peace has been signed. For, however great the burdens placed by the Peace Treaty on the conquered, the sacrifices entailed by the victorious peoples will be felt none the less, since everywhere now the chief interest will be turned from external problems to problems of home policy.

The opposition of the proletariat will, in such case, always assume more and more energetic forms, according as its self-consciousness increases. The German, and still more the Russian, Revolution has in this respect acted as an incentive. Whatever one may think of the Bolshevik methods, the fact that a proletarian government in a great State has not only come into power, but been able to maintain itself for nearly two years under the most difficult conditions conceivable, naturally increases the feeling of power among the proletariat of all countries. For the world-revolution therefore, in this respect, the Bolsheviks have rendered an enormous service, far more than they have through their emissaries and propagandists, who have been responsible for more harm to the proletarian cause than for any revolutionary achievement.

The proletariat of the whole world has now been set in motion, and its international pressure will be strong enough to cause all economic progress of the future to develop on Socialist, and no longer on capitalist lines.

In this respect, therefore, the world-war has made this epoch significant; for it has meant the end of capitalist and the beginning of Socialist development. Clearly, we shall not be able to leap at one bound out of a capitalist into a Socialist world. Socialism is not a piece of mechanism, which one can put together on a pre-conceived plan, and which, once it has been set in motion, can go on working in a regular manner. On the contrary, it is in reality a process of social co-operation, which has its own special laws just like any other form of social activity; which however, within these laws can assume the most varied forms, and is also capable of fuller development, the outcome of which it is impossible for us at the present moment to see.

We of the present day have no "ready-made Utopias to introduce by popular decision." What is now happening is the liberating of those elements that mark the beginning of Socialist development. If we care to call that the world-revolution, because this is happening throughout the world, then we are certainly confronted with a world-revolution. It will not proceed on the lines of a dictatorship, nor by means of cannons and guns, nor through the destruction of one's political and social adversaries, but only through democracy and humanity. In this way alone can we hope to arrive at those higher forms of life, the working out of which belongs to the future task of the proletariat.

Churchill on LENIN

'He is no Socialist who will not sacrifice his Fatherland for the triumph of the Social Revolution.'—LENIN.

'Ich bin der Geist der stets verneint.'
'I am the Spirit that evermore denies.'
                        —MEPHISTOPHELES in *Faust*.

From the circle of panoplied and triumphant states soon to gather from all over the world to the Peace Conference in Paris there was one absentee.

At the beginning of the war France and Britain had counted heavily upon Russia. Certainly the Russian effort had been enormous. Nothing had been stinted; everything had been risked. The forward mobilisation of the Imperial Armies and their headlong onslaught upon Germany and Austria may be held to have played an indispensable part in saving France from destruction in the first two months of the war. Thereafter in spite of disasters and slaughters on an unimaginable scale Russia had remained a faithful and mighty ally. For nearly three years she had held on her fronts considerably more than half of the total number of enemy divisions, and she had lost in this struggle nearly as many men killed as all the other allies put together. The victory of Brusilov in 1916 had been of important service to France and still more to Italy; and even as late as the summer of 1917, *after the fall of the Czar*, the Kerensky Government was

[From Winston S. Churchill, *The World Crisis—1918–1928: The Aftermath* (Charles Scribner's Sons, 1929). By permission.]

still attempting offensives in aid of the common cause. The endurance of
Russia as a prime factor, until the United States had entered the war,
ranked second only to the defeat of the German submarines as a final
turning-point of the struggle.

But Russia had fallen by the way; and in falling she had changed her
identity. An apparition with countenance different from any yet seen on
earth stood in the place of the old Ally. We saw a state without a nation,
an army without a country, a religion without a God. The Government
which claimed to be the new Russia sprang from Revolution and was fed
by Terror. It had denounced the faith of treaties; it had made a separate
peace; it had released a million Germans for the final onslaught in the
West. It had declared that between itself and non-communist society no
good faith, public or private, could exist and no engagements need be respected. It had repudiated alike all that Russia owed and all that was
owing to her. Just when the worst was over, when victory was in sight,
when the fruits of measureless sacrifice were at hand, the old Russia had
been dragged down, and in her place there ruled 'the nameless beast' so
long foretold in Russian legend. Thus the Russian people were deprived
of Victory, Honour, Freedom, Peace and Bread. Thus there was to be no
Russia in the Councils of the Allies—only an abyss which still continues
in human affairs.

* * *

A retrospect is necessary to explain how this disaster had come upon
the world, and to enable the reader to understand its consequences.

The Czar had abdicated on March 15, 1917. The Provisional Government of Liberal and Radical statesmen was almost immediately recognised
by the principal Allied Powers. The Czar was placed under arrest; the independence of Poland was acknowledged; and a proclamation issued to the
Allies in favour of the self-determination of peoples and a durable peace.
The discipline of the fleets and armies was destroyed by the notorious
Order which abolished alike the saluting of officers and the death penalty
for military offences. The Council of Soldiers and Workmen's deputies at
Petrograd so prominent in the revolution, the parent and exemplar of all
the soviets which were sprouting throughout Russia, maintained a separate existence and policy. It appealed to the world in favour of peace
without annexations or indemnities; it developed its own strength and
connections and debated and harangued on first principles almost continuously. From the outset a divergence of aim was apparent between this
body and the Provisional Government. The object of the Petrograd Coun-

cil was to undermine all authority and discipline; the object of the Provisional Government was to preserve both in new and agreeable forms. On a deadlock being reached between the rivals, Kerensky, a moderate member of the Council, sided with the Provisional Government and became Minister of Justice. Meanwhile the extremists lay in the midst of the Petrograd Council, but did not at first dominate it. All this was in accordance with the regular and conventional Communist plan of fostering all disruptive movements, especially of the Left and of pushing them continually further until the moment for the forcible supersession of the new government is ripe.

The Provisional Ministers strutted about the Offices and Palaces and discharged in an atmosphere of flowery sentiments their administrative duties. These were serious. All authority had been shaken from its foundation; the armies melted rapidly to the rear; the railway carriages were crowded to the roofs and upon the roofs with mutinous soldiers seeking fresh centres of revolt and with deserters trying to get home. The soldiers' and sailors' Councils argued interminably over every order. The whole vast country was in confusion and agitation. The processes of supply, whether for the armies or for the cities, were increasingly disjointed. Nothing functioned effectively and everything, whether munitions or food, was either lacking or scarce. Meanwhile the Germans, and farther south the Austrians and the Turks, were battering upon the creaking and quivering fronts by every known resource of scientific war. The statesmen of the Allied nations affected to believe that all was for the best and that the Russian revolution constituted a notable advantage for the common cause.

In the middle of April the Germans took a sombre decision. Ludendorff refers to it with bated breath. Full allowance must be made for the desperate stakes to which the German war leaders were already committed. They were in the mood which had opened unlimited submarine warfare with the certainty of bringing the United States into the war against them. Upon the Western front they had from the beginning used the most terrible means of offence at their disposal. They had employed poison gas on the largest scale and had invented the 'Flammenwerfer.' Nevertheless it was with a sense of awe that they turned upon Russia the most grisly of all weapons. They transported Lenin in a sealed truck like a plague bacillus from Switzerland into Russia. Lenin arrived at Petrograd on April 16. Who was this being in whom there resided these dire potentialities? Lenin was to Karl Marx what Omar was to Mahomet. He translated faith into acts. He devised the practical methods by which the Marxian theories could be applied in his own time. He invented the Com-

munist plan of campaign. He issued the orders, he prescribed the watch-
words, he gave the signal and he led the attack.

Lenin was also Vengeance. Child of the bureaucracy, by birth a petty
noble, reared by a locally much respected Government School Inspector,
his early ideas turned by not unusual contradictions through pity to revolt
extinguishing pity. Lenin had an unimpeachable father and a rebellious
elder brother. This dearly loved companion meddled in assassination. He
was hanged in 1894. Lenin was then sixteen. He was at the age to feel.
His mind was a remarkable instrument. When its light shone it revealed
the whole world, its history, its sorrows, its stupidities, its shams, and
above all, its wrongs. It revealed all facts in its focus—the most unwel-
come, the most inspiring—with an equal ray. The intellect was capacious
and in some phases superb. It was capable of universal comprehension in
a degree rarely reached among men. The execution of the elder brother
deflected this broad white light through a prism: and the prism was red.

But the mind of Lenin was used and driven by a will not less exceptional. The body tough, square and vigorous in spite of disease was well
fitted to harbour till middle age these incandescent agencies. Before they
burnt it out his work was done, and a thousand years will not forget it.
Men's thoughts and systems in these ages are moving forward. The solutions which Lenin adopted for their troubles are already falling behind
the requirements and information of our day. Science irresistible leaps off
at irrelevant and henceforth dominating tangents. Social life flows through
broadening and multiplying channels. The tomb of the most audacious
experimentalist might already bear the placard 'Out of date.' An easier
generation lightly turns the pages which record the Russian Terror. Youth
momentarily interested asks whether it was before or after the Great War;
and turns ardent to a thousand new possibilities. The educated nations
are absorbed in practical affairs. Socialists and Populists are fast trooping
back from the blind alleys of thought and scrambling out of the pits of
action into which the Russians have blundered. But Lenin has left his
mark. He has won his place. And in the cutting off of the lives of men
and women no Asiatic conqueror, not Tamerlane, not Jenghiz Khan, can
match his fame.

Implacable vengeance, rising from a frozen pity in a tranquil, sensible,
matter-of-fact, good-humoured integument! His weapon logic; his mood
opportunist. His sympathies cold and wide as the Arctic Ocean; his
hatreds tight as the hangman's noose. His purpose to save the world: his
method to blow it up. Absolute principles, but readiness to change them.
Apt at once to kill or learn: dooms and afterthoughts: ruffianism and
philanthropy: but a good husband; a gentle guest; happy, his biographers

assure us, to wash up the dishes or dandle the baby; as mildly amused to stalk a capercailzie as to butcher an Emperor. The quality of Lenin's revenge was impersonal. Confronted with the need of killing any particular person he showed reluctance—even distress. But to blot out a million, to proscribe entire classes, to light the flames of intestine war in every land with the inevitable destruction of the well-being of whole nations—these were sublime abstractions.

'A Russian statistical investigation,' writes Professor Sarolea, 'estimates that the dictators killed 28 bishops, 1,219 priests, 6,000 professors and teachers, 9,000 doctors, 12,950 landowners, 54,000 officers, 70,000 policemen, 193,290 workmen, 260,000 soldiers, 355,250 intellectuals and professional men, and 815,000 peasants.'[1] These figures are endorsed by Mr. Hearnshaw, of King's College, Cambridge, in his brilliant introduction to 'A Survey of Socialism.' They do not of course include the vast abridgments of the Russian population which followed from famine.

Lenin was the Grand Repudiator. He repudiated everything. He repudiated God, King, Country, morals, treaties, debts, rents, interest, the laws and customs of centuries, all contracts written or implied, the whole structure—such as it is—of human society. In the end he repudiated himself. He repudiated the Communist system. He confessed its failure in an all important sphere. He proclaimed the New Economic Policy and recognised private trade. He repudiated what he had slaughtered so many for not believing. They were right it seemed after all. They were unlucky that he did not find it out before. But these things happen sometimes: and how great is the man who acknowledges his mistake! Back again to wash the dishes and give the child a sweetmeat. Thence once more to the rescue of mankind. This time perhaps the shot will be better aimed. It may kill those who are wrong: not those who are right. But after all what are men? If Imperialism had its cannon food, should the Communist laboratory be denied the raw material for sociological experiment?

When the subtle acids he had secreted ate through the physical texture of his brain Lenin mowed the ground. The walls of the Kremlin were not the only witnesses of a strange decay. It was reported that for several months before his death he mumbled old prayers to the deposed gods with ceaseless iteration. If it be true, it shows that Irony is not unknown on Mount Olympus. But this gibbering creature was no longer Lenin. He had already gone. His body lingered for a space to mock the vanished soul. It is still preserved in pickle for the curiosity of the Moscow public and for the consolation of the faithful.

Lenin's intellect failed at the moment when its destructive force was

[1] Sarolea, *Impressions of Soviet Russia* [1924], p. 81.

exhausted, and when sovereign remedial functions were its quest. He alone could have led Russia into the enchanted quagmire; he alone could have found the way back to the causeway. He saw; he turned; he perished. The strong illuminant that guided him was cut off at the moment when he had turned resolutely for home. The Russian people were left floundering in the bog. Their worst misfortune was his birth: their next worst—his death.

Index